Women Across Cultures

Women Across Cultures
A Global Perspective

Second Edition

Shawn Meghan Burn
California Polytechnic State University

The McGraw·Hill Companies

Higher Education

WOMEN ACROSS CULTURES: A GLOBAL PERSPECTIVE
Published by McGraw-Hill, a business unit of The McGraw-Hill Companies, Inc., 1221 Avenue
of the Americas, New York, NY, 10020.

This book is printed on acid-free paper.

5 6 7 8 9 0 FGR/FGR 0 9 8 7

ISBN-13: 978-0-07-282673-9
ISBN-10: 0-07-282673-8

Publisher: *Phillip A. Butcher*
Sponsoring editor: *Sherith H. Pankratz*
Developmental editor: *Beth Kaufman*
Senior marketing manager: *Daniel M. Loch*
Project manager: *Jean R. Starr*
Senior production supervisor: *Rich DeVitto*
Associate designer: *Srdjan Savanovic*
Lead media project manager: *Marc Mattson*
Photo research coordinator: *Alexandra Ambrose*
Cover design: *Mona Grigaliunas*
Typeface: *10/12 New Baskerville*
Compositor: *Carlisle Communications, Ltd.*
Printer: *Quebecor World Fairfield Inc.*

Library of Congress Cataloging-in-Publication Data

Burn, Shawn Meghan.
    Women across cultures: a global perspective/Shawn Meghan Burn.—2nd ed.
        p. cm.
    Includes bibliographical references and index.
    ISBN 0-07-282673-8 (softcover: alk. paper)
    1. Women—Social conditions—Cross-cultural studies. 2. Women—Economic
conditions—Cross-cultural studies. 3. Women's rights—Cross-cultural studies. 4. Sex
role—Cross-cultural studies. 5. Sex discrimination against women—Cross-cultural studies.
States—Social conditions. 8. Discrimination—United States. I. Fiske-Rusciano, Roberta.
I. Title
HQ1161.B87 2005
305.42—dc22

                                                                2004053080

www.mhhe.com

Contents

Preface

In the last two decades, women's studies scholars embraced diversity when they realized that women's experiences are shaped by socioeconomic status, ethnicity, culture, sexual orientation, and age. This diversity is true not only in our own countries, but globally, and it tremendously influences gender equality efforts. Stimulated by the United Nations' Fourth Women's World Conference in 1995, other conferences, and by the Internet, awareness of the global diversity in women's experiences and equality struggles continues to grow. *Women Across Cultures: A Global Perspective* demonstrates this diversity and integrates it with feminist theory and practice. This international women's studies book documents women's low status and power, violations of women's human rights due to their gender, and hope in the form of courageous women organizing for change. This work addresses the diversity and similarity of women's experience worldwide. The book's content reflects the perspective that women's human rights and respect for cultural diversity are not mutually exclusive, and in fact, must go hand-in-hand.

In this book, I try to convey the scope of gender injustice and the variety of factors (e.g., economic, reproductive, political, religious) that contribute to it. Chapter 1 orients readers to a cross-national, multicultural approach to women's studies and summarizes some basic women's studies concepts, such as *patriarchy* and *empowerment*, for those who may be unfamilar with them. Chapter 2 provides an overview of women's status worldwide. From there I move on to a discussion of reproductive choice and its relationship to women's status, power, and health in Chapter 3. Chapter 4 focuses on lesbianism and how societal reactions to lesbianism exemplify many important feminist issues. Women's unpaid and underpaid labor are discussed at length in Chapter 5 as causes and effects of women's lower power and status. Women and development is the focus of Chapter 6, with the emphasis on feminist critiques of traditional development approaches and feminist efforts to bring women into the development process. Chapter 7, new to this edition, is on the ways that globalization has reshaped women's lives worldwide. Chapter 8 presents feminist critiques of religion as well as women's efforts to reform and reconstruct religions. Although all of the chapters to some extent focus on women's empowerment, the final three look more closely at women's political efforts. Chapter 8 examines women in national politics, Chapter 9 examines women's gender equality movements, and Chapter 10 examines the international women's human rights movement.

I hope that readers will be struck by the scope of gender injustice but equally struck by the scope of women's resistance and the possibilities for change. International women's studies can read like a study of women's victimization but in fact it is increasingly a study of women's empowerment cross-culturally. Throughout the book are many examples of women's actions—from the small grassroots effort, to the use of international law for attaining gender justice. These diverse actions demonstrate that there are many meanings of feminism based on the needs, issues, cultures, and goals of diverse women. Boxed material profiling activist women and organizations, and end-of-chapter websites further illustrate the scope of women's actions for gender equality. Opportunities for readers to take action are also provided at the end of each chapter.

There is a lot of information in the book. As a long-time teacher, I am sympathetic to students' concerns about how to read and master textbook content. To this end, I have included a number of pedagogical elements. Headings alert readers to upcoming content. Important terms and concepts appear in boldface in the text and appear in a glossary at the end of the book. Throughout each chapter are thought-provoking quotes as well as examples of sheroes in women's history. Each chapter includes examples of feminist thought and action from all over the world, including "Activist Profiles" and "Women Around the Globe" boxed material. Study questions are listed at the conclusion of each chapter. Students may use these to make sure they understand the major points of the chapter and to structure the study of text material. Discussion questions and activities follow the study questions. These are intended to stimulate critical and creative thinking and discussion. Instructors may use these as assignments or for class discussion. The book's chapters are organized by issues rather than by country or region, but an appendix provides an overall sense of women's status on a country-by-country basis using economic, educational, and health indicators. Students can use this information as the basis for country or regional reports on the status of women. This information may be enhanced by use of the end-of-chapter informational and activist organization websites.

Changes from the First Edition

This second edition of *Women Across Cultures* is the result of a major overhaul of the first edition. New research was conducted on every chapter and the chapters were rewritten to reflect current scholarship. Some chapters, such as the chapter on women and religion, are significantly different from the first edition; others enjoyed more minor organizational changes and updates. Using the book in the classroom with a wide variety of majors, as well as feedback from other classroom instructors, also showed me how to better explain and organize the material for reader understanding. This feedback also led to the addition of glossary items, action opportunities, and more examples from women globally. The introduction has been expanded to provide more of an orientation to the cross-cultural study of women. The book no longer contains a separate chapter on explanations for women's lower status. Instead, this information is spread throughout the text. Another change is the addition of a chapter on women and globalization—a new area in international women's studies and one suggested by a reviewer. All statistics have also been updated from the first edition. Although this process was somewhat tedious at times, it was also exciting to see improvement on some key indicators such as literacy, political representation, and domestic violence legislation. In the end, I hope the result is a "readable" text that clearly conveys challenging concepts and communicates my passion for the topic of international women's studies.

Acknowledgments

Writing a book is a time-consuming and somewhat insane endeavor. It is also something that few of us can do without support. My students, as always, inspire and teach me. For the first edition, special thanks to Janet Decatur and Toni Duganne, students in my women's studies class in winter, 1997, and to my wonderful research interns Jennifer Adams, Christine Bailie, Ann Lescoulie, Carey Moyles, Jeff Nielsen, Kelly Seefeldt, and Amy Tewell, all of whom helped with library research. Also deserving of accolades are Sallie Harlan, research librarian at Cal Poly State University, who taught me how to conduct web research in 1998, and her highly efficient colleagues from interlibrary loan. For the second edition, I would especially like to thank my spring 2002 women's studies students who told me, among other things, that the book would be improved by a glossary and by suggestions for activism. The librarians at California Polytechnic State University once again deserve my thanks—they always did what they could to help.

Of course the book seriously benefited from the critical eyes and minds of reviewers: Teri Ann Bengiveno, San Jose State University; Jill Borchert, Midway College; Carolyn Broadway, Empire State College; Gwyn Kirk, San Francisco State University; Letitia Ann Peplau, University of California, Los Angeles; Brenda Phillips, Texas Women's University; and Sheila Ruth, Southern Illinois University for the first edition, and Marie Pace, University of Connecticut; Susan Hinze, Case Western Reserve University; Jacquelyn Litt, Iowa State University; Lavinia Nicolae, University of New Mexico; and Marguerite Bouraad Nash, University of California-Santa Barbara who provided feedback for the second edition. My editors at McGraw-Hill, Sherith Pankrantz, Amy Shaffer, and Beth Kaufman, were delightful and open to my suggestions for improving the second edition, even when my ideas (such as a map) would cost money! I am grateful to my colleague Patrice Engle, currently working for UNICEF, who inspires and encourages my work in the area of international women's studies. I must also thank all those who are working to bring about women's equality and all the great scholars who appear on the pages here—these are my sheroes, and I feel I have been in the presence of greatness. Last, thanks to my husband, the always-supportive Gene Courter; my son, the brilliant and talented Kane Lynch; and my stepson, the sensitive and generous Colby Courter.

Women Across Cultures

Introduction to Cross-Cultural Study of Women's Issues

We must be courageous in speaking out about the issues that concern us; we must not bend under the weight of spurious arguments invoking culture or traditional values. No value worth the name supports the oppression and enslavement of women.

—Dr. Nafis Sadik, Fourth World Women's Conference, 1995

Women's activism occurs globally although the challenges women face and how they face them varies depending on culture.

This book is about women's issues and women's equality cross-culturally. It documents women's lower status and power relative to men and what is being done about it, and in that way the book is about empowerment. **Empowerment** includes the processes by which women gain greater power over their own lives both within and outside of the home, and their power to bring about change in situations of gender inequality (Datta & Kornberg, 2002). Empowerment is a key feature of feminism. Sen and Grown's (1987) understanding of feminism suits this book well. They said that, at its core, **feminism** entails a commitment to breaking down the structures that keep women lower in status and power.

Because feminism seeks social change it is considered subversive, therefore efforts are made to discredit it by labeling feminists "man-haters," "anti-family," or "lesbian." Participants in an African women's leadership conference made a list of terms used to describe feminists in their societies that included, "Lesbians, Power hungry, Emotionally deprived, Sexually frustrated, Unmarriageable, Against God's plan," or "Castrators." In the United States, feminists are often labeled as "Femi-Nazis." Unsurprisingly, many people are reluctant to call themselves feminists, although they agree with the primary goal of feminism: for women to be full and equal participants with men at all levels of societal life.

This book is also about the diversity of women. Women are the same and yet different cross-culturally. Their commonalities create connection and provide the basis for transnational feminist movements that span across multiple nations. However, their differences mean that women must be the architects of their own empowerment within their cultures since the path to gender equality is shaped by culture.

Cross-Cultural Similarities

Regardless of where they live, women have a lot in common. For example, they are expected to get married to men and to have children. They are more likely to experience sexual and domestic violence than are men. Women's role as "reproducers," that is, their ability to bear and nurse children is a particularly important thing that women share regardless of culture. Bearing and caring for children is a source of status and value for women as it is one of the only areas in which women are believed to excel over men. The role of "mother" is for most women, a major source of identity and how they define themselves. Women are also responsible for their children in ways that men are not, and this affects their daily lives dramatically, regardless of where they live.

One important thing that women have in common is that most of them live in patriarchal societies. Patriarchy is often defined as a social organization where men have the highest status in the family or clan, wives and children are legally dependent on fathers, and descent and inheritance are through males. In women's studies, **patriarchal societies** are defined as those

"Female subordination runs so deep that it is still viewed as inevitable or natural rather than as a politically constructed reality maintained by patriarchal interests, ideology, and institutions."
Charlotte Bunch

3

with economic, political, cultural, and legal structures that perpetuate gender inequality. Men generally control economies and political and legal systems, and this has great implications for women worldwide. More specifically, it often means that women do not have the resources to live independently of men, to leave situations of abuse, or to seek justice. It means that many countries do not have laws protecting women from gendered acts of violence and that those countries with such laws often fail to enforce them. It means that in many places, violence against women and the perception of women as men's property is common cultural practice and that women are conditioned to accept this. The fact that men typically control social systems means that women's issues, such as childcare, reproductive health care, and violence against women, are often a low priority. Finally, it means that it is challenging for women to occupy positions of power and for women to bring about changes in discriminatory practices.

These commonalities are an important topic of this book. The form and specifics of these commonalities may vary based on culture, but women undoubtedly share certain experiences due to their gender. These similarities form the basis for **transnational feminism,** feminism that cuts across cultures and unites women's struggles from many parts of the world. That women in cultures so different from our own face many of the same issues we face leads us to feel a great kinship with them. For instance, almost everywhere, women work extremely hard in both paid and unpaid labor, experience sexual harassment, get married, structure their lives according to their children's needs, worry about unplanned pregnancies, and are at some risk for gender violence such as rape, sexual assault, or domestic violence. As one of my American students wrote,

> Domestic violence. What can I tell you about that? I did not want to rehash the years of misery I spent at the hands of a batterer. He was a charming Christian man who came from a well-known upper-middle-class family in our community. He entered my life at a time when my self-esteem was in the pits. Little did I know it would go down a lot more before my decade of terror was over. I felt like a prisoner of war. He always kept one of the children with him so I wouldn't leave. I was a hostage. I will spare you the brutal details of the bloody rape and torture I endured. Had there been a women's shelter in the early years, maybe I would have been able to escape earlier. But there was not. Financially, I was stuck. I was only able to get away later with the help of the women's shelter and welfare.

Cross-Cultural Differences

While the majority of women worldwide live in patriarchal societies, there is great cross-cultural variation in the gendered challenges women face and how they face them. For instance among other things, activists in

Sor Juana Inés de la Cruz (1651–1695) was a brilliant Mexican poet and intellectual. To avoid marriage and to continue her self-education, Juana entered a Catholic convent. When told by a bishop to give up her writing, she spiritedly defended the right of women to engage in intellectual pursuits, saying in a 1681 letter, "Who has forbidden women to engage in private and individual studies? Have they not as rational a mind as men do?" Ultimately, she lost her battle and was forced to give up her writing and her books.

- The United States: work on increasing the number of women in Congress by giving money to women's campaigns and lobby Congress to make emergency contraception available without a prescription.
- Kuwait: seek women's right to vote in legislative elections through protest and lobbying male politicians.
- Israel: seek an end to Orthodox Jewish laws that allow only husbands to seek divorce.
- Japan: work to increase the number of shelters and community supports for battered women.
- India: fight for the enforcement of laws forbidding dowries where the bride's family must pay the groom's family.
- Nigeria: protest against multinational oil corporations whose practices have affected the environment and made it harder for women to provide for their families.
- Pakistan: aim to protect women from "honor killings," where male relatives murder women to protect the family honor for such offenses as being raped.
- Afghanistan: seek the prosecution of gunmen who have forced the closing of several girls' schools and have burned some down.
- The Dominican Republic, Brazil, Cambodia, Costa Rica, Burma, Thailand, and Cuba: work to prevent the "trafficking" of young girls and women into sexual slavery.
- Yugoslavia: strive to change the legal definition of rape so that marital rape is illegal.
- Mexico: push for the capture of a serial rapist-killer in Ciudad Juarez who has killed at least 88 women in the last decade. They have also set up women-only buses and escorts to protect women while traveling from work or school.

A truly **global feminism** recognizes this diversity and acknowledges that there are diverse meanings of feminism, each responsive to the needs and issues of women in different regions, societies, and times. As Sen and Grown (1987) noted, feminism's issues, immediate goals, and methods are defined by different groups of women *for themselves*. Throughout this book, you will see that there are many cross-cultural differences in how women conceive of their struggles as women. In Western nations such as the United States, workplace discrimination and reproductive rights have been primary focuses but Third World women often focus on issues that are directly related to the survival of their families such as the availability of clean water and arable land. Third World women also connect their struggle as women to the struggles of their communities against racism, economic exploitation, and imperialism. In short, women's issues vary by

"At certain points we may find that the idea of equality is unpalatable to ordinary people, beyond the pale of consensus. These are the raw nerves of the social construction of sex that, when tickled, arouse ridicule; the primal roots of gender roles that, when exposed, invoke a protest of incredulity and irritation."
Carmel Shalev

"We have never been in a democracy, we've always been in a phallocracy."
Francoise Parturier

Christine de Pizan (approximately 1365–1430), a Frenchwoman, was the most successful female writer of the Middle Ages. Furthermore, in her 1405 book *The City of Ladies*, she became one of the first to argue in writing against women's inferiority.

culture and culture determines the journey to gender equality. By the time you reach the end of this book, you will be well acquainted with this conception of global feminism.

The Study of Global Women: Rich and Rewarding, Shocking and Disturbing

The global study of women is rich and rewarding because it requires that we learn about different customs, religions, and forms of government and that we imagine what it would be like to be a woman in another culture. The study of women across cultures is an exciting and wonderful way to learn about life in other places. Studying women's lives in other cultures also inspires a profound appreciation for women. The great strength that women possess and the work they accomplish despite their customary lower status and power is truly amazing. For instance, after reading *Women in the Material World* (D'Alusio & Menzel, 1996) a photojournalistic essay on women from all over the world, one of my American students wrote in her journal,

"Man was not made a tyrant by nature, but had been made tyrannical by the power which had, by general consent, been conferred upon him; she merely wished that woman might be entitled to equal rights, and acknowledged as the equal of man, not his superior."
Lucretia Mott, speaking at the Women's Rights Convention at Seneca Falls, New York, 1848

Been thinking about the women in *Women in the Material World*. I think it's a huge chore to rinse and load the dishwasher. I detest even more having to unload it. In the book I see women who have to travel back and forth to bring water to their home to wash and cook and clean. Women that gather by the community water pump to clean their pots and pans.

It's cold today. I need to open my side door, reach out, bring in a log. In the book I see pictures of women who walk for miles to gather wood for their daily fires to warm their houses and cook their meals.

Good grief—it's laundry day again. I need to gather up the clothes. I might even have to reach under Josh's bed to find a dirty sock. In the book I see women that gather by a muddy stream to pound their family's laundry.

The kids are hungry again! I will go to my modern kitchen and place a dish of food in the microwave oven to reheat leftovers from last night's dinner. I see women in the book that squat over the floor to cook the family's meal on the floor.

Last week, I planted three packets of sunflower seeds in my garden. I see a woman who seems permanently bent as she follows her husband and the oxen to pick through the dirt clods for the weeds. And I think my life is demanding!

The study of women across cultures is rich and rewarding, but it is also very difficult. At times, it is shocking and disturbing. My students are often horrified, surprised, and angered at some of the gender-based abuses that continue today—in their own country as well as others. The saying, "The truth will set you free, but first it will make you mad" (and I might add, "sad"),

BOX 1.1   *Activist Profile: The Revolutionary Association of Women in Afghanistan (RAWA)*

RAWA, the Revolutionary Association of the Women of Afghanistan, is a good example of women's activism in the face of gendered oppression. RAWA began in Kabul, Afghanistan, in 1977 as an independent political/social organization of Afghan women fighting for human rights and for social justice. After the Soviet occupation of Afghanistan in December 1979, RAWA became directly involved in the war of resistance. RAWA also established schools with hostels for boys and girls, and a hospital for refugee Afghan women and children in Quetta, Pakistan with mobile teams. They also conducted nursing courses, literacy courses, and vocational training courses for women. One of RAWA's founders, Meena, was assassinated in 1987, possibly by the Soviets or by religious fundamentalists. Once the Taliban overthrew the Soviets in 1992, the focus of RAWA's political struggle became the Taliban's atrocities against the people of Afghanistan in general and women in particular. Under Taliban rule, RAWA worked to draw international attention to the oppression of women under the Taliban and continued to secretly educate girls and women despite laws outlawing it. RAWA continues to work on behalf of women in Afghanistan and runs an orphanage, schools and literacy programs, income generating projects for women, and a rehabilitation program for prostitutes. For more information on RAWA, go to www.rawa.org. Visit http://www.feminist.org/afghan/intro.asp for the Feminist Majority Foundation's Campaign for Afghan Women and Girls. There you will find letter writing campaigns and crafts made by Afghani women (all proceeds go to the women that produced them).

applies to the subject matter of this book. However, as you read the book realize that awareness is the first step toward change. We cannot improve the lives of women if we ignore the many offenses committed against them because these abuses are painful to consider.

Although there is plenty of bad news, there is also much about which to be hopeful. The study of global women is not about women as victims; it is about women as agents of change, as activists. Wherever women's rights are violated, there are women that resist and rally for change. Global women's study is about action and empowerment and in this way it is exciting, inspiring, and hopeful. In every chapter you will find examples of women coming together to achieve gender justice. In addition to efforts made by governments, there are literally thousands of nongovernmental organizations (NGOs) working for gender equality. These range from small, local grassroots organizations to large international organizations. In addition to the efforts of Western women, with which you may be familiar, there is a long history of struggle for women's equality in the Middle East, Latin America, Asia, and Africa. I will talk at length about efforts worldwide to increase the status of women. Starting with Chapter 2, at the end of every chapter you will also find a feature called "Action Opportunities," in case you'd like to focus your emotion in a constructive direction. Many of the websites listed at the end of each chapter also provide ways to help.

> "All human beings are born free and equal in dignity and rights."
> *United Nations Universal Declaration of Human Rights*

Respecting Diversity and Avoiding Ethnocentrism

The cross-cultural study of women requires a multicultural approach. Multiculturalism, or interculturalism, emphasizes helping people to understand, accept, and value the cultural differences between groups, with the ultimate goal of reaping the benefits of diversity (Ferdman, 1995). The goal is to both celebrate differences and emphasize the dimensions of commonality or inclusion that supersede these differences (Devine, 1995).

"It is good to swim in the waters of tradition but to sink in them is suicide."
Mahatma Gandhi

Multiculturalism goes against our natural human tendencies to reject people and cultures that are different from our own. Humans, it appears, come equipped with a number of tendencies that make diversity especially challenging to us. Indeed, people have a general discomfort of diversity that is driven by a natural inclination to categorize people as one of "us," or one of "them," and to prefer those that are similar to us. We like to believe that our culture's way of doing things is "right," and we like those things that are familiar to us. People are often ethnocentric—quick to think their culture's way is the right and only way and quick to judge and reject the way other cultures do things.

A feminism that fails to understand and appreciate cultural diversity will be a failure. A truly global or transnational feminism strives for "diversity-within-unity." The world is large and diverse, and women's experiences defy simple explanation. We want to acknowledge cross-cultural similarities regarding women's experience, while simultaneously acknowledging differences. We want to be critical of practices that are harmful to women, but understand that the issues of greatest concern to women in our country may not be the major issues of concern to women in other countries. We want to be culturally sensitive and avoid assuming that our way is the right way and that the path to gender equality is the same regardless of culture. We want to talk about women's lives in different cultures, but we must take care to acknowledge the wide range of women's experiences within any given culture—experiences often shaped by social class, ethnicity, region, and religion. We want to support international women's movements for equality while respecting the rights of women within particular countries to initiate their own movements in ways that work for them in their cultures.

As I chronicle some of the more dramatic instances of women's lower status and power, I do not want women from countries with subtler forms of gender discrimination to become complacent about sexism in their own countries. I also do not want to contribute to feelings of cultural superiority. All cultures are rich in tradition and beautiful in one way or another. Those cultural aspects that do not result in the oppression of women or others deserve our respect and appreciation. Conversely, all cultures permit the suffering of identifiable groups of people. It is our responsibility to be critical of our own cultures and to bring about change in them.

In summary, a multicultural approach to women's studies is not about judgment, cultural superiority, or the imposition of our ways on other cultures (what is sometimes called "cultural imperialism"). On the contrary, it is

BOX 1.2   *Country Profile: India*

India is a large, heavily populated country in southern Asia. Unlike most of the world's major religions, Hinduism, the dominant religion of India, has many powerful female deities. India was also one of the first countries to have a female head of state (Indira Gandhi became prime minister in 1966), but currently only 9 percent of the Indian Parliament is female. By law, employed women are supposed to receive 12 weeks of maternity leave during which they receive 100 percent of their wages. There are large caste differences in India that affect women's lives dramatically. For instance, women in the upper castes often have female servants from lower castes that assist with the household labor. A woman's primary role is viewed as that of wife and mother, and parents arrange most marriages. About 40 percent of women report being victims of domestic violence, 48 percent of married women use contraception, and the average woman has 3 children. Approximately 35 percent of women are illiterate compared to 20 percent of men. India has a vibrant women's movement working on such issues as the enforcement of laws prohibiting dowry (money paid to the groom's family by the bride's family), the prosecution of dowry deaths (when husbands or in-laws kill wives who do not bring enough dowry), and reducing sex-selective abortion (when parents abort female fetuses due to a preference for sons).

Source: United Nations, 2000

about understanding the influence of culture on women's issues and women's experiences, and accepting and transcending cultural differences with the goal of promoting women's human rights. It is about "looking in our own backyard" and bringing about change in our own societies as we support women in other cultures. It is about supporting the equality struggles of women worldwide without telling them what they must be concerned with and what they should do about it.

Women's Rights as Human Rights

Adding to the difficulty of our task is the great disagreement regarding the study of women cross-culturally. Some people suggest that cross-cultural women's studies cannot be done honestly because our own cultural biases inevitably lead to distortion. Others are uncomfortable with people from one culture making value judgments about the treatment of women in another culture when those judging cannot possibly understand the cultural context in which the treatment occurs. These concerns have some validity and caution is clearly required.

Sometimes people mistakenly assume that respecting cultural diversity requires that we accept all cultural practices without judgment. This book assumes a **women's rights as human rights perspective.** The idea is that regardless of culture and gender, people are entitled to certain basic rights such as freedom from violence, and political economic, and social freedoms. Human rights are protected under international law and are monitored and enforced by the United Nations. For example, the Universal Declaration of Human Rights adopted by UN member nations in 1948 stipulates that by virtue of being human, we are all entitled to full and equal rights (Articles 6 & 7); everyone has the right to life, liberty and security of person (Article 3); no one should ever be tortured or held in slavery (Articles 4 & 5); everyone has the right to freedom of movement (Article 13); everyone has the right to own property and to participate politically (Articles 17 & 21); and everyone has the right to an education, to work for pay, and to be compensated fairly (Articles 22 & 23). Many of the situations described in this book may be viewed as violations of these and other basic human rights and respect for cultural diversity should not be used to justify them. For instance, domestic violence and rape are never okay although many cultures may act as though they are. Domestic violence is a form of torture and rape violates women's freedom of movement and their right to security. The women's human rights perspective maintains that regardless of culture, it is unacceptable to deny women their human rights.

At first glance it may appear that advocating for women's human rights internationally and valuing cultural diversity are mutually exclusive. However, international women's studies and transnational feminism requires that we do both. The way to accomplish this is to recognize the cross-cultural variation in the challenges women face and to let women be the architects of change in their own countries. The best way to respect cultural diversity and advocate for women's rights is to focus on those practices of concern to women in their own countries and to support their efforts to do something about it. For example, Indian women's groups striving to stop bride burnings and dowries, Islamic feminists lobbying for interpretations of the Koran that promote women's equality, Kenyan women's groups attempting to stop female genital mutilation, Irish women's activists pursuing greater access to contraceptives, Brazilian women's groups fighting to reduce domestic violence, and Mexican feminists battling to reduce rape. Again, bringing about gender equality is something that women do for themselves in their own countries; it is not something we do for them by going into their countries and telling them what to be concerned with and what to do about it. We are most helpful when we share organizational strategies, help call international attention to abuses, lobby for international organizations to classify violations of women's rights as human rights violations, contribute money to their campaigns, and compare stories of struggle.

A Cautionary Word

One last thing: This small book cannot begin to convey the diversity of women's lives worldwide or to speak for all women everywhere. As Gross (1996, p. 51) says, "The more diversity is affirmed, the more difficult inclusivity becomes, simply because human diversity is almost infinite." Given the enormity of the task of studying women globally and the fact that information is still difficult to obtain, my job will be to give you some overall sense of the variety of issues affecting women and the variety of their responses, and how both of these are affected by culture and women's role as reproducers.

Overview of the Book

The book begins with an overview of women's status in the world today. Chapter 2 makes the case that women are indeed disadvantaged in today's world. The chapter briefly documents women's lower status and power, both politically and economically. The fact that most societies place higher value on males than females is also explored in a discussion of son preference and the greater value assigned to male activities. I also discuss the social stigma of divorce as a factor contributing to women's social and economic dependency on men—a dependency that makes it difficult to challenge men's control over women's lives. A major theme in the chapter is violence against women, women's sexual objectification, and how these relate to women's economic and political power.

The topic of Chapter 3 is reproductive choice, including women's ability to control the number and spacing of their children and their access to a range of birth control methods from which they may freely and knowledgeably choose. I discuss how women's reproductive choice is connected to women's status, power, and health and how issues of diversity must be considered in discussions of reproductive choice. One theme in the chapter is that women's reproductive choice typically lies in men's hands. In many countries, there are few contraceptive options, and women rely on abortions, often performed under life-threatening conditions. In some countries, women are coerced into using forms of contraception that are reliable but that have undesirable side effects. The global economy and international politics are also major players in women's reproductive choice. Ironically, when it comes to contraception, women's interests often come last. This means that the liberating and positive health potentials of birth control often go unrealized. There are many examples of women's activism around issues of reproductive choice.

Chapter 4 is on the topic of lesbians. The study of lesbians globally exemplifies many feminist issues. I document the incidence of lesbianism worldwide and how it varies within and across cultures. The chapter also discusses the issue of how, worldwide, lesbianism is viewed as a violation of the traditional female role and the severe consequences of that violation. I also discuss lesbian feminism as a worldwide political movement encompassing a range of lesbian struggles against patriarchy.

Chapter 5 investigates the topic of women's work. Feminists frequently point out that women's labor is typically unpaid or underpaid and that this is both a cause and an effect of women's lower power and status. Women's unpaid household labor is the first major theme of the chapter. I discuss how the burden of this work falls largely on women, even when they work full-time for pay. Despite the importance of this work to the well being of families, communities, and nations, its importance is masked, and it is not typically calculated as work by government statistics. Women's paid labor is the second major topic of Chapter 5. This discussion includes an examination of the worldwide gender pay gap, the glass ceiling, the responsibilities of women to home and family and how they impact their paid work, government maternity and child-care policies, and sexual harassment. I also discuss women's micro- and small-scale enterprises (their work in the informal sector). Throughout the chapter, I explore the role of legislation, women's cooperatives, and labor organizing as solutions to women's labor inequality. The chapter concludes by considering the relationship between women's paid and unpaid labor and their power in the domestic and public domains.

Feminists generally believe that economic development should be an agent of women's empowerment, not their subordination. Chapter 6 takes a close look at women in economically developing countries. The chapter begins by describing traditional approaches to economic development and common feminist critiques of the traditional development process. Next I consider in some detail the ways in which development efforts frequently fail to consider women and the effects of this on women's status and development goals. The chapter also explores feminist efforts to bring gender into the development process, and it chronicles the evolution of these efforts from those that simply include women in some way to those that attempt to empower women. The important role of women in sustainable development—development that meets the needs of the present without compromising the future—is one of the last topics explored in the chapter. Finally, I clarify the role of women's nongovernmental organizations (NGOs) in bringing about change.

Chapter 7, "Women and Globalization," describes how a world economy dominated by transnational corporations affects women. The chapter begins by explaining what globalization is and how structural adjustment programs and economic fluctuations impact women's labor and poverty. Globalization often leads women in search of work to alleviate poverty and provide for their families and this is a major chapter topic. Some women work in transnational corporate factories where conditions are poor and wages are low. Others migrate to other countries where there is a demand for low-wage workers, sending most of their wages back home. Migrant women's work in domestic service, sex work, and nursing and home health work are discussed, along with the phenomenon of mail-order brides. The trafficking of women and girls into prostitution as part of the global sex industry, including sexual tourism, is also presented as one of the effects of globalization. Last, one positive effect of globalization on women is considered. That is the growth of transnational feminism through the Internet, and national, regional, and international conferences as women resist the negative effects of globalization.

Chapter 8 tackles the subject of women and religion. Many feminists view religion as part of the social system that acts to keep women subordinate to men. Feminist critiques of religion and feminist theology are presented here. These include the male imagery and language used by most of the world's major religions, the divinely ordained subordination of women by many religious texts, and the exclusion of women from important religious ceremonies and positions. Hinduism, Buddhism, Islam, Judaism, and Christianity are examined through a feminist theological lens. Despite religions' negative influence on women's status, many feminists remain convinced that religion is profoundly important to women. Feminist efforts to reform existing religions or to create new women-centered religions are another major topic in Chapter 8.

Feminists agree that women's political activity is one key to their equality, and Chapter 9 examines women in national politics. This chapter explores the causes of and solutions to women's poor representation in political parliaments, congresses, and cabinets. As well, the chapter provides an analysis of female national leaders in the twentieth century. The common assumption that female politicians lead differently than male politicians is investigated. To this end, I try to determine whether female leaders are more peaceful, whether they are more likely to promote domestic policies favorable to women and children, and whether they typically pursue feminist agendas. The chapter concludes with a discussion of women's political activity in social protest movements. When we consider this form of political activity it is evident that women are more political than they might appear at first glance.

Chapter 10 investigates women's movements worldwide. The chapter begins by noting the many forces that operate against women's activism and how, despite these, women still frequently protest gender injustice. One of the main points of the chapter is that women's movements assume a variety of forms. In most countries you will find women's rights activist groups that focus on national policy, women's research groups that attempt to document the status of women and raise public awareness, and women's grassroots organizations that help women on a local level by providing shelter for battered women, providing credit for women-owned businesses, and so on. The chapter also points out that local and national political and economic conditions affect women's movements, both positively and negatively, throughout the world. The chapter concludes with a discussion of the successes and failures of women's movements.

Women's activists have also tried to bring about change by connecting women's rights to human rights, which are protected under international law and are monitored and enforced by the United Nations. This is the focus of Chapter 11. The chapter explores the role of the United Nations in global feminism, including the four international UN women's conferences and important treaties and conventions such as the Convention on the Elimination of All Forms of Discrimination Against Women (CEDAW). The challenges facing the global women's human rights movement are an important theme in the chapter. These challenges include the development of an inclusive women's rights agenda, such that the interests of diverse women are represented, and greater implementation and enforcement of international laws protecting the rights of women. Another challenge comes from cultural relativists who argue that there are no legitimate cross-cultural human rights standards—it is up to a given culture to determine what is right and wrong. The chapter ends with discussion of the cultural relativist position that the international human rights approach is incompatible with respect for cultural diversity. I conclude that the success of the movement requires women's political activity from the local to the global level, as well as an acknowledgment of both universal human rights and cultural difference.

Throughout each chapter, you will find quotes from women scholars and activists, as well as examples of "sheroes" and women's history. In addition to the "action opportunities" and websites mentioned earlier, the end of each chapter provides study questions, and discussion questions and activities. The study questions are intended to help you structure your studying of the information provided in the chapters. The discussion questions and activities are provided to stimulate your critical thinking on chapter topics.

The Appendix provides a summary, alphabetized by country, of women's status worldwide. This information was compiled largely from United Nations documents. In the appendix you will find information on the geographic location of each country and averages on age of females at marriage, educational level, life expectancy, rates of maternal death, deaths from abortion, contraceptive use, and number of children. Statistics are also provided on percentage of women who make up the paid workforce, percentage of women in professional and technical jobs and administration and management, and percentage of women in governmental legislatures and parliaments. Figures on violence against women are also listed by country. These data reminds us of the great diversity of women's status worldwide. However, information on the status of women is often hard to come by, as many governments do not compile accurate statistics, or, if they do, they may only release them periodically. This means that these statistics should be regarded cautiously, and it means that throughout the text you will frequently find statistics that are several years old.

Study Questions

1. What is the core idea behind feminism? What is empowerment?

2. What does it mean to say that women worldwide are "both the same and different"? What does this mean to the study of women cross-culturally?

3. What is multiculturalism? Why is it important to avoid ethnocentrism and to take a multicultural perspective when studying women cross-culturally? How does global or transnational feminism exemplify a multicultural approach?

4. What is the women's rights and human rights perspective and what does it say about cultural diversity and women's rights?

Discussion Questions

1. Do you agree with the chapter's claim that many people have a negative view of feminism but that most people agree with the aims of feminism?

2. The chapter emphasizes the importance of avoiding ethnocentrism when studying women cross-culturally but at the same time says that regardless of culture, women have basic human rights. Can you think of any cultural practices related to women that you are critical of? Should you override your ethnocentrism in regards to these, or are they violations of basic human rights?

3. According to the chapter, one of the risks of looking at some of the more dramatic instances of women's lower status and power is that it can foster feelings of cultural superiority. Why is this wrong, or is it?

2 Women's Low Status and Power

Although we are divided by race, class, culture, and geography, our hope lies in our commonalities. All women's unremunerated household work is exploited, we all have conflicts in our multiple roles, our sexuality is exploited by men, media, and economy, we struggle for survival and dignity, and, rich or poor, we are vulnerable to violence. We share our "otherness," our exclusion from decision making at all levels.

—PEGGY ANTROBUS, Coordinator of Development with Women for a New Era (DAWN) and Director of Women and Development at the University of the West Indies

The scope of gender injustice is striking, but equally striking is the scope of women's activism.

W orldwide, females are generally lower in status and power, relative to males. This may be called gender stratification, although it is sometimes referred to as gender inequality, sexism, patriarchy, and female disadvantage (Chafetz, 1990). This chapter provides a brief overview of the current status of women globally and introduces you to some of the gendered inequalities that exist in the world (refer also to the Appendix). Pay careful attention to the ways in which most modern societies are structured such that gender inequalities and patriarchy are enabled. In the sections that follow, it should become clear that societies are structured in ways that give men greater economic and political power and condone men's right to control women.

Males' Greater Economic Power

Many feminists view men's greater economic power and, correspondingly, women's economic dependence on men, to be at the heart of women's lower status and power. Once societies based on money evolved, men's labor appeared to have greater value because it was done for money or the exchange of goods. The important economic contributions that women make collecting fuel, taking care of animals, growing vegetables, doing laundry, preparing food, taking care of children, and so on are frequently forgotten or devalued as "natural." Research, both in the United States and elsewhere, consistently finds that women's power is related to their ability to make money. However, women's ability to make money has been constrained by their household responsibilities and by the designation of higher paying jobs as for men.

Worldwide, men control economies and resources, own more property, and occupy more positions of power in business and banking. This is true in virtually every country, including industrialized nations such as the United States. Men make more money than women, and even when they work the same jobs as women, this tends to be true. Women's labor is also undervalued relative to men's. On average, women have less leisure time than men do and they do more of the world's work than men. But because their labor is more likely to be unpaid or underpaid, women typically have less economic power. For example, employed women's earnings range between 50 and 95 percent of what men earn; on average they earn two-thirds of what men earn (International Labour Organization, 2003; United Nations, 1999). As you will learn in Chapter 5, "Women and Work," only part of this **gender wage gap** can be explained by differences in educational attainment and job experience.

Women's lack of economic power is related to their strong presence among the ranks of the poor. Poverty is said to have a "woman's face" because the majority of the 1.5 billion people living on one dollar a day or less are women (United Nations, 2000). The gap between women and men caught in the cycle of poverty has widened in the past decade, a phenomenon commonly referred to as the **feminization of poverty.** Chapter 6,

"Women and Development," and Chapter 7, "Women and Globalization," discuss the feminization of poverty in more detail.

Males' Greater Political Power

Politics is another arena in which women's low power and status are apparent. In the twentieth century, activists worked to gain women the right to vote (called **women's suffrage**). In most countries, voting rights have only been awarded to women in the last thirty years. Even in the United States, it was not until 1920 that women were granted the right to vote. By the year 2003, all countries that allow males to vote have granted women that same right, except for Kuwait. Box 2.1 discusses the efforts of women in Kuwait to gain the vote.

Huda Shaarawi (1879–1947) was the founder of the modern Egyptian women's movement and encouraged Egyptian women to participate in politics. She organized meetings of Arab feminists from other countries and led delegations of Egyptian women to international conferences.

Figures from the Inter-parliamentary Union (2003) show that only 15 percent of the world's lawmakers are female (although the good news is that this is up from 11 percent in 1995). The United States ranked fifty-ninth among the 125 countries with female representatives. The United States, France, and Japan all lag behind thirteen sub-Saharan countries in Africa. Fifteen countries had no female representatives: Armenia, Bahrain, Micronesia, Palau, Saudi Arabia, Solomon Islands, Tuvalu, Barbados, Kiribati, Libya, Nauru, Nigeria, Tonga, the United Arab Emirates, and Kuwait. The Nordic countries have the highest percentages of female representatives (39 percent) and the Arab states the lowest (5.9 percent; Inter-Parliamentary Union, 2003).

Women's presence in formal politics is important because male lawmakers are less likely to make laws that serve women and children's interests. Without the activism of women, most male lawmakers are not inclined to think about rape, domestic violence, women's health issues, and childcare. A current focus of activists is increasing women's political power by increasing the number of female lawmakers. For example, in 2003, in separate demonstrations, women's activists in India, Indonesia, and Jordan protested the failure of political parties to support woman candidates. They demanded that their governments require that 30 percent of representatives be female, a figure set by the United Nations as a goal for all countries by the year 2005.

Despite their somewhat poor representation in formal politics (parliaments, congresses, heads of state), women are often very political. In later chapters you will see that much of women's political influence comes from their activities in grassroots organizations that place pressure on formal political institutions. Chapter 9 focuses on women in politics and how women gain political power.

Males' Higher Status

Not only is women's work typically unpaid or underpaid, it is undervalued relative to men's work. Part of being the underclass is that your group is less val-

BOX 2.1   *Kuwaiti Women Seeking Political Rights*

Kuwait, a predominantly Islamic country, is located in the northwest corner of the Persian Gulf in the Middle East. By law, Kuwaiti women are assured equal rights in regards to pay and job opportunities, and women do serve in high-level appointed governmental posts. However, women make up only 16 percent of the workforce and occupy only 4 percent of administrative and management positions. Women in Kuwait are allowed to dress as they wish, although some favor the traditional *abaya* that covers them from head to toe. Law segregates public schools and universities by sex. Poor women from outside of Kuwait are imported from countries such as Bangladesh and the Philippines to serve as maids and sex workers. Human rights organizations have documented their harsh treatment.

During the occupation by Iraq in 1990 and 1991, Kuwaiti women courageously smuggled food, weapons, and information to resistance fighters and were surprised that after the war, they were not rewarded with political rights. Indeed, Kuwait is the only country in the world where men, but not women, are allowed to vote and hold political office. Resistance to women's voting rights is not religious, but social. Those opposed, such as law professor Abdrazzak Shayji, a law professor at Kuwait University, emphasize that in Kuwait, "the man speaks for the family," and "political differences between husbands and wives could damage the family." Others argue that politics would take women away from the home and their children.

Activists lobby politicians, hold silent protests, and have even attempted to register to vote. In November of 1999, 120 Kuwaiti women wearing t-shirts reading "Rise Up Women 2003" sat in the parliament's viewing gallery to encourage male politicians to vote in favor of women's suffrage. (The measure was defeated.) On February 1, 2000, the first day of the annual voter registration period in Kuwait, hundreds of women marched to the registration centers and demanded to be registered as voters. They were not allowed to register and subsequently filed several suits against the government. Kuwaiti feminists are hopeful that within the next several years their activism will result in the Kuwaiti parliament passing laws permitting them to vote and hold office. As Said Al-Habib, chief of cardiology at Kuwait Armed Forces Hospital said, "Women have more of a role to play than simply to cook and clean for men. We are here to contribute to society." She noted the irony of the fact that she clears the blockages to men's hearts but these same men block her from voting. Unfortunately, in July 2003, male Kuwaitis voted to keep parliament all male. The women that tried to force themselves into polling stations to vote were told to leave by security forces.

Sources: Lafferty, (2003), Perry (2003), Times Wire Reports (2003), United Nations (2003)

ued than the upper class, despite your group's contribution to the economy or culture. Margaret Mead, the famous anthropologist and one of the first scholars to pay serious attention to the activities of women, noted, "Whatever the arrangements in regard to descent or ownership of property, and even if these formal outward arrangements are reflected in the temperamental relations between the sexes, the prestige values always attach to the activities of men" (1935, p. 302). Likewise, anthropologist Michelle Zimbalist Rosaldo (1974) points out that what is striking is that male activities, as opposed to female activities, are always recognized as predominantly important, and cultures bestow authority and value on the activities of men. She notes, for example, that in parts of New Guinea where women grow sweet potatoes and men grow yams, yams are the prestige food distributed at feasts.

The influence of French feminist Simone de Beauvoir (1908–1986) may be seen in the work of many great feminist thinkers. She was one of the first to put forth the idea that women's lower status was linked to their role as reproducers and to make a distinction between biological sex and socially constructed gender. Beauvoir was also a women's rights activist.

"Daughters are not for slaughter."
Indian women's movement slogan

"The most gifted and beautiful girl is not as desirable as a deformed boy."
ancient Chinese proverb

Job prestige is one example of women's lower status. According to the UN, women worldwide are almost always in less prestigious and lower-paid jobs than men. As the level, prestige, and pay of a job increase, so does the numbers of men in those job categories (Burn, 1996). This is true even in countries you might think of as progressive. For example, in the United States, the majority of prestigious and professional jobs are held by men: 71 percent of computer scientists, 74 percent of doctors, 64 percent of college and university professors, 77 percent of architects, and 90 percent of engineers (U.S. Department of Labor, Bureau of Labor Statistics, 2002).

Not only are male activities valued over female ones, but in most countries, families value male children over female children, in what is known as **son preference.** All over the world, people greet the birth of boys and girls differently (Mosse, 1993). For instance, among the Turkana people of northern Kenya, great feasting accompanies the birth of a boy, but there is no feasting if the baby is a girl. According to the UN High Commissioner for Human Rights (2003), the areas most affected by son preference are South Asia (Bangladesh, India, Nepal, Pakistan), the Middle East (Algeria, Egypt, Jordan, the Libyan Arab Jamahiriya, Morocco, the Syrian Arab Republic, Tunisia, Turkey) and parts of Africa (Cameroon, Liberia, Madagascar, Senegal). Although son preference is not as obvious in the West, great value is still placed upon producing a male heir to carry on the family name. Girls are expected to grow up, marry, take their husband's name, and have babies. In many families, their only achievement is expected to be to have children, who, because they have their husband's name, are not credited as achievements to her family but rather to his. Conversely, a son's achievements—financial successes, property ownership, education, and so on—are credited to his family of origin. In the United States, most Americans express the wish that their first child be a boy and that if they have more than two children, that there be more boys than girls (Atwood, 2001).

In some countries, son preference means that girls are disadvantaged from birth, receiving less care and fewer resources than sons do. Every year, about 250,000 girls die because they experience disadvantage relative to boys (United Nations, 1998). Female children aged 1 to 4 are more likely to die than male children in all countries in southcentral Asia (India, Bangladesh, and Nepal) and in nearly three-quarters of the countries in northern Africa and western Asia even though males are genetically more susceptible to most causes of infant death (UN, 1998). In Latin America, there is evidence of abnormal sex ratios in infant mortality figures in Ecuador, Mexico, Peru, and Uruguay. Discrimination in the feeding and care of female infants and/or higher rates of morbidity and malnutrition have been reported in most of the countries already listed and also in Bolivia, Colombia, the Islamic Republic of Iran, Nigeria, the Philippines, and Saudi Arabia (UN High Commissioner for Human Rights, 2003). The UN attributes these differences to the better nutrition, health care, and support that male children receive in some countries. **Femicide** (female infanticide) is also a contributing factor in some cases. In extreme cases, son preference may even lead to discrimination prior to birth in the form of **sex-selective abortion.** In mainland China, Taiwan, South Korea, and India, some parents use amniocentesis and sonography (ultrasound) to determine fetal sex so that female fetuses can be aborted.

Femicide has significantly affected the sex ratio of the population in some parts of the world. According to the United Nations Population Fund (2003), worldwide it is estimated that more than 100 million girls are "missing" as the result of sex-selective abortion, infanticide, and neglect. India now has one of the most distorted sex ratios in the world; there are 927 females for every 1000 males when globally the average is 1060 females for every 1000 males. In two Indian states, northern Haryana and Punjab, it is even lower—793 girls for every 1,000 boys. The Women's Centre, a leading Bombay feminist group, was instrumental in passing legislation to ban tests for the use of sex determination in 1988 in the Indian state of Maharashtra and the federal government has requested that doctors not perform sex-selective procedures. The Women's Centre documented the growth of bargain clinics offering the service for low prices to the middle class and the poor. These clinics played on the fear of dowry with such slogans as "Better 500 rupees now than 500,000 later" (Bumiller, 1990). Despite legislation and government directives, son preference continues in India and women's activists continue their work to stop it.

According to the UN, the practice of son preference emerged with the shift from subsistence agriculture, which was primarily controlled by women, to settled agriculture, which is primarily controlled by men (UN High Commissioner for Human Rights, 2003). In the patrilineal landowning communities prevalent in the Asian region, the economic obligations of sons towards parents are greater. Sons are family pillars ensuring continuity and protection of family property. Sons are the source of family income and have to provide for parents in their old age. Sons bring prestige to the family. They are the interpreters of religious teachings and the performers of rituals, especially following the death of their parents. They are the holders of political power positions and high status jobs. They are the soldiers that protect the community. In contrast, daughters are expected to marry, leave the family, and have children. Consequently, they do not have the potential to enhance the family's economic or social position the way that sons do. Daughters in some cultures are viewed as wasted investments. For instance, an Indian proverb says, "Raising a daughter is like watering a shady tree in someone else's courtyard." Similarly, the title used to describe the female Muslim child translates to "another's wealth." This refers to the fact that any investment made in a girl is enjoyed only by her husband's family when she moves in with them upon marriage. Because she is in a sense a wasted investment, she will receive less attention and fewer resources than her brother (Goodwin, 1994).

In India, and other countries where it is expected that parents of daughters will pay a **dowry,** son preference is aggravated. A dowry consists of money or goods paid by the bride's family to the groom or his family. Dowry inflation is a problem in many countries, particularly Greece, India, and Pakistan. It costs more and more to marry off one's daughter as globalization increases the

---

BOX 2.2   *She Walked Away from Her Wedding Due to Dowry Demands*

In May 2003, Nisha Sharma, a 21-year-old computer student, became a role model to Indian women on the day of her wedding. As is common in upper middle-class Indian society, her parents found the bridegroom by placing a classified ad and interviewing prospective grooms. For dowry, her parents gave the groom's family two televisions, two home theater sets, two refrigerators, two air conditioners, and one car. On the day of the wedding, the musicians were playing, the 2,000 guests were dining, and the Hindu priest was preparing for the ceremony, when her about-to-be in-laws demanded an additional $25,000 in rupees. Outraged, Nisha picked up her cellphone and called the police to report a violation of the Dowry Prohibition Act of 1961 and called off the wedding. Sharma became an instant "shero," and television star. Interviewed on television and by newspapers, she posed wearing a sash reading "Anti-dowry," and encouraged other brides to walk away when in-laws request more dowry.

Sources: Devraj, 2003; Vasudev, Menon, Vinayak, David, & Muralidharan, 2003

---

consumerism of cultures and families with sons look at dowries as a way to increase family wealth and acquire material things. This makes daughters expensive, especially for those who are poor. In contrast, when a son marries, the family accrues wealth from the new daughter-in-law's dowry. Box 2.2 tells the story of an Indian woman who rebelled against demands for increased dowry.

Son preference is also common in cultures such as India and China where it is the responsibility of the son to take care of elderly parents, whereas daughters usually take care of elderly in-laws. For instance, in rural India, 90 percent of elderly men and 82 percent of elderly women live with their sons (Narayan, 1993). In many parts of China, families are restricted to one-child only and son preference has led to femicide and the abandonment of girl children. Interestingly, in the last decade, daughters' value has grown in some parts of the world as rural daughters go to work in the city and send their money home to the family. There is some evidence of this pattern in rural China, Mexico, and Guatemala. Some researchers have noted that girl children receive more intrahousehold resource allocations when they have moneymaking potential. Indeed, several studies suggest that in developing countries such as India, rural females' survival chances are increased by their participation in the paid labor force (Papanek, 1990). The suggestion is that the female's economic value to the family is higher in cases in which she may bring in money, and consequently, the family invests more resources in her survival.

Although you might expect that a scarcity of females due to femicide might also increase their value, this has not yet occurred despite shortages of females available for marriage in some parts of the world. In general, shortages are dealt with by importing poor women from other regions or countries. These women are willing to relocate for purposes of economic survival.

Females as Property

When people are thought of as commodities or property, they are diminished and dehumanized and do not have the power to make their own life choices. In many cultures, a female is property—first of her father and then of her husband. These men decide her fate and she is expected to obey. In Pakistan, a father may take his daughter to court if she marries without his permission; the court may nullify the marriage and even charge the couple with the crime of having sex outside of marriage. In some countries, women are still objects of exchange between families—used to enhance a family's social status, to gain resources, or to settle disputes. In the United Arab Emirates and northern Africa, women follow parental orders to marry cousins so as to keep property in the family (Goodwin, 1994; Mertus, 1995). In Pakistan's North West Frontier Province and the tribal territories, a practice called **swara** persists (Amnesty International, 2002; DAWN, 2003). The practice involves handing over young girls and women to rival partners in order to settle conflicts. The idea is to end feuds between enemies by establishing a blood tie. In many parts of Ethiopia, women and girls are viewed as the property of male family members who may exchange them as they wish. The Ethiopia Women Lawyers' Association reports such cases as:

> The sixteen year-old girl that sought protection from the EWLA from a forced marriage. The girl was given shelter, but the police forcibly took her home to be married off. EWLA sought support from all relevant government officials who ordered that the marriage be stopped. The parents were jailed. But in the meantime, other family members enforced the marriage.
>
> In Oromia region, a young girl was given to an 80 year-old man. Her father took the old man's daughter. The first girl ran back to her home. Her father sent her back to the old man. The pattern of running away and being sent back continued. In the end, the girl killed her father.
>
> The practice of making the first wife the wife of the family. All the male relatives of the bridegroom have sex with the bride on the first day of the wedding. If the bride does not conceive within the wedding period, the practice continues until she becomes pregnant.
>
> Women being expected to give sexual services to their brothers-in-law when they stay overnight as well as to her husband's friends.
>
> Wife inheritance. Another example from the Gambela region involved exchange marriage when a man inherited the wives of his late brother.
> (African Women's Development and Communications Network, 2001)

As mentioned previously, the paying of dowries, common in India and Pakistan and parts of Africa, Portugal, China, Greece, and Turkey, is also reminiscent of women as property. Hundreds of years ago, dowries were property of the bride and provided her economic protection within the marriage. Women could not inherit land from their parents, and dowry was viewed as their inheritance. However, as currently practiced, dowries consist of goods

"I am a poor man, and this is how I can feed my large family. What else could I do? Many others are doing the same thing."
Afghan man that sold his 9- and 10-year-old daughters to wealthy opium poppy growers, 2003

or money *given to the groom and his family* by the bride's family. For example, in India, the parents arrange approximately 90 to 95 percent of marriages, and the parents of the bride must typically pay a dowry to the parents of the groom if it is requested. These dowries usually consist of material goods such as televisions and personal items such as jewelry, but sometimes they include money and land. Although the Indian Parliament outlawed dowry in 1961, the practice has actually spread as a way for families of sons to increase their wealth.

Brideprice (sometimes called *bridewealth* or *lobala*) is also common in the majority of African ethnic groups and is also practiced in parts of Papua New Guinea, India, and Afghanistan. The practice involves the groom giving money, goods, or livestock to the parents of the bride in return for her hand in marriage. In South Africa, even those who are highly educated often condone the practice. For example, university students condone the practice believing that it increases a husband's appreciation of his wife's worth, and keeps the divorce rate low since marriage is so expensive (Mwamwenda & Monyooe, 1997). Critics point out that brideprice forces women to stay in abusive marriages because divorce means their families will have to pay back the brideprice. Also, when a man has paid brideprice, he may view his wife as property that he has purchased to do with what he will (Women's International Network News, 2000). One particularly sad consequence of brideprice is that poverty drives some families to sell their very young daughters into marriage. For instance, in war-torn, poverty-stricken Afghanistan, the practice is on the rise and parents are selling their girls, aged 8 to 12, for $300 to $800 (RAWA, 2003).

Physical Violence Against Women

Violence is often "gendered" in that types of violence, such as rape and domestic violence, are experienced disproportionately by women. Violence against women is used to reinforce men's power over women, to keep women in their place, to remind them that men are "boss." The fact that it is common, accepted (or at least ignored), and that police and legal systems frequently fail to intervene, is an indication of women's lower status and power.

The United Nations *Declaration on the Elimination of Violence against Women* (1993) defines violence against women as "any act of gender-based violence that results in, or is likely to result in, physical, sexual, or mental harm or suffering to women, including threats of such acts, coercion or arbitrary deprivation of liberty, whether occurring in public or in private life." Gender violence is broadly defined. The United Nations Fund for Women (UNIFEM) suggests that violence against women includes: prenatal sex selection in favor of male babies, female infanticide, sexual abuse, female genital mutilation, sexual harassment in schools and the workplace, trafficking, forced prostitution, dowry-related violence, domestic violence, battering, and marital rape. Violence against women and girls occurs in every segment of society—regardless of class,

"If a man wants to marry a woman, the man gets a delegation of about ten men who go to the woman's home. When they reach there, they find another delegation of men from the woman's side. The speaker from the woman's side says the number of cows, goats, and money that are 'worth' their daughter and the speaker from the man's side says what they are willing to pay, the process of 'please reduce and you must increase' continues as though they are in a commercial or political negotiation."
Woman from Uganda, 2000

"Through violence men seek both to deny and destroy the power of women. Through violence men seek and confirm the devaluation and dehumanization of women."
Rhonda Copelon, professor of law and Co-Director of the International Women's Human Rights Clinic

cthnicity, culture, or country. In this section, the focus is on domestic violence, dowry death, honor killing, and rape.

Throughout the book you will see how women's social, political, and economic subordination are not only issues in and of themselves but are interrelated and influential in a variety of women's issues. The remainder of this chapter, which focuses on physical and sexual violence against women, shows how these factors combine to produce a situation in which women's human rights are violated. You will see how the perception of women as men's property contributes to their abuse by husbands, to war rape, and to the selling of daughters into prostitution or marriage. Women's lack of political power means that legal and police protections against domestic and sexual violence are often absent or minimal. Women's lower status leads to an acceptance of violence against them by families and authorities. Women's lack of economic power leads to prostitution, to women marketing themselves as mail-order brides, and to women staying in situations of sexual and physical abuse. The trafficking of women into prostitution and mail-order brides are discussed in Chapter 7.

November 25th is International Day for the Elimination of Violence Against Women

Domestic Violence

Domestic violence includes bodily harm, usually accompanied by verbal threats and harassment, emotional abuse or the destruction of property as means of coercion, control, revenge, or punishment on a person with whom the abuser is in an intimate relationship (Human Rights Watch, 1995). Domestic violence is a concern of feminists worldwide because it is exists in all regions, classes, and cultures. Reported rates vary by country but range from between 10 and 80 percent. Box 2.3 shows the incidence of domestic violence in a sample of countries.

The World Health Organization reports that 40 to 70 percent of women murdered in the United States, Canada, Australia, and Israel were killed by their husbands or male partners and that in nine Caribbean countries, 48 percent of women surveyed said their first sexual experience was forced or "somewhat forced" (United Nations, 2002). In the United States, battery is the leading cause of injury to adult women; close to 700,000 cases are reported each year (U.S. Department of Justice, 2002). In the Japanese government's first nationwide survey of domestic violence in 1999, one in twenty women reported life-threatening abuse at the hands of their husband and four times as many had experienced some sort of domestic violence (Magnier, 2002). Official estimates from Russia are that 12,000 women die each year from domestic violence and the leading women's rights organization in Pakistan concludes that upwards of 80 percent of women in that country experience domestic violence (Human Rights Watch, 2000). Surveys from Kenya indicate that 42 percent of women had been beaten by their husbands; in Papua New Guinea, 67 percent of rural women and 56 percent of urban women report being victimized by their husbands (Human Rights Watch, 1995). A third of Egyptian women report that they are beaten at home, and

BOX 2.3   *Prevalence of Physical Violence Against Women by An Intimate Partner 1991–1999*

	Last 12 Months	Ever
Australia	22%	—
Bangladesh	19	47%
Canada	3	29
Chile	23	—
Columbia	—	19
Egypt	—	34
Ethiopia	10	45
Korea	38	—
Mexico	27	27
Nicaragua	30	52
Nigeria	—	31
Norway	—	18
Palestine	48	—
Peru	31	—
Puerto Rico	—	48
Switzerland	6	—
Turkey	—	58
United Kingdom	12	30
United States	1	22

Source: http://unstats.un.org/unsd/demographic/ww2000/table6c.htm
Note: The UN cautions that studies varied in how physical violence was defined and that psychological and verbal abuse were not included. As well, the report mentions that these numbers are likely underestimations as many women were unable to be interviewed in private.
The U.S. National Domestic Violence Hotline number is: 1–800–799–SAFE

the penalty for killing an adulterous wife is typically one to three years in jail (Daniszewski, 1997).

Carillo (1992) links domestic violence against women to the socially constructed dependency of women on men (Carillo, 1992). This dependency is frequently economic and results from a multi-layered system of sex discrimination. First, much of women's labor is unpaid and therefore not valued. Second, even in paid jobs, women work for longer hours for lower pay with fewer benefits and less security. Women's dependency on men is more than economic, however. Carillo points out that women are trained to believe that their value is attached to the men in their lives—fathers, husbands, and sons. They are often ostracized if they disobey these men, and frequently social norms equate being a good woman with being an obedient woman. Bradley (1988, in Carillo, 1992, p. 109) said, "Threats of violence control women's minds as much as do acts of violence, making women act as their own jailers. This means that a woman makes her choices not on what she wants to do or believes is best, but on what she thinks her husband will allow her to do."

Lerner (1986) also points out that women are socially dependent on men. She says that class for men was and is based on their relationship to the means of production: Those who owned the means by which things are produced can dominate those who do not. However, the class position of women is generally consolidated and actualized through their sexual relationships with men. It is through men that women gain or are denied access to the means of production and to resources. Cross-culturally, women share the "unfreedom" of being sexually and reproductively controlled by men, although there are "degrees of unfreedom" ranging from the slave woman whose sexual and reproductive capacity was commodified as she herself was; to the slave-concubine, whose sexual performance might elevate her own status or that of her children; then to the "free" wife, whose sexual and reproductive services to one man of the upper classes entitled her to property and legal rights. (Lerner, 1986, p. 215)

Women's socioeconomic and psychological dependency on men makes it difficult for them to leave situations of violence or sexual harassment (sexual harassment is discussed in detail in Chapter 5). Adding to this problem is the fact that in many countries it is difficult for women to obtain a divorce and there is great social stigma associated with divorce. In comparison to men, a woman's status is significantly reduced if she is divorced, and this increases her dependence upon the marriage and her husband's power over her. For instance, in India, women have no right to matrimonial assets upon divorce, divorce renders women social pariahs, and abused women have few alternatives to remaining in an abusive marriage (Jaising, 1995). In the United Arab Emirates and in Iran, a divorced mother is only entitled to custody of her children until they are 7. Men may take second wives and divorce their wives without their wives' knowledge (Goodwin, 1994; Mirhosseini, 1995). Israeli women are not allowed to divorce their husbands if the husband refuses to grant the divorce; a husband's abandonment, disappearance, or incompetence is also not grounds for divorce. However, husbands may be granted a divorce even if the wife refuses (Shalev, 1995). In the Sudan, the man has the right to unfettered divorce, and once he says the words "You are divorced," a divorce takes place (Abdel Halim, 1995). In contrast, a woman must go to court and prove she is entitled to a divorce. After the divorce, there is a three-month period in which the husband may change his mind

"Every woman thinking of leaving worries about finances. Women find themselves forced back into abusive marriages because they can't earn a living."
Ritsuko Nomoto, Japanese woman that opened a restaurant to give battered women jobs.

and order the woman back. She is expected to comply. In Ireland—a country strongly influenced by the Roman Catholic Church, which is opposed to divorce—divorces were not granted until 1997. At that time there were an estimated 80,000 to 90,000 separated people who had been unable to divorce. Although now legal, divorce remains difficult for several reasons, aside from its stigma: Couples must be separated for at least four years, they must complete a rash of paperwork, and the court may still deny the petition for dissolution if it is deemed harmful to the family.

It is also important to recognize that the majority of countries do not provide assistance for women who want to leave abusive situations, making it difficult for women to do so. For example, despite the prevalence of domestic abuse in Japan, as of 2002, only thirty-five shelters for battered women existed (Magnier, 2002). If women's families do not support their leaving and they have nowhere to go and no way to survive outside of marriage, of course they will stay.

Women's activists often seek legal reform. In many countries, neither government laws nor the police protect women from domestic violence; it is viewed as a private family matter and a husband's right. For example, following years of activism, Japan enacted its first law against domestic violence in 2001 and the number of women's shelters grew from five in 1995, to thirty-five in 2002. Kenya enacted its first domestic violence bill in 2002. In 2003, in Pakistan, the Progressive Women's Association (PWA) presented a resolution to the Supreme Court demanding legislation on domestic violence against women and held a rally outside the Parliament. Malaysia passed its first domestic violence bill in 1994 after ten years of activism (UNIFEM, 2001a). Bills making domestic violence illegal were also considered in Zimbabwe and Kenya in 2002, and in Indonesia in 2003.

Unfortunately, laws prohibiting domestic abuse are little protection when police refuse to take men into custody and judges refuse to punish them. One such example is Uzbekistan where Uzbek authorities, committed to maintaining a low divorce rate, refuse to prosecute cases of domestic violence and tell abused women to go home to their husbands (Human Rights Watch, 2001a). Often, following the passage of legislation, women's groups have to work for the laws' implementation and enforcement. For instance, the Malaysian Women's Aid Organization works to strengthen implementation of Malaysia's domestic violence law and to make it easier for victims of violence to make complaints and leave their abusers (UNIFEM, 2001). Prior to activism, women had to go to three different places to make their complaint, had to pay significant amounts of money, and had to endure officials that encouraged them to return to their husbands. Activists also call for documentation of the problem of domestic violence, lobby for and create legal and community services for battered women, and educate the public about the problem. Examples include the South African program that educates young people, educators, and parents about violence against women in dating relationships and in Peru, a program that broadcasts fictional stories based on real cases to generate discussion and increase awareness. In Japan, grassroots

BOX 2.4   *Activist Profile: Doris Solis Carrion, Vice-Mayor of the City of Cuenca, Ecuador*

"Violence against women has always been at the core of my work," says Doris Solis Carrion. "Six out of every ten women in Ecuador are victims of violence within their own households and the cost of such violence is enormous: it impacts women, children, and society as a whole. So from very early on it was clear to me that eliminating violence against women was the first step towards social development and poverty eradication in my country."

Born and raised in Cuenca, Ecuador's third-largest city, Ms. Carrion and her eight brothers and sisters, grew up with a university professor father active in a progressive political party, and a mother involved in the women's movement. At 15, Ms. Carrion became an activist, working with the indigenous population that constitutes 40 percent of her country's population and with the women's movement.

For years Ms. Carrion worked as executive director of the NGO SENDAS (which stands for Services for an Alternative Development in the South) and as co-founder of the Programme of Gender Studies at the University of Cuena. Two years ago she became the first woman to be Vice Mayor of the municipality of Cuenca where she was instrumental in instituting Cuenca's Equal Opportunities

Plan, which includes strengthening the system of social, legal, and health services for battered women, implementing education and sensitization campaigns for law-enforcement agencies, and drafting municipal laws committing the local government to eradicating violence.

"It took a lot of work just to create awareness of violence against women," explains Ms. Carrion, "and by 1995 the issue was addressed by a national law which later became part of Ecuador's constitution." But Ms. Carrion notes that despite this legal victory, "implementation is weak. Laws by themselves are not enough, what is needed is a comprehensive program to prevent and deal with the legal, psychological and health issues attached to violence." As a result of her efforts, the municipality of Cuenca established information and education programs, psychological assistance projects, a hotline and a shelter for abused women. "Today we have an Assessment of Gender Inequalities, an Equal Opportunities Plan and a wide-ranging plan to prevent violence against women," says Ms. Carrion.

Source: UNIFEM http://www.unifem.org/

women's organizations conduct and disseminate research on the problem, and conduct community forums, workshops, and exhibits. Box 2.4 profiles Doris Solis Carrion of Ecuador, an activist who has made a difference in reducing domestic violence.

Dowry Death

Dowry death refers to the murder of wives by husbands or in-laws in India and Pakistan. It occurs when the bride's family is unable to provide the agreed-upon dowry, when the husband's family wants to get rid of her so that they may get another dowry from a new bride to increase their family's wealth, or when a woman does not produce a son. Her husband or his family then stages her death.

In India, dowry deaths are sometimes called bride burnings because most victims are held over the cooking stove until their saris catch fire. In 2001, the Indian government reported over 7,000 of these fatalities. Forbes (1987) notes that dowry deaths are related to the historically low valuation of women and a modern consumerism (influenced by the West) that has produced a new way of exploiting women's dependency. Dowry deaths are also an example of viewing women as property. Seeing women as objects of exchange between two families is responsible for the killing of wives who do not bring enough money or material goods to the marriage (Mosse, 1993). Since the 1970s, dowry deaths have been a leading concern of Indian feminists. They have raised public awareness of the problem, and in 1986 won their battle to strengthen the Dowry Prohibition Act of 1961. Unfortunately, these activists must continue to fight for enforcement (Bumiller, 1990; Forbes, 1987; Ray, 1999).

Honor Killing

Rana Husseini, reporter for the *Jordan Times,* received the 1998 Reebok Human Rights Award at age 26. Despite the risk of serious physical harm, she continues to investigate and write about the practice of honor killing in Jordan.

In 1998, Sarhan Abdullah of Jordan shot his sister in the head four times. He murdered his sister because her brother-in-law raped her and she therefore brought shame to the family. He was released from jail after serving six months (Jamison, 2003). This is an example of **honor killing,** a tradition whereby a man is obliged to kill a close female blood relative if she does something that is believed to tarnish the honor of the family. The most common transgression is for an unmarried woman to have sex, but marital infidelity (or suspected infidelity), seeking a divorce, flirting, being raped, and dating without parental approval, can all be seen as offenses dishonoring the family. The United Nations Commission on Human Rights reports honor killings in Bangladesh, Brazil, Ecuador, Egypt, India, Israel, Jordan, Pakistan, Morocco, Turkey, Palestine, and Uganda (Mayell, 2002).

Because governments do not keep track of honor crimes, and because independent investigators face danger, the number of victims is unknown. However, the UN estimates at least 5,000 deaths annually (Jamison, 2003). Honor killings are seen as a way to keep moral stability and are therefore rarely punished and, when they are, the punishment is usually minimal. On average in Pakistan, there are two honor killings daily, but only 20 percent of cases are prosecuted; the law states that in murder cases, the family of the victim may compromise with the killer (who is in this case a relative) (Bonner, 2002; Pakistan Press International, 2003). Brazil still fails to prosecute and convict men who have commited honor killings because of alleged infidelity (Human Rights Watch, 2001b) and, in Jordan perpetrators of honor crimes receive sentences of three months to one year (Human Rights Watch, 2000). Jordanian women's and human rights activists have collected over 13,000 signature on petitions calling on Parliament to end honor killings and 5,000 people (mostly women) rallied at the Parliament for legal changes (Human Rights Watch, 2000; Jamison, 2003). Turkey recently repealed a law that reduced the sentences of those who commit honor crimes, hoping that it would help with their bid to join the European Union (Zaman, 2003).

Sexual Violence and Exploitation

Women routinely experience sexual assault in ways that have no immediate parallels for men (Chowdhury et al., 1994). Women are disproportionately sexually victimized (as in the case of rape) and sexually exploited (sexually abused for others' sexual gratification or for financial gain, as in the case of prostitution and pornography). This is further evidence of women's lower power and status, for if women and men were equal, women would not be sexually subjugated, and, if they were, there would be severe consequences. Barry (1995) summed it up well when she said that **sexual exploitation** objectifies women by reducing them to sex; this **sexual objectification** incites violence against women and reduces them to commodities for market exchange: "In the fullness of human experience, when women are reduced to their bodies, and in the case of sexual exploitation to sexed bodies, they are treated as lesser, as other, and thereby subordinated" (Barry, 1995, p. 24). When sex is treated as a thing to be taken, or to be bought, the human being is rendered into a thing, and her dignity and humanity are destroyed (Barry, 1995).

Rape

Rape haunts the lives of women on a daily basis: It is the stranger approaching on the street, the violent husband or partner at home (Niarchos, 1995). All over the world, you will find women's activists working to strengthen rape laws and their enforcement, educating men to see rape as wrong, training police in sensitive procedures for handling cases, and providing assistance to rape victims, largely through rape crisis centers.

The U.S. Department of Justice estimates that more than 350 rapes a year will occur on a college campus with a population of 10,000 female students.

Rape is a concern of feminists for five main reasons:

1. *Rape is a very real threat to women everywhere.* For instance, in the United States, one in four women experience a sexual assault in their lifetime and seventy-four women are raped every hour (National Sexual Violence Resource Center, 2003). In India, a woman is raped every thirty-five minutes and out of every hundred cases, only ten are reported to police (Vasudev & Renuka, 2002). For more information, see the Appendix while keeping in mind that rape is one of the most underreported of crimes.

2. *Rape laws are weak and poorly enforced.* Most of the world's rape laws conceive of rape as an act against the property of another man— either the father of the unmarried woman or the husband of the married woman (Mosse, 1993). Traditionally, rape is condemned as a violation of a man's honor and exclusive right to sexual possession of his woman/property, and not because it is an assault on a woman (Copelon, 1995). In most countries, rape victims receive little support and feel shamed and humiliated, which results in secondary

"Crimes against women will halve if they are careful about what they wear and know their limits."
R.S. Gupta, Police Chief of Delhi, India 2003, where rape is on the rise

victimization from family, the police, and the legal system. In extreme cases, like Pakistan, women may even be charged with the crime of having sex outside of marriage. As you read earlier, in some countries, victims may even be killed to preserve the family's honor. It is unsurprising then, that women often keep rape a secret; the woman who is raped is likely to be blamed for seducing her rapist, she brings shame upon her family, and may become unmarriageable because she is no longer a virgin.

3. *The threat of rape limits women's freedom of movement and denies them control over their sexuality.* More than any other crime, fear of rape leads women, consciously and unconsciously, to restrict their movements and their life choices or, alternatively, to prepare for battle (Niarchos, 1995).

4. *Many of the victims of rape are girl children and adolescents, often raped by an adult relative or acquaintance* (Neft & Levine, 1998). The problem is especially bad in parts of Africa, such as Zimbabwe and South Africa, where unscrupulous folk healers prescribe sex with a virgin to treat AIDS, and the practice has resulted in high infection rates in young girls (Murphy, 1998).

5. *The fact that men can and do rape women, whereas the reverse is not true, intimidates women and gives power to men.* Some feminists, such as Brownmiller (1986), view the threat of rape as the basis of men's power over women. Rape is an expression of dominance, power, and contempt, a rejection of women's right to self-determination (Niarchos, 1995). The threat of rape also makes women dependent on fathers, brothers, or husbands to protect them. This places women in a subordinate position to men. Brownmiller (1986) suggests that, historically, marriage and women's subjugation by men arose because women needed men to protect them from other men. Furthermore, says Brownmiller (1986), the price a woman paid for this protection was her male protector's exclusive ownership of her body.

War Rape

War magnifies the gendered structure of violence (Nikolic-Ristanovic, 1996). During times of war, women often experience great hardship. War often displaces women, and their dependent children, from their homes and makes them refugees, leaves them without husbands and fathers, and makes meeting basic needs difficult. If this weren't bad enough, they also face the increased prospect of rape.

Writings from as early as 420 c.e. document **war rape,** the rape of women during wartime. During World War II, Moroccan soldiers raped Italian women, Japanese soldiers raped Korean women, and Nazi soldiers raped Jewish women. In the 1970s, Pakistani soldiers raped Bengali women. In the

1980s, war rapes occurred in the Central American countries of El Salvador and Guatemala. In the 1990s, Bosnian Serb soldiers raped between 20,000 and 50,000 Muslim women in the former Yugoslavia. In Somalia's civil war, all factions raped women to punish rival factions. In Haiti the military raped female family members of male "subversives" and raped women's rights activists. Indian soldiers raped women in the rebellious Kashmir territory. In Peru, rapes were committed by government security forces as well as by their opposition (soldiers of the Shining Path resistance). An estimated 250,000 to 500,000 women and girls were raped during a civil war in less than 100 days in Rwanda in 1994. In 2003, reports from Liberia, Zimbabwe and Burma indicate that government soldiers used rape to terrorize and control groups opposing the government (Martin & Apple, 2003; Simmons, 2003; UN Integrated Regional Information Networks, 2003). A civil war in Congo also led to the rape of thousands of women in the period from 1998 to 2003; in fact, it is estimated that one in three women experienced gang rape (Wax, 2003).

The UN identifies four kinds of war rape, summarized in Figure 2.1 (UN Integrated Regional Information Networks, 2003). One type, **genocidal rape,** such as that seen in Rwanda and the Balkans, is intended to destroy an ethnic or political group perceived as the enemy. **Opportunistic rape** occurs when men take advantage of the breakdown of law and order that may occur during wartime to commit crimes against women, knowing it is unlikely they will face consequences. **Political rape** punishes individuals, families, or communities that hold different political views. When daughters or wives are raped to punish their male relatives, political rape is a variation on the woman-as-property theme. The desecration of the female is viewed as the torture of the male (Chesler, 1996). For instance, during the war in the former Yugoslavia, women were raped to "pay" for the attitudes and behaviors of their husbands, sons, brothers, or fathers (Nikolic-Ristanovic, 1996). The rape of women during wartime is not merely a matter of being in the wrong place at the wrong time (Chinkin, 1993). Women are the male enemy's property, and they are used as an instrument to defeat or punish the enemy (Brownmiller, 1986; Nikolic-Ristanovic, 1996). Many of the rapes occur in the presence of the victim's family, the local population, or other victims, and many involve sexual torture and sadism (Niarchos, 1995).

FIGURE 2.1 *Four Types of War Rape*

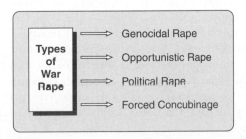

BOX 2.5   *The War Rape of Marijana*

I met Marijana in a hospital in Zagreb. Her doctor told me she had arrived from Bosnia several days earlier. Though our interview was difficult, 17-year-old Marijana was beyond tears: dry, tense little face, little child's body. She didn't exactly tell me what had happened; I had to coax the words out of her, one by one. One day in April, Serb irregulars came to the village, near Tesanj, in central Bosnia, where Marijana, a Muslim Croat, lived with her family. Marijana, her mother, and her 7-year-old sister were tending their vegetable garden. The soldiers raped Marijana and her mother there, then loaded Marijana on a truck, along with twenty-three other women from the village. This was the last time she saw her mother or her sister. Raping continued on the truck. The soldiers took the women to an improvised camp in the woods that operated as a military brothel. Women between the ages of 12 and 25 were kept in one room and raped daily. Marijana became pregnant in the first month. After four months, the soldiers let her and seven other visibly pregnant women go.

Source: Kuzmanovic, 1995.

Forced concubinage involves the kidnapping of girls and women to wash, cook, serve, and have sex with soldiers and militia. It takes the form of forced prostitution in "rape camps." For example, during World War II, the Japanese enslaved between 200,000 to 400,000 Korean, Filipino, Chinese, Indonesian, and Dutch women in "comfort stations" for sexual use by Japanese soldiers (Copelon, 1995). Ninety percent of these women died in captivity (Copelon, 1995). In Uganda in the late 1980s, rebels forced girls 12 years and older into sexual slavery; later these rebels received amnesty under a government program. Human rights organizations also documented military rape camps in Zimbabwe and Burma in the early 2000s (Martin & Apple, 2003; UN Integrated News Network, 2003). Box 2.5 offers an account of forced prostitution in the Bosnian conflict in the 1990s.

Until 1996, the UN postwar courts had never prosecuted sexual assault as a crime of war. Although postwar courts did hear evidence of rape, it was treated as secondary to other abuses. This changed on June 27, 1996, when a United Nations tribunal indicted eight Bosnian Serb military and police officers in connection with the rapes of Muslim women during the Bosnian war. The tribunal's chief prosecutor, Richard Goldstone, noted that "rape has never been the concern of the international community. . . . We have to deal openly with these abuses" (Simons, 1996). In 1998, the majority of the world's governments agreed to form the International Criminal Court (ICC), a permanent war tribunal. The ICC is to ensure redress for and protection against human rights violations committed in the course of war. Initially, the draft treaty did not acknowledge rape as a war crime. However, women's activists and legal experts worked to have women's concerns incorporated into the treaty establishing the ICC (Frankson, 1998). They formed the Women's Cau-

"Sexual violence constitutes a weapon of war."
Radhika Coomaraswamy, Special Rappoteur of the UN High Commisioner on Human Rights on the Issue of Violence Against Women

cus for Gender Justice in February 1997 and received the backing of more than 300 nongovernmental organizations from around the world. In 2001, the International Criminal Tribunal for the former Yugoslavia indicted eighty men for war rape, and in February 2002, three Bosnian Serbs were the first to be jailed for war sex crimes in a case involving sex enslavement (Taylor, 2002).

Prostitution

Prostitution is plainly about the sexual objectification of women, and it is clearly driven by economics. It is about women as commodities to be bought and sold and about how women's few economic options may force them into prostitution. The effect of prostitution on women is overlooked by governments such as Thailand, Korea, and the Philippines who use prostitution to boost tourism and their economies, and by militaries, such as the U.S. Army, who see "sexual recreation" as vital to the well being and morale of their troops. Although the prostitute herself typically earns barely enough to survive, an extended network of people profit from her body and her labor: The police and other government officials fine prostitutes or receive bribes to look the other way; pimps; bar, brothel, and hotel owners get a cut of her wages; airlines, travel agencies, and foreign customers also benefit. It is estimated that pimps control 80 to 95 percent of prostitution. These pimps find naive and needy young women, manipulate them into prostitution, and then take the majority of their money (Barry, 1995). Barry (1995) argues that prostitution is a form of sexual slavery because women and girls are held over time for sexual use and because getting out of prostitution requires escape. Worldwide, most prostitutes are women with no other economic choices because of multi-layered systems of sex discrimination. The greatest numbers of prostitutes are found in countries like Thailand, Brazil, and Hungary where there are few jobs for women and where **sexual tourism** is a major source of cash for economic development. Sexual tourism is discussed at greater length in Chapter 7, "Women and Globalization."

Activists say that cultural attitudes that consider prostitution a victimless crime, or that suggest women are sexual objects, must be changed. For instance, in Thailand, studies indicate that between 80 and 87 percent of Thai men have had sex with a prostitute and commercial sex is viewed as a legitimate form of entertainment and sexual release (Bales, 2002). Likewise, in the interest of keeping morale high, the U.S. Army permitted the **military sexploitation of women** in Southeast Asia. U.S. military bases in the Philippines, Korea, and in Okinawa, Japan, coordinated with government authorities and entrepreneurs to provide U.S. servicemen with sex (Enloe, 1996). The U.S. military often set up clinics where women were licensed and monitored for sexually transmitted diseases and received "sexual health" identification cards. In general, however, the women were not given information about contraception or the prevention of sexually transmitted diseases (Coronel & Rosca, 1993). In the Philippines alone approximately 50,000 children have

The persistence and painstaking research of Yoshiaki Yoshimi, a Japanese history professor, was instrumental in getting the Japanese government to admit that Japanese soldiers had used girls and women from Korea and China as "comfort women." The Japanese government had covered up the situation for more than forty years.

"Eradicating violence against women requires coordinated action and commitment by many actors; including governments, civil society, the judiciary, police, media, healthcare workers, educators, and the international community."
Noeleen Heyzer, Executive Director of UNIFEM

been fathered by U.S. servicemen over the past five decades (Coronel & Rosca, 1993).

In 2000, the U.S. military came under fire for allowing soldiers at Camp Casey in South Korea to frequent the dozens of clubs offering sexual services exclusively to U.S. soldiers (Demick, 2002). The women are mostly trafficked from the Philippines and the former Soviet Union. They are told they will be waitresses or entertainers, but shortly after arrival, find that they are expected to provide sexual services. Debt bondage is common, with most of their wages confiscated by club owners to pay for their plane ticket, rent, and food. They are held under slave-like conditions. The Korean Special Tourism Association lobbied the government to allow to the import of foreign women, saying that it was essential to prevent American GIs from harassing and raping Korean women.

Explaining Women's Low Status and Power

At this point in the chapter you are no doubt wondering why women are so disadvantaged economically, politically, legally, and socially relative to males. Why is it that despite women's respected role as childbearers and child-rearers, they are still so often treated as second-class citizens? No one is sure, but to some extent it appears to be an artifact of a gendered division of labor and the rise of economies based on exchange.

At one time, all cultures had no means of birth control and no infant formula. This, along with males' greater size and strength, made some types of work more appropriate for males, and some more appropriate for females. Women's work became concentrated in the **private sphere** or domestic domain of the home, and men performed the labor in the **public sphere** outside the home because they were not constrained by childcare (Sanday, 1974). In other words, a gendered division of labor arose and women ended up doing the work that was compatible with the unavoidable female life course of bearing and nursing children (Chafetz, 1990; Lerner, 1986).

"Clearly both men and women have the biological potential for many different kinds of behaviors. But like the external armor or shell that encases insects and other anthropods, androcratic social organization encases both halves of humanity in rigid and hierarchic roles that stunt their development."
Riane Eisler

Once a gendered division of labor arose, people then constructed **gender stereotypes** (beliefs about the qualities of each gender) and **gender norms** (social rules regarding what is appropriate for each gender to do). These were then passed on culturally (through legends and religious texts for instance) and taught to children in order to prepare them for adulthood. Conformity to gender-role expectations was maintained by granting social status and approval to conformers and by ostracizing violators. In short, people develop beliefs about the qualities of groups of people from what they see people in those groups doing and what they are told by their culture. Once people develop such beliefs, in this case beliefs regarding differences between females and males, the beliefs operate as expectations regarding appropriate roles for people from those groups (Ridgeway, 2001). The gender roles lead to gender stereotypes and the gender stereotypes promote gendered social roles that are maintained through social approval and disapproval (Burn, 1996; Eagly, 1987). These processes appear to operate in all

FIGURE 2.2 *The Reciprocal Relationship Between Gender Roles and Gender*

Gender Stereotypes ⟺ Gender Roles

cultures and explain how gender is socially constructed and maintained. Because gender is socially constructed, it can be changed if social structures are changed—admittedly something that is easier said than done.

It is true that a gendered division of labor is not in and of itself bad; sometimes it makes sense for females to do some things and males to do others. After all, men don't get pregnant and they can't breast feed infants. Unfortunately, over time, in most cultures, men's dominance in the public sphere led to them having greater property rights and political power, which they then used to sanction men's right to control the lives of women. Men's control of the public sphere, their greater size, and women's economic dependence on men meant that women couldn't do much about it, especially since they were occupied by their private sphere responsibilities.

Some theorists trace the development of patriarchy to the Neolithic period when agriculture developed and the labor of children was needed to increase production and further surpluses. At that point women came to be viewed as commodities—resources to be acquired, traded, and controlled (Lerner, 1986). Others have argued that males needed to control women in order to ensure that the children were theirs, as they did not want to support another man's children. The devaluing of women's work relative to men is linked to the development of societies based on money. Once this happened, men's labor appeared to have more value because women's labor was largely for the family's use (**private use value**) whereas men's labor yielded money or the exchange of goods, and thereby had **exchange value** (Glenn, 1992). Power and status, it seems, became increasingly tied to the ability to make money, and to control of material resources in the public sphere. Women's mothering and household duties consequently reduced their economic and political power as their energies were directed toward the children and home (Bem, 1993; Rosaldo, 1974).

Up until the late twentieth century, most anthropologists assumed that male-dominated societies had always been the norm. This belief arose out of a male bias in anthropology, one that viewed the world through patriarchal lenses. Slocum (1975) was one of the first to note a male bias in anthropology. According to her, historically, anthropologists assumed that most uniquely human behaviors—such as tool making, art, cooperation, and spoken language—arose out of early male hunting and that females contributed relatively little to human evolution. However, while males were out hunting and allegedly developing such skills as cooperation and inventing things such as language, tools, and weapons, females were hardly sitting around popping out babies and doing little else. Too little attention, Slocum says, has been

"To look for origins is, in the end, to think that what we are today is something other than the product of our history and our present social world, and more particularly, that our gender systems are primordial, transhistorical, and essentially unchanging in their roots."
Michelle Rosaldo

paid to the skills required for the gathering of food (important long before hunting) and the raising of dependent young. Tools were probably developed by females to dig up roots and tubers, to open nuts, and to free the hands while carrying a baby. And, just as males had to communicate in order to hunt together, females had to communicate in order to gather food and fuel together and to train their young.

Today's anthropologists generally agree that in the foraging societies of early history, which covered much more time than the 120,000 years or so from the Neolithic to the present, the sexes were probably complementary and of equal importance (Ehrenberg, 1989). As Gross (1996) says, it is difficult to imagine that humanity could have survived if early humans wasted female productivity and intelligence. Cultures in which women and men were basically equal were also common to hunter-gatherer and horticultural societies prior to colonization (Eisler, 1987; Kehoe, 1983; Leacock, 1981; Sacks, 1982; Sanday, 1981). Even today there are some cultures with egalitarian gender relations. Examples include the Ju/'hoansi people of the Kalahari Desert, the Mbuti Pygmies of Zaire, and the Vanatinai people who live on a small island southeast of Papua New Guinea (Bonvillian, 2001; Renzetti & Curran, 1995).

Some writers argue that in ancient times **matriarchies,** or societies in which women had greater power than men, were common (cf. Bachofen, 1967; Cavin, 1985; Davis, 1971; Diner, 1975). Archeologist Marija Gimbutas (1991) extensively catalogued archeological evidence in favor of the view that matriarchies were common during the Neolithic period in Old Europe. Paleolithic foraging societies, Chatal Huyuk (a village in what is now Turkey), Old Europe, ancient megalithic cultures, and especially Crete are often discussed by advocates of this position, because there is evidence (much in the form of sculptures) that numerous, powerful goddesses were worshiped (Gross, 1996).

Many feminists are attracted to the view that matriarchies or egalitarian societies were common at one time. They would like to show that a world where women have power is possible and that, despite patriarchy's current domination of social systems, patriarchy is not as natural as it may appear. As Eisler said in her popular 1987 book *The Chalice and the Blade,* evidence from art, archeology, religion, social science, history, and many other fields show that "war and the war of the sexes are neither divinely nor biologically ordained. And it provides verification that a better future is possible—and is in fact firmly rooted in the haunting drama of what actually happened in our past" (p. xv).

Bamberger (1974) points out that, to some, the fact that there are no *existing* matriarchal or egalitarian cultures is proof that these forms are ineffective. (Box 2.6 provides examples of matriarchal societies today.) Otherwise, the argument goes, these societies would not be extinct. Eisler (1987) responds to this by suggesting that the span of human cultural evolution is too short to make such a judgment. According to her view, patriarchy represents a 5,000-year maladaptive "detour"—maladaptive because patri-

"Men and women live on a stage, on which they act out their assigned roles, equal in importance. The play cannot go on without both performers. Neither of them 'contributes' more or less to the whole; neither is marginal or dispensable. But the stage set is conceived, painted, and defined by men. Men have written the play, have directed the show . . . assigned themselves the most interesting, most heroic parts."
Gerda Lerner

"The fact that some male-dominated religions have goddesses undercuts the thesis that there is a direct correlation between the presence of goddesses and high status for women."
Rita Gross

BOX 2.6   *Do Matriarchies Exist Today?*

In 1995, Juanita Darling, *Los Angeles Times* journalist, wrote that matriarchy flourishes in the town of Juchitán, Mexico. In the tradition of the pre-Colombian Zapotec empire, women dominate public economic activities, such as buying and selling products that are mostly produced by men. They also either make or participate in all decisions regarding the household and typically control the family money because men are believed to be incompetent when it comes to family finances. Unlike in most other parts of Mexico, women are not pressured to marry or to put up with a difficult husband. When a wife feels that her husband is not doing his share, she prefers to be alone. As one woman said, "The women in other places are submissive. They are tied to a man. Well, I am not going to beg a man to give me money to buy bread. Women here work. That is the base of our economy." Art, literature, and formal politics are seen as the domains of males. Politics are one of the few areas in which men occupy leadership positions.

Lugo Lake, in a remote corner of southern China, is another place that appears to have a matriarchal society. Property and names pass from mother to daughter, and the women rarely marry. Men engage in few productive activities; for the most part, it is the women who earn and control the money and grow the food. Men have no ownership of the children they father. The women of Lugo Lake like their traditions. They point out that their self-sufficiency means that they may choose men based on love, unlike outsider women who must choose based on whether prospective husbands can provide for them. As is the case in Juchitán, the men do hold most of the formal political posts, making decisions outside of the village but not within it.

Source: Darling, 1995; Farley, 1998.

archy's emphasis on dominance and violence may lead to the ultimate destruction of the earth and humankind. She further notes that cultural progression is not in fact linear, but rather has always been characterized by periods of advancement, and then regression. To solve our mounting global problems, Eisler (1987) believes that we must reject patriarchy and its emphasis on violence. Instead, we should choose to structure our societies in ways that are "more sexually egalitarian" and that emphasize the "life-generating and nurturing powers of the universe."

Many feminist anthropologists do not think that the anthropological evidence supports the idea that matriarchies and egalitarian societies were at any time common (Duley & Edwards, 1986; Ruth, 1995). For instance, Bamberger (1974) points out that the myths that tell of female-dominated societies typically conclude with women losing their power because of incompetence, unethical conduct, or weakness. In other words, the very myths that are often used as evidence of matriarchy can, upon closer examination, be used to deny women power. Or, as Rosaldo and Lamphere (1974) say,

> Elaborate female burial rituals might, for example, indicate a world in which women were the rulers; but they could equally be the remains of wives or mistresses, concubines of male elites, or women who became heads of state in lieu of male heirs in a royal family. Female sculptures may

represent goddesses, but there are historically documented and well-
studied contemporary societies that manifest female fertility cults while at
the same time placing political power in the hands of men. (p. 3)

To further illustrate, imagine that we are all vaporized by aliens who leave our
buildings and other creations intact. They land in the United States. There
they see billboards and magazines such as *Playboy,* videos, and so on plastered
with images of women. They might conclude from this that women dominated the society and were worshiped. However, the truth at time of vapor-
ization is that women in the United States held a minority of political and
business power positions—for example, only 13 percent of the U.S. Congress
and 4 percent of corporate executive officers are female. Although most
agree that the ancient world included many powerful and impressive goddesses, some believe that those in favor of the matriarchal hypothesis infer
more from the material artifacts than perhaps they should (Gross, 1996).

We will never know for sure whether matriarchies or egalitarian societies
were at any time common. As Eisler herself points out, the thousands of cave
drawings and sculptures depicting women could be ancient analogues for today's *Playboy* magazine, or they could be evidence of goddess worship and the
veneration of women's life-giving abilities. Eisler believes the latter. Furthermore, she makes the case that, in general, archeologists and anthropologists
have interpreted the evidence in ways that fit their stereotypes of prehistoric
peoples and that were consistent with their own views of man as dominator
and woman as secondary. Of course, we can also accuse Eisler of letting her
pro-female biases tilt her reading of the archeological record. However, even
if you disagree with Eisler's interpretation, remember that this does not mean
that we cannot move toward greater equality. Likewise, remember that even
if you agree with Eisler, this does not mean that steps toward gender equality
will occur without concerted effort. As Lerner (1986) says, "the creation of
compensatory myths of the distant past of women will not emancipate women
in the present and future" (p. 36). Regardless, activism, as well as a thorough
knowledge and understanding of modern cultures, is required to bring about
change.

Conclusion

This chapter documented women's lower power and status but is in no way
intended to suggest that men are by nature evil beings intent on the oppression of women. Rather, as you will see throughout the book, men's individual, intentional acts of dominance over women are the reflections of cultures'
overall systems of gender power relations. As Lips (1991) notes, the occurrence of many forms of routine oppression of women by men is mindless and
unintentional, often unrecognized by either the perpetrator or the victim. Individuals, more or less unaware of the structure of power that surrounds
them, participate in, maintain, and are limited by the power structures of

their societies. For instance, many cultures define masculinity in ways that encourage the denigration of women and define femininity in terms of submissiveness and subordination to men. Both females and males are socialized into cultures that emphasize men's power over women and are taught by their parents and other agents of socialization (such as peers), to participate in traditional gender systems.

It is also important to realize that it is not uniquely male to create groups in which some individuals have greater power and status than do others. Women often discourage their girl children from challenging traditional gender relations and they often participate in the social systems that oppress women. For instance, it is usually adult women that perform the physically traumatizing genital mutilations of girls common in some countries. Similarly, the brokers that trick young women into sexual slavery are sometimes women, and women of the upper classes often exploit women of the lower classes (especially those of other ethnicities) for household labor. As you will see throughout the book, to override the human inclination to exploit and dominate other humans and justify it by seeing the "victims" as "lesser" generally takes a great deal of political and social activism.

To suggest that women have limited power and status in comparison to men is not to overlook their great strength. Women are really quite remarkable—carrying on, often under conditions of great adversity, in order to keep their families going. Although their lives are frequently hard, they find pleasure in their friends and family, and pride in their strength. Also, despite barriers to their political activity, they fight for their rights, and they have brought about significant change in the last fifty years through their efforts. For instance, there are many organizations working on the issues discussed in this chapter. War Against Rape (WAR) is a Pakistani women's organization dedicated to providing legal, medical, psychological, and moral support to victims of rape; to creating awareness about violent crimes against women; and to keeping up the pressure on government and law enforcement in the prevention and handling of rape cases. WAR's activism was an important factor in the establishment of special women's police stations in Pakistan. Forum Against Oppression of Women (FAOW) is a group based in Bombay, India, which works on a variety of issues including rape, dowry, wife beating, and sexual harassment. FAOW networks with other women's groups, lobbies the government for change, raises consciousness, and helps individual women escape abusive situations. The Mifumi Project in Uganda has as its mission the reform of bride price. These are just a few examples.

The following chapters pick up on some themes started here. For instance, Chapters 5, 6, and 7 return to the topic of women's labor and the feminization of poverty. Chapter 8 shows how in some cases, religion is an agent of patriarchy. Chapters 9, 10, and 11 all explore aspects of women's political activity and empowerment. The next chapter, Chapter 3, explores how women's power and status are affected by their role as "reproducer" and the importance of reproductive freedom for the achievement of gender equality.

> "It's not governments or superheroes that will change the world—it's ordinary people who realize that governments and superheroes aren't doing anything."
> *Lauryn Oates, age 20, Canadian Human Rights Activist*

Study Questions

1. What is gender stratification?

2. What evidence does the chapter provide for the idea that women have less economic and political power than men? Why does this matter?

3. What evidence does the chapter offer for the idea that women are frequently viewed as the property of men? How is this an indicator of their lower status?

4. What is son preference? What are its effects, and why does it occur?

5. How common is domestic violence? How is domestic violence linked to women's social dependency on men, and why is it difficult for women to leave abusive situations?

6. Why are feminists so concerned about the rape of women?

7. How do the world's rape laws and war rape reflect the perception that women are the property of men?

8. What is sexual exploitation? How is the sexual exploitation of women evidence of their lower power and status? What is the role of economics in the sexual exploitation of women?

9. How is women's power in the home influenced by how much money they earn and legal and social views of divorce?

10. What does Lerner mean when she says that women share the unfreedom of being sexually and reproductively controlled by men but that there are "degrees of unfreedom"?

11. What is the likely explanation as to how patriarchy came about?

Discussion Questions and Activities

1. In most cultures, it is expected that women will take their husband's name upon marriage, and most women do (in the United States about 90 percent do). Does this tendency reduce a female's value in her family of origin because she doesn't "carry on the family name"? Does this practice contribute to the perception that a woman is the property of her husband and secondary to him? What do you think of the practice of women taking their husband's name upon marriage? How about how fathers "give their daughters away" at the wedding and how the family of the bride is expected to pay for the wedding?

2. The chapter stated that women are socialized to believe that their value is attached to the men in their lives and that this is one of the factors that contributes to women's abuse by men. Some researchers have suggested that women feel like they must have a husband or boyfriend to have any social value; therefore, women will put up with a lot rather than be

without a man. Do you know women who fit this model? How is your answer influenced by your culture? How is it influenced by your generation? Would it be different if you were older or younger?

3. Some researchers have argued that paradigms used to explain lower female status may reflect a Western cultural bias with its denigration of domesticity and the devaluation of informal power. What do you think? Are women really lower in status and power, or is their status and power just different from men's? Explain your answer.

4. This chapter discussed women's status in generalities, when in fact there is great diversity not only across countries but within them based on geographic location, religion, ethnicity, and social class. Interview a woman from another culture using questions developed from the topics covered in this chapter. Make sure you ask her how long she lived in the other culture, whether where she lived was rural or urban, and what social class she is from. Share with her the information about women's status in her country of origin (see the Appendix) and ask for her thoughts.

Activist Websites of Interest

Africa Feel Free Network

http://www.feelfreenetwork.org

UNIFEM's Global Campaign to Eliminate Violence Against Women

http://www.unifem.undp.org/campaign/violence

Informational Websites of Interest

WomenWatch

http://www.un.org/womenwatch

UN policy paper on various forms of violence against women

http://www.un.org/rights/dpi1772e.htm

UN's Declaration on the Elimination of Violence against women

http://www.umn.edu/humanrts/instree/e4devw.htm

Action Opportunities

1. Become a volunteer at your local rape prevention and crisis center or domestic violence shelter.

2. Get involved with a "Take Back the Night" demonstration. Held annually around the country in April during Sexual Assault Awareness Month, and often organized by women's university centers, these usually feature a nighttime walk followed by a rally with speakers. Contact your local women's center.

3. Contact your local domestic violence shelter and ask what types of donated goods they need. Common needs include toiletries and cleaning products. Giving people a list as they enter a store and requesting that they purchase one item to be dropped off to you when they leave is one strategy to easily collect these items.

4. Create wallet-sized cards that provide local statistics about violence against women and list local women's resources such as the local shelter and rape prevention and crisis center. Distribute in public places and get permission to leave small piles of them where they may be useful.

5. Be part of a letter-writing campaign by checking the Amnesty International and Human Rights Watch Web sites for campaigns (http://www.amnestyusa.org and http://www.hrw.org). Both organizations have campaigns on behalf of individual women and violence against women. For instance, in 2002–2003, more than 3 million letters were sent to the Nigerian government to protest the conviction of Amina Lawal, sentenced to be buried up to her neck and stoned to death for the crime of adultery (Lawal had a child out of wedlock but the father of the child did not face charges). In September 2003, Nigerian judges overturned the verdict and Lawal was released.

3

Reproductive Rights

". . . Good health is essential to leading a productive and fulfilling life, and the right of all women to control all aspects of their health, in particular their own fertility, is basic to their empowerment."

—United Nations Fourth World Conference for Women, Beijing Platform for Action, para. 92

Women in the U.S. demonstrate for reproductive rights. Reproductive choice is central to women's equality and health. © BRUCE ALLEN/Getty Images

The focus of this chapter is women's reproductive rights. Women's ability to bear and nurse children profoundly affects their lives. Yet, they frequently lack the freedom to control the timing and number of their children and to make informed decisions regarding their reproductive health. This is both a symptom and a cause of women's unequal rights and has a significant effect on women's health. Simply stated, reproductive freedom is critical to women's equality.

This chapter notes many contradictions when it comes to women's reproductive control. Women's status is simultaneously boosted and diminished by their role as reproducers. Safe and legal abortion too often goes hand in hand with poor contraceptive availability, resulting in women being forced to use abortion as a primary form of contraception. The most effective contraceptive methods are often those that require the closest medical monitoring, yet most of the countries that offer these methods do not provide the information and monitoring necessary to ensure effectiveness and safety. Governments miss the point when they attempt to reduce overpopulation by controlling women's fertility and fail to increase women's status and the likelihood that children will live to adulthood.

At the 1968 UN International Human Rights Conference, it was acknowledged that family planning is a human right, that is, that couples should be able to freely decide how many children they want and the spacing of those children (Dixon-Mueller, 1993). The reality, however, is that the majority of women worldwide do not have these reproductive freedoms. Women often bear unwanted children, are prevented from having wanted children, and have to bear children in desperate circumstances (Morgan, 1984). In some cases, decisions are made for them that have significant effects on their reproductive health. Women's reproductive rights are a critical transnational feminist issue because of the intimate relationship between women's reproductive choice and their status, power, and health.

> "Many of the data to measure the effect of family planning programmes focus on demographic and health objectives set by the government or by service providers, without taking into account the programmes' impact on individuals' reproductive rights."
> *Report of the International Conference on Population and Development, Cairo, 1994*

Reproductive Control as a Symptom of Women's Low Status

According to Jacobson (1992), a woman's reproductive control can be determined by her answers to the following questions: Can she control when and with whom she will engage in sexual relations? Can she do so without fear of infection or unwanted pregnancy? Can she choose when and how to regulate her fertility, free from unpleasant or dangerous side effects of contraception? Can she go through pregnancy and childbirth safely? Can she obtain a safe abortion on request? Can she easily obtain information on the prevention and treatment of reproductive illnesses? In countries where women are socially, politically, and economically disadvantaged, the answers to these questions are likely to be no, and high rates of reproductive illness and death are usually common.

> "Condoms are good enough, but there are men who don't want to use them. So it's men's consciousness that's lacking."
> *Motoko Katayama, age 20, Japan*

That women are often left out of the family planning equation when their interests should be central is yet another symptom of women's lower status. As you will learn, males, governments, and corporations often have a bigger influence on women's reproductive choice than do women themselves.

Lack of Reproductive Control Perpetuates Women's Low Status

Women's role as mother is frequently a source of social status. Without mothers, there would be no children to grow up to be workers, to continue family lineages, to fight wars. And although it is often believed that men are better suited for public sphere roles, it is commonly believed that women relative to men, excel in the private sphere, particularly in regards to children. In many societies, adult women attain status through marriage and children, particularly by giving birth to male heirs. It is ironic then that women's role as "reproducer" is a source of status yet plays a key role in their lower status. For example, because women get pregnant, and because men sought certainty regarding paternity, many societies have sought to control women's sexuality. For example, a high premium is placed on women's virginity and premarital virginity is sometimes ensured through various means such as female genital mutilation, honor killing, and by rendering non-virgins unmarriageable. Governments too recognize women's important role as reproducers. They have at times restricted women's access to contraception because they believed society would be served by a higher fertility rate and at other times coerced women into reducing their fertility when concerned about population size.

As you will learn in this chapter, many women lack reproductive control and cannot control the timing and spacing of their children. They have many children in close succession and spend most of their adult lives pregnant, nursing, and caring for small children. These important private sphere responsibilities limit their participation in the paid labor force and in the formal political sphere, and consequently, reduce their economic and political power. This means that without the ability to control the number and spacing of their children, many women often do not have the power or the time to contest cultural practices that are discriminatory to women.

Reproductive Control Impacts Women's Health

Reproductive control is also an important feminist issue because it is a major women's health issue. This section focuses on the relationship between reproductive control and maternal mortality, the safety of contraceptives, the health consequences of female genital mutilation, and the incidence of AIDS in women.

Reproductive control affects women's ability to determine the number, timing, and spacing of their pregnancies. When women do not have access to reliable contraceptives or their male partners prevent their use, women may experience unintended pregnancies, and have too many pregnancies spaced too closely together. This has major consequences for the health of millions of women.

Maternal Mortality and Pregnancy-Related Disability

Maternal mortality refers to the death of a woman while pregnant or within forty-two days of termination of pregnancy from any cause related to or aggravated by the pregnancy or its management. Every minute, a woman dies in pregnancy or childbirth—1400 each day, more than 500,000 a year from pregnancy-related causes, including 75,000 from unsafe abortion. These women leave behind 1 million orphaned children (United Nations Population Fund, 2003b). According to the United Nations Population Fund (UNFPA, 2003b), more than 80 percent of maternal deaths arise from five direct causes: hemorrhage, sepsis (systemic infection), unsafe abortion, obstructed labor, or toxemia (hypertensive disease brought on by pregnancy). Another 25 percent of maternal deaths are due to diseases that are more likely to be fatal in combination with pregnancy such as malaria, anemia, and AIDS.

For each woman that dies, another 30 to 100 survive but suffer from disabilities caused by complications from pregnancy or childbirth. One common disability is **obstetric fistula,** a condition arising from prolonged and obstructed labor, often in young women that are not physically mature. Torn tissues between the vaginal wall and the bladder or rectum results in incontinence, infections, and ulcerations. This neglected condition has severe physical and social consequences and affects at least 2 million women. Their babies usually die from the obstructed labor and the women are often ostracized and abandoned. To combat this problem, which has been all but eliminated in industrialized countries, UNFPA has launched an international campaign to prevent fistula and increase access to its surgical repair (UNFPA, 2002).

Most maternal deaths and disabilities due to pregnancy are preventable with greater access to contraceptives, prenatal care, and births assisted by medical personnel. Demographers estimate that about one-fourth of maternal deaths worldwide could be avoided if women's needs for family planning were met (Winikoff & Sullivan, 1987, in Dixon-Mueller, 1993). The more pregnancies a woman has, the more frequently she is subjected to risks associated with pregnancy and childbirth; risks are also increased by having children in close succession and by having children when one is under 16 or over 35.

The burden of having many children in close succession means that when women have the option, they seldom choose to have as many children as biologically possible. Unfortunately, this choice is not available to many women in the world. The quantity and quality of reproductive health care available to pregnant women—as well as women's knowledge of and ability to

> ### BOX 3.1 *Maternal Death Rates*
>
> A woman's lifetime risk of dying due to maternal causes is:
>
> - in Africa, 1 in 19;
>
> - in Asia, 1 in 132;
>
> - in Latin America, 1 in 188;
>
> - in more-developed countries, only 1 in 2,976.
>
> Source: United Nations Population Fund, State of the World Population, 2002

take advantage of the services that are available—are unequally distributed in favor of wealthier nations, urban locations, and social groups with higher incomes and education (Dixon-Mueller, 1993). In some parts of the world, such as Africa, many women will be pregnant and lactating for more than two-thirds of the time between the ages of 17 and 35 (Mosse, 1993). Deaths and illnesses from reproductive causes are highest among poor women everywhere, as Box 3.1 shows. Indeed, over 98 percent of these deaths occur to women in developing countries. The highest rates are in the African countries of Burundi, Ethiopia, Rwanda, and Sierra Leone (Seager, 2003).

Contraceptives and Women's Health

True **reproductive choice** involves offering women a broad range of birth control methods from which they can freely choose (Hartmann, 1995). But in most societies, reproductive choice lies not in the woman's hands but in her husband's or in the government's. The global economy and international politics are also players in women's reproductive choice—especially in terms of women's access to **contraceptives** or birth control methods (often referred to as reproductive technologies). So what seems like a very personal choice (the control of one's own fertility) is in reality greatly affected by economic, political, and social institutions. This is because reproductive technologies, like other technologies, are cultural objects enmeshed in social, political, and economic systems (Ginsberg & Rapp, 1995). Furthermore, these social, political, and economic forces tend to dominate whereas women's health, power, and status take a distant backseat. As Peterson and Runyan (1993) put it, "Here the personal is political in the sense that even women's most 'private' and intimate experiences are shaped by institutions and structures that privilege male-defined pleasures and masculinist principles" (p. 118).

Reliable and safe contraceptives are key to women's health. Unreliable contraceptives put women at increased risk for poorly timed or unwanted pregnancies that threaten their health. Some contraceptives have potentially serious side effects and without medical monitoring can endanger women's health. This is especially an issue when the government's main concern is population control. For instance, Naripokkho, a feminist activist group in Bangladesh, proved that Norplant, a hormonal contraceptive, is widely promoted to poor women without educating them as to side effects and without adequate follow-up. The IUD (intrauterine device) is another example. This small plastic or copper device is highly effective in the prevention of pregnancy, and once it is inserted into the uterus, pregnancy is usually prevented until its removal. The most common side effect is heavy bleeding and cramping; this is especially a concern for women who are nutritionally deficient and for those who have difficulty obtaining clean materials for menstruation. Women with IUDs run a much greater risk of pelvic inflammatory disease (PID). PID is an infection of the upper reproductive tract that may lead to sterility. This risk is heightened if the IUD is inserted under less than sterile conditions, which is more likely in developing nations where cost considerations sometimes lead to the purchase of unsterilized IUDs, poor training of personnel, and unsanitary conditions. Despite these problems, IUD use is roughly three times greater in developing nations than in developed ones. In the United States, it took several years of activism in order to get a particular type of IUD, the Dalkon Shield, off the market in 1974. This particular device was associated with a high incidence of PID and septic abortions (miscarriage accompanied by toxic infection). Fourteen deaths and 219 septic abortions were attributed to its use from 1971 to 1974 (Hartmann, 1995).

Box 3.2 provides an overview of the most common birth control methods, along with advantages and disadvantages. Note that there is often a trade-off between effectiveness and safety. Recall also that true reproductive freedom requires that women be able to make informed choices about a variety of birth control options. Unfortunately, governments, politics, and corporations often limit choices, a point we return to a little later in the chapter. Also consider that while the advent of hormonal methods has increased women's control over their fertility, men control the male condom, the most effective method for preventing sexually transmitted diseases.

Female Genital Mutilation

Another source of reproductive health problems for women is the practice of **female genital mutilation (FGM)** or **female genital cutting (FGC)**. FGC/FGM refers to all procedures involving partial or total removal of the external female genitalia or other injury to the female genital organs for cultural or other non-medical reasons (UNFPA, 2003). In some areas it is carried out during infancy (as early as a couple of days after birth), in others during childhood, at the time of marriage, during a woman's first pregnancy, or after the birth of

BOX 3.2   *Common Birth Control Methods*

Behavioral Methods

Abstinence—Continuous abstinence is not having sex play with a partner at all. It is 100 percent effective in preventing pregnancy and sexually transmitted infection. However, people may find it difficult to abstain for long periods of time, and women and men often end their abstinence without being prepared to protect against pregnancy or infection.

Predicting Fertility (Rhythm Method)—Uses calendars, cervical mucous, or temperature to chart the menstrual cycle. Abstinence or barrier methods are then used during the woman's fertile period. Can be effective with consistent and accurate monitoring but this is difficult for many women, especially those with irregular periods or those that are breast-feeding. Effectiveness is also reduced without men's commitment to abstain or use barrier methods during the fertile period. Provides no protection against sexually transmitted diseases.

Withdrawal—An unreliable method requiring that the man withdraw his penis from the vagina before or when he feels he has reached the point when ejaculation is likely. It requires great control and experience on the part of the man. It does not protect against sexually transmitted disease and pregnancy may still occur due to the possibility of semen in preejaculative secretions.

Barrier Methods

Reversible, with few side effects. These methods offer some protection against sexually transmitted diseases (STDs). They are highly effective in preventing pregnancy if used properly, but because many people find them inconvenient, their effectiveness is significantly reduced.

Diaphragm—Soft rubber shallow cup that holds spermicidal jelly or cream and fits over the cervix to block and kill sperm. Proper fitting requires the help of a health-care practitioner.

Female condom—Loose-fitting polyurethane sheath that lines the vaginal wall.

Male condom—The only temporary birth control method available to men, the condom is a thin sheath, usually of latex, which covers the penis during sex.

Cervical cap—Thimble-shaped rubber cap that fits over the cervix. Like the diaphragm, it is used with a spermicide to block and kill sperm and must be fitted by a health-care practitioner.

Hormonal Methods

Fifty percent of the world's women use these reversible and highly effective forms of birth control. Although they are effective, they offer no protection against STDs and may produce a variety of undesirable side effects. Some of the more common side effects are bleeding, weight gain or loss, breast tenderness, nausea, headache, change in sexual desire, and depression. Less common are blood clots in legs, lungs, heart, or brain, high blood pressure, and liver tumors, gallstones, and jaundice.

Birth control pills (the Pill)—synthetic hormones taken daily that prevent pregnancy primarily by preventing ovulation; a prescription drug in most countries.

Norplant—Synthetic hormones released gradually from match-size capsules inserted in the arm by a trained professional. Prevents pregnancy for up to five years by inhibiting ovulation and thickening cervical mucus (this impedes sperm activity). Removal is tricky and requires a skilled health-care practitioner. Removal after five years is important. Otherwise hormones may continue to be released and cause irregular periods without pregnancy prevention.

Depo-Provera—An injectable contraceptive that prevents pregnancy for up to three months by inhibiting ovulation and thickening cervical mucus.

Lunelle—A monthly injection of synthetic hormones (estrogen and progestin) that prevents pregnancy for one month.

The Patch (Ortho Evra)—A thin, plastic patch placed on the skin of the buttocks, stomach, upper outer arm, or upper torso once a week for three out of four weeks. The Patch releases synthetic estrogen and progestin to protect against pregnancy for one month. It works by preventing ovulation, thickening cervical mucus, or preventing implantation of a fertilized egg in the uterus.

continued

Box 3.2   Common Birth Control Methods continued

The Ring (NuvaRing)—A small, flexible ring inserted by a woman into the vagina once a month, left in place for three weeks, and taken out for the remaining week. The Ring releases synthetic estrogen and progestin and protects against pregnancy for a month. It works by preventing ovulation, thickening cervical mucus, or preventing implantation of a fertilized egg in the uterus.

Emergency Contraception (EC or the "Morning After Pill")—A small dose of birth control pills that if taken within 72 hours of unprotected intercourse can reduce the chance of pregnancy by 89 percent. EC works by delaying ovulation, preventing fertilization, or inhibiting implantation of a fertilized egg in the uterus. In some countries, like Chile, anti-abortion activists have tried to deny women's access to EC. However, because pregnancy occurs *after* implantation of the fertilized egg, and EC prevents this, it is not an abortifacient.

Intrauterine Devices (IUDs)

The most widely used form of reversible birth control in the world, the IUD is highly effective against pregnancy but provides no STD protection and has an array of possible negative side effects such as bleeding and infection. IUDs are small devices that fit in the uterus with a small string that extends into the upper vagina. Some contain copper or hormones. No one is sure exactly how it works to prevent pregnancy, but it works until removal. Must be inserted and removed by a qualified health-care practitioner.

Permanent Methods—Sterilization

This highly effective and permanent form of birth control is achieved through surgery. It is generally safe with few negative side effects if performed by a skilled professional in a sterile setting. In women, the fallopian tubes are blocked or cut in a procedure called a *tubal ligation*. Female sterilization is the most commonly used method of birth control in the world. In men, in a procedure called a *vasectomy,* the vas deferens is cut so that sperm cannot mix with the seminal fluid. A vasectomy can be reversed surgically in some cases.

Sources: Boston Women's Health Collective, 1992; Planned Parenthood, 2003.

her first child. The most typical age is between 7 and 10 years or just before puberty. It is estimated that over 130 million girls and women have undergone some form of genital cutting, and at least 2 million girls are at risk of undergoing the practice every year—6000 a day. FGM/FGC is most common in the African countries of Benin, Burkina Faso, Cameroon, Central African Republic, Chad, Cote d'Ivoire, Democratic Republic of Congo, Djibouti, Egypt, Ethiopia, Eritrea, Gambia, Ghana, Guinea, Guinea-Bissau, Kenya, Liberia, Mali, Mauritania, Niger, Nigeria, Senegal, Sierra Leone, Somalia, Sudan, Tanzania, Togo, and Uganda. It is also practiced by some ethnic groups in the Asian countries of India, Indonesia, Malaysia, and Pakistan; by some groups in Oman, Saudi Arabia, United Arab Emirates, and Yemen; and by certain immigrant groups in Europe, Israel, Australia, Canada, and the United States.

The World Health Organization (WHO, 2000) has identified four types:

- **Type 1:** Excision of the prepuce, with or without excision of part or the entire clitoris.
- **Type 2:** Excision of the clitoris with partial or total excision of the labia minora.

- **Type 3:** Excision of part or all of the external genitalia and stitching/narrowing of the vaginal opening (*infibulation*). Sometimes referred to as *pharaonic circumcision*.
- **Type 4:** Others. Includes pricking, piercing or incising, stretching, burning of the clitoris, scraping of tissue surrounding the vaginal orifice, cutting of the vagina, introduction of corrosive substances or herbs into the vagina to cause bleeding or to tighten the opening.

Types 1 and 2 are the most common, with variation among countries. Type 3, infibulation, constitutes about 20 percent of all affected women and is most likely in Somalia, Northern Sudan, and Djibouti. In most cases, a midwife or practiced village woman does female genital mutilations, although upper-class girls may be taken to a physician. Various tools may be used (knives, razors, scissors, rocks, glass), and they may or may not be sterilized. There is also variation in the use of anesthesia and antibiotics.

The health consequences of FGM/FGC are significant. Short-term medical consequences include pain, severe bleeding, and infection. There are some deaths from shock, bleeding, and infection. The long-term consequences are serious, especially in the case of Type 3 (infibulation). Due to the small size of the remaining opening, women have difficulty urinating, menstruating, having sex, and giving birth. Inadequate drainage is responsible for tears (fistulae) in the tissue separating the vagina from the urinary tract and the bowel, resulting in the leakage of urine and feces. Prolonged labor, harmful to both mother and child, is often a consequence. So that sex is possible, the husband or midwife cuts open the woman on her first night of marriage (de-infibulation). De-infibulation is further needed to make childbirth possible and re-infibulation is common after delivery. All forms of female genital mutilation negatively affect the sexual pleasure of women.

"Circumcision makes women clean, promotes virginity and chastity and guards young girls from sexual frustration by deadening their sexual appetite."
Female defender of FGM in Kenya

BOX 3.3   *The Genital Mutilation of Hannah from Sierra Leone*

"I was genitally mutilated at the age of ten. I was blindfolded and stripped naked. I was forced to lie flat on my back by four strong women, two holding tight to each leg. Another woman sat on my chest to prevent my upper body from moving. A piece of cloth was forced in my mouth to stop me screaming. I was then shaved. When the operation began, I put up a big fight. The pain was terrible and unbearable. I was genitally mutilated with a blunt penknife. The stuff they put on my wound stank and was painful. I was not given any anesthetic in the operation to reduce my pain, nor any antibiotics to fight against infection. Afterwards, I hemorrhaged and became anemic. This was attributed to witchcraft. I suffered for a long time from acute vaginal infections."

Source: Amnesty International (2003)

FGM/FGC is performed for a variety of reasons but it is not intended to harm girls and women. In some cultures, it is intended to control female sexuality by preserving virginity before marriage and fidelity after marriage. Sometimes FGM/FGC is performed because people believe that the female external genitalia are dirty or ugly and that the practice is hygienic and beautifies a woman. One of the difficulties in eradicating the practice is that it is often viewed as an important rite of passage and initiation into womanhood. Women who do not undergo the procedure may have difficulty finding a husband. The practice is also a major source of income and respect for those who perform it, often older women. Although religion is sometimes used to justify FGM/FGC, it predates Christianity and Islam. Historical evidence of it is found all over the world including in Africa, the Philippines, Mexico, and Australia. As recent as the 1950s, clitoridectomy was practiced in Western Europe and the United States to treat "ailments" in women as diverse as hysteria, epilepsy, mental disorders, masturbation, nymphomania, melancholia, and lesbianism (UNFPA, 2003c).

Major efforts are underway to eradicate FGC/FGM. The UN condemns the practice and has tried to reduce it by pointing out that it is incompatible with numerous international covenants such as the Convention on All Forms of Elimination of Discrimination Against Women. CEDAW, as it is called, proceeds from the assumption that all practices that harm women, no matter how deeply they are embedded in culture, must be eradicated. The World Health Organization also condemns the practice. In the last several years, twenty countries have passed laws against FGM/FGC and a few people have been prosecuted (Center for Reproductive Law and Policy, 2003a; UNFP, 2003c).

Critics point out that legislation without education and outreach is likely to drive the practice underground. Consequently, governments, the United Nations, and grassroots women's organizations sponsor education and outreach programs. For example, activists in Gambia broadcasted programs critical of FGM on state-owned radio and television stations, following a widely supported letter campaign (Brandell, 1998). Women's organizations work to transform the rite of passage. Kenyan women's organizations, along with the NGO Program for Appropriate Technology (PATH), are providing an alternative to FGM in the form of a new ceremony incorporating song, dance, and educational drama (Thomas, 1998). In Senegal, a movement to end FGM by educating women about the negative health consequences has almost ended FGM in 800 villages, saving an estimated 43,000 girls (Armstrong, 2003).

HIV/AIDS

Yet another threat to women's health is HIV/AIDS. Men's higher status and women's social and economic dependencies on men mean that women often lack the power to negotiate safe sex with their partners. This is especially serious since it is linked to the incidence of Acquired Immunodeficiency Syndrome (AIDS) in women. **AIDS**, caused by infection with the Human Immunodeficiency Virus (HIV), breaks down the body's natural defenses

> "FGM is one of the worst forms of violence against women."
> *Zipporah Kittony, Member of Kenya's Parliament*

> "Women are denied their right to free and accurate information about their bodies, and this greatly contributes to their inability to protect themselves from infection."
> *Lydia Cacho, a feminist and journalist in Mexico*

"Women's empowerment is one of the only AIDS vaccines available today."
UNIFEM (United Nations Development Fund for Women)

leaving it susceptible to disease and infection, and eventually death. There is no known cure or preventative vaccine. According to UNAIDS, of the people who died in 2000 due to AIDS, close to 52 percent, or 1.3 million, were women, thus increasing the total of women who have died of HIV/AIDS-related illnesses to over 9 million since the epidemic began (Macan-Markar, 2001). AIDS now ranks as one of the leading causes of death among women aged 20 to 40 years in several cities in Europe, sub-Saharan Africa, and North America (UNAIDS, 2003). The proportion of adults living with HIV/AIDS who are women has been steadily increasing and is largely due to women's lack of sexual decision-making power. For instance, most AIDS prevention programs emphasize reducing the number of sexual partners and promoting condom use, and women often do not have the power to get males to use condoms or be sexually monogamous.

The Agents that Control Women's Reproductive Choice

Male partners, governments, corporations, and religious organizations frequently determine the options available to women. In the public sphere, corporations and governments sometimes make women's health concerns a low priority in the marketing and availability of contraception. Governments concerned with population control, and corporations concerned with profit, of-

---

BOX 3.4 *A Gender-Based Response to HIV/AIDS*

"A gender-based response to HIV/AIDS and STDs focuses on how different social expectations, roles, status, and economic power of men and women affect and are affected by the epidemic. It analyzes gender stereotypes and explores ways to reduce inequalities between women and men so that a supportive environment can be created, enabling both to undertake prevention and cope better with the epidemic."

UNIFEM

• Improve the access of girls to formal schooling.

• Ensure women and girls have information about their own bodies, education about AIDS and the other STDs, and the skills to say "no" to unwanted or unsafe sex.

• Promote gender awareness in HIV prevention programs, and routinely provide sex-disaggregated figures for all service statistics and research.

• Multiply and strengthen existing training opportunities for women, women's credit programs, saving schemes and cooperatives, and link them with AIDS prevention.

• Provide alternatives to sex work, particularly in areas where migration of young women to enter sex work has become an established pattern, and in areas where sex workers operate.

Source: UNIFEM: Women, Gender, and HIV/AIDS in East and Southeast Asia, 2003b

ten endanger women's health and at the very least, restrict women's options. Powerful religious groups may also influence reproductive choice. Meanwhile, in the private sphere, male partners often restrict women's reproductive choices. Many women are socialized through religion, cultural taboos, and other social mechanisms to accept sexual subordination and even sexual oppression (UNIFEM, 2003). The result is that husbands make the decisions regarding the number and spacing of children and the use of contraception. All over the world, you will find women's activism around issues of reproductive choice. Women seek to take charge of their reproductive lives and reproductive health, because too often, the decisions that are made are not in their best interests.

Male Control of Women's Reproductive Choice

Cross-culturally, it is not uncommon for males to control sexual decision-making, including the use of contraception and the practice of safe sex. In parts of Bangladesh, Ethiopia, India, Korea, Nigeria, and Tunisia, women's bodies are viewed as the property of their husbands, and so it is husbands that decide the number and spacing of the children (Jacobsen, 1992). Many men fear that their partner's use of contraception will lead to her promiscuity, and they therefore oppose it. For instance, in Lesotho, men question their wife's loyalty if she is on the pill or has an IUD (intrauterine device). They believe that if she does not fear pregnancy, she may go with another man (Kanno, 1991). Many cultures believe that if women could enjoy sexual relations and could prevent pregnancy, then sexual morality and family security would be jeopardized (Cook, 1995). In some cultures, having many children is a sign of male virility and men in such cultures may oppose their partners' efforts to prevent this. The family planning literature documents that women's contraceptive use is inhibited by fear of male reprisal in the form of violence, desertion, or accusations of infidelity (Heise, 1995). In some countries, like the Philippines, Chile, and Lesotho, a husband's permission is typically required for a wife's sterilization, a surgical procedure that prevents pregnancy (Kanno, 1996; Macklin, 1996). In Chad, women must have spousal permission in order to get barrier or hormonal contraceptives. In over a dozen countries, such as South Korea, Honduras, Togo, and Turkey, a woman must have her husband's consent for an abortion (Seager, 2003).

As mentioned previously, male control of sexual decision-making has significantly increased women's risk for AIDS. Countries where it is common for married men to engage in extramarital sexual relations provide clear examples. In such places, both elite and working-class women frequently express powerlessness in the face of their husband's multiple partner relationships. As the wife of a government official in Zaire said, "I can't ask him to stop, but I wish he would use condoms. Use condoms with the other women, with me, whatever. But I just don't feel I can introduce the subject. It wouldn't do any good. My husband would just get angry and tell me to mind my own business" (from Schoepf, 1997, p. 322). In Zambia, a study found that fewer than

25 percent of women believed that a married woman could refuse to have sex with her husband, even if he had been demonstrably unfaithful and was infected. Only 11 percent thought that a woman could ask her husband to use a condom in these circumstances (UNIFEM, 2003a).

"Women are not expected to discuss or make decisions about sexuality and they cannot request, let alone insist on using a condom or any form of protection."
World Health Organization

Women are often unable to negotiate the use of a condom or discuss fidelity with their partners without physical violence or the threat of violence. This, along with the fear of abandonment, fuel the spread of AIDS to women (UNAIDS, 2003). Prevailing views about masculinity and manliness encourage men to demonstrate sexual prowess by having multiple sexual partners and by consuming alcohol and other substances that may lead to risk-taking and violence (UNAIDS, 2003). Rape, sexual abuse, and sex work arising from economic hardship also put millions of girls and women at risk of HIV infection. These are all situations in which women are unlikely to have the power to negotiate the terms of sex. Young women and girls are at greater risk of rape, sexual coercion, and sex trafficking because they are perceived to be more likely to be free from infection, or because of the erroneous but widespread belief in some regions that sex with a virgin can cleanse a man of infection.

Reproductive freedom is also enhanced by information but unfortunately, the widespread view that women should be virgins at marriage is often associated with the assumption that knowledge of sex indicates that she is a "bad" woman. This means that women often lack knowledge about their bodies and about how HIV is transmitted and prevented. For example, in Sub-Saharan Africa, teenage girls are five times more likely to be infected than boys, since girls are mostly infected not by boys their own age, but by older men. UNIFEM (2003) reports that in a study of several countries in Sub-Saharan Africa, almost half of all girls aged 15 to 19 did not know that a person who looks healthy could be infected with HIV and could transmit it to others. Sadly, in surveys in seventeen Sub-Saharan countries, over half of teenage girls could not name a method of protection against HIV transmission.

Government Control of Women's Reproductive Choice

As suggested earlier in the chapter, governments often control women's reproductive choices. This is done legislatively and through outright bans against some forms of contraception and abortion, through government regulation of contraceptives as pharmaceuticals, and through government family planning services that provide limited birth control options. For example, in May 2003 in Argentina, a federal judge banned the sale of oral contraceptives and IUDs, claiming that they were abortifacients that violate the constitutional right to life (Cabal, 2003). Sterilization is illegal in some countries such as Poland, Argentina, and Cote d'Ivoire. In Japan, the government banned hormonal contraceptives in the 1960s, saying that they were unhealthy and promoted promiscuity. This did not change until 1999, after thirty years of lobbying by women's activists.

Politics and political administration changes also significantly affect the reproductive choices available to women. Policies affecting women's reproductive rights are often made at the executive level, without legislative approval and this means that when governments change, policies often change as well. The U.S. approval of Mifepristone, a chemical alternative to aspiration abortion used in early pregnancy, is a good example. The drug became available in France in 1988 but activists opposed to abortion threatened that they would boycott its manufacturer Roussel Uclaf should it be marketed in the United States. By 1991, President Bush put the pill on a list of medications banned by the United States. In 1993, newly elected President Clinton called on the FDA to test the drug. Roussel Uclaf gave the rights to the drug to a non-profit group, the Population Council. This group had to raise millions of dollars to conduct clinical trials of the drug, because none of the major pharmaceutical companies were interested due to the controversial nature of abortion in the United States. Seven years later, the drug was approved for use in the United States, largely due to the efforts of activists who felt strongly Mifepristone should be available to American women (Bernstein, 2000).

The policies of the government of one country may even affect the reproductive choices of women in other countries. In his first act as President of the United States in 2001, George W. Bush reinstated the "Mexico City policy," or "Global Gag Rule." This policy restricts foreign non-governmental organizations (NGOs) that receive USAID family planning funds from using their own, non-U.S. funds to provide legal abortion services, lobby their own governments for abortion law reform, or even provide accurate medical counseling or referrals regarding abortion. In eighteen of the fifty-six countries that receive U.S. family planning funds, abortion is legal without restriction as to reason or on broad grounds, such as when a pregnancy results in socio-economic hardship and in cases of rape and fetal impairment (Center for Reproductive Rights and Policy, 2003b). Ironically, the administration's action may have increased abortion rates since reduced family planning services mean more unplanned pregnancies and poor women often resort to abortion when they cannot afford more children. Approximately 70,000 women die each year as a result of unsafe abortion—many of which would not have occurred if women had access to family planning services (Safir, 2002).

In 2002 the Bush administration also withheld $34 million pledged to the United Nations Population Fund (UNFPA) for family planning programs, claiming that the UNFPA supported coercive sterilization programs in China. Even after a State Department investigation disproved this, the Administration declined to provide the funds. This money was enough for the UNFPA to prevent two million unwanted pregnancies, 4,700 maternal deaths, nearly 60,000 cases of maternal illnesses, and over 77,000 cases of infant and child death (UNFPA, 2003c). Box 3.5 features two American activists with a campaign to make up for the lost funds.

Margaret Sanger (1883–1966) founded the birth control movement in the United States. Despite harassment and arrest, she successfully pushed the federal courts to change laws preventing physicians from providing birth control information and devices. In 1921 she founded the organization that would later become Planned Parenthood. Although Sanger was an important figure in the history of women's reproductive choice, she was a supporter of eugenics, a movement to limit the reproduction of undesirable groups.

"It is very little to me to have the right to vote, to own property, et cetera, if I may not keep my body and its uses, in my absolute right."
Lucy Stone, suffragist, 1855

"Women still face the dilemma that the safest contraceptives are not the most effective, while the most effective are not necessarily the safest."
Joni Seager, 2002, author of "The Penguin Atlas of Women in the World."

BOX 3.5   *Activist Profile: Jane Roberts and Lois Abraham of the United States*

In 2002, United States President Bush withheld the $34 million in funding to the United Nations Population Fund (UNFPA) previously pledged. American women Jane Keeney Roberts (age 62), a retired teacher from California, and Lois Abraham (age 70), a lawyer from New Mexico, got mad when they heard the news. After all, they each reasoned, family planning programs reduce the need for abortion and the UNFPA does not even engage in abortion-related activity. Independently, the women e-mailed everyone they knew and asked them to send $1 to the UNFPA. Eventually, the women heard

about each other and collaborated to continue what became known as the "34 Million Friends Campaign." Less than a year after they started, the UNFPA announced that it had received over $1 million in single dollar bills and small checks. In 2003, the women took their campaign global.

Sources: Farley, 2003; United Nations Population Fund, 2003c

"We won, we won! Never underestimate the women of the world."
June Zeitlin, Executive Director of the nonprofit Women's Environment and Development Program (WEDO), following successful protests to restore language promoting women's reproductive rights to the final document of the 2002 World Summit on Sustainable Development. Religious conservatives lobbied for the exclusion of the language.

Governments often control women's reproduction in the name of social needs or national interests. Poor women rely on government family planning programs for their contraceptive and reproductive health needs. Governments that use family planning programs for population control purposes frequently view women as targets, objects, and means to an end instead of as people with health needs capable of making dignified, informed choices (Fathalla, 2002). Countries with **pronatalist** policies seek to increase birth rates and do this by reducing or banning contraception and abortion. **Antinatalist** programs seek to reduce birth rates and strongly encourage or require that women limit their fertility. They tend to provide a limited range of contraceptive options, emphasizing those that are high in effectiveness but have greater health risks.

Pronatalist policies may be intended to replace wartime casualties. This was the case in Iraq in the 1980s. Following large casualties from its war with Iran, Iraq banned contraceptives, waged a campaign stressing motherhood, and encouraged men to take second wives in order to increase the number of children. Increasing the workforce is another common goal. The Romanian government outlawed contraception in the 1970s and 1980s because it was feared that population growth was too low to keep up with projected labor needs (note: contraception and abortion became legal and available in Romania in 1990).

Pronatalist policies may also be in response to falling birthrates. For example, since 1983, Singapore has offered tax incentives and child-care subsidies to encourage citizens to have more children. Fear that the population of ethnic minority groups or immigrants will outstrip the population of a dominant ethnic group can also motivate pronatalism. Jewish leaders in Israel have often voiced concern about losing the Jewish majority in Israel because the Arab population has a higher birthrate than the Jewish population. Government propaganda in the 1970s suggested that it was a woman's patriotic duty to reproduce and Israeli women's access to contraception and abortion has been limited by religious and pronatalist concerns (King, 2002).

More common than pronatalist programs are antinatalist programs. **Coercive antinatalism** typically occurs when concerns about reducing population growth eclipse concerns about women's health and control over their bodies (Dixon-Mueller, 1993). Women are persuaded, tricked, and even coerced into sterilization or contraceptive methods with the lowest failure rates, irrespective of the health risks these methods pose. They are often not told enough to make informed choices. And because non-medical personnel often administer population control programs and fail to screen and monitor women, the health risks of these methods are increased. These methods also do not protect women from sexually transmitted diseases. Antinatalist programs that incorporate persuasion, incentives, and targets for family planning workers have been documented in China, Indonesia, Thailand, Sri Lanka, Bangladesh, the Republic of Korea, Colombia, Mexico, Tunisia, and India (Dixon-Mueller, 1993).

Coercive antinatalism is sometimes selective within a country, targeting lower income women or women from an ethnic group deemed undesirable by government officials. For instance, in 1976, it was revealed that the U.S. government had sterilized 3,000 Native American women in a four-year period without obtaining adequate consent (Hartmann, 1995). In Slovakia, it is alleged that Romany (Gypsy) women are being sterilized without their consent in order to limit the Roma population, a growing and unpopular minority (Center for Reproductive Rights, 2003c; Yee, 2003). Following activism by women's groups, Slovakia reformed their medical system to reduce discrimination against Romany women (Center for Reproductive Law and Policy, 2003). In 2003, the Peruvian minister of health issued an apology for the forced sterilization of indigenous women that took place in the 1990s (Center for Reproductive Law and Policy, 2003). It is estimated that from 1996 to 2000, over 200,000 poor women were sterilized without their consent or were coerced through the use of various incentives (Women's Health Journal, 2002). In Australia, Depo-Provera, a controversial injected contraceptive, has been given by government agencies to Aboriginal women but only rarely to women of Anglo descent (Morgan, 1996).

China's one-child family policy, first instituted in the 1970s, provides one of the more dramatic examples of coercive antinatalism. In its early incarnation, parents were issued permits to have children, and those who had additional children could be fined, lose their jobs, land, or homes, or be demoted (Chow & Chen, 1994; Hartmann, 1987; 1995; Fang, 2003; Pan, 2002). There were also reports of forced abortion, and women could be fitted with an IUD after their first child and sterilized after their second (Pan, 2002). The one-child policy became law in 2003 and is credited by the Chinese government with preventing 300 million births in a twenty-year period (Fang, 2003). However, the fact that only 20 percent of children under 14 are only children shows that the plan was unevenly enforced and that it was resisted (Pan,

". . . Countries wishing for slower population growth will attain it by purely voluntary means. . . . Freedom of choice, backed by information and the means to make choices, will result in smaller families and slower population growth."
Dr. Nafis Sadik, Executive Director, UNFPA

2002). Due to son preference, the policy also led to the abandonment of thousands of infants, 90 percent of whom were girls. Sex-selective abortion contributed to a lopsided gender ratio.

Women's activists in China highlighted the conflicts between the government's family planning program and women's health care, the negative effects of certain contraceptive methods, abortion abuse, and the connections between the government's program and female infanticide (Zhang & Xu, 1995). International pressure was also exerted. In 1998, Chinese family planning officials agreed to implement UNFPA non-coercive programs in thirty-two counties and found that population growth remained stable when women were given information and choice about contraception. Birth permits, targets, and quotas, and the promotion of abortion as birth control have now stopped in many Chinese counties and half of women live in counties where they are allowed to choose what contraceptives to use (Pan, 2002). A law passed in 2002 gives each region the authority to decide how large fines will be and whether to allow some groups of people, such as farmers, or those without sons, to have more children (Fang, 2003). The one-child policy remains coercive but to differing degrees in different parts of the country and overall, it is not as coercive as it once was.

"When women are given a real choice, and the information and means to implement their choice, they will make the most rational decision for themselves, their community, and ultimately the world." Dr. Mahmoud F. Fathalla, Egyptian gynecologist and former president of the International Federation of Planned Parenthood

Governments often view coercive antinatalism as necessary to reduce poverty and promote economic development but demographers, the United Nations Population Fund, and women's activists strongly believe that these goals can be achieved without sacrificing women's reproductive rights. When women have higher status, when conditions are such that child mortality is low, when women have access to information and a variety of ways to control their fertility, they have fewer children (Dixon-Mueller, 1993; Fathalla, 2002; Hartmann, 1995). For example, the Indian state of Kerala achieved the fastest and greatest drop in fertility rates in the country by investing in women's development (Acharya, 2001). Kerala's fertility rate is similar to rates in Europe. More than 70 percent of Kerala's women are literate, three times India's national average. The average age at which women marry (22) is the highest in India. Kerala is also the only state in India where females outnumber males (remember that in many parts of India son preference has led to a lop-sided sex ratio). Women in Kerala also have greater economic and political power than they do in most parts of the country.

The Global Economy and Women's Reproductive Choice

Pharmaceutical companies play a large role in the reproductive technologies available to women and they are motivated primarily by profit, not by concerns about women's reproductive choice or health. For instance, in the United States, the Today Sponge, 250 million of which were sold from 1983 to 1995, was taken off the market when pharmaceutical giant Wyeth decided it didn't want to pay to upgrade its plant (Associated Press, 2003). The popular product was unavailable to American women until a small company bought the rights to it in 2003. Activists are also concerned that in an effort to keep research and development costs down and maximize profit, pharmaceutical companies emphasize benefits and downplay side effects and risks. For example, Corea (1991) showed that Upjohn, the developer of Depo-Provera, presented incomplete information from Depo-Provera drug trials in order to receive U.S. Food and Drug Administration approval. In addition, the common side effects of depression and loss of sexual arousal were portrayed as "minor" (Corea, 1991).

Pharmaceutical corporations from industrialized countries make contraceptives and aggressively market them to government-run population control programs in Third World countries with the goal of monetary profit. These agencies play a major role in advertising, promoting, and distributing pharmaceutical contraceptives developed in First World capitalist countries such as the United States (Hartmann, 1995). Owners and presidents of U.S. pharmaceutical companies even sit on the boards of international population organizations, donate money to them, and lobby Congress for population appropriations (Hartmann, 1987). In short, the local availability of different birth control technologies may depend very much on international politics and economics of other countries. This is an example of globalization, the topic of Chapter 7.

Religious Organizations' Control of Women's Reproductive Choice

Religious fundamentalism is often associated with the curtailing of women's reproductive rights (Heyzer, 2002). Fundamentalists typically favor traditional roles for women and see women primarily as mothers and reproducers. For instance, under the fundamentalist Islamic Taliban, Afghan women had virtually no access to contraception or abortion. In the United States, fundamentalist Christians opposed to abortion act politically to reduce its availability. Their activism has made it increasingly challenging for women to obtain abortions.

Worldwide, Catholicism has also had a strong influence on women's reproductive rights. With the exception of the calendar or rhythm method, the Catholic Church is officially opposed to the use of contraception. Currently, contraceptives are legal in Chile but are limited in availability due to resistance from the Catholic Church. Influenced by the country's bishops, the Supreme Court banned emergency contraception in 2002 (Meacham & Shallat, 2002). The Philippines, a largely Catholic country, has one of the highest birth rates in Asia. Local legislators are reluctant to allocate government funds for family planning programs due to resistance from the Catholic Church (Agence France Presse, 2002).

Almost all Catholic hospitals in the United States will not perform sterilizations, abortions, or emergency contraception, even in cases of rape (Cooley, 2003; Pyle, 2000; Stammer, 2001). Doctors in Catholic-owned medical buildings have complained that their leases prevent them from prescribing birth control, or doing vasectomies in their offices (Pyle, 2000). By 2001, more than one in ten U.S. hospitals and eight of the country's fourteen largest healthcare systems were Catholic (Stammer, 2001). Anti-abortion groups led by the Roman Catholic Church have been particularly influential in Poland, Slovakia, Lithuania, Italy, and Hungary. In the strongly Catholic country of Italy, many doctors and hospitals refuse to perform abortions. Although a first-trimester abortion has been legal since 1978, the law permits any health-care worker or administrator to claim conscientious objector status and to refuse to participate. In the first year, 72 percent of Italian doctors became objectors (Boston Women's Health Collective, 1992).

The Catholic Church explains that their opposition to contraception is based on the belief that it involves setting the will of individuals against God's will. However, some writers suggest that the church's opposition is partly due to its desire to maintain church authority over the traditional (patriarchal) family and to its declining numbers of religious adherents (Dixon-Mueller, 1993). Others argue that the Church's battle is about controlling women's sexuality since traditionalists believe that contraception leads to non-procreative sex (Meacham & Shallat, 2002). It should be noted that the influence of the Roman Catholic Church is not always enough to override government concerns for reducing birthrates and Catholics' desires to limit the size of their families. For example, 51 to 75 percent of Brazilian and Mexican couples use modern contraceptive methods including oral contraceptives, injectable contraceptives, IUDs, or sterilization (Seager, 2003), and the Catholic countries of France, Belgium, and Italy all have relatively liberal abortion laws.

Abortion

"Abortion is a parody of choice, when there is no contraception."
Janet Hadley

Many women's activists believe that the availability of safe and legal abortion is an important reproductive freedom. Approximately 50 percent of pregnancies are unintended, many due to poor availability and knowledge of contraception. Worldwide, approximately half of unintended pregnancies end in **abortion**. More than one quarter of pregnancies worldwide, about 52 million annually, end in abortion (UNFPA, 2003e). Most women that obtain abortions are married, or in a long-term union, and already have children (Seager, 2003).

Legal Abortion

Restricting legal abortion does not reduce the incidence of abortion (Alan Guttmacher Institute, 1999). When women cannot attain legal abortions, they often get illegal ones or travel to neighboring countries where abortion is legal. Some 21 million of the 52 million abortions performed annually occur in countries where abortion is illegal or allowed only to save a woman's life. In European countries, such as Ireland, where abortion is illegal, women travel to neighboring countries where it is legal. Between January 1980 and

December 2001, at least 98,565 Irish women had abortions in Britain (Irish Family Planning Association, 2003).

Although legality does not strongly influence the incidence of abortion, legality does strongly influence the safety of abortion. About 70,000 women die each year from unsafe abortion, and a much larger number suffer from infection, injury, and trauma (UNFPA, 2003e). Hartmann (1995) notes that, in general, legalization of abortion leads to reductions in mortality rates. In the United States, for example, prior to legalization in 1973, an average of 292 women died per year from illegal abortions. In 1973, the figure fell to 36. Romania legalized abortion in 1990 and its abortion-related mortality rate dropped one-third in one year. Beginning in 1998, South African women were able to have abortions during the first twelve weeks of pregnancy. Prior to the law, approximately 425 deaths occurred annually from illegal abortions. When abortion was legalized in Guyana in 1995, hospital admissions from complications following illegal abortions declined 41 percent in six months (Alan Guttmacher Institute, 1999). Although many people oppose abortion on moral grounds, the fact of the matter is that women will have them when they face the possibility of having a child they cannot support. Where abortion is illegal or difficult to obtain, women customarily rely on other women for information about where to obtain an abortion or what to take to induce one. Box 3.6 describes "Jane," a women's collective that served this purpose.

Sanctions against abortion historically originated on behalf of the family, tribe, state, or husband. The idea was that a woman did not have the right to deprive these agents of their "property" (French, 1992; Petchesky, 1984; United Nations, 1993). Abortion was illegal in almost every country until the second half of the twentieth century (Alan Guttacher Institute, 1999). In

---

BOX 3.6   *Women Helping Women: "Jane"*

In 1969, abortion was illegal in the United States, and many women with unwanted pregnancies resorted to illegal and often unsafe abortions. A Chicago women's group hired doctors to perform safe abortions and referred women to them. Clients paid $375. The abortion collective was called "Jane," and everyone associated with the clinic went by the name Jane in order to protect their anonymity. After a time, it was discovered that one of the doctors was not a doctor after all, although he had performed competently. The women who ran the collective decided that if he could do it, then they could learn too. At its peak, Jane performed 300 abortions a week for a price of $40. By 1973, when abortion was legalized in the United States, Jane had performed 11,000 abortions with a safety record comparable to legal abortions performed in medical facilities. No longer needed, Jane closed.

Source: Boston Women's Health Collective, 1992.

Women on Waves is a Dutch organization that promotes legal, safe abortion by operating a mobile clinic on a ship that sails to countries where abortion is illegal. Their mission is to provide reproductive health services, provide sexual education, and support local initiatives to further women's reproductive rights. In 2003, the ship visited Ireland and Poland at the invitation of local women's organizations.

2003, thirty-five countries forbid abortion under any circumstances. In most countries, it is permitted under special circumstances. In some countries, including Ireland, Egypt, Iran, and Guatemala, the only grounds are to save the woman's life and to preserve her physical health. The preservation of mental health is an additional circumstance in countries such as Kenya, Pakistan, Costa Rica, and Spain. In countries including Panama, Thailand, and Ghana, abortion is also permitted in cases of rape or incest. Fetal impairment is also grounds for abortion in countries such as Panama, Liberia, Israel, and New Zealand. Zambia, the United Kingdom, India, and Barbados are among the countries that also allow abortion in cases of social or economic hardship. Abortion is available "on request" (without justification) in fifty-two countries including South Africa, Cuba, Uzbekistan, Viet Nam, and France. In Mexico and Australia, abortion law is determined by local governments and may vary within the country. Western Australia for instance, has liberal abortion laws, the Northern Territories, Queensland, and South Australia limit abortion to fetal impairment and saving the life or health of the mother, and New South Wales permits it for social or economic regions. Mexican abortion laws show less variation and are generally limited to saving a woman's life or cases of rape.

The legal status of abortion does not fully reflect availability (Seager, 2003). Although few countries completely forbid abortion, legal abortions can still be difficult to obtain because abortion laws are frequently restrictive and complicated, and because doctors and clinics performing abortions may be limited. In Zambia, for instance, three doctors must approve the abortion, it must be deemed medically necessary, and it must be performed in a hospital. Most women there resort to illegal abortions. According to law in Mexico, women can obtain abortions in cases of rape, but the procedure is almost impossible to get. Some countries with seemingly liberal abortion laws have restricted abortion in other ways. For instance, in the United States there is a trend towards states passing legislation requiring extensive counseling and waiting periods prior to abortion. Such legislation is intended to discourage women from having abortions (Gold, 2003; Mestrel, 2003). Because of budget cuts, lack of medical personnel, and effective lobbying by anti-abortion groups, many clinics have closed in a number of countries including the United States, Britain, India, Poland, Slovakia, Lithuania, and Hungary. In the United States, 87 percent of counties have no surgical abortion providers (Mestel, 2003).

Activists favoring the liberalization of abortion laws often emphasize that illegal and restrictive abortion laws are human rights violations. Such laws threaten women's rights to autonomy in reproductive decision making since women are forced to carry unwanted pregnancies to term, threaten women's right to physical and mental health, and constitute a form of discrimination against women since they criminalize a procedure only women need (Center for Reproductive Rights and Policy, 2000). The number of countries legalizing abortion has grown dramatically in the last twenty years, largely due to women's activism. This is because where there are no safe and affordable abortions, almost all women have themselves experienced or know someone who has experienced the dangers of illegal abortion. Here is a sampling of examples from all over the world:

- In the 1970s, feminists in the United States and western Europe worked for legalization by lobbying legislatures and staging demonstrations and speak-outs (Jenson, 1995; Wolfe & Tucker, 1995).

- In Nigeria activists push for legalization of the procedure as well as for improved sex education and contraceptive availability (Simmons, 1998).

- In 1988, when Brazil was rewriting its constitution, Brazilian women's activists presented a petition to the government for an amendment to legalize abortion. The petition included 30,000 signatures. Although abortion was not legalized, activists felt that their efforts were successful in that the stricter penalties advocated by the Catholic Church were not adopted (Soares et al., 1995).

- In Poland, following the end of communist rule, the Catholic Church moved quickly to outlaw abortion. This led to the formation of hundreds of women's organizations established to exert pressure on Parliament to refrain from criminalizing abortion (Matynia, 1995). The Polish Parliament decided that only the physician performing the abortion was to be punished, not the woman undergoing it (Matynia, 1995).

- In Nepal, the Family Planning Association of Nepal successfully worked for the passage in the Nepalese Parliament of a bill that would legalize abortion. Prior to its legalization in 2002, women were imprisoned for having abortions. Activists now seek the release of women imprisoned for life under the previous law banning abortion.

- Because of feminist activism, in 1998 South Africa passed one of the world's most liberal reproductive rights laws.

- In 2004, Portuguese activists collected over 100,000 signatures in an effort to get Portugal's parliament to legalize abortion during the first ten weeks of pregnancy.

Reducing Abortions: Contraceptives and Sex Education

Women's activists do not view abortion as a form of contraception; they would prefer a dramatic reduction in the number of unwanted pregnancies. This is why they strongly favor increasing the availability of contraceptives and reproductive health education. Higher abortion rates are most strongly tied to a lack of contraceptive information and availability (United Nations, 1993). Better contraceptive services for all would greatly reduce abortions. In Bolivia, for example, only 7 percent of women hospitalized for abortion complications

"As long as it remains possible for a woman to become pregnant without wanting to be, abortion will be a necessity and its denial a punishment of women—for having sex."
Rosalind Petchesky

had ever used contraception, yet 77 percent said that they wanted to (UNFPA, 2003e). Women in many African countries face an especially difficult situation: Access to contraception is limited and abortion laws are restrictive. Almost 45 percent of deaths from illegal abortion occur in Africa, a continent where the majority of countries have restrictive abortion laws (Seager, 2003). The Netherlands' abortion rate is the lowest in the world, even though abortion is legal, free, and available upon request. The reason: Holland has one of the most extensive sex education and reproductive health programs in the world, and one of the highest rates of contraceptive use (Hadley, 1996). In the Netherlands there are only six abortions per one thousand women aged 15 to 44, compared to twenty-six abortions per one thousand young women in the United States (Center for Reproductive Rights, 2001).

Conclusion

A key theme of international feminism is that of diversity and, in particular, how women's issues and rights are affected by culture, ethnicity, and socioeconomic status (SES, or class). The study of reproductive choice illustrates this theme quite well. For example, reproductive choice is too often tied to socioeconomic status such that rich women are almost always guaranteed this choice whereas other women are not. Women in developing nations face greater reproductive health risks than women in more developed nations, but women in the most developed of nations still suffer from lack of reproductive choice. In some countries, the right to choose abortion and contraception is the issue; in others, the right to refuse it is the issue.

It is increasingly apparent that a broad range of reproductive health services is necessary because the best choice for a given woman is affected by many things—her health, her sexual relationships, the stage she has reached in her reproductive life, her status in society, her risk of suffering violence, her possible exposure to infected partners, and her access to education and information (Plata, 1994). For example, the likelihood of women's exposure to HIV from heterosexual contact varies significantly across cultures such that the effects of a contraceptive technology on HIV transmission may be more relevant in one culture versus another (hormonal methods do not reduce HIV transmission whereas barrier methods do).

"In a sane world, it would seem, humankind would place a high value on life and those able to provide it."
Marilyn Waring

The effectiveness and safety of different contraceptive technologies also may not generalize across cultures. As seen in the section on reproductive health, the danger of a given reproductive technology depends upon the information and medical care received. A good example is the contraceptive pill. In most Western countries, a physician prescribes the pill, and a woman must have a Pap smear once a year to get her prescription renewed. This permits screening for cervical cancer and allows the dosage to be adjusted if there are side effects. The prescription requirement also provides the opportunity for screening out those women for whom the pill is contraindicated, such as those with heart disease or diabetes and those who smoke. However, in some countries (including Brazil, Mexico, and Bangladesh), the pill is sold without a prescription in pharmacies and stores. Depo-Provera is sold over the counter in Nigeria and even along the roadside (Pearce, 1996). Long distances to health-care facilities often preclude the monitoring that increases the safety and effectiveness of contraceptive methods.

It is also the case that some side effects may be more tolerable in some societies than in others. Hartmann (1995) gives a number of such examples. For instance, the heavy bleeding that may accompany use of Depo-Provera and IUDs is especially difficult for poor women who face practical difficulties in coping with the bleeding, because they have only unsterile rags to use. Prolonged bleeding is also a problem for women in some Muslim countries where a woman's everyday activities are curtailed during menstruation for religious reasons (Jacobson, 1992). Conversely, one of the most common reasons cited for discontinuing hormonal methods of contraception is disruption of the menstrual cycle (Jacobson, 1992). To many women, such bleeding is a sign of good health and fertility, and in some cultures it is viewed as a cleansing of bad blood or spirits.

Reduced lactation caused by hormonal contraceptives containing estrogen is another side effect that affects women in some countries more than others. Hartmann (1995) suggests that it is one of the greatest dangers of the contraceptive pill in the Third World. For millions of infants, breast milk is the main source of nutrition for several years. Use of hormonal contraceptives during lactation can contribute to infant malnutrition and higher infant mortality rates. In short, greater attention needs to be paid to the variable social and biological circumstances of women's lives so that available methods can be appropriately applied (Snow, 1994).

Feminists generally feel strongly that women must be able to control the number and spacing of their children before they can achieve equality. However, this too must be placed in cultural context. As Dixon-Mueller (1993) points out, a reduction in fertility in the absence of other social changes can actually worsen women's status in societies where childbearing is their main source of satisfaction and claim to social consideration. Many cultures place a high value on a woman having a large number of children and on men who father large numbers of children. In many African countries, the women strive to bring to maturity at least six children and view childbearing as a primary responsibility (Mikell, 1997). In societies where women feel that they must be married in order to achieve any kind of respect, they may have children in order to bind their husbands more securely to them.

In this chapter you learned that reproductive control is both a reflection and a determinant of women's equality. In addition, it greatly affects women's health. These are the reasons why so many people all over the world have worked so hard for women's reproductive rights. Indeed, it is exciting and important to realize just how much progress has occurred from activism. Large non-governmental organizations like the Center for Reproductive Rights and the International Federation of Planned Parenthood, and thousands of small grassroots non-governmental organizations are devoted to providing women with control over their reproductive lives.

Study Questions

1. What is reproductive control?
2. In what way is a lack of reproductive control a symptom of women's low status and power?
3. How does women's lack of reproductive control perpetuate their lower status?
4. Why is reproductive control a major women's health issue?
5. What is female genital mutilation? Where is it practiced? What is its purpose? What health problems does it create? What is being done to stop it?
6. How is women's reproductive choice sometimes controlled by the men in their lives?
7. How do government population control programs frequently interfere with women's reproductive choice and health? What is pronatalism? What is antinatalism? What are some of the faulty assumptions underlying coercive antinatalist programs?
8. What role does profit making play in women's reproductive choice?
9. What influence does religion have on women's reproductive choice?
10. What are some of the factors influencing rates of abortion? Does legality affect the incidence of abortion? What is the relationship between legality and mortality rate? Why may abortion be legal but largely unavailable?
11. Why is it important to consider cultural diversity when considering reproductive rights?

Discussion Questions and Activities

1. Does feminist advocacy of abortion rights mean that feminists must condone the use of abortion for the sex selection of sons over daughters?
2. Why is it that women end up being largely responsible for contraception? To what extent is it symbolic of their lower power? Would leaving it up to men represent a loss of control over women's bodies?
3. First World countries often make financial aid to developing nations contingent upon their reducing population growth. To this end, the First

World countries often encourage the antinatalist programs of developing nations. Do First World countries have the right to do this?

4. Interview several people from another generation. Ask them about the contraceptive methods available when they were of childbearing age and ask what happened when unplanned pregnancies occurred. Were they able to decide how many children they wanted and the spacing of those children?

Activist Websites of Interest

RAINBO Research Action and Information Network for the Bodily Integrity of Women

http://www.rainbo.org

Feminist Majority Organization

http://www.feminist.org/rrights/index.asp

The Female Genital Cutting Education and Networking Project

http://www.fgmnetwork.org/volunteers/index.html

Stop FGM

http://www.stopfgm.org

Women on Waves

http://www.womenonwaves.org/index_eng.html

Catholics for Free Choice

http://www.cath4choice.org/

Informational Websites of Interest

The Center for Reproductive Law

http://www.crlp.org

International Planned Parenthood Federation (IPFF)

http://www.ippf.org

United Nations Population Fund (UNFPA)

http://www.unfpa.org

Global Reproductive Health Forum

http://www.hsph.harvard.edu/grhf/WoC/index.html

World Health Organization's Department of Reproductive Health and Research

http://www.who.int/rht/

Action Opportunities

1. Do a project to increase women's reproductive choice in your community. For instance, distribute wallet-sized cards on public transportation with the locations and numbers of family planning clinics in your area, or volunteer at a family planning clinic.

2. Why don't young women ask men to use condoms and how can this be changed? Develop a program to help young women develop the skills to request that male sexual partners use condoms. See http://www.plannedparenthood.org/bc/condom.htm for some things to say when men resist using condoms. Present your workshop in the dorms, at sorority meetings, or to at-risk teen girls.

3. All over the world activists work to increase the availability of emergency contraception and women's knowledge about it because they believe that it will reduce unwanted pregnancies and abortion. Get involved in a campaign to increase availability (numerous letter-writing and petition campaigns seek to make it available "over-the-counter"). Or, do an informational campaign to educate women in your community about emergency contraception and where it may be obtained.

4. U.S. women spend approximately 70 percent more money out-of-pocket than men spend on health care because their employer's health insurance plan does not cover prescription contraceptives. The issue of contraceptive equity gained momentum when most insurance companies decided to cover the male impotence drug Viagra but did not cover drugs and devices that would reduce the number of unwanted pregnancies. What is your state law regarding contraceptive equity? Go to http://www.crlp.org/st_law_equity.html to find out. Get involved in a federal or state campaign for contraceptive equity.

5. The United Nations Population Fund (UNFPA) and the International Federation of Planned Parenthood (IPPF) are major funders of family planning services worldwide. Such services allow women to control the timing and spacing of their pregnancies without resorting to abortion. Go to the UNFPA and IPPF websites (http://www.unfpa.org and http://www.ippf.org) to discover whether lobbying efforts are still needed to get the United States to restore the $34 million of funding cut by the Bush administration in 2002. Conduct a letter-writing campaign or petition drive to send to your congressional representatives. Or participate in a fund-raising campaign. For example, in 2003, a grassroots campaign was started to replace the monies denied by the U.S. government. Called the "34 Million Friends Campaign," the campaign requests that people send $1 or more to The United States Committee for UNFPA, 220 East 42nd Street, Suite 2800, New York, NY 10017 http://www.unfpa.org/support/friends/34million.htm.

6. RAINBO, the Research Action and Information Network for the Bodily Integrity of Women, is an international non-profit organization working to eradicate female genital cutting. They work with non-governmental organizations in Africa to promote alternatives to FGC and provide information to immigrant women and doctors. To help, you can: spread the word about their work and their website (http://www.rainbo.org), link your website to theirs, or make a financial contribution.

4

Lesbians in Cross-Cultural Perspective

No woman can determine the direction of her own life without the ability to determine her sexuality. Sexuality is an integral, deeply ingrained part of every human being's life and should not be subject to debate or coercion. Anyone who is truly committed to women's human rights must recognize that every woman has the right to determine her sexuality free of discrimination and oppression.

—Palesa Beverley Ditsie of South Africa, speaking at the 1995 Fourth World Conference on Women

Deepa Mehta (left), the director of the film "Fire," participates in a candlelight vigil outside the Regal Theater in New Delhi, India, in December 1998. "Fire" was pulled from theaters all over India after protests against the film's subject matter (a lesbian relationship) disrupted showings. Worldwide, lesbianism is viewed as a violation of the traditional female role and is often punishable.

This chapter focuses on lesbians cross-culturally. Simply put, **lesbians** are female homosexuals, women affectionally and sexually attracted to women. However, there are other definitions as well—some that focus on the politics of lesbianism and others that focus on self-identification as a lesbian. It is important at the outset to understand that lesbians are diverse. Some of this diversity stems from cultural differences and some of it from individual differences. There is no one way to be lesbian and some women switch back and forth in their sexual identity.

The inclusion of lesbianism in our topic of global women is important because it underscores themes common to the cross-cultural study of women. For instance, women's lives are heavily determined by traditional gender roles, and women do not typically have the option to stray from these. Most societies direct women toward a female role centered on heterosexual marriage and family. Women are expected to marry or pair with men, and women's social status is typically based upon their ties to men. Furthermore, in most societies, the work of adult women is unpaid or underpaid. Consequently, women are economically dependent upon marriage to men. This restricts the freedom of heterosexual and homosexual women alike but may be especially great for lesbian women who must falsely live a heterosexual life. Therefore, the struggle for lesbians' right to control their lives is part of women's general struggle to control their own lives.

Another theme throughout the book is that those who challenge traditional female roles often experience negative social consequences. The significant discrimination and hardship lesbians face worldwide exemplifies this. Societal pressure toward heterosexual marriage makes anything else seem deviant and unnatural. Yet another reason for including lesbians in our cross-cultural study of women is that it fits with the goal of including and valuing a wide range of women's experiences. Although allegedly committed to women's diversity, heterosexual feminists have regularly overlooked their lesbian sisters, despite the fact that many women are not heterosexual.

There is one more reason to include lesbianism in this book and that is that **homophobia** (fear of homosexuals) and **heterosexism** (prejudice against homosexuals) is often used as a weapon against feminism. For example, in Croatia, one of the most prominent women's human rights groups has been targeted by a newspaper-based campaign alleging that the group is comprised of "unnatural women without children, lesbians and women in league with the Serbian aggressors" (Amnesty International, 2001). Pharr (1988) suggests that homophobia, along with economics and violence against women, acts to keep sexism in place. These weapons threaten women with pain and loss should they challenge women's subordination to men. Women often distance themselves from feminism for fear of being labeled "lesbian" and the losses that this label entails (such as, in employment, approval of friends and family, community, children, and safety). Calling feminists lesbians is a way of ostracizing and disempowering feminism. It is a way to keep

"Enforced heterosexuality is tied to women's lack of economic power and the restriction of female activity to the domestic sphere. Further, the embeddedness of sexuality with gender roles in Western societies proscribes homosexual activity and defines women as male sex objects."
Evelyn Blackwood, anthropologist

"When any woman curtails her freedom or fails to take an action or say what she believes out of fear of being labeled a lesbian, then homophobia has denied her independence and sapped her strength."
Charlotte Bunch, Human Rights Lawyer

"What is important is not the gender of the two people in the relationship with each other but the content of that relationship. Does that relationship contain violence, control of one person by the other? Is the relationship a growthful place for those involved?"
Suzanne Pharr

women conforming with traditional gender roles and gender stereotypes lest they be called lesbian (Greene, 1994). As Pharr (1988) says,

> So what does one do in an effort to keep from being called a lesbian? She steps back into line, into the role that is demanded of her, tries to behave in such a way that doesn't threaten the status of men, and if she works for women's rights, she begins modifying that work. When women's organizations begin doing significant social change work, they inevitably are lesbian-baited; that is, funders or institutions or community members tell us that they can't work with us because of our "man-hating attitudes" or the presence of lesbians. We know that as long as the word lesbian can strike fear in any woman's heart, then work on behalf of women can be stopped; the only successful work against sexism must include work against homophobia. (p. 263)

It is interesting to consider this equation of feminism with lesbianism given the real facts of the matter. Indeed, it may surprise some readers to find that despite stereotypes to the contrary, mainstream feminism is at times guilty of ignoring lesbianism. Lesbian activists from Colombia, Hong Kong, the Philippines, Malaysia, Thailand, India, Germany, the United States, the United Kingdom, and Italy have all reported barriers to advancing lesbian rights within their feminist movements (Dorf & Perez, 1995; Mak et al., 1995; Nur, 1995; Rondon, 1995). Women's movements vary significantly in the extent to which they address issues of sexual orientation (Basu, 1995). It is not that heterosexual feminists are always unsympathetic to lesbian issues, but sometimes they are ignorant. Other times they want to enhance their credibility with the larger public and therefore distance themselves from lesbians. Basu (1995) notes that the stronger women's movements are, and the less worried they are about survival, the more likely it is that they will be inclusive and advocate for lesbian rights.

"If lesbians were truly perceptible, then the idea that women can survive without men might work itself into social reality."
Sarah Lucia Hoagland

Just as it is true that most feminists are not lesbians, it is also true that most lesbians are not feminists. Yes, it is true that lesbianism can be a feminist political statement and identity, a point discussed later in the chapter. But feminism is not the usual motivator of lesbianism. Indeed, for most lesbians, lesbianism is a quiet, personal matter that arises out of a natural sexual attraction to women or from falling in love with a woman. In most cases, lesbianism is not intended as a political statement. Lesbians, like heterosexual women, are diverse in their feminism and vary in their awareness of women's issues and in their activism for women's equality.

One last point before continuing. Although most societies currently view homosexuality and bisexuality as a sickness or deny their existence entirely, most psychologists and biologists believe that they are just instances of many human variations. Following significant lobbying by lesbian and gay political organizations, the American Psychiatric Association removed homosexuality from its list of mental disorders in 1974. The APA currently takes the position that it is no more abnormal to be homosexual than it is to be left-handed, which 15 percent of the population is. The World Health Organization removed homosexuality from its list of diseases in 1991. I will not dwell here on the causes of lesbianism, as I do not wish to add to the perception that it is an abnormality in need of explanation, prevention, or treatment. For instance, people generally do not ask why heterosexuals are heterosexual for it is viewed as normal and not in need of explanation. However, you should know that lesbians are not women that wish they were men, nor are they necessarily more "mannish" than heterosexual women. Also, research does not support the notion that women turn into lesbians because they are abused by men. Likewise, there is no support for the idea that women turn to other women because they are too unattractive to attract men, or because there is a shortage of men (Greene, 1994).

The Incidence of Lesbianism

Women in every culture and throughout history have undertaken the task of independent, nonheterosexual, women-connected existence (Rich, 1980). Examinations of ancient literature, art, and anthropology reveal that lesbianism has always existed and has not always been viewed as unacceptable and deviant. The designation *lesbian* comes from ancient Greece and the life of the lyric poet Sappho, who lived on the island of Lesbos (600 B.C.E.). Some of her poetry described her strong love for women. Cavin (1985) notes that it is ironic that lesbians are omitted from discussions of early society because, according to her, the earliest recorded history, art, and literature of Western society documents their existence: Lesbians in Sparta and Crete (400 B.C.E.); and among the Celts described by Aristotle. Lesbianism was also reported in Athens (450 B.C.E.) and in Rome (100 C.E.). Several ancient Chinese sexual handbooks also describe lesbian activities, and lesbian relationships are celebrated in a number of Chinese plays and stories dating from the tenth to the eighteenth centuries (Ruan & Bullough, 1992).

Anthropological accounts indicate that lesbianism was acceptable in a number of cultures prior to Western colonization (Allen, 1992; Blackwood, 1986; Greene, 1994). As Kendall (1998) says of her studies of lesbianism in Lesotho, an African country, "Love between women is as native to southern Africa as the soil itself, but . . . homophobia . . . is a Western import" (p. 224). Native American Paula Gunn Allen (1992), claims that colonizers of Native American tribes tried to make Native American culture resemble European patriarchy and the flexible and fluid sexuality found in many tribes did not fit this paradigm. Thus colonization is linked to the growth of prejudice against lesbians (Allen, 1986). Anthropologists also believe that Native American women from the Mohave, Maricopa, Cocopa, Klamath, and Kaska tribes could marry other women and make love with other women without being stigmatized (Blackwood, 1984).

In many cultures, female–female romantic relationships occur prior to heterosexual marriage. Faderman (1981) found numerous examples of female–female romantic love relationships among European women from the seventeenth through the early twentieth centuries when she studied their letters to each other and the poetry and fiction written by women at that time. Likewise, in Lesotho, it is not uncommon for women to have romantic relationships with each other prior to and even during heterosexual marriage (Gay, 1986; Kendall, 1998). However, it appears that the acceptability of such relationships is due in part to their not being defined as "sexual" relationships (because no penis is involved!). For instance, Faderman's exploration suggests that it was not until after World War I, when the possibility of their sexual nature was acknowledged, that these intense romantic friendships were stigmatized. Similarly, Kendall (1998) concludes that although lesbian or lesbianlike behavior is common among Lesotho women, it is not viewed as sexual, nor as an alternative to heterosexual marriage. Both Kendall (1998) and Gay (1986) note the decline of lesbianlike relationships in Lesotho women exposed to Western ideas.

Lesbian Invisibility

"For the lesbian of color, the ultimate rebellion she can make against her native culture is through her sexual behavior. . . . We're afraid of being abandoned by the mother, the culture, *la Raza,* for being unacceptable, faulty, damaged. . . . To avoid rejection, some of us conform to the values of the culture, push the unacceptable parts into the shadows."
Gloria Anzaldua

In most contemporary societies, lesbianism has been rendered invisible by cultures that cannot deal with it and by lesbians who keep their lesbianism to themselves. For instance, in China, where lesbians may be jailed or forced to receive electroshock or aversion therapy, lesbianism requires great secrecy (Dorf & Perez, 1995; Ruan & Bullough, 1992). This global tendency for **lesbian invisibility,** for lesbians to live quiet, hidden lives, makes it difficult for us to get an accurate picture of lesbian experience worldwide. Lesbian invisibility also makes lesbians invisible to each other. This makes it difficult for them to identify as lesbians and be part of an accepting community of other lesbians (Penelope, 1990).

Lesbianism is also underdocumented because most cultures prefer to deny its existence. For example, there is no word for lesbian in most Asian languages (Greene, 1994). One of India's top scientists insisted that homosexuality is alien to India because "there are laws against it" (Dorf & Perez, 1995). Likewise, some country representatives at the UN's Fourth Women's World Conference balked at resolutions designed to protect lesbian rights. They claimed that there were no lesbians in their countries and that lesbianism was a Western cultural notion. However, as a statement from Third World lesbians at the 1985 UN Women's Conference in Nairobi said, if it seems that lesbianism is confined to Western White women, it is only because Third World lesbians and lesbians of color face more obstacles to visibility (Bunch, 1995). Box 4.1 lists organizations working for lesbian human rights. A glance at this list makes it clear that lesbianism is a worldwide phenomenon.

BOX 4.1 *Women Around the Globe: A Sampling of Lesbian and Gay Organizations Working for Lesbian Rights*

Lesbians a la Vista is an Argentinean group demonstrating for lesbian rights as human rights.

Colectivo Ciguay is a group in the Dominican Republic working against discrimination and harassment in a country that considers homosexuality an "offense against morality."

Gays and Lesbians of Zimbabwe struggles against social and political discrimination, homophobia, and laws that outlaw homosexuality.

Afro Lesbian and Gay Club in Ghana works against laws that ban homosexuality as "unnatural carnal knowledge" punishable by up to three years in jail.

Gay and Lesbian Organisation of Witwatersrand works to ensure that South Africa's new constitution provides civil rights protection to lesbians and gays.

The Asian Lesbian Network includes Asian lesbian groups from Bangladesh, India, Indonesia, Japan, Malaysia, Singapore, Thailand, the United States, the United Kingdom, the Netherlands, and Australia. These groups work together to document and combat discrimination.

RFSL is a Swedish group that has successfully assisted gay and lesbian refugees from the Middle East, Asia, and Latin America in their quest for political asylum in Sweden.

AKOE is a lesbian and gay group in Greece that provides support, protests antigay acts, and networks with other Mediterranean lesbians and gays.

Fiida is a group of Black lesbians in the Netherlands that works to combat discrimination based on race and sexual orientation.

Lambda became the first official gay and lesbian organization in Poland in 1992.

Society for the Protection of Personal Rights is an Israeli group working for legislation to protect lesbians and gay men.

International Lesbian and Gay Association (ILGA) documents human rights abuses against homosexuals worldwide and builds international bridges among homosexual groups.

Source: Amnesty International, 1997.

In anthropology and the social sciences, lesbianism has received far less study than male homosexuality (Blackwood, 1986; Blackwood & Wieringa, 1999). Cavin (1985) examined the Human Relations Area Files, the main anthropological database, for studies of lesbianism. Her search led her to conclude that Western anthropologists have hardly addressed the subject of lesbianism and that widespread societal sanctions against lesbianism have inhibited the free flow of information regarding it. Even so, in the Human Relations Area Files, she found evidence of lesbianism in thirty different societies from all over the world. Lesbianism did not appear to be more common to any one type of economy, family or household type, marriage form, stratification system, or marital residence. In other words, lesbianism reaches across a number of societies and social categories.

The social stigma associated with lesbianism also means that accurate information is difficult to attain. For instance, although survey research in the United States reveals that between 8 and 17 percent of American women are sexually involved with other women (Stevens & Hall, 1991), these figures probably underrepresent the frequency of lesbianism because many women are reluctant to share this information with interviewers. Furthermore, as Rich (1980) points out, without the profound social pressures to live a heterosexual life, the occurrence of lesbianism would probably be a lot higher. We simply do not know the numbers of lesbians who have remained in heterosexual marriages for most of their lives (Rich, 1980).

Factors Contributing to Lesbian Invisibility

Although homosexuality has not always been viewed as aberrant and unacceptable, it is generally viewed as such by contemporary cultures. For example, in Western cultures, by the nineteenth century and through much of the twentieth, lesbianism was viewed as an illness in need of treatment. Confinement in mental asylums, clitoridectomy, and psychotherapy were at times considered appropriate treatments for lesbianism. The presentation of lesbianism in the medical literature further contributed to extreme and negative stereotypes of lesbians (Stevens & Hall, 1991). In some countries, such as Russia, lesbians are still subjected to "cures" such as involuntary psychiatric treatment and electroshock therapy.

Although the lesbian experience is diverse within and across cultures, one aspect is relatively consistent today; that is, lesbianism is viewed as a violation of the traditional female role, and the social consequences of such deviation are often quite severe. Simply stated, women are expected to enter and stay in heterosexual unions and to enact a specific role as adult women. Those who don't, face trouble. As feminist historian Gerda Lerner says in her book *The Creation of Patriarchy* (1986), for women historically, and in most societies today, class is mediated through their sexual ties to a man. It is through men that women have access to or are denied access to the means of production and to resources. It is through their sexual behavior that they gain access to class. Breaking the sexual rules can "declass" women and consign them to the lowest status possible.

Pharr (1988) outlines a variety of losses that threaten lesbian women in heterosexual society. For the reasons described later, lesbians most frequently stay in the closet, that is, hide their lesbian identity from others and sometimes from themselves. The stigma and risk associated with acknowledging one's lesbian identity make coming out of the closet a lifelong process. These potential losses are elaborated below.

Employment   According to Pharr, almost every lesbian who is not self-employed or in a business that does not require social approval fears loss of her job should her lesbianism become known. She asks us to consider whether we know any

FIGURE 4.1   *Losses That Threaten Lesbians in Heterosexual Societies*

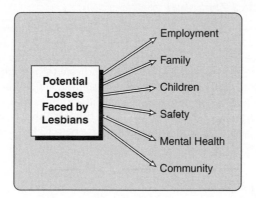

businesses that will knowingly hire and protect people who are openly gay or
lesbian. In thirty-seven states of the United States, it is still legal to fire someone
because they are lesbian or gay (Macleod, 2003). In Peru in 1987, police raided
a lesbian bar and then arranged to have the women's departure from the police station shown on the national news. Many of the women lost their jobs,
some were beaten by their families, and at least two were raped on their way
home from the police station (Dorf & Perez, 1995). In Brazil, the discovery of
a woman's lesbianism is also likely to lead to dismissal from her job (Martinho,
1995). In a 1993 survey of 800 British lesbians, 68 percent said that they had
concealed their sexuality from some or all of those with whom they work
(Palmer, 1995). In general, cross-culturally lesbians keep their sexual orientation hidden in order to hold onto their jobs. Lesbians also do not disclose their
sexual identities in fear that it will negatively affect relationships with cowork-
ers and interfere with their promotion and advancement (McLeod, 2003).

Family   The potential loss of family approval, acceptance, and love is another
threat faced by lesbians worldwide. Almost every lesbian struggles with when
and how (or if) to tell her family. In collectivist cultures where deviant behaviors bring shame on the family and people define themselves primarily in
terms of family and community, this is an especially big issue (see Box 4.2 for
an example from Zimbabwe). For many families, a daughter's heterosexual
marriage is an expected duty, and it is a social embarrassment to have an unmarried daughter over a certain age. The pressure to marry and have children
is explicit and intense and strict obedience to parents is expected (Greene,
1994). Daughters that do not marry men may be looked at as selfish since they
put their own happiness above the happiness of their family and dishonor the
family. Families are often angry and rejecting of daughters who disgrace them
by not conforming to this social program. In Brazil, for instance, Alice Dias
do Amaral was murdered by her lover's brothers after they found out about
their sister's lesbianism (Dorf & Perez, 1995). In many countries, lesbians are

Australia, Canada,
Netherlands, Slovenia,
Sweden, and the U.S.
have all passed laws to
reduce discrimination in
the workplace based on
sexual orientation.

BOX 4.2   *Activist Profile: Tina Machida of Zimbabwe*

Tina Machida is head of the GALZ, the Gay and Lesbian group of Zimbabwe. This is an act of bravery in a country where the president crusades against homosexuals and casts them as enemies of society. Machida's parents had her raped in the hopes that she would marry her rapist but she ran away and refused. Despite her pride in working openly for gay and lesbian rights, she feels guilty about its effects on her family.

> My parents are ignorant, and, like a lot of people, they think that homosexuality is unnatural and needs to be wiped out. At one point, a few years ago, I couldn't take it anymore, and I went to my mother and said I was going to kill myself. She said, "Good riddance to bad rubbish." I live with a lot of guilty feelings. I still believe in the traditions of my parents. Sometimes I wish I could go back into the closet but it is the satisfaction of walking through the gate here [GALZ headquarters] and seeing people laughing and talking—and knowing we are giving them something—that keeps me going.

Source: Amnesty International, 2001; Murphy, 1998

"In 1994 in Lima a very violent raid was carried out in the capital where about seventy-five lesbian women were beaten up and ill-treated by the police. Prostitutes get a very rough time in jail. But the treatment of lesbians was even worse. Lesbians were beaten up because, however degrading prostitution can be, it is still regarded as normal behavior, whereas lesbianism is seen as too threatening to the status quo."
Anonymous Peruvian witness

expelled from their homes, disowned, and subjected to physical and emotional abuse by their families.

In some countries families force their lesbian daughters to marry in an attempt to cure them. This is common in Thailand (Tarawan, 1995), Zimbabwe (Clark, 1995), Mexico (Perez & Jimenez, 1995), Iran (Vahme-Sabz, 1995), Turkey (Kilic & Uncu, 1995), and India (Cath, 1995). Many lesbians marry men to avoid family and social censure. For instance, most lesbians in Japan are married to men because remaining single is a social stigma (Ishino & Wakabayashi, 1995). Many Brazilian lesbians invent fictitious relationships with men or marry in order to avoid the rejection of parents and relatives (Martinho, 1995). Polish lesbians are also likely to be married to men because of pressure from their families and a desire to be accepted in society (Garnier, 1995).

Children   Lesbians must often keep their lesbianism secret for fear of losing their children. Most societies continue to believe that lesbians will create homosexual children or will sexually abuse them. In the United States, a 1995 court ruling in Virginia denied a lesbian woman custody of her son based on the presumption that the child would be harmed by growing up in a home where "active lesbianism" was practiced (Reske, 1995). In Germany, lesbian mothers are often denied custody of their children on the grounds of their "immoral lifestyle" (Duda & Wuch, 1995). This argument is used in a number of countries, including Mexico (Perez & Jimenez, 1995), the United States (Minter, 1995), and Uruguay (Martinez, 1995). Allegations of lesbianism, whether true or not, can result in a woman losing custody of her children in Serbia (Todosijevic, 1995) and in Nicaragua (Gonzalez, 1995).

These decisions are based on faulty assumptions. A number of recent research studies in the United States, Britain, and the Netherlands find no relationship between a mother's sexual orientation and her child's mental health, no evidence that homosexual parents are more likely to be sexually inappropriate with their children, and no evidence that their children are more likely to become homosexual (Brooks & Goldberg, 2001; Cooper, 1997; Patterson & Redding, 1996). Indeed, heterosexual adult males perpetrate approximately 90 percent of sexual abuse of children (Brooks & Goldberg, 2001). Despite this, lesbians are regularly denied their right to have children through artificial insemination and adoption and are refused custody of their biological children (Dorf & Perez, 1995; Patterson & Redding, 1996).

Safety   Lesbians worldwide may be subjected to physical and verbal attacks. This is yet another reason why lesbians typically keep their lesbianism hidden. Koen and Terry (1995), in a report on lesbians in South Africa, say that lesbians in South Africa are frequently targets of rape and assault. A recent survey of lesbian, gay, and transgendered students at American universities found that more than one-third said they experienced harassment in the past year and 20 percent said they feared for their safety because of their sexual orientation (Chronicle of Higher Education, 2003). Cases like that of 15-year-old Sakia Gunn of Newark, New Jersey fuel such fears. In 2003, Sakia was stabbed to death after telling a man that she and her friends were lesbians (Strunsky, 2003).

In many countries, police and legal systems offer little protection. In Zimbabwe, police decline to take a report if a victim of violence is homosexual (Murphy, 1998). Lesbianism is illegal in a number of countries, as Box 4.3 shows. For instance, in Malaysia, lesbians are whipped as punishment. In Iran, lesbians are executed after the fourth offense. In Nicaragua, the law specifies a penalty of one to three years of imprisonment for lesbianism. Lesbians are also regularly denied their basic rights to freedom from torture, punitive psychiatry, and arbitrary arrest and incarceration (Dorf & Perez, 1995). A handful of countries even punish homosexuality with death and since the 1990s, documented executions have occurred in Afghanistan, Iran, Sudan, Yemen, and Bahrain (Seager, 2003). Also, it should be noted that even when there are not laws specifically prohibiting lesbianism, there are often legal means by which to arrest lesbians. For instance, in Argentina, police may arrest and hold anyone while they check the person's police record, and they may arrest lesbians under an infraction known as "incitement to commit a carnal act in the public street" (Sarda, 1995).

Mental Health   In reading lesbians' accounts from around the world, one thing is evident: There is often a feeling of exile associated with being a lesbian. There are numerous sources of psychological stress for lesbians. First, lesbians experience great psychological conflict because of a conflict between their sexual orientation and the perceived ideals of society. Raised in homophobic societies, lesbians have often internalized the societal message that

> "Being comfortable with homosexuality in societies that view your life as being not only abnormal but in fundamental opposition to patriarchal notions of the family, love, and heterosexual norms of desire is never an easy process, no matter where one lives."
> *Kaushalya Bannerji*

> "Lesbians in Iran face violence and harassment not only from the state but also within their families and their communities; with no existing lesbian organizations and no attention to lesbian issues from women's groups or other organizations, lesbians who experience such violence have few places to turn."
> *Vahme-Sabz*

BOX 4.3   *Countries with Laws Criminalizing Lesbianism*

Afghanistan	Malaysia
Algeria	Mauritania
Angola	Mauritius
Bahrain	Morocco
Bangladesh	Mozambique
Barbados	Namibia
Benin	Nepal
Bhutan	Nicaragua
Brunei	Oman
Cameroon	Pakistan
Cape Verde	Qatar
Democratic Republic of Congo	Saint Lucia
Djibouti	Saudi Arabia
Eritrea	Senegal
Guinea	Seychelles
Guyana	Sierra Leone
Iran	Singapore
Kuwait	Solomon Islands
Lebanon	Somalia
Liberia	Sudan
Libya	Western Samoa
Malawi	Yemen
Mozambique	

Source: International Gay and Lesbian Human Rights Commission, 2003

---

homosexuals are bad. Consequently, they experience lowered self-esteem and shame, as well as guilt about maintaining a false image as a heterosexual (Friedman & Downey, 1995). The greater the invisibility of lesbians in a culture, the greater the problem this presents. Young lesbians who have never met another lesbian and are told that lesbianism is a sickness are especially likely to suffer. This may result in self-directed homophobia and can lead to isolation, passive acceptance of persecution, exile, and even suicide (Dorf & Perez, 1995).

Even in liberal countries, lesbians experience ongoing stress because of the effort required to conceal their sexual identity to avoid rejection, discrimination, and violence. Lesbians must continually decide who is safe to tell—that is, who is safe to "come out" to. They often worry about the negative reactions that may occur should their sexual orientation become known. This actual and expected harassment creates an emotional stress that seriously impedes personal development (D'Augelli, 1992). As Pharr says, an overtly homophobic world that permits cruelty to lesbians makes it difficult for lesbians and gays to maintain a strong sense of well-being and esteem.

Community and Credibility   Lesbians lose a sense of belongingness in their communities when they are rejected and ostracized by those with homophobic attitudes. Women who openly live as lesbians may no longer be respected, listened to, honored, or believed. They often become social outcasts. For instance, in the United States in 1992, in Mississippi, local citizens attempted to force two lesbians from their land using the state's antisodomy laws (Dorf & Perez, 1995).

The Perception of Lesbianism as Dangerous

What kinds of arguments are made against lesbianism? The most common seems to be that it is "unnatural." Some argue, for instance, that females and males are "designed" to have sex with one another for procreative purposes; therefore homosexual sex is unnatural. Heterosexuality may also seem natural because most adults appear to live heterosexual lives. Lesbian invisibility further contributes to this notion because we are generally unaware of the lesbians among us. Societies also emphasize heterosexual coupling as the norm and something to aspire to. For these reasons, homosexuality may appear abnormal, but the fact that it persists across time and culture despite societies' efforts to discourage it indicates that it is natural for many people.

Some feminists suggest that lesbians appear dangerous because lesbianism is a threat to men's control over women. Lesbians challenge notions of what constitutes a family, a household, and "normal" sexual relationships and this makes it subversive (Penelope, 1990; Seager, 2003). The general argument goes like this: To protect and sustain women's traditional heterosexual roles as wives and mothers, the culture stigmatizes and pathologizes lesbianism (Stevens & Hall, 1991). Were lesbianism to become acceptable and were women to believe that they could live independently of men, men would be less able to exploit women's sexuality and to use them as a source of unpaid labor. In short, men would have less control over women and would have sexual and emotional access to women only on women's terms. For example, Trujillo (1991) says that Chicana lesbians pose a threat to the

Chicano community because they threaten the cultural beliefs that women should define themselves in terms of men and should be subservient to men. The existence of Chicana lesbians, she says, is a threat to the established order of male control and oppressive attitudes toward women.*

One of the best-known feminists with this perspective is Adrienne Rich. In her classic book *Of Woman Born* (1976), she suggests that heterosexuality is "institutionalized." By this she means that most modern cultures require that a woman be legally married to a man, and anything, including lesbianism, that threatens this social order is viewed as deviant. Patriarchy, she says, could not survive without motherhood and sexuality in their institutional forms. Therefore, societies typically present wife and motherhood as "natural" and "unquestionable." This idealization of heterosexual marriage and romance can be seen in art, literature, media, advertising, and so on.

According to Rich (1980), taboos against homosexuality and the enforcement of heterosexuality are a means of assuring the male right to physical, economical, and emotional access to women. Economic systems enforce **compulsory heterosexuality** by providing women with few economic options outside of marriage. Men need the labor provided by women's compliance with the traditional female gender role. This is ensured by rendering the lesbian possibility pathological and by destroying historical records of its existence. Rich adds that heterosexuality is a social institution imposed, managed, organized, propagandized, and at times maintained by force. Lesbian existence has been written out of history and portrayed as a disease, and the realities of lesbian existence are hidden as a means of keeping heterosexuality compulsory.

Lesbian Feminism

At the beginning of the chapter it was mentioned that for some women, lesbianism is a political feminist statement. **Lesbian feminism** may be defined as a variety of beliefs and practices based on the core assumption that there is a connection between an erotic and/or emotional commitment to women and political resistance to patriarchal domination (Taylor & Rupp, 1993). For instance, Simone de Beauvoir in *The Second Sex* (1953) presented lesbianism as a deliberate refusal to submit to the coercive force of heterosexual ideology, a refusal that acts as an underground feminist resistance to patriarchy. Similarly, Rich (1980) suggests that lesbian existence involves the rejection of a compulsory way of life and is a direct or indirect attack on male right of access to women. As she puts it, "Woman-identification is a source of energy, a potential springhead of female power, violently curtailed and wasted under the institution of heterosexuality" (p. 267). Ferguson (1981) said, "The possibility of a sexual relationship between women is an important challenge to

---

* *Chicana* and *Chicano* are used by some Latin Americans instead of *Hispanic,* a term adopted by the U.S. government and rejected by some activists.

patriarchy because it acts as an alternative to the patriarchal heterosexual couple, thus challenging the heterosexual ideology that women are dependent on men for romantic/sexual love and satisfaction" (p. 164). Or, as Penelope (1990) put it, we live in heteropatriarchal societies where men are the ruling class and everyone is, or should be heterosexual. Heteropatriachies restrict the possibilities of women's lives through laws, religion, and social pressure to marry men and define their lives in relation to them.

Lesbian feminism is a political movement that combines an interest in the liberation of women with an interest in the liberation of lesbians. Keeping homosexuals in the closet is viewed as the core of lesbian oppression. Therefore, "coming out"—that is, being open about one's lesbian identity with others—constitutes a political act. The strategy is that if everyone came out of the closet, lesbians and gays could not be oppressed because "they are everywhere" (Cavin, 1985).

Cavin (1985) claims that in the twentieth century lesbian feminism has emerged twice as a political movement, first in Germany and later in the United States. In Germany, lesbian feminists were politically active in both the early feminist and homosexual rights movements (1924–1935). Their activities continued until the Nazi regime sent them to the concentration camps, where they were forced to wear a pink triangle (now a symbol of lesbian and gay rights). Over 200,000 homosexuals died in Hitler's camps. The second emergence of lesbian feminism as a political movement began in the United States around 1970. It was stimulated in part by the neglect of lesbians by both the feminist and gay rights movements. Political lesbians learned that they had better speak for themselves or else they would not be heard at all (Cavin, 1985). According to Cavin, lesbian feminism is a worldwide political movement of lesbians that broadly encompasses all degrees of lesbian struggle for liberation from patriarchy. The goals range from liberal lesbians' efforts to obtain lesbian civil rights within current patriarchal systems to the radical lesbian separatist goal of overthrowing world patriarchy in order to liberate all women.

Most lesbian activism is not explicitly focused on the dismantling of patriarchy. Instead, the focus is on attaining the human rights and freedoms accorded to heterosexuals—rights like safety and privacy, and legal rights. Because they are not heterosexual, lesbians face particular challenges not experienced by heterosexual women. Heterosexual women may be oppressed, but at least society grants them a legitimate place as part of the cherished cultural unit of husband and wife. In addition to the safety, family, and employment losses lesbians face, they are denied the heterosexual privileges of social, cultural, and legal recognition (Calhoun, 1995). Lesbian activism is intended to remedy these problems.

A small minority of lesbian feminists identify themselves politically as lesbian separatists. **Lesbian separatism** began in the United States and Britain in the early 1970s. The idea is that lesbian liberation requires females' noncooperation with the patriarchal system. This noncooperation ranges from a woman's choice not to be involved with men socially, emotionally, sexually,

In 2003, the United States Supreme Court struck down laws making gay and lesbian sex illegal. The ruling voided laws in thirteen states that prohibited sex between same-sex partners.

politically, or economically to physical separation from the institutions and jurisdiction of patriarchy (Cavin, 1985). Originally, lesbian "homelands"— free from sexism, racism, and ageism and embodying positive female values such as caring, compassion, and community—were seen as important in accomplishing these goals. In the 1970s and 1980s some women lived in alternative separatist communities but by the 1990s, these were all but extinct. American lesbian separatist Jackie Anderson (1994) says that separatists begin with the assumption that injustices against women are expressions of hatred and violence and that the way to respond to this is to separate from men to the greatest extent possible. They are pessimistic that justice for women will be attained through legal remedies and appeals to moral values, such as equity. They conceive of a future for women that does not include men and in which lesbianism is the norm (Anderson, 1994).

"If we come out, we are more often than not exiled by the community. If we don't come out, we still feel that sense of exile because we are unable to share a very real part of ourselves with them."
Pratibha Parmar

Lesbian separatists and lesbian feminist movements do not characterize the lesbian experience in most of the world. Most lesbians live in countries where lesbianism must be kept secret and lesbians must live as heterosexuals to avoid persecution and for economic survival. In some countries, the lack of a lesbian community precludes a political lesbian existence. In many places it is not possible for such communities and networks to develop. Lesbian publications are shut down, police harass women going into lesbian meeting places, and political activity on the part of lesbians is simply not allowed. Sometimes female same-sex practices are a normal part of some cultures though they may not be labeled as lesbian (Blackwood & Wieringa, 1999).

Wage earning, the ability to live separately from kin, and lesbian bars and gathering places all seem to be preconditions for the development of a more political lesbianism where lesbians see themselves as an oppressed minority with a right to exist. Indeed, lesbian feminist communities and organizations are more common in modern capitalistic societies, and in those, are more common among urban, educated lesbians. Blackwood (1986) suggests that in societies where women do not have control over their productive activities, and may not gain status independently of men, lesbian behavior is more "informal."

Lesbian Responses to Invisibility and Heterosexism

Embracing the Lesbian Label

Some lesbians feel that normalizing lesbianism and reducing negative stereotypes of lesbians requires that lesbians embrace the lesbian label and come out as lesbians. Staying invisible is thought to perpetuate the notion that lesbians are inferior. Poet Audre Lorde, a self-identified "black, feminist, lesbian," felt that lesbians in secure positions had the power to break the silence and encourage more women to empower themselves by speaking up (in Wekker, 1993).

Although it is not surprising that lesbians often choose invisibility because of fears of social disapproval, discrimination, and violence, this makes it easier for stereotypes of homosexuals to be maintained. For instance, when lesbianism is acknowledged by the larger heterosexual culture, it is often portrayed inaccurately. Swedish lesbian Rebecka Lindau (1993) writes about how it is only in the last few years that the existence of lesbians in Sweden has been acknowledged. Unfortunately, however, the attention given to lesbianism by the Swedish mainstream media consists largely of ridicule and pornographic portrayals of lesbians as bisexual and sadomasochistic. In a report on Hong Kong, Mak and her coauthors (1995) report that lesbianism primarily appears in pornographic films for heterosexuals. These films often end with the women turning straight. In India, lesbianism is receiving increased media attention but is still portrayed as a curiosity and abnormality (Cath, 1995). Lesbians are of increasing interest to the Japanese media, but they are often portrayed pornographically or as tragic figures who try to seduce pretty women and fail (Ishino & Wakabayashi, 1995). Contemporary portrayals of lesbians in China generally depict lesbians as ugly women who no man will have or as women who were so badly treated by men as to be uncomfortable with male sexuality (Ruan & Bullough, 1992).

In the 1990s a number of popular U.S. entertainers came out in an effort to increase lesbian visibility and the accuracy of perceptions of lesbians (comedian Ellen DeGeneres, singer k.d. lang, and musician Melissa Etheridge are examples). Likewise, in Mexico, a number of artists have publicly come out as lesbians in support of lesbian rights. These include theatrical director Nancy Cardenas, musical performer Chavela Vargas, writer/director/comedian Jesusa Rodriguez, and writer and poet Rosamaria Roffiel (Perez & Jimenez, 1995).

Not all lesbians agree on the need to come out and embrace the lesbian label. Some, such as Rupp (1997), even question whether the term should be used to describe women that would not use it to describe themselves. Some non-western lesbians find the label restrictive and disrespectful of cultural traditions that support woman-woman relationships without calling attention to them (see Box 4.4). Also, in some non-western cultures, lesbian is viewed as a western word. Its use reduces the credibility of non-heterosexual relationships since detractors claim that lesbianism is a western import or the result of western colonization.

Lesbian Communities and Organizations

Lesbians sometimes adapt to their outsider status by developing their own lesbian communities and cultures within the larger culture. Lesbian organizations exist in Argentina, Australia, Austria, Bangladesh, Belgium, Brazil, Canada, Chile, Denmark, the Dominican Republic, Estonia, France, Germany, Honduras, Hong Kong, India, Indonesia, Ireland, Italy, Japan, Mexico, the Netherlands, New Zealand, Norway, Peru, the Philippines, Russia, South

"Somebody that you know, probably somebody that you care about, is gay or is a lesbian. And are you willing, really, to say that that person should be treated differently because of their sexual preference? I am not willing to do that."
Anita Faye Hill, American attorney known for her testimony against Supreme Court Justice nominee Clarence Thomas

"The one thing that *most* lesbians seem to have in common is the more or less conscious rejection of the social imperative that women must define ourselves in relation to men. In fact, it is the indifference to men that society finds so threatening."
Diane Griffin Crowder

"... it is important to make a distinction between the secrets from which we draw strength and the secrecy which comes from anxiety and is meant to protect us. If we want to have the power for ourselves this silence must be broken. I want to encourage more and more women to identify themselves, to speak their name, where and when they can, and to survive."

Audre Lorde, American poet and self-identified black lesbian feminist

BOX 4.4 *Two Black Women Poets on the Lesbian Label*

"I do not call myself 'lesbian' and I do not want to be called 'lesbian' either. Life is too complex for us to give names not derived from us, dirty, conditioned words, to the deepest feelings within me. . . . Simply doing things, without giving them a name, and preserving rituals and secrets between women are important to me. Deeds are more obvious and more durable than all the women who say they are lesbian and contribute nothing to women's energy." Astrid Roemer, Suriname poet

Source: Wekker (1993)

"We want to live proudly and with dignity. But to want such things as Lesbians, is complicated and difficult because we live in cultures which have forbidden our existence, and scapegoated and murdered those of us they identified as Lesbians (or "unnatural," "sick," or "mad"). What might appear to be perfectly simple and reasonable desires are perceived by those who hate us as "unreasonable"; once they've defined us as subhuman, we can be denied the most basic of rights."

Julia Penelope and Susan Wolfe

Africa, Spain, Sweden, Taiwan, Turkey, the United Kingdom, the United States, and Uruguay (Seager, 1997). These groups are important for the formation of a positive lesbian identity in the face of social stigma. They provide a social arena where lesbians do not have to hide. The Internet has also stimulated the development of lesbian community. Lesbians have electronic access to a wide range of lesbian organizations and chat groups.

Some groups work to enhance lesbian visibility and serve a political function as well. Depending upon the country, lesbian activists (see Box 4.1) may work for laws prohibiting discrimination based sexual orientation, the right to marry (especially important because so many governmental and employment benefits are shared with spouses), legal acknowledgment of partnerships, the right to adopt, the right to custody of their children, and the repeal of laws punishing homosexuality. For instance, South Africa's constitution now includes protection from discrimination on the grounds of sexual orientation. South Africa, Canada, Denmark, Slovenia, Spain, France, Norway, New Zealand, the Netherlands, and Sweden all have national legislation banning discrimination based on sexual orientation. Austria, Belgium, Canada, Denmark, Finland, Germany, the Netherlands, Norway, Sweden, and the United States all have accepted sexual orientation as grounds for political asylum. The activities of these groups are acts of bravery, for in many countries, lesbian publications are shut down, members of lesbian organizations are harassed, and meeting places are raided and closed down. For instance, Irene Petropoulou, the lesbian editor of a Greek lesbian and gay magazine, was sentenced to five months in prison and fined 50,000 drachma for publishing so-called indecent materials (Dorf & Perez, 1995).

Lesbian political organizations also work to have lesbian rights acknowledged as international human rights. At the 1995 United Nations Fourth

World Women's Conference in Beijing, lesbian advocacy groups worked toward including lesbian rights in the Platform for Action, the document that outlines women's human rights. This chapter's opening quote is from one of the activists. Unfortunately, language specifically referring to lesbian rights was not adopted. Even the term "sexual orientation" was excluded from the platform although in the health section of the platform it states, "The human rights of women include their right to have control over and decide freely and responsibly on matters related to their sexuality, including sexual and reproductive health, free of coercion, discrimination, and violence" (Bunch & Fried, 1996).

Lesbians have been granted to right to full, legal marriage in Belgium, the Netherlands, and in the Canadian provinces of Ontario and British Columbia.

Recovering Lesbian Herstory

Efforts are being made all over the world to reclaim homosexuals' place in history and to create archives and libraries to render the lesbian experience visible. The idea is that recovering lesbian history (herstory) will support current lesbian culture and inspire continued resistance to compulsory heterosexuality. Scholars such as Lillian Faderman (1991; 1997; 1999) and Leila Rupp (1996; 1997) document the lesbian relationships of western women such as Jane Addams, Emily Dickinson, and Eleanor Roosevelt. Historian Vivien Ng (1996) looks for lesbians in Chinese history. Also, in the United States, there are the Lesbian Herstory Archives (LHA), the West Coast Lesbian Collections, and the Women's Collection held at the Northwestern University library. Another example is the United Kingdom's South Asian gay and lesbian organization, Shakti Khabar. It is in the process of documenting the historical presence of homosexuality in South Asia.

Recovering lesbian herstory is difficult because women who have loved women were often careful not to leave evidence of their relationships, or if they did, it was often suppressed or destroyed (Rupp, 1997). Also, because sexuality is greatly influenced by the social context, the lesbian experience in the past may look different than the lesbian experience of the present (Ng, 1996).

Conclusion

In many ways, the study of lesbianism cross-culturally mirrors our more general study of women cross-culturally. Like other topics covered in the book, the study of lesbianism points to the similarity and diversity of the female experience. Penelope (1990) points out that wherever a lesbian lives, whatever social or economic class she is born into, she lives in a heteropatriarchal society where men are the ruling class and everyone is supposed to be heterosexual. These heteropatriarchal societies deny lesbian existence, suppress evidence of lesbian life and struggle, and make lesbians invisible to one another. When lesbian existence is acknowledged, she says, lesbians are caricatured as pathetic, desperate creatures too flawed to find a man or as men's swaggering imitators.

The Lesbian rejects male sexual/political domination; she defies his world, his social organization, his ideology, and his definition of her as inferior. Lesbianism puts women first while the society declares the male supreme. Lesbianism threatens male supremacy at its core.
Charlotte Bunch

Despite this global commonality, there is remarkable **lesbian diversity.** The construction of lesbianism and the lesbian experience are greatly influenced by cultural context; there is no single way to be lesbian. There are a variety of lesbian experiences even within a country. First is the degree of invisibility lesbians must maintain. The repression of lesbians is more severe in some countries and subcultures than in others. In San Francisco, for example, there is a vibrant lesbian community, but in most places in the United States, lesbians remain closeted, and lesbian cultures are harder to identify. In cultures where it is acceptable for women to be unmarried or publicly close and affectionate, lesbianism is easier to carry off. For example, Estonian lesbian Lilian Kotter (1995) notes that because there is little stigma associated with being unmarried in Estonia, lesbians can live their lives in a climate of relative tolerance. Likewise, Thai lesbian Kanokwan Tarawan (1995) says that Thai culture allows two women to live together for extended periods of time, hold hands, hug in public, sleep in the same bed, and even raise a child together, without assuming the relationship is sexual. This makes it possible for lesbians to live together as long as they keep the sexual aspect of their relationship hidden.

Second, there is great lesbian diversity because other cultural and group identities, such as class and ethnicity, interact with lesbianism to produce a variety of complex lesbian identities. For instance, in Latin America, there is a key distinction between the *activos* who play a more macho role and the *passivos* who play a more feminine role (Ferguson, 1990). In Swaziland, lesbian couples frequently consist of a high-status wealthy woman and a low-status dependent woman (Ferguson, 1990). In the United States, middle- and upper-class lesbians typically eschew butch/femme roles, but working-class lesbians do not. Furthermore, the experience of Asian-American and African-American lesbians may be very different from Euroamerican lesbians as they may face the racism from outside their communities and heterosexism within. Culture so strongly influences same-sex practices between women that some theorists emphasize that the word "lesbian" does not have a coherent, unifying meaning across cultures (Blackwood & Wieringa, 1999). An edited volume by Blackwood and Wieringa (1999) illustrates the diversity of women's same-sex practices. It features anthropological accounts from Indonesia, Suriname, India, Lesotho, Peru, Tahiti, Mexico, and Malaysia—accounts that show great variety.

This chapter reminds us that most societies are structured to favor traditional gender roles, and those women who stray from these suffer the consequences. A good example of this is that, like heterosexual women, homosexual women frequently stay in heterosexual marriages in order to avoid losing their children and their social status. Another revisited theme is that of reproductive control. Compulsory heterosexuality is a denial of women's right to control their own bodies, to choose with whom they want to share their bodies. The denial of lesbianism is consistent with a societal tendency to deny women's sexuality or to define sex as being about men's and not women's pleasure. As Bunch (1995) points out, the defense of lesbian rights is integral to the defense of all women's right to determine their own sexuality, to work at the jobs they prefer, and to live as they choose with women, men, children, or alone.

Like other chapters, this chapter also points to the role of economics in women's oppression. The ability to lead a lesbian life is very much tied to economics. Denying women the ability to earn a living wage forces them into a heterosexual existence. An atypical example exists in Swaziland, where a high divorce rate coupled with the practice of women leaving property to their daughters created a situation in which 50 percent of women live independently of men. This has permitted the development of a lesbian subculture where lesbians live together and participate in an active lesbian social life (Ferguson, 1990). The role of economic power in bringing about women's equality cannot be underestimated. This is the focus of Chapter 5, "Women's Work."

Study Questions

1. Why is the study of lesbians important to the topic of women across cultures?

2. What is the relationship between mainstream feminism and lesbianism?

3. What evidence is given for the commonality of lesbianism?

4. What are the factors contributing to lesbian invisibility?

5. Why do so many societies view lesbianism as dangerous?

6. What does Adrienne Rich mean when she says that heterosexuality is compulsory and serves to maintain men's power over women?

7. What are some of the core beliefs and practices of lesbian feminism?

8. How have lesbians attempted to overcome lesbian invisibility?

9. What are some of the ways in which lesbianism differs cross-culturally?

10. How does the study of lesbianism cross-culturally mirror our more general study of women cross-culturally?

Discussion Questions and Activities

1. What would the world be like if homosexuality was not stigmatized? How would it affect children's play? How would it influence affection between those of the same sex? How would it affect what we wear? How would it affect what jobs we choose? How would it affect marriage?

2. Cavin says the predicament of the lesbian in heterosexist society is that of "unrecorded reality" and "recorded unreality." What did you know about lesbianism prior to reading this chapter? Where did you get your

information (TV, movies, family, church, personal experience)? Given lesbian invisibility and negative stereotyping, how accurate do you think your impressions are?

3. What do you think Rich meant when she said that "feminist research and theory that contributes to lesbian invisibility or marginality is actually working against the liberation and empowerment of women"?

4. Conduct an interview with a lesbian using questions developed from the chapter section on factors contributing to lesbian invisibility.

Activist Websites of Interest

International Lesbian and Gay Association

www.ilga.org

Human Rights Campaign

www.hrc.org

National Gay and Lesbian Rights Task Force

www.ngltf.org

Amnesty International OUTfront! Human Rights and Sexual Identity

www.amnestyusa.org/outfront

Informational Websites of Interest

Gay/Lesbian Politics and Law

www.indiana.edu/~glbtpol/organizations.htm

Matthew Shepard International

www.worldzone.net/international/mattshepard/gayles.html

Statement delivered by Palesa Beverley Ditsie of South Africa to United Nations Fourth World Conference on Women

www.hartford-hwp.com/archives/28/014.html

International Lesbian Information Service

www.helsinki.fi/~kris_ntk/ilis.html

The National Latina/O Lesbian, Gay, Bisexual & Transgender Organization

http://www.llego.org/

The Resource Center of the Americas

www.americas.org

Action Opportunities

1. Find out if your school has a gay-straight alliance. If so, get involved, if not, start one.

2. Volunteer for Parents and Friends of Lesbians (PFLAG). You can call the national organization at (202) 467-8180, write to 1726 M Street NW Suite 400, Washington, D.C. 20036, or go online to www.pflag.org for information and to locate your community's branch. You could also volunteer for the Trevor Project www.thetrevorproject.org, a hotline that provides information and support to lesbian, gay, bisexual, and transgendered youth.

3. Encourage your church or synagogue or school organization to reach out to lesbian and gay members. For instance, your organization can develop an anti-discrimination policy, or have a booth at the next local gay and lesbian pride event to show support.

4. Use strategies developed by the Gay, Lesbian and Straight Education Network to prevent heterosexism in the schools. www.glsen.org

5. Join a letter-writing campaign sponsored by Amnesty International www.ai-lgbt.org/lesbian_issue.htmor.

5

Women's Work

All women are working women whether they are engaged in market or nonmarket activities.

—Mary Chinery-Hesse, Deputy Director-General of the
International Labour Organization

Guatemalan women participate in the informal economy. Women's labor is critical to economies worldwide, and women do more of the world's work than men do. The undervaluing of women's work is both a cause and an effect of women's lower status.
© Dave G. Houser/Corbis

W omen have always worked, and work is a central part of women's lives all over the world. The woman who enjoys a leisurely life paid for by her husband is a worldwide rarity. The vast majority of mothers worldwide engage in both domestic and wage-earning work to meet their children's needs (Bruce, 1995). Paid or unpaid, most women work, and they work hard. Indeed, it may surprise you to find that if women's unpaid labor contributions are included, women do more of the world's work than men do (United Nations, 2000). For instance, according to the Food and Agriculture Organization (FAO, 2003a), in Africa and Asia, women work about thirteen hours more than men do each week.

You may also be surprised to hear that, according to the International Labour Organization (ILO, 2003a), worldwide the employment rate for women with children in the home is 53 percent and for women without children, 68 percent. Women now make up over 40 percent of the global workforce. Nearly 58 percent of African women hold paying jobs, 64 percent in Asia, 46 percent in Latin America and the Caribbean, 69 percent in Europe, 73 percent in North America, and 35 percent in the Arab world (ILO, 2003a).

Box 5.1 lists women in the paid workforce for a sample of countries. These cross-cultural differences are attributable to cultural factors and differences in fertility rates (International Labour Organization, 2003b). For example, in the Middle East and North Africa, women's work outside the home is often discouraged. In Latin America and Caribbean countries, high fertility rates and an emphasis on the traditional female role make participation in the paid work force less likely. In Scandinavian countries, where there are many government policies and programs for employed parents, women's labor force participation is especially high. Economic conditions make a difference as well—in transition economies for instance, poor economic conditions have decreased labor force participation.

Unfortunately, key indicators of gender equality in the workplace indicate that inequality of treatment marks virtually all aspects of women's working lives (ILO, 2003a). Women receive less pay than men do, even for the same work (the **gender pay gap**); they face barriers to promotion and advancement (the **glass ceiling**); and are often relegated to the lowest paying jobs under the poorest work conditions (the **sticky floor**). In addition, many women experience sexual harassment in the workplace.

"If women's work were accurately reflected in statistics, it would shatter the myth that men are the main breadwinners of the world."
Mahbub ul-Haq

Women's Work and Our Study of Women Across Cultures

The study of women's labor is an important part of our study of women across cultures because the undervaluing of women's labor is both a cause and an effect of women's lower status and power. Recall from Chapter 2 that women's lower pay and poorer representation in economic power positions is an indicator of women's lower status and power. Regrettably, it is still the

BOX 5.1 *Change in Percentage of Women in the Paid Workforce: A Global Sample*

	1990	2000
Developed Nations		
France	57	62
Greece	35	39
Ireland	36	46
Japan	50	49
Transition Nations		
Hungary	48	45
Poland	57	50
Romania	55	56
Russia	60	52
Caribbean		
Dominican Republic	34	41
Jamaica	62	58
Asia		
Hong Kong	47	48
Korea, Republic of	47	47
Bangladesh	65	56
Philippines	47	50
Latin and South America		
Brazil	44	53
Chile	32	36
Mexico	22	38
Peru	29	58
Africa		
Egypt	28	20
Ethiopia	58	72
Rwanda	83	85
Middle East		
Iran	21	10
Jordan	17	12
Syria	24	17

Source: International Labour Organization, 2003

case that women are discriminated against in the world of work. Moreover, up until the latter part of the twentieth century, few people questioned men's domination of the economic sphere.

Women's lower status and power are aggravated by the fact that their work tends to be unpaid or underpaid. Women often do work that is compatible with the female life course of childbearing and nursing. In particular, this means that women's work is often conducted in the private sphere of the home. Furthermore, historically women's work more typically had *private use value* (for the family's private use) rather than *exchange value* (something that could then be exchanged for money or other goods). In short, because women's labor was typically conducted in the private sphere of the home and was largely unpaid, its social and economic importance has been masked and, consequently, has contributed to the devaluation of women.

In her book *If Women Counted,* New Zealand feminist economist Marilyn Waring (1988) analyzes the fact that much of women's labor is left out of governments' systems of economic accounting. For example, Waring points out that dung is used in many parts of the world for fertilizer, fuel, and building. Women spend entire days collecting it in woven baskets carried home on their heads, but all the hours women spend gathering, transporting, and using it are not recorded as work. Waring notes that not only is much of women's labor unpaid household labor, but women's labor often takes place in the **informal labor sector,** which receives less attention from governments. Informal sector work includes small enterprises, trading and selling at markets, work done on a contract basis in the home (such as garment sewing), and "under the table" and "off the books" employment. The national accounting systems used by most governments define labor in terms of formal employment, in the **formal labor sector.** To understand the distinction, compare these two hair stylists. Sofia cuts the hair of neighbor women and children in her garage. She does not report her income to any government agency and therefore she would not count as employed according to her government. She works in the informal labor sector. In contrast, Gloria works out of a salon in busy city. She receives a paycheck and pays taxes on her income. She is in the formal labor sector and gets counted as employed by her government.

Feminist economists like Waring, and activist organizations such as the International Women Count Network, have pushed governments to include women's unpaid labor as part of government accounting systems. They argue that women should be recognized for their contributions to economies and that such recognition would benefit women. For instance, assigning unpaid work a value would make it more likely that homemaker women would be treated fairly in divorce proceedings. Also, in countries with pension systems it could lead to policies that provide homemakers with pensions or retirement benefits (currently such women rely on husbands' pensions). Including women's unpaid labor in labor statistics is additionally important because such statistics are used to design employment policies and programs. Because women's labor so often remains invisible in national accounting systems, and

"The international economic system constructs reality in a way that excludes the great bulk of women's work—reproduction (in all its forms), raising children, domestic work, and subsistence production."
Marilyn Waring

policy is so often based on national accounting figures, policymakers make fewer policies and spend less money on programs and policies addressing women's needs. As Waring says, systems cannot respond to values that remain unrecognized. In 2001, Noleen Heyzer, the executive director of the United Nations Development Fund for Women (UNIFEM), called on governments to engage in "gender responsive budget analysis" to see how national budgets impact women and girls differently than men and boys. Such analyses would measure government commitment to women's specific needs and rights and would require a focus on the unpaid care economy in which much of women's time is spent (UNIFEM, 2001b).

> "A woman's work is never counted."
> *Peggy Kome, Canadian Activist*

This point, that governments typically overlook women's labor when designing programs and policies, is further illustrated in Chapter 6 on women and economic development. That chapter examines in some detail how women's labor has been largely ignored by programs designed to bring about economic development. Most development programs focus on men's labor. The result is that development programs do not usually enhance women's status, and women's lives are often made even harder. Furthermore, broader goals of development, such as increased quality of life, are not achieved when women's labor contributions are overlooked. This is because women are major family providers—growing and collecting food and fuel for family consumption and providing sanitation and health care to family members. Add to this the fact that when women work for pay, they devote more of their income to family subsistence than do men, who spend more on themselves (Blumberg, 1995). Despite this, most development programs have focused solely on men's wage earning.

Once again, the fact that women's work is frequently unpaid or underpaid, and therefore rendered invisible, is closely linked to women's lower power and status, for it leads to the perception that women do less work and are therefore less important to societies. It is also true that those who control the money generally have greater power and status. This is one reason why women's activists worldwide have focused on women's economic empowerment. Many Marxist feminists view women's economic dependence on men as the primary basis of patriarchy (Chafetz, 1991; Hartmann, 1984; Vogel, 1983). Economic empowerment, though, is about more than just women's economic independence from men; it's also about equal pay for equal work, women's access to traditionally male jobs, women in business power positions, and eliminating sexual harassment. Many women do work for pay—especially those who are single heads of households because of widowhood, desertion, or divorce. However, even when women work for pay, their low wages often interfere with translating this into greater power and status.

The relationship between women's status and power and paid employment is complex, but the importance of economic power cannot be denied. Blumberg (1991) suggests that for women, economic power is probably more achievable than other sources of power. Women rarely possess the *power of force* (both at the individual violence level and the organized social force level), seldom possess *political power,* and infrequently possess *ideological power* (the power that comes from social beliefs that one's group is superior). As Blumberg says, "Only with respect to *economic* power does women's position run the full range from near-zero to near-total control of the local economy" (p. 29).

Women's Unpaid Labor

Worldwide, who does the laundry, shopping, cooking, child care, and looks after the family's medical needs and aging parents? In countries where water and fuel must be gathered and families must grow much of their own food, who takes care of these tasks? The answer is, of course, women. Although there are cross-cultural variations in the jobs that men and women do, in every society women continue to do most of the daily, routine household labor (Batalova & Cohen, 2002; Chafetz, 1990; Seager, 2003). This is true in both industrialized and developing countries. For example, in the United States, women spend on average twenty-seven hours a week on housework compared to men's sixteen hours; in Sweden the ratio is thirty-three hours for women and twenty-four for men; and Japanese men spend a meager four hours a week on housework compared to Japanese women's twenty-nine hours (Seager, 2003). In developing countries, women spend between thirty-one and forty-two hours a week in unpaid activities, versus five to fifteen hours for men (ILO, 1996a). **Gender-based household divisions of labor** begin early, in childhood chores (Whiting & Edwards, 1988). For instance, in Mexico, El Salvador, Argentina, South Africa, Peru, the United States, and Pakistan, it is customary for girls to cook, clean, do laundry, and care for younger siblings while boys do "outside" work such as yard chores.

One major household task for which women are unpaid is childcare. The presence of small children increases the work of women substantially more than it does the work of men (United Nations, 2000). Worldwide, women are largely responsible for the care of the children (Chafetz, 1990; Ishii-Kuntz, 1993; Jankowiak, 1992; Leslie, Anderson, & Branson, 1991; Munroe & Munroe, 1992; Nsamenang, 1992; Sanday, 1981; Roopnarine & Ahmeduzzaman, 1993; Tulananda, Young, & Roopnarine, 1994). The general worldwide pattern is that fathers spend approximately one-third of the time mothers do in providing child care (Engle & Breaux, 1994), although there are a few exceptions such as the hunter-gatherer Aka pygmies of the southern Central African Republic and the northern People's Republic of the Congo (Hewlett, 1992). Lamb (1981) suggests that this sex-based division of child-care labor is aggravated by industrialization, which requires fathers to leave the home for large parts of the day in order to work at jobs where children's presence is viewed as inappropriate.

It is ironic that the unpaid work women do is of tremendous importance to the well-being of families, communities, and nations and yet is poorly measured in official statistics (United Nations, 2000). According to the ILO (1995), if the household duties performed by women were calculated as productive activity in the various systems of national accounting, the value of the world's GDP (gross domestic product) would increase by 25 to 30 percent. The UN's

BOX 5.2   *Feminist Economist Lourdes Beneria on Unpaid Labor*

Lourdes Beneria is a professor at Cornell University. She is the author of half a dozen books, and serves on the editorial board of the journal "Feminist Economics."
The challenge of accounting for women's unpaid work first surfaced for me in 1978 when I visited the picturesque town of Chechaouen in northern Morocco while I was working at the International Labor Office. . . . Statistics showed that the labor force participation rate for men and women in Morocco differed widely—more than 75 percent for men and less than 10 percent for women. But what I saw in the streets of Chechaouen told me a very different story. I saw many women moving about the busy streets, some carrying dough on their heads to bake bread in public ovens, others carrying wood on

their backs or clothes to be washed in the brook bordering the town; still other women were carrying baskets or bags on their way to shopping, often with children at their side. The men were less busy—men were sitting outside the town's shops, idle and chatting, perhaps waiting for the tourist season to increase the demands for the beautiful crafts sold in the stores. I immediately thought something was wrong with the statistics I had seen. It was the first time I had thought about this type of discrepancy, but I soon found out how prevalent it was across countries and regions.

Source: Beneria, 1998.

International Research and Training Institute for the Advancement of Women (INSTRAW, 1995) states that the measurement of women's unpaid labor would make clear the value of household production to economies worldwide. It would also show that the burden is disproportionately carried by women, who almost match men hour for hour in paid labor and who outwork men 2 to 1 in nonmarket activities (INSTRAW, 1995). Box 5.2 provides further insight on this point from feminist economist Lourdes Beneria.

Why is it that women's work remains uncounted and devalued? Mosse (1993) suggests that it is because so much of women's work is seen as "natural." After all, she says, only women can become mothers and suckle their children, but this biological or natural ability has often meant that all of women's work in maintaining life—nurturing children, collecting fuel and water, growing the family food and marketing the surplus, caring for those who are sick or elderly— is also seen as "natural" rather than as "work," which is what men do. Chafetz (1990) points out that in gender-stratified societies, men fill most elite positions, and therefore it is men who determine what work is valuable. Not surprisingly, they produce ideologies and norms that emphasize the value of what they do.

Another reason why women's unpaid labor so often remains uncounted is because it is challenging to collect data. The most accurate measures involve time-use surveys that show what women and men do throughout the day. Since 1995, only seven countries have provided such data to the United Nations (Australia, France, Japan, Latvia, Netherlands, New Zealand, and the Republic of Korea). Based on these data, the International Labour Organization (2003) reports that women spend 50 to 70 percent as much time as

"Before I leave home, I have to work. When I get home, I have to work."
Irene Ortega, Mexican woman who joined a one-day household labor strike. She normally puts in 10-hour days selling music cassettes and does all the household labor.

men on paid work, but almost twice as much or more time on unpaid work. The differences were especially pronounced in Japan and the Republic of Korea where women's unpaid work is about eight times that of men's. In the seven countries studied, more than half of women's total work time is spent on unpaid work. A **leisure gap** was also evident: men have between one to seven more hours of leisure time a week than women.

There are three common explanations for gender differences in household labor, as shown in Figure 5.1. The **time availability perspective** on gender divisions of household labor suggests that because women spend less time in the paid workforce, they have more time to perform household tasks (Bianchi, Milkie, Sayer, & Robinson, 2000). For instance, in the United States, men are doing more housework but employed women still do more household labor than men do. However, women have reduced their in-home labor by lowering their standards and when they can afford it, by "outsourcing," such as buying prepared food and hiring home cleaning services (Bianchi et al., 2000). This suggests that as women have less time due to employment, they devote less time to household tasks. However, it is true that research from a variety of countries indicates that employed women still do significantly more household labor than their male partners (Anson, Levenson, & Bonneh, 1990; Blumberg, 1991; Charles & Hopflinger, 1992; Dubisch, 1993; Frisco & Williams, 2003; Ghorayshi, 1996; Ilyas, 1990; Kerig, Alyoshina, & Volovich, 1993; United Nations, 1991b). Employed women frequently work one shift in the paid work and another unpaid **second shift** at home before or after paid work (Hochschild, 1989). If it were only a matter of time availability, we would expect more equal allocations of labor in the home.

The **relative resources perspective** emphasizes that the division of household labor reflects the relative economic power of women and men. Women, then, do more household labor because they must make up for their smaller monetary contribution to the household (Bianchi et al., 2000). Since women rarely match or exceed their husbands in pay, even where women do earn money, they must still work a second shift at home. Some studies find that the smaller the income gap between an employed woman and her husband, the

FIGURE 5.1   *Explanations for Gender-Based Household Divisions of Labor*

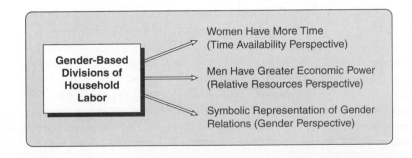

smaller the gender household labor gap (Batalova & Cohen, 2002; Blumstein & Schwartz, 1991). However, Sanchez (1993) found that wives' material conditions and relative resources had no consistent, significant effect on husbands' household labor in the five countries she studied (Indonesia, South Korea, Philippines, Taiwan, and the United States).

The **gender perspective on household labor** argues that household labor is a symbolic representation of gender relations, not merely a matter of who has time and who has the money (Bianchi et al., 2000). The idea is that husbands and wives display proper gender roles through the activities they perform in the home. Household labor and childcare are viewed as "women's work," stereotyped female activities. Socialization in childhood reinforces this perception. Women's employed work is seen as secondary to their primary role as wife and mother, and men's higher status is such that they have refusal power (Blumberg, 1991; Burn, 1996). Women often accept household labor as "their work" and may act as "maternal gatekeepers" that limit men's involvement in the home (Allen & Hawkins, 1999). Because gendered divisions of household labor arise out of traditional gender ideologies, it follows that more egalitarian beliefs about the genders should lead to more egalitarian divisions of household labor. Indeed, one study of twenty-two countries found that gender empowerment (as measured by the number of women in government, administration, and professional careers) was related to more egalitarian divisions of household labor (Batalova & Cohen, 2002).

Internationally, there are a number of campaigns devoted to increasing recognition of women's unpaid labor. For instance, Wages for Housework is a network of women from a number of countries. They seek to draw attention to the gendered organization of household labor, women's disproportionate share of this work, and the need for women to be compensated for this work through the reduction of military spending. A key success of the network came in 1995 when the 189 countries participating in the UN's Fourth World Women's Conference in Bejiing committed to "the recognition of the economic value of women's work in the home, in domestic food production and marketing, and in voluntary activities not traditionally renumerated" (Karides, 2002).

Women's Paid Labor

The Gender Pay Gap

Equality of opportunity and treatment for women in employment has yet to be achieved anywhere in the world. *Michel Hanseene, Director-General of the UN's International Labour Organization*

Women have entered the paid workforce in record numbers, but their economic power is diminished by the fact that they frequently receive less pay for their work than do men. Worldwide, women on average earn two-thirds what men earn (ILO, 2003). Fortunately, many countries have significantly reduced their **gender pay gap** in the last fifteen years. For instance, the gap fell the most in the United States where it declined by 38 percent, and in France, where it fell 34 percent. Box 5.3 shows how women's wages as a percentage of men's in manufacturing have improved since 1990; however, it also shows that women continue to earn less than men in all countries.

BOX 5.3   *Narrowing of the Gender Pay Gap: Women's Earnings as a Percentage of Men's in Manufacturing*

Country	1990	1997
Australia	82	85
Bangladesh	49	50
Brazil	54	54
Costa Rica	74	76
Egypt	68	74
Ireland	69	75
Jordan	57	62
Latvia	84	89
Mexico	50	71
Portugal	69	69
Sweden	89	90
Swaziland	73	71

Source: United Nations, 2000

Why is it so common for women to be paid less than men are? There are three explanations most commonly offered: (1) Women are segregated and concentrated in lower-paying, female-dominated jobs, (2) the high percentage of women working part-time, and (3) outright gender wage discrimination. Figure 5.2 summarizes contributors to the gender pay gap.

Gender Job Segregation

Historically, females and males have had different jobs in almost every culture (Almeida Acosta & Sanchez de Almeida, 1983; Davidson & Thomson, 1980; Munroe & Munroe, 1975). According to the United Nations (1991b), everywhere in the world the workplace is segregated by sex, and **gender occupational segregation** is one reason why women earn less than men (ILO, 1995; 2003). This refers to the fact that men and women tend to work in different sectors of the economy and hold different positions within the same occupational group. Simply, most jobs are designated as being either for males or for females.

FIGURE 5.2   *Contributors to the Gender Pay Gap*

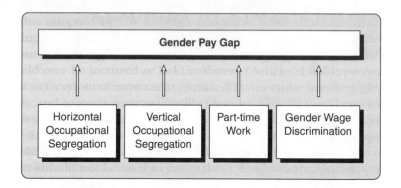

Horizontal occupational segregation refers to the tendency for occupations mainly held by men to have substantially higher pay rates and status as compared to those mainly held by women. Men are more likely to be in core or regular and better paid positions, whereas women are often in peripheral, insecure, less-valued positions. Women generally work in such sectors as secretarial work, sales, and domestic services whereas men generally work in industry and transportation; women engage in teaching, care services, and subsistence agriculture whereas men are found in management, administration, and policy (ILO, 1995). Countries vary in how horizontally segregated they are but half of all workers in the world are in jobs dominated by one gender (Anker, 1998). Some of the lowest levels of horizontal segregation are in the United States (37 percent), Russia (35 percent), Hong Kong (40 percent), and Thailand (25 percent) (where percentages refer to the percentage of the labor force that works in a gender dominated occupations). Some of the highest rates are found in Iran and Pakistan where 85 and 93 percent, respectively, work in gender dominated jobs (ILO, 2003).

Recruitment practices that favor men, or barriers in the promotion or career development of women, have the effect of excluding women or "segregating" them into certain jobs (ILO, 2003a,b). In most countries women find it hard to be hired into the better-paying jobs customarily held by men. Research indicates that women are less likely than equally qualified men to be hired for nontraditionally female jobs (Kawashima, 1995; Olson & Frieze, 1987). Kawashima's (1995) report surveying Japanese firms exemplifies this. Of the firms surveyed, 48 percent answered that they hired and assigned women to jobs that "fit their special attributes." In many countries, such as Japan and Hong Kong, many job advertisements still specify a particular sex (WIN, 1993). In Hong Kong, employers refuse to employ women when the job being advertised is high in pay and is managerial or technical (WIN, 1993). A study in Argentina found that professional women required more than sixteen years of seniority over male job candidates in order to be considered qualified for the same job (Neft & Levine, 1997). In short, in most countries, jobs are earmarked as male or female jobs, and typically women can only get traditionally female jobs—jobs that pay less than male jobs.

In the 1980s and 1990s, horizontal segregation fell in most countries (ILO, 2003b). On the face of it, the reduction of horizontal occupational segregation should reduce the gender pay gap. However, women still receive less pay than men do when working in the same job. For example, in Australia, female nurses earn 89 percent of what male nurses earn and in China, female accountants earn 65 percent of what male accountants earn (ILO, 2003b). Some of this is due to **vertical occupational segregation.** Vertical segregation refers to how within occupations there is a hierarchy of jobs and women tend to be represented in lower ranks than men are within the same occupation. In short, men generally occupy the better-paid ranks and more powerful positions (ILO, 2003b; United Nations, 2000).

Part-Time Workers

The gender pay gap is partially due to women's large presence in part-time work. In all countries, women comprise the majority of part-time workers (ILO, 2003a,b). Overall, about one in four employed women are part-time workers, and women constitute about two-thirds of all part-time workers (Thurman & Trah, 1990). The ILO (1995) suggests that the main reasons for women's high rates of part-time employment are that they cannot find full-time jobs, or they must work part-time to simultaneously satisfy family demands such as childcare and household labor. Indeed, in most countries, married women have a higher incidence of part-time work than do other groups (Blau & Kahn, 1996). Employers have discovered the benefits of part-time workers. Part-time workers are generally paid substantially less than full-time workers, they can be easily laid off during slow periods, and, in many countries, they are not paid nonwage labor costs such as Social Security contributions (Thurman & Trah, 1990).

Gender Wage Discrimination

There are other explanations for the gender pay gap but these too fail to explain the entire gap. One of these explanations, the **compensating differentials** approach to the gender pay gap, suggests that women's jobs pay less because these jobs offer pleasant work conditions, good social relations, the opportunity to serve others, flexible hours, or easy work (Filer, 1985, 1989). However, there is scant research support for this hypothesis (Padavic & Reskin, 2002). For example, according to research in the United States, female jobs do not offer more flexible hours, lower levels of exertion, and other characteristics that would facilitate parenting (Glass & Camarigg, 1992). In fact, Glass and Camarigg (1992) found that the opposite is true: Greater concentrations of females in professional and blue-collar jobs is related to less flexibility, greater supervision, and less control over the timing and pacing of tasks. An analysis of 1,600 U.S. jobs by Jacobs and Steinberg (1990) suggests that female-dominated jobs involve somewhat different, but not necessarily fewer, undesirable working conditions than male jobs. Women's jobs are

In Ireland, until 1973, the government, banks, and most companies had a "marriage bar" that prohibited married women from employment.

more likely to involve working with difficult clients, cleaning others' dirt, mindless repetition, and low autonomy (lack of control over one's work). Furthermore, they found that undesirable working conditions typically have a *negative* effect on wages for both men's and women's jobs because unpleasant jobs tend to be held by those who are low in power and cannot command the higher wages needed to offset the unpleasant work conditions.

Another explanation for gender difference in pay is called the **human capital approach** (Blau & Ferber, 1987; Jacobsen, 2003). Human capital refers to any attributes a person has that contribute to her productivity including education, skills, and focus. The idea is that women get paid less because they are less skilled, less educated, or less experienced workers than men typically are. These differences originate in gender discrimination in education and training, and also because many women enter and leave the workforce due to childbearing and rearing. Also, the thought is that the costs of employing women are higher because they get pregnant and take time off when their children are sick and are less focused on their work due to family concerns. According to research, the factors identified by the human capital approach explain from 4 to 50 percent of the male–female earnings differential, depending on the country (Jacobsen, 2003). For instance, women may have less work experience due to taking time out to have children or due to lack of training. In some countries, women's educational level is lower than men's. However, excepting some African and South Asian countries, the gender gap in primary and secondary schooling is narrowing worldwide, and women's enrollment in higher education also equals or surpasses that of men. And yet, women continue to hold lower-paying occupations than men with equivalent education and work experience (ILO, 2003b).

The gender pay gap cannot be explained away by suggesting that the jobs women tend to hold are easier or require fewer skills and, it exists even when women and men work in the same job and have the same qualifications. This leads to the conclusion that some of the gender wage gap is due to outright **gender wage discrimination**—paying women less just because they are women. Gender wage discrimination appears to have three main sources. One is the traditional devaluation of women's work. In general, women have been devalued and so has their work—if women do it, it is worth less than if it's done by men. Second, in some cultures, it is assumed that a woman can be paid less because her income is merely a supplement to her husband's and that her paid job is secondary to her unpaid job as wife and mother (Padavic & Reskin, 2002). For instance, Kawashima (1995) says that in Japan, employers view women as secondary or supplementary workers and as secondary breadwinners in the household. She also cites a survey of Japanese women suggesting that many accept low wages because of a belief that their wages are supplementary to the household income. Some might argue that paying women less has been a way to keep women in the wife/mother role (with few economic options women must depend on men). Last, paying women less often has to do with employers' simply wanting to make more money. When employers can get away with paying women less, they often do—because saving on women's wages increases employers' profits.

Remedies to the Gender Pay Gap

Many countries have laws prohibiting gender pay discrimination. One example is the Equal Pay Act of the United States. Passed in 1963, it says that women's pay should be equal to men's when their positions are equal. Other countries with equal pay laws include Brazil, Britain, Canada, China, Cyprus, France, India, Israel, Italy, Japan, Mexico, New Zealand, the Philippines, and Sweden. Unfortunately, although it is a good start, **equal pay legislation** does not by itself bring about gender pay equality. In many countries, there are no penalties for violation of equal pay laws, and in others there is no enforcement of such penalties. Although some countries such as Ghana, the United States, and Hong Kong, have specialized enforcement bodies to investigate and prosecute gender pay discrimination, they are limited in funding and staffing (ILO, 2003b). In the United States, for example, complaints first go through federal, state, or local agencies, which are horrendously backlogged (Crampton, Hodge, & Mishra, 1997). The U.S. federal Equal Employment Opportunity Commission (EEOC) received 25,167 sexual discrimination complaints in the year 2000 alone (Hersch, 2003).

Equal pay legislation also does not typically do much to address the sources of gender pay inequalities, such as gender occupational segregation. For instance, most of the countries that have equal pay laws make it illegal to pay women working the *same* job as men less money, but the truth of the matter is that occupational segregation means that in most countries, women are not found in the same jobs as men. Take Japan as an example. Japan's Equal Employment Opportunity Law officially prevents companies from discriminating against women in hiring. However, many companies get around the law by using a two-track hiring system (Kawashima, 1995; Lazarowitz, 1997). The *sogoshoku* track leads to managerial positions but requires the possibility of working overtime and accepting geographic job transfers. Men are automatically placed on this track. The *ippanshoku* track is a secondary track where the work is routinized, promotions are limited, but transfers and overtime are not required. About 98 percent of Japanese women are placed on this track (Lazarowitz, 1997). According to Kawashima (1995), women are given the option of choosing either track but are expected to choose the *ippanshoku* track. Kawashima suggests that this is partly because *sogoshoku* women are expected to fit into a male workplace that does not welcome women. Furthermore, their heavy share of responsibility at home remains unchanged, which makes success in the *sogoshoku* track difficult.

The International Labour Organization notes that in addition to equal pay legislation, governments need to undertake other measures to bring about gender pay equality. For instance, governments can design programs and policies that promote the entrance of women into better-paying, traditionally male jobs (**affirmative action**). Or governments can raise the wages of traditionally female jobs by increasing the minimum wage. Data from Poland, the Netherlands, the United Kingdom, and the United States suggests that women account for the majority of workers who benefit from minimum wage laws.

Comparable worth policies may also be used to compensate for gender occupational segregation. Using detailed classification systems, this approach permits the comparison of different jobs on skill, effort, responsibility, and working conditions (United Nations, 1994). So-called female and male jobs could be compared and people would be compensated based on the skill, experience, and stress involved in the job, instead of whether the job was customarily held by women or men. The 1994 United Nations' Commission on the Status of Women agreed to promote the idea of comparable worth. The ILO is also a proponent of comparable worth and views it as potentially reducing the gender wage gap because it can deal with wage differences due to occupational segregation (Gunderson, 1995).

Cross-Cultural Variation in the Gender Pay Gap

Government commitment to equal pay for the genders is one important factor in cross-cultural variation in the gender pay gap (ILO, 2003b). In a study of the gender pay gap in eleven industrialized countries, Blau and Kahn (1996) found that countries with strong centralized unions and government participation in wage setting tended to have the smallest pay gaps. For example, in 1991, Russian women earned 75 percent of men's wages, but this proportion fell to 40 percent with the move from centralized communism to a decentralized market economy (Neft & Levine, 1998). Another important factor explaining cross-cultural variation in the gender pay gap is the extent to which traditional stereotypes of the genders still prevail (ILO, 2003b). When traditional gender stereotypes are culturally pervasive, a gender-segregated workforce and lower pay for women is more likely. It is also the case that under these cultural conditions, child-care options for employed women are fewer, and the men do less work in the home. This makes it harder for women to dedicate themselves to the work organization in the same way that men can. Consequently, women may be less likely to apply for jobs that make it difficult to satisfy their domestic role.

The Glass Ceiling

Further evidence of gender discrimination in paid employment comes in the form of a **glass ceiling.** This term is used to refer to the various barriers that prevent qualified women from advancing upward in their organizations into management power positions. According to the United Nations (2000), in most parts of the world, women make up approximately 30 percent of the administrative and managerial workforce. At the current rate of progress, it is estimated that it will take a couple of centuries for men and women to achieve equal representation at higher levels in organizations (ILO, 1995).

Admittedly, the picture is quite variable and has improved considerably in the last twenty years. For instance, in Australia, Finland, Italy, Norway, Portugal, Sweden, and the United Kingdom, women hold between 26 and 40 percent of administrative and managerial jobs. However, they hold 10 percent or less in Algeria, France, India, Indonesia, Iran, Nigeria, Pakistan, Singapore, Sudan, and Turkey (Seager, 1997). Box 5.4 gives a regional sampling of the percentage of women in administrative jobs. Keep in mind, however, that combining administrative and managerial positions, as governments so often do, paints a somewhat rosier picture than that seen without the inclusion of administrative positions. Women are still very much the minority at senior levels of corporations. For example, only 1 to 3 percent of top executives and board members in the largest German corporations are women; in Brazil, only 4 percent; and in the United States, women hold just over 5 percent of senior corporate positions in the 500 largest companies (United Nations, 2000). Consider also that in many countries some women face the dual burden of racism and sexism in organizations, leading to a **concrete ceiling** (Nkomo & Cox, 1989). For instance, in the United States, of the 3 to 5 percent of women that occupy top management positions, 95 percent are white (U.S. Department of Labor, 1997).

Research on the glass ceiling does not support the idea that there are few women in higher status positions because women have personality traits or behavior patterns that make them ill-suited for managerial positions (Burn, 2004; Eagly, Karau, & Makhijani, 1995; Hooijberg & DiTomaso, 1996). Instead, the main culprits appear to be stereotypes that suggest that women are inappropriate for leadership positions, and organizational barriers such as a lack of mentoring and training of women for leadership positions. This is an important point. As Geis (1993) notes, if we are under the impression that there is equal opportunity for women and men, then we may falsely conclude that

BOX 5.4 *Share of Female Administrators by Region in 2000*

Region	Percentage of Female Administrators
Developed countries	27.6
Transition economies	32.9
Asia and the Pacific	15.3
Latin America and the Caribbean	32.8
Middle East and North Africa	28.1

Source: International Labour Organization, 2003

FIGURE 5.3 *Contributors to the Glass Ceiling*

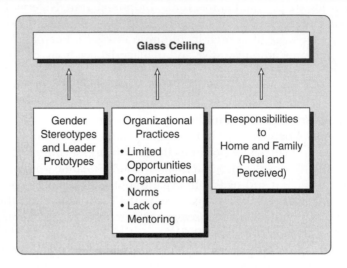

women's lower pay and power are reflections of women's inadequacies. Likewise, the ILO (1998) states, "The assertion that an insufficient number of qualified women exist to fill more top jobs is rapidly becoming outmoded. While gender differences still exist in professional study choices, women worldwide are demonstrating their intellectual ability and are approaching the levels of men in educational attainment" (p. 2). Three common explanations for the glass ceiling are represented in Figure 5.3 and are discussed below.

Gender Stereotypes

When you think of a leader, what types of qualities do you imagine? In your culture, are these qualities typically associated with males or females? Gender stereotypes are one contributor to the perception that women are inappropriate for leadership and managerial positions. If it is believed that a woman's place is in the home or that women are ineffective as leaders and decision-makers, then women will be denied leadership positions (Stevens, 1984). Common stereotypes of women suggest that women cannot lead. For example, many people hold stereotypes of women as emotional and indecisive—qualities that are clearly undesirable for a leader. A number of studies find that successful managers are believed to have personality traits that are more consistent with male rather than female stereotypes (Brenner, Tomkiewicz, & Schein, 1989; Heilman et al., 1989; King, Miles, & Kniska, 1991; Massengill & DiMarco, 1979; Powell & Butterfield, 1984; Schein, 1973, 1975; Schein, Mueller, & Jacobson, 1989). Schein and Mueller (1992) found males in the United States, Great Britain, and Germany to believe this. Females in Germany sex-typed the managerial positions almost as much as males in Germany do. British females also sex-typed it but not as much as the German females. However, American women see women and men as equally likely to possess the traits needed for effective management.

Another way to look at it is that whether you are perceived as leadership material depends in part on whether you fit the **leader prototype** common in your culture. **Leadership categorization theory** suggests that matching an observed person against an abstract prototype stored in memory plays an important role in the attributions of leadership (Lord & Maher, 1991). The better the fit between the perceived individual and the leader prototype, the more likely the person will be seen as a leader (Offermann et al., 1994; Foti & Luch, 1992). Gender and ethnic stereotypes affect whether we perceive individuals from various social categories to be suitable candidates for leadership roles.

According to several studies in the United States, our beliefs that women are inappropriate for leadership positions are so strong, that contrary data are often ignored in managerial selection and other managerial decisions affecting women (Freedman & Phillips, 1988; Heilman & Martell, 1986; Ilgen & Youtz, 1986; Morrison & Von Glinow, 1990). Cejka and Eagly (1999) found that gender-stereotypic images of occupations corresponded to sex segregation in employment. Glick (1991) found that jobs are generally seen as "masculine" or "feminine" and that job applicants are seen as more or less suitable for different jobs depending upon the applicant's sex. Likewise, in a study of job applicants and job interviewers in the Netherlands, Dutch researchers (Van Vianen & Willemsen, 1992) found that gender stereotyping influenced hiring decisions. Gendered leader prototypes, combined with the fact that there are relatively few women in positions of power, may make it hard for some people to imagine a woman in a leadership position in the public sphere.

> "I was kept in the lowest position no matter how many years I worked. And I was really working hard."
> *Noriko Narumi, Japanese woman who successfully sued her employer of thirty-eight years in a landmark case*

Organizational Practices

Gender stereotypes are but one cause of the glass ceiling. Another is that common organizational practices generally dictate the hiring and promotion of males, rather than females, into management positions. If social and organizational norms do not explicitly advocate hiring women into high-level positions, then those doing the hiring are likely to follow standard operating procedures and hire a man (Burn, 1996). In some cases social norms clearly communicate that women are not appropriate for high-level positions. Individuals within the organization may then comply with these norms regardless of their personal feelings regarding the appropriateness of women in leadership positions (Larwood, Szwajkowski, & Rose, 1988). Similarly, a qualified woman may not be promoted if upper management feels that employees' or clients' stereotypes might interfere with her effectiveness—for instance, they won't be comfortable taking orders from a woman or won't find her a credible authority.

Another problem is that within the organization, women may not receive the experiences needed to advance in the organization. Most organizations have entry-level jobs that lead up the organizational ladder. According to economist Bergmann (1989), these jobs are typically earmarked for men. Kanter (1976) argued that women are usually placed in jobs with less power and limited mobility, and in this way, they are "structurally disadvantaged" in the organization. In the United States, Baron and co-workers (1986) analyzed job ladders (jobs that provide promotion opportunities as opposed to so-called dead-end jobs) in 100 organizations. Jobs in these organizations were pervasively segregated by sex (only 73 of the 1,071 jobs studied had both female and male incumbents), and men exclusively occupied 71 percent of the promotion ladders in the sample. Women in prestigious male-typed organizations are usually segregated into female-typed specialties that offer fewer resources for power or are hired into departments with little power (ILO, 1998; Ragins & Sundstrom, 1989).

Women's progress may also be limited by their relative lack of access to the political network and lack of mentoring. Mentoring occurs when a senior organizational member helps guide the career of a junior member by sharing knowledge about how to succeed in the organization. Mentoring is important because protégés receive more promotions, better compensation, and greater career mobility (Ragins, 1999). Women are less likely than men to receive personal support, job-related information, and career developmental support from their supervisors (Cianni & Romberger, 1995). Because of their gender and concerns about intimacy and sexual attraction, women are often excluded from the informal social relationships shared by their male counterparts in which power transactions and mentoring often occur (Bhatnagar, 1988; Nelson et al., 1990; Noe, 1988; Powell & Mainiero, 1992). In many countries, it is socially inappropriate for women to interact closely with men who are not husbands or family members. In others, the seclusion of women is accepted practice among some ethnic and religious groups. This is the case in parts of Afghanistan, Bangladesh, Cameroon, Eritrea, India, Iran, Morocco, Niger, Nigeria, Oman, Pakistan, Saudi Arabia, Tunisia, the United Arab Emirates, and Yemen (Seager, 1997).

Responsibilities to Home and Family

Finally, women's responsibilities to home and family, real and perceived, may prevent upward mobility in the organization. This can happen in two ways. First, when a woman is married and/or has children, employers often *assume* that her family responsibilities will interfere with her work commitment, and, consequently, they will not promote her into positions of responsibility. Second, for some women, home and family demands do mean that they are unable to put in the extra hours or travel time necessary for advancement in the organization.

Childbearing and women's primary responsibility for child rearing also affect women's pay and promotion in the workplace because many women take leaves of absence from their jobs in the formal sector while their children are small. For example, in Japan, advancement in the organization is highly dependent upon uninterrupted service to the organization and seniority. Japanese mothers with small children generally do not participate in the paid sector because of difficulty reconciling the wife/mother role with the demands of paid employment (Tanaka, 1995). Women who interrupt their careers because of pregnancy or who leave the workforce while their children are young are disadvantaged upon their return (Kawashima, 1995). Indeed, in Japan, unwritten policies have generally prevented the hiring of women older than 30 or 40 (Lazarowitz, 1997). As Tanaka (1995) points out, marriage is more costly to a woman's career because only women are called upon to reconcile the competing demands of work and family responsibilities. Men are able to rely on wives to take care of the household responsibilities, and this frees them to concentrate on work responsibilities. Research in the United States also indicates that women are significantly more likely to interrupt their careers for family-related reasons than men and that such interruptions affect later job advancement and career decisions, especially for women (Powell & Mainiero, 1992).

Because high work involvement is incongruent with the traditional female gender role, employed women often experience anxiety and guilt (Burke & McKeen, 1988), and this may affect their career choices. Few men see marriage or family as a constraint on the emphasis they place on their careers, whereas multiple and conflicting role demands related to parenthood frequently affect women's career choices (Powell & Mainiero, 1992). They may choose not to pursue the career track that takes them away from their families. Many choose part-time work that, although compatible with family responsibilities, is largely incompatible with pay increases and climbing the promotion ladder.

State Maternity Leave and Child-Care Policies

Maternity leave and childcare are prerequisites for women's full participation in the labor force (ILO, 2003b). This is because it is common for women get pregnant and have babies, and because women have primary responsibility for children. As an ILO report said in 1995, women workers still have to juggle numerous roles with considerable difficulty and stress, and few countries provide adequate support—child-care facilities, parental leave, family-friendly workplaces—for workers with family responsibilities.

Most countries have laws guaranteeing women maternity leave benefits and, typically, women receive all or part of their wages during the covered period (United Nations Statistics Division, 2003). These wages are usually paid by the state's social security systems, but in some countries, employers pay them entirely or partially. The Scandinavian countries of Sweden, Finland, and Denmark have the most comprehensive family policies. In Sweden, parents have their jobs guaranteed by law for several years if they wish to stay home with their children, and they may receive 80 to 90 percent salary compensation for fourteen months (Haavio-Mannila, 1993; ILO, 2003b). In Argentina, federal law entitles women to a ninety-day maternity leave. They cannot be fired during this time and receive Social Security payments equivalent to their full salary; however enforcement is lax (ILO, 2003b; Neft & Levine, 1998). Likewise, Indian and Bangladeshi women are entitled to paid maternity leave for twelve weeks; Italian women may take a five-month paid maternity leave, and Mexican women receive twelve weeks of paid maternity leave (Neft & Levine, 1998). Only a handful of countries guarantee women the right to maternity leave without wages. These include the United States, Australia, New Zealand, Swaziland, and Papau New Guinea. In the United States, where parental leave is unpaid and guaranteed only to women working in firms with 50 or more employees, 64 percent of workers with family responsibilities do not take the full twelve weeks because they cannot afford it (ILO, 2003b).

Affordable childcare also remains a significant problem for working parents. In many countries, such as the United States and the United Kingdom, childcare is viewed as the responsibility of parents, not the state. In such places, the greatest difficulties obtaining quality childcare are experienced by low-income and single parent households—ironically, the ones that need it the most (ILO, 2003b). Again, Sweden is one of the best countries for working parents. A Swedish law passed in 1985 guarantees a place in a day-care center for every child between the ages of 1 and 6, and a place in a "leisure time" center for every child between the ages of 7 and 12 (Neft & Levine, 1998). France also provides government sponsored childcare for children over age 3 (Morgan, 1996).

In summary, laws promoting paid maternity leaves and childcare are a good start. However, many family and work laws are not enforced. Another problem is that in many countries they are limited to women that work for companies with 50 or more employees (for example, the United States, Pakistan, Argentina, and Bangladesh). The policies often do not apply to women working in the service and informal sectors. Some of these benefits also work against women when employers must pay all or part of the costs. In such cases, employers may choose to hire men or make women prove that they are not pregnant before hiring them (Morgan, 1996; Neft & Levine, 1998).

Sexual Harassment

Sexual harassment is yet another problem facing employed women worldwide. For example, in the 1990s, women at the U.S. Mitsubishi automobile plant in Normal, Illinois were subjected to repeated and unwelcome physical and verbal abuse. Among the host of harassing behaviors were obscene graffiti demeaning to women, men exposing themselves to women and grabbing women's breasts, and men taunting women with crude names and pressuring them to have sex (Braun, 1998; Cray, 1997).

Defining Sexual Harassment

Fitzgerald's **tripartite model of sexual harassment** identifies three behavioral dimensions of sexual harassment, represented in Figure 5.4 (Fitzgerald, Swan, & Magley, 1997). **Gender harassment** refers to verbal and nonverbal behavior that convey insulting, hostile, and degrading attitudes toward women. Displaying pornography, calling women bitches or whores, and obscene gestures are in this category of sexual harassment. **Unwanted sexual attention** is just what it sounds like. It includes suggestive comments about a woman's body as well as unsolicited and unreciprocated sexual advances such as repeated requests for a kiss, a date, or sex. Last, **sexual coercion** refers to requiring sex as a condition of employment or job rewards. Legally, it is often called **quid pro quo sexual harassment.**

Sexual harassment may be defined behaviorally using the tripartite model but it is also important to have definitions recognizing that sexual harassment is a stressful and often traumatic experience. Psychological definitions of sexual harassment emphasize that it is perceived by victims as annoying, offensive, upsetting, embarrassing, stressful, and frightening (Fitzgerald et al., 1997). Depression, anxiety, shame, helplessness, and post-traumatic stress syndrome are possible mental health consequences (Dansky & Kilpatrick, 1997). Sexual harassment often results in emotional and physical stress and stress-related illnesses (Gutek & Koss, 1993; ILO, 1995; Schneider, Swann, & Fitzgerald, 1997). It is also potentially costly to organizations. Research in the United States indicates that harassment can lead to increased absenteeism, job turnover, requests for transfers, and decreases in work motivation and productivity (Knapp & Kustis, 1996).

"The señor wanted to take advantage of me, he followed me around . . . he grabbed my breasts twice from behind while I was washing clothes . . . I yelled, and the boy came out, and the señor left. I didn't tell the señora, because I was afraid. I just quit."
Maria Ajtún, domestic worker in Guatemala City

Prevalence of Sexual Harassment

It is only within the last twenty years that industrialized countries have identified sexual harassment as a workplace problem, and U.S. researchers have

FIGURE 5.4   *Fitzgerald's Tripartite Model of Types of Sexual Harassment*

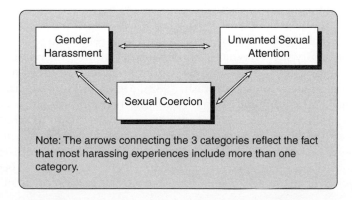

Note: The arrows connecting the 3 categories reflect the fact that most harassing experiences include more than one category.

conducted most systematic research on the dynamics of harassment. In areas where women have only recently entered the formal workforce, there is still denial of the problem and reluctance to report incidents (Bullock, 1994). Japan is a good example. Until 1989, when the country's first sexual harassment case was brought before the courts, there was no Japanese word for sexual harassment (it is now called *sekahura*). Statistics on the occurrence of sexual harassment worldwide are hard to obtain, although available statistics suggest that sexual harassment is prevalent. After reviewing cross-cultural research on sexual harassment, Gruber (1997) estimated that sexual harassment probably affected about half of all employed women in the United States, Canada, and Europe in the 1990s. Barak (1997) reviewed available studies on prevalence in twenty-two countries and reported figures ranging from 90 percent to 11 percent (much of this variation appeared to depend on how women were asked). The ILO (1995) reports that between 15 and 30 percent of employed women surveyed in industrialized countries say they have experienced frequent, serious sexual harassment such as unwanted touching, pinching, offensive remarks, and/or requests for sexual favors.

Although the prevalence of sexual harassment varies cross-culturally, research suggests that there is universality in the types of sexual harassment experienced. Gruber and colleagues (1996) reviewed existing research on cultural differences in types of sexual harassment. Their findings provide evidence of cross-cultural similarity in sexual harassment experiences. In studies with American, French, Spanish, Canadian, and Russian women, the most frequent form of harassment was verbal abuse and suggestive comments, followed by "sexual posturing" (including sexually suggestive looks or gestures, touching, following, and leering). Next were repeated requests for dates, sex, or a relationship; and last was outright sexual assault and coercion.

Causes of Sexual Harassment

The three main sources of sexual harassment are shown in Figure 5.5. At its simplest, sexual harassment is a consequence of traditional power relationships between the genders in larger society and gender power differences within organizations. For instance, sexual harassment is about power relations within a society in that who sexually harasses who depends on which groups have the greatest power. In other words, sexual harassment is a manifestation of the greater status and power of men relative to women. **Sex-role spillover** theory suggests that traditional expectations and relationships between the genders overflow into the workplace although they are irrelevant or inappropriate (Gutek & Morash, 1982). Men, used to perceiving women in sexual and traditional terms, carry this behavior into the workplace. Women, trained to interpret male attention as flattery and to avoid conflict, put up with it. Sexual remarks and behaviors towards women are normalized and therefore not perceived as problematic (Fitzgerald et al., 1997).

From a feminist perspective, sexual harassment is about power, because like other forms of gendered violence, it arises from and reinforces the subordinate

"Frankly speaking, sexual harassment for many women in Korea is something that they have grown up with. Having been raised in this situation, women have tended to view sexual harassment as something they had to endure rather than something they had to protest. More women, especially in younger age groups, have started to raise the issue privately and publicly."
Korean woman

FIGURE 5.5   *Causes of Sexual Harassment*

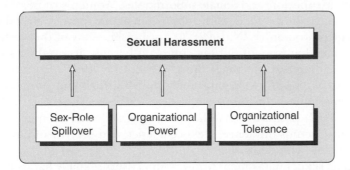

position of women in society (Cleveland & McNamara, 1996; Fitzgerald, 1993; Pagelow, 1992). By intimidating and discouraging women from work, male dominance occupationally and economically is assured (Tangri, Burt, & Johnson, 1982). Indian researchers Shobha Menon and Suresh Kanekar (1992) suggest that sexual harassment—like wife beating, dowry, sati (when widows throw themselves on their husband's funeral pyre), feticide, and rape—is a manifestation of the power differential between men and women and its misuse by men. Also like wife battering, rape, and incest, sexual harassment is considered to be a consequence of gender-role socialization processes that promote male dominance, the sexual objectification of women, and the cultural approval of violence against women (Cleveland & McNamara, 1996).

Research suggests that women who are numerical minorities are at greater risk for sexual harassment than women in jobs in which women predominate or are members of the dominant ethnic group (Gutek, Cohen, & Konrad, 1990). This is because their gender is especially noticeable and leads to processing of them based on gender stereotypes. Furthermore, women who are ethnic minorities in the workplace may be targeted because minority group status denotes marginality and lack of power within the workplace (Murrell, 1996). Additionally, such women may be susceptible because racism toward female ethnic minorities may be expressed as sexual aggression and harassment (Collins, 1990). It is interesting to note, for instance, that sexual harassment of women is reportedly widespread in factories owned by transnational corporations. This appears to be especially true when the supervisory staff is male and from a different country than the female subordinates. Murrell (1996) adds that the sexual harassment of ethnic minority women should be viewed as a form of racial discrimination because the sexual harassment of such women is often fueled by race-based stereotypes of women. Ethnic minority women are also likely to see their harassment as arising from their minority status (Collins, 1990; Murrell, 1996). This dual experience of racism and sexism, or sexual racism, may exacerbate the negative experience of sexual harassment (Murrell, 1996).

Sexual harassment is also about power because it frequently involves the abuse of **organizational power.** Men are often privileged in organizations and abuse their organizational power to sexually coerce or intimidate women (MacKinnon, 1979). For instance, most cases of sexual harassment occur between male superiors and female subordinates. Women's vulnerability to unemployment allows men with decision-making power to take sexual advantage of women (WIN, 1992). At Mitsubishi, many of those who experienced sexual harassment did not complain because it was their supervisors who were doing the harassing (Braun, 1998; Cray, 1997). Ironically, according to the company's sexual harassment policy, sexual harassment complaints were supposed to be made through these very supervisors (Cray, 1997). Livingston (1982) points out that the relative social and economic power of harassers and victims influences the occurrence and severity of harassment as well as victims' responses.

Not all sexual harassment involves supervisors sexually harassing subordinate females. Male peers also harass female peers, especially when the organization gives them to power to do so by its inaction. Researchers and activists agree that organizational climate is a strong determinant of sexual harassment. More specifically, **organizational tolerance,** the degree to which an organization is perceived by employees to be insensitive or tolerant of sexual harassment, affects its frequency and severity (Hulin, Fitzgerald, & Drasgow, 1996). In organizations that are tolerant of sexual harassment, complaints are not taken seriously, perpetrators are not meaningfully punished, and there is risk to women reporting harassment (Fitzgerald et al., 1997). Pryor and colleagues (1995) note that men predisposed to harass women do it when such behavior is tolerated, modeled, and encouraged in the organization, thereby becoming an acceptable norm. One study in Japan found that organizational tolerance was correlated with the incidence of sexual harassment of Japanese working women (Kakuyama, Onglatco, Tsuzuki, & Matsui, 2003).

Organizational tolerance is also manifested in the organization's treatment of the sexually harassed. According to sexual harassment researcher Louise Fitzgerald, research indicates that 95 percent of those who experience sexual harassment do not report it because they fear losing their jobs and sabotaging their careers (Murray, 1998). Research suggests additional reasons for low rates of reporting as well. These include victims' fears of retaliation, fears they won't be believed, and fears they will be blamed for it (Cleveland & McNamara, 1996; Gutek & Koss, 1993). These fears have basis in reality. For example, in the Mitsubishi case referred to earlier, women who lodged complaints were subjected to hostile phone calls, the threat of rape, and stalking (Cray, 1997). Studies of *maquiladoras,* assembly plants in Mexico owned by multinational corporations, reveal that sexual harassment, including rape, is common and is used to control female employees. Few women report it because they fear reprisals and feel shamed and humiliated (Nauman & Hutchison, 1997). *The Asian Women's Newsletter* reports that in Asia women do not dare speak out about sexual harassment for fear of being labeled as "loose women," because people still believe that decent women do not get harassed (WIN, 1992). Hong Kong researchers Chang, Tan, and Chang (1999) link reluctance to report incidents to collectivist cultures that emphasize harmonious relationships with others. They suggest that in addition to fears of retaliation and loss of privacy, sexually harassed victims in Hong Kong wish to avoid the negative label of "troublemaker."

Sexual Harassment Interventions

Sex-role spillover theory suggests that sexual harassment will decline with increased societal gender equality. As more women enter the paid workforce and occupations traditionally dominated by men, sexual harassment should subside as women's presence in the workplace becomes more "normal" and women are seen as capable of occupying non-traditional roles. Men will get used to relating to women on the basis of their work roles rather than on the basis of traditional gender roles where men are the sexual pursuers and women are the sexually pursued. In a more gender-equal world, women will also be more likely to be assertive regarding the unacceptability of sexual harassment. They will not accept it is as natural for males to harass and as part of their lot as females to put up with it. They will not try to minimize it by considering it a compliment, nor blame themselves for being too friendly or for wearing the wrong clothes. They will not hesitate to assert themselves out of a fear of not being nice or creating conflict. Of course, we do not yet have gender-equal societies so in the meantime, governments and organizations need to enact policies and programs that censure sexual harassment and make it easier for women to stop it.

Unsurprisingly, sexual harassment declines when organizational tolerance for it is reduced. Companies can put into place mechanisms that prevent men from abusing their organizational power. Although many organizations have adopted sexual harassment policies, the majority of organizations in the world have neither policies against sexual harassment nor procedures for handling it. This is unfortunate since sexual harassment is reduced when there are clear procedures to support victims and punish harassers and when there is a clear and consistent statement from management that sexual harassment will not be tolerated. One U.S. study found that the presence and effectiveness of sexual harassment policies and procedures reduced the incidence of harassment (Hesson-McInnis & Fitzgerald, 1995, reported in Hulin et al., 1996). Sexual harassment training, designed to prevent harassment from occurring, may also be effective *if* it is accompanied by strong managerial support. Unfortunately, sexual harassment training is often offered without procedures for ensuring that complaints will be taken seriously. Once again, the Mitsubishi plant in Normal, Illinois, serves as an example. The company's standard disciplinary measure was to require the harasser to watch a thirty-minute sexual harassment video and to place a memo in the person's file (Cray, 1997). Watching the film reportedly became a companywide joke.

The majority of countries in the world have no laws against sexual harassment in the workplace. Some of the few countries with laws against sexual harassment include Australia, Canada, Cuba, Denmark, France, Greece, India,

Portugal, South Korea, Sri Lanka, and the United States. Laws in other countries, such as Britain, Ecuador, Finland, Japan, Norway, Pakistan, and Sweden, can be interpreted to include sexual harassment. Of course, once again, laws are of limited impact when they are vague or not enforced, and this is definitely the case when it comes to sexual harassment law. In the countries that have laws, violations rarely make it to court. This is partly because sexual harassment laws are often more progressive than the societies in which they are enacted. Despite laws, sexual harassment is not taken seriously by male-dominated legal systems or viewed as a crime by societies. Thus, there is relatively little motivation for prosecution. Sexual harassment law is also new and confusing, and legal systems are not yet prepared to handle sexual harassment complaints. This means that not only are there few attorneys familiar with it, but that it is often unclear what legal evidence is necessary to prove harassment. Women often have difficulty finding legal counsel willing to take these cases. Some countries require that complaints first be registered through underfunded and backlogged government agencies. For instance, in Canada, the Human Rights Commission handles complaints, and there is typically a backlog of two and a half years (Morgan, 1996).

Given this state of affairs, women frequently see little point in pursuing legal avenues of redress, especially given the high personal and financial costs of doing so. However, some courageous women pursue their cases despite this, and eventually their efforts may have the effect of reducing organizational tolerance and increasing awareness. For example, in June 1998, Mitsubishi was ordered by the U.S. courts to pay $34 million to 486 female workers at its Illinois plant. This is the largest such settlement on record in a corporate case. In Japan, following the passage of a law in 1999 banning sexual harassment, a 21-year old campaign worker groped by a political candidate, was awarded $100,000. In 2003, 100 women at the Dial Soap plant in Illinois received settlements averaging $100,000 each. The women were groped, called crude names, and subjected to pornography. The company will pay a total of $10 million to settle the federal sexual harassment suit. Such cases are important because they send a message that sexual harassment is unacceptable and potentially expensive to employers.

Self-Employed Women

In contrast to the formal sector, the organized and visible economic sector, is the informal sector, or the **self-employed sector.** The Cuban woman who runs a beauty shop on the roof of her apartment building, the Peruvian woman who sells vegetables from her garden by the roadside, the South African woman who brews and sells her own beer, the Filipino woman who does others' laundry for pay, the American woman who gets paid for watching her neighbor's children, and the Mexican woman who sews sweatshirts in her home for the subcontractor of a transnational corporation, all work in the informal sector. Informal sector work includes petty trade, food processing, and domestic work. Informal sector work is paid, but unstructured and unregulated (Seager, 1997). Women in self-employment rely on the skills and experience they already have, and so food processing and trading, sewing, and domestic and personal services are all common (Bullock, 1994). Home-based work done for subcontractors is also part of the economic strategy of women (Beneria & Roldan, 1987; Tinker, 1995). In most cases, women are paid by the assembled piece ("piece rate"). In such cases, work at home is part of the chain of production in the formal sector, demonstrating the blurry line between formal and informal sectors.

Women generally make up at least half and sometimes more, of the informal sector (Dignard & Havet, 1995). In the last decade, the number of women in the informal sector has increased dramatically (ILO, 2003a). Latin America alone has seen women's participation grow from 29 percent to 44 percent. There are more women in the informal sector in some countries than in others. Some countries with high rates of women in the informal sector are Zambia (72 percent), Gambia (62 percent), the Republic of Korea (41 percent), and Indonesia (65 percent) (ILO, 1996a). In some sub-Saharan African countries, most of the female labor force is in the informal economy—for example, 97 percent in Benin, 95 percent in Chad, 85 percent in Guinea, and 83 percent in Kenya (ILO, 2003a).

More women than men are found in the informal economy (ILO, 2003a). Women dominate informal sector work for several reasons. One is that it is often the only work they can find because formal manufacturing enterprises and state (government) bureaucracies have failed to create enough jobs (Dignard & Havet, 1995; ILO, 1996a). Another reason is that it permits the combining of paid work with family and household responsibilities and poses less of a challenge to the "male breadwinner ethos" (Bullock, 1994; Tinker, 1995). Remember, in many cultures a woman's primary role is to care for her home and family, and a man's role is to be the cash provider. Informal sector work, particularly home assembly work, allows women to work for pay without defaming the family or threatening men's masculinity.

Bullock (1994) notes that the concept of the informal sector has been challenged on the grounds that the word *informal* belies the importance of these economic activities and women's role in paid economic life. She reports that the Self-Employed Women's Association (SEWA), which works to protect and organize women in the informal sector in India, recommends use of the term *self-employment* out of respect for this type of work. As Bhatt (1995), one of the founders of SEWA said, "It is contradictory to describe such a vast, active work force in terms that relegate it to a peripheral position, while in reality it is central to the economy. In my view, in order to properly characterize this work force, it should be called the 'self-employed sector' or 'the self-employed'" (p. 87). Another designation gaining acceptance is **women's micro- and small-scale enterprises** (WMSEs) (Dignard & Havet, 1995). Box 5.5 features some self-employed women from Uganda.

BOX 5.5   *In Their Own Words: Self-Employed Ugandan Women*

"I eat and drink from my business. I built a house so that I no longer rent. I bought my plot from my earnings. I have been able to educate my children. That is very important—an even better achievement than building a house."
Betty Nakiganda, 48, widowed with eight children, sells mangos

"Through my business I have achieved a lot. I managed to construct a house, buy things for it, buy a vehicle, and open two more shops like this one. I believe there is nothing men can do that we cannot do."
Teddy Birungi, 36, married with five children, wholesales beer, soda, and whiskey

"I started what they were calling *magenda* (informal trade) in those days, that is, buying sweets and selling them, making a little profit to add to my salary. Later I baked buns and that was more rewarding. . . . I started looking for a shop. I got a small place in Kisura, but I lived in Nakaserto, so it took me a long time to commute. I had to run the shop after office hours. At 5 p.m., I would collect my children, take them home, given them tea, run through their homework, then rush to the shop."
Alice Karaugaba, 50s, separated with four children, owns two furniture and soft-goods stores

Source: Coughlin, 2002

The way that women are able to scrape together an income on the basis of almost no inputs but their own labor and ingenuity inspires admiration and respect (Bullock, 1994). Despite this, economists see these activities as "economically marginal" because women micro-entrepreneurs do not always use their profits for business growth (Tinker, 1995). Instead, women often return their profits to the family in the form of better food and living conditions, to what is called the "human economy" (Tinker, 1995). As noted earlier, women's work in the informal sector is also literally devalued by its exclusion from national accounting systems, although some efforts are being made to remedy this.

One problem facing self-employed women is that they do not usually have the advantage of being represented by unions. This means that collective action to redress labor wrongs is less available to them. Another problem is that the invisibility of women's work in the informal sector, along with it not fitting standard definitions for economically successful business, mean that women entrepreneurs have had difficulty getting credit (loans) from banks, governments, and development agencies. Berger (1995) summarizes some of the constraints on credit access for women micro-entrepreneurs. One of these is lack of collateral. This is a key problem as women often do not have clear title to land or property. This is compounded by the widespread practice of registering property in the man's name and by inheritance systems that favor men. Bank practices, such as those that require a male cosigner, also discourage women. In addition, many poor women, especially those with little education, have difficulty completing the complicated application

BOX 5.6   *Activist Profile: Ela Bhat of the Self-Employed Women's Association (India)*

Ela Bhat, born in 1933 in India, is known as the founder of the Self-Employed Women's Association (SEWA). Bhat's work as a lawyer for the textile industry brought her into contact with thousands of self-employed women workers such as street vendors and home-based piece rate workers. She realized that because the women were not organized, they were easily exploited and because they worked in the informal labor sector, they could not appeal to the government for economic protections, and there were no unions to represent them. As Bhat once said, "Personally, I don't think there can be any greater injustice to anybody in the world than to have one's work contribution negated. . . . Who is the backbone of any economy in the country? It's the poor! Yet they are not recorded as workers in the national census. They are described as non-workers!" Bhat recognized that these women could be organized to demand better pay and work conditions, and that by pooling their resources they could provide loans to women's micro-enterprises that would otherwise be unable to obtain funding. With these goals, she founded SEWA in 1972. Today SEWA has 250,000 members and empowers women to have greater control of their economic lives. SEWA is the model for thousands of women's cooperatives worldwide.

forms required by lending agencies. Consequently, for credit purposes women micro-entrepreneurs frequently rely on moneylenders (who charge high interest rates), family, and friends (Berger, 1995).

Self-employed women have learned to create their own solutions to these problems. For example, there are a number of self-employed women's unions such as the South African Domestic Workers' Union (SADWU) and the Union of Domestic Workers of Brazil. Perhaps the best-known self-employed women's union is SEWA of India, begun in 1972. One of SEWA's principal activities is the organization of cooperatives through which labor problems are addressed. Bhatt (1995) gives a number of examples. SEWA helped the "pushcart vegetables cooperative" to fight for women's right to receive vending licenses; it helped the "paper pickers cooperative" to set up their own collection network so that they could sell directly to the paper factories and avoid middlemen; and it helped the "cane and bamboo cooperative" to upgrade their skills and receive a greater share of their state government's harvested bamboo at a reasonable price. In addition, the SEWA Bank provides capital for women's small-scale businesses. Before the SEWA Bank, self-employed women had to obtain capital at high interest rates from moneylenders. As of 1992, SEWA had forty-four different cooperatives, 46,000 members, 22,000 savings accounts, over a million U.S. dollars in working capital, and over 860,000 U.S. dollars in loans with a repayment rate of 96 percent (Bhatt, 1995). A brief biography of Ela Bhat, founder of SEWA, appears in Box 5.6.

Madam C. J. Walker (1867–1919), the first self-made woman millionaire in the United States, demonstrates the entrepreneurial spirit of African American women. She helped other women gain economic independence by hiring them to work at excellent wages for her hair-care products business.

In industrialized nations, the number of **women entrepreneurs,** women who start their own businesses, is also rising, although their businesses tend to be part of the formal sector and directed toward growth. In Canada, women comprise almost a third of all self-employed workers and have been starting their own businesses at three times the rate of men (Neft & Levine, 1998). In Thailand, nearly 40 percent of businesses are now owned or operated by women (ILO, 2003a). According to the ILO (1996b), in developing countries women start their own micro-enterprises as a matter of survival, whereas in industrialized countries women do so in order to be masters of their own fate. In other words, in contrast to the small-scale enterprises run by women in developing nations to provide for their families' basic needs, women in industrialized nations start their own businesses to be their own bosses and to escape the glass ceiling. However, it should be noted that poor women in the United States also start small businesses in order to provide for their families' basic needs. One thing experienced by women entrepreneurs all over the world is limited access to credit. In the United States for instance, where women owned almost 40 percent of small businesses and employed 20 million workers, they received only 12 percent of the credit provided to small firms (Dickerson, 2000). Another commonality is the role of alternative economic organizations such as women's banks, networks, and cooperatives in women's entrepreneurship all over the world.

Conclusion

One recurring theme in this book is that governments often respond to gender inequality by passing legislation but then fail to enforce or implement it. Most nations have national laws or have signed international documents supporting gender equality in work. For example, the ILO is a branch of the United Nations that deals with international labor standards. Box 5.7 summarizes International Labour Organization (ILO) conventions that specifically concern women's labor. Member nations that sign ILO conventions agree to follow the declarations stated therein. The majority of UN member nations have ratified the Equal Renumeration Convention and the Discrimination Convention (United Nations, 2003b) and yet as you read earlier, gender equality in the workplace has not occurred. This is because governments frequently fail to enforce laws and conventions.

Bullock (1994) points out that one of the problems is lack of **legal literacy.** As she puts it, a law that no one knows about does not really exist. People need to know their rights according to the law and should have the means to defend and enforce them. Bullock (1994) suggests that the transformation of the situation of working women rests on three pillars: laws that establish equality principles, women's active participation in workers' organizations, and women's understanding of their rights. Workers' organizations along with other NGOs are important in pressing for the ratification of interna-

BOX 5.7 *International Labour Organization Conventions Relevant to Women*

The Equal Remuneration Convention, 1951, provides for the equal remuneration (pay) for men and women for work of equal value.

The Discrimination (Employment and Occupation) Convention, 1958, promotes equality of rights between men and women in the workplace.

The Workers with Family Responsibilities Convention, 1981, aims to create effective equality of opportunity and treatment for men and women workers with family responsibilities.

The Part-Time Work Convention, 1994, aims to ensure protection for part-time workers in areas such as access to employment, working conditions, and Social Security.

The Home Work Convention, 1996, aims at improving the situation of home workers who are largely unrecognized in labor statistics and unprotected by legislation.

Maternity Protection Convention, 2000, Provides maternity protection for women at work through leave, benefits, health care, employment security, and non-discrimination.

Source: International Labour Organization (2003)

tional labor standards and their implementation, as well as promoting women's legal literacy (Bullock, 1994).

As already noted, one customary way to advocate for workers' labor rights is through the organization of labor unions that collectively bargain for workers. The International Confederation of Free Trade Unions (ICFTU) reports that 34 percent of its membership worldwide is female (Bullock, 1994). Historically, unions have paid relatively little attention to labor rights specific to women, such as violence against women, sexual harassment, child-care facilities, and gender job segregation. According to the ILO (1997), male dominance, along with the way unions are typically structured, hinder the promotion of women's labor rights. For instance, unions frequently hold meetings at night, and women's family responsibilities make it difficult for them to attend. Also, strong male networks tend to dominate, making it difficult for women to participate. Furthermore, because women tend to hold lower status jobs, they are unlikely to be elected to important committees and bargaining teams. The ILO views labor unions as essential ingredients in women's workplace equality and in recent years has attempted to educate and encourage unions to do a better job of including women. Their recommendations to unions include such things as removing sexist language in union material; sensitizing men to the role women play in daily life; setting up a women's commission to keep attention focused on women's needs; reserving

Mary "Mother" Jones (1830–1930), an Irish American, was a labor organizer for fifty-nine years. Her passionate speeches along with the dramatic marches and confrontations she organized brought attention to the plight of child laborers and coal and railroad workers.

a certain number of seats for women in decision-making bodies (ideally providing extra seats so that men don't feel threatened); setting goals such that, within a certain period of time, a specific number of women occupy decision-making posts; and having meetings at times when women can attend.

Dolores Huerta (1930–) is the co-founder of the United Farm Workers Union in the United States. The mother of eleven has worked tirelessly for thirty years to gain a living wage and safe working conditions for farmworkers. Her recent focus is on the right of female farmworkers to work without sexual harassment and assault. She also works to get Latina women into leadership positions in unions and in politics.

Alexandra Kollontai (1872–1952; Russian) believed strongly in women's right to work for wages, their right to sexual freedom, and their right to control their fertility. She felt that women's equality with men required their economic independence from men. She organized women workers and played an important role in establishing the concept of women's rights in the newly developing USSR.

The ILO's efforts, along with women's growing union membership and the work of activists and women's leaders, has resulted in some progress. For instance, Bullock (1994) reports that over 90 percent of ICFTU affiliates reported having a special structure and/or officer responsible for women's and equality issues. In cases in which mainstream trade unions have not responded to women's needs, women have often formed their own associations. India's SEWA, discussed earlier in the chapter, is one example. The Working Women's Co-operative Society (WWCS) and its offshoot, the National Union of Working Women, are other Indian examples. Also, there are the Grassroots Women Workers' Centre in Taiwan, the Korean Women Workers' Association, the South African Domestic Workers' Union, and the Union of Women Domestic Employees in Brazil.

Most feminists view women's **economic empowerment** as the key to women's equality, but there is some debate on the effects of paid work on women. On the one hand, earning money buys some freedom and some power in the home. On the other hand, this is often offset by the difficulties of balancing work and family, low wages, glass ceilings, and poor work conditions, including sexual harassment. The prevailing opinion is that employment is a necessary but not sufficient condition of high female status (Tinker, 1990). Indeed, Tinker notes that in some societies, women's social status is enhanced when they are economically dependent on husbands and don't have to work, and many poor, hard-working women would welcome such a situation. Furthermore, the extent to which women get to keep or control the income they generate varies greatly worldwide (Blumberg, 1991). Mere work in economic activities or even ownership of economic resources does not translate into benefits if the person has no control over them (Blumberg, 1991, 1995). The more a society's political, economic, legal, and ideological systems disadvantage women, the less a woman gets her "hypothetical dollar's worth of economic power for every dollar she brings to the household" (Blumberg, 1995, p. 213).

It should be apparent after reading this chapter that women's disproportionate responsibility for household labor and child care features prominently in their continued subordination. Chafetz (1991) summarizes the thinking on this point by showing the interrelationships between women's paid and unpaid labor and their power in both the domestic and public domains (which she respectively calls "micro" and "macro" levels of power). The argument goes like this: Societies designate household labor (including child care) as women's work. This, combined with men's greater power in the home (**micro power**), means that men are able to avoid household labor, regardless of the other work women might do. In addition, the double workday experienced by wage-earning women reduces women's ability to compete for better-paying jobs, and this reinforces men's micro power advantages. Men's micro power can also be used to prevent women from entering the paid labor force or may restrict them to part-time jobs (for example, husbands may forbid their wives from working for pay at all or from working full-time). This further reinforces males' micro power advantage because they continue to be the major providers of money. Chafetz points out that even when women do earn wages, their husbands' micro power is not totally eliminated because women can rarely match or exceed their husbands in the provision of economic resources. The fact that men generally enjoy greater **macro power** (public sphere power) plays into this as well. This power permits men—as employers, lawmakers, and so on—to segregate women into low-paying jobs, to restrict their opportunities to acquire skills and credentials needed for better jobs, or to even prevent them from paid employment altogether. Men's macro power is then reinforced as women tend to lack the resources to challenge it. For example, in Afghanistan the Taliban government did not permit women to work unless they were widows with no other source of income. Girls were not allowed to work or go to school. In Yemen, women must have their husband's permission to have a job.

Chafetz's model suggests that changing societal conceptions of household labor as "women's work" would remove one barrier to women's achievement of higher paying work roles. This would then positively impact both their micro and macro power levels. Many feminists believe that gender roles are unlikely to change until the division of labor in the home changes. Current gender-based divisions of labor in the household are viewed as symptomatic of continuing gender inequality and gender-role socialization (Blair & Lichter, 1991). As Braverman (1991) points out, "The allocation of housework and childcare reflects in microcosm the power inequities between men and women in society at large" (p. 26). Traditional divisions of household labor may also perpetuate the lower status of females. It is apparent to the child that the person who works all day and who must then come home and cook and clean is of lower status than the one who works all day and does not have these duties when he returns home. Children may then infer that females must really be inferior, or they wouldn't have this lower status.

Traditional divisions of household labor lead children to develop gender stereotypes and to learn different skills based on their gender. When children see males and females in different roles, they assume that males and females have different qualities that make them better suited for these differing roles (Burn, 1996). These gender stereotypes then act as social norms, or prescriptions, for behavior. In other words, children come to believe that men and women should occupy different roles and have different psychological qualities.

Another implication of Chafetz's model is that women's achievement of higher paying work roles should increase women's micro power. This is why activism toward the goal of gender pay and promotion equity is so important. The model also suggests that male macro power results in gender ideologies, norms, and stereotypes that support a gendered division of labor and reinforce male power and privilege. This is one of the reasons that feminists work to increase the number of women in governmental and business power positions. Chapter 9 addresses how women come to occupy powerful political positions. In general, though, women are a minority in formal political positions.

Despite women's low power and few material resources, they do organize, mobilize, challenge, and change macro power institutions. This chapter presented evidence of this in the form of changed laws and union activity. Chapter 10 examines in more detail the dynamics of gender equality movements. Chapter 6 focuses on women in developing economies and Chapter 7 discusses women and globalization. All of these chapters provide additional examples of change brought about by women's activism.

Study Questions

1. Why is the study of women's labor important to a study of women across cultures?

2. What evidence is there that women's labor is undercounted and undervalued? Why is this the case?

3. What are gender-based household divisions of labor? Why do they occur?

4. What is the gender pay gap? How common is it? What explanations for it were given in the chapter? What accounts for cross-cultural variation in the gender pay gap? What can be done about it?

5. What is the glass ceiling? How common is it? What causes it?

6. Why are state maternity and child care policies important but sometimes ineffective?

7. What is the tripartite model of sexual harassment? What groups of women are especially vulnerable to sexual harassment? Why does it occur? How can it be reduced?

8. Why do women make up such a large percentage of the self-employed? In what way do economists devalue women's informal sector work? What are some of the difficulties facing self-employed women, and what have they done about them? How are self-employed women in industrialized nations somewhat different from those in less industrialized ones?

9. What does it mean to say that the effects of paid work on women are somewhat paradoxical? In what ways does working for pay benefit women?

10. How has legislation been used to remedy workplace gender inequalities such as the gender pay gap, the glass ceiling, sexual harassment, and inequalities arising from pregnancy and childcare responsibilities? Why has such legislation been less than effective?

11. How is the fact that women are largely responsible for child care and household labor related to the gender pay gap, the glass ceiling, and women's micro and macro power?

Discussion Questions and Activities

1. Choose two jobs. One should be a "man's" job and one a "woman's" job. For each, make a separate list of the hazards, skills, and work involved, how heavy or light the work is, whether the work requires few or many decisions, whether the skills required are high or low, and whether the responsibility is high or low. Use your lists to decide the value of each job. Which is higher status? Which is paid more? What might you conclude about fairness? (adapted from Bullock, 1994)

2. What would happen if women in heterosexual cohabitating or married relationships went on strike and did not perform the unpaid labor they normally do?

3. Discuss how the fact that women get pregnant, have children, and retain primary responsibility for children interferes with equal employment opportunities. This is a case in which women's differences from men mean that they need to be treated differently from men. Is this consistent with feminists' desire for women to be treated equally to men?

4. Discuss with others whether they have experienced sexual harassment in the workplace. Ask them to describe the type of harassment, how it affected their productivity, and its emotional and physical effects. How did they handle it and why? How did the answers of females and males differ? Summarize your findings.

Activist Websites of Interest

Mothers are Women (Meres et Femmes) Canadian organization dedicated to the recognition of women's unpaid labor.

http://www.mothersarewomen.com

Global Fund for Women

http://www.globalfundforwomen.org

Informational Websites of Interest

International Labour Organization

http://www.ilo.org

Feminist Majority's Sexual Harassment Information Page

http://http://www.feminist.org/911/harasswhatdo.html

World Association of Women Entrepreneurs

http://www.fcem.org

American Federation of Labor and Congress of Industrial Organizations (AFL-CIO) (access to branches outside of the United States is also available at this address)

http://www.aflcio.org

Action Opportunities

1. Hold a bake sale in a public place to draw attention to the gender pay gap. List your prices by gender (charge men one dollar for each item and women seventy-five cents). Explain to puzzled customers that your pricing scheme reflects the fact that women make approximately 75 percent of what men make. When they argue that your pricing is not fair, remind them that the gender pay gap is not fair either. Donate your proceeds to a worthy women's cause such as UNIFEM, the United Nations Fund for Women.

2. Suzanne Doerge is a Canadian educator who teaches economics to women. She once said that making women's unpaid work visible is key to increasing the perception of its value. Develop a project to increase the visibility of women's unpaid work. For instance, staff a table at a public event (activists call this "table-ing") where you have a display and pass out information. If you and your female friends tend to do all of the household labor for the males in your life, consider going on a strike for a day.

3. What is your university's policy on sexual harassment? What do students do if they wish to report being sexually harassed? Educate your campus about what sexual harassment is and what to do about it. Write an article for your school newspaper, pass out information in your student union, design a web page and advertise the address, or post your information on bulletin boards on campus.

4. Check the Amnesty International and Human Rights Watch websites for campaigns related to working women's rights. Or, write letters to the U.S. Department of Labor and the International Labour Association encouraging them to stay focused on women's labor issues.

5. Use your labor and ingenuity to create your own short-term micro-enterprise and donate all or part of your profits to The Global Fund for Women. The Global Fund for Women is an organization that uses monetary donations to fund women's micro-enterprises and empowerment all over the world. Recently, they have given grants to women's projects in Sierra Leone, Mexico, India, Russia, and Rwanda. Learn more about the Global Fund for Women at http://www.globalfundforwomen.org. Explain what the project taught you about self-employed women.

6

Women and Development

Development was to be a liberating project—a project for removal of poverty and leveling of socio-economic inequalities, based on class, ethnicity, and gender. While the dominant image of "development" persists as a class and gender neutral model of progress for all, the experience of "development" has been the opposite, polarizing the dichotomizing society, creating new forms of affluence for the powerful, and new forms of deprivation and dispossession for the weak.

—Vandana Shiva

Women in Zimbabwe collect water from the village well in the Eastern Highlands for their families. Women play an important, though often neglected, role in world development. © Robert Holmes

M illions of the world's women live in developing countries. This chapter takes a close look at women in developing countries and how they are affected by economic development efforts in their countries. As you will see, historically, gender equality has largely been ignored in development efforts. The result is that women's inequality was often untouched, and sometimes aggravated, by development projects. The study of women and development is also another story of successful activism. After three decades of struggle by women's activists and scholars, gender is finally acknowledged as an important and central part of development.

The study of women and development is an important part of internationally oriented women's studies (Staudt, 1995). Women constitute 70 percent of the world's 1.3 billion poor who live on less than $1 a day (ILO, 2003a) and development projects are intended to promote economic development and reduce poverty. Previous chapters have touched on the subject of women in developing countries. For instance, in Chapter 3, it was noted that family planning efforts, which are often a part of development programs, frequently fail to improve women's reproductive choices. In Chapter 5 the idea that governments typically overlook women's labor when designing programs and policies intended to bring about economic development was touched on. The point was made that most development programs focus on men's labor. Consequently, development programs do not usually enhance women's status, and women's lives are often made even harder.

"The impact of economic development on gender equality is often neither automatic nor immediate. Nor is it sufficient."
World Bank

Background

Development Terminology

An introduction to development terminology is necessary first. The terms **Third World** and **developing nation** are usually used to describe the less or nonindustrialized nations of the world. The United Nations identifies approximately 128 nations in Africa, Latin America, and Asia as "developing." The forty-nine identified as "least developed" are listed in Box 6.1. The majority of these are in the region known as sub-Saharan Africa where 50 percent of the population lives on less than $1 a day, over one-third of the population is malnourished, and only 60 percent have a primary education (United Nations Development Programme, 2003). The **First World** countries are those such as the United States that are industrialized and market based. In recent years, the terms **northern** and **southern countries** (see *First World Nations* and *Third World Nations* in glossary) have gained acceptance based on the relative geographic location of the industrialized nations in the north and developing nations in the south (Mermel & Simons, 1991; United Nations, 1997a).

In a nation, **development** is the process of growth that may include the following: emphasis on large-scale economic growth; focus on small-scale

BOX 6.1 *Countries Identified as "Least Developed" by the UN*

Southern Asia
Afghanistan
Bangladesh
Bhutan
Maldives

Southeastern Asia
Cambodia
Laos
Myanmar
Nepal

Western Asia
Yemen

Oceania
Kiribati
Tuvulu
Vanuatu
Samoa (Western)
Solomon Islands

Caribbean
Haiti

Sub-Saharan Africa
Angola
Benin
Burkina Faso
Burundi
Cape Verde
Central African Republic
Chad
Comoros
Democratic Republic of Congo
Djibouti
Equatorial Guinea
Eritrea
Ethiopia
Gambia
Guinea
Guinea-Bissau
Lesotho
Liberia
Madagascar
Mali
Mauritania
Mozambique
Niger
Rwanda
Sao Tome and Principe
Senegal
Sierra Leone
Somalia
Sudan
Tanzania
Togo
Uganda
Zambia

Source: United Nations Conference on Trade and Development, 2001.
Note: Classified as least developed based on income, level of economic diversification, and human resources such as life expectancy, caloric intake, and literacy.

community development projects aimed at increasing individuals' self-reliance; creation or improvement of national infrastructures such as roads; provision of credit, training, or services that enable people to participate more fully in the economic, political, and social lives of their communities; improvement in access to health care; mechanisms for increasing agricultural yield; increased access to education for women and children; and expanded opportunities for political development (Mermel & Simons, 1991). Development programs are often funded through foreign aid, from the government of one country to the government of another country (called **bilateral aid**) such as that provided by USAID, or through **multilateral aid** funded by the World Bank, the IMF (International Monetary Fund), and other UN agencies. Nongovernmental development organizations such as OXFAM and the Global Fund for Women also fund development projects.

Colonial History

Many of the countries in the south spent years as colonies of northern countries, some well into this century. For example, the developing nation of Sri Lanka (formerly Ceylon) is an island country off the coast of India. Europeans dominated it for more than 400 years, first the Portuguese in the sixteenth century, then the Dutch, and later the British, who controlled it until 1948. Only two countries in Africa were never colonies (Liberia and Ethiopia). Belgium, Britain, France, Portugal, Holland, Germany, and Spain controlled the other African countries until a lengthy decolonization period following World War II. As colonies, these countries were exploited as sources of cheap labor and resources. Typically, profits were not shared with the natives.

Colonization permanently altered cultural features such as language and economies and, some would argue, negatively impacted women's status and power. Many feminist development scholars argue that colonization replaced egalitarian gender arrangements by removing women from the political decision-making spheres, limiting their access to and control over resources, and interfering with their legal rights and privileges (Boserup, 1970; Duley & Diduk, 1986; Sen & Grown, 1987). For example, Western patrilineal notions of land ownership contributed to a situation in which women own hardly any of the world's land. Industrialization, which necessitated the movement of families into cities, increased women's dependence upon men for their livelihoods because offices and factories hire far fewer women than they do men, and urban work is often incompatible with traditional female roles.

Colonial experiences also affect how developing nations interpret Western attempts to "help" them. This fact is relevant to our study here. Colonizers often defended their behavior on the grounds that they were doing native cultures a favor by remaking them in the Western image. The result, of course, was the loss of many native traditions and suspicion of

Western intervention. Consequently, efforts to promote gender equality as part of development are often resisted with the charge of Western cultural imperialism.

Conditions in Developing Nations

People in developing nations are poor, not just in income, but in terms of their limited choices and opportunities for living a tolerable life (United Nations, 1997a). It is important to consider gender when we consider poverty because the experience of poverty depends in part on gender. As previously mentioned, the feminization of poverty is especially marked in developing countries where 70 percent of those in poverty are women (ILO, 2003a). Also, as the poorest of the poor, women in developing countries work extremely hard for the basic survival of their families. The main responsibility of managing poverty falls on women; it is their labor and their personal austerity that typically compensates for the family's restricted resources (Seager, 2003). Box 6.2 leads you through an exercise so that you can imagine what it is like to live in a developing country.

Poverty goes hand in hand with limited educational opportunities and poor quality of life, and these too disproportionately affect women. Nearly half a billion people are illiterate, two-thirds of them women (United Nations, 2000). In the southern countries, 60 percent of the illiterate are women, and female wages are only three-fourths of male wages. Well over a billion people lack access to safe water, and 60 percent do not have access to adequate sanitation and it is women who generally manage sanitation and water resources for their families. Most women in the least developed countries can expect to die before age 60. Nearly two-thirds of those infected with the AIDS virus live in developing countries and AIDS now ranks as one of the leading causes of death among women ages 20 to 40 years in sub-Saharan Africa (UNAIDS, 2003). A third of married women in developing countries are battered by their husbands. More than half of the pregnant women in southern countries suffer from anemia, which leads to low birth weights and maternal illness. Over 98 percent of women's deaths and illnesses from reproductive causes occur to women in developing countries. Life expectancy, educational attainment, and income are especially low for women relative to men in the southern countries of Sierra Leone, Niger, Burkina Faso, Mali, and Ethiopia (United Nations, 1997a).

Feminist Concerns with the Development Process

Historically, most development programs focused on economic growth and a conversion to capitalist market economies. This focus is commonly associated with **modernization theory,** so-called because other systems were viewed as backward, and urban-based market economies were viewed as modern and

BOX 6.2 *Life in a Developing Country*

Heilbroner (1963) suggests that to understand economic development, we must have a picture of the problem with which it contends. Here is a condensed version of his attempt to take us there. Strip your house of its furniture and linens, except for a few blankets, the kitchen table, and a wooden chair. Empty your closet of clothes except for your oldest dress or pants and shirt. Empty your kitchen of appliances and food save for a box of matches, a few onions, and a dish of dried beans. Cut off the running water and the electricity. Now take away the house or apartment and move to a toolshed. You have no newspapers, books, or television (you can't read anyway). There are no government services, no hospital nearby. There is a clinic, but it is ten miles away and you have no transportation. This is what you have although you work 12 to 14 hours every day.

desirable. For example, following the Second World War until the 1970s, development policies focused on the introduction of high-yielding varieties of seeds and the transfer of modern technology to developing nations (United Nations, 1999). Modernization proponents believed that modern capitalism and other forms of development go hand in hand. That is, if we transformed the economy of a developing country, then political and social development would follow. Theoretically, then, economic development should increase women's status by providing more opportunities for them to participate in paid work, thus reducing the gendered division of labor. To the extent that economic development increases public services such as healthcare and reliable food and fuel sources, then women's workloads should be reduced (World Bank, 2001). Traditional development programmers saw no need to consider gender since they believed that what benefited the economy would benefit both men and women.

Sadly, economic growth does not necessarily increase the status of women nor reduce their considerable workloads. Indeed, it can lead to increased income inequalities and can leave social and political inequalities untouched. The results of economic growth do not always trickle down; instead, the gap between the haves and the have-nots often increases (UN, 1999). Women are among the many social groups that frequently suffer severe economic and social dislocation as a result of development plans and projects (Howard, 1995; UN, 1999). The fact that some southern countries outperform richer industrialized countries in gender equality in political, economic, and professional activities also demonstrates that economic development does not necessarily lead to increased gender equality. For instance, Barbados is ahead of Belgium, Italy, and Greece on indicators of gender equality; Trinidad and Tobago outrank Portugal; the Bahamas does better than the United Kingdom; France is behind Suriname, Colombia, and

"It is not possible to address society's needs at any level while ignoring the perspectives, priorities, and knowledge of more than half of the world's population."
Rosina Wilshire of UNDP

BOX 6.3   *Common Feminist Criticisms of Traditional Development Programs*

- Neglect women's labor in and out of the home, helping them little.

- Often increase women's workloads through environmental degradation, taking water and land for cash crop production, and taking men away for wage earning.

- Do not benefit women head of households or reduce gender inequality since development resources are channeled through men, and male wage earning is the goal.

- In cultures where they were important producers, may erode women's status by directing women into homemaking roles.

Botswana; Japan is behind China, Guatemala, and Mexico (United Nations, 1997a). This shows that gender equality can be achieved at different stages of development and that economic development is no guarantee of women's equality.

In the 1970s, things started to change when feminists began voicing their concerns about the invisibility of women in development (Anand, 1993). A 1970 book by Ester Boserup, *Women's Role in Economic Development,* stimulated the debate as the first major text in the women and development literature (Mosse, 1993). As Boserup says in the opening sentences of the book, "In the vast and ever growing literature on economic development, reflections on the particular problems of women are few and far between" (p. 5). Boserup's research fostered an understanding of the dual aspects of colonial and contemporary development policies, which belittled women's economic contributions while relying on and exploiting their labor (Acosta-Belen & Bose, 1995). She also showed that economic development has a differential impact on men and women and that the impact on women was often negative (Beneria & Roldan, 1987).

Boserup's book stimulated a number of feminist critiques of development programs, summarized in Box. 6.3. One common criticism is that the programs fail to acknowledge that women's work both inside and outside the home is vital to development. The absence of women in the public sphere, along with an emphasis on their role as homemakers and mothers, has led to a devaluing of their productive labor in the development process (Anand, 1993). Because work is viewed in terms of participation in the paid labor force, all the productive labor women perform in and around their households is not considered work and therefore is not targeted for development assistance (Mosse, 1993). For instance, in Bangladesh, women care for family livestock and poultry, grow, harvest, and store vegetables, and are responsible for obtaining the family's fuel (wood collected from the forest), yet this work is considered "noneconomic" (FAO, 2003a).

"Experience shows that investing in women is one of the most cost-effective ways of promoting development. As mothers, as producers or suppliers of food, fuel, and water, as traders and manufacturers, as political and community leaders, women are at the center of the process of change."
Gro Harlem Brundtland, Former Prime Minister of Norway and Head of the World Health Organization

One serious consequence of the failure to consider women's work is that it is vital to the survival and ongoing reproduction of people in all societies (Sen & Grown, 1987). Therefore, successful development must take into account women's roles as the principal providers of basic needs (fuel, water, health care, sanitation, and so on). For instance, although rural women in most of the developing world are the main food producers for their families, agricultural research and education programs generally target cash crops grown by men. However, this focus often does not reduce periods of famine or food shortages because these cash crops do not produce food for family consumption. As the FAO put it, "Neglecting women as agricultural producers and resource managers inhibits the attainment of food security goals" (FAO, 1997b). Many water resource development and agricultural irrigation projects have also failed due to the exclusion of women's important role in water management (FAO, 1997f). Similarly, the relationship between women's status and important development goals such as the reduction of child malnutrition is also increasingly obvious. As Ramalingaswami, Jonsson, and Rohde (1996) note, it is all but impossible for a woman to provide high-quality childcare if she herself is poor and oppressed, illiterate and uninformed, anemic and unhealthy, lives in a slum or shanty, has neither clean water nor safe sanitation, and lacks necessary support either from health services, her society, or the father of her children. Mothers also devote more of their income than do fathers to family subsistence, holding back less for personal consumption (Blumberg, 1995). As Amin and Li (1997) note, because women are more likely to look to the interests of their children, any measure that puts resources directly into the hands of women or strengthens their autonomy is likely to improve children's health and well-being. Their research shows that the children of NGO credit members in Bangladesh had higher immunization rates and lower infant and child mortality rates.

Another consequence of the failure to consider women's work in the development process is that in most cases, development projects have not positively influenced women's considerable workloads. In many regions, women spend up to five hours a day collecting firewood and up to four hours a day preparing food (FAO, 2003a). Box 6.4 gives you an idea of the average workday for a woman in the developing nation of Sierra Leone. You can probably readily think of development projects that could significantly reduce her work burden. Women's work as the primary household food producers and preparers, and as water and fuel gatherers, has gone largely unappreciated and unaided even as this workload grows because of resource depletion and pollution. For instance, in rural Africa, women have to travel longer and longer distances to collect clean water, and they must spend more and more time coaxing crops from depleted soils (Bryceson, 1995). Development projects focusing on irrigation systems for cash crops (crops grown for cash rather than local food production) are another good example of how development projects often negatively impact women. Such projects often divert water away from home gardens and other domestic uses, making it more difficult for women to provide for their families' food and water needs.

BOX 6.4   *One Women's Day in Sierra Leone*

4:00 A.M. to 5:30 A.M.	Fish in local pond.
6:00 A.M. to 8:00 A.M.	Light fire, heat washing water, cook breakfast, clean dishes, sweep compound.
8:00 A.M. to 11:00 A.M.	Work in rice fields with four-year-old son and baby on back.
11:00 A.M. to 12:00 P.M.	Collect berries, leaves and bark, carry water.
12:00 P.M. to 2:00 P.M.	Process and prepare food, cook lunch, wash dishes.
2:00 P.M. to 3:00 P.M.	Wash clothes, carry water, clean and smoke fish.
3:00 P.M. to 5:00 P.M.	Work in the gardens.
5:00 P.M. to 6:00 P.M.	Fish in local pond.
6:00 P.M. to 8:00 P.M.	Process and prepare food, cook dinner.
8:00 P.M. to 9:00 P.M.	Clean dishes, clean children.
9:00 P.M. to 11:00 P.M.	Converse around the fire while shelling seeds and making fishnets.
11:00 P.M. to 4:00 A.M.	Sleep.

Source: Food and Agriculture Organization, 2003.

The focus of traditional development programs on men's labor is not only based on the faulty assumption that unpaid work is not work, but on the assumption that what benefits men trickles down to benefit women. Traditional development programs often assume a gender-role arrangement in which men are breadwinners and women are homemakers. Consequently, the programs focus on fostering wage earning by male heads of household and on adult women in domestic homemaking roles. For instance, through much of the 1970s, development efforts targeted at women viewed women primarily as mothers by focusing on mother–child health programs, feeding schemes, family planning, food aid, and so on. Many such programs continue today. Moser (1989) calls this the **welfare approach.** As Mosse (1993) points out, these programs do not do much to create independence and self-reliance among women, but they are politically safe in that they do not challenge women's traditional roles.

The assumption that males should be heads of households and that all households have a male to do so also led to the channeling of development resources through men (Youseff, 1995). This has led to a situation in which women without husbands are doubly disadvantaged because they often lack even indirect access to development resources (Bryceson, 1995). This focus on males means that development programs have typically increased males' but not females' access to important sources of development such as land, credit, cattle, and technical know-how. All these things maintain women's dependence on men. It also means that divorced, widowed, or abandoned women are particularly vulnerable to poverty. Female-headed households are on the rise all over the world, and female-headed households are the poorest group in every country. Women already head over a fifth of households in Africa and Latin America, and a third of households in the Caribbean (United Nations, 2000).

Yet another problem is that by encouraging or assuming a Western version of gender-role arrangements, development programs have contributed to erosions in women's status. The development projects of the 1960s and 1970s were predicated on the notion that a male breadwinner and female housewife was a desired goal. This mentality pervaded national and international agents of development, and that, combined with local patriarchal beliefs, contributed to women's continued lower status and power relative to men. Rogers (1980), in a highly influential book called *The Domestication of Women,* argues that development efforts up to this time were designed to encourage women's conformity to Western middle-class notions of the housewife role. By failing to provide incentives for women as producers, development projects eroded what had been a source of power and status for women. For instance, in many developing nations it is women who traditionally engage in improving and innovating plant and animal varieties. This important source of status and control for women is lost when development projects give men, but not women, access to improved seed varieties and other farming technologies, as is typically the case (FAO, 1997e). According to the Food and Agriculture Organization of the United Nations (FAO), the introduction of high-yielding varieties of rice in Asia also displaced women's wage-earning opportunities through mechanization.

As Mosse (1993) notes, many development projects resulted in women changing from being independent producers and providers to being housewives economically dependent upon men as controllers of cash income. Furthermore, with cash, men gain access to banks and other modern institutions, leaving women further behind (Mosse, 1993). The idea that progress involves the promotion of the male breadwinner/female

"The evidence indicates that . . . women micro-entrepreneurs . . . tend to do their utmost to succeed. They benefit (although they may increase their workday and self-exploitation), their children benefit, the credit project benefits, and the planet's equity account becomes a little less tilted toward power, privilege, and patriarchy."
*Rae Lesser Blumberg,
American Sociologist and
Gender Stratification
Expert*

homemaker roles also interferes with the extension of loan moneys to women entrepreneurs, although their high rates of repayment are well documented.

Women are also disadvantaged because development programs often provide resources on the basis of land ownership. Land can be used as collateral for loans, and it is assumed that those who own the land also have the power to implement development suggestions. In short, secure access to land often goes hand in hand with access to development credit and training, and because laws and local practices typically disfavor women's property ownership, women are often denied development resources. In Asia, this is largely due to laws that favor male inheritance. Similarly, in many Latin American countries (such as Chile, the Dominican Republic, Ecuador, Guatemala, Mexico, and Paraguay), according to law it is the husband who is the administrator of the conjugal property. In Africa, land was traditionally "owned" collectively in the sense that it was shared by a community. As the notion of private ownership of land has developed, it has largely excluded ownership of land by women under the assumption that women will be provided for by male kin. Having little access to land for purposes of collateral, women are often unable to obtain cheap credit. This makes it difficult for them to develop economically. Likewise, lack of access to cattle ownership significantly reduces the economic power of rural women in developing nations, and development programs generally do not provide draft animals to those who are not landowners. Draft animals, which pull plows through fields, are particularly important in terms of increasing agricultural yields. Profits go down when there is no access to draft power or when it must be borrowed, exchanged, or hired.

Extension programs, in which out-of-school educational services are offered to rural producers, have largely ignored the needs and priorities of women. According to the Food and Agriculture Organization (FAO) of the United Nations, extension workers bypass women because women often do not own or control the land they farm and are therefore unable to obtain the credit to put extension education into action (FAO, 2003b). Women receive a mere 5 percent of extension resources worldwide (FAO, 2003b). In Africa, this may be seen in development projects in which male extension workers deliver technical information to a male clientele and in which the focus is on the production of cash crops. Because women typically farm for cultivation of food for the family rather than for sale, their farming does not generally receive rural development moneys and attention. For example, although women manage almost 80 percent of Africa's agriculture, they are not considered to be the farmers (Anand, 1993). In Asia, women provide 40 to 50 percent of the labor for rice production, and in Latin America, women do 30 to 40 percent of the agricultural work. The FAO (2003b) has demonstrated that there are significant benefits to including women in extension efforts. Following a national project targeting women in Kenya, corn yields increased by 28 percent, beans by 80 percent, and potatoes by 84 percent.

"If you want to see which way a country is headed, look at the country's budget and how it allocates resources for women and children."
Pregs Govender, Member of South African Parliament

"Women are community managers, farmers, water collectors, entrepreneurs, caretakers of fragile ecologies, and as mothers they daily create and maintain life. Only when their expertise and value are realized will development initiatives have half a chance of succeeding."
Julia Mosse

Cultural and religious customs further reduce women's access to extension workers. The majority of extension workers are men, and in some cultures it is socially unacceptable for women to interact closely with men who are not family members. In Egypt, for example, women account for 53 percent of agricultural labor yet only 1 percent of Egyptian extension workers are female (FAO, 2003b). Some efforts have been made to solve this problem through hiring and training more female extension workers, but male extension workers still outnumber female ones. Another problem is that women's workloads are such that they cannot get to the demonstrations or take part in the training courses (FAO, 2003b).

Women in Development Approach

Feminist criticisms of traditional development programs did have some impact. For example, in 1973 the U.S. Congress enacted the Percy Amendment to the Foreign Assistance Act. It required that bilateral programs "give particular attention to those . . . activities that tend to integrate women into the national economies of foreign countries, thus improving their status and assisting the total development effort" (World Resources Institute, 1994–1995). The **women in development (WID)** approach emerged, an approach that emphasized the inclusion of women in development projects. WID demanded increased attention to women's development needs and emphasized women's productive labor. WID projects may be classified into three general types: (1) income-generating projects, (2) projects that provide labor-saving technologies, and (3) projects that improve women's local resource access (see Figure 6.1).

Income-Generating Projects

In the 1980s, development efforts directed at women turned away from a home economics approach and began focusing on fostering women's economic participation in the public sphere. The thought is that women enhance family well-being and their own power within the household and society when they earn money, thereby increasing their status (Acevedo, 1995; Bryceson, 1995). **Income-generating projects** remain one of the most common types of women's projects under the WID approach.

Buvinic (1995) summarizes the effects of development projects in enhancing women's income-earning opportunities as "negligible at best, and perverse at worst" (p. 220). The typical income-generating project for women focuses on traditional female skills such as sewing, embroidery, and handicrafts—all low in marketability and profit in comparison to the skills taught to men (Bryceson, 1995; Youseff, 1995). The projects are often unsuccessful because they are launched before it has been determined that there is a market for the goods produced and because they fail to take into account the work women must also do in the household. As Bryceson (1995) put it, women's overbooked working day is a major stumbling block to their involvement in commodity production

Song of an African Woman

I have only one request.

I do not ask for money

Although I have need of it,

I do not ask for meat . . .

I have only one request,

And all I ask is

That you remove

The road block

From my path.

From the Acholi poem, Song of Lawino *by* Okot p'Bitek

FIGURE 6.1   *Three Types of Typical Women in Development Projects*

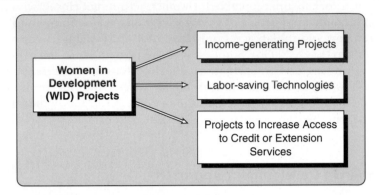

for pay, or in its improving their quality of life. It is increasingly evident that the process of development benefits women only if and when it addresses the double burdens of production and reproduction carried on by women (Afshar, 1991). Or as Buvinic (1995) says,

> The perverse effects from such poorly conceived income-generation projects for women are magnified when not only are the women unable to generate income as a result of the training, but the training itself has imposed additional demands on their time, thus negatively affecting the welfare of both the women and their children. (p. 220)

Another problem is that this type of income-generating program frequently fails to include women in the project design process. Women are typically presented with the program instead of being asked to generate their own ideas. Involving women directly in the development process would increase the likelihood that there would be a market for the item produced and that the choice of item could be produced within the constraints of women's workload. It would also give women organizational skills and a sense of empowerment that would last long after the donor has left the area. Under these conditions, income-generating projects can positively contribute to women's status and power. Mosse (1993) tells of such a project in Bangladesh. Each member of a women's group saved a handful of rice a week, which they pooled and sold for cash. After a year, the women had enough cash as a group to take over the lease of a piece of land. The women grew rice on the land and generated more money. This experience gave the women even more confidence to effect changes around them. They successfully lobbied to have the road to their village repaired and to reduce the amount of dowries.

Although development programs sometimes still include small-scale income-generating development projects for women, particularly in rural areas, the trend since the mid-1980s is toward the employment of women by transnational corporations. As discussed in Chapter 7, these corporations have significantly increased profits by having much of their product assemblywork done by low-waged women workers in developing nations. Indeed, women's work for transnationals constitutes a growing proportion of women's work in currently developing countries, especially in Asia, Latin America, and the Caribbean (Ward & Pyle, 1995). This situation is encouraged by international development and financial institutions such as the World Bank and the International Monetary Fund (IMF) as a way to generate income to pay off development loans.

This situation demonstrates that wage earning per se is no guarantee of a better life for women. The women working for transnational corporations frequently face harsh and unsafe working conditions, sexual harassment, and discrimination. In some places, such as Colombia and Indonesia, women are paid less than a subsistence wage because it is assumed they live with their family or a husband (Ward & Pyle, 1995). This situation keeps them from economic independence. Furthermore, efforts to organize for better conditions or wages often result in corporations relocating to other low-wage countries. "Homework," assemblywork done in the home, has also increased throughout the world and is often chosen by women who seek to combine wage earning with domestic responsibilities. Homeworkers are typically paid far less than factory workers are paid. In short, women in low-level, dead-end jobs with low wages and high household workloads relative to men do not necessarily benefit from wage earning. However, traditional measures of development success, such as increased gross national product (GNP) and per capita income, may lead to the perception that development based on providing low-cost labor to transnationals is an effective development strategy.

Labor Saving Technologies

Women's quality of life in developing countries is significantly affected by the lack of technologies, including relatively simple tools. Therefore, it is certainly logical that labor saving technologies are an important aspect of development projects targeted toward women. A number of development projects have reduced women's labor loads by providing such things as grinding mills, pumps, or cooking stoves. The main criticism of these projects is that they have disseminated only a narrow range of devices that only begin to address the reality of women's multitask responsibilities (Bryceson, 1995). Also, because development agencies frequently fail to consult the women whom they wish to reach, the tools are often unsuccessful. For example, in Ethiopia, where women are the primary water collectors, women were not consulted in the design of a water development program. Because of this, a pump that required two hands to operate was installed. Due to the traditional round-bottomed water jar used for collection, this meant that two people were required to collect the water (Mosse, 1993).

Women's Access to Development Resources

The UN's Convention on the Elimination of Discrimination Against Women (CEDAW) specifically addresses the rights of women in development. Article 14(9) of the convention promises women the right to "have access to agricultural credit and loans, marketing facilities, appropriate technology and equal treatment in land and agrarian reform as well as land resettlement schemes." As already noted, women's access to credit and loans is inhibited by the fact that they are unlikely to own land to use as collateral. This also affects women in the informal economic sector. For instance, women micro-entrepreneurs do such things as run beauty parlors out of their homes or make tortillas or clothing and sell them in the marketplace. In the 1980s and 1990s, aiding micro-entrepreneurs in the form of small loans became a popular form of development aid; however, male entrepreneurs are more likely to receive aid than females (Blumberg, 1995). This is partly due to the faulty assumptions that women are not serious entrepreneurs, that they would default on their loans, and that their businesses have no growth potential.

Loan practices also make it more difficult for women to obtain loans. For instance, many programs prohibit loaning money for certain types of activities or require a male cosigner for women (but permit men to be sole signers). Forrester (1995) points out that the reluctance to lend to women is ironic given that women have a repayment rate of 90 percent, even when interest rates are over 20 percent. Evidence from Bangladesh, the Dominican Republic, Guatemala, and Indonesia indicates that women micro-entrepreneurs have a payback record at least as good or better than men's (Blumberg, 1995). Furthermore, Blumberg's (1995) research in the Dominican Republic, Ecuador, and Guatemala found that women's micro-enterprises often produce as many or more jobs than men's and often grow faster than men's do.

Although women are excluded from most conventional lending schemes, there are some programs that do extend loans to women for small-scale economic enterprises. The best known is probably Bangladesh's Grameen Bank, which grants small loans to help women set up micro-enterprises. The bank now has 3 million members in 37,000 villages. Nearly half of the women who have received their grants are no longer living in poverty, according to the United States Agency for International Development (Wright, 1995a). At least five other nongovernmental agencies in Bangladesh have adopted the collateral-free loan system of the Grameen Bank (Amin & Li, 1997). Now literally thousands of nongovernmental organizations throughout Asia, Africa, and Latin America use revolving credit funds and lend disproportionately to women (Fisher, 1996). For instance,

BancoSol in Bolivia makes small loans of about 100 to 200 U.S. dollars for micro-enterprises, has a zero default rate, and has approximately 45,000 female clients (Buvinic, 1995). Women's credit programs benefit women in many ways. Studies indicate that women's credit programs positively impact on their contraceptive use and nutritional status via the mechanisms of increased empowerment and autonomy (Amin & Li, 1997).

Gender and Development Approach

In the 1980s, yet another approach to women and development arose. Called the **gender and development approach (GAD),** it focuses explicitly on improving women's status. The inclusion of the word "gender" in place of the word "women" reflects an emphasis on looking at the overall power relationships of women and men and their importance to development. Critics of the WID approach pointed out that despite increased attention to women in development, development programs for the most part failed to increase women's status. WID makes it seem as though women are not being left out of the development process when in fact, the inclusion of women in traditional development projects does not usually further women's rights (Howard, 1995). For instance, Rogers (1982), in a study of Tanzania, wrote that the failure of development programs to increase women's status is traceable to ignoring the basic structure of gender relations. Likewise, Howard (1995) argued that WID projects are ineffective in promoting women's equality because they aim at increasing economic growth and not at changing the traditional cultural beliefs that underlie women's subordination. Changes in the political and ideological spheres, as well as the economic, are needed. Howard recommends the specific allocation of development moneys for women's development in the areas of education and politics. In this way, women would have the tools to advocate for their equality. She notes that although this type of development activity would not directly increase economic growth, it would likely ensure that women's rights are furthered.

The GAD approach takes into account women's lives and labor, both inside and outside of the home. In addition, it emphasizes a bottom-up approach in which women are not as much integrated into development, as they are the architects of their own development. Projects based on a GAD approach involve encouraging women to bring about positive change through women's organizations and activism. Mosse (1993) suggests that GAD differs from other approaches to women and development in that it sees the goals of development for women in terms of self-reliance and strength. GAD emphasizes empowering women to work to change and transform the structures that contributed to their subordination (a bottom-up approach). Moser (1989) terms this approach the **empowerment approach** (see *Gender and Deevelopment Approach* in glossary) because of its emphasis on the full equality of women and their action in bringing it about. Box 6.5 summarizes the differences between the WID and GAD approaches.

"There is a need to reconceptualize a development paradigm that can promote equity, social justice, sustainability, and self-determination."
Filomina Steady

BOX 6.5   *Comparison of WID and GAD Approaches to Development*

Women in Development (WID)	Gender and Development (GAD)
Focus: Improve women's welfare.	*Focus:* Transform society to create gender equality.
How: By providing income-generating projects, labor-saving technologies, access to development resources like credit and extension services.	*How:* By encouraging women's empowerment through women's organizations and activism, participation in politics, and decision making.
Top-down approach: Services determined and offered by development organizations. Women are passive recipients of aid.	*Bottom-up approach:* Women are architects of their own development. Women are active participants of aid.
Criticisms: Usefulness impeded by failure to consult women. Does not increase women's status or empowerment.	*Criticisms:* Difficult to translate into specific policies and programs. Resistance due to its "revolutionary" nature.

GAD as Envisioned by Southern Hemisphere Feminists

"Empowerment is the process of gaining control over the self, over ideology and the resources that determine power."
Srilata Balliwala

Feminists from the south, in particular those in the organization DAWN (Development with Women for a New Era), have embraced GAD (Braniotti, Charkiewicz, Hausler, & Wieringa, 1994; Sen & Grown, 1987). DAWN, launched as a Third World initiative in 1984, includes representatives from Asia, Africa, Latin America, the Pacific, and the Caribbean. Many influential Third World feminists are members. DAWN's main purpose is to mobilize opinion and to create a global support network for equitable development (Dankelman & Davidson, 1988). DAWN works to make sure that a gender perspective is included in development efforts (this is called gender mainstreaming) and has established a presence at most major development conferences and meetings. Brandiotti and colleagues (1994) summarize the DAWN position as follows:

1. Rejecting the separation of the private and public domains.
2. Promoting women's empowerment through larger international and societal changes.
3. Advocating equitable development based on the values of cooperation, resistance to hierarchies, sharing, accountability, and commitment to peace.

4. Acknowledging that women's empowerment can only come about by examining the interrelationships between gender, race, class, and nationality.

5. Emphasizing political mobilization, consciousness-raising, and popular education as crucial to women's empowerment.

Development Agencies and GAD

Development agencies are still in the process of determining how to use GAD to create specific policies and programs. In the 1990s, the leading development agencies began by adding GAD-sounding rhetoric to their mission or goal statements. As the UN's 1997 *Human Development Report* points out, if development is not "engendered it is endangered," and if development strategies "fail to empower women, they will fail to empower society." Or consider these three very GAD-sounding strategic objectives of the UN's Food and Agriculture Organization Plan of Action for Women in Development (1996–2001):

1. To promote gender-based equity in the access to, and control of, productive resources.
2. To enhance women's participation in decision and policy-making processes at all levels.
3. To promote actions to reduce rural women's workload and enhance their opportunities for remunerated employment and income.

By 2000, development agencies had embraced **gender mainstreaming** as a way to incorporate gender in the development process. Gender mainstreaming strays from the original call of GAD proponents to promote women's activism for gender equality but it does contribute to the empowerment of women. Gender mainstreaming requires a gender analysis to make sure that gender equality concerns are taken into account in all developmental activities. It also requires women's active participation in the development process. The United Nations Development Programme (UNDP, 2003a) in a document on gender mainstreaming in water management, said that gender is about power, subordination, and inequality, and gender mainstreaming is about changing these to secure greater equality. This requires that programmers and analysts understand the differences and relations among and between women and men in each specific context and that this information be incorporated into project design. Participatory approaches that involve both men and women are to be used and when possible, projects should reduce gender inequality. The UNDP has created training programs and documents to assist programmers. The UNDP's gender mainstreaming tools advise programmers to incorporate gender specialists and representatives of women at all levels, to identify gender issues relevant to each project, to take all possible steps to ensure gender balance in project staff, and involve

"Women are indeed great, as I learn that they are better fighters against poverty than their men, have more calculative, stable, forward looking strategies to deal with their own environment. Everywhere in the country, we found that women were the most committed proponents of our future."
Ela Bhatt, Self-Employed Women's Association, India

"We have learned that when women gain economic autonomy, the health, nutrition and education of other members of the household, especially children, improve at the same time.
Noleen Heyzer, Executive Director of UNIFEM

". . . governments and other actors should promote an active and visible policy of mainstreaming a gender perspective in all policies and programmes, so that, before decisions are taken, an analysis is made of the effects on women and men, respectively."
Beijing Platform for Action, Fourth World Conference on Women

women's nongovernmental organizations (NGOs) in project identification, formulation and appraisal. Checklists, examples, practice case studies, and evaluation tools are provided.

OXFAM, one of the world's leading nongovernmental development aid organizations, is also in the process of making changes consistent with a gender and development approach. In 1985 the gender and development unit was created to ensure that OXFAM's development and relief programs improve the quality of women's lives. OXFAM's gender policy states a commitment to the following: promoting the empowerment of women, confronting social and ideological barriers to the improvement of women's status, promoting women's independent access to development resources, helping women exercise their rights over their bodies and protect themselves from violence, and promoting initiatives with a gender focus. However, as was the case with other development agencies, it took some time for OXFAM to figure out how to put these ideas into practice.

In the 1990s, OXFAM incorporated gender mainstreaming in a number of different ways. In India and Serbia they provided funding to local programs devoted to making gender violence against women visible and unacceptable and provided women with options in cases of violence against them. Another OXFAM example is that of a program designed to help families displaced by civil conflict in rural Andean Peru. Initially, OXFAM supplied seed, llamas for breeding stock, and agricultural training to male heads of households although 40 percent were female-headed. Also, the initial program did not support the labor contributions that women make to their families. OXFAM brought in a team of gender advisors who noted that women were being disempowered by the way aid was being provided. The program was altered to include support for communal vegetable gardens (so that women could feed their families); funds for small livestock production (to be consumed by the family or sold and traded); training in agricultural production, nutrition, and project management; and the strengthening of women's organizations. By 2001, OXFAM recognized that what they were doing still looked more like the WID approach than the WAD approach (OXFAM, 2002). They were not, they concluded, doing enough to promote gender equality. The main problem was that despite a commitment to the GAD approach, managers and staff did not really understand how to integrate gender equality concerns. OXFAM is currently training staff how to address gender equality issues (OXFAM, 2003).

Gender mainstreaming represents notable progress and contributes to women's empowerment. However, so far it hasn't stimulated the greater transformations necessary for gender equality. Perhaps this is because it strayed from the original GAD vision of development as being about women's organizations and activism. Gender mainstreaming may be viewed by traditional development agencies as a good way to incorporate gender concerns with traditional development concerns. It may also be seen as a "safe" way to include gender in the development process since GAD is viewed with suspicion by many aid agencies and Third World governments. This suspicion has to do with developing nations' past history with colonialism (Mosse, 1993). Western donor

"Think equality to end poverty."
Slogan from Women Environment and Development Organization's campaign to increase the number of women in politics

BOX 6.6   *Activist Profile: Joyce Banda of Malawi*

Joyce Banda is an influential activist, entrepreneur, and educator in Malawi, one of the poorest countries in Africa. Through her work, thousands of Malawi women have been empowered by becoming economically self-reliant. Banda founded the National Association of Business Women to boost the status of all women—by giving them access to credit, training, information, markets, and appropriate technology. So far, NABW has mobilized 15,000 women countrywide, disbursed $2,000,000 in loans, and trained 12,000 women to run their own businesses. Here is an excerpt from her acceptance speech for the 1997 Africa Prize for Leadership.

> I fully agree with what the UNDP Human Development report says when it states that the economic empowerment of the women, especially those living in poverty is one of the foundations on which sustainable human development must be built. Together with the political and social empowerment of women, it is the surest and only means of not only alleviating poverty in the short run but also of eradicating it and world hunger in the long term.

I count myself fortunate that I have had the opportunity to work with many women and witness their growth from a point of not knowing where to get the next meal to feed their family to levels of financial independence that have placed them in the mainstream of business and this allows them to provide all the needs for their business, and families; moving them from being abused wives to respected mothers, wives, and partners. I have watched these same women start sharing in decision making for their families. I have seen these women slowly reach out to help their families and neighbors. This often has resulted in their building enough confidence to stand for elections in other activities in their communities and quickly move all the way up to the policy formulating tables on national organizations, parliamentary seats, and state corporations.

Source: The Hunger Project (1997)

agencies have to proceed cautiously to avoid charges of cultural imperialism and cultural insensitivity. Consequently, donor agencies often play it safe by funding more traditional women in development projects or by using the more subtle gender mainstreaming approach. Box 6.6 describes the work of Malawi activist Joyce Banda. Her organization exemplifies a GAD approach.

Women, the Environment, and Sustainable Development

In the mid-1980s, the United Nations, environmentalists, and policy makers concerned with the environment called attention to the environmental consequences of traditional development. Their main charge was that development, in both the north and the south, was not sustainable. Sustainability can be defined a number of ways, but the general idea is that **sustainable development** "meets the needs of the present without compromising the ability of future generations to meet their own needs" (World Commission on Environment and Development, 1987). Another good definition comes from Rosina Wilshire, manager of the Gender in Development Program of the United Nations Development Programme. She defines sustainable development as "development that promotes human well-being and human dignity while regenerating and protecting the natural resource base so that the issues of empowerment and equity are central to development, which cannot be equated with economic growth per se" (1995, pp. 127–128). (You will appreciate Wilshire's definition as you read further.) This section explores women's role in promoting sustainable development, but first, some sustainability basics are in order.

Sustainability Basics

Environmental indicators suggest that much of the development in both northern and southern nations is not sustainable. It is a fact that economic development has environmental consequences, many of which may significantly impact human health and survival. The environment is called an eco*system* for a reason: Like other systems, change in one part affects the others. Take the case of deforestation, a problem faced on almost every continent but especially in developing nations. Trees hold soil in place, and, consequently, deforestation contributes to soil erosion. Agricultural yields are significantly decreased when valuable topsoil washes away. But the animal waste often used for fertilizer may be burned for fuel when there are no trees left. This means that petrochemical fertilizers must be used to increase agricultural yields. However, over time these build up and increase the salinity of the soil. This results in desertification, which means that nothing will grow. Runoff of agricultural fertilizers pollutes waterways, thus reducing the amount of drinkable water and killing fish. Deforestation also contributes to global warming as trees are major consumers of deadly carbon dioxide gases. These are only a few of the many effects of deforestation. The bottom line is that shortages of the basics of life, such as food, water, and clean air, may occur when development is not sustainable.

It may seem clear that development should be conducted with regard to the future. However, the role of the north in southern development clouds the situation. Development in the southern countries is often guided and in many cases controlled by the northern countries that supply the capital for development. These northern countries, such as the United States, gain many of the benefits and bear few of the costs of development in the south. The northern countries benefit from higher profits from lower labor and materials costs, weaker environmental laws, and lower priced goods, thus permitting the continuation of high-consumption lifestyles. The environmental costs are borne largely by the citizens of the southern countries, especially the poor, who are disproportionately women and children.

You may not understand why the southern countries accept this type of development, but this too is complex. First, you must remember that some of the fault lies at the doorstep of the economic development strategies encouraged by traditional development programs. These programs encourage the replacement of small, localized economies with market-based economies that produce goods for export to generate cash. International development programs arrange large loans (sometimes in the millions and billions of dollars) but in return often dictate what type of development is to occur. Funding is based on projects' money-making potential, and environmentally sustainable development is often perceived as at odds with this goal. Remember also that economic progress is typically measured in terms of short-run economic goals, such as increases in per capita income and gross national product. Developing nations must demonstrate this type of progress in order to receive more aid.

To make matters worse, what has often happened is that the cash generated goes to pay the interest on the loans. A high debt burden results and is aggravated when international markets fluctuate and prices fall. To come up with the money simply to pay the interest on their loans, governments are often forced to sell goods at bottom prices and to exploit fragile natural resources. Transnational corporations are increasingly part of this equation. Their primary interest in their own profit and growth strategies frequently means that they are largely unconcerned with the effects of their practices on local environments and people. The people lose: They remain poor because they often cannot eat or use the commodity produced for export, and their health suffers as governments cut down on food subsidies and government health services to repay development loans. Furthermore, the environmental resources on which the people depend are often degraded in the process.

I said earlier that there are serious questions about the sustainability of development in both the north and the south, but you should note some important differences. The north's contribution to environmental degradation arises out of a consumer lifestyle. Consider this evidence of consumption: Northern families spend an average of $9 billion a year on video games for their children and $7.5 billion to care for their lawns (World Resources Institute, 1994–95). The north's heavy diet of fossil fuels and nonrenewable resources (once they're gone, they're gone) contributes to *global* environmental problems such as ozone depletion and global warming. These are problems that degrade the global commons—the environmental resources we all share. In contrast, in the developing nations of the south, the major damage is to local renewable resources such as water and land. Furthermore, unlike in the northern countries, the damage is done in the quest to meet basic needs, not to sustain a consumer lifestyle. Currently, about half of the world's poorest people earn their livelihoods in ecologically fragile areas. Such people often have little choice for survival other than to contribute to resource depletion and pollution.

Effects of Environmental Degradation on Women

Feminist environmentalists emphasize that the consequences of unsustainable development in the south fall largely on the shoulders of the poor, especially the women. This is because women are the primary cultivators and gatherers of food, water, and fuel for family consumption in southern nations, and environmental degradation significantly increases the amount of time that must be spent on these tasks. Because poor women rely heavily on natural resources, they are among the first to notice and feel the effects of environmental stress (Steady, 1995).

Environmental degradation often increases women's workloads. Women must work harder and harder to coax crops from tired soils. They must travel farther and farther to collect fuel, fodder, and water. For example, in the state of Gujarat, India, women now spend four or five hours a day collecting fuelwood, where previously they sought fuel once every four or five days (UNFPA, 2001). Similar cases are found in other parts of India, Peru, and in Africa (Dankelman & Davidson, 1988). Some 30 percent of women in Egypt walk over an hour a day to meet water needs, and in some parts of Africa, women and children spend eight hours daily collecting water (FAO, 1997f). In El Salvador, where 80 percent of the natural vegetation has been destroyed and 77 percent of the soil has been lost or degraded, it is increasingly difficult for peasant women to find firewood and food (Lorentzen & Turpin, 1996). Contaminated water supplies also increase women's work because it is usually women who care for those who are sick with diarrhea and other diseases caused by unclean water. Increased workloads from environmental degradation interfere with the attainment of gender equality because it reduces women's time and opportunities for education, literacy, and income-generating activities (UNDP, 2003b).

Women's health is also affected by environmental degradation (Steady, 1995). For example, poor women must often cook with wood, crop residue, and animal dung, often in enclosed spaces, and suffer respiratory diseases, anemia, and cancer as a result (Chant, 2003; World Resources Institute, 1994–95). Carrying heavy loads of wood, often on their head, for long distances damages the spine and causes problems with childbearing (Dankelman & Davidson, 1988). As the primary water carriers and managers, they have the most contact with polluted water and are therefore most vulnerable to water-related diseases (INSTRAW, 1991). Because it is women that care for the sick, they are more susceptible to contracting diseases from others (Chant, 2003). The longer hours women work because of environmental degradation also increase their susceptibility to health problems. For example, a study of Sri Lankan women concluded that they suffered from persistent sleep deprivation because of their multiple roles (Lorentzen & Turpin, 1996).

The Role of Women in Sustainable Development

Women of the south play a critical role in sustainable development for two main reasons. First, in many cases they are the main managers of local natural resources. According to the Food and Agriculture Organization, women are often the principal caretakers and guardians of the forest. In developing nations, they are the ones who collect fuel, fodder, and food from trees and other plants. In the south, women are also largely responsible for collecting, supplying, and managing water. A World Bank review of 121 rural water projects found that women's participation was one of the variables most strongly associated with project effectiveness (UNDP, 2003a). Also, in most of the developing world, women are significant agriculturists. Unfortunately, acknowledging the role that women play in resource use has sometimes led to blaming them for environmental degradation. However, it is important to realize that Third World women often have no choice but to exploit natural resources in order to survive, even though they may have the knowledge to promote sustainability (Dankelman & Davidson, 1988). Furthermore, evidence shows significantly more ecological damage results from development practices such as commercial logging and high-tech agricultural practices. For example, the main contributor to deforestation is commercial harvesting and the clearing of land for large-scale agriculture, not women collecting fuelwood (Brandiotti et al., 1994; Elliot, 1996). Indeed, as Shiva (1996) suggests, development projects have impaired the productivity and renewability of nature by removing land, water, and forests from women's management and control.

A second reason why women are important to sustainable development is that they often possess important knowledge about sustainability in their environments. For instance, they often know which varieties of seed will yield drought- and pest-resistant plants and which seeds do not require petrochemical fertilizers. They often know which trees are easiest to grow and have the most practical value in their culture as sources of food, fuel, and medicine. Their knowledge of water sources and water quantity and quality during wet and dry seasons makes them important sources of information when water resources are being developed. Many ecofeminists see this knowledge as evidence of women's interconnectedness with nature. They draw a parallel between the desire of industrialization to conquer nature and the desire of men to dominate women (Tinker, 1994). Box 6.7 briefly discusses **ecofeminism** and Vandana Shiva, an ecofeminist leader in India.

Environmental degradation is now recognized as a critical development problem, and women are increasingly acknowledged as important contributors to sustainable development. This is reflected in a number of official reports and declarations that originated in the work of women's environmental conferences and activism. The 1991 World Women's Congress for a Healthy

"In the Third World, because women have remained in intimate contact with nature, they often give the early warning signals that something is wrong with the environment."
Vandana Shiva, Indian physicist and ecofeminist

"Women do not want to be mainstreamed into a polluted stream. We want to clean the stream and transform it into a fresh and flowing body. One that moves in a new direction—a world at peace, that respects human rights for all, renders economic justice and provides a sound and healthy environment."
Bella S. Abzug, U.S. Congresswoman and WEDO co-founder

BOX 6.7   *Ecofeminism*

Simply put, ecofeminism suggests that the domination of women and the domination of nature are intricately connected and that women are particularly suited to lead ecological movements to save the planet (Sachs, 1997). That being said, in truth ecofeminism is an umbrella term for a variety of approaches that bridge feminist and environmental concerns (Donash & Seager, 2001; Merchant, 1992; Sachs, 1997; Sturgeon, 1997). For example, *cultural ecofeminists* suggest that menstruation, pregnancy, and childbirth bring women closer to nature and are a source of women's power and environmental activism. In contrast, *social ecofeminists* emphasize how capitalism and patriarchy are used to dominate both women and nature. The idea is that economic development generally entails the devaluing and conquering of nature and that women's association with nature dooms them to conquering as well. Despite the range of ecofeminist perspectives, one underlying theme is a commitment to illuminating the role of gender, class, and race in environmental issues (Donash & Seager, 2001).

Because of some of the more radical and theoretically problematic versions, many feminist scholars and activists currently distance themselves from ecofeminism (see Sturgeon, 1997, for discussion). Some prefer to call themselves *feminist environmentalists, ecological feminists,* or *feminist political ecologists* (Donash & Seager, 2001). For instance, Biehl (1991) criticizes ecofeminism for rejecting rationalism and for worshiping goddesses. Critics of ecofeminism also charge it with "essentialism,"

that is, with saying that there are essential differences between women and men. Such essentialism rubs many feminists the wrong way for essentialism has historically justified discrimination against women. However, the essentialism charge is more relevant to some ecofeminisms than others.

Vandana Shiva, trained as a theoretical physicist, is a well-known Indian ecofeminist. She works closely with the Chipko movement as well as other rural environmental movements in India. Her 1989 book *Staying Alive: Women, Ecology and Development* is already a classic for Third World ecofeminism. The book, along with later writings, argues that Western science and Western economic development have created both environmental destruction and the marginalization of women through the "death of the feminine principle." This feminine principle arises from direct experience with nature and is holistic, caring, cooperative, intuitive, nonhierarchical, welcoming, and supportive of diversity (Sachs, 1997). This feminine principle is "not exclusively embodied in women but is the principle of activity and creativity in nature, women, and men" (Shiva, 1989, p. 52). Shiva also suggests that Third World women are uniquely suited to environmental activism: "Because of their location on the fringes, and their role in producing sustenance, women in Third World societies are often able to offer ecological insights that are deeper and richer than the technocratic recipes of international experts or the responses of men in their own societies" (Shiva, 1994, p. 1).

Planet, organized by the Women's Environment and Development Organization (WEDO) laid the foundation for a number of important documents. For instance, the 1992 UN Conference on Economic Development (UNCED), sometimes called the Earth Summit, yielded a document known as "Agenda 21." It calls for specific agreements by governments to strengthen the role of women in creating and implementing sustainable development strategies (Steady, 1995). Women and sustainability are also mentioned in the Rio Declaration from the conference, which states "Women have a vital role in environmental management and development. Their full participation is essential to achieving sustainable development." Keep in mind that women's groups worked hard for these things. The truth is that gender issues were given very little attention in the preparatory committees for UNCED and were only taken up after intense lobbying by women's NGOs (Brandiotti et al., 1994; Elliot, 1996).

The United Nations Fourth World Conference for Women's Platform for Action, adopted unanimously by 189 delegations in Beijing in September 1995, also includes a section on women and the environment. This resulted from feminist environmental advocacy. Three strategic objectives are detailed: (1) involve women actively in environmental decision-making at all levels; (2) integrate gender concerns and perspectives in policies and programs for sustainable development; and (3) strengthen or establish mechanisms at the national, regional, and international levels to assess the impact of development and environmental policies on women. However, some feminist environmentalists were disappointed because the terms "environmental justice" and "environmental racism" were left out. These terms would have clearly reflected the fact that a disproportionate share of the burden of environmental degradation is experienced by the poor and by ethnic and indigenous groups that are low in power.

According to Steady (1995), there are four main obstacles to increasing women's involvement in the promotion of sustainable development. One of these is the debt problem facing developing nations that has led to the promotion of export-led growth at the expense of the environment. A second problem arises from development programs and policies dominated by men who are not always aware of the gender implications of program planning and implementation. For instance, the fact that women are marginalized into the private sphere means that their close connection to ecosystem health is overlooked and undervalued (Elliot, 1996). The low level of participation by women in decision-making positions is a third obstacle Steady identifies. Women are not only underrepresented in the formal institutions of states, but in development agencies and nongovernmental development organizations as well. A fourth obstacle is the dominant ideology that development should be propelled by the domination of nature. Current patterns of development and the use and management of natural resources are in line with male values that see the relationship with nature as one of control (Elliot, 1996). Steady (1995) suggests that these barriers mean that women's environmental organizations and movements hold the key to sustainable development in many countries.

Women and Environmental Activism

It is easy to view women as victims of ecological crisis. However, women often organize to prevent ecological destruction. It is women who are usually the first to become environmental activists in their communities because they are in direct contact with the natural environment and because environmental degradation affects their family's health (Donash & Seager, 2001). As Shiva (1988) says, "I know for certain, no matter where you go, that if there is a

"Women give life. We have the capacity to give life and light. We can take up our brooms and sweep the earth."
Isabelle Letelier

scarcity of water, women have protested; if there has been an overfelling of trees, women have resisted it." Women's mobilization for the environment demonstrates the courage women have shown in the battle against the growing ecological degradation that surrounds them and against the traditional power structures that subordinate their needs (Sontheimer, 1991). As Elliot (1996) notes, women must not just be seen as victims of environmental degradation but as agents who must participate equally in the solution to these problems.

Women have had trouble gaining leadership positions in mainstream and radical environmental organizations and women's environmental issues have customarily been a low or non-existent priority (Donash & Seager, 2001). Consequently, much of women's activism for the environment is the result of women's nongovernmental organizations (NGOs). Indeed, according to Fisher (1996), NGOs now serve as principal institutional resources for sustainable development in the Third World, both because of their own activities and because of their impact on governments. Fisher suggests that NGOs take two general forms: the **grassroots organizations (GROs),** locally based groups that work to develop and improve the community; and **grassroots support organizations (GRSOs),** nationally or regionally based development assistance organizations, usually staffed by professionals, that channel funds to grassroots organizations and help communities other than their own to develop.

"Come arise, my brothers and sisters,

Save this mountain . . .

Come plant new trees, new forests,

Decorate the earth."

Song of the Chipko movement

The Chipko movement in the forests of Uttar Pradesh, India, is a famous example of a GRO. In 1974 conflict escalated between logging companies supported by the state and the natives who depended upon the forest for food and fuel. The villagers were also aware that previous logging by commercial interests had resulted in erosion and flooding from which they had suffered dearly. The village men were away on the day the contractors arrived to cut 2,500 trees, but the village women took action. They wrapped themselves around the trees (*chipko* means "hug") and refused to move until the contractors left. The contractors did leave, and Indira Gandhi (the Prime Minister of India at the time) issued a fifteen-year ban on commercial logging in the forests of Uttar Pradesh (Dankelman & Davidson, 1988). The Chipko movement has spread throughout the Himalayas in India, Nepal, and Bhutan (Jain, 1991). The Chipko message is spread through sustainable development camps that meet twice a year (Fisher, 1996). This shows how GROs sometimes become GRSOs, which then support grassroots organizations elsewhere. In addition, Chipko-based resistance is now used throughout India to protest environmentally irresponsible road building, mining, and dam projects (Seager, 1993).

The Greenbelt movement in Kenya is a well-known example of the role of GRSOs in sustainable development involving women. The movement was begun in 1977 by Wangari Maathai, an ardent feminist, environmentalist, and scholar in microbiology, in conjunction with the National Council of Women of Kenya. By the 1970s, severe deforestation and soil erosion had created a shortage of fuelwood and food. The movement organized women to plant and manage trees for fuelwood and to guard against erosion. Maathai explains her focus on women by noting that it is women who use wood fuel for cooking and who also till the land (Katumba & Akute, 1993). More than 20 million trees have been planted and the movement now includes some 1,500 tree nurseries with more than 50,000 women participants. The women learn important leadership skills and gain economic power by the income generated by the sale of seedlings. In the last ten years, more than 7 million trees have been planted. The project also promotes organic farming and organizes workshops and seminars on sustainable development. The movement has been replicated in twelve other African countries.

Other GRSOs with a sustainability focus include the Secretariat for an Ecologically Sound Philippines, which addresses environmental problems affecting women, farmers, youth, and minorities, and KENGO, a Kenyan organization that hosted the Kenya Assembly of Women and the Environment in May 1993. International GRSOs with a sustainability focus exist as well. Some examples include the Women's Environment and Development Organization, which organized the World Women's Congress for a Healthy Planet in 1991 in preparation for the Rio Earth Summit; the International Women and Environment Network, which formed in 1989 in Managua, Philippines; and the Earth Council, formed after the Rio Earth Summit.

Wangari Maathai, Kenyan microbiologist, feminist, and environmentalist, is considered the founder of the Greenbelt movement. In 1999, Maathai was injured by government forces when she organized women to plant trees in a forest scheduled for demolition.

Conclusion

Feminists generally favor the gender and development approach to development because it integrates development, gender equality, and women's empowerment. It also specifically emphasizes that women themselves should set the agenda for women's development. Contrary to the belief that women in southern countries are content with their position, when given opportunity and support, women seek out ways of challenging and changing their situations (Mosse, 1993). Numerous cases show that local women are capable of being the agents of their own development (Moser, 1995). While development agencies may be timid about promoting women's activism, this hasn't stopped women from organizing themselves. Local women have exerted pressure from the bottom up with some success (Moser, 1993). For instance, in many countries women are entitled to own land, but local customs prevent them from assuming ownership. This, as previously noted, prevents them from obtaining development loan moneys because they have no property for collateral, and it keeps them from receiving extension training. Women's NGOs in Thailand, China, Nicaragua, Malaysia, and Cuba have fought for women's land rights. According to Fisher (1996), over 200,000 grassroots organizations exist in Asia, Africa, and Latin America, over half of them organized by women. Additionally, her research indicates that there are 30,000 to 35,000 grassroots support organizations active in the Third World.

Women's activism is largely responsible for the changes in development programs we've seen so far. Women in local grassroots groups often demand

"Gender equality is more than a goal in itself. It is a precondition for meeting the challenge of reducing poverty, promoting sustainable development and building good governance".
Kofi Annan, United Nations secretary general

inclusion in development projects and national and international women's organizations like DAWN and WEDO won't let development agencies forget to include women. This activism will continue because, to borrow a phrase from Jahan (1995a), development agencies and organizations have only tinkered with the constraints on women's equality. They have yet to come forward with bold policies and adequate budgetary allocations. Networking and political pressure from a variety of women's organizations, which build on what happens at the local level, scale out the impact of women's NGOs at the grassroots level and scale up their impact on policy (Fisher, 1996).

Study Questions

1. What is a "developing nation" and what is the process of development?

2. How does a past history of colonialism affect development efforts?

3. How is the experience of poverty affected by gender? That is, what are conditions like for many women in developing countries? How are these different from the male experience of poverty?

4. Did modernization and welfare approaches to development help women's status?

5. What are some common feminist criticisms of traditional development programs?

6. What is the "Women in Development (WID)" approach to development? What are the three types of typical WID projects? What criticisms are made of the WID approach?

7. How does the "Gender and Development (GAD)" or empowerment approach differ from WID? What is gender mainstreaming and why have development agencies adopted it?

8. What is sustainable development? Why are women important to sustainable development? What obstacles stand in the way of including women in sustainable development strategies? How have GROs and NGOs like the Chipko movement and the Greenbelt movement acted for sustainability?

Discussion Questions and Activities

1. If southern women followed the footsteps of U.S. women, would they gain or lose? What cultural biases or values underlie your answers? (adapted from Duley & Diduk, 1986)

2. Do international development agencies have the right to intervene in the gender arrangements of a country? Is it morally wrong for them not to?

BOX 6.8   *United Nations Millennium Development Goals (MDG)*

1. Eradicate extreme poverty and hunger.
2. Achieve universal primary education.
3. Promote gender equality and empower women.
4. Reduce child mortality.
5. Improve maternal health.
6. Combat HIV/AIDS, malaria, and other diseases.
7. Ensure environmental sustainability.
8. Develop a global partnership for development.

Source: UNDP's Human Development Report, 2003b.

3. Consider this quote from DAWN's Peggy Antrobus: "We must never lose sight of the fact that the women's movement and the environmental movement are primarily *revolutionary* movements. If we give up that political challenge to the dominant paradigm, there is no hope for change." What do you think she means and do you agree?

4. The UNDP has also explicitly included gender in its "Millennium Goals" shown in Box 6.8. All 191 UN member nations have pledged to meet the goals by the year 2015 and all major UN agencies have programs designed to help nations reach the goals and track progress. Look at the Millennium Development Goals and explain the importance of women to attaining each one.

Activist Websites of Interest

Heifer International
http://www.heifer.org/about_hpi/faq.htm
Future Harvest
http://www.futureharvest.org/people/women
Association for Women in Development (AWID)
http://www.awid.org

Development with Women for a New Era (DAWN)

http://www.dawn.org

Women's Environment and Development Organization (WEDO)

http://www.wedo.org

Informational Websites of Interest

World Food Organization (FAO)

http://www.fao.org/gender

World Bank Gender Home Page

http://www.worldbank.org/gender

United Nations Division for Sustainable Development
  Agenda 21

http://www.un.org/esa/sustdev/documents/agenda21

United Nations Fourth World Conference on Women Platform for Action:
  Women and the Environment

http://www.un.org/womenwatch/daw/beijing/platform

Action Opportunities

1. Heifer International is a nonprofit organization that combats poverty and restores the environment by providing appropriate livestock, training, and related services to small-scale farmers worldwide. Heifer has a gender equity program called "WiLD" (Women in Livestock Development) that funds projects with women's groups. To help Heifer International help women, you can raise money so that Heifer can buy an animal for a project (the cost of different types of animals for projects are listed on their website). You can also make an individual donation, or instead of holiday gifts to family and friends, make a donation in their names (Heifer will send a gift acknowledgment for each gift of $10 or more). Heifer International was featured on the Oprah television show in 2002. http://www.heifer.org

2. OXFAM is one of the world's leading nongovernmental, non-UN development organizations and has a GAD focus. Join an OXFAM letter-writing or fund-raising campaign. http://www.oxfam.org/getinvolved.htm

3. One focus of this chapter was poverty. Take action locally or globally to reduce poverty. Locally, do a canned food drive for your local food bank, or volunteer at community organizations that serve low-income women.

Globally, you can raise money for a nongovernmental organization that recognizes the role of women's empowerment in alleviating poverty, such as The Hunger Project (http://www.thp.org/overview/index.html). Or in October you can participate in the "Trick-or-Treat for UNICEF" program. UNICEF provides medicine, immunizations, nutrition, clean water and sanitation, education, and emergency relief to children in 158 countries. By asking people for their spare change for UNICEF, you can probably raise $100 in a few hours. See http://www.unicefusa.org for information.

Women and Globalization

Global economic and trade policies are not "gender neutral." Women comprise 70 percent of the world's 1.3 billion absolute poor. Worldwide, they bear the brunt of economic and financial transition and crisis caused by market forces and globalization. Yet, women's issues are not considered in trade liberalization policy making and analysis. The failure of governments and intergovernmental organizations to formulate and evaluate trade policies from a gender perspective has exacerbated women's economic inequity.

—Women's Environment and Development
Organization (WEDO)

Globalization often leads poor women to migrate to affluent countries where they do low-wage work as nannies, maids, janitors, and health workers. Some become mail-order brides or sex workers. © CATHERINE KARNOW/CORBIS

This chapter discusses the ways that globalization has reshaped women's lives worldwide. In this chapter you will learn how the growing trend toward a world economy dominated by transnational corporations impacts women. You will also learn that globalization has stimulated transnational feminism. Feminist activism has become increasingly transnational, aided by the Internet, international conferences, and regional meetings.

By the year 2000, it was increasingly likely that the goods consumed by people in one country were grown, produced, or assembled in a multitude of other countries. Americans dine on fruit grown in Central America and wear clothes assembled in Vietnam or the Dominican Republic. Russians wear American-brand clothes manufactured in developing countries. South Africans smoke American cigarettes and drink Coca-Cola. Europe is dotted with Pizza Huts and Starbucks. An economic crisis in one country affects the economies of other countries. These are examples of globalization. **Economic globalization** refers to the integration and rapid interaction of economies through production, trade, and financial transactions by banks and multinational corporations, with an increased role for the World Bank and the International Monetary Fund, as well as the World Trade Organization (WTO) (Moghadam, 1999). **Cultural globalization** refers to the transnational migration of people, information, and consumer culture.

Critics of globalization are alarmed by the fact that the benefits of globalization are not evenly distributed across nations. For example, more affluent northern governments provide subsidies to their farmers so that they can afford to sell their products for less in the global market. Farmers from southern countries where subsidies are unavailable are unable to compete and become poorer. Northern governments also frequently impose tariffs and import limits on goods from other countries. This keeps "cheaper" goods out of the home market and protects the profits of corporations in the home country. Liberalized trade agreements have eroded workers' rights and unionization. Environmental sustainability is compromised when poor countries, desperate for a piece of the global economic pie, let transnational corporations exploit or pollute their natural resources. Protests at world trade meetings are frequent, large, and often dramatic.

"In the international women's movement, 'globalization' is a negative word because it has brought great harm to many women—by facilitating the systematic exploitation of women as a source of cheap domestic and migrant labor."
Jessica Neuwirth, founder of Equality Now, an international women's human rights organization

The Effects of Globalization on Women

Feminists' attention to the negative effects of globalization on women was stimulated by financial crises in the 1980s. At that time, Third World commodity prices dropped, interest rates rose, and many developing nations could not make payments on their development loans. Debtor countries in Africa and Latin America were forced to ask for more money from the International Monetary Fund (IMF), the UN's international banking agency, and from wealthy First World countries. The new loans were made contingent upon a series of reforms since the lenders believed that without reforms, debt would continue to grow and economic development would be hindered. Governments imposed these conditions, part of what are called **structural adjustment programs (SAPs),** to save and raise money.

Structural adjustment programs are government belt-tightening measures. In the 1980s they required that governments in debt to bilateral or multilateral donors focus on a single goal: earning foreign exchange to service their debt (Miller, 2002). This means that production for domestic use was discouraged and cash crops and goods for exports were encouraged. Structural adjustment programs also typically entailed cuts for social services, schools, hospitals, nutrition programs, public transportation, and utilities. Many of these SAP impositions affected women more than men (Chang, 2000). Cuts in wages and social services and rises in the costs of basic goods and services have a greater impact on women because women are normally responsible for providing food, water, and healthcare for family members (Blumberg, 1995; Chang, 2000; Lorentzen & Turpin, 1996; Mosse, 1993; World Resources Institute, 1994–95). For example, women are typically responsible for taking care of ill family members so when medical services are cut, women's workload increases. If water service is unreliable, it is women and children who have to walk longer distances or stand in longer lines. When food is in short supply, men and boys generally suffer less than women and girls, who are expected to limit their consumption so that the males can eat (Miller, 2002; Mosse, 1993).

Structural adjustments did not go away with the 1980s. The integration of world economies requires that countries become flexible; they must be able to adjust to changes in world markets as well as to economic recessions and collapses in other countries that affect the world economy (United Nations, 1999). This **flexibilization** of the economy, as it is called, sometimes requires that governments make structural adjustments to stay solvent and remain competitive. Once again, women's unpaid labor increases as government services are cut and women must provide more care for children, elderly parents, and the sick (Chang, 2000; Desai, 2002). The price of household goods, especially food, often rises as government subsidies are removed. Women must make do with less, becoming more vulnerable to malnutrition since they often wait to eat until other family members are finished (Desai, 2002). These government austerity measures often coexist with high rates of unemployment and inflation such that life is very difficult. It is ironic that when women most need a government safety net, it is most likely to be taken away.

Flexibilization also means that countries become flexible in regard to the environment. Agricultural land for local food production may be converted to use for export crops. As men become increasingly involved in the production of cash crops or wage employment, women become responsible for the household agricultural work previously done by men (United Nations, 1999). To keep the costs of production down, and profits up, countries may not require environmentally sustainable agriculture or manufacturing. To look attractive for the siting of transnational factories (needed for jobs and cash), governments often relax environmental laws. This has a large impact on women who depend directly on their environments for their family's survival. As mentioned in the previous chapter, this type of economic development often increases women's workloads as they must travel further and further for water and have less access to arable land to grow food for their families. Women in poor, urban neighborhoods find their communities polluted by toxic chemical wastes and human wastes (Desai, 2002). In short, the costs of economic adjustment and change fall largely on the shoulders of women already burdened by poverty. Figure 7.1 summarizes the effects of globalization on women's unpaid labor.

Under globalization, many women make do with less and work more to keep their families afloat (Chang, 2000). Globalization has had mixed effects on women's employment though for the most part, it is associated with increases in women's paid employment. The economic shifts that come with globalization create some jobs for women, particularly low-paid factory and domestic work. Women need jobs to help families weather the effects of SAPs and economic transitions. When women increase their unpaid labor and paid labor but are still unable to sustain their families, they may have no viable option but to leave their families and migrate for work (Chang, 2000). Many women in countries hard-hit by the negative economic effects of globalization must turn to sex work (prostitution), or migrate to other countries to provide for themselves and their families.

Although globalization is believed to increase women's paid employment, it should be noted that in times of economic downturns and transitions, women are often the first to lose their jobs. For example, in the transition economies of the countries that made up the former Soviet Union, the change to a free-market economy has increased women's unemployment. An estimated 26 million jobs were lost in the region from 1990 to 1995, 14 million of which were held by women (Desai, 2002). In large firms, women are often the first fired in an effort to protect male "breadwinners" (United Nations, 1999). In many countries, such as Muslim countries in Northern Africa and the Middle East, women have difficulty getting hired in the private sector and are

FIGURE 7.1   *Effects of Globalization on Women's Unpaid Labor*

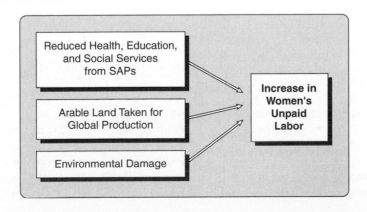

employed primarily by the government in clerical and social services types of jobs. When economic times get tough, governments shrink their budgets through layoffs and reduced services, thus increasing women's unemployment and reducing their job opportunities (Posusney & Doumato, 2003).

In some cases globalization has negatively impacted the women's income from informal sector work. For example, in the Caribbean, the cultivation of nontraditional export crops has reduced the production of food for the local market. This has negatively impacted women, the traditional producers and marketers of food for the local market (United Nations, 1999).

Women's Work in the Transnational Factory

In the global economy, knowledge-intensive aspects of the production process often remain in western countries but labor-intensive activities are subcontracted to factories in developing countries where cheap female labor is abundant (Naples, 2002; Stearns, 1998). The United States was the first to relocate labor-intensive factory work such as garment-making, footwear, and electronics to lower wage sites in the Caribbean, East Asia, and Latin America (United Nations, 1999). **Free trade zones (FTZs)** or **Export Processing Zones (EPZs)** have been established in many Third World countries to attract transnational factories. In these zones, companies are generally exempt from labor, health and safety, and environmental laws and pay few, if any, taxes. More than sixty countries have established EPZs (Domosh & Seager, 2001). In Honduras alone there are eleven FTZs with 200 factories employing 100,000 people (Mendez, 2002).

Women's relatively cheap labor is the basis of export-oriented industrialization and international competition for many developing countries (ILO, 1996a). Women constitute over 80 percent of the workers in EPZs in Mexico, Taiwan, Sri Lanka, Malaysia, and the Philippines, and more than 70 percent in South Korea and Guatemala (Domosh & Seager, 2001). Women are the preferred labor supply because they can be hired for lower pay and under less desirable working conditions than men can (United Nations, 1999). Women's manual dexterity and docility (conditioned by culture), their desperation for work, and their seemingly limitless supply have made them the choice factory workers of transnational corporations worldwide. Some theorists argue that women's low-wage labor for transnational corporations fuels global production and is at the heart of corporate profits (Fuentes & Ehrenreich, 1983; Salzinger, 2003).

"I want my job and value it, because even though it tears me apart and exploits me, with my job I am able to feed my kids."
Nicaraguan Maquila Worker

With few options for paid work, many women must work for low pay in **sweatshops**—businesses that violate wage, child labor, and safety standards. Many factories in EPZs are little more than sweatshops. Sweatshop workers are unlikely to complain because they need the work despite the conditions. These jobs are desirable because in developing countries there are few modern wage jobs for women and because most of the jobs are concentrated in farming, domestic service, and the informal sector (Lim, 1990). The odds are good that the majority of your clothes, shoes, toys, and electronics were created with women's sweatshop labor in countries such as Bangladesh, Burma, China, the Dominican Republic, Haiti, Honduras, Indonesia, Guatemala, Malaysia, Mexico, Nicaragua, the Philippines, and Vietnam.

Recently, transnational corporations have begun employing women to do clerical work in offshore "electronic sweatshops," mostly in the Caribbean. These jobs in the *infomatics* industry include telemarketing, but are mostly data-entry jobs for banks, insurance companies, and airlines (Bullock, 1994; Freeman, 2000; United Nations, 1999). For instance, at one Barbados infomatics location, 100 women sit at clustered computer stations and daily enter 300,000 ticket stubs for one airline's 2,000 daily flights; one floor below, an equal number of women enter medical insurance claims data from one of the largest U.S. insurance companies (Freeman, 2000).

The *maquiladoras* (also called *maquilas*) of Mexico's border towns are another example of women in the transnational corporate factory. There, over 2,000 multinational corporations employ over a half million workers, two-thirds of them women, who get paid between $3.75 and $4.50 a day (Nauman & Hutchison, 1997). In El Salvador, women employees of the Taiwanese *maquilador* Mandarin are forced to work shifts of 12 to 21 hours during which they are seldom allowed bathroom breaks; they are paid about 18 cents per shirt, which are later sold for $20 each (Jeffrey, 1996). Mandarin makes clothes for the Gap, J. Crew, and Eddie Bauer (Herbert, 1995). In Bangladesh, women sewing clothing at Disney's contract plants are paid 5 cents for every $17.99 Winnie-the-Pooh shirt they assemble; workers describe 14-hour days, seven-day work weeks, and beatings if they do not meet quotas (Gentile, 2002). In Vietnam, 90 percent of Nike's workers are females between the ages of 15 and 28. Nike's labor for a pair of basketball shoes (which retail for $149.50) costs Nike $1.60, 1 percent of the retail price.

Contrary to popular beliefs, these wages are generally insufficient to escape poverty. For example, sweatshop workers in Nicaragua average from $55 to $75 a month when the average family needs $165 a month to make ends meet (Stark, 1996). In Indonesia, the government estimates that the minimum wage there is equal to just 67 percent of what is required to meet minimum physical needs, and many companies do not pay even that much (Wallace, 1992). Wages at Mexican *maquiladoras* are sufficient to provide for only one-fourth of the needs for a typical worker's family (Nauman & Hutchison, 1997). In Vietnam, a living wage is estimated to be $3 a day, but Nike workers make only $1.60 a day (Herbert, 1997). Nike's chief executive officer, Philip Knight, is one of the richest men in the world.

Health problems are reportedly common because of harsh working conditions such as inadequate ventilation, chemical exposures, and repetitive motion. However, most governments have generally failed to collect information or to carry out studies to document their severity. At the Dynamics factory in Bangkok, Thailand, where Mattel makes Barbies, over 75 percent of the 4,500 female workers suffer severe breathing problems from the inhalation of dust (Foek, 1997). In the Lamphun province in northern Thailand,

"Just don't buy it."
Slogan of the Global Exchange's Boycott Nike Program

female factory workers at electronic production factories use lead and other solvents to clean electronic components. The accumulation of toxic metals in the workers' bodies is contributing to high levels of chronic illness and deaths. The government is reluctant to attribute the high rate of illness and death to occupational causes out of fear that foreign investors will go elsewhere if the costs of doing business in Thailand should rise (Rajesh, 1997). In Mexico, several studies found acute health effects due to chemical exposures as well as reproductive effects such as babies with lower birth weights (Nauman & Hutchison, 1997). In short, health and safety hazards are common, and government protections are few.

Women workers in the transnational factory typically have little choice other than to accept these questionable work conditions. Often from rural areas and unaware of their rights, they are afraid of losing their jobs should they assert themselves (Nauman & Hutchison, 1997). Many are underage and work with forged birth certificates (LaBotz, 1993). There are few other jobs available for women, making the situation a desperate one (Bullock, 1994). The women at the Dynamics factory, for example, come from northeastern Thailand where the poverty is so bad that parents sometimes sell their daughters into sex slavery or as cheap labor (Foek, 1997). In Guatemala, war and conflict in the countryside have led to migration to the cities, and people must take any work they can find. In the United States, illegal immigrants desperate for employment have little choice but to take what work they can. Many work in garment industry sweatshops or perform home-based sewing and assembly of garments.

Corporations may expect female workers to be cheap and docile but they only take so much abuse before they organize themselves for better pay and work conditions. As Louie (2001) put it, they transform themselves from sweatshop workers to sweatshop warriors. Strikes and efforts to organize for better work conditions and pay are increasingly common, but are often swiftly and harshly punished. At a Nike subcontractor in Indonesia where more than 9,000 women work, workers who organized a protest of pay and working conditions were fired (Herbert, 1996). Likewise, eighteen Sony workers at a Mexican *maquiladora* were fired for union organizing. When workers protested these firings by stopping work and blocking the road to the factory, Sony brought in riot police who beat the workers (Bacon, 1997). After South Korean women successfully unionized at Nike plants in the 1980s, Nike and its subcontractors began shutting down their South Korean factories, moving them to Indonesia and Vietnam (Enloe, 1995a). Governments generally participate in the suppression of labor organizing. Competition with other economically struggling countries for foreign investment is stiff. In order to attract and keep foreign operations in their country, they must guarantee that there will be no labor conflict and little regulation.

Corporations choose to locate in countries where the unemployment is high and the people are desperate for work. As the chairman of the only union in Indonesia noted, the union is weak because there is an oversupply of labor—every year there are approximately 2.5 million new workers look-

"Solidarity among workers should cross the border as easily as companies move production."
Mary Tong, Director for the Support Committee for Maquiladora Workers

"Jobs, Yes . . . but with Dignity!"
Campaign Slogan of the Network

ing for jobs. Governments are hesitant to intervene, needing the jobs and foreign currency to pay off loans and knowing that transnational corporations will move their operations to other countries that do not enforce labor regulations. They feel that the multinationals give them no choice. The companies argue that they are doing nothing wrong because the people are better off than they would be if they had no jobs. International free trade agreements such as GATT (General Agreement on Tariffs and Trade) and NAFTA (North American Free Trade Agreement) have aggravated poor labor conditions by making it easier for corporations to ask for and receive exemptions from laws that ostensibly interfere with free trade. These treaties have encouraged the development of export processing zones.

Some labor unions have begun to actively support their exploited counterparts in transnational industries. For instance, in 1993, Honeywell workers in Canada, Mexico, and the United States protested the firing of Mexican employees in Chihuahua (Nauman & Hutchison, 1997). Labor unions and NGOs in both northern and southern countries are urging the inclusion of "social clauses" in trade agreements to protect the rights of workers (Bullock, 1996). Nongovernmental organizations, such as the United States' Multinational Monitor, the London-based Women Working Worldwide, and the Dutch group SOMO, have launched awareness campaigns, organized consumer protests, and monitored working conditions in transnational factories. In 2002, a three-year legal battle brought by activist groups against twenty-six of America's biggest clothing retailers was settled. The companies agreed to improve work conditions, pay $20 million in back wages, and to create a monitoring system to prevent labor abuses in Saipan factories (Collier & Strasburg, 2002).

> "It is unacceptable that any zone or enterprise should be outside the labour laws of the country where it is situated and similarly, that it should flout international labour standards."
> *Susan Bullock*

The Global Economy and Women's Migration

People have always migrated from one location to another for purposes of survival and in an effort to increase their quality of life. People from areas where there is a labor surplus often migrate to areas where there is a labor deficit—this is nothing new. But what is new is how globalization has affected women's migration.

This section focuses on how globalization makes economic survival difficult in some countries, leading poor women migrate to more affluent countries where there is a strong demand for low-wage workers. There they service the upper-income and corporate beneficiaries of globalization. Many leave children behind in the care of family members. They typically send anywhere from half to nearly all of what they earn home to their families (Ehrenreich & Hochschild, 2002). Governments in some countries, such as Sri Lanka and the Philippines, encourage women to migrate because the money sent home contributes to the economy and reduces poverty (Chang, 2000; Ehrenreich & Hochschild, 2002).

The work women migrants do in the global economy is often a reflection of traditional gender roles. They are janitors, maids, and nannies, "hostesses"

> "We see migration as the result of structural adjustment programs—we give up our lands, our products, and finally people."
> *Eileen Fernandez of Malaysia, speaking at the Fourth World Women's Conference NGO Forum on Women*

and "entertainers" (sex workers), nurses and home health workers, and sometimes brides to American and European men seeking traditional marriages. They often face prejudice and discrimination as well as poor work conditions. Language, cultural barriers, and economic desperation interfere with migrant working women asserting their rights as women and workers. For undocumented workers without legal work papers and workers who live where they work, it is even more difficult since they face deportation or homelessness if they complain.

It is estimated that there are approximately 60 million legal and illegal women migrants (Ehrenreich & Hochschild, 2002). Scholars now speak of the "feminization of migration" because in many cases, women migrants outnumber men migrants. According to Ehrenreich and Hochschild (2002), there are four main migratory "streams" for women. One stream of migration goes from Southeast Asia to the oil-rich Middle East and Far East—from Bangladesh, Indonesia, the Philippines, and Sri Lanka to Bahrain, Oman, Kuwait, Saudi Arabia, Hong Kong, Malaysia, and Singapore. Another stream goes from the countries of the former Soviet Union to Western Europe. These are the women from Russia, Romania, Bulgaria, and Albania who travel to work in Scandinavian countries, Germany, France, Spain, Portugal, and England. A third migratory stream is in the Americas, from south to north, including Mexico to the United States. A fourth stream moves from African countries to Europe. France, for example, receives many female migrants from Morocco, Tunisia, and Algeria while Italy receives many from Ethiopia, Eritrea, and Cape Verde.

Domestic Service

Domestic service is one of the largest fields of employment for female migrants. The increased demand for domestic workers in affluent countries is partly due to the entry of educated women in northern countries into the workforce. Globalization has created more jobs for them. Gender role changes and the rise of female-headed households have also increased the number of women in the paid workforce. At the same time, advertising has created a consumer culture that often requires two incomes to sustain. Consequently, even married women with children often work for pay. As middle- and upper class women enter the professional workforce and have less time to devote to household labor, they seek help with the traditional household duties typically done by women. For the most part, men have not provided this help. Indeed, research indicates that women's entry into the workforce has barely impacted the amount of childcare and household labor performed by men (Ehrenreich & Hochschild, 2002). The result: a booming market in affluent countries for **domestics**—maids, childcare providers, and caregivers for the elderly and disabled. The use of migrant domestics has also increased among affluent families with stay-at-home wives and mothers. Anderson (2002) suggests that for some people, having hired help is a status symbol. Domestics also maintain the extravagant lifestyles of their

BOX 7.1   *Rosemarie Samiego: Filipino Nanny Working in Italy*

"When the girl I take care of calls her mother 'Mama' my heart jumps all the time because my children also call me 'Mama.' I feel the gap caused by our physical separation especially in the morning when I pack lunch because that's what I used to do for my children. . . . I begin thinking that at this hour I should be taking care of my very own children and not someone else's, someone who is not related to me in any way, shape, or form. . . . The work I do here is done for my family but the problem is that they are not close to me but far away in the Philippines. . . . If I had wings, I would fly home to my children. Just for a moment, to see my children and take care of their needs, help them, then fly back over here to continue my work."

Source: Parrenas, 2002.

employers—help is needed to take care of the huge house, to care for the furniture, art, and knick-knacks. Increased demand in combination with poor economic conditions in southern countries has fueled Third World women's migration to richer countries to work as domestics.

At first glance, you might think that the migration of Third World women to First World countries to perform domestic work is an arrangement that meets the needs of all parties involved. However, you may wish to consider the children that many migrant women leave behind. Many, if not most, migrant women workers have children and express guilt and remorse about leaving them to care for the households and children of others (Hochschild, 2002). Box 7.1 describes the painful predicament experienced by many migrant mothers that work as nannies.

Domestic work is neither socially nor intellectually fulfilling but is chosen for economic reasons (Parrenas, 2001). Domestics clean up the dirt and mess of non-family members. They provide love and care to the children of others while their own children are cared for by their family members in another country. They must quietly do whatever they are asked, no matter how nasty or degrading. They work long, physically demanding hours in other people's homes where they must act invisible. Due to their long hours in others' homes, there are feelings of isolation and loneliness. Many are educated but can make more money as migrant domestics than they can as professionals in their own country.

Migrant domestic workers are also sometimes subject to harsh treatment. As migrants from other countries, they are often viewed as "lesser" by prejudiced employers who do not treat them as fully human. Because domestic work is done in the home, unfair work conditions are not visible and subject to regulation. Additionally, migrant domestic workers are non-citizens or partial citizens, dependent on employers' sponsorship to stay in the country. Kalayaan, an organization in Britain that works for justice for migrant

"The lifestyles of the First World are made possible by a global transfer of the services associated with a wife's traditional role—childcare, homemaking, and sex—from poor countries to rich ones."
Barbara Ehrenreich and Arlie Hochschild

"It is hard to make a living back home. Working here and sending money home to my family is the only way I can take care of my family."
Dominique, New York City nanny from Trinidad

domestics, conducted interviews with 775 migrant domestics in Britain. They found widespread abuse of domestic workers from Brazil, Columbia, Ghana, Nigeria, the Philippines, and Sri Lanka (Chang, 2000). Verbal and physical abuses were common. Many did not receive regular food and had no bedroom; many were not allowed to leave the house. Almost all of them worked at least 17 hours a day with no time off and were paid less that what was agreed upon in their contracts.

Some of the worst reports of abuse come from Kuwait. Rape, physical assaults, illegal confinement, and nonpayment of wages have led over 2,000 Asian maids annually to seek shelter in their home country's embassies (Human Rights Watch, 1995). According to Human Rights Watch (1995), the Asian maids have little choice; they are not protected under Kuwaiti law, and the government denies exit visas to maids seeking to leave without their employer's permission. Escape is further discouraged by several other practices. For instance, it is customary for employers to take the women's passports upon arrival in Kuwait. Yet, if they are caught without a passport, they are subject to immediate arrest, detention, or fines. Also, law enforcement agencies refuse to investigate or prosecute maid abuses and usually return maids to their employers.

It is easy to scapegoat middle- and upper class women for the exploitation of southern women and to think that their selfish entry into the paid workforce is responsible for their neglect of children, the elderly, and household tasks. However, as Ehrenreich and Hochschild (2002) point out, this is not quite fair. First, they remind us that the demand for domestic service would not be so great if men increased their household labor contributions. As they say, "the presence of immigrant nannies does not so much enable affluent women to enter the workforce; it enables affluent *men* to continue avoiding the second shift" (p. 9). Second, in many industrialized nations like the United States, governments have not done a good job of providing or subsidizing childcare, after-school care, or paid maternity and family leave. Because many nations do not provide support for women's entry into the paid workforce, women often have little choice but to turn to migrant domestics. Third, were economic conditions not so bad for migrant women in their home countries, they would not be motivated to leave home in search of domestic jobs. As Hochschild (2002) points out, while women choose to migrate, they choose it because economic pressures all but coerce them to do so. These arguments point in the direction of some solutions. In industrialized nations we need to:

- Increase male's contributions to household labor.
- Provide government-subsidized childcare.
- Support "family friendly" workplaces.
- Regulate the "servant industry" to prevent and prosecute abuses.

- Provide ways for migrant domestics to leave abusive employment situations.
- "Forgive" at least some of the debt of Third World countries such that severe SAPs do not create a situation where migration is necessary.

In the developing nations that supply migrant domestics we need to:

- Develop the economy such that women can support their families without migration.
- Recognize and reduce the impact of SAPs on women.
- Improve the status of women such that they do not need to migrate to flee domestic violence or to have more control over their lives as women.

A number of migrant workers' organizations work to expose abuses, and fight for workers' rights. These include the British organization Kalayaan mentioned earlier, INTERCEDE in Canada, and in the United States, the Campaign for Migrant Domestic Worker Rights.

Mail-Order Brides

Another example of women migrating due to poverty is the phenomenon of mail-order brides. Women in poor economic circumstances from newly developing and economically underdeveloped countries are marketed as brides to men in advanced capitalist countries. **Mail-order brides,** as they are called, use commercial organizations to arrange introductions and broker marriages with foreign men. Mail-order brides are often substitutes for women in industrialized countries who resist conventional forms of marriage (Kojima, 2001). By the 1990s, mail-order bride agencies marketing women from the Philippines, India, Thailand, Eastern Europe, and Russia were established throughout Europe, the United States, Japan, and Australia. Potential customers can peruse hundreds of Internet mail-order bride sites and catalogues complete with photos and brief biographies. They may pay a fee for addresses and then exchange a series of letters before a visit is arranged. Some companies have package tours to countries, like Russia and the Philippines, to meet prospective brides. The industry promotes stereotypes and exploitative relationships on both sides. To prospective brides, they emphasize the wealth of foreign husbands, and to prospective husbands, they emphasize the obedience and subservience of foreign women.

No firm statistics exist on the practice. However, in the United States, immigration officials estimate that more than 200 international matchmaking services operate, annually arranging 4,000 to 6,000 marriages between U.S. men and foreign women mostly from the Philippines and former Soviet

"The Russian woman has not been exposed to the world of rampant feminism that asserts its rights in America. She is the weaker gender and knows it."
Chance for Love Matchmaking Service Website

Union (Associated Press, 2003). In Japan, in 1995 alone, more than 19,500 Japanese men married women brought over from Korea, China, the Philippines, Brazil, and Peru (*Los Angeles Times,* 1997). Japanese feminists see these arranged marriages as reflecting Japanese men's desire for a subservient bride, referred to as *o-yome-san*—a role that Japanese women are increasingly reluctant to accept. In the Philippines, where the majority of mail-order brides originate, there is a law prohibiting advertisement by mail-order bride companies (McClelland, 2003). However, since the companies are based outside of the Philippines, they are not prosecuted.

Barry (1995) argues that mail-order bride selling is not only a form of trafficking in women but also a kind of prostitution whereby men buy women for sexual as well as domestic service. The industry targets women who are so impoverished that marriage to a stranger and immigration to a foreign land are seen as their best chance for survival. Discrimination against women in the labor market, growing unemployment among women, lower wages, lack of skills and training—essentially, the feminization of poverty—all contribute to the growing number of young women willing to take their chances by searching for opportunities and a better life in a foreign country (UN High Commissioner for Human Rights, 2002).

Some mail-order marriages satisfy the participants but many of the marriages are problematic. Mail-order brides may be disappointed to find that their husbands are not rich and husbands may be disappointed when wives are not obedient and subservient. Some brides find themselves at the mercy of violent and tyrannical husbands. Evidence is growing that mail-order wives frequently suffer domestic violence. In Japan, for example, mail-order wives do not have full legal status and considerable evidence suggests that they are abused by both their husbands' and their husbands' families (Sassen, 2002). The murder of Anastasia King, a mail-order bride from Kyrgystan, by her husband Indle King, an American man with a history of domestic violence, prompted the U.S. Congress to draft a bill that would provide prospective brides with a criminal background check (Associated Press, 2003). As of this writing, the bill has not yet come up for vote.

Nongovernmental organizations, such Gabriela, a Philippine-American women's organization and the Global Alliance Against Trafficking in Women (GATW), are working on this issue. Domestic violence shelters in regions where mail-order brides are more common are also adapting their services to help those that experience domestic violence.

Women's Work in the Global Sex Trade

Sex work connected to tourism is known as **sexual tourism.** Sexual tourism is another effect of globalization and is made possible by a globalized system of communication and transportation (Cabezas, 2002). It arises out of a globalized economy that makes sex work one of the only ways for some women to earn a living wage. Governments that need the money brought by international tourism are willing to encourage, or at least ignore, sexual tourism. First-world men that exoticize dark-skinned native bodies, buy sex in developing countries for cut-rate prices (Brennan, 2002). Sexual tourism is yet another example of how the effects of globalization are not gender-neutral.

Sexual tourists are the hundreds of thousands of men, many of them businessmen, who travel to other countries for sex holidays. Sex tourists come primarily from Australia, Canada, France, Germany, Japan, Kuwait, New Zealand, Norway, Qatar, Saudi Arabia, Sweden, the United Kingdom, and the United States (Seager, 1997). Their main destinations are Brazil, Cambodia, Costa Rica, Cuba, the Dominican Republic, India, Indonesia, Hungary, Kenya, Morocco, the Philippines, and Thailand. Racial stereotypes and economic disparity between the developed, and developing worlds, characterize the sexual tourism industry (Brennan, 2002).

Some workers in the sex industry choose their work as a survival strategy and an economic advancement strategy. Research in the Dominican Republic suggests that some women perceive sex work as a possible stepping-stone to marriage to a foreigner and migration to a better life in another country (Brennan, 2002; Cabezas, 2002). Sex work pays a lot more than work as a domestic or factory worker in an EPZ. For instance, in the Dominican Republic, the occupations available to women other than sex work yield less than 1,000 pesos a month whereas one sexual encounter with a foreign client yields 500 pesos and a chance to build a modest savings account (Brennan, 2002). Some Dominican sex workers attempt to persuade European tourists to send them money or marry them. They keep in touch with clients through global communications such as telephones, faxes, wire transfers, and the Internet (Brennan, 2002; Cabezas, 2002). Box 7.2 features a quote from the Dominican sex worker organization Movimiento de Mujeres Unidas (MODEMU). The group advocates for the right of sex workers to control their bodies and achieve social respect.

The majority of sex workers are forced by economics, and often, single motherhood, into prostitution, but it is economics, not others, that forced them. For example, it is estimated that more than 50,000 Dominican sex workers have traveled to Western Europe, the Middle East, and Asia to work in the sex industry. Most of these women knew they would be doing sex work and chose to go so that they could support families and buy a home upon return (Cabreza, 2002). In stark contrast are the millions of sex workers coerced or tricked, and even sold into sexual slavery and taken away from their home countries. They are part of the multi-billion dollar **sex trafficking industry.** As the UN Protocol to Prevent, Suppress and Punish Trafficking in Persons defines it, trafficking in persons means "the recruitment, transportation, transfer, harbouring or receipt of persons, by means of threat or use of force or other forms of coercion, of abduction, of fraud, of deception, of the abuse of power or of a position of vulnerability or of the giving or receiving of payments or benefits to achieve the consent of a person having control over another person, for the purpose of exploitation" (UN High Commissioner for Human Rights, 2002).

"Far too many men, in Sweden and the rest of the world, see women as objects, as something that can be bought and sold. . . . A woman's body is not the same as a glass of brandy or an ice cream after a good dinner."
Swedish Deputy Prime Minister Margareta Winberg

"From 1970 I had been involved in initiating radical feminist action against rape, but until I learned of the traffic in women and explored pimping strategies in prostitution, I did not fully grasp how utterly without value female life is under male domination. Women as expendables. Women as throwaways. Prostitution—the cornerstone of all sexual exploitation."
Kathleen Barry

BOX 7.2   *Prostitution as Work: The Dominican Republic's Sex Worker Organization, MODEMU*

MODEMU uses a human rights framework to claim sex workers' rights as women, workers, and citizens. MODEMU emphasizes that the term "prostitute" is disrespectful and that the term "sex worker" recognizes that it is a job rather than a disgrace. These quotes are from MODEMA's first national conference.

"What does the term 'prostitute' mean to sex workers? We unanimously reject the term 'prostitute' for being pejorative and referring to us as devalued women and human beings. . . . We have the right not to be seen as criminals. Not to be abused, persecuted, or mistreated.

Not to be exploited; by person or groups in the business of trafficking in women; to have the opportunity to form labor unions and alternative forms of employment. Respect for our right to decide over our bodies and our lives. The right to raise our children. That our children are not discriminated for being the children of sex workers. That authorities rightly attend to our complaints when our rights are violated."

Source: Cabezas, 2002, p. 53.

Josephine Butler (1828–1906) of Great Britain was one of the first Western women to organize against prostitution and the trafficking of women. Despite threats of violence against her, she proved that the state-licensed brothels were participants in White slave traffic and the sale of children for prostitution throughout Europe.

Typically, an agent uses the offer of work to entice poor women to illegally immigrate to other countries. They may be told they will work as maids, waitresses, or entertainers. Sometimes they are lured through false marriage offers. Upon arrival, however, their agent or "fiancé" sells them to a brothel or "club." Poverty-stricken parents in rural Thailand, Burma, and Laos may even sell their daughters to brothel brokers and agents, in most cases believing that the girls will work as maids, waitresses, or dishwashers, but sometimes understanding the work will be as a prostitute (Bales, 2002). According to Human Rights Watch, the recruiters often take advantage of families known to have financial difficulties and recruit during lean times before the harvest.

Thailand is one of the most obvious offenders. Thailand specializes in sexual tourism, with men from all over the world traveling there to take advantage of the brothels. This industry generates approximately $10 billion annually (Bales, 2000). Bales (2002, p. 212) shares the following case from his study of brothels in Thailand:

Siri's case was typical. A broker, a woman herself from a northern village, approached the families in Siri's village with assurances of well-paid work for their daughters. . . . After some negotiation they were paid 50,000 baht (U.S. $2,000) for Siri, a very significant sum for this family of rice farmers. This exchange began the debt bondage that is used to enslave the girls. The contractual arrangement between the broker and the parents requires that the money be paid by the daughter's labor before she is free to leave or is allowed to send money home. . . . In addition, Siri later learned of other payments she would be required to make, including rent for her room, at 30,000 baht per month, as well as charges for food and drink, fees for medicine, and fines if she did not work hard enough or displeased a customer.

Women in forced prostitution can rarely escape the life (Bales, 2002; Barry, 1995; Human Rights Watch, 1995; Pyne, 1995). These uneducated, unpaid, or underpaid women in an unfamiliar land do not know how to return home. Almost all are controlled through **debt bondage.** They must first repay with interest the money given to their family at the time of recruitment. This debt mounts as they are charged for food, shelter, and clothing. Should they try to leave the brothel without paying their debt, they are likely to experience physical punishment by the brothel owner or the police. To keep them there, they are threatened with harm to their parents and with being arrested as illegal immigrants. Lack of familiarity with the local language or dialect puts them at a further disadvantage. Because trafficked women are often in the country illegally, law enforcement agencies respond to them as lawbreakers rather than as victims. To make things worse, they may be prosecuted for illegally leaving their own country should they attempt to return home.

Women forced into prostitution are exposed to significant health risks in the forms of violence and disease (Bales, 2002; Human Rights Watch, 1995, 2000; Pyne, 1995). Rapes and beatings are used to ensure compliance. Multiple daily clients, and the occasional sadistic client, inflict more pain. In brothels, women are exposed to sexually transmitted diseases, such as AIDS, because they are not allowed to negotiate the terms of sex and are forced to have sex with as many as twenty clients a day. Although condoms may be available to clients, the client has the choice of whether or not to use them. The case of Lin Lin, a young woman from Burma (Myanmar) is described in Box 7.3 and illustrates these points.

The United Nations estimates that as many as 4 million people are trafficked every year, half of them children (Lochhead, 2003). The practice of luring, abducting, and tricking young women into sexual slavery occurs in India with the trafficking of Nepalese women and girls to Indian brothels, and in Pakistan with Bangladeshi women and girls trafficked to Pakistani brothels (Human Rights Watch, 1995). The number of girls trafficked from Burma to Thailand is estimated to be 10,000 a year (Human Rights Watch, 1995). It is estimated that 50,000 girls and women have been trafficked from Thailand into Japan, where many endure slave-like conditions in the Japanese sex industry (Bales, 2002; Human Rights Watch, 2000).

Women are also trafficked to Europe. Up to 10,000 Nigerian women are trafficked to Europe, especially Italy, every year (*The Herald,* 2003). Hundreds of thousands of women from all over the Balkans (Croatia, Bosnia-Herzegovina, Yugoslavia, Kosovo, Macedonia, and Albania) are trafficked into Europe (Zimonjic, 2002). About 3,000 women, mainly from the former Soviet Union, are sold annually into Israel's sex industry (*Times Wire Reports,* 2002). Kuwait and Saudi Arabia also have sex industries. Poor women from

BOX 7.3   *Forced Prostitution: The Case of Lin Lin*

Lin Lin was thirteen years old when she was recruited by an agent for work in Thailand. Her financially destitute father took 12,000 baht (equal to $480) from the agent with the understanding that his daughter would pay the loan back out of her earnings. The agent took Lin Lin to Bangkok, and three days later she was taken to the Ran Dee Prom brothel. Lin Lin did not know what was going on until a man came into her room and started touching her breasts and body and then forced her to have sex. For the next two years, Lin Lin worked in various parts of Thailand in four different brothels.

The owners told her she would have to keep prostituting herself until she paid off her father's debt. Her

clients paid the owner 100 baht ($4) each time. If she refused a client's requests, she was slapped and threatened by the owner. On January 18, 1993, the Crime Suppression Division of the Thai police raided the brothel, and she was taken to a shelter run by a local nongovernmental organization. She was fifteen years old and tested positive for HIV.

Source: Pyne, 1995.

Bangladesh, India, the Philippines, and Sri Lanka believe they are accepting jobs as maids or domestic laborers only to be tricked into working as prostitutes (Neft & Levine, 1998). Brazil also has a thriving sex tourism business that includes an estimated 500,000 girls under the age of fourteen (Neft & Levine, 1998). In the United States women and children are trafficked from Latin America and the U.S. State Department estimates that every year, 50,000 to 75,000 children are trafficked into the United States (Lochhead, 2002).

Although international and national laws prohibit the trafficking of women, such laws are unevenly enforced. Under the terms of a 1949 international treaty, the Convention on the Suppression of Traffic in Persons and the Exploitation of the Prostitution of Others, state parties agree to "punish any person who, to gratify the passions of another, procures, entices or leads away, for purposes of prostitution, another person." In 2000, the UN's Office of the Commissioner of Human Rights began working to develop protocols for governments to identify and assist victims of trafficking in southeastern Europe. This area was targeted because over 100,000 women from central and Eastern Europe are trafficked each year (Office of the High Commissioner for Human Rights, 2002).

The globalization of the sex trade makes stopping it difficult. International organized crime networks are increasingly involved in the trafficking of women (Sassen, 2002). U.S. Attorney General John Ashcroft points out that prosecuting traffickers is challenging because it involves large numbers of victims, language barriers, multiple investigating agencies, overseas investigations, and severe sexual and physical trauma of victims and witnesses (Lochhead, 2003). Human Rights Watch provides a number of recommendations to governments, to the United Nations, and to countries that loan money or conduct business with the offending countries. For instance, it is suggested that all governments bring their countries into compliance with international treaties pertaining to the trafficking of women and that they educate women regarding the dangers. The United Nations is advised to develop programs and strategies to curb such practices and ensure accountability. Donor countries are advised to use every opportunity to raise the issue of trafficking publicly and in official meetings. Organizations such as Shared Hope International with outreach efforts in the United States, India, Nepal, and Jamaica, and Safe House for Women in Yugoslavia, rescue women and provide them with medical treatment and counseling. These are good and noble efforts. However, like the situation of migrant domestics, mail-order brides and sex trafficking are unlikely to abate until poverty is reduced.

Conclusion

In this chapter you learned that globalization has increased women's paid employment but that the costs of economic adjustment are often borne by women—especially women who are already poor. Such women are hit harder by economic downturns and are more likely to directly experience the effects of environmental degradation. Because they have few economic choices, they can be exploited in the global labor marketplace. This suggests that the effects of globalization on women are largely negative. However, throughout the book you have read that employment has the potential to increase women's power and status so you might ask, "Is it possible that globalization has in fact benefited women by increasing their paid employment?" There is not a simple answer to this oft-debated question; it depends on the conditions under which the work is offered and on how much control women have over the money they earn.

Lim (1990) found that women in developing countries often cite such benefits of employment as the ability to earn independent income and spend it on desired consumer purchases; the ability to save for marriage or education; the ability to help support their families and "repay" their debt to parents; the opportunity to delay marriage and childbearing and to exercise personal choice of a marriage partner; and the opportunity to enjoy some personal freedom, the companionship of other women, and to experience more of what life has to offer, such as a "widening of horizons." Chant (1997), in a study of Mexican women working in the tourist industry in Puerto Vallarta, Mexico, also suggests that the ability to earn an independent income reduces the pressure on women to marry. However, she notes that some men take their wives' money and that women are still left with the majority of household labor tasks.

According to Blumberg (1995), data from Third World women indicates that a woman's absolute and relative income is tied to increases in self-esteem and confidence, greater leverage in fertility decisions, and greater leverage in other household economic and domestic decisions. Other studies (Blumstein & Schwartz, 1991; Engle, 1993; Lips, 1991; Stroh, Brett, & Reilly, 1992) also suggest a link between women's paid employment and their power in the home. In particular, the greater a woman's control of income, the greater her say in other household economic and domestic decisions and the greater her "voice and vote" in the marital relationship (Blumberg, 1991, 1995).

Safa's (1995) research on globalization and women in Cuba, the Dominican Republic, and Puerto Rico led her to conclude that the key to understanding the effects of wage earning on women's power is whether they are viewed as "breadwinner" or "supplementary wage earners." When they are perceived as supplementary wage earners whose primary responsibility is as wife and mother, they are confined to poorly paid, unstable jobs, and their wage labor adds to the burden of their domestic chores. However, when their monetary contribution exceeds or approaches men's, they then are able to challenge male dominance.

On the one hand then, perhaps globalization has increased the autonomy of some women and increased their economic power. This is more likely if her income comprises a significant portion of the family income and if she has control over how it is spent. On the other hand, however, difficult work conditions, job insecurity, low wages, and the continued responsibility for household labor may mean that the lives of many women are not improved by the increased employment created by globalization. Much of the work is in export processing zones with no job security, is part-time, or is "homework" done in the home and paid for by the unit or piece. Social security, such as unemployment payments, do not apply to such temporary workers. We also cannot forget the high price that some women pay for their participation in the global economy—such as relocation to another country as a mail-order bride, housekeeper, or nanny. When we consider these cases, the jobs provided to women by globalization appear to be yet another example of women's subordination. We need, as Hochschild (2002) noted, to develop a global sense of ethics to match emerging economic realities. We must ask what kind of a world globalization has created when working in a sweatshop, sex work, migration to work as a domestic, and becoming a mail-order bride are rational economic choices. These may appear to be individual choices but they are not really free—they are the result of economic globalization.

Some people hope that cultural globalization will benefit women by promoting the development of neoliberal democratic governments. The thought is that democratic models of government will provide women with greater rights and opportunities. However, it should be noted that democratic forms of government are not necessarily inclusive of women, although they may provide more space for women to fight for their rights. Additionally, in some cases, the economic crises brought on by globalization and cultural crises brought on by the homogenization of world culture have contributed to the development of conservative and fundamentalist religious movements. The products, technologies, and capitalism associated with globalization all reflect the Western cultures in which they originate. This influx of Western culture often produces a conservative cultural reaction that includes calls for a return to traditional gender roles (Posusney & Doumato, 2003).

Many scholars and activists studying the effects of globalization on women embrace one particular effect of globalization: its effects on transnational feminism. The "silver-lining" of the globalization "cloud" is that in many cases globalization has inadvertently led to women's empowerment as women organize to combat its negative effects. For instance, as you saw in the chapter, women organize and protest poor work conditions in the transnational factory. Fueled by the dynamics of globalization itself, women all over the world fight the negative effects of globalization and use the transnational political stage to press for social, economic, environmental, and political justice (Cabezas, 2002; Naples & Desai, 2002). As Valentine Moghadam (1999, p. 384) said:

> In my view, the singular achievement of globalization is the
> proliferation of women's movements at the local level, the emergence
> of transnational feminist networks working at the global level, and the
> adoption of international conventions such as the *Convention on the
> Elimination of All Forms of Discrimination Against Women* and the *Beijing
> Declaration and Platform for Action of the Fourth World Conference on Women*.

Transnational networks of activists play an increasing role in international and regional politics and may have progressive effects on policies regarding women, human rights, and the environment (Karides, 2002; Keck & Sikkink, 1999). They can expose injustices in an international arena. This is globalization from below, rather than from above. They use electronic communication and international and regional conferences to share information and expand political participation. For instance, the Network is an organization that links Mexican and Central American groups that work on issues pertinent to women in *maquila* factories (Mendez, 2002). WFAN (Women, Food, and Agriculture Network) is a transnational network of rural women based in the United States. They oppose globalization and transnational trade agreements such as NAFTA by supporting cross-border organizing of women workers and activists (Wells, 2002). WFAN uses information technology to share information about factory conditions and their local campaigns as well as to provide public information about the factories. Box 7.4 provides additional examples.

"Entering the labor market for a woman does not automatically mean that she will have greater control over income; it may mean, instead, increased work burdens, greater drudgery, and multiple responsibilities as she is caught up in a global assembly line over which she has little control."
Gita Sen

BOX 7.4   *Sampling of Transnational Feminist Networks*

DAWN. Development Alternatives with Women for a New Era was formed in 1985. Its focus is Latin America, the Caribbean, South Asia, and Southeast Asia. Leading figures are Peggy Antrobus in Jamaica, Gita Sen in India, and Neuma Aguiar in Brazil. One of the founding members is Noeleen Heyzer of Malaysia, now the head of UNIFEM. DAWN is very active in international economic circles.

WLUML. Women Living Under Muslim Laws is an international network of individuals and groups that monitors the status of Muslim women. It is a secular, anti-fundamentalist organization emphasizing women's human rights issues. Its leading figures, including Marie-Aimée Hélie-Lucas (born in Algeria) and Farida Shaheed (Pakistani) are often invited to expert-group meetings held by the UN or by European governments.

WIDE. The focus of the Network Women in Development Europe is on development assistance and the global economy, with a feminist critique of economic theory and of European and U.S. trade and foreign aid policies. It is based in Brussels, Belgium.

WEDO. The goal of the Women's Environment and Development Organization is "to make women more visible as equal participants, experts, and leaders in policy making from the community to the international level, and in formulating alternative, healthy, and peaceful solutions to world problems." WEDO is based in New York and has co-chairs in Brazil, Guyana, Norway, Egypt, Kenya, Nigeria, Costa Rica, India, and New Zealand. WEDO is currently engaged in monitoring the implementation of the Beijing Platform for Action around the world and increasing the number of women in elected politics.

Source: Adapted from Moghadam, 1999.

The effects of globalization are relevant to our next topic of women and religion. Under conditions of economic stress and Western cultural penetration, people often seek certainty and a return to old times. This makes them more open to conservative and fundamentalist religious ideas that are detrimental to women's status. Chapter 8, "Women and Religion," shows how religion is sometimes an instrument of patriarchy. It also shows how women seek to reclaim and reform their religions, and create their own spiritual traditions.

Study Questions

1. What is globalization? What are structural adjustment policies? What are the effects of globalization and SAPs on women's labor?

2. What are sweatshops, and why do women work in them? How well paid are the women who work in them? What are the working conditions like? How can corporations get away with the way they treat these workers? How do workers respond?

3. How does globalization influence women's migration? What does it mean to say "the work women migrants do is often a reflection of traditional female roles and stereotypes"?

4. How does globalization influence the supply of and demand for migrant women domestics? Why should we be concerned about this trend? What can be done?

5. What are mail-order brides? What countries do they come from and why?

6. What is sexual tourism? How is it related to the differential effects of globalization based on gender, class, and race? Who are these "sexual tourists" and what are their destinations?

7. What is the sexual trafficking industry? How does it work? What are the effects on women? What is being done to stop it?

8. What are some of the possible positive effects of globalization for women?

Discussion Questions and Activities

1. How is your life affected by globalization?

2. How do migrant women contribute to your community? Which countries do they come from? What are the economic conditions in those countries that contribute to their migration? What types of work do they do—is it the care work traditionally done by women? Alternatively, interview a recent woman migrant using questions developed from the chapter.

3. Where were your clothes made? Choose an article of your clothing. Write a short story about the life of the woman who made it. To make it realistic, use the information in the text on women in the global factory and information in the Appendix on the status of women in that country.

4. Locate websites that advertise mail-order brides (just type "mail-order brides" into a basic search engine and you'll find hundreds of sites). What countries do most potential "brides" come from? Do some research on women's economic conditions in those countries. What are the economic conditions in those countries that make women turn to this option?

5. As discussed in the chapter, sex work is sometimes voluntary and sometimes coerced. The case of coerced sex work and trafficking in women is clearly a violation of women's human rights, but what about voluntary sex workers—the ones that choose sex work as an economic advancement strategy? Is sex work always exploitative or should it be acknowledged as a real job that deserves respect and is part of a woman's right to control the use of her body?

Activist Websites of Interest

Coalition Against Trafficking of Women
http://www.uri.edu/artsci/wms/hughes/catw.htm
Global Alliance Against Traffic in Women
http://www.inet.co.th/org/gaatw/
Standing Against Global Exploitation
http://www.sageprojectinc.org
Shared Hope International
http://www.sharedhipe.org
International Justice Mission
http://www.ijm.org

Informational Websites of Interest

Third World Network (TWN)
http://www.twnside.org/sg/women.htm
WEDO's Primer on Women and Trade
http://www.wedo.org/global/wedo_primer.htm
Women's International Coalition for Economic Justice
http://www.wicej.addr.com/

Action Opportunities

1. The Fair Labor Association is a relatively new consortium of apparel and footwear firms and nonprofit groups that monitors factory conditions. Over 150 colleges nationwide have signed on to help ensure that merchandise bearing their logos is made without sweatshop labor. Find out whether your college or university has a "no sweatshop policy" for

their apparel. If they do, find out how it came about and how compliance is assured. If they don't, find out how you can help bring such a policy about.

2. Go to Sweatshop Watch at http://www.sweatshopwatch.org and join one of their campaigns to end sweatshop labor. The website also provides a list of sweatshop-free retailers so that you can shop responsibly.

3. Join the Global Alliance Against Trafficking in Women (http://www.thai.net/gaatw/membership_terms.htm).

4. Help your local women's shelter develop a program to reach out to migrant women who experience abuse from male partners or employers.

Women and Religion

Now what about Islam? And what of the other great religions? When we think about religions in general, it seems to me that, more or less, they are the same. They all have a general human call for the equality of people—regardless of color, race, or sex. One finds this conception of equality in all of the religions, as well as in Marxism or existentialism. But when we come to the specifics, when we come to the daily lives of men and women, rich and poor, one race and another, this general sense of equality does not seem to be in evidence. Here we find oppression, including the oppression of women. So we must not have illusions about religion, because religion is used, and it is used often by those in power.

—NAWAL EL SAADAWI, 1987

A Jewish girl holds a tambourine at a feminist seder in the United States. Women called to serve God often reconstruct their religious traditions so that the traditions no longer support the subordination of women. © *Los Angeles Times/*IRIS SCHNEIDER

This chapter considers the relationship between religion and women's subordination. It is also a chapter on **feminist theology** (theology is the study of religious doctrines). As King (1994) said, feminist theology seeks to accomplish both a negative and positive task. The negative task is the critique of and struggle against the oppression of women whereas the positive task is one of reform and reconstruction. King (1994) suggests that feminist theology is always dynamic and pluralistic—including and expressing the voices, experiences, and approaches of many different women in very different situations and societies.

Religion is one of the cultural agents that shapes gender ideologies—our conceptions of female and male. We are not born believing that females and males should differ in specific ways and are destined to do different things. We learn this from our culture, and one important cultural messenger for most people is their religion. Therefore, when considering the various forces that contribute to women's lower power and status, it is important to consider religion. Feminist theologian Rosemary Ruether (1974) suggests that religion is the most important shaper and enforcer of the image and role of women in culture and society. Likewise, feminist theologian Mary Daly (1978) and anthropologist Susan Sered (1999) say that religion often plays a critical role in presenting patriarchy as inevitable, inescapable, and ultimately correct.

At the outset it is important to realize that it is difficult to generalize about entire religious traditions. Many variants exist within all of the world's major religious traditions, some of which are more supportive of women's equality than are others. It is primarily the conservative and fundamentalist strains of the world's religions that most vociferously promote traditional roles for women and attempt to limit women's rights. Although all religious fundamentalisms express great concern and respect for family and childrearing, all are also associated with the patriarchal control of women and their sexuality (Pollit, 2002; Rose, 1999; Ruether, 2002). Box 8.1 summarizes the common features of religious fundamentalist groups.

Despite the recent media focus on Muslim fundamentalists in countries like Afghanistan, other religious fundamentalisms—including Judaism, Buddhism, Hinduism and Christianity—also seek to control women (Armstrong, 2000; Helie-Lucas, 1999). However, as you will see in this chapter, other strains of the very same religions pull equally hard in the other direction. Ruether (2002) notes that it is a mistake to think that religiousness is authentically represented only by patriarchal, misogynist religious traditions; there are progressive, egalitarian principles within religious traditions.

Also, bear in mind that smaller indigenous religions often give women a greater role than do the world's major religions. In many indigenous traditions there are strong female mythological figures, female rituals, and no doctrine of male superiority and dominance (Gross, 1996; Sered, 1994, 1999). Mbon (1987) illustrates this in a discussion of African religion. In many traditional African religions, women play active roles as *diviners* (who foretell the future) and as *healers* of physical and psychological illnesses. In some parts of

"Unquestionably 'religion' or 'spirituality' defined by and in the service of patriarchy is a force against freedom, vitality, and survival. But patriarchy's definition of religion is not the only one."
Sheila Ruth

Although the Greek goddess Pandora is known for unleashing the world's evils, in earlier history she was known by the name Gaea and worshiped as the embodiment of earth and the giver of all.

BOX 8.1   *Common Features of Religious Fundamentalism*

1. Assert that the society needs to be rescued from the secular society.

2. Reject norms of universal human rights and display intolerance for others.

3. Are committed to the authority of ancient scriptures.

4. Hold religion to provide a total worldview inseparable from politics.

5. Rely on an idealized past.

6. Are selective in drawing from an idealized past for religious traditions and orthodox practice.

7. Center that idealized past in a patriarchal framework mandating separate gender spheres and a "pristine morality" emphasizing women's modesty and subordination.

8. Reject outsiders and the concept of pluralism.

9. Are committed to activism and fighting for social, political, and legal change.

Source: Anwar, 1999.

Africa, women also occupy a central place in the practice of witchcraft, and this is a source of power for them. There are also many rituals and ceremonies that cannot be performed without women. In addition, in most traditional African religions, God is neither exclusively male nor exclusively female; God is both. It is also the case that in so-called marginal or non-mainstream religions, women often have more power and autonomy (Gross, 1996; Sered, 1994; Weissinger, 1993). Sered (1994) examines twelve contemporary woman-dominated religions in depth. (Box 8.2 gives a sampling of her research.) These religions are interesting in that they often exist alongside of mainstream religions and frequently emphasize the appeasement of spirits for purposes of healing and bringing good tidings.

Common Feminist Critiques of Religion

According to Peach (2002), almost all religions are patriarchal in origin, development, leadership, authority, and power. Feminist critiques of religion propose that the majority of the world's religions depict men's greater power

BOX 8.2   *Some Contemporary Woman-Centered Religions*

Afro-Brazilian Religions (Brazil)
These combine elements of African tribal religions, Amerindian religions, Catholicism, and Kardecism (French Spiritism). The main features are curing and public rituals in which female mediums are possessed by spirits. They coexist with Catholicism.

Black Carib Religion (Central America)
This religion is centered around numerous rituals to honor and appease ancestral spirits and to protect the living against evil spirits and sorcery. Old women are the spiritual leaders. Most Black Caribs are also Roman Catholic.

Burmese Nat Religion (Upper Burma)
This religion centers around the appeasement of spirits called *nats*. These *nats* are also called upon to prevent and cure illness and to bring good luck. Most rituals are performed by women, and almost all shamans are women as well. The religion exists alongside Buddhist practices.

Christian Science (United States)
This religion was founded by Mary Baker Eddy in the nineteenth century. Christian Scientists believe that healing comes about through study and prayer.

Feminist Spirituality Movement
This is discussed at the end of this chapter.

Korean Household Religion
Korean women make offerings to gods for the well-being of their households and consult female shamans for guidance. This coexists with Buddhism.

Sande Secret Society (West Africa)
Adolescent girls are initiated into the societies at lengthy all-female retreats. At this time, they are taught about childbirth and other skills women are expected to know. Sande societies also control the supernatural and sacred realm. This coexists with male secret societies called *Poro*.

Za–r (parts of Africa and the Middle East)
Za–r are spirits that attack and possess women. Women then join za–r cults in which they participate in rituals to appease the possessing spirit and turn it into an ally. Women's za–r activities often serve as a counterpart to men's involvement in official Islamic practices.

Source: Sered, 1994.

and status relative to women as appropriate and acceptable. The common presentation of God as male, traditions of male leadership, the exclusion of women from major religious rituals, and religious texts that leave out the female experience and legitimize men's authority over women, all legitimize and reinforce patriarchy (see Figure 8.1). In this way, religion makes it more difficult to see through the injustices of the patriarchal system (Daly, 1974).

Masculine God-Language

Feminist critiques of religion often cite the male imagery used by so many of the world's religions and regard it as both a source and a reflection of

FIGURE 8.1 *Negative Task of Feminist Theology: Critique of Religion*

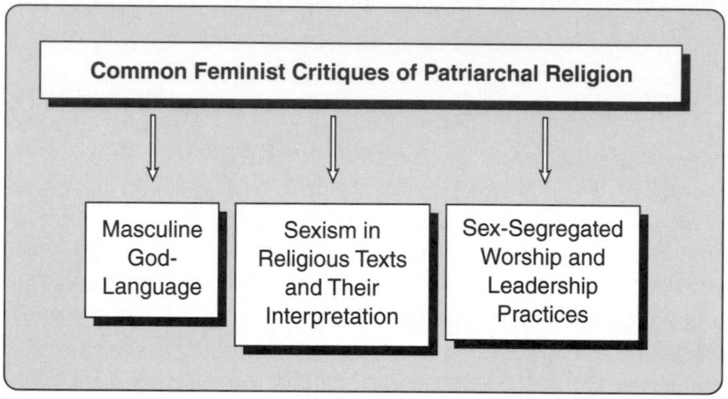

Common Feminist Critiques of Patriarchal Religion

| Masculine God-Language | Sexism in Religious Texts and Their Interpretation | Sex-Segregated Worship and Leadership Practices |

"If we do not mean that God is male when we use masculine pronouns and imagery, then why should there be any objections to using female imagery and pronouns as well?"
Rita Gross

"Consider the impact on your self-image of being 'in the likeness of God,' like Jesus, the Pope, and the 'Brothers of the Church' and contrast it with never finding yourself reflected in the sacred pronoun. Utter: God, He . . . ; God, Him. Now say: God, She. . . . Imagine the experience of seeing oneself reflected in the sacred images of power."
Sheila Ruth

patriarchy. For instance, God or Allah is typically presented using male imagery and language. Theologians are often quick to point out that God is not to be considered in sexual terms at all, despite such terminology. However, the actual language they use daily in worship and prayer conveys a different message and gives the impression that God is thought of in exclusively masculine terms (Pagels, 1976). That it is frequently considered daring, degrading, or alienating to speak of God using female pronouns and imagery perhaps indicates something about the way women and the feminine are valued (Gross, 1979). In other words, **masculine God-language** is not as innocuous as it may appear, for linguistic conventions do indeed shape our perceptions of reality.

Many feminists argue that referring to God using terms like "Our Heavenly Father" and "He" suggest that on earth, men can be the only true gods. After all, God is the ultimate male and in this way deifies male power. God as male is also a stern, commanding ruler, and an image that represents only one aspect of humanity: maleness (Ruth, 1995). The thought is that as long as God is only the God of our fathers and not our mothers, men will be perceived as having both a closer relationship with God and a higher religious status (Umansky, in Cantor, 1995). In addition, God's main messengers on earth are typically male. For instance, Jesus (Christianity), Muhammad (Islam), and the Buddha (Buddhism) are all male. This too is viewed by many feminist theologians as contributing to the common cultural view that men are above women.

The effects of this on women are also an issue to feminist theologians. Ruth (1995) suggests that the sexist and masculine focus of religion makes being a religious woman analogous with maintaining a stoic attitude about one's lower status. Or as Daly (1973) puts it, the males' judgment having been metamorphosed into God's judgment, it becomes the religious duty of women to accept the burden of guilt, to see the self with male chauvinist eyes, to accept male dominance.

Sexism in Religious Texts

Another focus of feminist criticism of religion is sexism in religious texts. One key issue for feminists regarding the scriptures is the relative absence of females and female experience. Put simply, most of the stories are about men and male experience, and when women appear it is usually as characters in stories told by and about men or as objects of male concern such as the control of female sexuality. As Ruether (1985) suggests, although women's experience may be found between the lines of religious texts, for the most part the norm presented for women is one of absence and silence. When women are portrayed, it is as objects praised for obedience or admonished for disobedience to men.

A second key issue for feminists with regard to the scriptures is that most of these texts sacralize patriarchy (present it as sacred). As Gross (1996) puts it, the study of religious scriptures is important because scriptures are so often used to support traditional notions of women's roles. Feminist theologian Mary Daly (1985) notes that the endorsement of traditional gender roles in religious texts acts to convince women to accept their lower status. As she puts it, "ecclesiastical propaganda" seems to put woman on a pedestal by emphasizing her value as a wife and mother, but, in reality, it prevents her from genuine fulfillment and full participation in society. Religion, she notes, makes women feel guilty or unnatural if they rebel against the role prescribed to them, and this condemns women to a restricted existence in the name of religion.

Religious stories and texts often contain four common messages that perpetuate women's lower status and power. These are: (1) Female sexuality is dangerous and must be suppressed; (2) female religious figures are subordinate to male religious figures (they are typically portrayed in relationship to males); (3) females should be subservient wives, mothers, and homemakers; and (4) women's lower status is punishment for their sinful nature. It is hard to say with certainty why these themes are consistently found in the world's religions. However, Prusak (1974) suggests that the men who created these stories were puzzled by the power of the sexual drive and birth. Through the creation of stories that connected women with evil, they could explain why women bled every month and why they experience the pain and inconvenience of pregnancy and childbirth. By connecting women with evil, they also had a theological explanation and justification for male dominance and female subservience. As an added bonus, they were able to explain evil by identifying women as its source.

It is important to realize that it is not the scriptures themselves that lead to women's subordination; it is how people interpret them. **Hermeneutics** is the study of the principles of interpretation for religious texts. Whether one interprets a text literally (as the word of God), allegorically (as stories from which moral lessons are to be learned), or historically (as reflections of the times in which they are written) has important implications for women.

"If Jews believe that all of us, male and female are created in the divine image, then why doesn't our liturgy reflect this basic theological conviction?"
Ellen Umansky

At the beginning of the chapter you were cautioned that it is hard to generalize about any religion since there are many variants, some more supportive of women's equality than others. Fundamentalist strains are more likely to interpret texts as the literal word of God. Therefore, the traditional relationships between men and women found in the scriptures are seen as prescriptions for modern life as well. More liberal strains of the same religion will look at scriptures metaphorically and consider the historical context in which they were written. This hermeneutic provides more room for selectivity; passages that condone women's subordination can be seen as historical reflections rather than as role models for current gender relationships. It is interesting, however, that even so-called literal interpretations are selective, for no religion takes all of the passages found in its scriptures literally. For instance, those who argue that male dominance is required according to the scriptures do not generally argue that slavery is also required, although the scriptures of the three main monotheistic religions (Christianity, Islam, and Judaism) all allow and condone it (Gross, 1996).

As the chapter proceeds it will be evident that most religious texts also have passages that may be interpreted in ways favorable to women's equality. Some (such as the Sikh religious texts of India) explicitly call for the equal treatment of women. However, as Holm (1994) notes, historically in all major religions, it is men who have composed, transmitted, and interpreted the sacred writings. Over time these writings and their interpretations increasingly reflected men's activities, achievements, and power as well as societal views of male superiority.

It is also interesting to note that it appears that women had greater status in at least four religions (Islam, Christianity, Hinduism, and Buddhism) in the religions' formative years. In all of these religions it appears that once the original leaders died, new writings and interpretations emerged that justified the continuation of existing patriarchal traditions. Once again, as el Saadawi (1987) says, those who have power change religion according to their own interests, not according to the interests of the people. It is then up to the people to redirect attention back to the founder's intent.

Sex-Segregated Religious Practices

A number of the world's religions have different religious rituals and forms of worship based on gender, that is, they have **sex-segregated religious practices.** Many Hindu women, for instance, perform rituals of self-denial, such as fasting, in order to create positive energy and power for their husbands. The self-sacrifice of a woman for her husband is understood to be a religious offering. Men do not perform such rituals for their wives. There are also domestic rituals performed by females for fertility that are not found in Hindu texts but are passed down orally from woman to woman (Young, 1987). In general, the religious practices of males are more public (for example, in the church, temple, or synagogue) and the practices of women are conducted in the home.

Another instance of sex-segregated religious practices is that leadership roles in religions are usually reserved for males. Thus, female ministers, bishops, priests, rabbis, gurus, mullahs, or sadhus (holy people) remain rare or nonexistent in most religious traditions, even today (Eck & Jain, 1987). As Gross (1996) suggests, the ordination of women is not the only important indication of whether or not women have genuine membership in their religion, but it is a way to quickly assess the status of women in a given religion.

Religious texts are often used to justify why women should not hold religious leadership positions. For instance, this passage from the Bible has historically been used as a proof text for why women shouldn't hold priestly and liturgical roles: "Women should keep silence in churches. For they are not permitted to speak, but should be subordinate, as even the law says" (I Cor. 14:34–35) (Parvey, 1974, p. 128). Many religions also keep women theologically illiterate, and thus they are unqualified to hold high positions within the religion. For instance, women may not be permitted to study religious texts, attend important religious ceremonies, or have access to theological education. Likewise, higher rates of illiteracy among females, and the lack of schooling in the languages of the texts, are in some cases obstacles. In most of the world's major religions (for instance, Christianity, Islam, and Buddhism), God's messengers on earth are male, and it is often said that only males may represent them. Some religions also maintain that women are spiritually inferior to men and that they are therefore unsuitable for religious leadership.

> Clare of Assisi (1193–1254) was a disciple of St. Francis of Assisi and led the first female Franciscan order.

> "If God had not intended that Women shou'd use their Reason, He wou'd not have given them any, for He does nothing in vain. If they are to use their Reason, certainly it ought to be employ'd about the noblest Objects, and in business of the greatest Consequences, therefore in Religion."
> *Mary Astell, 1705*

Reformist Efforts in Feminist Theology

Although modern religion is often an agent of women's oppression, religion is profoundly important to many feminists. As feminist theologians Christ and Plaskow (1979) say, for many women, the discovery that religions teach the inferiority of women is experienced as a betrayal of deeply felt spiritual and ritual experience. Indeed, religious women who wanted to serve God but were limited in their efforts because they were female have sought to reform and transform existing religions. For instance, women who felt called to be rabbis, priests, and ministers and found themselves barred from these vocations have fought for the right to become religious leaders (Christ & Plaskow, 1979).

Although there is great diversity in how feminists reform and reconstruct religion (see Figure 8.2), according to Gross (1996) feminist theologies agree on two basic things. First is that human experience is the source of and authority for authentic religious expression. Second is that religious expressions, expressions worthy of surviving for centuries and millennia, must promote the full humanity of women as well as men. Efforts to reform the world's major religions are typically based on the belief that deep down these religions are supportive of women's equality. Reformists assume that although it is generally the case that religion has contributed to the oppression of women, this does not

> "I heard the gospel long before I heard of the women's movement."
> *Nancy Hatch Wittig, one of the first women to be ordained as an Episcopal Priest in 1974 on "being called" to the priesthood.*

"The first step in the elevation of woman to her true position, as an equal factor in human progress, is the cultivation of the religious sentiment in regard to her dignity and equality, the recognition by the rising generation of an ideal Heavenly Mother, to whom their prayers should be addressed, as well as to a Father."
Elizabeth Cady Stanton,
The Women's Bible, *1895*

have to be so. Reformers argue that feminist reforms bring religion closer to its true heart and core of equality and freedom (Gross, 1996).

One common reformist effort centers on the changing of God and prayer language to be more female inclusive. Both Jewish and Christian feminists have tried, with some success, to address God as "She" or at least to leave out masculine references such as "He" or "our Father." The idea is that without de-emphasizing the masculine face of God, women cannot be fully equal in the religious community. Reformists also work to reduce sexism in religious practices. This includes working for women's ordination and leadership within their religious traditions as well as their rights to read sacred texts and perform sacred rituals.

Another reformist effort centers on the reexamination of religious texts and history in order to promote women's equality. A distinction is made between those aspects of the tradition that support women's empowerment and those that do not (Gross, 1996). As Carmody (1979) says in her book on women and world religions, the task "is to winnow the wheat of authentic religion . . . from the religion's sexist chaff" (p. 14). This, like so many things, is easier said than done. In reality, the analysis of religious texts is a complex scholarly enterprise requiring archeological, historical, and linguistic study (Gross, 1996). Not only are religious scriptures often self-contradictory, but they have usually undergone numerous interpretations and translations over time. The Bible, for instance, was originally written in an ancient language

FIGURE 8.2 *Goals of Reformist Efforts in Feminist Theology*

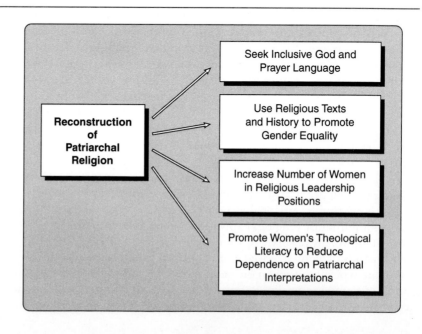

that is no longer used. Likewise, as Gross (1999) points out, finding women in the historical record of a religion can be difficult because once patriarchy became common, the records typically preserved more information about men than women.

Women and The World's Major Religions

So far you have learned that religion can be an agent of patriarchy. Religious language, scriptures and texts (a religion's **canon**), sex-segregated religious practices, and masculine God-language, contribute to traditional gender ideologies and are sometimes used to support the subordination of women. You have also learned that many women are do not believe that God, or the founders of their religion, intended for their religions to be used in this way. These women, along with supportive men, seek to reform their religions. They resist fundamentalist interpretations that call for women's return to the private sphere. This next section applies these ideas to each of the world's five main religions.

Hinduism

Hinduism, practiced primarily in India for 6,000 years, is the only major polytheistic religion in the world and is also the only one that worships female as well as male deities (Carmody, 1974; Gross, 1996). This means that masculine God-language is not the issue it is in the world's other major religions. Hinduism also has no single founder or single prophet—no male Son of God such as Jesus, or male prophet such as Muhammad. Although the *Vedas* (written from 1750 to the sixth century B.C.E.) are the primary Hindu scriptures, there is no single authoritative scripture, no one sacred text (Carmody, 1991; Narayanan, 1999). Relative to many other religions, local customs, festivals, and rituals are far more important to the practice of Hinduism than the scriptures, which are written in Sanskrit, a language that most Indians cannot read (Narayanan, 1999; 2003). Early Hinduism was more supportive of women's equality than later Hinduism. Women lost much of their freedom in seventh century B.C.E. when Hindu law, in particular the *Laws of Manu,* codified patriarchy (Gupta, 1991).

On the face of it, Hinduism is not a masculinist religion in that females figure prominently in the form of goddesses. Some of these goddesses suggest great female power. These include *Durga* who rules strength and protection and is believed by some devotees to be the Supreme Being, *Sarasvati,* Goddess of Learning, *Lakshmi,* Goddess of Prosperity, and *Kali,* "the Dark One." Many Hindus celebrate and worship goddesses during a ten-day fall festival called *Navaratri.* In some communities, women put up temporary altars and make elaborate displays of dolls that represent the goddesses (Narayanan, 2003). Like most Hindu festivals, songs and dances are used to honor the divine.

Although there are powerful female goddesses in Hinduism, some critics point out that female gods are often portrayed as dangerously passionate, capable of giving and taking life, and needing the control of male gods so that they do not produce chaos (Carmody, 1989). In general, the unmarried goddesses are more likely to be presented as the dangerous ones. The married ones such as *Savitri, Sita, Parvati,* and *Lakshmi* are viewed as more virtuous and are more likely to be held up as models for women. For example, Savitri, a prominent female figure in Hindu mythology, is so devoted to her husband that she sacrifices her life for his. Similarly, another major female figure, Sati, wife of the god Siva, commits suicide by walking into a fire to avenge her husband's honor. Fire and the preservation of the husband's honor also figure in the story of Sita. Sita is kidnapped from her husband, Rama, by the demon Ravana. She is twice victimized—first, by the terror of abduction and captivity, and again, when she is rescued by Rama and must prove to him that she remained pure and faithful to him. She steps into a sacrificial fire but emerges unscathed because she was virtuous. Sita risked death to protect the honor of her husband (Robinson, 1985).

Like other religions, Hindu religious rituals differ depending on gender. The theme of *pativratya,* or husband devotion, is important to the practice of Hinduism for women in many Indian communities. Key concepts of Hinduism are reincarnation and karma, the idea that one's present life is the result of actions taken in previous lives. Many believe that good karma comes to those women who are good and loyal wives. Men gain good karma, and therefore a higher level of rebirth, through the study of the Vedas and through meditation (Carmody, 1989). Traditionally, ideal Hindu wives ended their lives by throwing themselves on their husband's funeral pyre, a practice called *sati* or *suttee*. Although outlawed during the British colonial era, some Hindu fundamentalists defend the practice. A few isolated incidents of *sati* such as the 1987 case of Roop Kaneer have occurred in recent years. In this case, a young widow, encouraged by her in-laws and a crowd, threw herself on her husband's funeral pyre.

Women are extremely important to the practice of many Hindu rituals. Women maintain household religious shrines requiring daily attention and perform rituals, including fasts, on behalf of their families' well-being. Because Hinduism views women to be polluted when menstruating, they have often been prohibited from full participation in public sphere religious activities such as those in temples (Narayanan, 1999). Hindu temple rituals and rites of passage are still performed by male priests, and most Hindu teachers (gurus) remain male (Young, 1987). The classical Hindu texts, especially the *Vedas* and early *Upanishads,* seem to suggest that women could receive religious education and perform religious ceremonies, but as time went on, these were closed to women (Carmody, 1991; Leslie, 1983; Narayanan, 1999). In some areas of India, there are still restrictions on women's study of the *Vedas* (Narayanan, 1999).

Hindu women who seek to reform their religion often look to the epic figure Draupadi, who does not allow men to dictate to her, and to the god-

"Although Hindu traditions are portrayed, and quite correctly in some instances, as being patriarchal, the system has built-in mechanisms to allow for dynamic reinterpretation."
Vasudha Narayanan

dess Kali, who inspires terror and awe and is a model of female power (Gupta, 1991; Sugirtharajah, 1994). They seek to recast Hindu goddesses and religious figures as spiritual beings who show their devotion independent of husband devotion (Narayanan, 1999). They refer to the evidence that women contributed to the development of Hinduism, for example, composing hymns and performing rituals in the Vedic period (Peach, 2002). They study the ancient texts that support women's equality and point out how it was only over time that Hindu texts came to support the subordination of women. (Box 8.3 provides a sampling of Hindu scriptures that celebrate the feminine divine.) Many note how colonization by the British gave Hindu legal texts supportive of male power greater precedence than those that were more liberal in their attitudes toward women (Narayanan, 1999). They resist Hindu fundamentalism and its demands that women be restricted to their roles as wives and mothers, and its insistence that women not read the Vedas. Hindu women seeking reform also work toward women's inclusion as spiritual leaders. Until recently, one barrier to women's leadership in Hinduism was that only males could study Sanskrit, the language of the religious texts. However, today the university study of Sanskrit is more likely to be undertaken by women since men pursue more lucrative professions. In recent years, some women have become ascetics and gurus, study the *Vedas*, recite the *Vedas*, and perform Vedic rituals (Narayanan, 1999; Young, 1994).

> "When men know that spiritually we are the same as they are, they will have to judge us on our merits and our ability and not on what someone said thousands of years ago."
> *Reverend Master Jiyu Kennett Roshi ("Roshi" means Zenmaster), one of the few female heads of a Buddhist monastery in the United States*

Buddhism

Buddhism began in India in the fifth or sixth century B.C.E. after Siddhartha Gautama attained enlightenment and became the "Buddha" or the "awakened one" (Peach, 2002). Very generally, Buddha counseled that spiritual enlightenment requires devoting oneself to understanding and ending suffering, getting rid of ego and desire, seeking spiritual depth, and behaving morally (e.g., no killing, stealing, lying, gossiping, no intoxicants). Forms of Buddhism are found in Burma, China, Hong Kong, Japan, Sri Lanka, Nepal, Taiwan, Thailand, Cambodia, Laos, Tibet, and in the United States, Canada, and Europe.

Although the Buddha is male, Buddhism is nontheistic; consequently there are no gendered Absolute or Supreme Beings and no masculine God-language. However, like the world's other major religions, we find evidence of sexism in some Buddhist scriptures that describe women as filled with evil desires and as harmful obstacles to men's attainment of enlightenment (Uchino, 1985). Buddhist popular thought often regards women as impure, as having a more sinful karma than men (thus their poor situation), and as being unable to attain Buddhahood (the highest level of enlightenment) unless they are reborn as a man (Gross, 1999, 2003; Uchino, 1985). This is accomplished by being good wives and mothers.

Although some texts in every period in Buddhist history cast women in a negative light, there are also ones in every period that clearly state otherwise. On balance, the Buddhist *dharma* (central truth or spiritual path) does not

BOX 8.3   *Some Hindu Scriptures Venerating the Divine Feminine*

I am the Queen, source of thought,

knowledge itself!

You do not know Me, yet

you dwell in Me. I announce Myself in words both

gods and humans welcome.

From the summit of the world,

I give birth to the sky!

The tempest is My breath, all living creatures are My life!

Beyond the wide earth,

beyond the vast heaven,

My grandeur extends forever!

From the Devi Sukta

Great Goddess, who art thou?

I am essentially Brahman [the Absolute]

From me has proceeded the world comprising Prakriti [material substance] and Purusha [cosmic consciousness], the void and the Plenum.

I am bliss and nonbliss.

Knowledge and ignorance are Myself.

I am the five elements and also what is different from them,

The panchabhutas

And tanmatras.

I am the entire world.

I am the Veda

as well as what is different from it.

I am unknown.

Below and above and around am I.

From the Devi Upanishad

The Divine Mother revealed to me in the Kali temple that it was She who had become everything. She showed me that everything was full of Consciousness. The Image was Consciousness, the altar was Consciousness, the water-vessels were Consciousness, the door-sill was Consciousness, the marble floor was Consciousness—all was Consciousness.

I found everything inside the room soaked, as it were in Bliss—the Bliss of Satchidananda. I saw a wicked man in front of the Kali temple; but in him also I saw the Power of the Divine Mother vibrating.

That was why I fed a cat with the food that was to be offered to the Divine Mother. I clearly perceived that the Divine Mother herself had become everything—even the cat.

From The Gospel of Ramakrishna

support patriarchy. As Gross (1999, p. 83) says, "the weightier texts, stories, and teachers argue that dharma is neither male nor female" and "there have always been important Buddhist thinkers that clearly said discrimination against women in Buddhism is inappropriate and un-dharmic." Barnes (1987) argues that most of the main schools of Buddhism thriving today are egalitarian in doctrine and that the problems faced by women in Buddhist countries have more to do with social values that were not originated by Buddhist theorists.

It important to know that there are several forms of Buddhism and that these also differ in terms of their male-centeredness. The literature of Theravada (Hinayana) Buddhism is the one most likely to view women as obstacles to spiritual progress and to suggest that women are inferior spiritual beings. In contrast is Mahayana Buddhism, which stresses that all human experience, male or female, is the source of enlightenment and that all things share one life because nothing can stand on its own. This is known as the Supreme Wisdom, Prajnaparamita, or the feminine principle (Bancroft, 1987). Tantric Buddhism—another though less popular form—is even more female-centered and includes the presence of strong, sexually active female sacred beings (Gross, 1996).

Perhaps Buddhist dharma does not distinguish between females and males as spiritual beings, but in practice, Buddhism has. The pursuits most honored in the Buddhist tradition—teachers, students, monastics, and meditators—have favored men (Gross, 2003). It has been expected that women show devotion through their domestic duties as wives and mothers, lay devotional practices, and by feeding monks (monastic rules prohibit them from farming or handling money). Leadership in the Buddhist tradition has also been predominantly male. In traditional Buddhism, the main religious leaders are the male monks, or *bhikkhu*. The female counterpart is the *bhikkhuni*, sometimes translated as "nun" although it is really the female form of the word *bhikkhu*. At first women were not allowed to enter the monastic order and attained this right through protest, possibly one of the first cases of organized female protest against male supremacy in a religious order anywhere in the world (Goonatilake, 1997). Five hundred women with shaved heads and saffron robes walked 100 miles to plead with the Buddha. After the third time, he granted permission.

In some Buddhist countries—such as Burma, Cambodia, Laos, Tibet, Thailand, Sri Lanka, Nepal, Bhutan, and Burma—there are no orders of fully ordained *bhikkhuni* (although the Dalai Lama of Tibet is supportive of their ordination). Most of these countries practice the more gender-conservative Buddhist school of Theravada, which does not ordain nuns, or does so under limited conditions (Bancroft, 1987; Barnes, 1994). In these countries, there are women who shave their heads as nuns and live as Buddhist devotees (Barnes, 1994). For instance, in Thailand, women may become *bhikkhuni* that are not fully ordained, called *jis,* but they receive no public or governmental support and have low social status. Male monks administer all religious rituals and instruction. Thai Buddhist monastic rules forbid close association with women, and the Buddhist tradition is taken to be the sphere of men (Kabilsingh, 1987). These practices have the effect of removing women from their religious heritage and rights (Kabilsingh, 1987).

In contrast to Theravada Buddhism, the Mahayana (Zen) school gives women greater freedom as religious teachers. In Taiwan, Buddhist nuns, or ascetics, have their own monasteries and enjoy social and financial support from the public. In Japan, nuns are ordained and may even perform some priestly duties in some sects. Uchino (1987) discusses how this came about in an article tracing the status elevation process of Soto sect nuns in modern Japan. Changes began in the early 1900s when Buddhist schools for nuns were established. Nuns who studied at these schools later became leaders in the nun equality movement. Beginning in 1925, the nuns held conferences and issued demands for increased equality in the world of Buddhism. Changes toward nun's equality occurred gradually over the next fifty years due to continued political pressure on the part of the nuns' organization.

In general, though, Buddhist nuns have not fared as well as Buddhist monks in any period of history (Gross, 2003). There are fewer nunneries, fewer opportunities for economic support, and less family support since having a nun in the family does not bring the respect that having a monk does. Barnes (1994) describes some of the restrictions placed on nuns relative to monks. The ordination process is more difficult for nuns, and nuns' lives are more closely regulated than monks' lives. Nuns must also adhere to eight regulations spelling out their lower status relative to male monks. These regulations are alleged to have come from the Buddha himself and require that nuns treat all monks as their superiors; nuns are required to seek out monks for instruction but not to instruct or admonish them (Bancroft, 1987; Willis, 1985). However, many Buddhist historians think that these regulations were improperly attributed to the Buddha (Carmody, 1991; Gross, 1999).

Reform efforts in Buddhism include a review of Buddha's history and conclude that it was not his intention to restrict women's participation in Buddhism (Kabilsingh, 1987). They also show that essential Buddhist teachings state that women and men have equal potential for enlightenment. Rita Gross's work (1993; 1996; 1999; 2003) is an excellent example of showing how Buddhism is fundamentally compatible with feminism. Buddhist reformers work to discredit the orthodox Theravada view of women's inferiority by showing that the scriptures were not written down until 400 years after the Buddha's death (Bancroft, 1987). Box 8.4 offers some of the Poems of Enlightenment that are attributed to female disciples of Buddha. Reformists in the Buddhist tradition also point out that the fundamental concepts of Buddhism (the Four Noble Truths, Practice, and the attainment of nirvana) are applicable to both sexes. Buddhist reformists direct attention to those stories and texts supportive of women's equality and work toward equal participation within their religion, particularly greater respect and support for nuns.

Reformist efforts have created new possibilities for women in Buddhism. Several recent Buddhist sects give women an equal place with men and have women in top administrative positions. Won Buddhism (begun in Korea and found in Taiwan and in the United States) is one example (Holm, 1994). The old distinction between cleric (monks) and laypeople is now rejected by many, and this has increased the number of Buddhist female leaders and teachers. Among the most influential of these are Ayu Khandro and Ani Lochen (Tibet), Achan Naeb (Thailand), Daw Panna (Burma), Ruth Denison and Maureen Stuart (United States), Jiyu Kennett Roshi (United King-

BOX 8.4   *Writings of Female Disciples of Buddha*

Sakyadhita, the International Association of Buddhist Women, maintains that the predominant role of males in the history of Buddhist societies has no Buddhist doctrinal support. The organization researches and promotes knowledge of Buddhist women and fosters communication on issues of relevance to Buddhist women. Here are some Poems of Enlightenment from the society that are attributed to female disciples of Buddha.

> While the breeze blows
>
> cool and sweet-smelling,
>
> I shall split ignorance asunder,
>
> as I sit on the mountaintop.
>
> *Therigatha 544*

Awareness of impermanence

practiced and developed,

exhausts all desire,

exhausts all ignorance

and removes all conceit.

> *Therigatha 717*

I am friend to all,

companion to all,

sympathetic to all beings,

and I develop a heart full of love,

delighting in non-harming.

> *Therigatha 648*

dom, now in the United States), and Ayya Khema (Sri Lanka, originally from the West). The recently developed American version of Buddhism, and a number of the lay versions developed in Japan and Korea, frequently have women leaders believed to possess spiritual powers (Bancroft, 1987; Barnes, 1994). Furthermore, laywomen in some Theravada countries and in Europe and America have assumed new roles as the teachers of meditation as a means to nirvana (Barnes, 1994).

Islam

Islam began in the eighth century C.E., when Muhammad recorded the **Koran** (also spelled Qur'an). Muslims believe that the Koran is the unadulterated word of God as transmitted to Muhammad via the Angel of Gabriel (Hassan, 2003). Muhammad is seen as the final prophet of God, the last of a lineage beginning with Adam, and including Moses, Abraham, and Jesus (Peach, 2002). All Muslims are expected to observe the "Five Pillars of Islam." They are to profess faith in God's oneness, accept Muhammad as God's prophet, pray five times a day, fast during the holy month of Ramadan, give alms, and make a pilgrimage to Mecca at least one time. Although Islam opposes the used of gendered imagery for the Divine, Allah (God) is typically referred to as "He."

The Koran is considered to be the primary source of Islam but there are other sources to which Muslims refer (Hassan, 2003). These include the *Sunnah* (the practices of Muhammad) and the **Hadith** (sayings attributed to Muhammad). These sources of Islam have been interpreted almost entirely by men who have used them to justify patriarchy (Hassan, 2003). This is particularly true of the Hadith. Many ahadith are of questionable authenticity and yet recommend extremely traditional practices regarding women. This has great implications for women because religious law (called *shari'ah* or *sharia*) is based on the Hadith.

> "In tandem with mass female education and the entry of women into the formal work force, the expanded activities of women's organizations will be the strongest challenge to patriarchy, the neopatriarchal state, and the Islamist agenda."
> *Valentine Mogahadam*

Islam is the fastest growing religion in the world. It originated in the Middle East and is now a major religion not only there, but also in Asia and Africa. Although **Muslims** throughout the world identify the Koran as their major religious text and are expected to observe the Five Pillars of Islam, Islam and its impact on women is not the same everywhere. Some countries, to counter "Westernization," have embraced "Islamization." Adherents of these movements reject the "fundamentalist" label and call themselves "Islamists." **Islamists** often seek governments that rule according to shari'ah. However, they base their laws on ahadith that restrict women's rights since women's emancipation is associated with Westernization. This trend has been seen in many Muslim countries including Pakistan, Algeria, Nigeria, Yemen, and Iran. For instance, it was under shari'ah, adopted by Nigeria in 1999, that Amina Lawal was sentenced to death by stoning for having sex when she was unmarried. Another especially extreme example is Afghanistan under the Taliban. Women were relegated entirely to domestic roles and girls were not allowed to go to school. In public, women had to wear the *burqua,* a cumbersome tent-like garment that completely covered them so they could not tempt men (they could peer out only through a small, screened area around their eyes). The governments of other Muslim countries, like Syria and Turkey, do not base law on Islamic texts and women have greater freedom (Moghadam, 2003).

Many Muslims feel that relative to other religions, Islam is favorable to women. Muhammad abolished practices such as female infanticide, slavery, and levirate (the requirement that a widow marry her husband's brother). He also guaranteed women the right to inherit and bequeath property. He even said, "Men and women are equal as two teeth on a comb." Women also were important in the development of Islam. Khadija, his first wife, was a successful international trader, fifteen years his senior, and was the first person to accept his prophetic mission. Women also served in key spiritual leadership roles in early Islam. After Khadija's death, Muhammad married A'isha and clearly said that she was to be accepted as an authority on the ahadith ascribed to him (Hassan, 2003). She, and her daughter, Fatima, carried the word of Muhammad long after his death. Women's authority as scholars and teachers of Islam was accepted and respected in early Islam (Shaaban, 1995). Rabi'a, a female saint is also an important figure in early Islam.

For centuries, Muslim women enjoyed greater rights and assumed a wider variety of roles than other women (Moghadam, 2003; Shaaban, 1995). This is ironic given that many Muslims now use the Koran to justify men's superiority and women's relegation to the domestic sphere. For instance, the following passage is popularly interpreted as textual proof that men are superior to women:

> Men shall protect and maintain women because God has made some of them excel others, and because they support them from their means. Therefore the righteous women are obedient, guarding the intimacy which God would have them guard. As for those women whose rebellion you justly fear, admonish them first; then leave their beds; then beat them. Then if they obey you, seek no harm against them for God is most High, Exalted, Great.

Another Koran verse, "Tell the believing women to lower their gaze and be modest, and to display of their adornment only that which is apparent, and to draw their veils over their bosoms" is used by some Muslims to justify the seclusion of women (called *purdah*) and the veiling of women.

In Islam women and men show their devotion to God in distinctly different ways. Women play an important role in the practice of religious rituals in the home. Also, unlike men, many women show devotion through Islamic dress. Some wear the *hijab,* a headscarf that allows no hair to show (sometimes called a veil), or the *abaya,* a long dress or coat and a headscarf. (It should be noted that controversy about whether Islam truly calls for veiling has occurred for over 100 years. Although there are clearly cases where Islamic dress has been oppressively imposed on women, some women choose it as an expression of faith and appreciate that it frees them from sexual objectification.) For women, there are also ritual ways of washing after menstruation and after sex. Also, in contrast to men, menstruation restricts women's participation in some "public" religious practices. Because menstruation is considered a kind of pollution, women are not allowed to enter mosques or touch the Koran until their period is over and they have taken a ritual bath. Mosques are also segregated by gender so that men and women are not distracted from prayer. Despite women's importance as spiritual leaders in early Islam, there are now few opportunities for women's leadership outside of female groups that worship together. A hierarchy of *mullahs* (low-level religious officials) and *mojaheds* (high-ranking religious officials) serve as religious leaders and with only a few exceptions worldwide, these are men (Peach, 2003).

Many Muslim women are concerned about Islamist movements and the reduction of women's rights in the name of Islam. They take action locally and transnationally. Moghadam (2003) describes many of these efforts. For instance, Women Living Under Muslim Laws is an international solidarity

"If women's rights are a problem for some modern Muslim men, it is neither because of the Koran nor the Prophet, nor the Islamic tradition, but simply because those rights conflict with the interests of a male elite."
Fatima Mernissi

network formed in 1984. This transnational network continues to monitor laws affecting Muslim women and publicizes gender-related acts of violence and oppression. The Algerian feminist organization, Rassemblement Algerien des Femmes Democrates (RAFD), formed in 1993, is an example of local action against Islamist movements. In 1994, they organized a protest involving tens of thousands Algerian women. They were responding to increased violence against women. Unveiled women, women living alone, and feminist activists were being attacked and in some cases killed, apparently with the support of the government.

Because Muslim feminists' efforts for gender equality are often greeted with charge that they are "Westernized" and untrue to Islam, many ground their arguments in Islam rather than the language of human rights or social justice values (Mogahadam, 2003). Some activists work for women's literacy, feeling strongly that women's dependence on men for the interpretation of texts interferes with their ability to know their rights under Islam. Egyptian feminist Leila Ahmed (2002, p. 120) put it this way: "Just because they were powerful, privileged in their societies and knew how to write, does this mean they have the right to forever to tell us what Islam is or what the rules should be?" As Nilofar Ahmad, the director of Daughters of Islam, a women's organization in Pakistan, said, "If I have any message for Muslim women it is that they must study their religion for themselves, learn what it really says, not accept someone else's idea. Only then will they be able to fight for their rights with the very weapon currently used against them—the Koran" (in Goodwin, 1994, p. 75). Those seeking an Islam more favorable to women emphasize the religious heritage of Islam and that Muhammad intended equality and dignity for women as well as men (Hassan, 1991, 1999, 2003; Mernissi, 1987). They point to Khadija, Ai'sha, Fatima, and Rabi'a, early leaders of Islam. Muslim feminist theologians such as Riffa Hassan of Pakistan (1999; 2003) provide alternate interpretations of apparently sexist passages from the Koran and draw attention to passages that clearly do not distinguish between women and men in Islam. Box 8.5 profiles Shirin Ebadi of Iran who in 2003 won the Nobel Peace Prize for her work for women's rights and democracy in Iran. She exemplifies those devout Muslim women who use the Koran to show that Islam is compatible with women's rights.

Judaism

Judaism is among the world's oldest religions. By 700 C.E., the Jewish tradition achieved most of the major features that it has today (Peach, 2002). Judaism is a strongly textual religion and studying sacred texts is very important. Of the world's major religious traditions, some consider Judaism as possibly the most sexist (Gross, 1996; Heschel, 2003). This distinction stems from the strong masculine image of God (Yahweh), the paucity of female images in Judaism, the specific sexism of some religious texts, and because women are often excluded from the study of important texts, from leadership positions in

"What is it after all that Jewish women seek? They do not ask to be excused or exempt. They do not wish to turn their backs on the tradition, to wash their hands of it and walk away. Rather, they desire to enter it more fully. They long to share a greater part of the tradition, to partake of its wealth of knowledge, to delight in the richness of ritual. For these reasons, their efforts should be welcomed, not scorned."
Blu Greenberg

BOX 8.5   *Activist Profile: Shirin Ebadi of Iran*

Shirin Ebadi is the first Iranian and the first Muslim woman to win the Nobel Peace Prize. A lawyer, Ebadi became Iran's first female judge in 1970 and in 1980s began battling Islamists regarding the rights of women and children. Ebadi defended many of the democratic activists that protested against the government in 1999 and served jail time for publicizing evidence that the government attacked pro-democracy forces. She has been instrumental in the successful drive to get women to elect candidates favorable to women's equality, including President Mohammad Khatami in 1997. Ebadi grounds her arguments for women's equality in the law and in the Koran. She insists that the true spirit of the Koran is consistent with women's rights.

_____

Source: Moaveni and Rotella, 2003.

the faith, and from participating in important rituals. However, Judaism is not monolithic and in practice the effects of this religion on women vary dramatically depending on whether you refer to Orthodox, Reform, Conservative, or Reconstructionist Judaism. Orthodox Judaism is the oldest and most prominent as well as the most traditional regarding women's roles, whereas Reconstructionist Judaism is the most progressive in regards to women's equality.

The two most important Jewish texts are the *Torah* (the first five chapters of the Old Testament), and the *Talmud* (a sixty-three volume of legal and theological teachings centering on the meaning of the Torah and the practice of Judaism). The keeping of the Torah's commandments is the pride of Jewish life, yet very few of the 613 religious injunctions in the Torah apply to women (Carmody, 1994). The central concern of the *mitzvot*, the commandments of the Bible and the Talmud, is the religious life of Jewish men (Heschel, 2003). The Talmud generally restricts women's study of the Torah and their public religious worship, and parts also portray women as sexual temptresses who distract men from prayer (Heschel, 2003).

Judaism is also based on various other texts, stories, and prayers not found in the Bible and these often contain negative images concerning women. For instance, a legend from *Genesis Rabbah* in the Midrash (a record of rabbis' biblical exegeses from 200–600 C.E.) explains that menstruation is one of women's punishments for Eve's sins (Schulman, 1974). One Orthodox Jewish prayer is the male's daily morning prayer: "Blessed art thou, O Lord our God, King of the Universe, who has not made me a woman." Heschel (2003) points out that although there are Jewish prayers for all sorts of bodily experiences, there is no prayer for giving birth. She provides this as an example of how the theological literature of Judaism was composed by men concerned primarily with the religious life of men, not women.

Traditionally, Judaism has strongly delineated between the roles of women and men within the faith. This is still true of Orthodox Judaism, which requires much studying and praying on the part of men. However, these activities can interfere with the running of the household. Therefore, women are excluded from the majority of religious activities that take place outside of the home. The spiritual domain belongs to men; women's participation is through following the laws required to ensure the ritual purity of their homes. These included keeping the laws of family purity such as the ritual bath seven days after menstruation, preparing kosher food and doing the ritual work for home-centered religious holidays and the weekly Sabbath dinner. In Orthodox Judaism, women do not count as members of the *minyan,* the quorum of ten males required for public religious services. Women are also segregated from men in orthodox synagogues. Orthodox Judaism also does not permit the ordination of women as rabbis.

Orthodox Judaism is the only form of Judaism that still prevents women from leading services. Women can't lead services in part because they are not allowed to read from the Torah. Indeed, the Talmud (the sixty-three volume explanation of the Torah) says: "Let the words of Torah rather be destroyed by fire than imparted to women." At the Wailing Wall in Israel, Orthodox Jewish men will not worship beside women and in 1994, the Israeli Supreme Court dismissed a petition requesting that women be allowed to pray out loud at the wall. The petition was viewed by religious authorities as an outrageous act of rebellion and a usurpation of the male claim to exclusive communion with God (Shalev, 1995). In 1997, a group of Conservative and Reform Jewish women and men carried a Torah scroll to the wall to worship together. They were pelted by bags of stones and excrement hurled by Orthodox Jews shouting "Nazis! Nazis!" ("World in Brief," 1997).

Some Jewish women do not necessarily see women's separate religious role as lesser, feeling that women's private sphere religious responsibilities connect them closely to their religion. However, because prayer and study are at the heart of traditional Judaism, many Jewish women see women's exclusion from these activities as rendering women subordinate and inferior (Umansky, 1999). Over the last thirty years, Jewish feminists have successfully pressed for changes that would grant them greater permission to participate in the public sphere of religious life (Heschel, 2003). In the United States, where the greatest number of Jews live, women participate equally in most non-Orthodox synagogues. The reform, reconstructionist, and conservative Jewish traditions now permit women to be rabbis and cantors (directors of music and prayer in the synagogue), although it should be noted that they still face sexism in hiring and promotion. In Israel, however, Orthodox Judaism is the official state religion and most synagogues exclude women from leadership positions and active participation in worship, and still segregate females and males (Peach, 2002). Orthodox Judaism also prevails in Europe (Heschel, 2003).

Jewish theologian Judith Plaskow (1991) once said "Half of Jews have been women, but men have been defined as normative Jews, while women's

> "The fact that, in traditional Judaism, women are not counted in a *minyan* (quorum required for public prayeer) or called to the Torah amounts to our exclusion from the public religious realm."
> *Judith Plaskow*

voices and experiences are largely invisible in the record of Jewish belief and experience that has come down to us. Women have lived Jewish history and carried its burdens, but women's perceptions and questions have not given form to the scripture, shaped the direction of Jewish law, or found expression in liturgy" (p. 1). Jewish feminists seek to remedy these shortcomings. They try to change masculinist religious language, for example by changing "Blessed Are You, Lord Our God, King of the Universe" to "Let us bless the source of life," and adding the names of the foremothers Sarah, Rebecca, Leah, and Rachel to those of the forefathers Abraham, Isaac, and Jacob in Jewish prayer books (Cantor, 1995; Gross, 1996; Umanksy, 1999). They have created feminist liturgies and rituals (Heschel, 2003; Umansky, 1999). They have looked to history for evidence women held important roles as prophets, judges, and leaders during early Judaism (Heschel, 2003; Peach, 2002). They point out that the Talmud also contains protections against the exploitation of women and advanced the status of women over what was common when it was written (Heschel, 2003). They emphasize the strong female figures in the Old Testament such as Deborah, Jael (Yael), Esther, and Naomi (see Niditch, 1991 for a discussion). They pressure rabbinic authorities to change religious laws detrimental to women such as the one that says only a husband can initiate divorce (Umansky, 1999). With the exception of Orthodox Judaism, they have brought about profound changes in Judaism.

Christianity

Christianity arose out of Judaism around the first century C.E. and is based on the life, death, and resurrection of Jesus of Nazareth. The main text of Christianity is the **Bible,** both the Old and New Testaments. The New Testament tells of Jesus and his followers and was composed between 50 C.E. and 90 C.E., long after Jesus' death (Gerhart, 2003). Most Christians believe that Jesus is the Son of God, and God personified on Earth. Disagreements over biblical interpretation and practice led to two main forms of Christianity, Catholic and Protestant (Peach, 2002). As well there are dozens of different Protestant denominations. In some versions of Christianity, most notably Latin American Roman Catholicism, Jesus' mother, Mary, is an important religious figure and model of womanhood. Mary is also presented as the perfect mother and a spotless virgin, ideals that some Catholic women have noted are difficult to live up to (Cisernos, 1996; Drury, 1994). There are also a number of female saints in Catholicism.

The different forms of Christianity vary considerably in their promotion of patriarchy; some are far more liberal about women's roles than are others. For instance, evangelical (fundamentalist) Christianity is explicitly antagonistic to feminism and promotes the traditional patriarchal family (Rose, 1999). The Catholic Church also emphasizes women's role as wife and mother. The official position of the Catholic Church is to prohibit abortion, contraception, sterilization, to limit divorce and remarriage, and to deny the rights of gays and lesbians, although many Catholics do not agree (Kissling,

Elizabeth Cady Stanton (1815–1902), one of the founders of the American women's movement, wrote and lectured on a variety of women's issues, including religion. Her *Women's Bible*, published in 1895, was the major nineteenth-century feminist interpretation of the Bible.

"The Christian tradition is by no means bereft of elements which foster genuine experiences and intimations of transcendence. The problem is that their liberating potential is choked off in the surrounding atmosphere of the images, ideas, values, and structures of patriarchy."
Mary Daly

1999). Many Christian denominations with more traditional views of women rely heavily on canonical scripture and use a literal hermeneutic (they read the Bible as the literal word of God). Scriptural content regarding women's roles is seen as God's intent for women rather than as a reflection of the historical times in which the scriptures were written. Other Christian denominations, such as the Episcopal Church, do not look at the canon this way and are decidedly more progressive regarding women's roles.

It should be noted that there were a handful of nineteenth-century Christian movements in the United States that challenged conventional notions of the family and of men and women's roles. These include the Oneida community, the Shakers, Christian Science, and the Theosophy movement. Some scholars suggest that these movements and the large numbers of women who joined them arose in part out of a rebellion against women's lower status in Protestant churches and American culture (Gross, 1996). Women founded several of these, such as the Christian Science movement and the Theosophy movement.

Because the Bible uses masculine God-language and the majority of stories are the stories of men, many feminists view the Bible as a patriarchal document of a patriarchal society (although this does not necessarily mean that they recommend its complete abandonment). For instance, in Genesis (2:24), Eve is created as a companion ("help-meet") to Adam from his rib. This part of the story is often used to legitimate a husband's power over his wife in the most persuasive of ways—it is presented as divinely ordained. The story of Adam and Eve's fall from grace (Gen. 1:3) is frequently cited by feminist theologians as one of the most influential biblical stories affecting women's status because it has so often been used to justify women's subordination to men. Here, Eve is punished for eating from the tree of knowledge of good and evil. She is responsible for human's banishment from paradise, and because of her transgression, God tells her, "in sorrow thou shalt bring forth children; and thy desire shall be to thy husband" (Gen. 3:16).

Christian and Catholic feminists sometimes refer to the barriers in the way of women's progression through the church hierarchy as the "stained glass ceiling." In the late 1960s and early 1970s, feminists pointed out how males monopolized all visible roles in Christianity beyond singing in the choir, baking, and teaching young children (Gross, 1996). Activism from this time on has led to the ordination of women and to the occupation by women of other church positions traditionally held by males, such as deacon. In the 1990s, women made up more than one-third of the student body at theological seminaries (Gross, 1996). But, change has been uneven (Eck & Jain, 1987). For instance, the Lutheran Church of America, the United Church of Christ, the United Methodist Church, the Presbyterian Church, and the Episcopal Church, all ordain women. The United Methodist has ordained over 5,000 women, more than any other church. However, despite the removal of official barriers to ordination in many Christian denominations and the surge of women graduating from seminaries, women are still only 21 percent of clergy leading mainline Protestant congregations. Many still find that they are confined to lower status positions such as assistant or associate pastor (Duin, 2001; Sullins, 2000).

There are Christian churches that still do not ordain women, including the Latter-day Saints (Mormons), the Anglican Church, and the Catholic Church. Those opposed to the ordination of women often point to 1 Timothy 2:12 which states that women should not teach or usurp the authority of men (Duin, 2001). All women in the Catholic Church are laity, including nuns, because ordination to the clerical state is denied to women. Pope John Paul II defended this on the grounds that Jesus had no women among his twelve apostles and that because Jesus is male, only another male may represent him. However, approximately 4 percent of Catholic churches are led by nuns or female lay ministers who are permitted to do everything but deliver the sacraments.

Ruether (1999) outlines Christian feminist reformist efforts in all regions of the world. In addition to trying to break the stained glass ceiling and develop gender-inclusive liturgical language, Christian feminist theologians reexamine Christian texts and history to reveal those aspects that support women's equality. They refer to the Bible to show that Jesus is portrayed as freely talking to women, assigning them roles in his parables, and thinking of them as good friends and followers (Gross, 1996). They translate and interpret ancient documents that provide less sexist versions of biblical stories (Arthur, 1987). They point out that Jesus' role as the Son of God was first revealed to a woman as was his resurrection. They point to passages such as the one where the apostle Paul said, "There is neither Jew nor Greek, there is neither slave nor free, there is neither male nor female; for you are all one in Christ Jesus" (Gal. 3:28). They emphasize that women were major figures in the founding and spread of Christianity in its early years, and provide evidence that women were among Jesus' disciples (Fiorenza, 1979; French, 1992; Gerhart, 2003; Stark, 1995).

Christian feminist theologians also reinterpret biblical literature. For example, they show how the story of Adam and Eve can be reread in a way that is not hostile to women (Trible, 1973). Asian Christian and Latin American Christian "Mariologists" reclaim and redefine Mary, the mother of Jesus Christ, as a model of liberation, suffering, and struggle (Gebara & Bingemer, 1994; Singapore Asian Christian Women's Conference, 1994).

Sonia Johnson (1936–) was excommunicated from the Mormon Church for supporting the Equal Rights Amendment in 1979. Despite this, she founded Mormons for ERA and in 1981 wrote about her experiences in the book *From Housewife to Heretic.*

Revolutionary Feminist Theology

Some feminists question that equality for women can be found through revision of the world's major religions. They believe that the essential core of the world's major religions is so fundamentally sexist that reform efforts are all but hopeless. One example is Daphne Hampson of Britain who worked tirelessly for reform in the Church of England. The resistance she faced eventually convinced her that that Christianity was incompatible with feminism. Hampson (1987; 1990) concludes that real equality for women cannot come from the Christian church because it is based on religious texts from the past that are, for the most part, supportive of leaving gender relations the way they are. The medium, she says, is the message, and the Bible is not read as just any book but rather as one that conveys what is normative for humans and how we should think about God. She notes that it is clear that the biblical language for God is male (he is Father, King, Lord, Judge) and that women are, in the biblical world, subordinate to men. As Daly (1971) says, if God in *his* heaven is a *father* ruling *his* people, then it is in the nature of things and according to divine plan and the order of the universe that society be male dominated.

Seeking to reconcile their beliefs in God with their beliefs in women's equality, these feminists choose to look at God differently. For instance, Daly (1971) calls for a recasting of the God concept away from the "divine patriarch" and toward something that is transcendent and immanent yet not reducible or able to be represented by such expressions as *person, father, supreme being*. A God that is not objectified in this way cannot be easily used to legitimate oppression, she argues. Or as Hampson (1987) says, women are at a very creative point and have the possibility of creating a new feminist spirituality that conceives of God as spirit who moves among us, between us, and within us.

Some feminists who believe that the world's major religions are fundamentally sexist work to create new traditions. For example, a number of feminist theologians have made efforts to develop a new textual base for religion that makes women's experience visible and central. Rosemary Ruether's efforts are particularly well known in Christian feminist theology. In her 1985 book *Womanguides: A Reader Toward a Feminist Theology,* she looks to the past for sources of a **revolutionary feminist theology** and begins the process of developing new texts. She notes that although there is no canon of an alternative feminist religion of ancient times, we are not left without sources for our own experience in the past. Women, she says, can read between the lines of patriarchal texts and find fragments of their own experience that were not completely erased. They can also find, outside of canonized texts, remains of alternative communities that reflect either the greater awe and fear of female power denied in later patriarchy or questionings of male domination in groups in which women did enter into critical dialogue (Ruether, 1985).

Some revolutionary feminist theologians favor an entirely new canon, one not based on existing religions but based on women's experience. Theologians such as Daly (1974) feel that the reformation of patriarchal religion is not enough and is doomed to fail given that these religions are the products of men and are designed to serve the needs of sexist societies. In general, revolutionary feminist theologians favor grounding a new theology in women's experience. Feminist experience, traditional women's experience, women's experience past and present are all potential starting points for a new feminist theology. Recurrent themes are women and nature, the significance of community with other women, women-centered stories and rituals, and the use of female imagery and symbolism (Christ & Plaskow, 1979).

"Jesus Christ cannot symbolize the liberation of women. A culture that maintains a masculine image for its highest divinity cannot allow its women to express themselves as the equals of men."
Naomi Goldenberg

"There is no way to find any feminist value in the Qur'an. If people say it is found, then either they lie, or they try to interpret the verses differently to make it suitable with the present day."
Feminist Bengali Physician and Writer Taslima Nasrin

Revolutionary feminist theologians share the belief that we must look to women's experiences as the basis of a new women's religion. However, they differ as to whether they look for this female experience in the present or in the past. Daly (1974) is an example of looking to the present. For example, she emphasizes that the bonding phenomenon among women has deeply spiritual dimensions and is an important source of a new women's religion. For her, the unfolding of women's consciousness is an intimation of the endless unfolding of God. Revolutionary feminists of this sort propose that this unfolding occur in a community of women who use dreams, stories, and women's literature to recover and discover women's experience.

Other revolutionary feminist theologians locate women's experiences in paganism, an umbrella term for a wide variety of pre- and nonbiblical religions that include female images of the divine (Gross, 1996). These ancient religions are rich sources of positive female imagery and have the advantage of being rooted in tradition (Christ & Plaskow, 1979). According to Gross (1976), collectively, these groups are known as the **feminist spirituality movement.** However, others prefer the term **women's spirituality movement.** Many of these religions fall under the heading of **goddess spirituality** since the focus is on goddess worship, although there is a lot of variation in how these groups envision the goddess (Griffin, 2003; King, 1987). Writers such as Starhawk (1979), Eisler (1987), Gimbutas (1991), and edited works such as that by Olsen (1983) point to archeological artifacts and myths showing the important role of the goddess in early religion and civilization. For instance, feminine sacred beings (goddesses) were popular in the Greco-Roman traditions that co-existed with early Christianity and remain common in many indigenous African and Native American traditions as well as in Hinduism (Gross, 1996). This quote from Starhawk (1979) gives us a feel for the important role of the goddess in women-centered religion:

> The importance of the Goddess symbol for women cannot be overstressed. The image of the Goddess inspires women to see ourselves as divine, our bodies as sacred, the changing phases of our lives as holy, our aggression as healthy, our anger as purifying, and our power to nurture and create, but also to limit and destroy when necessary, as the very force that sustains all life. Through the Goddess, we can discover our strength, enlighten our minds, own our bodies, and celebrate our emotions. We can move beyond narrow, constricting roles, and become whole. (p. 9)

Wicca is a form of spirituality based on ancient wiccan (witchcraft) traditions (note: this type of witchcraft is not to be associated with Satanism and devil worship). There are numerous versions of Wicca, some of which are more explicitly feminist than are others. Feminist wicca is rich in group and meditative rituals that emphasize women's connectedness with the earth and nature. In the United States, Starhawk is one of the best-known feminist

"Womanist is to feminist as purple is to lavender."
Alice Walker, African American writer and womanist

spiritualists and has written several feminist Wiccan guides. Starhawk (1979) emphasizes female- and earth-centered, nature-oriented worship that venerates the goddess and that flourished before the advent of Christianity. One of the founders of Dianic witchcraft, Zsuzsanna Budapest, a Hungarian immigrant to the United States, is also an important person in the Wicca tradition. Vivianne Crowley is another important figure in the modern development of Wicca. Her nine books, her teaching, and organizing efforts have been especially influential in Europe (Griffin, 2003).

Those in the Wiccan movement often emphasize that in the years 1560–1760, ancient witchcraft traditions were eradicated by the Christian church through a campaign of persecution that constituted an attack on women's power. Historian Anne Barstow (1994) says that approximately 100,000 women were killed in European witch hunts during this time period and 200,000 were accused. Old single women, seen as burdens, were especially likely to be accused, as were outspoken women and those who stepped out of the traditional female role. Accusations of witchcraft are still used today against women who displease others and are too powerful. For instance, Amoah (1987) writes about how witchcraft accusation is used in contemporary Ghana to deal with women's power. Women who are educated and successful in business are especially likely to be accused. In the United States, politician Pat Robertson declared that supporting the Equal Rights Amendment was a "socialist, anti-family, political movement that encourages women to leave their husbands, kill their children, *practice witchcraft,* destroy capitalism, and become lesbians" (Barstow, 1994 [italics added])!

Barstow suggests that the European and American witch hunts had a number of effects on women's power. One is that fear of being accused of witchcraft kept women quiet and obedient. Another is that the campaign took away a source of power for women. Previously, witches had a lot of power as the village healers who delivered babies, performed abortions, set bones, and prescribed and administered herbal medicines. The attack on witchcraft had the effect of taking the practice of medicine away from women. The European and American witch hunts also essentially destroyed the religion of witchcraft. Indeed, remnants of that smear campaign remain today in common perceptions of witches as casting evil spells and worshiping Satan, although these were not part of the religion of witchcraft. For this reason, women from this tradition often call their religion the **womanspirit movement** rather than witchcraft.

Conclusion

This chapter suggested that the world's religions play a role in women's oppression, yet your experiences with religious women may suggest that these women do not seem to feel oppressed. This could be due to theological illiteracy in the sense that women may not have the tools to critique traditional theologies. It could be because they accept their religion's portrayal of the gender order. Or, as Carmody (1989) suggests, it may be because, in practice, women do not always accept the designations of their nature and roles as laid out in their religions' orthodox teachings. For instance, she says that Hindu women may believe that it is not necessary to be reborn as a man to gain salvation, despite what they are taught. Christian women denied the right to be ministers can take pride in the other work they do for the church and know that the church is losing out on some great leadership. Women also adapt by developing their own rituals conducted by and for women. For instance, an important part of the lives of many Muslim women is the practice of healing and semi-magical practices (Smith, 1987).

The Jewish theologian Judith Plaskow (1987) also points out that traditional religious women do not necessarily experience themselves as oppressed. Religious women often have a sense of importance in their religions from the knowledge that without them, those parts of religious traditions that take place in the home would not occur. Women's religious roles frequently provide the support necessary for the growth and maintenance of the tradition (Peach, 2002). Sered (1994) also maintains that even in many highly patriarchal cultures women sacralize their domestic lives through holiday food preparation. In many cultures, food is one of the few resources controlled by women, and it plays a central role in women's religious lives (Sered, 1994).

Many religious women maintain that just because women's role in religion is largely a private one, it is not a lesser one. Ahmed (2002) suggests that women's limited public role in Islam means that "women's Islam" is more spiritual and mystical than the "men's Islam" that focuses on religious texts and what some male religious leader says. It is also interesting that in virtually every culture the heart of the religious tradition, at the local level and in the home, is performed, maintained, and transmitted by women (Eck & Jain, 1987). For instance, in most American Christian homes, it is the mother who gets the children ready for church and who prepares all religious holiday meals. Plaskow (1987) suggests that one benefit of the sex-segregated nature of religion is that it provides women with a common life, or **womanspaces,** where power and integrity come from their shared experiences and visions as women. For instance, in India it is not uncommon for a married woman to live with her in-laws, and a household may consist of a number of sisters-in-law as well. Together these women run the household, and this domestic space is frequently a source of feminine support and friendship. Indeed, most of us can remember our mothers spending many hours working together with other women preparing for religious celebrations. Many of us have done this ourselves and can recall the special times spent with other women as we shared intimacies as we worked to prepare for elaborate meals and rituals (and then cleaned up afterward).

Looked at this way, women's differing role in religion does not seem quite so bad. After all, the practice of religion would grind to a halt without the work of women, and women do have some special times with other women as a result of the sex-segregated nature of most religions. However, as Plaskow cautions, perhaps these womanspaces are simply preserving an unjust system by rendering it bearable and providing shared self-validation. Also, as Eck and Jain (1987) note, here again we confront an old and pervasive disjunction: the indomitable presence and influence of women at the domestic level and the virtual absence of women at the public level. The problem with this is twofold. First is that the appearance of this arrangement in religious hierarchies suggests its appropriateness in other life arenas. In other words, it is as if this arrangement is sacred and ordained by God. As Daly (1971) suggests, the situation provides images of the rightness of male rule. A second problem is what it communicates to women about themselves. A number of people suggest that the exclusion of women from religion's public spaces conditions women to view themselves as inferior to men and to accept subordination. For instance, the French feminist Simone de Beauvoir (in Daly, 1985) writes:

> God's representatives on earth: the pope, the bishop (whose ring one kisses), the priest who says Mass, he who preaches, he before whom one kneels in the secrecy of the confessional—all these are men . . . . The Catholic religion among others exerts a most confused influence upon the young girl.

Likewise, South African Anglican Bishop Desmond Tutu once said when speaking about resistance to the ordination of women into the priesthood, "A child of God subjected to that kind of treatment, actually gets to doubt that he is, or she is, a child of God" (in Hampson, 1987, p. 140).

Religion plays a paradoxical role in the lives of women. In some ways it has contributed to women's oppression. In other ways religion often renders women's suffering more bearable by suggesting that the traditional women's role is a form of worship that will be amply rewarded at some later date. Eck and Jain (1987) note yet another paradox. They suggest that religion is both a problem (or *the* problem) where its structures of dominance have oppressed women and a solution where its vision of liberation or equality has generated powerful movements of social change. They also note that the same religion may be both a problem and a solution. Mosse (1993) makes a similar point when she says that although religion has been used to oppress women, it has also brought women together to fight oppression. She provides the example of Rigoberta Menchu, an Indian Guatemalan peasant woman who is an important leader in her country, and quotes from her autobiography (*I, Rigoberta Menchu,* 1984):

> At the end of 1977, I decided to join a more formal group—a group of peasants in Heuheutenango . . . and yet, I still hadn't reached the rewarding stage of participating fully, as an Indian first, then as a woman, a peasant, a Christian, in the struggle of my people. That's

when I started to get more involved. . . . I began traveling to different areas, discussing everything. . . . Why do they reject us? Why is the Indian not accepted? Why is it that the land used to belong to us?. . . Why don't outsiders accept Indian ways?. . . I started to work as an organiser. No one taught me to organise because, having been a catechist, I already knew. We began forming groups of women who wanted to join the struggle. . . . Our main weapon. . . is the Bible. We began to study the Bible as a text which represented each one of us. We tried to relate them to our Indian culture. We took the example of Moses for the men, and we have the example of Judith, who was a very famous woman in her times. She fought hard for her people. . . . We feel it is the duty of Christians to create the kingdom of God on earth. . . . This kingdom will exist only when we all have enough to eat, when our children, brothers, parents don't have to die from malnutrition.

As this chapter ends, women's diversity must once again be acknowledged. In this case, the last thirty years have brought forth a multiplicity of feminist theologies. Feminist theological voices have been heard in North America and Europe since the late 1960s, but Third World feminist theologies and feminist theologies of women of color are more recent and much less known (King, 1994). King (1994), in a book on feminist theology from the Third World, notes the ways in which First World feminist theology and **Third World feminist theology** are similar and different. As King views it, feminist theology is in general an advocacy theology concerned with the liberation of women from oppression, guided by the principle of seeking to achieve the full humanity of women.

Liberation theologies are activist theologies focused on justice and equality for all people. The above paragraph from Rigoberta Menchu is an example of liberation theology because religion is used to motivate struggles for social justice. Feminist liberation theologies respond to not only women's marginalization as women, but their marginalization due to nationality, culture, race, and economics. In the Third World context, feminist theology is much more of a liberation theology, as it develops where the oppression of women and the denial of their full humanity is often much greater and women face multiple oppressions based on race, economics, and gender.

This is also true of theologies developed in the First World by women from traditionally oppressed groups. For instance, **Womanist theology** is a newly developing African American Christian feminist theology. Womanist theology brings Black women's social, religious, and cultural experiences into the theological discourse (Williams, 1994). Womanist theology is a liberation theology in that it emphasizes justice for women and the oppressed and is envisioned as an instrument for theological and social change. Likewise, *Mujerista* **theology,** a Latin American feminist theology, has as its goal the liberation of Hispanic women and all people and the changing of church

---

BOX 8.6   *Firsts for Women in Religion in the United States*

1970   First female Lutheran minister—Elizabeth Platz

1972   First female Reform rabbi—Sally Preisand

1974   First Reconstructionist rabbi—Sandy Eisenberg

1976   Episcopal Church votes to allow the ordination of women as bishops and priests

1980   First female Methodist bishop—Majorie Swank Matthews

1984   First female African American Methodist bishop—Leotine Kelly

1985   First female Conservative rabbi—Amy Eilberg

1989   First female Episcopal bishop—Barbara Harris

1991   First female Lutheran bishop—April Ulring Larson

1993   First female Diocesan Episcopal bishop—Mary Adelia McLeod

1994   First female senior rabbi of a large Reform congregation—Laura Geller

1994   First Catholic altar girls

1996   First female evangelical minister in the Christian Reformed Church—Lesli van Milligen

1996   First chairwoman of the Methodist World Council—Frances Alguire

---

structures such that Hispanic women may participate fully in them (Isasi-Diaz, 1994). *Mujerista* theology also emphasizes the discovery and affirmation of God in Hispanic women's daily lives and communities.

Once again it is important to acknowledge women's activism, for it is through such activism that progress toward gender equality in religion is made. In virtually every religious tradition women have called their lower status into question. The last thirty years of the twentieth century evidenced remarkable change toward greater gender equality in many of the world's religions. (Box 8.6 gives some examples of important firsts for women in U.S. religions.)

Women who question patriarchy within their religions and work actively to promote change show great courage. Calling for equality is especially difficult for religious women who have been socialized to think that virtuous religious women are quiet and long-suffering. Those who do this work face many obstacles. They must work to change old and entrenched organizational structures that typically exclude women. Their opponents point to tradition and to religious texts as evidence that things should not change. Calls for equality are also typically met with the response that change represents an assault on the traditional family, and therefore women's equality poses a threat to the religious group's survival. Women calling for change are likely to be ignored, and if they persist, threatened with abandonment or branded as traitors and betrayers to their religious community.

This chapter, like the ones that preceded it, illustrates the persistence and prevalence of patriarchy. It also reminds us of the courage displayed by those who work for change and who defy tradition. Once again there is evidence of positive results from women's activism. This theme is a major focus of the remaining chapters, which center on women's political activities.

Study Questions

1. Why is it difficult to generalize about religion and its effects on women? What features of "fundamentalist" and conservative religious variants contribute to traditional views of women?

2. What are the common feminist critiques of religion?

3. Why do hermeneutics matter in feminist theology?

4. What basic assumptions underlie reformist efforts in feminist theology? What are some common reformist efforts?

5. For each major world religion examined in the chapter, briefly explain whether the canon is supportive of gender equality.

6. For each major world religion examined in the chapter, briefly review the sex segregated religious rituals and practices.

7. What basic assumptions underlie revolutionary feminist theology? Why have some abandoned reformist efforts in favor of new traditions? What are some common features of these new traditions?

8. What are womanspaces? In what way are they beneficial? In what way are they problematic?

9. What are feminist liberation theologies and why have they developed?

Discussion Questions and Activities

1. Are traditional religions (Christianity, Islam, Hinduism, Judaism, and Buddhism) fundamentally sexist or have they merely been misinterpreted? Is it feasible that traditional religions can be reconceived or reinterpreted in a way that permits gender equality? Or will it be necessary for women to develop their own religions in order to achieve equality?

2. Does the use of "He" to refer to God and the exclusion of women from most religious hierarchies condition women to view themselves as inferior to men?

3. Make a list of masculine adjectives that describe God and another list of feminine adjectives that describe God. What does this tell you about your conceptions of God? Is God male?

4. Interview a woman minister or rabbi, a practitioner of feminist spirituality (for instance, a witch), or a traditional religious woman, using questions developed from the chapter.

Activist Websites of Interest

Sawnet: South Asian Women's Network

http://www.umiacs.umd.edu:80/users/sawweb/sawnet/

Sakyadhita, International Association of Buddhist Women

http://www.Hawaii.edu/~tsomo

Jewish Feminist Website

http://www.cddc.ut.edu/feminism/jewam.html

WATER, Women's Alliance for Theology, Ethics, and Ritual

http://www.his.com/~mhunt

Catholic Network for Women's Equality

http://www.sarnia.com/groups/cnwe

Maryam's Net: Muslim Women and Their Islam

http://www.maryams.net

Muslim Women's League

http://www.mwlusa.org

Sisterhood is Global

http://www.sigi.org/index.htm

Informational Websites of Interest

Women and Religion Bibliographies Websites

http://www.academicinfo.net/religwombibs.html

http://www.nd.edu/~archives/lau_bib

Celebration of the Feminine Divine

http://www.acu.edu/academics/cas/music.html

Hulda: Feminist Theology Website
http://www.dike.de/hulda/english.html
Marian Research Center (Studies the role of Mary in Christian life)
http://www.udayton.edu/mary/
Women in African Religions
http://isizoh.net/afrel
Covenant of the Goddess
http://www.pinn.net/~swampy/gdstudy.html

Action Opportunities

1. If you worship regularly as part of an organized religion, lead a scripture study of passages suggestive of women's subordination to men. Be prepared to discuss their textual and historical context and whether they are otherwise consistent with the religion's conception of God.

2. If you are a member of an organized religion and you are dissatisfied with the treatment of women within your tradition, lead a change effort. For instance, you can lead a petition drive in favor of women being allowed to hold positions such as deacon, minister, or bishop or to change liturgical language to be more gender neutral. You can also meet with your rabbi, priest, or minister, or other, and ask that they devote more time to presenting stories about women in the tradition and what they have to teach us.

3. Check the chapter websites for feminist activist efforts specific to your religion.

4. Go to http://www.Amnesty.org and http://www.HRW.org to participate in a letter-writing campaign for cases involving the persecution of women due to Sharia.

5. Do something to counteract religious conservatives' assault on women's rights in your country or community. Write letters to editors and your representatives in Congress about a particular policy area of concern to you such as the restriction of women's reproductive rights or the prohibition of sex education. In the United States, People for the American Way (pfaw.org) may help you identify where religious fundamentalists stand on women's issues of concern to you. Enlist progressive clergy to speak out to counter people that use religion to promote gender inequality.

Women in Politics

> Political space belongs to all citizens, but men monopolize it.
>
> —United Nations Human Development Report, 1995

Mary Bourke Robinson, former president of Ireland, United Nations Human Rights Commissioner, and currently executive director of the Ethical Globalization Initiative. Women as national and international leaders are still uncommon. However, women are very political and have a long history of involvement in economic, environmental, revolutionary, and peace and justice movements. LAURENT GILLIERON/AP Photo/Wide World

In their book on women and politics worldwide, Chowdhury and her colleagues (1994) conclude that *in no country do women have political status, access, or influence equal to men's.* The sweep of women's political subordination encompasses the great variety of cultures, economic arrangements, and regimes in which they live (Chowdhury et al., 1994). Over ten years later, this subordination remains true and noteworthy because women's political empowerment is key to gender equality. Women's underrepresentation in politics signifies their continued lower status and perpetuates it by posing a barrier to women's issues advocacy. Like the domination of the economic sphere by men, male domination of the political sphere both reflects and perpetuates women's lower status and power.

When people think of politics, they often think of activities such as registering to vote, voting, running for and holding political office, and lobbying elected officials. The political sphere is also typically viewed as a masculine one and politicians as male. This is not surprising given that the majority of formal political positions continue to be held by men (see Box 9.1, *Women Around the Globe: Political Power Worldwide*). Also, politics are a public activity, and the public sphere is associated with male activities. Add to this that media coverage of politics tends to be almost exclusively focused on male political actors. As well, political science has centered on male political activity and leaders.

A feminist might note several things about these perceptions. First is that the domination of formal politics by men perpetuates the notion that politics are the domain of men and therefore discourages women from participating. This notion is, as Ruth Lister (2003) says, an affront to the ideals of democracy and justice.

It is also important to recognize the domination of formal politics by men and to increase women's representation because laws made by men often do little to address gender inequality. Likewise, policies that explicitly address the needs of women and children are less likely because male lawmakers are often unaware of these needs. Researchers consistently find a positive relationship between the number of female legislators and the amount of legislation favorable to women, children, families, education, and medical and welfare needs (Davis, 1997; O'Regan, 2000; Rule, 1994; Swers, 2002; Thomas, 1994; WEDO, 2003). For instance, women state legislators in the United States are more likely than male legislators to emphasize issues that affect women and children (Beckman & D'Amico, 1995; Swers, 2002). Major childcare and equal rights legislation has passed in Sweden and Norway once women occupied over a third of the seats in parliament (WEDO, 2003). The United Nations estimates that women need to constitute at least 30 percent of a legislative body in order to exert a meaningful influence on politics (UNDP, 1995).

A feminist perspective on politics also recognizes that by limiting our definition of politics to electoral activities and offices, women seem less political

"It is only when there is a critical mass of women in all their diversity in every country of the world in both appointed and elected decision-making positions and in all international bodies, that gender issues will be addressed in the policy agenda and the goals of equality, development, peace and human rights for all can be realized in the 21st century."
Women's Environment and Development Organization (WEDO)

"The gendered division of power makes possible not only the relative denial of formal power to women in the international system but also the exclusion of women's struggles and 'women's issues' from the world politics agenda."
V. Spike Peterson and Anne Sisson Runyan

BOX 9.1   *Women Around the Globe: Political Power Worldwide*

In 2003, worldwide,

- There were twelve female heads of state.

- Of the 179 countries with legislatures, women were leaders of twenty-three legislatures (9.5 percent).

- Women comprised about 14 percent of the membership of national parliaments and congresses.

- The following countries had the highest percentages of women in national legislatures: Rwanda (45 percent), Sweden (45.3 percent), Denmark (38 percent), Finland (37.5 percent), Norway (36.4 percent), Cuba (36 percent), Belgium (34 percent), Costa Rica (35 percent), and the Netherlands (33 percent).

- Industrialized nations do not necessarily exhibit greater gender parity in legislatures: The United States (14 percent), Britain (17 percent), France (11.7 percent) and Japan (10 percent) lag behind many less economically developed countries including Mozambique (30 percent) and Vietnam (27.3 percent).

- Some countries have no women representatives including Bahrain, Kuwait, Micronesia, Palau, Saudi Arabia, Solomon Islands, Tuvalu, and the United Arab Emirates.

Sources: Inter-Parliamentary Union, 2003a; WEDO, 2003.

"50/50 by 2005: Get the Balance Right!"
Campaign Slogan of WEDO's 50/50 Campaign to increase the number of women in formal politics

than they actually are. In fact, if the definition of political activity is broadened to include women's involvement in social movements and protests, women are a lot more political than they appear to be at first glance. As Lister (2003) notes, a distinction should be made between the level of women's political *representation* and women's political *activity.* Women, for instance, have a long history as key players in antiwar and peace movements, revolutionary movements, and economic movements (Peterson & Runyan, 1999). Unfortunately, women's political activity is rarely recognized or documented by political scientists because it is more apt to be in the context of social movements and protests ("power from below"), and politics tend to be narrowly defined in terms of participation in **formal politics** such as representation in elected political bodies ("power from above") (West & Blumberg, 1990). Women, as I've remarked before and will demonstrate in this and the final two chapters, do act politically despite significant obstacles. That so many women overcome the barriers to their participation, at least to some extent, is a testimony to their commitment to the ideals of political citizenship (Lister, 2003). This commitment is especially evident in the sphere of **informal politics,** which include local community-based action and national and international social movements (Lister, 2003). This chapter begins with a consideration of women's participation in formal politics including voting, representation in parliaments and congresses, and women as heads of state. From there, it moves to a discussion of women's participation in social movements and protests (informal politics).

BOX 9.2 *Women Around the Globe:*
A Sampling of Women's Suffrage

Years	Countries
1893–1919	Australia, Canada, Finland, Germany, Greenland, Iceland, New Zealand, Norway, Russia, Sweden, Turkey
1920–1944	Brazil, Burma, Ecuador, France, Ireland, Lithuania, Philippines, Spain, Thailand, United Kingdom, United States
1945–1959	Argentina, Bolivia, Chad, Chile, China, Columbia, Costa Rica, El Salvador, Ethiopia, Guatemala, Honduras, India, Japan, Mali, Mexico, Morocco, Nicaragua, Niger, Pakistan, Portugal, Senegal, Venezuela, Vietnam
1960–1979	Algeria, Angola, Iran, Kenya, Libya, Nigeria, Paraguay, Peru, Sudan, Zaire, Marshall Islands
Since 1980	Hong Kong, Iraq, South Africa, Western Samoa, Vanuatu, Liechtenstein, Central African Republic, Namibia, Samoa, Kazakhstan, Moldova

Source: Inter-Parliamentary Union, 2003a.

Women Voters, Legislators, and Cabinet Members

Voting

Female voting, or **women's suffrage,** was a major aim of the early feminist movement from the mid-1880s through the first half of the twentieth century. Voting rights for women were hard-won, and women activists (suffragettes) were arrested and harassed while demonstrating for this right. In 1907, Finland became the first country to elect women to public office. See Box 9.2, *Women Around the Globe: A Sampling of Women's Suffrage,* for a sampling of countries and the year women's suffrage was attained. Keep in mind though that there were often restrictions on *which* women could vote. For example, Native American women were not allowed to vote until 1924, four years after other American women, and in Australia, White women won the vote in 1902 but Aboriginal women had to wait until 1967 (Seager, 1997). Qatar was one of the last countries to grant women suffrage. On March 8, 1999, International Women's Day, women in Qatar, a prosperous, small country of 150,000 citizens on the Persian Gulf, were permitted to run for political office and to vote for the first time. Today, Kuwait is the only country with elected representatives that denies women voting rights.

Although there is little research on how women vote in comparison to men, there is evidence from a handful of countries (France, Germany, Russia, and the United States) that women, more than men, favor liberal or left-wing parties (Seager, 1997). Public opinion polls in the United States indicate that relative to men, women favor increased social spending and social programs, are more opposed to U.S. military intervention in other countries, and are more supportive of restrictions on firearms (Center for American Women in Politics, 1997).

Voting does not by itself guarantee equality of opportunity in politics (Abukhalil, 1994). In some countries, women's fathers, brothers, or husbands may interfere in their voting choices or discourage them from voting at all. Women's ability to exercise their voting rights freely is also impaired in those countries where there are discrepancies in the adult literacy rates of women and men. Perhaps it is not surprising, then, that in many countries women vote at a lower rate than men. Also, in some countries, voting is a token gesture intended to ratify choices made by tyrannical rulers. In certain countries, women's independent political organizations are not even permitted.

> "We've never been in a democracy, we've always been in a phallocracy."
> *French feminist Françoise Parturier*

Parliaments, Congresses, and Cabinets

Women's voting is only one form of political involvement. Although many years have passed since women in most countries first obtained voting rights, women remain underrepresented in political power positions. Unfortunately, political systems, whatever the ideology and form, rest on the virtual exclusion or marginalization of women from formal politics (Chowdhury et al., 1994). As Rule (1994, p. 15) put it,

> "There is no democracy in our beautifully democratic countries. Why? Women have not the same part in decision making as men have."
> *Vigdis Finnbogadottir, President of Iceland*

> Government of the people, by the people, and for the people—Abraham Lincoln's concept of democracy—is an ideal unachieved in the world. Democracy falls short when women of whatever color or ethnic group cannot vote or cast an effective vote, cannot expect success in electing representatives of their choice or in being elected to the legislative bodies, and have little hope for enactment of laws they believe are critically needed.

> In 1949, Rachel Kagan became the first feminist to be elected to the Israeli Parliament (the Knesset).

Governments are complex organizational structures consisting not only of heads of state but of other formal political actors such as members of **parliaments and congresses.** As is evident in Box 9.1, *Women Around the Globe: Political Power Worldwide,* women only rarely serve as heads of government and are consistently underrepresented in parliaments and congresses. As the Appendix illustrates, on average, women hold approximately 14 percent of formal government positions worldwide. Within parliaments and congresses, women infrequently occupy top leadership positions. They constitute only 9.5 percent of presiding heads of national parliaments or houses and the committees they chair tend to be minor or so-called "women's committees" (Rodriquez, 2003; WEDO, 2003).

> In 1997, Yeh Chin-Fong became the first Taiwanese woman to serve in the important cabinet position of interior minister.

Women are even more rare as cabinet members. **Government cabinets** consist of advisors to the head of state who frequently lead specific government agencies and wield considerable policymaking power. In many countries, cabinet members are called ministers (as in Minister of Finance), but in some, such as the United States, they are called secretaries (as in Secretary of Labor). On average, women hold about 8 percent of cabinet positions worldwide (United Nations, 2000). In most cases, cabinet ministers are drawn from the ranks of parliamentarians, especially those that have served on important committees or who have otherwise distinguished themselves, such as through finesse in parliamentary debate (Davis, 1997). In addition, appointments are often given as rewards for loyal party service. The assignments and positions that lead to cabinet appointments are most often given to men.

This is not to say that there has not been improvement. In 1986, Norway became the first country to have a cabinet with close to half of its members women (Bystydzienski, 1994). An analysis of cabinet appointments in western Europe shows that the number of women in parliamentary cabinets increased from 1968 to 1992 in all of the countries studied, except Portugal (Davis, 1997). There were, however, wide variations across countries and within countries over time (the researcher suggests that this is because cabinet appointments change with administration changes, and some administrations appoint more women than others). In the Nordic countries of Norway, Finland, and Sweden, the representation of women approached parity with men. In contrast, in continental Europe (Austria, Belgium, Germany, France, and the Netherlands), representation ranged between 10 and 20 percent. In the United Kingdom and Spain, the levels of representation were between 5 and 10 percent, and in southern Europe, they were at or below 5 percent. Women are typically appointed to cabinet positions in the areas of family, social affairs, health, and education and rarely to economic and defense positions. For instance, when elected in 1994, President Zedillo of Mexico appointed a record three women to his cabinet but he assigned them to somewhat secondary ministries such as tourism, environment and fisheries, and comptroller (Rodriquez, 2003).

Barriers to Women's Presence in Formal Politics

There are many barriers to women's occupation of formal political posts and these echo the reasons given in Chapter 5 for the glass ceiling: gender stereotypes and leader prototypes, responsibilities to home and family, and organizational practices (see Figure 9.1).

Gender stereotypes and leader prototypes reduce both the supply and the demand for female political leaders. The dominant image of women in most cultures is that of the wife–mother who is competent in the private sphere of life, not the public one. Politics is stereotyped as a male domain, and as part of gender conformity, men are more likely to pursue formal politics than are women. As Peterson and Runyan (1999) suggest, women are socialized into domestic roles that are antithetical to public political sphere activities, and the traits associated with political efficacy (ambition, aggression, competitiveness, authority) are seen as distinctly *un*feminine. The result is that women are not comfortable in conventionally defined politics, and men and women have

In 1997, Madeleine Albright, former U.S. ambassador to the United Nations, became the highest-ranking woman in the history of the U.S. government when she became U.S. secretary of state.

In 1999 Sweden became the first country to have more female than male ministers in the cabinet.

"We have a ghetto in my country called the Ministry of Gender, Labor and Social Development. It has few resources, and five powerful women have been dumped there. So we are saying 'no.' We want to see women having real power—over budgets, over bureaucracies."
Winnie Bayanima, member of the Constituent Assembly in Uganda

"The hand that rocks the cradle may be too tired to rule the world."
Carole Wade and Carol Tavris

"But what is true I think, is that women who want and need a life outside as well as inside the home have a much, much harder time than men because they carry such a heavy double burden . . . and the life of a working mother who lives without the constant presence and support of the father of her children is three times harder than that of any man I have ever met."
Golda Meir, 1975

"A woman's place is in the house, and in the Senate."
American feminist proverb

"If you have only a few women, they are forced to concentrate their efforts in a few areas associated with women, usually education, health and social systems. If you have a large number of deputies and women in power, it is not possible to confine them to traditional women's issues."
Karin Junker, executive board of Germany's Social Democratic Party, member of the European Parliament

FIGURE 9.1 *Obstacles to Women's Presence in Formal Politics*

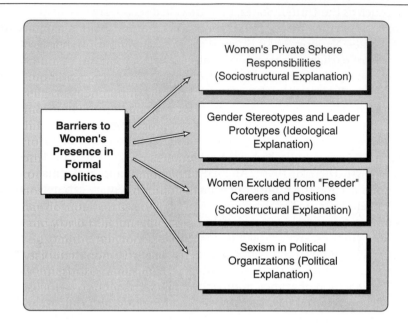

trouble accepting women as political agents (Peterson & Runyan, 1999). Sometimes these types of explanations are called **ideological explanations for gender differences in political representation** because traditional gender ideologies are used to justify women's exclusion from politics. As Paxton and Kunovich (2003) explain, ideological beliefs influence women's choice to pursue politics (thereby affecting supply) and also influence voters' and political parties' support of women candidates (thereby affecting demand).

Sociostructural explanations focus on how the structure of social systems impacts the "supply" of female candidates (Paxton & Kunovich, 2003). For instance, horizontal occupational segregation reduces the pool of women qualified to run for and hold office. In many countries, women have been largely excluded from law schools and high-level military positions and yet most elected politicians are lawyers or former military officers. The jobs that often lead to formal political office are also ones that are gender-typed as male (law, military, career civil service, big business) (Peterson & Runyan, 1999). Women's private sphere roles and responsibilities are another sociostructural barrier to their political participation. When we consider women's paid and unpaid labor, women generally have less time to pursue political careers than men do. Moreover, it is not only women's longer workday that interferes, it is their lack of control over when they will be available and whether (how) family obligations will interfere with political pursuits (Peterson & Runyan, 1999). Combining family responsibilities and political office are largely a problem *for women only;* men are not forced to make these choices because their political activities are considered separate from their domestic relations (Peterson &

Runyan, 1999). As long as the sexual division of labor keeps women tied closely to the private domestic sphere, only a minority of women will be able to enter the formal political sphere (Lister, 2003).

Political explanations emphasize how political systems are often closed to women (Paxton & Kunovich, 2003). The culture and processes of formal political institutions (especially political parties) are major barriers to women's equal participation in institutional politics (Chowdhury et al., 1994). Women, in general, have not been welcome in the fraternity of formal politics. What Chowdhury (1994) says in regard to politics in Bangladesh is true in general: Women's participation in electoral politics is illustrative of male control of party organizations; men have a greater ability to build viable constituency and party support in favor of nominations; women lack access to the kind of money and patronage needed to win elections; and the aggressive electioneering tactics often employed discourage women's entrance into the fray—especially the threat of character assassination and innuendo that is damaging to women's honor. Women experience vertical occupational segregation within political environments when they are assigned to the least powerful positions and committees. In other words, they are often structurally disadvantaged in political organizations by assignments that do not give them the opportunity to garner the experiences necessary to move up the political ladder. They are also less likely to be groomed and mentored for political power positions by powerful people within political organizations.

Female Heads of State

Although somewhat rare, powerful female leaders may be found throughout history. Women like Cleopatra (Egypt), Catherine the Great (Russia), Yaa Asantewaa (Ghana), and Tz'u-Hsi (China) acquired their positions through hereditary monarchies in countries where women were deemed largely incapable of exercising political power. Historian Antonia Fraser writes of many of these queens in her book *The Warrior Queens* (1988). Currently three Western countries have reigning queens: Queen Elizabeth II, queen of the United Kingdom of Great Britain and Northern Ireland (since 1952); Margrethe II, Queen of Denmark (since 1972); and Queen Beatrix of the Netherlands (since 1980). In the twenty-first century, however, these queens wield little power and coexist with democratically elected governments. The true heads of state are considered to be the democratically elected or appointed presidents or prime ministers of their respective countries.

In 2003 only twelve women were heads of state (see Box 9.3, *Women Around the Globe: Women Heads of State in 2003*) but despite their small number, female prime ministers and presidents still interest us. First there is the question of how women come to occupy such visible and customarily male leadership positions. In other words, what is the path to power for female heads of state? This is an important question to feminists concerned with increasing women's power. Second, women as national leaders are interesting because their existence often masks the problem of sexism in world politics. In this section, you will see that not only does sexism persist in countries with

"The challenge for Filipino women is to enter the rarified environment of politics or to remain forever on the sidelines of policy-making and implementation. We face many obstacles, but four of the more prevalent are stereotyping, the nature of the political beast, a rigid electoral system, and apathy."
Daisy Avance Fuentes, first woman deputy speaker in the Philippines House of Representatives

"We can't be certain that women would make different decisions than men, but they might if there were enough of them to affect the decision process and its environment."
Jeanne Kirkpatrick, first female U.S. ambassador to the UN, 1981–1985

In August, 1997, Masoumeh Ebtekar became the first woman vice president in Iranian history.

In 1872, Victoria Clafin Woodhull ran for U.S. president on her own Equal Rights Party ticket.

BOX 9.3   *Women Around the Globe: Women Heads of State in 2003*

Prime Minister Begum Khaleda Zia (Bangladesh)

Premier Jennifer Smith (Bermuda)

President Tarja Halonen (Finland)

President Mary McAleese (Ireland)

President Vaira Vike-Freiberga (Latvia)

President Mireya Moscoso (Panama)

Governor-General Pearlette Louisy (St. Lucia)

President Chandrika Kumaratunga (Sri Lanka)

Prime Minister Helen Clark (New Zealand)

President Gloria Macapagal-Arroyo (Philippines)

President Megawati Sukarnoputri (Indonesia)

Prime Minister Maria das Neves Ceita Batista de Sousa (Sao Tome and Principe)

In 2003 Finland became the first European country to have women as both president and prime minister.

female heads of state but also, as it turns out, gender plays a large role in the election, appointment, and retention of female leaders. Last, another interesting question has to do with whether female world leaders lead differently than men. Feminists frequently assume that things would be better for women, and for the world, if there were more female leaders. Therefore this section also examines the evidence to see whether female leaders are less likely to lead their countries into war, whether they are more likely to pursue domestic policies friendly to women and children, and whether they typically pursue feminist agendas.

Paths to Power

Political Surrogate Path to Power.   According to D'Amico (1995), most women who govern are the daughters of privilege and politics. They are disproportionately from the upper classes and in many cases follow the "widow's walk" to power. In other words, they are **political surrogates** (stand-ins) for husbands killed by natural or political causes and, as such, are expected to act as their husbands would. Likewise, a handful of female leaders come into power as stand-ins for their deceased political fathers when there are no male offspring to assume this role. However, in contrast to the widows, the daughters of political martyrs typically have extensive political party experience. Their political pedigree helped them to get their foot in the political party door where they eventually became political "insiders." It also gave them a credibility that aided in their election. However, once elected they often stray significantly from their father's leadership style and policies. Box 9.4, *Women Around the Globe: Political Surrogates,* lists some of the political surrogates of the past half-century.

BOX 9.4 *Women Around the Globe: Political Surrogates*

Leader/Year Appointed or Elected	Country/Position	Surrogate for
Corazon Cojuangco Aquino, 1986	Philippines, president	Husband
Sirimavo Ratwatte Dias Bandaranaike, 1959	Sri Lanka, prime minister	Husband
Benazir Bhutto, 1988	Pakistan, prime minister	Father
Violeta Barrios Torres de Chamorro, 1990	Nicaragua, president	Husband
Indira Nehru Gandhi, 1966	India, prime minister	Father
Maria Estela "Isabelita" Cartas Martinez de Peron, 1974	Argentina, president	Husband
Aung Sun Su Ki, Myanmar (Burma)	expected head of state should military rule be suspended	Father
Begum Khaleda Zia,* 2001	Bangladesh, prime minister	Husband
Mireya Moscoso, 1999	Panama, president	Husband
Megawati Sukarnoputri,* 2001	Indonesia, president	Father
Gloria Macapagal-Arroyo,* 2001	Philippines, president	Father

Source: Partially derived from D'Amico (1995).
*Zia's path has "insider" elements, and Sukarnoputri and Macapagal-Arroyo's paths have "outsider" elements.

In the case of most surrogates, the husband or father was assassinated and subsequently martyred by the citizenry as a persecuted leader of democratic change or national independence. When it appeared that the government was going in the direction of pre-struggle politics and there were no electable alternative candidates, political strategists sought the next best thing to the successful but now deceased challenger—his male offspring. Lacking a son of the right age, his widow or daughter would have to do. During the campaign, references to the achievements and martyrdom of the husband/father were made repeatedly, and it was implied that the female candidate would serve as a stand-in for the cherished leader. With all but a few exceptions, these women were well educated and came from wealthy, political families. Most had little political experience when drafted by a political party.

The world's first woman prime minister, Sirimavo Bandaranaike of Sri Lanka (1960–1965, 1970–1977, 1994–2000), took the widow's walk to power.

She came from an aristocratic, well-off family. Her husband, Solomon Dias Bandaranaike, was a popular political leader largely because of his nationalism. Following centuries of colonial rule, he campaigned to make Buddhism the national religion and Sinhalese the national language (replacing English), and he was part of the movement to gain independence from Britain. He became prime minister in 1956, only to be assassinated in September 1959. New elections were set for March 1960, and Sirimavo Bandaranaike was asked to campaign on behalf of her husband's political party, the Sri Lankan Freedom Party (SLFP). In May 1960, she reluctantly accepted headship of the SLFP, and the party won the majority of seats in the House of Representatives. As head of the party, she became prime minister. Like many women who walk the surrogate path to power, prior to her husband's death, Sirimavo Bandaranaike was active in service organizations and did not aspire to political office. At the beginning she acted as a surrogate for her dead husband, carrying out his political plans. However, over time she became a politician in her own right. In 1994 she was again appointed prime minister—this time by her daughter, President Chandrika Kumaratunga. Bandaranaike retired in 2000 at age 84 and died a few months later, only hours after voting in a public election.

In countries where attitudes toward women are especially traditional, the surrogate path appears to be the most likely route to female national leadership. In such countries, women are expected to serve devotedly and assist men and to have few ideas of their own. Consequently, it seems safe to expect women to serve as political surrogates for departed husbands or fathers. Violeta de Chamorro, president of Nicaragua (1990–1996) is a good example of this. According to Saint-Germain (1993), Nicaraguan women are expected to derive their identities from their male relatives and are respected to the extent that they sacrifice and submit to the demands of men. The line between public (political) and private (home) spheres is clearly demarcated, and women are expected to stay within the home sphere. Given this dual gender system, it is difficult for women to be political. To do so, they must typically present their political activity as an extension of their role in the home. Thus, during elections, and even once elected, their wife and mother roles are emphasized. For instance, during Chamorro's campaign she said she was not a feminist but rather a woman dedicated to her home, as "taught" by her husband, Pedro Chamorro. She stated she was not a politician but was running "for Pedro and for her country." At one point she said that she was "marked with the Chamorro branding iron." Violeta Chamorro's advisors modeled her image after the Virgin Mary, the ultimate long-suffering maternal mother in Nicaraguan culture. The idea of a national mother who could bring together war-torn Nicaraguans appealed to voters. This, in combination with U.S. promises to provide aid and stop encouraging the Contras should she be elected, resulted in her election to president in 1990. (The Contras were a rebel military force that launched numerous attacks across the country to topple the democratically elected Sandanista government.)

Benazir Bhutto, prime minister of Pakistan (1988–1990, 1993–1996), is another example of how in gender-traditional countries, women's political activism is tolerated when it appears as though they are acting on behalf of male relatives. Bhutto was the first woman to head a Muslim country and almost certainly would not have been elected in the conservative country of Pakistan were it not for the popularity of her martyred father, Zulfikar Ali Bhutto. Following her father's imprisonment and her brothers' political exile abroad, Bhutto took over the male role in her family.

Bhutto was extremely close to her father and dutifully carried on his struggle against the authoritarian regime of General Mohammad Zia. Her father was eventually put to death by Zia, and Benazir was imprisoned. This treatment only cemented the Pakistanis' adoration of the Bhuttos. In time, international and domestic pressure led Zia to release Benazir, and, in 1988, Zia allowed elections. His timing, however, was suspect for he called the elections to coincide with the birth of Benazir's first baby—not that this stopped Benazir from campaigning. She used her father's image skillfully, referring repeatedly to him in speeches and being photographed with his image in the background (Anderson, 1993). Although Zia was killed in a plane crash right before the election, his successor allowed the elections to go on. Benazir's party, the Pakistan People's Party, won the majority of seats in the National Assembly, and Benazir became prime minister. In 1990, President Izhaq Khan dismissed Bhutto on charges of nepotism and corruption. She ran for office and won again in 1993, but three years into her five-year term she was dismissed by President Farooq Leghari, again under charges of corruption.

Political party officials frequently assume that once elected or appointed, the female head of state will act as a figurehead and will leave the governing to party officials. For instance, although Chamorro was often portrayed as strong-willed, others within her administration took most substantive action (in particular, her son-in-law Antonio Lacayo) without her involvement. Indeed, it appears that few party officials had any intention of actually having Chamorro lead. As one of her brothers-in-law said, "We are not looking for someone to run the country. We are looking for someone who represents the ideal [of democracy]." One of her political advisors said, "Violeta wasn't chosen for her abilities as a president. Violeta was chosen to win" (Saint-Germain, 1993, p. 84). Likewise, the Pakistani political party chose Benazir Bhutto to head the party because she was a Bhutto and had suffered political persecution by Zia. However, the party elders assumed that she would serve primarily as a symbol and had a difficult time accepting her leadership (Anderson, 1993).

Political Insider/Climber Path to Power.   A second path to power for female leaders is that of **political insider** or **climber** (D'Amico, 1995). Such leaders work their way up through a party hierarchy over a number of years. D'Amico (1995) hypothesizes that this is an infrequent path to power for women because women are statistically underrepresented in the professions that

BOX 9.5   *Women Around the Globe: Insiders/Climbers*

Leader/Year Elected or Appointed	Country/Position
Agatha Barbara, 1982	Malta, president
Kim Campbell, 1993	Canada, prime minister
Eugenia Charles, 1980	Dominica, prime minister
Tansu Ciller, 1993	Turkey, prime minister
Edith Campion Cresson, 1991	France, prime minister
Indira Nehru Gandhi,* 1966	India, prime minister
Golda Mabovitz Meir, 1969	Israel, prime minister
Milka Planic, 1982	Yugoslavia, prime minister
Mary Bourke Robinson,* 1990	Ireland, president
Margaret Roberts Thatcher,* 1979	United Kingdom, prime minister
Chandrika Kumaratunga,* 1999	Sri Lanka, president
Tarja Halonen,* 2000	Finland, president

Source: Partially derived from D'Amico (1995).
*Gandhi and Kumaratunga's paths have elements of "surrogacy," and Robinson, Thatcher, McAleese, and Halonen's paths have elements of "outsider."

serve as political stepping-stones (that is, the law, military service, and business). Therefore, relatively few women are in the typical apprentice pool for political leadership. However, over the last decade the number of women heads of state that have served in parliaments, congresses, and cabinets has increased. Even many "surrogates" are strong politicians in their own right that have paid major political party dues and can also be considered insiders. Box 9.5, *Women Around the Globe: Insiders/Climbers,* lists some examples of women leaders who took the insider path to power.

Indira Gandhi of India is one example of a leader who took the insider path. She became a member of the Congress Party in 1948, was elected to its Working Committee in 1955, to its presidency in 1959, to the upper house of Parliament in 1964, and served an appointed position as Minister of Information and Broadcasting before assuming the presidency of India in 1966

(Carras, 1995). Although she certainly presented herself as a political surrogate (especially early on), her party granted her power in part because she had earned her status within the party hierarchy. Similarly, Margaret Thatcher of Great Britain began working for the Conservative Party in the 1950s, was elected to the House of Commons in 1959, became Parliamentary Secretary to the Ministry of Pensions and National Security in 1961, became Secretary of State for Education in 1970, leader of the Conservative Party in 1975, and finally, prime minister in 1979.

Golda Meir, prime minister of Israel, was clearly a political insider. Her government service to Israel began in the state's formative years. As a teenager in the United States, she became a Zionist, organizing and raising funds for an independent Jewish state in Palestine. In 1921, she moved to Palestine. For a time, she lived on a kibbutz, a communal experience dedicated to Zionism. In 1928 she took a position as secretary of the Women's Labor Council. Meir raised hundreds of millions of dollars for the fledging Israeli state. She spent a good part of the 1930s and 1940s traveling the world raising funds for the Jewish settlers in Palestine. She was active in the formation of the Mapai political party and served in many positions. She was responsible for settling the thousands of immigrants arriving from Europe in the late 1940s and orchestrated the building of thousands of homes. She served as the first Israeli ambassador to the Soviet Union, secretary of labor, foreign minister, head of the Mapai Party, and finally in 1970 as prime minister.

Women who take the insider path to power appear to function more as honorary males than women who take other paths to power. They appear more likely to dismiss the relevance of gender to their leadership and to see themselves as one of the political boys. Indira Gandhi once said, "As Prime Minister, I am not a woman. I am a human being" (quoted in Everett, 1993). Likewise Golda Meir (1975) said, "The fact is that I have lived and worked with men all my life, but being a woman has never hindered me in any way at all. It has never caused me unease or given me an inferiority complex or made me think that men are better off than women—or that it is a disaster to give birth to children. Not at all." Perhaps without these attitudes these women would not have been able to rise through the party ranks.

Despite having paid their political dues through party service, a confluence of factors must occur before insider women are considered seriously as possible heads of state. In particular, it appears that most are compromise candidates in the case of a divided political party (D'Amico, 1995). For example, it is generally agreed that Indira Gandhi may not have come to power at all were it not for the unexpected death of Prime Minister Lal Bahadur Shastri, a divided political party, and a desire to prevent a particular individual (Morarji Desia) from becoming prime minister (Carras, 1995; Everett, 1993). Likewise, Margaret Thatcher became head of the Conservative political party because the person expected to run for the post refused to run, and there was a shortage of qualified competitors. It was, to use the words of Kenneth Harris (1995, p. 61), "almost a bombshell of surprise and certainly an extraordinary achievement" and was testament to the "strength of her character and the quality of her political instincts." Thatcher benefited from a remarkable sense of timing. As Genovese (1993) suggests, Thatcher's first election to prime minister had more to do with the failure of the Labour Party to solve severe domestic and trade union problems than it did with her policy proposals or charisma.

In 1982, Rosario Ibarra Piedra became the first woman to run for president in Mexico.

Likewise, Golda Meir may never have become prime minister of Israel were it not for a series of unusual events. She had retired from government service in 1968, but in 1970, Israel's Prime Minister Levi Eskol died suddenly from a heart attack. It was a bad time for Israel. Tensions and violence were mounting between Israel and Egypt, and the prospect of war loomed. Increased defense expenditures taxed the economy. There were profound disagreements within Eskol's coalition cabinet about how to respond to these problems. Clearly, selecting a leader from the cabinet would be divisive and disruptive. It seemed to make sense to appoint the steady Meir as an interim prime minister rather than engage in political infighting when Israel was on the verge of war. During her term as interim prime minister, she emerged as a highly visible, action-oriented leader. This, combined with her history as a Zionist pioneer, led to her popularity and her national election to prime minister in October 1970 at age 72.

"I ran for office because I wanted to play an active part in developing my community and my country, and because I knew one route to gender equality is providing young girls with role models. The young girls of Namibia are encouraged to run for elections and become leaders themselves when Namibian women hold leadership positions."
Priscilla Beukes, mayor of the town of Marientao and President of the International Union of Local Authorities in Namibia

Political Outsider Path to Power.   A third path to power described by D'Amico (1995) is that of **political outsider.** These candidates are more likely to enter politics from grassroots citizen movements. They are often elected at a time when citizens perceive insider politicians as corrupt and are looking for honesty and change. Because of the unusualness (statistically speaking) of female politicians, they are easily perceived as outsiders and as a departure from politics as usual. It should be noted that some insider political women got elected in part because of public perceptions of their outsider status. For instance, Margaret Thatcher presented herself as an outsider although she had served for years in a variety of positions in the British Conservative Party and was apt to toe the party line.

Outsider/activist women politicians seem to be one of the few cases in which stereotypical female gender stereotypes are beneficial. The common gender stereotype of women as other-centered may be valuable when citizens are reacting against corruption. Likewise, as D'Amico (1995) suggests, women tend to be seen as caring, compassionate, and accessible. These qualities are advantageous when the issues facing a country involve healthcare and domestic economic and social issues.

In 1993, Agathe Uwilingiyimana became the first female prime minister of Rwanda but was assassinated in 1994.

In some cases, the election of a woman to a presidential position is not as daring as it first appears, for in many countries, presidents have few executive powers. For instance, the presidency in Iceland, which has been held by two women (Vigdis Finnbogadottir from 1980 to 1996 and Tarja Halonen 2000 to present), is a nonpolitical office in which the president has little power over domestic issues. Likewise, the Irish Constitution prevents the

Irish president from participating in politics. However, as former president of Ireland Mary Robinson once said, "I feel I can change perceptions about equality. . . . This office allows me to be more symbolic, more reflective, to engage in lateral thinking, to do the unexpected" (Orth, 1992, p. 122). Many outsider/activist women leaders have used the symbolic power of their offices to promote social reform. They may not have much official power, but they may be empowering.

Liberal civil rights lawyer Mary Robinson's election as the first female president of Ireland in 1990 is a good example of the outsider/activist woman national leader. Robinson served a twenty-year term in the Irish Senate, where she championed causes considered radical in Ireland, such as the legalization of contraception and divorce, the removal of discriminatory taxation against working married women, and the overhauling of the Irish jury system to allow women the right to serve on juries. She was not expected to win the presidential election, and Dublin oddsmakers listed her as a 1,000 to 1 underdog. Her opponent, Brian Lenihan, was one of the most popular politicians in the country, and her ardent feminism seemed a liability in a country fiercely devoted to traditional women's roles. She campaigned tirelessly and made some progress in the polls, although Lenihan maintained the lead for most of the campaign. However, the electoral tides changed in the final weeks of the campaign with a political scandal involving Lenihan. In the end, none of the three candidates won the majority of votes. Under Irish law, in such cases the second preference votes of the minor candidates are tallied with the first preference votes to determine the winner. This resulted in Robinson's winning the election with 52 percent of the vote.

Robinson was a popular president despite and because of her feminism and femininity. A female symbol of Ireland is in some ways a comfortable one, for the Irish used feminine names to refer to Ireland when the ruling British forbade them to mention Ireland. Mary Robinson's popularity may have been due in part to her transformation of the image of Mother Ireland as a land of the dispossessed and forlorn to one of strength and pride. Many commentators have noted that Robinson represented change in a country ready to change (Orth, 1992). Furthermore, as a skilled politician and lawyer, she was able to present feminist ideas in ways that were acceptable to the electorate and that mirrored their own opinions and concerns. For instance, she was critical of a feminism that devalues homemaking and bringing up children, saying "If we do not sufficiently value these activities and the skills involved in them, how can we persuade society as a whole of their value and the importance of ensuring that these activities are more evenly shared between parents?" (Frank, 1991).

After her term as Ireland's president, Mary Robinson became an international leader. Robinson assumed the role of the United Nations Human Rights Commissioner from 1997 to 2002. She is currently executive director of the Ethical Globalization Initiative (EGI), a project intended to bring human rights norms and standards into the globalization process.

Leadership Style

Accepting the characterization of aggressiveness and authoritarianism as male traits, many feminists have assumed that women world leaders would govern in a more peaceful and democratic way than do male leaders. However, evidence indicates that this is not necessarily true. Indeed, there is great variability in leadership styles in women, just as there is in men. Simply put, it is difficult to generalize about women leaders. Their policy agendas and styles of leadership are diverse and often challenge gender-based notions of feminine values and behavior (D'Amico, 1995). As Gonzalez and Kampwirth (2002) concluded in regard to Latin American women in politics, the evidence does not support the position that men are inherently more violent and women inherently more peaceful.

Contrary to our images of women as nurturers and peacemakers, women leaders do not appear less likely to use their militaries to resolve conflicts. Many of the women profiled in this chapter did not hesitate to use the military against domestic protesters and to go to war to defend territorial interests. Indeed, Fraser (1988) suggests that many women leaders "have found in the crucible of war—if successfully survived—the fiery process which has guaranteed them passage into the realms of honorary men" (p. 10).

The world's first female prime minister, Sirimavo Bandaranaike of Sri Lanka, increased defense spending, bought armaments from all over the world, and used them to control rebellion against her government. The military was used to squash ultra-leftists, who felt Bandaranaike was not moving quickly enough, and to combat the Tamils, a minority group who revolted when she decreed Buddhism the national religion and Sinhalese the national language. Indira Gandhi oversaw the most ambitious program of military buildup in India's history, presided over India's first underground nuclear explosion, built up the navy to become the principal naval power in the region, and went to war with Pakistan over East Pakistan's desire to become an independent state (Bangladesh).

> "Women are not inherently passive or peaceful. We're not inherently anything but human."
> *Robin Morgan*

Margaret Thatcher sent British forces to the Falkland Islands in 1982 to reclaim them from the Argentinean government. She did not hesitate to use the police in strike situations and showed little sympathy for the citizens injured (Genovese, 1993). Eugenia Charles, prime minister of Dominica, appealed to U.S. president Ronald Reagan for assistance in invading Grenada in 1983 following a political coup. Charles believed that if the coup succeeded the whole Caribbean would be susceptible to Communist takeover.

Golda Meir was quite willing to use force in conflicts with Israel's neighbors, seeing it as necessary to the establishment and preservation of a Jewish state in Palestine. As foreign minister she was ready to use force against Egypt in 1956, and she supported the Six-Day War of 1967 with Egypt. That she did not launch a preemptive strike against Egypt and Syria prior to the Yom Kippur War of 1973 (called the October War by Arabs) is attributed to faulty military intelligence and poor advice from the United States rather than to an aversion to military solutions (Thompson, 1993).

Tansu Ciller, the first female prime minister of Turkey (1993–1996) is yet another example of the fact female leaders are often no more gentle, peaceful, and ethical than male leaders. While Ciller was prime minister, tensions between Greece and Turkey over the island of Cyprus escalated following the killing of a Greek protester who had tried to tear down a Turkish flag on the island. Ciller reportedly warned that anyone who tried to tear down the Turkish flag would have their hands broken. During her administration, human rights activists repeatedly called attention to the imprisonment and torture of political opponents and the evacuation and destruction of over 1,000 Kurdish villages. Ciller also introduced a law allowing the seizure and government sale of land that did not have a title issued since the last coup. Ciller personally benefited from such land seizures. Kurdish rebellion, economic instability, and charges of corruption led her to step down in 1996. She has remained active in politics, first as foreign minister, then as a member of parliament, and currently as leader of the True Path Party.

Of course, some women world leaders do fit the feminist image of peacemaker. These include such leaders as Corazon Aquino, Violeta Chamorro, and Mary Robinson. These leaders worked hard to resolve major domestic conflicts without the use of military force. Aquino, president of the Philippines from 1986 to 1992 and a political surrogate for her martyred husband, Benigno Aquino, emphasized economic development and the peaceful resolution of long-standing internal conflicts (Boudreau, 1995; Col, 1993). She granted amnesty to guerrillas, declared cease-fires with rebels, and released political prisoners (Col, 1993). Chamorro, much to the chagrin of the UNO party that ran her as a candidate, cooperated with the defeated yet powerful FSLN party. This she did by appointing General Humberto Ortega, a director of the FSLN, to be her senior military officer. By cooperating with the FSLN and the Contras, she undoubtedly quelled some civil strife. In a country torn for many years by civil war, she consistently advocated consensus and reconciliation over confrontation and vengeance (Williams, 1995). Mary Robinson is another example. She has consistently worked for a peaceful solution to the conflict in Northern Ireland.

As the evidence currently stands, female leaders are also not more likely than male leaders to exhibit a democratic leadership style. Some are, but it appears that many, like Turkey's Tansu Ciller, are described as combative, insensitive, arrogant, and power mad. It is all too easy to find autocratic female leaders. These leaders have strong convictions regarding the directions that their countries should take, and they believe that only they are qualified to lead their countries there. For instance, in 2003, President Chandrika Kumaratunga of Sri Lanka suspended parliament and deployed troops around the capital while her prime minister and arch-rival Ranil Wickremesinghe was out of the country. She did this in part to signal her displeasure with his willingness to negotiate with Tamil rebels to end a twenty-year civil conflict that has left 65,000 dead. Margaret Thatcher and Indira Gandhi are some of the best-known examples of women leaders that did not exhibit a democratic leadership style and they shared the moniker "Iron Lady." Their external gentle appearance was at odds with their shrewd and ruthless leadership style. Indira Gandhi, for instance, tolerated little dissent from political advisors and cabinet members. When threatened with public opposition, she imposed martial law and used the military against Indian citizens to repress dissent. For this she was ultimately killed. Gandhi authorized a military operation (resulting in at least 576 deaths) against a Sikh temple from which alleged terrorist activities were conducted. Several months later, she was assassinated by two of her Sikh security guards.

As the privileged and doted-upon daughter of a national hero, Benazir Bhutto was reputedly an arrogant and imperious leader who surrounded herself with family members who had proven their loyalty (Anderson, 1993). Contrary to the notion of women leaders as democratic and ethical, she lost her office amid charges of autocratic rule and corruption. As Zahid Hussain, a respected Pakistani journalist, said, "Instead of strengthening democratic institutions, which have been weakened by long periods of autocratic rule, Ms. Bhutto has virtually set out to destroy them" (Dahlburg & Bearak, 1996). Bhutto routinely bypassed parliament and awarded high positions in her administration to corrupt politicians, including her husband. In addition, many believe she was behind the death of her brother and political rival, who was ambushed and killed by police. In a country where the average person earns $1.18 a day, she proposed $1.1 billion in new taxes while she was in the process of purchasing a $4 million mansion in Britain (Dahlburg & Bearak, 1996).

Margaret Thatcher was also known for an aggressive leadership style and chose cabinet members based on their loyalty to her. As Genovese (1993) says, Thatcher's style was highly personalized and imperious. She did not believe in listening to divergent viewpoints within her cabinet, nor did she believe in seeking consensus. As she herself once said, "I am not a consensus politician, I'm a conviction politician" (Jenkins, 1988, p. 3), and on taking office, "It must be a conviction government. As prime minister I could not waste time with any internal arguments" (Genovese, 1993, p. 197). She believed in getting her way and did it by arguing, bullying, intimidating, and threatening, and was unapologetic about it. Genovese (1993) quotes her as saying, "I am not ruthless, but some things have to be done, and I know that when they are done one will be accused of all sorts of things" (p. 199). Like Indira Gandhi, she chose her cabinet based on loyalty and obedience and regularly shuffled her ministers in order to maintain control.

Although less extreme than Gandhi or Thatcher, Golda Meir was also known for being tough, especially when it came to international relations. As an ardent international champion of Israeli interests, she became known for her confrontational style and her uncompromising opposition to concessions in the Arab-Israeli conflict. Like her prime minister predecessors, Meir employed a consultative decision-making style with her cabinet. Indeed, a cabinet subgroup of her allies and advisors would often meet in her kitchen the night before cabinet meetings. A number of biographical accounts describe Meir making and serving cookies and coffee as policy issues were discussed. On the face of it, the "Kitchen Cabinet," as it was dubbed, appears to be evidence of a democratic leadership style. However, she set the agenda, she invited the participants, and she announced the decisions to the full cabinet the next day (Thompson, 1993).

Corazon Aquino is one of the few female national leaders who was clearly consensus oriented and democratic in her leadership style. She came to power during a time when Filipinos were tired of the dictatorship of Ferdinand Marcos and longed for democracy. After nineteen years of rule by Marcos, wealth and power were concentrated in the hands of a powerful few, and the people were angry. Cory Aquino represented human rights, civil liberties, and democracy. As leader of the Philippines, she sought to develop a political culture ruled by law, tolerance, and participation. In her commitment to democratic participation, she made decisions only after elaborate and lengthy consultations with as many people and groups as possible (Col, 1993). Although criticized as incompetent and indecisive, she remained committed to a democratic style of leadership.

At this time it is difficult to say why women national leaders lead remarkably like men. Many feminists believe that there are no clear-cut leadership differences because female leaders are so aware of their precarious hold on power that they feel compelled to lead as men would. Carras (1995) points out that in time this may change as the number of women leaders increases and as they feel less bound by the male rules of the current power game. Perhaps then the prediction that women leaders are more cooperative and community oriented in their approaches will be borne out. On the other hand, the fact that the behavior of female world leaders is not strikingly different from male behavior could be because leadership, male or female, is more influenced by situational factors and personality than it is by gender. Similarly, the customary ways of gaining, wielding, and holding on to power may erroneously be believed to be male ways of power because most power is held by males. If this is the case, the absence of a gender difference in world leader behavior is likely to persist regardless of women's increased presence in world politics. It may be that, regardless of gender, getting and maintaining political power may require a certain ruthlessness and defensiveness.

Whatever the case, at present it is true that in most political systems, obtaining and holding on to power require playing by those "male" rules. Therefore, at least for now, women may have to follow these rules before they will be allowed to play the political game. Once they have earned status and respect for doing so, they will probably stand a greater chance of being able to deviate without a loss of power. As Boudreau (1995) notes, perhaps we should not ask whether women bring new perspectives to politics, but whether they can defend those perspectives—when they exist—against the established political order.

"Many women do not want to be mirror images of men in similar positions, but at the same time they must show authority or they will simply be swept aside."
Margaret Anstee, 1993, first woman to head a UN peacekeeping mission

"I accept that women are gentler at the moment, but if they had the same amount of power as men, they wouldn't be more virtuous."
Lynne Segal, 1987

"And I know, in the depth of my being and in all my knowledge of history and humanity, I know women will struggle for a social order of peace, equality, and joy."
Joan Kelly, 1982

Advocacy of Women's Issues

Many feminists believe that adding women to existing power structures will put women's issues on policymaking agendas (Peterson & Runyan, 1993), and I have noted that there is some evidence for this position. However, this gender difference is not so clear at the international head-of-state level, probably because most female heads of state are aware that being seen as a "women's leader" would quickly result in the loss of their already tenuous hold on power. Recall that most of these women gained power under very unusual circumstances. Also, women typically come into power during economic and political transitional periods. Therefore, it is not surprising that women's issues are frequently subordinated to other seemingly more pressing concerns, particularly economic ones affecting all citizens. Keep in mind as well that most female heads of state came into office without "feminist consciousness." Only a few such as Mary Robinson, Vignis Finnbogadottir (president of Iceland), and Gro Harlem Brundtland (prime minister of Norway), had a prior record of commitment to women's issues and organizations.

There appear to be some women's advocacy variations based upon the different paths to power we've discussed here. It is, for example, uncommon for political surrogates to advance women's issues. Surrogates generally do not come to their leadership roles with any feminist agenda. They are often gender-role traditional, reluctantly leading only because they are pressured to do. For example, Megawati Sukarnoputri, president of Indonesia and a daughter of that nation's first president, has done little for women's rights in her country since her election in 2000. For most of her adult life she was a homemaker, entering politics in 1998 at the urging of her husband and the populist Indonesian Democratic Party. Violetta de Chamorro appointed no female ministers until three years into her term. She also suspended governmental support for feminist organizations, reduced funding for programs designed to address women's and children's needs, and eliminated programs for the rehabilitation of prostitutes and street children. Isabel Peron, the third wife of President Juan Peron, became president of Argentina in 1974 after her husband's death. Like Violetta de Chamorro, she was also unsympathetic to feminist issues. One example of this is that after the Argentinean Congress passed a law giving mothers, as well as fathers, authority over their children, Isabel Peron vetoed it (Navarro, 2001).

The fact that political surrogates typically come to power in gender-role-traditional cultures is also relevant to their women's issues advocacy. In gender-traditional countries, calls for gender equality are unlikely to be met with encouragement. Thus, even those sympathetic to women's issues such as Benazir Bhutto must tread lightly or compromise what power they have. Although Bhutto made women's rights a major theme of her campaign and in writings favored a feminist interpretation of Islam, she was nonetheless criticized by feminists as being more concerned with political power than with women's rights (Anderson, 1993). Her arranged marriage as well as the fact that she never appeared without the traditional Islamic head covering for women (the dupatta), further dismayed Islamic feminists. However, Islamic fundamentalism was on the rise at the time, and many were antagonistic to the idea of a woman leader—especially a Western-educated one. Further-more, Bhutto's party did not have a majority in the congress, and there were laws limiting the prime minister's power. Given these constraints, she may have had little choice other than to soft-pedal her women's rights agenda. Even so, Bhutto made some improvements for women. For instance, women could appear in public without the dupatta. More importantly perhaps, Bhutto prevented passage of an amendment that would have reexamined all laws in terms of their conformity to Islam. (Movements in this direction un-der Zia's Islamization programs resulted in the severe repression of women.)

Political insiders and "honorary men"—such as Indira Gandhi, Margaret Thatcher, Edith Cresson, and Golda Meir—are also disinclined to pursue a feminist agenda. Women like these who worked their way up through their political party's ranks were socialized by these experiences to act in accor-dance with their party's political strategies and ideologies. They were allowed to advance precisely because they minded their manners and proved to the party that they would advance a party line, not a feminist agenda. Margaret Thatcher once said, "The battle for women's rights has largely been won," and "The days when they were demanded and discussed in strident tones should be gone forever" (quoted in Harris, 1995). Her policies, which dras-tically decreased funding for education and social programs, disproportion-ately affected poor women and children, earning her the nickname "Maggie Thatcher the Milk Snatcher." As "honorary male" politicians, insiders seem no more likely than male politicians to encourage the appointment and elec-tion of females to political posts. For instance, Indira Gandhi appointed no women to her cabinet, and the number of women in the British cabinet de-creased under Thatcher. As Enloe (1989) says, "When a woman is let in by the men who control the political elite it is usually precisely because that woman has learned the lessons of masculinized political behavior well enough to know not to threaten male political privilege" (pp. 6–7).

Outsiders seem the most likely to be openly feminist, to have explicitly feminist agendas, and to increase the number of women in government po-sitions. Gro Harlem Brundtland, prime minister of Norway, appointed seven women of seventeen posts in her first cabinet and eight of eighteen in her sec-ond (D'Amico, 1995). She also extended maternity leave to twenty-four weeks, supported changing Norway's Constitution to include female inheri-tance of the throne, and was instrumental in the Labor Party's requirement that at least 40 percent of the party's candidates in any given election be fe-male. Vignis Finnbogadottir, president of Iceland from 1980 to 1996, pro-moted feminist causes and had a long history with Iceland's feminist movements as a member of parliament and as a member of the Women's Al-liance Party (Peterson & Runyan, 1999). Mary Robinson, Ireland's former president, was a vocal supporter of rights for women, greater reproductive freedom for women, and reform in family laws that limited women. As a member of the Irish Parliament, she introduced legislation to legalize contraception in Ireland (1969) and divorce (1976)—daring moves in a country dominated by the Roman Catholic Church. On February 15, 1980, in the *London Times Literary Supplement*, she wrote, "Equality of employment cannot become a reality in a country which has not yet fully legalized the sale of contraceptives; where there is no divorces, no maternity legislation, and virtually no state creche [day care] or nursery facilities."

Role of Gender in the Perception of Female World Leaders

Wilma Mankiller was the first woman elected chief of an American Indian tribe (the Cherokee Nation), in 1987.

Rosaldo (1974) argues that cultures emphasize women's maternal role, and because of this, there is a near-universal opposition between domestic and public roles. Because of the confining of women to the domestic sphere, women view the exercise of power as illegitimate. Thus, she says, the ways that women gain prestige and a sense of value are shaped and limited by women's association with the domestic world. This is indeed true. Politics are generally a game played out in the public sphere by those with stereotypically masculine qualities such as aggressiveness. Also, as mentioned earlier, women's confinement to the domestic sphere generally means that there are fewer in the apprentice pools of leadership. In addition, the strong association of women with the domestic sphere affects the perception and evaluation of female leaders.

It is important to note, though, that women heads of state often manage to turn gender stereotypes to their advantage, especially when campaigning. For example, many of the women discussed in this chapter came to power in war-torn or politically corrupt countries where the image of women as peaceful, selfless, and dedicated to others helped them gain power. The "ironfisted, velvet-gloved" Margaret Thatcher and Indira Gandhi used their femininity to disguise their ruthless accrual of power. These nice middle-aged motherly looking ladies were not expected to be so single-mindedly political, and this served them well, at least until everyone caught on. This could also be said of Tansu Ciller, reputedly the most beautiful female world leader. Her good looks, Western education, and Western clothing led to the assumption that she would behave democratically and that corruption and human rights violations would decrease in Turkey. As increasing evidence surfaced regarding her involvement with drug cartels, death squads, and tax evasion, she battled for political survival.

For the most part it appears that any political advantage there is to being female is not long lasting. Eventually, it seems, gender stereotypes are used against women leaders. If they are aggressive and decisive, they are chided for being "men"; if they are democratic, they are criticized for being weak and for not being in control. Women must do what is not expected of them while doing enough of what is expected of them to gain acceptance (Morrison, White, & Van Velsor, 1987). It was this very dilemma that led Benazir Bhutto to make the very political decision to marry a man chosen by her family. In

Pakistan, it is highly unusual for a woman in her thirties to be unmarried. There was constant speculation about her private life, she required a chaperone, and was under surveillance by the opposition party, who hoped to catch her in a sexual liaison. Her male colleagues were uncomfortable interacting with an unmarried woman. Her unmarried status became a political liability and her arranged marriage afforded her respectability and made her seem more normal. In short, female leaders must be careful not to trigger those gender stereotypes that suggest they cannot lead; yet they must also avoid stepping too far outside of their gender role lest they be rejected or ridiculed.

The dominant response to powerful women has tended to be first violence, then hostility, then indifference and dismissal (Lips, 1991). Powerful women are frequently attacked and vilified, threatened and demeaned. Edith Cresson, prime minister of France for a mere ten months in 1991 and 1992, could testify to this. Despite her credentials and experience, it was repeatedly implied in the French press that she must have been sleeping with President Mitterand to obtain the appointment. French feminists commented that women who succeed in politics are commonly believed to have done so through seduction and that a media hate campaign with sexist overtones was partly responsible for Cresson's problems (Opfell, 1993).

Another example is Benazir Bhutto. Her gender made her less threatening initially such that she was not forced into exile like her brothers and she was trusted to be a representative of her father. However, over time being a female leader in a conservative country reduced her power as it was not seen as legitimate. One popular joke following the birth of her second child in 1990 was that as prime minister all she had been able to deliver was a baby (Anderson, 1993).

Those seeking the ouster of Margaret Thatcher demeaned her with such nicknames as "Attila the Hen" and "Her Malignancy," and slogans such as "Ditch the Bitch" (Genovese, 1993). Note that these attacks are gendered. Research indicates that when a woman is a numerical minority in a job category, we are more likely to judge and evaluate her according to gender stereotypes (Burn, 1996; Ragins & Sundstrom, 1989). As Vignis Finnbogadottir, president of Iceland, said, "Women must be very cautious when embarking on a leadership path. . . . If you make a mistake you will be attacked with the strongest weapon—mockery. . . . Unlike men, mistakes made by women inevitably reflect on their entire gender" (Jones, 1992).

> "Critical mass will make a difference—we know now that having more women in the federal parliamentary arena or in decision-making bodies leads to policies and legislation that are more likely to reflect the concerns and interests of women."
> *Natasha Stott Despoja, deputy leader of the Australian Democrats*

Increasing Women's Participation in Formal Politics

Women positively influence policymaking regarding women's issues but this effect is often constrained by their small numbers (Davis, 1997; Saint-Germain, 1989; Swers, 2002; Thomas, 1994). Because of this, feminists seek a "critical mass" of female representatives in formal politics. Such a critical mass is also seen as the antidote to a masculinist political culture where the behavioral traits deemed suitable for success are stereotypically masculine ones, and the meeting times and locations, as well as networking activities, are convenient for men's, not women's, schedules (Lister, 2003; Peterson & Runyan, 1993). Too often women are disadvantaged by the fact that political systems are run on the assumption that those who participate have no family responsibilities (Norris & Lovenduski, 1995).

"Women's participation in all aspects of any democratic society is crucial to the quality of democracy itself."
Nikki Craske

Chowdhury et al. (1994) conclude that significant improvements in women's presence in formal politics are unlikely in the absence of changes within the organizational cultures of parties and the electoral rules of the game. Research clearly suggests that **electoral system reform** increases women's legislative representation. The electoral system (the procedures by which representatives are elected) explains almost 30 percent of the varying proportions of women in democracies' national legislatures (Rule, 1994). Rule (1994) demonstrates this in an analysis of twenty-seven long-established democracies. The system that yields the greatest number of female parliamentarians is the **party list/proportional representation system** (PL/PR). It has these characteristics: Seats are allocated roughly in proportion to the votes each party receives; there are five or more representatives per district (multi-member districts); three or more parties prepare lists of candidates for election from each district (party lists); and the voter may choose candidates from the lists. Under this system, parties see an advantage in having some female candidates to attract more female voters and gain more seats.

The PL/PR system is used in the majority of the countries with the highest percentages of female legislators—Sweden, Denmark, Finland, Norway, Netherlands, Iceland, Germany, New Zealand, Mozambique, and South Africa. Paxton and Kunovich (2003) in a cross-national study of women in legislatures also found that proportional-representation party systems were more effective for getting women into politics. Many newly developing democracies have chosen PL/PR systems with positive effects for women's representation. The new democracy of Namibia adopted a PL/PR system in 1989. A total of fourteen women appeared on candidate lists, and women were elected to 6.9 percent of assembly seats. Although this may not seem significant, this was only the second election in which Namibian women were eligible to vote and run for office. By 2003, Namibian women representatives comprised 26 percent of the lower house and 7.7 percent of the upper house. Rwanda and South Africa are other examples of countries where the PL/PR system has had positive effects for women's representation. In 2003, 45 percent of the Rwandan parliament was female and in South Africa, 28 percent.

Female political representatives are far fewer in what are called **single-member district systems** (SMD). About 40 percent of the world's countries have these nonparty list/nonproportional representation systems that require winning candidates obtain an absolute majority vote or a plurality in any one constituency. SMD systems are "winner-take-all" systems where there is usually only one seat per district, and the person who gets the most votes wins. Unsurprisingly, parties will usually choose and support only those candidates believed capable of winning the required number of votes. They usually believe that a male candidate gives them the best chance of winning the district and that it is too risky to run a female candidate. SMD systems are one reason why nations like the United States and the United Kingdom have relatively low numbers of females in their legislatures.

It is clear that PL/PR systems are most advantageous for increasing the number of women legislators. However, some changes can overcome the disadvantages of the SMD system for women. Australia provides a good example of the role that political parties in SMD systems can play in increasing the number of female representatives. Sawer (1994) describes how changes in Australian political parties increased the percentage of female parliamentarians from 2 percent in 1972 to 18 percent in 1997. It began with the Labour Party's desire to gain power. Party leaders figured out that if they could get 8 percent of the women's vote, they could gain control of the government (voting is mandatory in Australia so women's votes can make a big difference). The problem was that women generally did not vote Labour, because of its image as the working man's party. In 1981, the party adopted an affirmative action policy aimed at increasing women's representation at all levels of the party to approximately 25 percent. In addition, they also promoted some women-centered policies such as a sex discrimination bill. Their strategy was successful, and by 1983 they were able to take control of the government. Since 1985, the other political parties (the Liberal, National, and Australian Democratic parties) have also been fielding more female candidates. The Australian Democrats have the largest number of female parliamentary representatives as well as females occupying top leadership positions within the party.

In the SMD system of the United States, feminist groups have attempted to increase the number of female candidates by funding their campaigns. EMILY's List (the acronym stands for Early Money Is Like Yeast) is one such example. In the United States, the average cost of a congressional campaign in a district without an incumbent is over half a million dollars (in California, Senators Dianne Feinstein and Barbara Boxer spent $8 and $10 million, respectively, in the 1992 election). Compared to most other electoral democracies, American election districts cover large populations and vast geographic distances. At an average size of 550,000 residents, many U.S. congressional districts are larger than the entire populations of many nations (Lauter, 1995). U.S. congressional candidates must therefore reach voters through the mass media, but this of course costs big money. When women are able to run for congressional office, they win at the same rate as men. Unfortunately, fewer women run for office because they lack access to the traditional business, professional, and political networks that allow male candidates to raise funds (Lauter, 1995). Begun in 1985 by feminist Ellen R. Malcolm, EMILY's List helps female candidates by introducing them to a network of donors who provide funds. EMILY's List has helped to elect seven women governors, eleven women to the United States Senate and fifty-five women to the U.S. House of Representatives. In the 2002 elections, EMILY's List and its almost 73,000 members contributed nearly $9.7 million to pro-choice Democratic women candidates (Emily's List, 2003).

Quotas are one of the most effective electoral reforms for increasing the number of women in formal political positions. Without a doubt, there are more women in elected politics in countries that reserve a certain number of seats for women in parliament or congress, or that have political parties that require that a certain percentage of party candidates be female. For instance, the PL/PR countries of Finland, Sweden, the Netherlands, Norway, Denmark, and Iceland (each of which has women in at least one-third of positions in the lower or single house of parliament), all have some type of quota system. National laws in the Latin American countries of Argentina, the Dominican Republic, Venezuela, Bolivia, Ecuador, Brazil, Panama, Costa Rica, and Peru require political parties to reserve 20 to 40 percent of candidacies for women (WEDO, 2003). Bangladesh reserves 30 of its 330 seats for women and Eritrea reserves 10 out of 105 seats (WEDO, 2003). In 2003, Rwanda earned the honor of coming closer to achieving gender parity in national parliament than any other country in the world (Inter-Parliamentary Union, 2003b). The new Rwanda Constitution has a quota of twenty-four seats for women in the lower house and an additional fifteen women were elected to non-reserved seats. In the Senate, the constitutional quota of six women was also met. Women now comprise 45 percent of parliament; prior to the new constitutional requirements, women accounted for 25.7 percent of parliament members.

Quotas are also often the result of women's activism (Rule, 1994; WEDO, 2003). For example, in the PL/PR country of Argentina, a law passed in 1991 stipulated that female candidates must occupy 30 percent of the upper-level positions on party lists. Argentina's law was the result of a bill introduced by Senator Margarita Malharro and Representatives Norma Allegrone de Fonte and Florentina Gomez Miranda. On the day of the parliamentary debate, huge numbers of women from different social classes and different ideologies mobilized in the gallery, the Chambers, and in the streets and squares near the Congress (Bonder & Nari, 1995). The first election following implementation of the law made an immediate difference in the number of female federal district senators: Of the fifty-four senators elected, nineteen (35 percent) were female (Molinelli, 1994). The quota law also increased women's representation in the Chamber of Deputies from 5.5 percent in 1991 to 12.8 percent in 1993, and in 1994 resulted in the election of eighty women representatives (26.4 percent) to the constitutional assembly (Feijoo, 1998). The percentage of women in the House of Representatives rose from 5.4 percent in 1991 to 13.3 percent in 1993 (Bonder & Nari, 1995).

Quotas are not foolproof solutions to the problem of women's lower representation in elected politics. France provides an interesting illustration. With one of the lowest percentages of female representation in parliament in

Europe, in 2000 the French parliament decreed that political parties had to field an equal number of male and female candidates. Although this increased the percentage of women to a record 11.7 percent from 6 percent, in many cases, the new law failed to significantly change the male–female ratio of elected officials. Women were relegated to low spots on party tickets, or endorsed for elections they could not possibly win (Bryant, 2003).

As Chowdhury (1994) points out, "a policy of protection hardly ever guarantees equality unless it is intended as a temporary device and orchestrated with measures designed to eliminate the factors that warrant the protection" (p. 99). Reserving a certain number of parliamentary seats for women may increase women's numbers, but it does not necessarily increase women's political power. In Bangladesh, for instance, 30 out of 330 seats are reserved for women, but the way it works is that women are indirectly elected—the party obtaining the largest number of parliamentary seats gets to nominate women for the seats. Women's participation in the parliament is almost entirely dependent upon the male elite in power, and this accentuates women's political dependence and subordination (Chowdhury, 1994). Similarly, some feminists in Argentina remain skeptical about the increased number of women in their parliament. They are concerned that male politicians have filled the positions with their own female supporters, friends, and relatives (Bonder & Nari, 1995; Feijoo, 1998). There is also a concern that many of the women elected are not committed to gender issues (Bonder & Nari, 1995). As Bonder and Nari (1995) noted after anonymous interviews with Argentinean women legislators, the quota law in Argentina is not a point of arrival but rather one of departure, an effort that requires constant monitoring so that its original significance will not be lost.

Achieving greater formal political power also depends on women achieving greater **political literacy.** Getting elected is a complex, expensive, and bureaucratic process. Without the backing of those who know and understand complex election rules, it is typically difficult to run for office. Unfortunately, the political insiders and parties familiar with the process are often hesitant to mentor women through it. In some places, women's organizations have stepped in to close this gap. For example, Korean women's organizations such as the Women's Research Association, the Korean Research Institute for Women and Politics, and the Center for Korean Women in Politics work to educate and train potential female candidates (Darcy & Hyun, 1994). UNIFEM partnered with Kenyan women's organizations to provide media advocacy and training for women running for election; for the first time six women were appointed to the cabinet and the number of women in parliament rose 3 percent (WIN, 2003). Box 9.6, *Activist Profile: Hazel Brown on Increasing Women's Political Literacy in Trinidad and Tobago,* features a first-hand description of a political literacy campaign in Trinidad and Tobago.

Norway provides one of the most successful cases of women's activism and political literacy. In the 1970s, a coalition of women's groups mobilized women to run for office, worked through political parties, and taught voters how to use

"Everyone knows what a woman must suffer who undertakes to act against bad men. My reputation has been assailed, and it is done so cunningly, that I cannot prove it to be unjust."
Sarah Winnemucca, 1855, American Indian rights activist

BOX 9.6   *Activist Profile: Hazel Brown on Increasing Women's Political Literacy in Trinidad and Tobago*

Here Hazel Brown, Coordinator of the Network of NGOs of Trinidad and Tobago for the Advancement of Women, describes a campaign in the Caribbean for increasing women's political literacy and empowerment:

We decided to work together with women across the Caribbean, and exchange ideas on increasing women's participation locally. We developed eight strategies:

First, focus on cross-partisan activities. In the last local government elections in Trinidad and Tobago, of 100 who ran for office, 48 won. Getting 100 women to run was very difficult, but we wanted women on all the councils. To increase the number of women running, we played each party against the others. When one party gave us a list with thirty-one women, we went to the other party and said, "Can I have your list please?" That list came up with forty-four women. We went back to the first party and said, "This party has forty-four—you can't go out there with thirty-one."

Second, women need consistent, supportive networks. For example, women often say campaigns can't be run without money. So how do we get the money? Cocktail parties are one way. A cocktail party at the British High Commission included many men with money. I slid up to one and said, "We are running this campaign for women candidates, would you be willing to support it?" And surprisingly, men are willing to support women's campaigns. Some of them said, "I'm not giving my money to any party candidates," but we were able to promise to give their money to independent women candidates. We shared the pool of money raised equally among all the women who participated.

Our third strategy was to produce a manual on how to dress, how to read a speech, how to handle security, how to make eye contact with an audience, where to campaign, how to plan ahead, what to do about caring for your children, what you do about your husband. Everything was written down.

Fourth, we recommend using professional media. All of us who are activists think that we have brilliant messages that everybody understands. But everyone doesn't understand. When we used professional media, we found ways to help ordinary people understand our messages. For example, a media professional translated our long message on how good it is to have women candidates into: "If the hand that rocks the cradle rules the world, then it is time for more of those hands to help." Everybody understood it, and it can run on the radio over and over again.

Fifth, build alliances—with church people, union people, business people—with anybody who supports your cause.

Sixth, target young voters. We found that it was young people who were willing to come out and work for our new paradigm. But most women in political parties don't appear to have a strategy for encouraging either youth or women voters.

The seventh strategy relates to sustainability after the elections. It is not enough only to get women elected, because nothing in the system supports them. After the election, we formed local government women's forums—combinations of women across each party, including those who won, lost, and worked on the campaigns. They now understand the dynamics of working together and the forum can be a valuable resource for women inside the political system.

The eighth strategy is to build links between women activists and politicians. Too often, politicians from the women's movement forget about us after they assume power; therefore we need to strengthen communications.

Source: Women's Environment and Development Organization, 2003 http://www.wedo.org/5050/trinadad.htm.

FIGURE 9.2   *Conditions Leading to More Women in Parliaments, Congresses, and Cabinets*

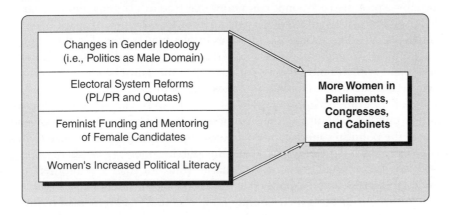

flexible voting rules (the system permits the writing in of names on ballots) (Bystydzienski, 1992b, 1995). Activists went door-to-door telling women how they could ensure the election of women by crossing out men's names on the voting lists and replacing them with female candidates (Bystydzienski, 1994). This technique proved so successful that male politicians subsequently limited voters' ability to alter ballots. Fortunately, Norwegian activists also convinced political parties to nominate women candidates and accept gender quotas, and female parliamentary representation has remained high. The result was the quadrupling of female political representation locally and nationally in a period of two decades. According to Bystydzienski (1994), Norway exemplifies the fact that although a PL/PR system is helpful for women's representation, only in combination with a strong, organized women's movement can the number of women representatives be significantly increased. Figure 9.2 summarizes the conditions leading to greater female representation in formal politics.

Women in Informal Politics: Social and Protest Movements

Although relatively few women are official "state actors" and politics continues to be stereotyped as a male domain, women all over the world are political, active, challenge gender dichotomies, and change world politics by their political agency (Peterson & Runyan, 1999). As stated early in the chapter, the invisibility of women's political activity is in part due to defining politics narrowly as participation in formal politics. Women's political activity is especially high when we take into account local, community-based actions in which women are a driving force (Lister, 2003).

West and Blumberg (1990) suggest that there are four general types of issues that draw women into **social protest:** (1) issues linked to the economic survival

The Northern Ireland Peace Women were awarded a Nobel Peace Prize in 1977.

of themselves and their children; (2) issues related to nationalist and racial/ethnic struggles; (3) issues addressing broad humanistic/nurturing problems; and (4) issues identified as women's rights issues. They also note that these may overlap—a protest of economic conditions may lead to a larger, nationalist struggle as was the case when women's demands for food helped to spark both the French and Russian revolutions. Other examples may be found in the fact that peace and environmental causes are often part of the agendas of feminist movements, and women's movements, particularly in the Third World, may connect their struggles as women to their struggles against racism.

Much of women's informal political activity can be viewed as an extension of their traditional feminine roles. Women who might be otherwise uncomfortable in the political sphere can use **maternalism** as a way to rationalize the expansion of their nurturing roles into the public sphere (West & Blumberg, 1990). As Lister (2003) says, it is primarily (but not solely) as mothers that women transgress, and feel justified in transgressing, the public-private divide in their struggle to protect their families and communities. Women who do not generally see themselves as political may take political action when their families and communities are threatened. It is interesting to think of this in private sphere–public sphere terms. In short, when public policies and conditions make it difficult for women to meet their private sphere responsibilities, they may act publicly on behalf of private sphere concerns such as the food, shelter, and safety needs of their families. This has been called **accidental activism** (Hyatt, 1992), wherein women are often the active citizens of deprived communities. One cross-national study found that "concern with care, health, and education of children is a unifying thread" in women's local political action (Chanan, 1992, p. 86). However, motherhood is not the only motivation for women's political participation and it is a mistake to reduce women's political participation to maternalism. To do so is to possibly contribute to women's marginalization within politics, a situation where they will be seen as credible political actors only within the context of women and children's issues (Pateman, 1992). It is also exclusionary in the sense that it may leave no room for political women who are not mothers or are not motivated by maternal concerns (Lister, 2003). Emphasizing maternalism also runs the risk of reinforcing women's traditional roles (Dietz, 1985; Segal, 1987; Strange, 1990).

Although social protest actions taken by women as extensions of their nurturing wife–mother roles are viewed as less of a gender violation than women's participation in the formal political sphere, they are still somewhat dangerous. Women's political activism is frequently punished. This is perhaps not surprising when you consider that to be political activists, women violate their gender role and challenge male-dominated institutions of power. Violence as a consequence of women's social protest is well documented, and this punishment is frequently gendered in the sense that it may involve verbal sexual slurs, rape, sexual torture, and violence against their children (Amnesty International, 1990). Women also face criticism from their husbands and families, who may see them as stepping out of their proper role at the expense of their husbands and children.

West and Blumberg (1990), as well as others, have noted the historic invisibility of women in protest movements. In other words, the historical record does not often reflect the important roles that women have played. It seems that women often initiate movements at the local level, but once they expand to higher levels men assume formal leadership. Likewise, women often play important roles but do so quietly with men occupying the official leadership roles.

The first three types of social protest described by West and Blumberg (1990) are examined below. The fourth type, political action for women's rights, is the focus of the final two chapters of the book.

Women's Action Around Economic Issues

Women's protests in regard to economic conditions are one of the most durable and pervasive examples of women as political actors (Peterson & Runyan, 1999). Women have led and taken part in food riots, welfare protests, labor struggles, tenants rights, and other similar actions (West & Blumberg, 1990). In our chapter on women and work, women's labor organizing around the world was noted. In the chapter on women and economic development, I discussed women-organized grassroots organizations dedicated to promoting women's economic development. Many of women's actions in this category fit with what I said above about political activity often being an extension of women's maternal, private sphere role. For instance, Nigerian women have staged a series of protests against multinational oil companies in Nigeria. Since 2002, they have taken over numerous oil facilities, refusing to leave until their demands are met. In one case in 2002, over 150 Nigerian women took over a Chevron facility for eight days, resulting in a loss to the company of 500,000 barrels of oil a day (BBC, 2002). They did not leave until Chevron promised to hire locals and to build schools, water, and power facilities. In 2003, a group of eighty Nigerian village women, ranging from 25 to 60 years old, took over a Shell Oil pipeline station (Mbachu, 2003). Their action was precipitated by the company's moves to build a chain-link fence around the station—preventing the women from drying the vital local staple, manioc, in the heat of gas flares, an unwanted byproduct of oil. They called for employment opportunities, infrastructural development, and microcredit lending programs from the multinational corporation and accused the company of exploiting the environment and neglecting the country's poverty. The women occupied the pumping station after driving employees out and replacing the locks. Shell was forced to shut down facility operations, resulting in a daily loss of 40,000 barrels of crude oil.

Women's Action Around Nationalist and Racial/Ethnic Issues

Throughout history, women have initiated and joined protests and movements demanding liberation and equality (West & Blumberg, 1990). In the United States, Black women were important organizers of civil rights actions, and Rosa Parks, famous for refusing to give her bus seat up for a White man, was a long-term activist in the NAACP, a major civil rights organization (West & Blumberg, 1990). Millions of women have participated in countless uprisings, guerrilla movements, and revolutions—ranging from the French, American, Russian, and Chinese revolutions to the more recent revolutionary struggles throughout Latin America, the Caribbean, Africa, and the Middle East (Peterson & Runyan, 1999). For example, women were visible participants in the political opposition to military rule in Argentina, Brazil, Chile, and Peru (Jaquette & Wolchik, 1998). Additional examples of women's roles in independence movements are found in the next chapter on women's movements, as many women's movements originate in nationalist liberation struggles.

Women's Action Around Humanistic/Nurturing Issues

Women have been leaders and mass participants in movements that address such issues as peace, environmentalism, public education, prison reform, mental health care, and hospices (West & Blumberg, 1990). Their actions in these arenas are sometimes extensions of their wife–mother roles. In the chapter on women and development, the role of women in the environmental sustainability movement was illustrated using the Chipko movement and the Greenbelt movement. In the United States, women have taken leadership roles in the movement against hazardous wastes. For example, Lois Gibbs of the United States uncovered the contamination of her home community (Love Canal in New York state), organized collective action to protect those living there, and now runs an organization that helps other women fight pollution in their communities.

Another example is the Argentinean group, Mothers of the Plaza de Mayo. A military junta took over the government in 1976 and began a terrorist regime in which an estimated 30,000 citizens (thought to be a political threat to the government) were kidnapped and killed (Feijoo, 1998; Navarro, 2001). People were taken without warning, and families were unable to obtain any information about the whereabouts of their loved ones, who came to be known as the "disappeared" or *desaparecidos*. The mothers (and grandmothers) marched defiantly and silently with photographs of their disappeared loved ones; they talked and made tapestries to share the truth about their loved ones; they used drama, speech, and other art forms to publicize their political message (West & Blumberg, 1990).

Women have been the backbone of peace movements worldwide (West & Blumberg, 1990), and their protests against war are often maternally inspired (Strange, 1990). One example of women's organized resistance to war occurred in 1915, when 1,500 women from twelve countries met at the International Congress of Women in The Hague to discuss women's role in ending World War I. They linked women's suffrage with peace, arguing that if women were allowed greater political participation, war would be less likely.

After the meeting, envoys from the conference visited leaders in fourteen countries and called for peace and mediation by neutral countries. There is evidence that these women had a positive effect on the peace process (Stienstra, 1994).

More recent examples include women in Northern Ireland, like Mairead Corrigan and Betty Williams, who won the Nobel Peace Prize in 1977 for their efforts to stop the bloodshed between Protestants and Catholics, and the Sri Lankan Voice of Women for Peace, which called for the end of the civil war between the Sinhalese and Tamils (Peterson & Runyan, 1999). In 2002–2003, American women took a leading role in protesting the U.S. war in Iraq. Women in Black chapters held candlelight vigils all over the country to draw attention to the human costs of war. At protests the women dressed in black to signify mourning for the war dead. Code Pink, a women's peace organization that uses the color pink in their demonstrations, staged creative demonstrations in many major U.S. cities and handed out "pink slips" to legislators who supported the war in Iraq. PeaceWomen, an "international league for peace and freedom" has contacts for hundreds of women's organizations worldwide dedicated to promoting peace (http://www.peacewomen.org).

Women's groups have also been an important part of the movement against nuclear weapons' deployment and proliferation. In the 1980s, women's activist antinuclear groups emerged in Australia, Canada, Holland, Italy, the United States, the United Kingdom, and West Germany (Peterson & Runyan, 1999). Their activism here also appears to be strongly connected to their maternal roles; you can't, they declare, "hug children with nuclear arms" (Strange, 1990).

Although the motivation of much of women's activism against war and the military has been their association with and responsibility for mothering, many mothers support the war effort. Not all women are maternalist pacifists opposed to war (Strange, 1990). Maternalism and patriotism are often linked, and women frequently see their role as calling for their support of military operations (Strange, 1990). Women, like men, are not innately peaceful and have always served militaries and supported wars (Peterson & Runyan, 1999). Also, women do take up arms and support national liberation struggles, evidence that women are not naturally peaceful (Peterson & Runyan, 1999). For example, in 2003, female suicide bombers killed themselves (and many others) for the cause of nationalism (in Russia, the cause was Chechen independence and in Israel, Palestinian independence).

Conclusion

In this chapter you saw that there is more to women's political involvement and power than their presence in formal government decision-making bodies. Ordinary women act politically when they organize and put pressure on established power systems from the bottom up, and the results of these efforts

Jody Williams of the United States won the Nobel Peace Prize in 1997 for leading the international movement to ban landmines. Left after wartime, landmines maim or kill approximately 26,000 people a year. Williams has built a coalition of 1,000 nongovernmental organizations.

We choose pink,

the color of roses,

the beauty that like
    bread is food for life,

the color of the dawn of
    a new era

when cooperation and
    negotiation prevail
    over force.

*Code Pink, U.S. Women's
Peace Organization*

BOX 9.7   *Women Around the Globe: International Documents Enshrining Women's Political Rights*

Most countries have signed the majority of these international agreements.

Universal Declaration of Human Rights (1948)
http://www.un.org/rights/50/decla.htm

Convention on the Political Rights of Women (1952)
http://www.ipu.org/wmn-e/planactn.htm#14

International Convenant on Civil and Political Rights (1960)
http://www.pch.gc.ca/ddp-hrd/english/iccpr/CN_1.htm

Convention on the Elimination of All Forms of Discrimination Against Women (1979)
http://www.Gopher://gopher.un.org/00/ga/cedaw/convention

The Beijing Platform for Action (1995)
http://www.un.org/womenwatch/daw/beijing/platform/decision.htm

Beijing +5 (2000)
http://www.un.org/womenwatch/daw/followup/finaloutcome.pdf

---

are significant. As D'Amico and Beckman (1995) note, a feminist perspective on women in world politics sees women as engaged in politics when they are working to prevent rape, to stop female circumcision and dowry deaths, and to influence how development aid is allocated. That being said, the value of informal politics does not provide an alibi for the continued underrepresentation of women and minority groups in the formal structures of power (Lister, 2003). Indeed, when we think about the true purpose of representative democracy, we should become alarmed that although they make up approximately half of the population, women typically comprise only 5 to 14 percent of legislatures and only rarely occupy chief political posts. As Lister (2003) suggests, increasing women's political representation is particularly important because women have special interests, some in conflict with men's interests, which need to be articulated directly by women in political debate and decision making. Of course, not all women representatives advance women's causes, but in sufficient numbers (at least 30 percent), they do appear to make a difference.

The story of women in politics is a story of a glass "half-full" of remarkable progress, and "half-empty" with staggering disappointment. It is exciting that each year gives us a new first for women in politics—a country's first female prime minister, the world's first national parliament over 45 percent female, a country's first domestic violence legislation. In the last decade most governments have pledged to reach a goal of 30 percent female representation (see Box 9.7, *Women Around the Globe: International Documents Enshrining Women's Political Rights,* for international agreements). However, most governments and political parties have fallen far short in making changes that would fully include women. Male political control often poses significant barriers to women's rights advocacy. Also, too many women remain politically illiterate, unable to participate fully in politics and advocate for their rights. So, although there is room for cautious optimism, continued progress requires the transformation of the social structures and gender ideologies that interfere with women's full political participation. The next two chapters, one on women's movements and the other on women's rights as human rights, focus on the mechanisms for such transformations.

Study Questions

1. Why do we perceive politics as a masculine domain? Why is this perception of concern to feminists?

2. When did most of women's struggles to gain the vote occur? Why doesn't voting alone guarantee gender equality in politics?

3. On average, what percentage of formal government positions are held by women?

4. What are ideological explanations for gender differences in political participation?

5. What are sociostructural explanations for gender differences in political participation?

6. What are political explanations for gender differences in political participation?

7. Why do feminists wish to achieve a "critical mass" of females in formal politics? According to the UN, what percentage of women is needed in formal politics to make a difference?

8. What are the three paths to power for female heads of state? Describe.

9. What is the role of gender in the perception of female world leaders? Do female heads of state lead differently than male ones?

10. What factors influence whether female heads of state engage in women's issues advocacy?

11. How does "maternalism" affect women's activity in informal politics? Why should we be careful not to reduce all of women's informal political activity to maternalism?

12. What are the four general types of issues that draw women into social protest? Describe.

13. In the chapter conclusion it is said that the story of women and politics is cause for optimism and pessimism—what is meant by this?

Discussion Questions and Activities

1. Do you agree that were it not for the fact that women leaders must act like men to get and stay in office that they would lead differently than men? Why or why not?

2. The use of quotas, in which political parties must give a certain percentage of their political seats to women, are one of the main means of getting women into political office worldwide. Some have argued that such quotas are a necessary first step because without them women would not get a chance to show that they have what it takes to hold political office. Others argue that quotas don't help to generate a situation in which women are equal partners in politics because it is assumed that "quota women" are not as capable as those elected without the help of quotas. What is your position regarding the use of quotas to increase the number of women holding political office?

3. Do a biographical essay on one of the women leaders listed in the boxes on paths to power but not discussed in the chapter. Explain how the woman you profile rose to power and whether she was an advocate for women's issues.

Activist Websites of Interest

Women's Environment and Development Organization (WEDO) 50/50 Campaign

http://www.wedo.org/5050/

EMILY's List

http://www.emilyslist.org/home.htm

International Institute for Democracy and Electoral Assistance (IDEA)

http://www.idea.int/gender/index.htm

Informational Websites of Interest

Online Women in Politics

http://www.onlinewomeninpolitics.org/suffrage.htm

Inter-parliamentary Union

http://www.ipu.org

Center for American Women in Politics (CAWP)

http://www.rci.rutgers.edu/~cawp/index.html

Center for Women's Global Leadership

http://www.feminist.com/cfwgl.htm

Worldwide Guide to Women in Leadership

http://www.guide2womenleaders.com/index.htm

Action Opportunities

1. Join WEDO's 50/50 campaign. Launched in New York on June 8, 2000, during the five-year review of the Beijing Platform for Action, the campaign's goals are to increase the percentage of women in local and national politics worldwide. Since it began the 50/50 campaign has been adopted by 154 organizations in 45 countries. Go to http://www.wedo.org/sign.htm to sign a petition indicating your support, and go to http://www.wedo.org/5050kit.htm for a 50/50 campaign kit including fact sheets and strategies.

2. Do something to increase women's political literacy. For example, teach students how to use absentee ballots, or help females run for campus elected offices by explaining the process. Educate your local or campus women's group on political tactics such as "tabling," petitions, and running for student offices. Remember that your mission will be to teach others the specifics of participation in a political system.

3. Do some campaigning or fund-raising for a female political candidate.

4. Women in social protest movements frequently face government persecution, such as imprisonment without due process. Participate in an Amnesty International letter-writing campaign on behalf of one or more female political prisoners (http://www.amnesty.org).

10 Gender Equality Movements

While gender subordination has universal elements, feminism cannot be based on a rigid concept of universality that negates the wide variation in women's experience. . . . There is, and must be, a diversity of feminisms, responsive to the different needs and concerns of different women, and *defined by them for themselves.*

—GITA SEN AND CAREN GROWN of DAWN

Muslim women students in Jakarta, Indonesia, protest government policies that negatively impact women. In every society, in every generation, women protest gender injustice.

T his chapter focuses on contemporary women's efforts to address women's issues and bring about gender equality. These efforts occur cross-nationally and assume a variety of forms. The chapter begins with a consideration of the forces that operate against women's activism and empowerment. The remainder of the chapter focuses on women's movements worldwide, emphasizing the many different forms women's movements may take and how history, politics, culture, and current realities shape them.

> "Never doubt that a small group of thoughtful, committed citizens can change the world—indeed, it's the only thing that ever has."
> *Margaret Mead*

Forces Operating Against Women's Activism

People are sometimes puzzled that women put up with gendered abuses and seem to accept lower power and status. Many people simply proclaim that it could all be stopped if women would just stand up for themselves. There is a small truth in this since the system of patriarchy can function only with the cooperation of women. However, as Lerner (1986) points out, this cooperation is secured by a variety of means: gender indoctrination, educational deprivation, denying women their history of struggle and achievement, dividing women from one another, restraints and outright coercion, discrimination in access to economic resources and political power, and awarding class privileges to conforming women. In other words, standing up for women's rights is not such a simple matter after all.

It is important to understand the perils of women's activism. One danger in speaking out is the possible loss of social belongingness and social approval. Questioning tradition and seeking social change is one of the surest ways to trigger the wrath of others and their rejection. Socially speaking, it is a risky business to speak out on behalf of gender justice and many people are inhibited by a desire to fit in and be accepted by others. Even in Western, individualistic countries such as the United States, simply identifying oneself as a feminist or calling attention to sexism is often enough to be labeled a "Feminazi" or "Manhater"—labels women want to avoid.

In some cultures, the social rejection that accompanies women's activism can be quite severe. In Algeria, in the 1980s and 1990s, women's activists were threatened and killed (Moghadam, 2003). Box 10.1, *Activist Profile: Taslima Nasrin of Bangladesh,* tells the story of a Bangladeshi physician turned novelist who faces death due to her feminist beliefs. In many countries, rebelling against traditional gender practices makes women unmarriageable, a devastating consequence when there are few economic options for women outside of marriage. For instance, in cultures that practice female genital mutilation, a woman's marriageability is increased by the procedure. Further consider that social rejection may be experienced especially severely in collectivist cultures that emphasize the subordination of individual goals for the sake of the community. In collectivist cultures, people's identity is strongly rooted in family and community. Conformity is often stronger in these cultures because individuals do not want to bring shame upon their family or village.

> "The women's movement, not only here in the U.S., but worldwide, is bigger and stronger than ever before and in places where it has never been. It has arms. It has legs. And most importantly, it has heads.
> *Bella Abzug, U.S. Congresswoman and co-founder of Women's Environment & Development Organization (WEDO)*

> "It has been difficult for me as an indigenous woman to find the confidence to speak publicly, particularly since we were raised to believe that the only role for women is to maintain a household and to bear children. If you broke with this role, you were seen as abandoning tradition and you would lose the respect of the people."
> *Rigoberta Menchu, Guatemalan winner of the Nobel Peace Prize*

263

BOX 10.1   *Activist Profile: Taslima Nasrin of Bangladesh*

Taslima Nasrin was born in August 1962 to a Muslim family in Bangladesh. She began writing when she was 15 years old, publishing poetry in the literary magazines. She continued to write even while in medical school. After receiving her medical degree in 1984, she worked in public hospitals for eight years. Starting in 1986, she has published twenty-four highly acclaimed books of poetry and literature. Taslima's critical writings about religion and women's oppression make her a controversial figure in Bangladesh. By 1990, Islamic fundamentalists began an intimidation campaign against her that included demonstrations and physical assaults that made it impossible for her to appear in public. In 1993, a fundamentalist organization set a price on her head because of her criticism of Islam, and she was confined to her house. The public unrest stirred by her writing led the government to ban her books and force her to leave the country. In 1998, without the permission of the government, she risked death to return to her country to be with her ailing mother. Again, fundamentalists demanded she be killed and again she was forced to leave Bangladesh. Since that time, she has lived in exile in Europe. Her most recent book, *Dwikhandito,* or *Split in Two,* an autobiography, was banned in Bangladesh in 2003. Here is an excerpt from her response to this recent development (on her website http://taslimanasrin.com/).

What is the bottom line, and why the objections to my books?
Patriarchal minds object.

I am not supposed to write about equality and justice for women.
Patriarchal minds object.

I must not talk about the enjoyment of sex, if what I write includes showing the enjoyment of sex by women.
Patriarchal minds object.

I must not dare to challenge patriarchy.

For if it were to tumble down women would no longer be able to be treated as slaves, as sexual commodities, and men would have to make a shift in their viewpoints and actions.

I am a proud nonconformist. I accept the good from the past and reject the bad. But I do not accept the view that it is bad to express oneself freely. Women are being oppressed everywhere, are they not? Well, this oppression simply has to stop!

Sources: Filkins, 1998, and Taslima Nasrin's official website (http://taslimanasrin.com/).

"Women have been taught for centuries that they are the slaves of men. I started writing because I wanted to wake them up."
Taslima Nasrin

Individuals generally have little doubt about the gender norms and roles of their culture. The distinct differences between women's and men's roles in most societies clearly communicate that what is expected of individuals is based in part on their sex. Starting in early childhood we become aware of our identity as a male or female and notice that different things are expected of each sex. We then model the behaviors of same-gendered others in a tendency psychologists call **differential modeling** (Burn, 1996). Add to this that children are reinforced for behaviors depending upon the behavior's gender appropriateness. This is called **differential reinforcement** and has been documented cross-culturally (Low, 1989; Rogoff, 1981; Whiting & Edwards, 1988). In particular, there is a greater emphasis on nurturance, obedience, and

FIGURE 10.1   *Bandura's Self-Efficacy Model*

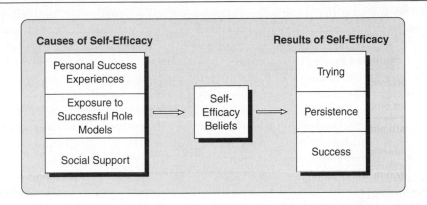

responsibility for girls, and achievement and self-reliance for boys, especially in societies in which women have little control over resources (Low, 1989). As a result of **differential socialization** by gender, gender-inappropriate behavior is not within the individual's behavioral repertoire. For females socialized to be obedient and submissive, challenging gender customs is especially foreign. For instance, in many parts of Mexico, the ability to put up with things, *aguantar,* is a mark of feminine virtue (Darling, 1995).

Williams and Best (1990a) once said that beliefs concerning the psychological makeup of men and women are absorbed into myth and religion, into oral history and written literature. A culture's gender stereotypes typically function as gender norms—prescriptive social rules specifying appropriate behavior based on gender. They are also taught as part of childhood socialization. For instance, in the United States, there are sayings such as "Girls are made of sugar and spice and everything nice" and "Boys are made of frogs and snails and puppy dogs' tails." In short, societies have beliefs regarding how males and females are different and typically model and reinforce behaviors consistent with gender stereotypes. Wanting acceptance and approval from adults and peers, we conform to these gender roles and stereotypes and become more comfortable performing gender-appropriate behaviors (Burn, 1996). This makes it difficult to behave in a way counter to one's gender role.

Another reason why women often do not resist is that their low power leads them to believe that there is not much point in defiance. Women often lack **self-efficacy** (the belief that they will be effective) in regards to challenging the traditional gender order. Self-efficacy matters because if you are skeptical about your chances of success, then you are unlikely to try, or to persist if your efforts are not immediately fruitful (Bandura, 1986). As depicted in Figure 10.1, self-efficacy is based on personal success experiences with the task, seeing people like yourself succeed at the task (role models), and on receiving social support and encouragement (Bandura, 1986). Looked at this way, it is not surprising that women sometimes put up with gender inequality.

Particularly in cultures with rigid gender roles that tolerate little deviation, females learn early that efforts to rebel are unlikely to be successful. It is also the case that in female-repressive societies, females are unlikely to have ever seen females like themselves successfully step outside of their gender place. Instead, they have seen such individuals ostracized and otherwise punished. As Lerner (1986) points out, when there is no precedent, one cannot imagine alternatives to existing conditions. We must also consider that in female-repressive societies, others are unlikely to socially support deviation. This is because conformity is equated with survival. Given that there are few options for women outside of conformity to traditional roles and knowing that punishment is the likely result of deviation, the loved ones of potential "deviates" encourage conformity.

By communicating to women that they are empowered or disempowered as women, societal and family norms also affect women's perceived self-efficacy. The laws, religion, and cultural practices of a society communicate to its people the relative status and power of women and men. These societal values regarding male and female are enacted in the family in the form of resources and decision-making power. In this way, the norms of the society and of the family act together to determine a woman's power to make and carry out decisions. In other words, it is not surprising that women who have little power may be more passive and accepting of their lower status. Not only may they be unaccustomed to acting independently because it is discouraged and even punished, but because of their low power, attempts at independent action may not have much effect. Consequently, their inclination to act is reduced. Passivity may be especially marked for women who are exposed to numerous uncontrollable life stressors—in particular, high indoor and outdoor density, poverty, poor sanitation, or other factors beyond their control. Such uncontrollable events further contribute to the perception that action will make little difference.

The amazing thing, then, is not that women don't always protest gender injustice, but that *they often do.* Indeed, in every society, in every generation, there have been efforts by women to fight their lower status. For instance, Fatimah Umm Salamih, who lived in Persia (now Iran) in the nineteenth century, fought for the equality of women. Murdered in 1852, thrown in a well, and covered with rocks, her last words were recorded as "You can kill me as soon as you like, but you cannot stop the emancipation of women" (Tomasevski, 1993).

Salima Ghezali is a feminist activist and editor of Algeria's major newspaper, *La Nation,* now banned for criticizing the government and the Islamic extremists for their part in the violence that terrorizes Algeria. In hiding, she continues to write articles in an effort to draw international attention to human rights violations in Algeria. Ghezali also founded the Association for the Emancipation of Women and the feminist journal *Nyssa.*

Early Assumptions About Women's Movements

Until recently, Western feminist academics dominated the study of women's movements. Typically, they focused on movements in the United States and Europe and rarely on movements in postcolonial countries (Basu, 1995). These analyses often overemphasized the role of middle-class women, the role of economic development, and particular types of activities. This probably occurred because to Western scholars, the most visible feminist movements were those in industrialized nations dominated by middle- and -upper-class women engaged in campaigns to gain equal rights under the law (such as the right to vote). These features of Western women's movements were overgeneralized and led to a narrow definition of women's movements. This narrow definition excluded the many different ways in which women struggle against gender inequality, and, as noted by Basu (1995), defined out of existence those movements from which the middle class is absent or unimportant.

As Basu (1995) and others (Bystydzienski, 1992a) point out, there is a long history of struggle for women's equality in the Middle East, Latin America, Asia, and Africa; economic development is no guarantee of a strong women's movement; and women's movements comprise a range of struggles by women against gender inequality. Women's movements may be independently organized or affiliated with political parties, they may be of short or long duration, they may rest on a narrow social base or on multiclass coalitions, they may focus on one issue or multiple issues, and they may be local or national (Basu, 1995). To exclude any of these forms is to restrict our understanding of a rich and multifaceted phenomenon (Basu, 1995).

Diversity in Use of the Feminist Label

Some women's movements embrace the feminist label such as the Association of Women for Action and Research (Singapore), Action India, the Feminist Majority (United States), and Bat Shalom (Israel). However, many women's organizations that do the work of the women's movement avoid the feminist label. One reason for this avoidance is that feminism has a negative connotation in many cultures. In countries with a history of colonization (many African countries) or other antagonistic relationships with Western countries (many Muslim countries), the effectiveness of openly feminist organizations may be compromised by the public perception that feminism is a Western, imported notion. In other countries, antifeminist groups have successfully given feminism a negative image such that many with feminist leanings do not call themselves "feminists." For example, in the United States, many women's activists and organizations are "covertly" feminist because of the perception that support for women's policies and programs is reduced by association with the feminist label. Indeed, research in the United States finds that terminology affects support for feminist policies (Breinlinger & Kelly, 1994; Buschman & Lenart, 1996; Jacobson, 1981).

In a number of Latin American countries where socialist struggles have resulted in democratization, feminism is associated with the bourgeoisie (the middle and upper class) and imperialism. In Chile, for instance, feminists are considered bourgeois and elitist and insufficiently committed to the interests

"Believe not those who say

The upward path is smooth,

Lest thou should stumble on the way

And faint before the truth."

Anne Brontë (1820–1849), British writer

"Every country has women's rights groups." *Mahnaz Afkhami*

"If particular care and attention is not paid to the ladies, we are determined to foment a rebellion and will not hold ourselves bound by any laws in which we have no voice or representation." *Abigail Adams, wife of U.S. President John Adams, and perhaps America's first feminist*

of the working class (Frohmann & Valdes, 1995). In Bolivia, feminism is viewed as alien to the working class and as divisive to the labor movement (Salinas, 1994). Similarly, feminist activists in Nicaragua often avoid the feminist label because feminism is often portrayed in the media as antifamily and anti-male, and the traditional Latin American political left believes feminism to be bourgeois and inappropriate for women in a poor country like Nicaragua (Chinchilla, 1994).

Third World women may avoid the feminist label because the term *feminism* is frequently associated with a narrow, Western view of women's issues and strategies. Women in some countries, including Poland, Russia, and Honduras, distance themselves from Western feminism because it is not seen as relevant to their own social and economic conditions (Sekhon & Bystydzienski, 1999). Many Third World women feel that their struggle as women is connected to the struggles of their communities against racism, economic exploitation, and imperialism and believe that Western or First World feminism does not address this. For instance, Black South African feminism is based on Black women's experience of multiple oppressions and includes issues, such as access to clean water and housing, that have not traditionally been defined as feminist (Kemp, Madlala, Moodley, & Salo, 1995). Or as Oyeronke Oyewumi (2003, p. 3) says, "In its various guises and disguises, feminism continues to be the most avid manufacturer of gender consciousness and gender categories, inevitably at the expense of local categories such as ethnicity, seniority, race, and generation, that may be more locally salient."

In other words, First World feminism is viewed by many Third World women as too singularly focused on the struggle against gender discrimination when their oppression cannot be limited to gender alone (Johnson-Odim, 1991). As Mohanty (1991) says, "To define feminism purely in gendered terms assumes our consciousness (or identity) of being 'women' has nothing to do with race, class, nation, or sexuality, just gender. But no one becomes a woman purely because she is female. Ideologies of womanhood have as much to do with class and race as they have to do with sex" (p. 12). Or, as Kemp and colleagues (1995) say in a chapter on Black South African feminism,

> The challenge especially for Black feminists, has been to shape South African feminism based on three central assumptions. First, our identities as women are shaped by race, class, and gender, and these identities have molded our particular experiences of gender oppression. Second, our struggles as feminists encompass the struggle for national liberation from a brutal white state. Furthermore, the liberation of Black people as a whole is a feminist issue. Third, we have to challenge and transform Black patriarchies even though Black men have been our allies in the fight for national liberation. (p. 133)

Third World women distance themselves from Western feminism for other reasons as well. They are often aware, for example, that First World

Meena (1957–1987) of Kabul, Afghanistan, dangerously campaigned against the occupying Soviet forces, began a feminist women's magazine, founded the Afghan feminist organization RAWA, advocated against Islamic fundamentalist views of women, and established schools for Afghanistan refugee children in Pakistan and micro-enterprises for their parents. She was assassinated in 1987 by the Soviet secret service (KGB) and their fundamentalist accomplices.

"Feminism in Mexico, as elsewhere, is not expressed in a single voice."
Victoria Rodriquez

women participated in the oppression of Third World women (Johnson-Odim, 1991; Kemp et al., 1995). It is sometimes difficult for Third World women to think of Western feminists as their sisters when Western women received privileges on the backs of non-white women (Oyewumi, 2003). As Chase, a Black Namibian activist says, "The minute you hear about feminism one immediately puts it in the connotation of the European and North American women's struggles. These are women from societies which have long been independent—people who . . . support the governments that . . . support our oppression. I could never feel solidarity with that. . . . I think there will be a different feminism coming out of Africa" (in Kemp et al., 1995, p. 141). Third World women's activists are also cognizant of the fact that racism was present in the early Western women's movement and that, up until recently, First World feminists have dominated international women's conferences (Johnson-Odim, 1991).

Feminist concepts developed in Western and European cultures may not be exportable to cultures with different social organizations and logic (Oyewumi, 2003). For this reason, Third World feminists seek their own feminisms. As I've already suggested, African feminisms are shaped by African women's resistance to Western hegemony (domination) and by African culture. This means that some of the concerns that have driven Western feminism, such as female control over reproduction and choice within human sexuality, are not characteristic of African feminisms. Indeed, African feminism is "distinctly heterosexual, pro-natal, and concerned with bread, butter, culture and power issues" (Mikell, 1997, p. 4). Motherhood is central to many Latin American, South American, and African feminisms in contrast to Western feminisms that often distance themselves from women's role as mother and see that role as oppressive (Oyewumi, 2003). Third World feminisms are often rooted in a pre-colonial past in which women played strong roles and were high in status. For example, the creation of the first woman, according to the indigenous people of the Philippines, was simultaneous with the creation of the first man. Filipina feminists refer to this to show that as a person born whole and separate from man, the Filipina owns her body and self and can chart her own history and destiny (Santiago, 1995).

Western feminism is also frequently dismissed as an instrument of colonialism in Muslim countries. Islamic feminists often argue that Western feminism, with its emphasis on equality in the labor force and White middle-class women, is irrelevant to the majority of the world's women, who seek an honored place as wives and as mothers (Afshar, 1996). Like African feminists, women working toward equality in Muslim countries frequently distinguish themselves from Western feminists to avoid charges that they have been influenced by "foreign" ideologies (Moghadam, 1991). These efforts are centered around recovering their own women's history (which includes Muslim women rulers and theologians) and showing that women's equality is consistent with Islam (Moghadam, 1991; 2003).

The bottom line is that there is great diversity in the origins and character of women's movements worldwide. As noted by Margolis (1993), we must

"This demonization of feminism as Western totally Ignores the fact that for more than two decades women of Asia, Africa, Latin American, and the Middle East have been creating their own contextualized forms of feminism and speaking about their rights and demands in their own voices."
Rosemary Ruether

"In Islam and the Arab world, and in all our cultures, we must claim those things that are positive and discard without hesitation those things that are negative. In Egypt we have a long tradition of women in power. For thousands of years, for example, we have had the Goddess Isis, and her tradition. Thank God, thank Goddess, we still have her spirit with us."
Nawal el Saadawi

Ichikawa Fusae (1893–1981) led the women's suffrage movement in Japan, founded one of the first feminist organizations in 1919 (the New Woman's Association), and was elected to the House of Councillors in 1952, where she continued her work on women's issues and served until her death.

guard against the ethnocentric assumption that all gender equality movements will happen in the same way. Because cultures differ, the issue that stimulates the women's movement in one country may hurt it in another. Margolis (1993) gives the example of family planning. In the West, family planning and abortion have served as major mobilizing forces for the women's movement, but such programs often arouse suspicion and opposition from Third World women, who may see these as attempts to limit the populations of their ethnic groups. This approach also does not make sense to women in countries where women's status is enhanced by having lots of children or where women need lots of children to help with the labor. Similarly, Basu (1995) acknowledges that women's movements often address common feminist issues in very different ways. For example, with regard to reproductive rights, Irish women struggle for freer access to contraception, Bangladeshi women fight antinatalist government policies, Chinese women emphasize the connection between the one-child policy and female infanticide, and Filipino women's groups organize for prostitutes' rights, access to a greater range of contraception, and education to prevent AIDS.

"Hum Bharat ki nari hain, phool nahin, chingari hain." ("We, the women of India, are not flowers, but fiery sparks.")
Indian feminist slogan

Because feminist struggles occur in unique cultural contexts unable to be fully understood by outsiders, women in their own cultures create the most effective women's movements. It is these women who know how to frame women's rights in cultural context. Also, associations with "outsiders" often compromise the legitimacy, and correspondingly, the effectiveness of movements. Feminist outsiders mean well when they try to change practices in other cultures, but they may unwittingly interfere with gender progress and other women's right to self-determination. In a critique of Western attempts to eradicate female circumcision in Africa, Obiora (2003) says those who are best suited to engineer and bring about lasting reform are women in their own cultures. Box 10.2, *Women Across the Globe: Differences Between Western and other Feminisms*, summarizes the reasons why Western feminisms are not easily exportable to non-Western cultures.

Different Strands of Women's Movements

"Can an outsider be so arrogant as to assume that she is omniscient or omnipotent enough to unilaterally appropriate a lead role and articulate a viable reform agenda?"
L. Amede Obiora

Nationally and cross-nationally, women's movements may take many forms. The term women's movement describes a sum of campaigns around issues of importance to women—campaigns that feed into a network of women's groups and increase awareness of women's problems and rights (Kumar, 1995). The women's movement is not a distinct organizational entity worldwide, or even in most countries; within a single country, the movement has broad ideological variety and a range of organizational expressions (Katzenstein, 1987). Indeed, it is inaccurate to talk of *a* women's movement; it is far more accurate to speak of women's movement*s*. Box 10.3, *Women Around the Globe: Diversity in Women's Activism*, provides a sense of this variety. Consider also this example from Alvarez (1994) describing the Brazilian women's movement of the 1970s and 1980s:

BOX 10.2   *Women Across the Globe: Differences Between Western and Other Feminisms*

- Western feminism may not apply to cultures with different economic and social conditions.

- Third World feminism is tied to other struggles (e.g., racism, poverty, imperialism) that are seen as equally important.

- Third World women do not always trust First World feminists because they have historically excluded Third World women from international conferences and come from countries with a history of imperialism.

- Motherhood is often central to Third World and Arab feminisms.

- Third World feminisms often rooted in pre-colonial past.

- Arab feminisms are often rooted in Islam.

- Western feminism is viewed suspiciously as a possible effort to impose Western culture.

- Association with Western feminism often hurts Third World and Arab feminist efforts.

Women spearheaded protests against the regime's human rights violations; poor and working-class women crafted creative solutions to meet community needs in response to gross government neglect of basic urban and social services; women workers swelled the ranks of Brazil's new trade union movement; rural women struggled for their rights to land that were increasingly being usurped by export-agribusiness; Afro-Brazilian women joined the United Black Movement and helped forge other organized expressions of a growing antiracist, Black-consciousness movement; Brazilian lesbians joined gay males to launch a struggle against homophobia; young women and university students enlisted in militant student movements; some took up arms against the military regime, and still others worked in legally sanctioned parties of the opposition. By the 1980s, thousands of women involved in these and other struggles had come to identify themselves as feminists (p. 13).

Bystydzienski (1992a) suggests that in countries with a women's movement, there are generally two branches: an established older branch made up of organizations that have become institutionalized and that are more or less accepted as the mouthpiece for women's rights; and a younger, noninstitutionalized branch made up of small, loose groups outside of the mainstream. The older branch, she maintains, tends to be more ideologically liberal or moderate and essentially struggles for changes in laws and policies within the existing society. This branch also tends toward a hierarchical structure with some role specialization and formal rules. In contrast, the younger branch is

BOX 10.3   *Women Around the Globe: Diversity in Women's Activism*

- In 1978 in Spain, as part of a national campaign in support of women on trial for having abortions, a thousand women publicly proclaimed in a written document that they too had had abortions and should be tried. In a second document, both men and women stated that they had participated in abortions and insisted that they too be judged.

- In 1984, women in Iceland protested gender wage discrimination by jamming grocery stores and markets and insisting that they should only have to pay sixty-six cents on the dollar for purchases. Their reasoning was that if they were only paid sixty-six cents for every dollar men earned, they should only have to pay 66 percent of the price of consumer goods.

- The Centre de Promotion des Femmes Ouvrières (CPFO) was founded in Port-au-Prince, Haiti, in 1985. CPFO's work focuses on the rights of women workers, women's literacy, women's reproductive health, and legal counseling and assistance. They serve a population of about 30,000 women workers.

- In the United States in the 1990s, feminists established centers for research on women, staged protests and demonstrations, developed policy and legislation, lobbied Congress, and developed service programs to meet women's needs.

- In 1990, forty-seven veiled Saudi Arabian women protested the law prohibiting women from driving cars on the King Abdul Aziz Highway in Riyadh.

- The National Women's Lobby Group (NWLG), formed in Zambia in 1991, aims to promote the end of laws and customs that discriminate against women, to increase women's education and political participation, and to put women in political decision-making positions. The NWLG intensely campaigns in order to get women's issues on the government agenda, forms alliances with other NGOs, and does outreach to educate women as to the law and their rights.

- The Zena Zenama (Woman to Woman) Association was founded in Mostar, Bosnia-Herzegovina, in 1997, by a Serb woman and two Muslim women. Working out of a crowded apartment, they engage in a number of activities such as helping elderly women try to recover their homes, assisting battered wives, running support groups for survivors of ethnic massacres and war rape, and providing voter education.

- The Sri Lanka Federation of University Women (SLFUW) was formed almost fifty years ago by a handful of graduate women. Today the organization's focus is on helping women graduates and undergraduates and on training programs to enhance women's employment opportunities. The organization networks with a number of other organizations both nationally and internationally.

- In 2003, hundreds of Iranian women rallied for equal social and political rights in Tehran on International Women's Day. This was the first women's public protest since the 1979 Islamic Revolution.

more ideologically radical and seeks transformation of existing societies according to feminist principles. It consists of small, local groups, often linked by informal networks, and avoids formal rules and hierarchies. The activities of the younger branch focus on building alternatives outside of the system, such as cooperatives run by women, economic enterprises, women's shelters, health clinics, and daycare centers.

Three major strands of women's movements (see Figure 10.2) are found in many countries: women's rights activist groups that raise women's issues at

FIGURE 10.2   *Three Common Types of Women's Movements*

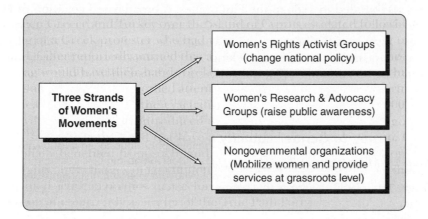

the national policy level; women's research and advocacy organizations that raise public awareness; and nongovernmental organizations that work to raise women's awareness and mobilize women at the grassroots level (Jahan, 1995b). Furthermore, these different types of groups often build coalitions in order to create change. Jahan (1995b) describes these three major strands in Bangladesh in her discussion of campaigns to eliminate violence against women in Bangladesh (from the late 1970s to early 1980s). Researchers documented violence against women, grassroots groups started intervention programs, and women's organizations pressured the government to enact laws against that violence.

Large, national organizations focused on legislative change are perhaps the most visible of the three "strands." For example, from the early to mid-twentieth century, women's organizations on every continent won women the right to vote. Another example of change sought by a large, national women's organization is Bangladesh's largest women's organization, Mahila Parishad. This organization collected 17,000 signatures and lobbied parliament for an antidowry law, which was passed in 1980. Likewise, the Concertación Nacional de Mujeres por la Democracia (National Coalition of Women for Democracy, or CNMD), a coalition of women's organizations in Chile, successfully lobbied to include women's issues on the agenda of the new democratic government formed in 1990.

Despite the visibility of large national women's organizations, the vitality of women's movements lies primarily in small, local-level activist groups (Basu, 1995; Katzenstein, 1987). These grassroots organizations (GROs) include small, local-level groups that provide services such as shelter to battered women or credit to female micro-entrepreneurs, or engage in local protests or awareness campaigns. Grassroots support organizations (GRSOs) are another type of nongovernmental organization characteristic of women's movements worldwide. GRSOs are nationally or regionally based assistance

"Power is not something people give away. It has to be negotiated, and sometimes wrested from the powerful."
Devaki Jain, Indian writer and activist

"The women's movement in Iran is very misunderstood by the West. If you could break the image that we are all one black mass under the hijab, you would understand women in Iran. What we care about is not what we wear on our heads, but much more important issues, more profound issues of law that affect our lives."
Mehranguiz Kar

organizations that channel funds and information to grassroots organizations; GRSOs are usually staffed by professionals. For example, GABRIELA is a GRSO founded in 1984 in the Philippines. A broad-based coalition of Filipino feminist organizations, GABRIELA rallies women and organizes campaigns against violations of women's rights in the home and workplace, sexual harassment, and sex trafficking. In every chapter you have encountered many examples of GROs and GRSOs that respond to women's issues.

The Journey to Gender Equality Differs Cross-Culturally

Women's Movements in Response to Different Issues

Molyneaux (1985) suggests that women's movements may arise out of either "practical gender interests" or "strategic gender interests." **Practical gender interests** are usually in response to an immediate perceived need and do not generally have as their goal women's emancipation or equality. In contrast, **strategic gender interests** arise out of an awareness of a generalized patriarchy and a desire to challenge and change it. Both types of movements are important and necessary for easing, and eventually eliminating, women's oppression. Peterson and Runyan (1993) propose that movements arising out of practical gender interests tend to be attempts at reforms of an existing system whereas movements arising out of strategic gender interests are oriented toward larger transformations.

Peterson and Runyan (1993) also suggest that most women's activism arises out of local and immediate conditions that are perceived as obstacles to the realization of practical interests, but that as activists become aware of the relationship between local struggles and the overall system of gender subordination they often move toward system-transforming politics. In this way, they say, participation in local resistance actions can lead to participation in (or at least support for) larger and sometimes global social movements. This point is driven home in the next chapter, on global feminism. It appears, however, that strategically motivated movements may also become more practically oriented. This seems to happen as activists discover just how deeply embedded gender inequality is in established social systems. They then focus on bringing about progress in recalcitrant social systems through incremental change. For example, Tanaka (1995) writes that the Japanese feminist movement that emerged in the 1970s changed from one that sought to "transform the whole set of cultural values" to one in the 1990s focused on "concrete social changes" and "women's assimilation into the male-dominated system" (p. 351).

"This is a common story in many women. We began with the social struggle, and little by little we moved toward the struggle of women."
Gilda Rivera, one of the founders of the Honduran Women's Organization Centre de los Derechos de la Mujer

Effect of Local Political and Economic Conditions

Local political and economic conditions also affect women's movements, both positively and negatively, and as these conditions change, women's movements change also. On the positive side, women's movements frequently arise out of other political struggles. These include working-class struggles, movements opposing state repression, and civil rights struggles. For instance, Nigeria's first women's activist association, the National Women's Union, was begun in 1947 by Funmilayo Ransome-Kuti, leader of a large women's march to protest the colonial power's taxation policies and those prohibiting assembly (Abdullah, 1995). Basu (1995) suggests that what initially motivates many women to organize is not necessarily a belief in the distinctive nature of their problems but rather a sense of shared oppression with other groups that have been denied their rights. West and Blumberg (1990) suggest that women's consciousness is also raised when they begin to see the contradictions in ignoring their own oppression while fighting other injustices. They add that in the course of participating in these other struggles, women also gain valuable leadership training, skills, and confidence.

Women's Movements Arising from Class Struggles

India in the 1970s provides numerous examples of women's organizations arising out of political movements fighting class differences. These include the Self-Employed Women's Association (SEWA), founded in 1970 in Gujarat by trade unionist Ela Bhatt; the Progressive Organization of Women (POW) of Hyderabad and the Stree Mukti Sangathana (Women's Liberation Organization) of Bombay, both of which arose out of the Maoist communist movement; and Mahila Samta Sainik Dal (League of Women Soldiers for Equality) of Maharashtra, which was associated with the anticaste *dalit* movement (Kumar, 1995). (Those born into the *dalit* or untouchable social class have the lowest status in India's caste system.) In many Latin American countries, the origin of women's movements are easily traced to efforts by the working class to organize, unionize, and struggle for better wages and working conditions. In Chile, for example, women workers began organizing around both class and gender issues in the early 1900s (Frohmann & Valdes, 1995).

Women's Movements in Tandem with Nationalist Struggles

Historically, women have played important roles in movements for national liberation, and women's activists frequently promote women's rights in tandem with other nationalist struggles for freedom. One example is Huda Sha'rawi, an important Egyptian feminist of the early twentieth century who actively involved women in the nationalist debate against the British in 1919. Women's public participation in a nationalist march empowered women to take a more public stand on women's rights, including the formation of feminist organizations and political activities on behalf of women (Sherif, 2001). Likewise, the rise of women's activism in India is traced to their involvement in the nationalist campaign against British colonialism (Desai, 2001).

New republics based on democracy, secularism, and equitable resource distribution also lend themselves to the inclusion of women's rights. These new governments often recognize women's important role in the national liberation movement and see gender discrimination as incompatible with their desire to move toward a modern, democratic society. Such new republics sometimes grant women equal rights, at least in the public sphere, although this occurs generally after some strong reminders from women's activists. In Egypt, which gained independence in 1952, and India, which gained independence in 1934, women had learned the language of political rights in the nationalist movement and insisted that the full economic and political equality of women be guaranteed by the new constitution (Desai, 2001; Sherif, 2001).

In the east African nation of Eritrea, which gained independence from Ethiopia in 1993, women fought alongside men in the thirty-two years of armed conflict. In exchange for women's participation in the fight for independence, the Eritrean People's Liberation Front (EPLF) promised that women would be equal partners in a new independent Eritrea. The new constitution guarantees women equal legal, political, and economic rights, and many laws, such as those that made it difficult for women to own land, were abolished. However, after independence many Eritreans resisted gender equality. As a result, the independent Eritrea has not fulfilled its promise to women, and women's organizations such as the National Union of Eritrean Women (NUEW) must continue to lobby for women's interests at both the local and national level (Leisure, 1999).

Spain is another example. The modern Spanish women's movement coincided with the end of a long struggle for democratic rule in 1975. Most of the movement leaders at this time were members or ex-members of leftist political groups who had struggled against the authoritarian rule of General Franco. Following the death of the dictator in 1975, Spanish feminists had to persuade the newly developing government that women's liberation was part of the task of building democracy and socialism (Threlfall, 1996). According to Threlfall (1996), the emerging movement was protected and encouraged by that fact that 1975 was the United Nations' International Women's Year. Feminists essentially got in on the ground floor of the newly developing government. From there, they encouraged the eradication of discriminatory legislation and the passing of legislation favorable to women. In 1983, the government set up the Instituto de la Mujer (Institute of Women). It is currently one of the largest women's public administrations in Europe and carries out functions similar to those that an independent feminist group might undertake, if it had the resources (Threlfall, 1996).

South Africa is yet another example of how feminism may emerge in the space created by national liberation. The British and the Dutch colonized South Africa. By 1948, the Dutch-descended Afrikaners controlled the government and the country. The Afrikaans government restricted the rights and movements of all non-White citizens under a system called apartheid. All Black opposition parties were banned, and individuals who violated this ban were arrested. The majority of Blacks were forced to live in desolate "homelands" called *bantustans,* were not allowed to own property, and when in White areas, were required to carry passes proving they had permission to be there. It wasn't until 1992, following years of national and international protest, that apartheid was outlawed and a new constitution granted equal rights to all South Africans. As was the case in Spain, from the beginning women's organizations in South Africa played an important role in the struggle for national liberation. They organized protests and other grassroots challenges to the state. National Women's Day, a public holiday on August 9, commemorates one particularly famous example. On August 9, 1956, despite the discouragement of male comrades, 20,000 South African women marched on the Union Building in Pretoria to protest the extension of "pass laws" to Black women and their children (Kemp et al., 1996).

As South African women's level of political awareness and experience grew, they demanded that women's issues be addressed in the national agenda. As Asha Moodley of the Black Women's Federation said,

> Having taken on co-responsibility for waging the political struggle, for sustaining and conserving it when it was really embattled, there was no way women would continue their silence . . . their suspension of the gender struggle. When they said then that the liberation of women was "inextricably linked" with the national liberation of the country, they did not mean that political liberation meant overall freedom for women. It was to imply a warning that at some time in the future, when deemed it fit to do so, there would be also a direct confrontation with patriarchy (in Kemp et al., 1995, p. 138).

This was no empty promise. Following the fall of apartheid, new women's organizations formed and old ones emerged from hiding. In 1992, the Women's National Coalition (WNC), representing eighty-one diverse women's organizations, was formed to ensure that women's rights were represented in the new constitution. Because the WNC represented a broad range of women's perspectives and was strongly activist, it was able to add women's issues to the national agenda of the postapartheid government. In 1996, the new South African Constitution, which provides equality between women and men as well as protection for lesbian and gay rights, was ratified.

The Philippines also fit this model of the newly liberated country sympathetic to women's issues. As was the case in Chile, Spain, and South Africa, from the beginning Filipino women played important roles in the labor and liberation movements. Santiago (1995) shows that feminist organizing and consciousness have a long history in the Philippines. Beginning in the early 1900s, *feminista* organizations campaigned to achieve political equality. Philippine suffragists campaigned in the Philippine Assembly, in the media, in schools, and at gatherings, and in 1937 they became the first women in Asia to win the right to vote. During the liberation movement of the 1970s and 1980s, *feministas* became an integral part of the struggle and insisted that a feminist perspective be part of the national agenda. In 1984, they founded a feminist political party and the feminist coalition GABRIELA mentioned earlier in the chapter. In 1985, when dictator Ferdinand Marcos declared victory in the national elections, feminist organizations were central in challenging the election results. This challenge toppled the Marcos dictatorship and affirmed Corazon Aquino as president. The Filipino women's movement today is strong and consists of a large variety of women's organizations working on a wide variety of issues, including reproductive rights, eliminating violence against women, employment, and the dismantling of U.S. military bases (Santiago, 1995). However, as is so often the case, traditional gender attitudes make the struggle ongoing and poor economic conditions often take precedence over social reforms for gender justice.

The involvement of women in nationalist struggles stimulates women's activism in yet another way. When women work hard in the battle for liberation only to discover the patriarchy within the very liberation movement in which they are working, their feminist consciousness is often raised. For example, Elaine Salo, of the South African United Women's Congress (UWC), recalls how the UWC was called upon to provide the tea and snacks at a national conference on the media instead of being a full participant (in Kemp et al., 1995). Likewise, many of the present leaders of the Bangladeshi women's movement became aware of gender discrimination as a result of the war for independence from Pakistan. Despite their role in the national independence movement, the new government marginalized women. They responded by organizing the first autonomous women's research organization in Bangladesh (Women for Women). Their reports on the status of women provided the basis for much of women's activism from the mid-1970s onward (Jahan, 1995).

Nationalist Struggles May Not Enhance Gender Equality

Although the fall of oppressive governments may lead to the adoption of reforms favorable to women and to climates supportive of feminist activism, this is not always the case. The countries of the former Soviet Union demonstrate this. Yes, it is true that most Soviet women were required to participate in the paid labor force for less pay and in lower status jobs than men, *and* to do most of household labor (Gottlick, 1999), and an independent feminist movement was not allowed. However, women did receive some economic protections and reproductive rights, and female political representation was guaranteed by "set-asides" for women. For the most part, these rights for women have been abandoned in the former Soviet republics, and women's political representation has declined significantly. Although there is variation, generally speaking, women of the countries that made up the former Soviet Union have lost ground. Women now constitute a higher proportion of the poorest, most disadvantaged sector of society, prostitution is on the rise, daycare is increasingly unavailable, and reproductive choice has been curtailed (Gottlick, 1999; Matynia, 1995; Waters & Posadskaya, 1995). The new "masculine democracies" that have arisen in countries of the former Soviet Union give little space to women's needs, interests, civil rights, and organization in the policy process (Molyneaux, 1996). For instance, in Russia, politicians from across the political spectrum have omitted women's equal rights from their list of legitimate and desirable goals (Waters & Posadskaya, 1995).

Initially it is puzzling that the falls of oppressive governments in Spain, the Philippines, and South Africa have led to positive development for feminism but not in the former Soviet republics. However, there are important differences. First, in the former countries, recall that there were politically active feminists who played key roles in the nationalist struggle and were able to link the liberation of women to the national liberation of the country. In other words, there was already a fairly strong feminist consciousness and familiarity with political advocacy. This was not the case in the majority of the Eastern bloc countries, although the countries with the most active women's movements (such as Poland) did have a longer history of organized rebellion against the Soviet Union.

Second, unlike the Spanish democracy that arose during the International Decade for Women and that was responsive to feminist requests for inclusion, the new democracies of the 1980s and 1990s arose in a climate emphasizing free markets and minimal government protections (Molyneaux, 1996). These combined issues mean that there is no mechanism for protecting women's rights and that women do not yet have the feminist consciousness and activist skills to push for the inclusion of women's rights in the new national agendas. The transition to market economies in Eastern Europe have also created inflation and unemployment and many women's issues have been subordinated to these economic concerns. Many women's groups channel their energies into providing services the communist state once provided (Aulette, 1999; Gottlick, 1999).

Third, unlike Spain, the Philippines, and South Africa, the former Soviet republics had a bad taste in their mouth with regard to feminism. These new republics illustrate how a large, repressive state bureaucracy can taint impressions of feminism. Unfortunately, many people in Eastern Europe associate feminism with Soviet communism. Consequently, the very fact that the Soviet regime espoused the idea of women's equality is now enough to bring it under suspicion (Molyneaux, 1996; Waters & Posadskaya, 1995). Similarly, in the former Soviet republics of Czechoslovakia, Slovakia, Poland, and Hungary, women have been slow to organize. Matynia (1995) suggests that large, nationwide organizations are still associated with the image of the *sodruzka*, the communist token woman. Her interviews also suggest that many women favor a return to traditional roles because "Soviet-style" gender equality forced women into the workplace without providing any relief at home, and because the pre-Soviet past is romanticized. The former Soviet republics are also a case of women's issues being subordinated to economic concerns. The transition to market economies has led to economic instability. Governments are focused on this and other pressing matters. In these situations, women sometimes feel that everyone is suffering and it is inappropriate for them to raise issues specific to women.

Successful nationalist struggles may also interfere with women's equality when they lead to states where conservative religious laws became state laws. This type of nationalism often seeks inspiration from an imaginary past and usually advocates redomesticating women and controlling their sexuality (Basu, 1995). Religious states and traditional women's roles are presented as necessary to preserve centuries-old cultures in the face of globalization and the importation of Western values and culture. The battle between those who desire a secular modernist state and those favoring a traditional religious state continues to be waged in many countries including Iran, Iraq, and Afghanistan. Who wins will greatly affect women's lives.

The traditional religious state won for a time in Afghanistan, where a nationalist religious movement succeeded in ending ten years of Soviet occupation. Prior to that, chaos reigned for almost nine years as the freedom fighters turned against one another. It was the nationalist Taliban group who brought peace. However, the ruling Taliban government enforced an extreme version of Islam that prohibited women from working outside the home, prevented girls from going to school, and required that women in public be completely covered by a garment called a *burqa*. The Taliban were overthrown following U.S. intervention in 2001. In 2003, the Loya Jirga (Grand Council) released a draft constitution that did not recognize women's rights as equal to men's nor did it grant women the right to vote. Due to the activism of women's rights advocates in Afghanistan and internationally, the final version passed in January 2004 explicitly states that men and women have equal rights under the law, pledges to promote education for women, and guarantees women a place in government. However, the Constitution also states, "no law can be contrary to the beliefs and provisions of the sacred religion of Islam." Women's rights activists are concerned that this leaves women's rights vulnerable. Inadequate funding for reconstruction, political instability and violence, and traditional Islamic views also interfere with the enforcement of Afghan women's rights (Maloney, 2004; Moghadam, 2003).

Iran is yet another case in which women's rights were significantly curtailed following a nationalist religious revolution. In Iran, a 1979 revolution led to an Islamist state. The new government restricted women's activities and rights, and Iranian women fought to regain the ground they lost (Afshar, 1996; Mir-Hosseini, 2001). They did this by anchoring their arguments in favor of women's rights in the teachings of Islam. As Afshar (1996) says, "Given the Islamic nature of the national political discourse, which posits the government as the defender of the faith, women were able to take the Republic to task for failing to deliver on its Islamic duty" (p. 203). They referred to parts of the Koran that favor respect for women and support for females' education and training. Islamic women also referred to educated and powerful female role models such as Muhammad's wives Khadija (politician and businesswoman) and A'isha (politician and religious expert). Consequently, in the 1990s, Iranian women successfully argued for the removal of many of the barriers placed upon educating women, women practicing medicine and law, and women owning and running businesses. They also successfully sought representation in parliament and hoped to change laws such as those that require women have their husbands' permission to work and that say a woman's word in the courts counts for half of a man's. However, in winter 2004 the Guardian Council, a judicial council of conservative clerics, banned more than 2,000 reformist candidates, including 87 members of parliament, from running for election to the 290-seat assembly. As a result, conservative candidates were able to gain a majority in the parliament. This is expected to result in the rollback of reforms favorable to women.

Following the overthrow of Saddam Hussein by U.S. forces in 2003, Iraq struggled to design a government that would satisfy those preferring a progressive democratic government enshrining the rights of women and those desiring a government based on the precepts of Islam. Initially, the U.S.-backed Governing Council passed a resolution that put family law under sharia (recall that sharia is Islamic religious law and is often interpreted in ways that promote gender injustice). U.S. and Iraqi women's activists lobbied the Bush administration not to approve the interim constitution with this provision. Eventually, the Governing Council agreed to tone down the language to say that Islam would be *a* source of legislation, rather than *the* source. However, this compromise still leaves the door open for future leaders to apply sharia to family law, and it is unclear whether a new government will rewrite the constitution once the U.S. leaves. At this writing, fundamentalism is on the rise in Iraq and there are many that view women's rights as an affront to Islam. Some are willing to use violence to discourage challenges to traditional gender roles and efforts to empower women. Fern Holland, a women's activist who worked for the U.S.-led Coalition setting up women's centers across south-central Iraq and who helped draft the women's rights section of the interim constitution, was assassinated in March 2004 two weeks after the constitution was signed. Given the political organization of Islamists, their resistance to women's empowerment, and the dangers facing women's activists, it is still to be determined how much women will benefit in the post-Saddam Hussein era.

Gender Equality Is Often Subordinated to Other Issues

Women's movements occur in the context of complex socioeconomic and political factors that determine their fate. Reforms intended to promote gender equality are often "put on the back burner" while other pressing social and economic matters are attended to.

War, for example, typically causes struggles for women's rights to put on hold. To illustrate, from the early 1900s until 1937, the women's movement was strong in Japan. Women such as Kishida Toshiko, Fukuda Hideko, Ishimoto Shizue, and Ichikawa Fusae spoke against the oppression of women, advocated women's rights, organized women's groups, and joined political parties (Ling & Matsumo, 1992). However, when Japan invaded China, the Japanese women's movement was prohibited, feminist leaders were forced to cooperate with the war effort, and those who persisted in feminist organizing were arrested and some killed (Fujieda, 1995; Ling & Matsumo, 1992). Likewise, Black South African women began protests against "pass laws" in 1912, but the campaign was suspended at the outbreak of World War I (Kemp et al., 1995). In the 1990s, war in Bosnia-Herzegovina also left little attention on women's rights (Wilkinson, 1998).

Economic crisis may also interfere with the struggle for women's rights (Margolis, 1993). Slovakia, once part of the Soviet Union, is a case in point. Matynia (1995) reports that in Slovakia, women feel that most of the problems they face are not specific or exclusive to women but are family problems caused by the economic transformation. Feminism may be seen as a luxury when the majority of the people are hungry. Similarly, Chowdhury (1994) states that women's issues are not perceived as major issues in Bangladesh, hidden as they are behind the country's poverty and underdevelopment.

Likewise, during times of political turmoil and repression, women's resistance of male oppression is often relegated to the margins, separated from other class and national struggles and subordinated to the wider and presumed higher cause of national liberation (Acosta-Belen & Bose, 1995). In Iran, in the late 1970s through the 1980s, women's demands for equal rights coincided with anti-colonial and nationalist discourses; any criticism of the patriarchal aspects of Muslim culture were seen as betrayals (Mir-Hosseini, 2001). In cases in which the state is highly repressive, the vast majority of men also experience oppression, and it is therefore difficult for women to present a case that they are particularly oppressed (Bystydzienski, 1992b). As a case in point, under Soviet communism, Polish, Hungarian, Czech, and Slovak women *and* men felt equally repressed by the state, and the energies of every social movement were directed toward activities with the potential for large-scale change (Matynia, 1995). In some cases, feminists believe that gender progress will not occur until authoritarian governments are overthrown, and so they work for other social changes under the assumption that women's liberation will follow. This was the case in the Philippines from 1950s until the 1970s. Many feminists joined the nationalist movement against dictator Ferdinand Marcos, believing that national liberation would bring about women's equality (Santiago, 1995).

Another example comes from India. The newly developing Indian women's movement of the 1970s was interrupted by the declaration of a state of emergency by Prime Minister Indira Gandhi in 1975. Most political organizations were driven underground, and those that remained focused on civil rights such as freedom of speech and association and the right to protest (Kumar, 1995). Kemp and colleagues (1995) describe a similar phenomenon in regard to Black South African feminism in the twentieth century. In the 1950s, women's activism was banned along with other opposition to the White, separatist government. In the 1970s, a resistance movement reemerged, but the immediacy of the state's attack on Black people and the constant bannings and detentions of Black activists meant that the debate over issues of gender and women's oppression had to wait until the battle for national liberation was won.

The State and Feminism

State Feminism

This section examines the relationship between governments and women's movements. Many governments have responded to women's activism and international pressures (such as pressure from the United Nations) by adding offices, commissions, agencies, ministries, committees, and advisors to deal with women's issues. Here are some samples: Office of the Status of Women (Australia), Canadian Advisory Council on the Status of Women (Canada), Danish Equal Status Council (Denmark), Frauenbeauftragte (Women's Affairs Offices, Germany), Ministry of State for Women's Affairs (Ireland), Equal Status and Equal Opportunity National Commission (Italy), Women's Bureau (United States), National Women's Service (SERNAM, in Chile), and the Better Life for Rural Women Programme (Nigeria). These have been called "women's policy machinery," and assume a variety of forms at many levels of government, ranging from temporary advisory commissions to permanent ministries (Mazur, 2001). The female bureaucrats who work as part of these government structures have been called "femocrats" (Stetson & Mazur, 1995). State feminism refers to activities of government structures that are formally charged with furthering women's status and rights (Stetson & Mazur, 1995).

Debate About the Role of the State

The role of the state (government) in promoting a feminist agenda is subject to debate. Some feminists and feminist groups look upon state feminism favorably and cultivate relationships with the state under the assumption that the best way to create change is from within (Gelb, 1989; Steinberg, 1988). The focus of these individuals and groups is often on changing laws and integrating women into the public sphere (this approach is often associated with liberal feminism). Some feminist critics of this approach, such as MacKinnon (1989), point out that no matter how many laws are passed or how many women hold public office, the state reflects, promotes, maintains, and responds to a hierarchy of male prerogative and female subordination (Stetson & Mazur, 1995). According to MacKinnon (1989), this is why women haven't made that much progress, despite legal changes.

Other critics concede that states should play a role in solving women's problems but remain concerned that many governments undermine change by co-opting women's organizations and weakening them, such that they become part of the system rather than a challenge to it. For example, in Mexico during the 1930s, the United Front for Women's Rights was founded and had more than 50,000 women members from different social classes and ideological viewpoints. The movement was incorporated into the official party, Partido Revolucionario Mexicana (predecessor of today's ruling Partido Revolucionario Institutional). Its activities were then restricted, ostensibly to prevent "political instability" (Pablos, 1992).

Basu (1995) also points to cases in which governments created women's organizations so that that they could control women's activism. These governments required that women's interests be pursued through these organizations and not independently. The problem is that under these conditions, governments decide what women's problems are and how to solve them. The result is the appearance of progress despite the fact that key women's issues are ignored, and traditional gender relations and gender power differentials remain largely intact. A number of examples come from Latin America. In Chile, SERNAM, the main governmental organization devoted to women's issues, is perceived by many feminists to be too cautious and conservative, as an instrument through which the women's movement has been co-opted, and to have failed to establish good links with grassroots women's organizations (Frohmann & Valdes, 1995). Grassroots feminists in Brazil make similar charges regarding state women's organizations (Alvarez, 1994).

> "A true feminist agenda challenges the state."
> *Hussaina Abdullah*

It is important that state feminist inclusion of societal actors empower those interests without co-opting or dominating them (Mazur & Stetson, 1995). As Mazur and Stetson (1995) caution, "If interests become overly dependent on the state, not only is their autonomy threatened, but their own fortunes become intertwined with those of the policy offices, and these are often linked to the fate of a governing party coalition" (p. 276). The United States is a typical example. In general, feminist organizations have worked to cement alliances with the Democratic Party, and when this party is in power, more policies consistent with feminist interests are made. However, some ground is lost when the Republicans control the government. For instance, it was very difficult to get equal rights legislation passed under Republican presidents Ronald Reagan, George H. W. Bush, and George W. Bush. By the early 1990s, some of the gains made in the 1970s were significantly weakened by these three administrations. For instance, the Reagan administration prohibited public health-care providers who receive federal funds from discussing abortion as an option (Brenner, 1996).

Nicaragua provides yet another example of how feminist-government alliances are somewhat risky because governments change and state feminist machineries may be dismantled. As was the case in many Latin American countries, a nationalist struggle for independence from a dictatorship stimulated the growth of the women's movement. Nicaraguan women played an important role in the overthrow of the Somoza dictatorship and, in the process, honed their political skills and confidence and earned the right to inclusion in the new Sandinista government. AMNLAE (Asociación de Mujeres Louisa Amanda Espinosa) became the Sandinista-affiliated women's organization and by 1985 played an aggressive role in educating Nicaraguan society about women's issues. The Sandinista government also funded a number of significant feminist research projects and created a Women's Legal Office, located in the President's Office, in order to participate in strategic planning (Chinchilla, 1994). In 1990, however, the Sandinistas lost the election to the conservative UNO party, and, as you may recall, Violeta de Chamorro became president. Once in power, the fundamentally conservative and antifeminist character of the Chamorro government became evident when the government advocated traditional gender roles and the rhythm method as the only acceptable form of birth control, and when it cut services that benefited women (Chinchilla, 1994). These events stimulated intense discussion within the Central American women's movement about the meaning and importance of autonomy for feminist organizations (Chinchilla, 1994). Although the Nicaraguan movement remains divided on this issue, it is a large and diverse movement. AMNLAE remains active; there are research and service centers, neighborhood women's groups, feminist collectives such as the Women's Radio Collective of Matagalpa, gay and lesbian groups, a university women's studies program, women's newspapers and foundations, and NGOs with a gender focus (Chinchilla, 1994).

There are many dangers inherent in state feminism including the possibility of the state co-opting women's movements, defining women's interests, and failing to bring about real change in the underlying social norms that support women's lower status and power. This has led some feminists, such as Abdullah (1995), to argue that real change requires women's movements independent of the state. This is certainly true to a point. However, Ferree (1987) in an analysis of the West German women's movement demonstrates the limits of strict autonomy. Although feminists there have played a leading role in the running of shelters for battered women, their fear of co-optation and desire for autonomy have made them reluctant to work for legislative and political changes. West German feminists now reluctantly acknowledge that their concerns with boundaries and independence have reduced their influence on the lives of most women. The movement is currently struggling to develop alliances with political groups without sacrificing their autonomy. Achieving this balance seems to be key to the success of women's movements.

Examples of State Feminism

In truth, whether the state helps or hinders women's movements depends on which state you are talking about. States might or might not allow independent women's organizations to participate in policy formation and implementation. States might or might not successfully co-opt and dominate women's organizations such that their influence is weakened. States might or might not provide state funds to independent organizations that advance women's

"Women hold up half the sky."
Chinese saying

interests. States might or might not have their own state-run women's bureaus or commissions, and these may be powerful or weak, focused on gender equality or on maintaining traditional women's roles. States might or might not require that women's organizations be state-run organizations. State women's policy machinery might or might not contribute to feminist policymaking and provide women's advocates with access to the policy process. The cases of China, Kenya, and Norway illustrate the point that state feminism varies quite a bit.

China Some countries do not have much of an independent women's movement, and almost all advocacy for women is done by government commissions and government-sponsored women's organizations. In Egypt, for example, all nongovernmental organizations have to be registered and supervised by the state (Sekhon & Bystydzienski, 1999). China is another example of a state feminism in which a doctrine consistent with women's rights is professed, little independent political activity is permitted, and women's organizations must register and be linked to a governmental administrative unit (Hom, 2001).

The contemporary women's movement in China developed alongside the country's political movement in the early part of the twentieth century. The movement away from dynastic rule involved the rejection of traditional culture and the Confucian philosophy that had so strongly influenced gender relations. In the 1920s, the move toward socialism involved a new Marxist ideology that linked women's oppression to the rise of private ownership and a class society and viewed women's liberation as part of socialist revolution (Zhang & Xu, 1995). Within this context arose many women's activist groups who promoted the rejection of traditional practices such as foot binding. By 1949, the Chinese Communist Party (CCP) ruled the country. To maximize the people's commitment and involvement in the revolution, the CCP established organizations to connect society to the state.

According to Zhang and Xu (1995), the All-China Women's Federation (ACWF) was set up to mobilize and represent the interests of Chinese women. Early campaigns focused on helping women to see that they had been oppressed and to convince them that support of the CCP would bring them equality. Campaigns against traditional practices such as forced marriage and bride-price were initiated. In 1956, China declared the socialist process virtually complete, and the ACWF, as a wing of the CCP, had to go along with the idea that women's equality had been reached as well. Women's issues were essentially buried, and the ACWF was actually abolished in the years from 1966 to 1978. In 1978 the government reactivated the ACWF as evidence of forced marriage, female infanticide arising from population control policies, and prostitution became harder to ignore.

The ACWF remains the primary way in which women's interests are addressed in China, and over time it has become more militant and independent in advocating for women's interests (Zhang & Xu, 1995). The ACWF currently documents women's inequality and pushes for the protection of women's rights and interests. In the 1990s the ACWF achieved some notable success in getting legislation favoring women's rights passed, in mobilizing state resources to work for women's benefit, and in encouraging the study of women's issues. As of 1994, the ACWF had over 98,000 employees. Since the early 1980s other women's organizations have arisen as well. These are of two types: women's professional and occupational organizations and women's organizations led by women intellectuals to bring attention to women's issues. However, these organizations are required by law to have a formal link with a state agency to supervise their activities. In short, women's activism in China is very much controlled by the government, but some significant gains in women's status have been made since 1949. Furthermore, the growth of women's studies as an academic discipline and the increasing number of women's publications and literature are evidence of an emerging women's movement independent of the state (Zhang & Xu, 1995).

Kenya Kenya appears to be an example of what Abdullah (1995) calls **state pseudofeminism,** a situation in which state-controlled women's organizations reinforce a conservative image of women as wives, mothers, and secondary income earners and prevent real changes in women's roles. She suggests that state pseudofeminism's effect on women is far from emancipatory because women are not empowered to resist patriarchy, their ability to earn independent income is not enhanced, and they are prevented from becoming a credible political force. On the face of it, however, the state has the appearance of attending to women's issues. According to Bystydzienski (1992a), when women have little access to government structures and the overall culture is unsupportive of women's equality, women develop other strategies for empowerment derived from women's culture. Kenya is a good example of how women organize themselves into groups that address their oppression and help them respond to it, even when societal conditions are not exactly conducive to women's activism.

Kenya remains a very patriarchal country where the constitution and courts continue to uphold traditional practices that discriminate against women. For instance, female genital mutilation is still practiced among the Kikuyu, Masai, Kisii, Meru, and Kalenjin peoples despite laws forbidding it (Morgan, 1996). Bride-price and polygamy continue as well, and there is no law against marital rape. Given the potential power of a unified women's movement to challenge male dominance, the state uses tactics to divide diverse groups of women such as those from different classes, religions, and tribes. The government is also a repressive one and stifles political dissent by permitting torture and ill treatment, including rape, by the police. This means that women's activists must proceed carefully lest they be intimidated, harassed, and imprisoned. Consequently, women in Kenya try to gain equal rights by helping one another become self-sufficient. This fits in with Kenyan women's traditions. Indeed, traditionally, much of Kenyan women's resistance was conducted through nonconfrontational artistic methods such as song, poetry, and dance.

There is no national organized feminist movement in Kenya, and the women's movement there is synonymous with the emergence of women's groups (Oduol & Kabira, 1995). Indeed, there are over forty registered national women's organizations and over 6,000 local women's groups in Kenya (Arungu-Olende, 1996). One of the first national women's organizations, Maendeleo Ya Wanawake (MYWO), dates back to colonial rule and was founded by White settlers' and administrators' wives. MYMO currently coordinates over 3,000 registered women's groups, but critics say its close association with the repressive ruling government reduces its effectiveness.

Other formal organizations in Kenya have programs that reinforce women's traditional roles (through welfare activities such as childcare, family nutrition, and hygiene) but also work for women's empowerment. The National Council of Women of Kenya (NCWK) is one example. Although the NCWK offers home economics programs, it also launched the National Committee on the Status of Women to educate women on democracy and their political rights. In addition, it also launched the Greenbelt movement to combat desertification in Kenya and was instrumental in the national women's conventions of 1992 and 1993, at which women from all over the country were brought together to strategize and demonstrate their solidarity in the struggle against gender-based oppression (Oduol & Kabira, 1995).

Much of Kenyan women's activism is conducted at a small grassroots level. These women's groups have a long history. Kenyan women's self-help groups have historically helped women cope in a male-dominated society that has denied them resources. For example, thousands of women's groups engage in business enterprises, community projects, and loan programs. The Kenyan Women Finance Trust, founded in 1983 by women professionals to provide loans for female-owned business ventures, is one such case (Morgan, 1996). Another example is the Kayole Women's Self-Help Group in Nairobi. Members of this group produce building materials, such as cinder blocks, for use in construction (Oduol & Kabira, 1995).

"We do not want a piece of the pie; we want to change the basic recipe of the pie."
Birgit Brock-Utne

Norway   Stetson and Mazur (1995) suggest that state feminism does the most for women when the state is culturally defined as the site of social justice, has the structural capacity to institutionalize new demands for equality, and sustains widely supported feminist organizations that challenge sexual hierarchies through both radical politics from outside the government and reform politics in unions and parties. These conditions exist in the state of Norway, considered to be one of the most progressive countries in the world with regard to women's issues. Box 10.4 profiles Gro Harlem Brundtland, Norwegian feminist and Norway's first female prime minister.

Norway serves as an example of a positive state feminism with centralized offices that have successfully integrated gender equity principles into many policy areas and that have fostered the empowerment of women's groups

BOX 10.4   *Activist Profile: Gro Harlem Brundtland of Norway*

In 1998, the World Health Organization (WHO) of the United Nations appointed Dr. Gro Harlem Brundtland as its new director. She was the first woman to head the agency, just as she was the first woman to be elected prime minister of Norway (she served from 1981 to 1997). Brundtland, a committed feminist and an outspoken advocate of abortion and reproductive rights, is well known for publicizing the link between poverty, health, and the environment. In 1987 she chaired the

UN's World Commission on Environment and Development, producing an influential document on sustainable development now known as the "Brundtland Report." Brundtland finished her term in 2003, and was credited with streamlining the WHO bureaucracy and changing its reputation from an ineffective organization to one effective in addressing world health problems.

(Stetson & Mazur, 1995). Although the Equal Status Council (ESC) remains the main agency focused on gender equality, the goal of equal status has been mainstreamed into most state agencies. The state actively promotes women's equality through publicly appointed committees, boards, and councils, quotas to increase the number of women in the civil service and in male-dominated occupations, childcare subsidies, and parental leave.

Bystydzienski (1992b; 1995) explains that part of the success of Norwegian state feminism is due to Norway's commitment to the values of equality and justice, as well as to a belief in the role of the government in equalizing economic and social differences. However, its success is also clearly due to women's activism. Norwegian women have always been strong and political, and this is reflected in Norwegian literature dating back to the tenth century (As, 1996). Bystydzienski (1992b; 1995) emphasizes the role of Norway's active women's movement in creating a state responsive to women's needs. The modern movement has its roots in the 1800s, when the Norwegian Association for the Rights of Women worked to improve women's education and the legal rights of married women, the Association for Women's Suffrage worked toward women's suffrage, and women's labor unions were formed (Morgan, 1996). In the 1920s, women's organizations focused on contraception and abortion rights, the election of women to parliament, and legislation regarding the family (Morgan, 1996).

During the 1960s and 1970s, women representing traditional women's organizations and the so-called new feminists formed a successful coalition that raised public consciousness regarding women's disadvantaged status and called on the government to respond. In the 1970s, they united on the issue of abortion, and the Storting (the Norwegian Parliament) gave women the right to abortion within the first twelve weeks of pregnancy. One particular goal of the feminist coalition that significantly impacted state feminism was to increase the number of women in public office (as discussed in Chapter 9). The growing responsiveness of the Norwegian government to feminist activists clearly coincides with the increased number of women in public offices, for many of these women received their political training in the women's movement and were sympathetic to feminist demands. As more women entered government, the state became more responsive to women's demands from below, and women began to participate in forming state policy. Because of the influence of feminist organizations, the major political parties have all adopted sex quotas for political campaigns (at least 40 percent female and 40 percent male in any given election). The case should not be overstated, however. Men are still advantaged in Norway, and Norwegian feminists face a dilemma of how to remain committed to the promotion of women's interests while participating fully in male-created and dominated institutions (Bystydzienski, 1995).

Conclusion

Women's struggles for equality are by no means new, but this fact, combined with women's continued lower status and power, suggests that these struggles have been less than effective. Indeed, the record of success is mixed. On the one hand, significant gains have been made. You can see this by the increase in national laws favorable to women (such as the dowry prohibition laws in India), the growth of international laws (the topic of our next chapter), increased women's services, and women's greater gender consciousness. Success is also evident in the sheer number of grassroots women's organizations worldwide. Although less visible than large national organizations, these groups have significantly improved the quality of women's lives through the provision of information, services, and organization for change. Basu (1995) suggests that the success of women's movements must also be gauged in terms of women's increased cultural visibility. For instance, feminist expression is increasingly found in theater, dance, music, and literature. Basu also sees the growth of women's studies and centers for the study of women and gender as gains of the women's movement.

It is true, however, that women's movements have not achieved many of their legislative demands, such as the legalization of abortion in Brazil, the passage of the Equal Rights Amendment in the United States, and the reform of family law in Kenya, India, and Bangladesh (Basu, 1995). It is also true that when legislation is passed, it is frequently unenforced. Indeed, Jahan's (1995) statement regarding the success of the women's movement in Bangladesh has broad applicability: While public pronouncements on the importance of including women are common, and women's participation at all levels has increased, no serious effort has been made to change the social structures and institutions perpetuating women's inequality. According to Jahan, the

Bangladesh government seeks to "contain" the discourse on women's rights in narrow channels that keep traditional notions of womanhood intact. Unfortunately, this is true of many governments.

Many explanations have been offered for the uneven success of women's movements. One thought is that many middle-class women's movements have failed because they did not mobilize poor women and assumed that class interests could be subordinated to gender interests (Basu, 1995). For example, in the case of women of color in the United States and Australia and in the Third World, the most pressing concerns may be freedom from starvation and ethnic discrimination, not gender inequality. Similarly, Australian Aboriginal women frequently feel that talking about women's rights is irrelevant when they are oppressed by racism and poverty and when the destruction of Aboriginal society deprives men, more than women, of status and self-respect (Sawer, 1994). Likewise, women's national, cultural, or ethnic identities may be of equal or greater concern to women, and many women may not support movements that fail to take this into account. LaFromboise, Heyle, and Ozer (1990) note that Native American women are at least as concerned with the preservation of their race and culture as they are with women's equality. They also suggest that Native American gender equality movements will differ from non-Native movements as Native women seek a feminism that works within the context of Native American families, their nations, and their cultures.

Countermovements against feminism often challenge the success of women's movements. These arise as women's movements begin to influence women's attitudes. Such **backlashes against feminism** were well in evidence in the 1980s and 1990s in a number of countries. In 1980s India, for example, Indian feminists were accused of being Westernists, colonialists, and cultural imperialists. Feminists worked against dowries, sati (a widow's immolation on her husband's funeral pyre), and arranged marriage. Irate families, the police, and the courts, which ruled against feminist positions, attacked them (Kumar, 1995). In 1980s India, Hindu nationalist women feared that feminist activism would erode traditional religious practices and agitated in *favor* of women's right to sati (Kumar, 1995).

In the United States, feminists are accused of being manlike and man-haters, and antifeminists actively work to limit women's reproductive rights. Women often fear that change threatens women's power in the private familial sphere and are unsupportive of feminist goals (Rowbotham, 1996). Antifeminist movements often draw attention to their female members and then charge that feminists do not represent the true interests of women and are forcing women into change that they do not want. As Basu (1995) points out, the opposition to women's equal rights is often better funded and better organized and often has the weight of the state, and tradition, behind it. Changing deeply entrenched gender ideology is a long-term process, particularly in the face of resistance and hostility from conservative and extremist groups using religion to legitimize a bid for social and political control (Jahan, 1995b).

Women's movements sometimes face significant challenges from within, as feminist groups differ about what they see as critical issues and about how to go about solving them. Consider the case of Brazil. There the women's movement was torn apart in the 1980s because of profound differences between feminist groups on which party to support during the election and controversy regarding whether the movement should remain autonomous from the state (Alvarez, 1994; Soares et al., 1995). Simply put, there are a variety of feminisms, often within one country, and these differences frequently threaten the solidarity that it takes to challenge entrenched systems. In Muslim countries, for example, Islamic feminists differ in their support of veiling. Some women openly rebel against it whereas others maintain that it is a positive expression of religious devotion, that it protects women from sexual objectification and sexual harassment, and that it liberates them from the dictates of fashion. Likewise, some feminists in Muslim countries try to promote a liberation theology as a way toward gender equality whereas others fight for secularism (a separation of religion and state) as a way to gain equality (Moghadam, 1991). In short, success often depends on feminist groups finding issues on which they can agree and putting aside differences in order to build movements with sufficient size and strength.

This chapter focused in particular on challenges to the traditional gender roles of a community by women in that community (that is, national and local movements). In contrast, the next chapter focuses on international legal instruments as a means for change. These two approaches to gender equality are not mutually exclusive and, in fact, are mutually supportive. Positive changes in international law frequently result from the coordinated efforts of grassroots women's movements. Furthermore, without the influence of grassroots movements, international law may not have relevance in the day-to-day lives of women and may coerce cultural variety into a false unity (Toro, 1995).

International laws regarding the equality of women also serve grassroots movements by legitimizing their struggles and providing mechanisms for change where women's movements are suppressed. By building regional and international linkages, women's ability to develop effective political and legal strategies for their local struggles are enhanced (Human Rights Watch, 1995). International laws also strengthen feminism worldwide by placing pressure on governments to respond to women's movements (Basu, 1995). Ideally, international law would allow women whose domestic legal systems fail to protect them to submit complaints to the United Nations for investigation and enforcement (Human Rights Watch, 1995).

Study Questions

1. What factors operate against women's activism? What are women up against when they ask for equal rights?

2. What early (and false) assumptions were made about women's movements by Western feminist scholars?

3. Why do some women's movements distance themselves from the feminist label? What are some differences between Western and other feminisms?

4. What does it mean to describe women's movements as having broad ideological variety and a range of organizational expressions? What are the three major strands of women's movements found in most countries?

5. How do cultures differ in terms of what stimulates the development of a women's movement?

6. How may local political and economic conditions affect the development of women's movements, both positively and negatively?

7. What are some specific examples of how women's movements may arise out of nationalist struggles for liberation? What factors seem to explain those cases in which struggles for national liberation do not foster women's equality?

8. What is state feminism? What are some of the concerns about state feminism? What are some examples of state feminism not doing much to help women's equality and some examples of it helping? What accounts for the difference?

9. What gains have been made by women's equality movements?

10. What are some of the explanations given for the uneven success of women's movements?

Discussion Questions and Activities

1. Choose a local women's issue that concerns you and sketch out a plan to do something about it. For example, is women's safety an issue on your campus?

2. Considering the broad definition of women's movements given at the beginning of the chapter, identify the various GROs and GRSOs in your community and what they do.

3. Why is it that governments enact legislation and sign conventions supportive of women's rights but frequently fail to enforce them? What can be done to change this?

4. What do you think of the feminist label? Would you identify yourself as feminist? Why or why not? Alternatively, ask a number of people these same three questions, along with others (such as age, gender, and religion) that you think may correlate with their answers.

5. One of the themes of the chapter is that women's movements vary cross-culturally and that gender social change is something that women in a

culture do for themselves. If this is true, how can feminists in one culture assist feminists in another culture, or can they?

6. The chapter discussed the cases of Iran, Iraq, and Afghanistan. In 2004, in all three countries, women's rights were uncertain as those favoring an Islamist government and traditional gender roles conflicted with those favoring a more progressive government and society. What has happened since? What is the current status of women's rights in those countries?

Activist Websites of Interest

Feminist Majority

http://www.feminist.org

National Organization for Women

http://www.now.org

All India Democratic Women's Association

http://www.aidwa.org

Informational Websites of Interest

National Council of Women's Organizations

http://www.womensorganizations.org

SAWNET South Asian Women's Organizations

http://www.umiacs.umd.edu/users/sawweb/sawnet/orgn.html

International Council for Research on Women

http://www.icrw.org

Action Opportunities

1. Volunteer your time to help a women's organization in your community. If you don't want to make a long-term commitment, many can use occasional office help or assistance with annual fund-raising efforts.

2. There are many specific types of feminist groups, including feminist groups for different religions and dedicated to different issues. Identify a feminist organization that fits you, or, participate in a campaign related to a women's issue that concerns you.

3. The Dupoto Women's Group of Kenya has a program to economically empower Masai women so that they can earn money to send their girl children to school. Unlike girls who are not in school, those attending school are not circumcised and then married off at a young age. To purchase beadwork made by Masai women to fund girls' education, go to http://www.beadsforeducation.org.

4. Afghanistan is a good example of how women's issues may be subordinated to other issues during the reconstruction that follows war. One problem is that Afghanistan has received only half of the funding promised by other countries; another problem is that more international peacekeeping forces are needed until democracy is restored. Most of the country is still under the control of warlords opposed to women's equal rights and women have been punished for "un-Islamic behavior" and girls' schools have been destroyed. Visit http://www.feminist.org for ways to help.

11

Women's Rights
as Human Rights

Challenging prevailing concepts of, and reinterpreting the movement for, human rights from a feminist perspective is not merely a matter of semantics. It is about the lives and deaths of individual women, everywhere, everyday. . . . Yet even as the international human rights community has begun to recognize gender-based violations as pervasive and insidious forms of human rights abuse, we must work further to see that concerted actions against such practices are taken. . . . Only through community responsibility and state accountability, day by day, place by place, will we counter the massive violation of women's human rights in the world.

—CHARLOTTE BUNCH (1995),
Center for Women's Global Leadership

Women at the UN's Fourth Women's World Conference in Beijing, China (1995).
The United Nations has promoted international feminism by holding four world
women's conferences on the status of women.

The last chapter focused on women's movements in different countries. Here the focus is on the international women's movement, or as it is sometimes called, **global** or **transnational feminism.** Transnational feminist movements span across multiple nations and have at their core the belief that women are entitled to the same rights as men, regardless of where the women live, their ethnicity, and their social class. However, global feminism recognizes diversity and acknowledges that there are diverse meanings of feminism, each responsive to the needs and issues of women in different regions, societies, and times.

Global feminism is not new. Indeed, in 1887, American suffragists Elizabeth Cady Stanton and Lucretia Mott called a meeting of the International Council of Women to be held in Washington, D.C., in 1888. Their call recognized the "universal sisterhood" of women and noted, "The position of women anywhere affects the position of women everywhere." They expressed the hope that the international council would "devise new and more effective methods for securing the equality and justice of women" and would help them realize their power in combining together to these ends (Fraser, 1987). This meeting resulted in the first formal international women's organization, the International Congress of Women (ICW) (Stienstra, 1994). Some of the first international women's organizations emphasized women's suffrage (right to vote). For example, in 1904, U.S. feminists Elizabeth Cady Stanton, Susan B. Anthony, and Carrie Chapman Catt formed the International Women's Suffrage Alliance (IWSA) with the goal of securing women's right to vote. Following World War I, international women's groups worked to ensure that the newly forming League of Nations (later the United Nations) included women's representatives and issues affecting women and children. Other early international feminist organizations include the Women's International League for Peace and Freedom (1905) and the International Alliance of Women (1926). Women's international nongovernmental organizations were also instrumental in the establishment of the United Nations in 1945 (West, 1999).

The modern transnational women's movement uses electronic communication and international and regional conferences to share information and to strategize. International law is used as the basis for asserting women's rights. The Universal Declaration of Human Rights (adopted by the United Nations in 1948) states that everyone is equally entitled to human rights such as life, liberty, and freedom from torture, and equal treatment under the law—regardless of gender. Women's rights activists frame gender inequalities and abuses in terms of these inalienable rights to motivate change for gender equality.

Women's Rights as Human Rights

According to the concept of **universal human rights,** everyone has certain inalienable rights simply by virtue of being human. This means that all humans

Our starting point is that there can be no human rights without women's rights. . . .
UN Office of High Commissioner for Human Rights

Former U.S. congresswoman Bella Abzug (1920–1998) was a pioneer of the U.S. women's movement and of global women's organizing. Abzug also fought to make governments accountable for their promises to promote women's equality. Toward this end, Abzug issued annual report cards to 187 nations, grading them on their progress toward women's equality. Abzug was also the founder of WEDO (Women's Environment and Development Organization). A few days before she died, she said, "This is the time to declare, as we approach the great millennium, that women must be made free."

March 8 is International Women's Day (IWD). Celebrated since 1901, it was originally intended to highlight the struggles of working-class women and to promote women's suffrage. The idea is that on this day, every year, women would speak together with one voice. In many countries, IWD is a day for rallies and marches to call attention to women's economic, political, and reproductive rights.

"Women's rights are human rights."
Slogan of women's human rights movement

"The recognition of such issues as human rights abuses raises the level of expectation about what can and should be done about them."
Charlotte Bunch and Samantha Frost

"Isn't it revealing that women's human rights need to be discussed?"
Isabel Allende

are born free and equal in dignity and rights, which no one, including governments, can deny them. In theory then, women have the same economic, political, civil, and social rights as men but as previous chapters suggest, practice is another matter altogether.

The idea behind the women's human rights approach is to wed women's rights to human rights, which are protected under international law and are monitored and enforced by the United Nations. This lends legitimacy to political demands because it is already accepted by most governments and brings with it established protocols for dealing with abuses (Friedman, 1995). Whether used in political lobbying, in legal cases, in grassroots mobilization, or in broad-based educational efforts, the idea of women's human rights has been a rallying point for women across many boundaries and has facilitated the creation of collaborative strategies for promoting and protecting the rights of women (Bunch & Frost, 2000). Describing a particular discriminatory act as a human rights violation gives it an importance that it cannot obtain by simply calling it unfair; it also opens the way for the affected women to seek redress and helps to prevent further violations (Tomasevski, 1993).

The **women's human rights perspective** views the unequal status of women and abuses against women as human rights violations. For example, the Universal Declaration of Human Rights clearly declares that freedom from torture and slavery are basic human rights. The women's human rights approach characterizes domestic violence as a human rights violation since it is a form of torture that often includes imprisonment in the home, either physically or psychologically, through terrorization (Bunch, 1995). Women are held involuntarily in slavery for prostitution and pornography, and domestic servants are beaten and raped. These abuses can be viewed as violations of international laws forbidding slavery. There are also international laws barring the use of torture and terrorism. Sexual assault is a form of terrorism, and rape is a form of torture. Female infanticide and neglect are forms of female genocide.

Framing discrimination against women as a violation of their human rights has not been easy. Human rights law has traditionally focused on violations in the public spheres of life, in particular violations committed by government agents (such as the imprisonment or torture of political dissenters). As Bunch (1995) notes, this is not surprising given that the Western-educated propertied men who first advanced the cause of human rights most feared the violation of their civil and political rights in the public sphere. They did not fear violations in the private sphere because they were the masters of that territory. In contrast, the most common violations of women's rights often occur in the private sphere of the family and are condoned by religious and cultural practices. As a result, these violations have traditionally been viewed as outside the scope of human rights law (Bunch & Frost, 2000; Mertus, 1995; Sullivan, 1995).

As advocates for women's rights point out, though, the public/private distinction breaks down upon examination because "private" behaviors such as wife murder, battery, and rape result from a public toleration of the subordination of women (Charlesworth, 1995). Governments condone abuses when they inadequately prosecute wife abuse, rape, and sexual harassment. Therefore, they are accountable for these abuses (Friedman, 1995). Furthermore, using the public/private distinction to justify states' lack of involvement with women's human rights abuses is hypocritical considering that marriage and family law is monitored by the state (Kerr, 1993).

Global feminists work to ensure that human rights instruments and mechanisms provide avenues for challenging the systemic abuse of women. Ideally, governments would implement laws against gender-based violations and increase the sensitivity of agencies handling these issues (Bunch, 1995). Already, significant pressure is placed on countries that violate human rights through torture, imprisonment, and the killing of those with opposing political views from those in power. However, rarely is it acknowledged that women, by virtue of being female, are routinely subjected to torture, starvation, terrorism, humiliation, mutilation, and even murder, simply because they are female (Peters & Wolper, 1995). Gender-based abuses such as these need to be seen as human rights abuses so that international pressure can be applied to countries that permit them. The United States has occasionally refused to trade with a country or to loan money because of human rights abuses. But never has a country, including the United States, based its aid and trade decisions on the treatment of women (Bunch, 1995). Indeed, in 1991, the United States fought Iraq to defend Kuwait—a country where women are not allowed to vote or run for political office, where top female students are ineligible for government grants to study abroad, where male polygamy is encouraged but female polygamy outlawed, and where the abuse of domestic servants is permitted.

Governments frequently support human rights by providing asylum to those who flee persecution in their own countries. Under international law, refugees seeking relocation must prove a "well-founded" fear of persecution due to race, religion, nationality, political opinion, or membership in a particular social group. Though gender is not explicitly included as a category, the UN High Commissioner for Refugees (UNHCR) declared that a gender-sensitive interpretation should be applied to asylum considerations. The UNCHR identifies two broad categories of gender-related claims: those in which the persecution constitutes a *type* of harm that is particular to the applicant's gender, such as rape or genital mutilation; and those in which the persecution may be imposed *because of* the applicant's gender, for example, because a woman has violated societal norms regarding women's proper conduct. Britain, Australia, New Zealand, Sweden, Ireland, South Africa, the United States, and Canada all recognize some gender-based asylum claims.

Activism and legal challenges by human rights activists and lawyers have been important in developing human rights policies based on gender. In one well-known case, it was only after numerous appeals by human rights lawyers and activists that a 17-year-old woman from the West African nation of Togo was permitted to stay in the United States. Fauziya Kasinga was ordered by her family to enter into a polygamous marriage to a 45-year-old man following

Rhonda Copelon is a U.S. law professor and international human rights activist. She is at the forefront of the use of international law to prevent and prosecute crimes against women such as war rape.

"My responsibility as UN High Commissioner is to adopt and to foster a rights-based approach across the whole spectrum of 'civil, cultural, economic, political, and social rights, to promote and protect the realization of the right to development and specifically to include women's rights as human rights.'"
Mary Robinson

her ritual genital mutilation (she was to become the fourth wife). She escaped to the United States, and upon her arrival at the airport, she requested asylum on the grounds that she faced genital mutilation should she return. She was sent to prison to await a hearing. The immigration judge said her story was not credible and that she did not have a well-founded case of persecution. Human rights lawyers rallied. In 1996, two years later, the Board of Immigration Appeals heard her case and Fauziya was released from prison and granted asylum.

Since that time, the courts, human rights activists and lawyers, and U.S. attorney generals have battled over what will count as legitimate grounds for gender-based asylum. Following a lengthy court case that granted asylum to Rodi Alvarado, a Guatemalan woman who fled to the United States after suffering a decade of severe domestic violence, Attorney General Janet Reno decided that gender should be included under the social group category in the refugee convention. By Reno's criteria, domestic violence could also be a basis for asylum. However, the new regulations were not yet in place when President George W. Bush took office. His attorney general, John Ashcroft, questioned the idea that gender should be included under the social group category although his policy considered forced abortions and involuntary sterilization as grounds for asylum on the basis of persecution on account of political opinion.

The United Nations

Most people agree that international human rights law owes its development to the United Nations and its institutions. This section focuses on global feminism through an examination of the four UN international conferences on women and international human rights law. The United Nations is a key player in a human rights approach to women's equality.

General Description

The **United Nations (UN)** is an international organization established in 1945 immediately following the end of World War II. Its purposes are the maintenance of international peace and security, the development of international law, and the correction of international economic, social, and humanitarian problems. The UN is a large, complex, and political organization with many specialized agencies, including the World Bank, the World Health Organization (WHO), and the United Nations Children's Fund (UNICEF). UN organizations publish many reports of social and economic statistics, fund development projects throughout the world, and lend technical and informational assistance to member governments. The UN also has many commissions including the Commission on Human Rights, which figures prominently in this chapter.

The General Assembly, which meets at least once a year, includes representatives from all member states, appoints councils, creates commissions,

FIGURE 11.1   *The UN and Gender Equality*

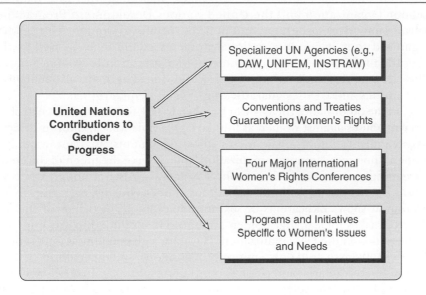

and receives reports from UN organizations. The UN commissions, as well as the General Assembly, may draft conventions, resolutions, and treaties that are legally binding as part of international law when ratified by member states. They may also draft and vote on declarations that are not legally binding but serve as international guidelines and general commitments. Each member nation, regardless of size and power, has one vote. Declarations, programs for action, and other nonbinding documents are often drafted and voted on at UN conferences.

The UN's Contribution to Gender Equality

The UN's contribution to gender equality is mixed. On the one hand, what the UN has accomplished is remarkable given that it is a male-dominated organization and that many member nations are resistant to UN efforts to increase the worldwide status of women. In fact, the UN has contributed to gender progress. Refer to Figure 11.1 for a summary of UN contributions to gender equality. The Commission on the Status of Women (CSW) was one of the first UN bodies to specifically address the concerns of women. Established in 1946, the CSW monitors the situation of women and promotes their rights. It is involved in setting universal standards regarding the status of women and assumes a leading role in bringing women's concerns to the attention of the UN specialized agencies. Some UN agencies such as UNIFEM (United Nations Development Fund for Women), INSTRAW (International Research and Training Institute for

Women), and DAW (Division for the Advancement of Women) are dedicated to women's issues. Other agencies, including the International Labour Organization and the United Nations Development Programme, include initiatives, programs, and policies specific to women. The UN has organized four major international women's conferences as well as the "Decade for Women" that drew international attention to women's status. The UN provides statistics on women worldwide. There are also many UN conventions and treaties guaranteeing women's equal rights.

On the other hand, the UN can be taken to task for its reluctance to characterize abuses against women as human rights violations and for its difficulties in ratifying important women's rights documents. In some ways, it is women's nongovernmental organizations that deserve the much of the credit for getting women's concerns on the UN agenda. Also, although UN commissions, documents, and policies call for gender equality, even the UN organization shows indications of sexism. For example, Article 8 of the UN Charter makes it clear that women are not to be excluded in any way from participation in the UN organization. However, a glass ceiling is well in place at the UN. Women hold only a minority of positions, and the majority of these are low-level secretarial and clerical jobs (D'Amico, 1999). In 2003, only four women headed UN delegations,* and approximately 35 percent of senior management positions held by women. Another concern has to do with the fact that the number of female ambassadors to the United Nations usually ranges between 3 and 5 percent. As Charlesworth, Chinkin, and Wright (1991) point out, it is significant that men are the main actors in the major institutions of international law (see Box 11.1). Because men are not usually the victims of domestic violence, sex discrimination, sexual degradation, and violence, these important human rights matters are often ignored.

The UN's World Women's Conferences

The United Nations designated 1975 as International Women's Year and 1975 to 1985 as the Decade for Women. During the Decade for Women, the UN, through the creation of national and international forums for action, the gathering of data about women, and holding three world women's conferences, promoted international feminism. These international conferences on the status of women (1975—Mexico City; 1980—Copenhagen, Denmark; 1985—Nairobi, Kenya) catapulted the international connections among women to a qualitatively different level as women from very different backgrounds worked together on committees, caucuses, and networking (Chowdhury et al., 1994). A fourth world conference was held in Beijing, China, in 1995. In 2000, the United Nations held a special session in New York City of-

---

*Four women run UN agencies: Carol Bellamy (UNICEF); Anna Tibaijuka (UN Centre for Human Settlements); Noeleen Heyzer (UNDP, UNIFEM); and Thoraya Obaid of the Population Fund.

BOX 11.1 *Women Around the Globe: Women Senior Managers as a Percentage of All Senior Managers at the UN*

Food and Agriculture Organization (FAO) 2%

General Agreement on Tariffs and Trade (GATT) 0

International Monetary Fund (IMF) 8

UN Center for Human Settlements (UNCHS) 0

UN Children's Fund (UNICEF) 22

UN Development Programme (UNDP) 16

UN Environment Programme (UNEP) 11

UN Population Fund (UNFPA) 28

World Health Organization (WHO) 10

Source: Seager, 2003.

ficially called Women 2000: Gender Equality, Development and Peace for the Twenty-First Century. This conference is popularly known as Beijing +5.

Because UN world conferences are media events, these conferences and the declaration of United Nations Decade for Women (1975–1985) publicized the low status and power of women in the world. In some cases this publicity led to increased grassroots activism. The international women's conferences and UN Decade for Women also encouraged national commitments to increase the status of women through the development of women's bureaus and commissions and through legal and constitutional changes. Preparations for the first international women's conference held in 1975 in Mexico City revealed that the UN had very little information on the status of women worldwide. As a result, the UN pushed for the collection of statistical data and now publishes regular reports on the status of women.

Member nations sent delegates to the women's conferences to discuss proposals regarding women's rights. For example, at the first women's conference in Mexico City in 1975, 133 delegates reached agreement on the "World Plan of Action," agreeing to work to end discrimination against women. In 1985, at the Third World Conference on Women in Nairobi, Kenya, 1,899 delegates reached agreement on the "Nairobi Forward-Looking Strategies for the Advancement of Women." This document set goals to be reached by the year 2000. The "Platform for Action" was the product of the Fourth World Conference on Women (FWCW) held in Beijing, China, in

"Unless the human rights of women, as defined by international human rights instruments, are fully recognized and effectively protected, applied, implemented and enforced in national law as well as in national practice in family, civil, penal, labour and commercial codes and administrative rules and regulations, they will exist in name only."
Beijing Platform for Action, 1995

1995. The Platform, negotiated by 5,000 delegates from 189 countries, identifies "critical areas of concern" such as the feminization of poverty, inequalities in education, politics, and the economy, violence against women, and persistent discrimination against and violation of the rights of the girl child. It is called the Platform for Action because for each critical area of concern, it specifies strategic objectives and actions to be undertaken by governments. In 2000, at the Beijing +5 conference, delegates from 180 countries approved the Political Declaration. This declaration included a statement agreeing to eradicate "harmful customary or traditional practices" and one that stated "women have the right to decide freely and responsibly on matters related to their sexuality . . . without coercion, discrimination, and violence." The Political Declaration also affirmed governments' responsibility to implement the Beijing Platform for Action.

The UN women's conferences illustrate the complexities of international politics and cooperation regarding women's rights. All four of the conferences became bogged down at some point by international politics that had little to do with the status of women. The 1980 conference in Copenhagen was perhaps the worst in this regard; the official conference agenda was superceded by resolutions dealing with nationalist concerns (Jaquette, 1995; West, 1999). Language issues and the fact that the UN uses a consensus model of decision making also make for difficulty. The final conference documents are usually somewhat unwieldy because the language must be translated into all of the languages of the UN system and because each government wants to make sure its viewpoint is included (Fraser, 1987). For instance, at the Fourth World Conference, voting on the 149-page "Platform for Action" was delayed by wording difficulties. There were translation problems with the word *gender,* which does not exist in some languages, as well as terms such as *gender-neutral* and *feminization.* Some countries had problems with the phrase "universal human rights," arguing that human rights are relative to the culture. Ultimately this issue was resolved by dropping the word *universal.* Likewise, it took sixteen hours of debate before a subcommittee could accommodate the contrary views of countries who believe that sex education encourages risky youth sexual behavior and those who insist such education reduces youth risk. Beijing +5 was also marked by strong disagreement. Wider protection of women's reproductive rights and protections for lesbians and gays were blocked by some Catholic and Islamic delegations.

The evolving character of the four women's conferences and Beijing +5 also symbolize the development of women's issues within the UN. For instance, at the 1980 Copenhagen convention, male dominance was evident. Indeed, it became a joke that male delegates always replaced women delegates occupying the lead delegate chair during important votes and debates. By the end of the Nairobi conference in 1985, however, women delegates dominated (Fraser, 1987). Similarly, male delegates took over the early women's conferences to complain about issues they had with other countries (Bernard, 1987). By the Fourth World Conference on Women, political issues unrelated to women's status finally took a backseat.

BOX 11.2   *Women Around the Globe: Two Women's Impressions
of the Beijing Conference's NGO Forum*

"The vast majority of Chinese women attending the NGO forum in Huairou saw or heard the slogan, "women's rights are human rights," there for the first time. . . . On arriving at the site of the 1995 NGO forum, Huariou, a banner with the slogan, "Look at the world through women's eyes," flew high above the road. This was a reminder, a resounding call. . . . We were used to seeing the world through the class struggle, now we are getting used to seeing it from the perspective of a commodity economy; women have almost never thought about how to use their eyes to see the world."

Journalist Chuan Renyan of China

"On a hill above the Beijing suburb of Huairou, the Older Women's Tent of sweeping yellow canvas welcomed over 2,000 women from every continent. This Tent was one of seven "diversity tents" designated for special issues, such as disabled, indigenous, refuge, youth, and lesbian women. . . . Over the subsequent days, older women succeeded in putting aging concerns on the international NGO agenda. They built a strong Older Women's Caucus that met daily at both the Tent and the Government Conference in Beijing. Each day, women crowded under the Tent to hear speakers and hold debates on a wide range of issues. . . . On the last day of the Forum at the Tent, women decided to build a global older women's network. Despite differences of culture and economy, many core issues are the same across regions: elder rights, economic security, and a desire to participate fully in the life of society."

*Susanne Paul, Coordinator of the
Older Women's Tent at Beijing*

International attention and commitment to women's rights and status were important outcomes of the UN women's conferences. However, an equally important outcome is the contribution of the conferences to the transnational feminist movement. At conference "nongovernmental forums," thousands of representatives from nongovernmental organizations (NGOs) around the world shared information and networked. In contrast to the formal political spaces of the official conferences, the NGO forums were "counter-political spaces" mixing serious political discussion, networking, and coalition building with women's cultural events and shopping (West, 1999). Box 11.2, *Women Around the Globe: Two Women's Impressions of the Beijing Conference's NGO Forum*, shares the experiences of two women that attended the conference.

The growth of the NGO forums from the first women's conference to Beijing +5 reflects the growth of transnational feminism. For example, approximately 6,000 people attended the NGO forum in 1975 at Mexico City, approximately 8,000 attended in 1980 at Copenhagen, and approximately 14,000 attended in 1985 at Nairobi (Fraser, 1987). In 1995 at Beijing, this number grew to 30,000 (West, 1999). Hundreds of women's NGOs held sessions at Beijing +5. Fraser (1987) suggests that this growth is more than merely numerical. By the time of the Nairobi conference, women had moved from the consciousness raising and outrage of the early conferences to collective activism. The growth of the forums also sends a message to the world that there is determination and solidarity among diverse women (Fraser, 1987). For instance, at the Fourth World Conference on Women in Beijing, tens of thousands of people, mostly women, participated in the Non-Governmental Organizations Forum on Women despite its location in the hard-to-reach suburb of Huairou, 35 miles from the conference site. Originally, the NGO forum was supposed to be in Beijing but Chinese officials hoping to prevent human rights protests moved it in an effort to discourage attendance and reduce its visibility.

Some Important UN Conventions and Treaties Regarding Women's Rights

The **Convention on the Elimination of Discrimination Against Women,** sometimes called the Women's Convention and sometimes called **CEDAW** (although the monitoring committee also goes by this acronym), is viewed as one of the most far-reaching and important women's right documents. It is essentially an international bill of rights for women. The 1979 treaty, developed during the UN's Women's Decade, defines discrimination against women as "any distinction, exclusion, or restriction made on the basis of sex which has the effect or purpose of impairing or nullifying the recognition, enjoyment or exercise by women, irrespective of their marital status, on a basis of equality of men and women, of human rights and fundamental freedoms in the political, economic, social, cultural, civil, or any other field."

> "... the full and complete development of a country, the welfare of the world and the cause of peace require the maximum participation of women on equal terms with men in all fields."
> *From the Convention on the Elimination of All Forms of Discrimination Against Women (CEDAW)*

Nations that ratify the Women's Convention agree to eliminate discrimination against women in employment, education, and politics. Every four years they are supposed to submit reports on their progress to the CEDAW Committee, a group comprised of twenty-three women's rights experts. This committee monitors compliance with CEDAW and issues recommendations. Because there have been so many overdue reports, the UN has begun to offer technical report assistance to those countries that seem to have trouble meeting this treaty requirement. The Optional Protocol to CEDAW, adopted by the General Assembly in 1999, offers two mechanisms to hold governments accountable for their obligations under CEDAW: (1) a communications procedure, which provides individuals and groups the right to lodge complaints with the Committee on the Elimination of Discrimination Against Women (CEDAW Committee), and (2) an inquiry procedure, which enables the CEDAW Committee to conduct inquiries into serious and systematic abuses of women's rights. These procedures apply only to countries that have ratified the Optional Protocol.

As of 2003, 174 countries have signed and ratified CEDAW. See Box 11.3 for a list of nations that have not yet ratified it. Box 11.4 discusses why the United States has not yet ratified CEDAW. It is important to note that many of the countries that ratified CEDAW did so only with "reservations" (when governments enter a reservation to a treaty, it means that they will not be bound to particular

BOX 11.3 Countries That Had Not Ratified CEDAW as of October 2003

Europe and North America

Monaco

United States

Middle East/West Asia

Iran

Oman

Qatar

United Arab Emirates

Asia Pacific/Central Asia

Brunei Darussalam

Cook Islands*

Kiribati*

Marshall Islands

Micronesia (Federated States of)*

Nauru*

Palau

Tonga*

Africa

Somalia

Sudan

Swaziland

*Non-member state of the United Nations.

BOX 11.4 The United States and CEDAW

In our country—where we have worked so hard against domestic violence, where we have worked so hard to empower women—it is to say the least, an embarrassment that the U.S. has not ratified CEDAW.

U.S. President Bill Clinton, 1996

It [ratifying CEDAW] would be like an equal rights amendment enforced by the UN. I don't believe in giving power over U.S. laws to a UN body.

Phyllis Schlafly,
U.S. conservative and antifeminist, 1996

The United States is one of a minority of UN members that has not yet ratified CEDAW. President Carter signed it in 1980, but the U.S. Senate has not yet ratified it due to resistance from political conservatives. Neither the

Reagan nor Bush (George H. W. and George W.) administrations even sought Senate ratification. In 1993, sixty-eight senators signed a letter asking President Clinton to support ratification of CEDAW but a group of conservative senators blocked a Senate floor vote on CEDAW. Conservatives object to CEDAW claiming that it will give the UN too much power over U.S. laws. Also, they say that ratifying CEDAW would be giving in to "special interests" (read: feminists). Some claim that it would force the United States to keep abortion legal.

In June 2002, the Senate Foreign Relations Committee held a hearing on CEDAW. On July 30, 2002, the Committee voted twelve to seven in favor of sending CEDAW to the full Senate for ratification. It still has not come up for a vote and is unlikely to as long as Senator Bill Frist remains the Senate Majority Leader.

parts of that treaty). In fact, fifty-six countries registered a total of 177 official reservations to CEDAW, most based on religious or cultural grounds. This is the highest number of reservations recorded for any international convention. For instance, Israel filed a reservation to Article 16, which states that parties undertake to eliminate discrimination against women in all matters relating to marriage and family relations (Shalev, 1995). As we discussed in earlier chapters, Israel's religious laws give men greater power in marriage and the family. Likewise, Bangladesh, Egypt, Libya, and Tunisia all invoked Islam as the reason for their reservations to the Women's Convention (Mayer, 1995a). Charlesworth and colleagues (1991) suggest that the CEDAW process shows that the international community is ready to acknowledge the considerable problem of women's inequality only if they are not required to alter the patriarchal practices that subordinate women. The fact that the international community tolerates these reservations, many of which are incompatible with the purpose of the CEDAW, further underlines the inadequacy of current international law regarding women's human rights (Charlesworth et al., 1991).

The Optional Protocol has been ratified by fifty-seven nations as of December 2003. This is far less than those that have ratified CEDAW. This may be partly due to the time it takes for government bodies to ratify UN documents through their domestic legal and legislative systems. However, it may also be due to the Protocol's emphasis on accountability. It is one thing for governments to support women's rights in theory; it is yet another thing for them to agree to take responsibility for women's rights violations in an international venue.

In 1993, women's rights advocates from all over the world organized and cooperated to get the United Nations World Conference on Human Rights to include discussions of women's human rights. The conference organizer did not intend to include a specific discussion of women's human rights on the agenda but at least 300,000 people from 123 countries signed a petition demanding that the conference address women's human rights. This effort was orchestrated by the women's human rights organizations, the Center for Women's Global Leadership, and the International Women's Tribune Center. Out of that conference came the **Vienna Declaration and Programme of Action,** which documents women's rights abuses in five areas: abuse within the family, war crimes against women, violations of women's bodily integrity, socioeconomic abuses, and political participation and persecution abuses. The document also includes recommendations for the reduction of such abuses although it does not adequately address the problem of compliance with these (Friedman, 1995).

Also in 1993, the General Assembly of the United Nations finalized the **Declaration on the Elimination of Violence Against Women.** It defines violence as "any act of gender-based violence that results in, or is likely to result in, physical, sexual, or psychological harm or suffering to women, including threats of such acts, coercion or arbitrary deprivation of liberty, whether occurring in public or private life." This document is a notable addition to the legal definition of the human rights of women because it condemns specific forms of violence against women in and out of the home and holds states re-

"The human rights of women and the girl-child are an inalienable, integral and indivisible part of universal human rights. Gender-based violence and all forms of sexual harassment and exploitation, including those resulting from cultural prejudice and international trafficking, are incompatible with the dignity and worth of the human person, and must be eliminated."
Vienna Declaration and Programme of Action, 1993

"[s]tates should condemn violence against women and should not invoke any custom, tradition, or religious consideration to avoid their obligations with respect to its elimination."
Declaration on the Elimination of Violence Against Women

BOX 11.5 *Article 2 of the United Nation's Declaration on the Elimination of Violence Against Women*

Definition of violence against women:

a. Physical, sexual and psychological violence occurring in the family including battering, sexual abuse of female children in the household, dowry-related violence, marital rape, female genital mutilation and other traditional practices harmful to women, non-spousal violence and violence related to exploitation.

b. Physical, sexual and psychological violence occurring within the general community, including rape, sexual abuse, sexual harassment and intimidation at work, in educational institutions and elsewhere, trafficking in women and forced prostitution.

c. Physical, sexual and psychological violence perpetrated or condoned by the state, wherever it occurs.

Source: United Nations, http://www.un.org/womenwatch/resources/documents/gad-RES-48-104.htm.

sponsible for averting and punishing it (see Box 11.5). Unfortunately, however, the document is not a treaty and therefore is not legally binding.

Box 11.6 profiles women's human rights leader Charlotte Bunch of the Center for Women's Global Leadership.

Challenges to a Women's Human Rights Agenda

The global movement for women's human rights has made impressive progress. Because of the efforts of women's activists, major human rights groups such as Amnesty International and Human Rights Watch now document violations of women's rights (before 1989, these organizations paid little attention to women's human rights). Also, the United Nations has begun to pay even greater attention to women's human rights. Still, there are many significant challenges to be met. These are summarized in Figure 11.2.

Moving from Visibility to Accountability

One challenge is that *we must move from visibility of abuse to actual accountability of abuse* (Thomas in Friedman, 1995; emphasis added). It is remarkable that

"If we consider women's rights to be human rights, then we must work to make the reality of our lives match the ideals laid out by the rights standards that international law extends to all human beings."
Ilka Tanya Payan, 1995

BOX 11.6   *Activist Profile: Charlotte Bunch of the Center for Women's Global Leadership*

Charlotte Bunch of the United States has been advocating for women's rights for over thirty years. In 1989 she founded the Center for Women's Global Leadership (CWGL), an organization dedicated to including gender and sexual orientation on the international human rights agenda. Under her leadership, CWGL was instrumental in mobilizing women worldwide to successfully demand the inclusion of women's rights at the 1993 Vienna Human Rights Conference. CWGL remains one the world's leading organizations in the effort to advocate for women's human rights internationally. CWGL promotes networking internationally for women rights, provides training, and organizes international campaigns to promote women's human rights in international law. CWGL's 16 Days of Activism Against Gender Violence is an international campaign originating from the first Women's Global Leadership Institute sponsored by the Center for Women's Global Leadership in 1991. During the annual campaign women all over the world take action to protest gender violence. Bunch is the author of many books and reports, the founder of a feminist journal, *Quest,* and the recipient of many awards, including the Eleanor Roosevelt Award for Human Rights. She is currently Executive Director of CWGL and a professor in the Women and Gender Studies Department at Rutgers University.

virtually all of the abuses documented in this book can be seen as violations of human rights according to *existing* UN conventions and treaties. Yet there is no question that these abuses continue. At this point the UN has issued some strongly worded "women's conventions," which specifically address violations of women's human rights. However, unlike treaties, conventions are not legally binding (they are more like suggestions). (Box 11.7 lists some conventions adopted by the UN General Assembly dealing with the rights of women.) The choice to go the convention route was made in part because the legally binding treaties would have to be considerably weakened before many member states would agree to ratify them. The UN Committee for the Elimination of Discrimination Against Women (CEDAW) monitors compliance with these conventions. This monitoring is done largely by the examination of reports submitted by member states and by dialogues with government representatives. However, this committee has not yet declared a government in violation of women's human rights conventions despite evidence to the contrary.

FIGURE 11.2   *Challenges to a Women's Human Rights Agenda*

Challenge 1	Moving from Identifying Abuses to Accountability for Abuses
Challenge 2	Incorporating Women's Human Rights into the Mainstream Human Rights Agenda
Challenge 3	Creating an Inclusive Women's Rights Agenda

BOX 11.7 *Conventions Adopted by the UN General Assembly Dealing with the Specific Rights of Women*

A convention is an international instrument subject to ratification that legally binds the ratifying governments to give full effect to all provisions contained in its text.

- *Convention on the Political Rights of Women* (1952). State parties to the convention undertake to grant women full political rights: the right to vote and to be eligible for election to all publicly elected bodies, and to be entitled to hold public office and to exercise all public functions on equal terms with men, without any discrimination.

- *Convention on the Nationality of Married Women* (1957). This convention provides for the general principle that men and women have equal rights to acquire, change, or retain their nationality.

- *Convention on Consent to Marriage, Minimum Age for Marriage and Registration of Marriages* (1962). The purpose of this convention is to ensure by national legislation equal rights for both spouses in connection with marriage. Marriages should be entered into with the free and full consent of both spouses. A minimum age for marriage is to be established, and all marriages are to be registered.

- *Convention on the Elimination of All Forms of Discrimination Against Women* (1979). This convention is a broad affirmation of a commitment to ensure equal rights for women in all fields of life: political, economic, social, and cultural.

Other conventions and covenants adopted by the General Assembly containing provisions concerning the status of women include: Convention for the Suppression of the Traffic in Persons and of the Exploitation of the Prostitution of Others; Supplementary Convention on the Abolition of Slavery, the Slave Trade, and Institutions and Practices Similar to Slavery; International Covenant on Economic, Social, and Cultural Rights; International Covenant on Civil and Political Rights; Optional Protocol to the International Covenant on Civil and Political Rights.

Source: United Nations,
http://www.un.org/womenwatch/un/iinstrum.htm.

The current truth of the matter is that there is very little litigation nationally and internationally concerning the violation of women's human rights (Tomasevski, 1993). There is a lack of proper implementation machinery and lack of women's awareness of that machinery that would empower them (Coomaraswamy, 1994). Indeed, one of the demands women's groups presented at the Vienna conference on human rights was that the UN appoint a Special Rapporteur on Violence Against Women. The UN responded to this demand by appointing Radhika Coomaraswamy from Sri Lanka. Her job is to collect information, make recommendations, and draw attention to human rights violations against women.

Several other obstacles hinder implementation. Many countries have an ideological resistance to human rights for women. Although the UN documents relevant to women's rights clearly imply that gender equality is a desirable value, this universal value is not so universal after all. Indeed, local customs and national and religious laws often contradict the treatment of women required by UN conventions and declarations. Furthermore, because of beliefs in state and cultural sovereignty, those local customs and national laws are usually given precedence.

Implementation of international laws and conventions is also hampered by the fact that in some cultures, talk about rights is not meaningful. Particularly in cultures with a history of colonialism, such as India, the human rights movement is disrespected, virtually ignored, and viewed as another tool of the West to eradicate indigenous cultures (Coomaraswamy, 1994). This may mean that unless movements *within* a society cause human rights values to take root, women's human rights will not be enforced (Coomaraswamy, 1994). If a country's own people demand change, these attempts to change things cannot be as easily resisted with accusations of cultural insensitivity. On the other hand, it is helpful to local women's groups to be able to appeal to international treaties. For instance, Plata (1994) explains how the Colombian government began to take women's groups seriously once they emphasized that their requests were consistent with Brazil's signing of the Convention on the Elimination of Discrimination Against Women. As Coomaraswamy (1994) says, civil society is necessary for creating the conditions for law to be relevant, but without law, any human rights activist will only be tilting at windmills.

Bringing Women's Rights into Mainstream Human Rights

A second challenge to an international approach to women's human rights is that *women's issues must become part of the mainstream of the human rights agenda such that they will be considered at every level of human rights discussions rather than marginalized* (Thomas in Friedman, 1995; emphasis added). The long-term male domination of all-powerful political bodies nationally and internationally means that issues of concern to men are seen as general human concerns whereas women's concerns are relegated to a specialized and marginalized sphere (Charlesworth, 1995). One way to bring women's human rights into the mainstream is to show how UN conventions and treaties can be interpreted in ways that include women's human rights violations. For instance, Copelon (1994) shows how domestic violence meets many of the criteria for torture according to international law. Still, this approach will only work if applied with great vigilance. Otherwise, as was evident from the 1993 UN Human Rights Conference, women's human rights will not receive a seat at the human rights discussion table.

Stamatopoulou (1995) suggests that the creation of specialized bodies for addressing women's issues within the United Nations has contributed to their marginalization. Because there are specific UN groups designated to deal with women's issues, the more powerful, mainstream organs of the UN, such as the Commission on Human Rights, have paid little attention to women's human rights violations such as rape, forced marriage, transboundary trafficking of women, honor killings, and genital mutilation. These special women's agencies have resulted in the treatment of women's rights as "lesser rights" (Stamatopoulou, 1995) and have created a "women's ghetto" within the UN (Reanda, 1992). On the other hand, prior to separate institutional mechanisms for dealing with women's issues, women's human rights violations were still ignored. It is not that specialized agencies devoted to women's issues are necessarily bad. The problem is that they are chronically under funded, given little authority, and often excluded from power bodies within the UN.

Respecting Cultural Diversity While Promoting Universal Human Rights

A third and especially "tricky" challenge is that *we must continue to work and organize for an inclusive women's human rights agenda so that the interests of diverse women worldwide are represented* (Thomas in Friedman, 1995; emphasis added). At the heart of the women's rights as human rights endeavor is **universalism**—the idea that all humans share the same inalienable rights. Both the Universal Declaration of Human Rights and CEDAW specify the international human rights standard of legal and social equality between women and men. However, such notions of universality are frequently undermined by beliefs that respect for cultural and religious diversity provides exceptions to human rights law. Claims for universality are even sometimes rejected as imperialistic and as a way to uphold Western economic interests (Chinkin, 1999). The claim that international human rights are incompatible with respect for cultural diversity must be carefully considered. Cultural diversity and human rights must be balanced. Cultural diversity should not be used to excuse human rights violations; nor should a claim for universal values be used to justify the eradication of unique cultural practices that do not violate human rights. This issue is particularly acute in international law, which is concerned with transnational standards (Charlesworth, 1994).

Cultural relativism is the notion that right and wrong are determined culturally. Cultural relativists and human rights activists most disagree on women's rights and every international conference discussing women's rights has seen conflict between feminists and cultural relativists (Coomarswamy, 1999). The most radical cultural relativists argue that there are no legitimate cross-cultural human rights standards and that the human rights endeavor, arising as it did out of the European Enlightenment, is by its very nature inapplicable to non-Western cultures (Coomaraswamy, 1999). In regard to women's rights, these cultural relativists suggest that Western condemnations of gender discrimination in other regions are insensitive and ethnocentric and are a version of cultural imperialism (Mayer, 1995a). For instance, El-Bakri and Kameir (1983) object to holding the role of women in the Middle East and Third World countries to the standards of Western democracies.

Other cultural relativists are more selective, taking issue with only some of the rights specified in human rights documents or their interpretation (Coomaraswamy, 1999). For instance, cultural relativists often emphasize that the treatment of women is often prescribed by a culture's religious practices;

Maryam Rajavi is president-elect of the National Council of Resistance of Iran. Rajavi uses UN women's human rights documents to critique what she calls the "gender apartheid" of Iran. Now living in exile, Rajavi continues to give speeches refuting the fundamentalists' use of the Koran to support their oppression of women. Rajavi emphasizes that democracy and world peace depend on the advancement of women.

"Torture is not culture."
Alice Walker

therefore calls for change are instances of religious intolerance (Jaising, 1995). As noted earlier, many of the countries that have ratified CEDAW did so only after registering "reservations" to those elements that they felt were contrary to important cultural or religious practices. This problem for CEDAW symbolizes a problem that plagues the whole women's rights and human rights endeavor.

Human rights and feminist values may conflict with traditional customs, and it is a legitimate question to ask which should be privileged when this occurs (Katzenstein, 1989). We certainly do not want to be so presumptuous as to impose our worldview on others. Just because a culture is different from our own does not mean that it is wrong. Furthermore, there is no question that historically, Western imperialists and colonialists destroyed native cultures and defended their actions based on the superiority of Western cultural practices. On the other hand, we can go too far in the worship of cultural difference. Nussbaum (1992) cites a number of examples of scholars who defend disturbing cultural practices out of reverence for the culture at hand. As philosopher Rachels (1993) points out, it does not stand to reason that just because cultures differ, that right and wrong are matters of opinion. If we were to take cultural relativism too seriously, we would have to agree that all sorts of questionable behaviors were not immoral because those countries in which they occur do not define them as immoral. Domestic violence is, for example, an accepted practice in many cultures.

It is true that we shouldn't reject cultural practices just because they are not our own and that we should not presume to understand the experiences of those in another culture. And it is true that many cultural practices are nothing more than what Rachels (1993) calls "social conventions," which, objectively speaking, are neither right nor wrong and about which we should keep an open mind. But should we accept cultural practices that obviously result in serious harm to large segments of a society out of respect for the existing culture or tradition? If this had been the case in the United States, slavery would not have been abolished, women would not have been allowed to vote, and civil rights legislation would not have been passed. As Rachels says, moral progress cannot occur if we take cultural relativism too far.

Another problem with the cultural relativist's position is that it implies that there is a homogeneous culture upon which there is agreement. However, "culture is not a static, unchanging, identifiable body of information," but rather is a "series of constantly contested and negotiated cultural practices" (Rao, 1995). For instance, Mayer (1995b) points out that contrary to the view of a monolithic Islamic position on human rights, Muslims actually espouse a wide range of opinions regarding international human rights. These range from the assertion that international human rights are fully compatible with Islam to the claim that international human rights are products of alien, Western culture and represent values contrary to Islam. Libya, Tunisia, and Algeria are all examples of Islamic countries that have found it prudent to make concessions to citizen demands for the observance of inter-

BOX 11.8 *Activist Profile: Sima Samar of Afghanistan*

While the Taliban were in power, Sima Samar's *Shihuda* organization ran three hospitals and twelve clinics for Afghani women and girls across the border in Pakistan. Samar also sponsored schools for girls after the Taliban banned education for girls. When the Taliban government fell, Samar was named Minister for Women's Affairs and deputy prime minister in the new president's cabinet. She criticized the Taliban's interpretation of Islam and its effect on women and advocated for women's rights to be included in the new constitution. Within a few months, conservative Muslims pushed for her dismissal. Despite support from moderate Islamic scholars, she was forced to step down amid death threats. Rather than leave the country, Samar stayed. She became head of the Independent Afghanistan Human Rights Commission and works to prevent extreme interpretations of Islam from threatening Afghan women's human rights.

Afghanistan is a good example of the point that, contrary to the view of a monolithic Islamic position on human rights, Muslims have a wide range of opinions regarding international human rights. Afghanistan is torn between those sympathetic to conservative interpretations of Islam, and those favoring moderate interpretations. Samar is one of many people who believe Islam is consistent with a women's rights as human rights approach, but others strongly disagree. Samar's work is critical in a country where girls' schools are attacked (in 2003, over thirty girls schools were violently attacked) and the new constitution does not explicitly give women rights as citizens.

Source: Williams, 2003.

national human rights (Mayer, 1995b). See Box 11.8 for a profile of Afghani activitist Sima Samar. Samar argues that Islam is compatible with a women's human rights perspective.

When pressured about international human rights, repressive governments often hide behind insincere claims of cultural imperialism as a way to remove the pressure. Their insincerity is evident when they show little respect for cultural diversity within their own nations and when internal demands for the recognition of international human rights show there is no cultural agreement. As Peters and Wolper (1995) say, when considering local, national, or international rulings, one must ask questions about context: What is the status of the speaker? In whose name is the argument from culture advanced? To what extent have the social groups primarily affected participated in the formation of the cultural practices being protected?

Some people doubt that it is possible to universalize feminism given the wide variety of women's experiences, and they question the usefulness of the international legal approach to women's rights. However, supporters of the international human rights approach point out that regardless of differences, women worldwide share the experience of patriarchy and the

"Women from every single culture and every part of the world are standing up and saying we won't accept cultural justification for abuses against us anymore. We are human, we have a right to have our human rights protected, and the world community must respond to that call and throw out any attempts to justify abuse on the grounds of culture."
Dorothy Q. Thomas, director of the Women's Rights Project of Human Rights Watch

devaluing of women and all that encompasses (such as violence against women). They say we can respect cultural diversity *and* promote human rights as long as we recognize that cultural and class difference affect women's experience and how male domination may be contested. As Walters (2001) explains, culture determines the specifics of international human rights violations. For instance, she says that dowry deaths are an Indian manifestation of the international problem of domestic violence. To address the problem of dowry deaths, both the specific cultural context and the fact that they are a violation of women's human rights must be addressed. As noted throughout the book, this consideration of the cultural context is something that is best done by people in their own cultures. We can agree on human rights standards but to be empowered and effective, people must be the architects of change within their own cultures.

Conclusion

You have seen in this chapter both the hope and challenges associated with a human rights approach to women's equality. The success of the women's human rights movement requires embracing both universal human rights and cultural difference. It is important to emphasize the separate identities and histories of groups of women based on religion, ethnicity, nationality, sexual orientation, and economic position while at the same time avoiding a dangerous fatalism of unbridgeable differences among women (Chowdhury et al., 1994). We must agree that regardless of culture it is unacceptable to deny women their equal rights, yet we must acknowledge the diversity of women's experiences to make our efforts relevant. We must respect those cultural features that do not lead to the oppression of women (and others) so as to preserve cultural diversity. We must understand the nuances of a culture because they will affect the ease with which human rights mechanisms are applied. We must create approaches that avoid cultural relativist excuses for oppression, as well as ethnocentric forms of universalism (Walter, 2001).

Finally yet importantly, to paraphrase Charlesworth and colleagues (1991), we must remember that the formal acknowledgment of women's rights as human rights by governments does not in and of itself resolve problems of inequality. That will require economic and cultural change that is unlikely to occur without women's political activity. As Bunch and Fried (1996) point out, the UN documents that affirm women's equal rights (such as CEDAW and the Beijing Platform for Action) are only tools. The potential of these tools can only be realized through vigorous leadership, difficult political dialogue among different groups of women, and women's political activity at all levels—from the global to the local.

Study Questions

1. What is transnational feminism? How do "global feminists" work together?

2. Is global feminism new? When were the first international women's movements founded, and what was their focus?

3. What are universal human rights?

4. What is the "women's rights as human rights" approach? How do human rights activists cast discrimination against women as a violation of their human rights? Why has this been difficult to do given the traditional focus of human rights laws? How can human rights instruments and mechanisms be used to challenge the abuse of women?

5. What contributions has the UN made to gender equality?

6. How have the four women's conferences contributed to transnational feminism? How have the conferences evolved since the first one in Mexico City? What is the role of NGOs in the conferences?

7. What is CEDAW? How do the problems in ratifying CEDAW represent a problem that plagues the whole women's rights as human rights endeavor?

8. What three challenges face the women's human rights movement?

9. What is the nature of the cultural relativist criticism that international human rights are incompatible with a respect for cultural diversity? How do universalists respond to cultural relativists' criticisms of the human rights approach?

10. How does the success of the women's movement require that we embrace both universal human rights and cultural difference?

Discussion Questions and Activities

1. What should be done when local customs and national and religious laws contradict the treatment of women required by UN conventions and declarations?

2. Are you optimistic or pessimistic about the UN's role in bringing about women's equality?

3. Charlesworth and colleagues (1991) suggest that it is significant that men people the major institutions of international law. Do you agree or disagree with their assertion that until there are more women in UN leadership roles, women's human rights will not receive the attention needed? Can and will men advocate for women's human rights?

Activist Websites of Interest

Center for Women's Global Leadership
http://www.cwgl.rutgers.edu
B.a.B.e. Be Active, Be Emancipated (Budi aktivna, Budi emancipirana)
http://www.babe.hr/eng
Creating Resources for Empowerment in Action (CREA)
http://www.creaworld.org
Equality Now
http://www.equalitynow.org
Human Rights Watch—Women's Rights Division
http://www.hrw.org/women
Madre
http://www.madre.org
Amnesty International—Women's Program
http://www.amnestyusa.org/women

Informational Websites of Interest

UN Conventions and Declarations relevant to women's rights
http://www.un.org/womenwatch/un/iinstrum.htm
UN High Commissioner of Human Rights (OHCHR)
    Women's Rights Are Human Rights
http://www.unhchr.ch/women/
Facts About CEDAW
http://www.womenstreaty.org/facts_home.htm
Human Rights Internet (HRI)
http://www.hri.ca

Action Opportunities

1. Join a campaign to ratify CEDAW by the United States. Go to http://www.womenstreaty.org/take.htm or http://www.hrw.org/campaigns/cedaw.

2. The 16 Days of Activism Against Gender Violence is an international campaign originating from the first Women's Global Leadership Institute sponsored by the Center for Women's Global Leadership in 1991. Participants chose the dates, November 25, International Day Against Violence Against Women and December 10, International Human Rights Day, in order to symbolically link violence against women and human rights and to emphasize that such violence is a violation of human rights. This sixteen-day period also highlights other significant dates including December 1, which is World AIDS Day, and December 6, which marks the Anniversary of the Montreal Massacre. Go to http://www.cwgl.rutgers.edu/16days/about.html for specific information on how to participate.

3. Participate in a campaign to help refugees seeking asylum based on gender persecution. Go to the Center for Gender and Refugee Studies at http://www.uchastings.edu/cgrs.

4. Do something to celebrate or inform on International Women's Day, March 8. Every year on this day, women around the world hold rallies and marches to call attention to women's economic and political rights. Hold a press conference, write a newspaper article or a letter to the editor, or have a table at a public venue.

Appendix: Statistical Indicators of Women's Status Worldwide

This appendix provides data by country for the following:

1. Country's relative geographic location
2. The average age at which women marry
3. Education (the percentage of women who are literate [able to read], the percentage of female college students, and in some cases, the percentage of girls who do not attend school)
4. Female life expectancy
5. Maternal deaths per 100,000 births (includes women who die from unsafe abortion, pregnancy-related illness, and women who die in childbirth)
6. Average number of children per woman
7. The percentage of contraceptive use among married women
8. Abortion law (as of December 2003)
9. Percentage of women in non-agricultural wage employment
10. Percentage of female administrators or managers
11. Percentage of parliament or congress that is female (as of October 2003)
12. Violence against women: includes incidence of domestic violence and sexual assault, absence of legislation making domestic violence, rape, and marital rape illegal; and presence of other forms of violence against women such as honor killings, female genital cutting, or dowry deaths

Notes: Most data is from government reports to the United Nations from 1995 to 2003. Data collection methods and years may vary across countries. Many countries lack the human and economic resources to reliably collect and analyze data on women's issues and status, so statistics must be interpreted cautiously. Statistics are particularly poor in regards to violence against women and when available are usually based on limited samples. A systematic study of violence against women is currently underway by the World Health Organization; check the website for reports.

Sources include the CIA Factbook (http://www.cia.gov/cia/publications/factbook), United Nations Statistics Division (http://www.unstats.un.org/unsd), Seager (2003), Center for Reproductive Law & Policy (http://www.crlp.org), Inter-Parliamentary Union (http://www.ipu.org), Weldon (2002), UNIFEM (http://www.unifem.org). Most of these sources update their information regularly; check for updates.

Country	Afghanistan	Albania	Algeria	Angola	Argentina
Location	Southern Asia, north and west of Pakistan, east of Iran	Southeastern Europe, bordering the Adriatic Sea and Ionian Sea, between Greece and Serbia and Montenegro	Northern Africa, bordering the Mediterranean Sea, between Morocco and Tunisia	Southern Africa, bordering the South Atlantic Ocean, between Namibia and Democratic Republic of the Congo	South America, bordering the South Atlantic Ocean, between Chile and Uruguay
Average age at marriage	17.8; polygamy legal	22	24	17.9	23
Education	20% literacy	77% literacy	51% literacy	No data	97% literacy
Life expectancy	44	77	72	47	78
Maternal deaths per 100,000 births	820	31	150	1300	85
Average number of children	7	2.3	2.8	7.2	2.4
Contraceptive use (% of married women)	No data	No data	52	No data	74
Abortion law	Only to save life of mother	On request	Health reasons; rape; incest	Prohibited	Health reasons; rape; incest
% in non-agricultural wage employment	4.7	41	12	42	43
% of administrative/ management positions	14%	No data	6	6	6
% of parliament or congress	Transitional Government; Elections to be held in 2004	6	8	16	31
Violence against women	Domestic violence reportedly common;rape/ sexual assault common due to lawlessness; attacks on women for "immodest" dress; no domestic violence, rape/ sexual assault, or marital rape laws.	Domestic violence reportedly common (46%); no domestic violence or marital rape laws; one shelter for battered women; 41 rapes reported to police annually; sex trafficking of Albanian women a problem.	Rape/sexual assault and domestic violence reportedly common; attacks on women for "immodest" dress; some women's activists have been killed; no domestic violence or marital rape laws.	Domestic violence reportedly common; no domestic violence or marital rape laws; no rape/sexual assault or domestic violence data.	Domestic violence reportedly common but no rape/sexual assault or domestic violence data; no marital rape laws; 5,000–7,000 rapes estimated to occur each year; only a 10% conviction rate for rapists.

Country	Armenia	Australia	Austria	Azerbaijan
Location	Southwestern Asia, east of Turkey	Oceania, continent between the Indian Ocean and the South Pacific Ocean	Central Europe, north of Italy and Slovenia	Southwestern Asia, bordering the Caspian Sea, between Iran and Russia, with a small European portion north of the Caucasus range
Average age at marriage	23	27	26	23
Education	98% literacy; 56% of college students	99% literacy; 51% of college students	99% literacy; 49% of college students	96% literacy; 44% of college students
Life expectancy	76	82	81	75
Maternal deaths per 100,000 births	29	6	11	37
Average number of children	1.1	1.8	1.2	1.5
Contraceptive use (% of married women)	61	76	51	56
Abortion law	On request	Health reasons; rape; incest; socioeconomic grounds; 26 legal abortions per 100 pregnancies.	On request	On request
% in non-agricultural wage employment	46	48	43	45
% of administrative/ management positions	No data	24	22	No data
% of parliament or congress	5	27	31	11
Violence against women	Domestic violence reportedly common; no domestic violence or marital rape laws; 27 rapes reported to police annually.	23–38% have experienced domestic violence; over 14,000 rapes reported to police annually; 20% of women report having been sexually abused as girls.	Government reports domestic violence is a significant problem; 949 rapes reported to police annually.	37% have experienced domestic violence; no domestic violence or marital rape laws; 66 rapes reported to police annually.

Country	Bahrain	Bangladesh	Belarus	Belgium
Location	Middle East, archipelago in the Persian Gulf, east of Saudi Arabia	Southern Asia, bordering the Bay of Bengal, between Burma and India	Eastern Europe, east of Poland	Western Europe, bordering North Sea, between France and the Netherlands
Average age at marriage	26	18	22; 68% divorce rate	25
Education	87% literacy; 57% of college students	29% literacy; 20% of college students	99% literacy; 53% of college students	99% literacy; 50% of college students
Life expectancy	76	61	74	82
Maternal deaths per 100,000 births	38	600	33	8
Average number of children	2.3	3.6	1.2	1.5
Contraceptive use (% of married women)	62	54	50	78
Abortion law	On request	Only to save life of mother	On request; 62 legal abortions per 100 pregnancies	On request
% in non-agricultural wage employment	13	23	56	45
% of administrative/ management positions	21	5	No data	13
% of parliament or congress	8	2	18	34
Violence against women	No domestic violence or rape/sexual assault data; no domestic violence or marital rape laws.	47% have experienced domestic violence; no data on rape/sexual assault; no law against marital rape; honor killings occur.	No domestic violence data; 577 rapes reported to police annually.	68% have experienced domestic violence; 1,684 rapes reported to police annually.

Country	Belize	Benin	Bhutan	Bolivia	Bosnia-Herzegovina
Location	Middle America, bordering the Caribbean Sea, between Guatemala and Mexico	Western Africa, between Nigeria and Togo	Southern Asia, between China and India	Central South America, southwest of Brazil	Southeastern Europe, bordering the Adriatic Sea and Croatia
Average age at marriage	No data	18; 50% polygamous	No data	23	23
Education	93% literacy	24% literacy; 22% of college students; 43% of girls not in school	35% literacy	79% literacy	88% literacy
Life expectancy	76	56	65	65	77
Maternal deaths per 100,000 births	140	880	500	550	15
Average number of children	2.9	5.7	5.1	3.9	1.3
Contraceptive use (% of married women)	47	16	19	48	No data
Abortion law	Health reasons; fetal impairment; socioeconomic grounds	Health reasons; rape; incest; fetal impairment	Prohibited	Health reasons; rape; incest	On request; parental authorization required for minors
% in non-agricultural wage employment	41	51	11.9	36	43
% of administrative/ management positions	No data	6	No data	24	No data
% of parliament or congress	3	6	9	18	12
Violence against women	No domestic violence or rape/ sexual assault data.	No domestic violence or rape/ sexual assault data; no domestic violence or marital rape laws; female genital cutting practiced.	No domestic violence or rape/sexual assault data; no domestic violence law.	62% report domestic violence; no rape/ sexual assault data; no marital rape laws.	No rape/sexual assault or domestic violence data.

Country	Botswana	Brazil	Brunei	Bulgaria	Burkina Faso
Location	Southern Africa, north of South Africa	Eastern South America, bordering the Atlantic Ocean	Southeastern Asia, bordering the South China Sea and Indonesia	Southeastern Europe, bordering the Black Sea, between Romania and Turkey	Western Africa, north of Ghana
Average age at marriage	No data	23	25	23	19; 51% polygamous
Education	80% literacy; 40% of college students	98% literacy; 60% of college students	88% literacy; 59% of college students	98% literacy; 60% of college students	13% literacy; 69% of girls not in school; 23% of college students
Life expectancy	No data	75	79	75	49
Maternal deaths per 100,000 births	No data	23	22	23	1400
Average number of children	3.9	2.2	2.5	1.1	6.8
Contraceptive use (% of married women)	33	77	No data	86	12
Abortion law	Health reasons	Health reasons; rape; incest	Only to save life of mother	On request; 55 legal abortions per 100 pregnancies	Health reasons; rape; incest; fetal impairment
% in non-agricultural wage employment	No data	46	46	50	12.5
% of administrative/ management positions	No data	37	18	31	14
% of parliament or congress	17	9	No data	26	12
Violence against women	13–29% have experienced domestic violence; no rape/sexual assault data; no domestic violence or marital rape laws.	No rape/sexual assault or domestic violence data; no marital rape laws; honor killings occur.	No rape/sexual assault or domestic violence data.; no marital rape law.	No domestic violence data; 774 rapes reported to police annually.	No rape/sexual assault or domestic violence data; no domestic violence or marital rape laws; female genital cutting practiced.

Country	Burundi	Cambodia	Cameroon	Canada	Cape Verde
Location	Central Africa, east of Democratic Republic of the Congo	Southeastern Asia, bordering the Gulf of Thailand, between Thailand, Vietnam, and Laos	Western Africa, between Equatorial Guinea and Nigeria	Northern North America, bordering the North Atlantic Ocean on the east, North Pacific Ocean on the west, and the Arctic Ocean on the north, north of United States	Western Africa, group of islands in the North Atlantic Ocean, west of Senegal
Average age at marriage	23	21	20; 33% polygamous	26	26
Education	40% literacy; 54% of girls not in school; 26% of college students	58% literacy; 16% of college students	69% literacy	99% literacy; 53% of college students	37% literacy
Life expectancy	41	59	51	82	73
Maternal deaths per 100,000 births	1,900	590	720	6	No data
Average number of children	6.8	4.8	4.7	1.6	3.2
Contraceptive use (% of married women)	9	24	19	75	53
Abortion law	Health reasons	On request	Health reasons; rape; incest	On request; 22 legal abortions per 100 pregnancies	On request
% in non-agricultural wage employment	10	52	24	49	50
% of administrative/ management positions	13	No data	10	43	23
% parliament or congress	19	4	8.9	21	11
Violence against women	No rape/sexual assault or domestic violence data; no domestic violence or marital rape laws.	16% have experienced domestic violence; no rape/sexual assault data; no marital rape law.	31% have experienced domestic violence; no rape/sexual assault data; no domestic violence or marital rape laws; female genital cutting practiced.	29% have experienced domestic violence; no rape/sexual assault data; 13% of women report having been sexually abused as girls.	No rape/sexual assault or domestic violence data; no domestic violence or marital rape laws.

Country	Central African Republic	Chad	Chile	China	Colombia
Location	Central Africa, north of Democratic Republic of the Congo	Central Africa, south of Libya	Southern South America, bordering the South Pacific Ocean, between Argentina and Peru	Eastern Asia, bordering the East China Sea, Korea Bay, Yellow Sea, and South China Sea, between North Korea and Vietnam	Northern South America, bordering the Caribbean Sea, between Panama and Venezuela, and bordering the North Pacific Ocean, between Ecuador and Panama
Average age at marriage	19; 20% polygamous	17; 39% polygamous	23; divorce is illegal	22	23
Education	34% literacy; 55% of girls not in school	41% literacy; 61% of girls not in school	95% literacy; 46% of college students	77% literacy; 36% of college students	92% literacy; 52% of college students
Life expectancy	46	47	79	74	75
Maternal deaths per 100,000 women	1200	1500	33	60	120
Average number of children	4.9	6.3	2.4	1.8	2.6
Contraceptive use (% of married women)	15	4	30	84	77
Abortion law	Prohibited	Rape; incest; fetal impairment; to save mother's life	Prohibited	On request; but sex-selective abortion illegal	Prohibited
% in non-agricultural wage employment	30	6	36	80	49
% of administrative/ management positions	9	No data	19	12	35
% of parliament or congress	7	6	10	22	11
Violence against women	No rape/sexual assault or domestic violence data; no marital rape laws; female genital cutting practiced.	No rape/sexual assault or domestic violence data; no marital rape laws; female genital cutting practiced.	26% have experienced domestic violence; no marital rape laws; 615 rapes reported to police annually; 20,000 rapes estimated to occur each year.	No domestic violence data; Some sex-selective abortion and female infanticide; no marital rape law; 40,699 rapes reported to police annually.	19% have experienced domestic violence; no marital rape laws; 1,423 rapes reported to police annually.

Country	Comoros	Congo	Costa Rica	Cote d'Ivoire	Croatia
Location	Southern Africa, group of islands, about two-thirds of the way between Madagascar and Mozambique	Western Africa, bordering the South Atlantic Ocean, between Angola and Gabon	Middle America, bordering both the Caribbean Sea and the North Pacific Ocean, between Nicaragua and Panama	Western Africa, bordering the North Atlantic Ocean, between Ghana and Liberia	Southeastern Europe, bordering the Adriatic Sea, between Bosnia and Herzegovina and Slovenia
Average age at marriage	22; 25% polygamous	22	22	20; 37% polygamous	25
Education	No data	74% literacy	96% literacy	38% literacy; 82% of college students	97% literacy; 51% of college students
Life expectancy	62	54	80	48	78
Maternal deaths per 100,000 births	No data	1,100	35	No data	18
Average number of children	5	6.7	2.7	4.6	No data
Contraceptive use (% of married women)	21	22	75	15	No data
Abortion law	Health reasons	Prohibited	Health reasons	Only to save life of mother	On request; parental authorization needed for minors
% in nonagricultural wage employment	50	32	40	20	46
% of administrative/ management positions	23	5	27	10	24
% of parliament or congress	No data	10	35	9	21
Violence against women	No rape/sexual assault or domestic violence data; no domestic violence or marital rape laws.	No rape/sexual assault or domestic violence data; no domestic violence or marital rape laws.	54% have experienced domestic violence; no marital rape laws; no rape/sexual assault data; rapist may go free if he agrees to marry victim; 32% of women report having been sexually abused as girls.	No rape/sexual assault or domestic violence data; no domestic violence or marital rape laws; female genital cutting practiced.	No rape/sexual assault or domestic violence data; 107 rapes reported to police annually.

Country	Cuba	Cyprus	Czech Republic	Denmark	Djibouti
Location	Caribbean, island between the Caribbean Sea and the North Atlantic Ocean, 150 km south of Key West, Florida	Middle East, island in the Mediterranean Sea, south of Turkey	Central Europe, southeast of Germany	Northern Europe, bordering the Baltic Sea and the North Sea, on a peninsula north of Germany	Eastern Africa, bordering the Gulf of Aden and the Red Sea, between Eritrea and Somalia
Average age at marriage	20	23	23	30; 35% divorce rate	19
Education	96% literacy; 60% of college students	95% literacy; 75% of college students	99% literacy; 48% of college students	99% literacy; 54% of college students	13% literacy
Life expectancy	79	81	79	79	42
Maternal deaths per 100,000 births	24	No data	14	15	520
Average number of children	1.6	1.9	1.2	1.7	5.8
Contraceptive use (% of married women)	70	No data	69	78	18
Abortion law	On request; parental authorization required for minors; 59 legal abortions per 100 pregnancies.	Health reasons; rape; fetal impairment; socioeconomic reasons	On request; parental authorization required for minors	On request; parental authorization required for minors; 20 legal abortions per 100 pregnancies	Health reasons
% in nonagricultural wage employment	38	43	47	49	No data
% of administrative/management positions	19	10	No data	20	2
% of parliament or congress	36	11	16	38	11
Violence against women	No rape/sexual assault or domestic violence data; no domestic violence or marital rape laws.	No rape/sexual assault or domestic violence data.	No rape/sexual assault or domestic violence data.	Government reports that domestic violence is a significant problem; 435 rapes reported to police annually.	No rape/sexual assault or domestic violence data; no domestic violence or marital rape laws; female genital cutting practiced.

Country	Dominican Republic	Ecuador	Egypt	El Salvador	Eritrea
Location	Caribbean, between the Caribbean Sea and the North Atlantic Ocean, east of Haiti	Western South America, bordering the Pacific Ocean at the Equator, between Colombia and Peru	Northern Africa, bordering the Mediterranean Sea, between Libya and the Gaza Strip, and the Red Sea north of Sudan, and includes the Asian Sinai Peninsula	Middle America, bordering the North Pacific Ocean, between Guatemala and Honduras	Eastern Africa, Bordered by Sudan and Ethiopia
Average age at marriage	21	22	22	22	17
Education	84% literacy; 57% of college students	90% literacy; 40% of college students	44% literacy; 42% of college students	76% literacy; 51% of college students	40% literacy; 52% of girls not in school
Life expectancy	70	74	70	74	54
Maternal deaths per 100,000 births	110	210	170	180	1100
Average number of children	2.7	2.8	2.9	2.9	5.3
Contraceptive use (% of married women)	64	66	56	60	5
Abortion law	Prohibited	Health reasons; rape; incest	Prohibited	Prohibited	Health reasons
% in non-agricultural wage employment	34	41	19	31	43
% of administrative/management positions	28	26	16	25	12
% of parliament or congress	15	16	3	11	22
Violence against women	No rape/sexual assault or domestic violence data; no marital rape laws.	No rape/sexual assault or domestic violence data; honor killings occur.	34% have experienced domestic violence; no rape/sexual assault data; honor killings; no domestic violence or marital rape laws; female genital cutting practiced.	No rape/sexual assault or domestic violence data; no marital rape laws.	No rape/sexual assault or domestic violence data; no marital rape laws; female genital cutting practiced.

Country	Estonia	Ethiopia	Fiji	Finland	France
Location	Northern Europe, south of Finland, north of Latvia, bordering the Baltic Sea	Eastern Africa, west of Somalia	Oceania, island group in the South Pacific Ocean, about two-thirds of the way from Hawaii to New Zealand	Northern Europe, bordering the Baltic Sea, Gulf of Bothnia, and Gulf of Finland, between Sweden and Russia	Western Europe, bordering the Bay of Biscay and English Channel, between Belgium and Spain, southeast of the UK; bordering the Mediterranean Sea, between Italy and Spain
Average age at marriage	21; 63% divorce rate	17	23	28; 56% divorce rate	25
Education	99% literacy; 53% of college students	32% literacy; 19% of college students; 70% of girls not in school	91% literacy	99% literacy; 53% of college students	99% literacy; 55% of college students
Life expectancy	76	44	72	82	83
Maternal deaths per 100,000 births	80	1800	20	6	20
Average number of children	1.2	6.8	3	1.6	1.8
Contraceptive use (% of married women)	70	8	40	77	75
Abortion law	On request	Health reasons	Health reasons; socioeconomic grounds	Health reasons; rape; incest; socioeconomic reasons; 15 legal abortions per 100 pregnancies	On request; 18 legal abortions per 100 pregnancies.
% in non-agricultural wage employment	52	40	38	50	46
% of administrative/management positions	No data	8	9	25	10
% of parliament or congress	19	8	6	38	12
Violence against women	No domestic violence data; 97 rapes reported to police annually.	45% have experienced domestic violence; no rape/sexual assault data; no domestic violence or marital rape laws; no rape data; rapist may go free if he agrees to marry victim; female genital cutting practiced.	No domestic violence data; no domestic violence or marital rape laws; 100 rapes reported to police annually.	52% have experienced domestic violence; 468 rapes reported to police annually.	Government reports that domestic violence is a significant problem; 8,200 rapes reported to police annually.

Country	Gabon	Gambia	Georgia	Germany	Ghana
Location	West Africa, bordering the Atlantic Ocean at the Equator, between Republic of the Congo and Equatorial Guinea	West Africa, bordering the North Atlantic Ocean and Senegal	Southwestern Asia, bordering the Black Sea, between Turkey and Russia	Central Europe, bordering the Baltic Sea and the North Sea, between the Netherlands and Poland, south of Denmark	West Africa, bordering the Gulf of Guinea, between Cote d'Ivoire and Togo
Average age at marriage	No data	No data	25	28; 41% divorce rate	21
Education	62% literacy	30% literacy; 36% of college students	98% literacy; 53% of college students	99% literacy; 43% of college students	31% literacy; 22% of college students
Life expectancy	54	49	78	81	58
Maternal deaths per 100,000 births	620	1100	22	22	590
Average number of children	5.4	4.8	1.4	1.3	4.2
Contraceptive use (% of married women)	33	12	41	75	22
Abortion law	Only to save life of mother	Health reasons	On request	On request; 14 legal abortions per 100 pregnancies	Health reasons; rape; incest; fetal impairment
% in non-agricultural wage employment	43	24	49	45	57
% of administrative/ management positions	No data	No data	No data	19	10
% of parliament or congress	10	13	7	31	9
Violence against women	No rape/sexual assault or domestic violence data; no domestic violence, rape, or marital rape laws.	No rape/sexual assault or domestic violence data; female genital cutting practiced.	50% have experienced domestic violence; No domestic violence laws; forty-one rapes reported to police annually.	Government reports that domestic violence is a significant problem; 6,636 rapes reported to police annually.	No rape/sexual assault or domestic violence data; no marital rape laws; female genital cutting practiced.

Country	Greece	Guam	Guatemala	Guinea	Guyana
Location	Southern Europe, bordering the Aegean Sea, Ionian Sea, and the Mediterranean Sea, between Albania and Turkey	Oceania, island in the North Pacific Ocean, about three-quarters of the way from Hawaii to the Philippines	Middle America, bordering the North Pacific Ocean, between El Salvador and Mexico, and bordering the Gulf of Honduras (Caribbean Sea) between Honduras and Belize	Western Africa, bordering the North Atlantic Ocean, between Guinea-Bissau and Sierra Leone	Northern South America, bordering the North Atlantic Ocean, between Suriname and Venezuela
Average age at marriage	25	24	21	16; 50% polygamous	No data
Education	96% literacy; 48% of college students	99% literacy	61% literacy	27% literacy; 11% of college students	98% literacy; 58% of college students
Life expectancy	81	77	69	49	67
Maternal deaths per 100,000 births	2	No data	270	1,200	150
Average number of children	1.2	4	2.4	5.8	2.3
Contraceptive use (% of married women)	No data	No data	38	6	No data
Abortion law	On request; parental authorization required for minors	No data	Only to save life of mother	Health reasons; rape; incest; fetal impairment	On request
% in non-agricultural wage employment	40	42	39	30	45
% of administrative/ management positions	12	41	32	No data	No data
% of parliament or congress	9	?	9	19	20
Violence against women	Government reports domestic violence is a significant problem; no marital rape laws; 166 rapes reported to police annually.	No rape/sexual assault or domestic violence data.	49% have experienced domestic violence; No rape/sexual assault data no rape or marital rape laws.	No rape/sexual assault or domestic violence data; no marital rape laws; female genital cutting practiced.	No rape/sexual assault or domestic violence data; no rape or marital rape laws.

Country	Haiti	Honduras	Hong Kong	Hungary	Iceland
Location	Caribbean, between the Caribbean Sea and the North Atlantic Ocean, west of the Dominican Republic	Middle America, bordering the Caribbean Sea, between Guatemala and Nicaragua and bordering the North Pacific Ocean, between El Salvador and Nicaragua	Eastern Asia, bordering the South China Sea and China	Central Europe, northwest of Romania	Northern Europe, island between the Greenland Sea and the North Atlantic Ocean, northwest of the UK
Average age at marriage	24	20	28	24	30
Education	46% literacy; 54% of girls not in school	72% literacy; 42% of college students	No data	99% literacy; 53% of college students	99% literacy; 58% of college students
Life expectancy	56	69	83	76	82
Maternal deaths per 100,000 births	1100	220	No data	23	15
Average number of children	4	3.7	1.2	1.2	1.9
Contraceptive use (% of married women)	28	62	86	77	No data
Abortion law	Prohibited	Prohibited	Health reasons; rape; incest; fetal impairment	On request; 42 legal abortions per 100 pregnancies	Health reasons; rape; incest; fetal impairment; socioeconomic grounds
% in non-agricultural wage employment	39	52	46	46	52
% of administrative/management positions	33	39	18	58	No data
% of parliament or congress	9	6	Chinese territory	10	30
Violence against women	No rape/sexual assault or domestic violence data; no marital rape laws.	No rape/sexual assault or domestic violence data; no marital rape laws.	No domestic violence data; 74 rapes reported to police annually.	No domestic violence data; 392 rapes reported to police annually.	No rape/sexual assault or domestic violence data.

Country	India	Indonesia	Iran	Iraq	Ireland
Location	Southern Asia, bordering Arabian Sea and Bay of Bengal, between Burma and Pakistan	Southeastern Asia, archipelago between the Indian Ocean and the Pacific Ocean	Middle East, bordering Gulf of Oman, Persian Gulf, and Caspian Sea, between Iraq and Pakistan	Middle East, bordering the Persian Gulf, between Iran and Kuwait	W. Europe, occupying five-sixths of the island of Ireland in the North Atlantic Ocean, west of Great Britain
Average age at marriage	20	22	21	22	28
Education	39% literacy	82% literacy; 31% of college students	70% literacy; 35% of college students	41% literacy	99% literacy; 52% of college students
Life expectancy	65	69	71	66	80
Maternal deaths per 100,000 births	440	470	130	370	9
Average number of children	3	2.3	2.8	4.8	1.9
Contraceptive use (% of married women)	48	57	73	14	No data
Abortion law	Health reasons; rape; incest; fetal impairment; socioeconomic reasons	Only to save life of mother	Prohibited	Prohibited	Only to save life of mother
% in non-agricultural wage employment	17	30	18	13	46
% of administrative/ management positions	2	17	2	13	17
% of parliament or congress	9	8	4	Transitional government	14
Violence against women	26–40% have experienced domestic violence; some sex-selective abortion and female infanticide; 7,000 dowry deaths reported in 2001; honor killings; no marital rape law; 15,330 rapes reported to police annually.	12% have experienced domestic violence; no rape/sexual assault data; no marital rape law.	No rape/sexual assault or domestic violence data; no domestic violence, rape, or marital rape laws.	No rape/sexual assault or domestic violence data; no domestic violence, rape, or marital rape laws.	18% have experienced domestic violence; no rape/sexual assault data.

Country	Israel	Italy	Jamaica	Japan	Jordan	Kazakhstan	Kenya
Location	Middle East, bordering Mediterranean Sea, between Egypt and Lebanon	Southern Europe, a peninsula extending into the central Mediterranean Sea, northeast of Tunisia	Caribbean, island in the Caribbean Sea, south of Cuba	Eastern Asia, island chain between the North Pacific Ocean and the Sea of Japan, east of the Korean Peninsula	Middle East, northwest of Saudi Arabia	Central Asia, NW of China; a small portion west of the Ural River in eastern-most Europe	Eastern Africa, bordering the Indian Ocean, between Somalia and Tanzania
Average age at marriage	24	27	29	27	25	22	21
Education	94% literacy; 52% of college students	98% literacy; 54% of college students	91% literacy; 38% of college students	99% literacy; 44% of college students	84% literacy; 42% of college students	96% literacy; 53% of college students	76% literacy; 28% of college students
Life expectancy	81	82	78	85	73	71	50
Maternal deaths per 100,000 births	8	11	120	12	41	80	1300
Average number of children	2.7	1.2	2.4	1.3	4.3	2.0	4.2
Contraceptive use (% of married women)	No data	60	66	59	53	66	39
Abortion law	Health reasons; rape; incest; fetal impairment	On request; spousal / parental authorization required	Health reasons; parental authorization required	Health reasons; socio-economic grounds; spousal authorization required; 13 legal abortions per 100 pregnancies	Health reasons	On request	Only to save life of mother

Country	Israel	Italy	Jamaica	Japan	Jordan	Kazakhstan	Kenya
% in non-agricultural wage employment	48	41	46	40	21	50	38
% of administrative/ management positions	19	54	No data	9	6	48	No data
% of parliament or congress	15	10	14	10	6	19	7
Violence against women	32% have experienced domestic violence; no marital rape laws; 519 rapes reported to police annually; honor killings occur.	No domestic violence data but over 100 shelters for battered women; 1,582 rapes reported to police annually.	No domestic violence data; no rape or marital rape laws; 1,900 rapes reported to police annually.	59% have experienced domestic violence; no marital rape laws; 1,657 rapes reported to police annually.	No domestic violence data; no marital rape laws; 92 rapes reported to police annually; honor killings occur.	No domestic violence data; no law against marital rape; 1,687 rapes reported to police annually.	42% have experienced domestic violence; no law against marital rape; no rape/sexual assault data; female genital cutting practiced.

Country	Kiribati	Korea, North	Korea, South	Kuwait	Kyrgyzstan
Location	Oceania, group of 33 coral atolls in Pacific Ocean, straddling the equator; about one-half of the way from Hawaii to Australia	Eastern Asia, northern half of the Korean Peninsula bordering the Korea Bay and the Sea of Japan, between Sea China and South Korea	Eastern Asia, southern half of the Korean Peninsula bordering the Sea of Japan and the Yellow Sea	Middle East, bordering the Persian Gulf, between Iraq and Saudi Arabia	Central Asia, west of China
Average age at marriage	22	No data	25	25	27
Education	No data	99% literacy	96% literacy; 32% of college students	80% literacy; 67% of college students	96% literacy; 52% of college students
Life expectancy	No data	68	79	79	72
Maternal deaths per 100,000 births	No data	35	20	25	80
Average number of children	No data	2.6	1.5	2.7	2.3
Contraceptive use (% of married women)	No data	62	81	50	60
Abortion law	Only to save life of mother	On request	Health reasons; rape; incest; fetal impairment; socioeconomic grounds; spousal authorization required	Health reasons; fetal impairment; spousal/parental authorization required	On request
% in non-agricultural wage employment	No data	50	41	23	45
% of administrative/ management positions	9	4	4	5	No data
% of parliament or congress	4.8	20	6	0	7
Violence against women	No rape/sexual assault or domestic violence data; no domestic violence, rape, or marital rape laws.	No rape/sexual assault or domestic violence data; no domestic violence, rape, or marital rape laws.	38% have experienced domestic violence; some sex-selective abortion; no marital rape laws; 5,327 rapes reported to police annually.	No rape/sexual assault or domestic violence data; no marital rape laws.	No domestic violence data; no law against marital rape; 1,482 rapes reported to police annually.

Country	Laos	Latvia	Lebanon	Lesotho	Liberia
Location	Southeastern Asia, northeast of Thailand, west of Vietnam	Eastern Europe, bordering the Baltic Sea, between Estonia and Lithuania	Middle East, bordering the Mediterranean Sea, between Israel and Syria	Southern Africa, an enclave of South Africa	Western Africa, bordering the North Atlantic Ocean, between Cote d'Ivoire and Sierra Leone
Average age at marriage	No data	24	23	No data	20; 38% polygamous
Education	50% literacy; 33% of college students	99% literacy; 60% of college students	80% literacy; 41% of college students	94% literacy; 60% of college students	37% literacy
Life expectancy	56	76	75	76	57
Maternal deaths per 100,000 births	650	70	130	530	1000
Average number of children	4.8	1.1	2.2	4.5	6.8
Contraceptive use (% of married women)	32	48	61	24	6
Abortion law	Prohibited	On request; 54 legal abortions per 100 pregnancies	Only to save life of mother	Prohibited	Health reasons; rape; incest; fetal impairment
% in non-agricultural wage employment	42	53	29	40	28
% of administrative/ management positions	No data	No data	2	33	11
% of parliament or congress	23	21	2	17	11
Violence against women	No rape/sexual assault or domestic violence data; no marital rape laws.	No domestic violence data; no domestic violence, rape, or marital rape laws; 119 rapes reported to police annually.	No rape/sexual assault or domestic violence data; no domestic violence or marital rape laws; rapist may go free if he agrees to marry victim.	No domestic violence data; no marital rape laws; 1,080 rapes reported to police annually.	No rape/sexual assault or domestic violence data; no domestic violence, rape, or marital rape laws; female genital cutting practiced; war rape.

Country	Libya	Liechtenstein	Lithuania	Luxembourg	Macedonia
Location	Northern Africa, bordering the Mediterranean Sea, between Egypt and Tunisia	Central Europe, between Austria and Switzerland	Eastern Europe, bordering the Baltic Sea, between Latvia and Russia	Western Europe, between France and Germany	Southeastern Europe, north of Greece
Average age at marriage	19	26	23	26	23
Education	68% literacy; 46% of college students	No data	99% literacy; 56% of college students	99% literacy	88% literacy; 55% of college students
Life expectancy	73	No data	78	81	76
Maternal deaths per 100,000 births	120	No data	27	No data	No data
Average number of children	3.3	No data	1.2	1.8	1.5
Contraceptive use (% of married women)	40	No data	59	No data	No data
Abortion law	Only to save life of mother; parental authorization required for minors	Health reasons	On request	Health reasons; rape; fetal impairment; socioeconomic grounds; parental authorization required for minors	On request; parental authorization required for minors
% in non-agricultural wage employment	19	No data	51	38	42
% of administrative/ management positions	No data	No data	No data	12	16
% of parliament or congress	0	12	11	17	18
Violence against women	No rape/sexual assault or domestic violence data; no domestic violence, rape, or marital rape laws.	No rape/sexual assault or domestic violence data.	No domestic violence data; no domestic violence or marital rape laws; 166 rapes reported to police annually.	No rape/sexual assault or domestic violence data; government funded battered women shelters; no domestic violence or marital rape laws.	No rape/sexual assault or domestic violence data; no domestic violence or marital rape laws.

Country	Madagascar	Malawi	Malaysia	Maldives	Mali
Location	Southern Africa, island in the Indian Ocean, east of Mozambique	Southern Africa, east of Zambia	Southeastern Asia, peninsula and northern one-third of the island of Borneo, bordering Indonesia and the South China Sea, south of Vietnam	Southern Asia, group of atolls in the Indian Ocean, southwest of India	Western Africa, southwest of Algeria
Average age at marriage	20	19; 21% polygamous	24	19	19; 44% polygamous
Education	59% literacy; 46% of college students	47% literacy; 25% of college students	84% literacy	96% literacy	33% literacy; 60% of girls are not in school
Life expectancy	55	39	76	67	53
Maternal deaths per 100,000 births	580	580	39	390	630
Average number of children	5.7	6.3	2.9	5.4	7
Contraceptive use (% of married women)	19	31	55	No data	7
Abortion law	Prohibited	Only to save life of mother; spousal authorization required	Health reasons; rape; incest	Health reasons; spousal authorization required	To save life of mother; rape; incest
% in non-agricultural wage employment	26	12	36	37	36
% administrative/ management positions	No data	8	16	14	20
% of parliament or congress	6	9	15	6	10
Violence against women	No rape/sexual assault or domestic violence data; no domestic violence or marital rape laws.	No rape/sexual assault or domestic violence data; no domestic violence, rape, or marital rape laws.	No domestic violence data; no marital rape laws; 1,429 rapes reported to police annually.	No rape/sexual assault or domestic violence data; no rape or marital rape laws.	No rape/sexual assault or domestic violence data; no domestic violence or marital rape laws; female genital cutting practiced.

Country	Malta	Marshall Islands	Martinique	Mauritania	Mauritius
Location	Southern Europe, islands in Mediterranean Sea, south of Sicily (Italy)	Oceania, group of atolls and reefs in the North Pacific Ocean, halfway between Hawaii and Australia	Caribbean, island between the Caribbean Sea and North Atlantic Ocean, north of Trinidad and Tobago	Northern Africa, bordering the North Atlantic Ocean, between Senegal and Western Sahara	Southern Africa, island in the Indian Ocean, east of Madagascar
Average age at marriage	22; divorce is illegal	No data	31	23; 18% polygamous	24
Education	No data	87% literacy	No data	29% literacy; 18% of college students	81% literacy; 47% of college students
Life expectancy	81	No data	82	54	76
Maternal deaths per 100,000 births	No data	No data	No data	870	45
Average number of children	1.8	No data	1.7	6	1.9
Contraceptive use (% of married women)	No data	No data	No data	8	75
Abortion law	Prohibited	Prohibited	No data	Prohibited	Prohibited
% in non-agricultural wage employment	31	No data	55	43	39
% of administrative/ management positions	No data	7	No data	8	No data
% of parliament or congress	8	3	No data	4	6
Violence against women	No rape/sexual assault or domestic violence data; no marital rape laws.	No rape/sexual assault or domestic violence data; no domestic violence, rape, or marital rape laws.	No rape/sexual assault or domestic violence data.	No rape/sexual assault or domestic violence data; female genital cutting practiced.	No domestic violence data; no laws against marital rape; 32 rapes reported to police annually.

Country	Mexico	Micronesia	Moldova	Mongolia	Morocco
Location	Middle America, bordering the Caribbean Sea and the Gulf of Mexico, between Belize and the United States and bordering the North Pacific Ocean, between Guatemala and the United States	Oceania, island group in the North Pacific Ocean, about three-quarters of the way from Hawaii to Indonesia	Eastern Europe, northeast of Romania	Northern Asia, between China and Russia	Northern Africa, bordering the North Atlantic Ocean and the Mediterranean Sea, between Algeria and Western Sahara
Average age at marriage	21	No data	22	No data	22
Education	89% literacy; 48% of college students	71% literacy	98% literacy; 54% of college students	99% literacy; 60% of college students	36% literacy; 41% of college students
Life expectancy	76	No data	70	66	71
Maternal deaths per 100,000 births	65	No data	65	65	390
Average number of children	2.5	No data	1.4	2.3	3
Contraceptive use (% of married women)	67	No data	74	60	50
Abortion law	Determined at state level; usually prohibited	Prohibited	On request	On request	Health reasons; rape; incest; spousal authorization required
% in non-agricultural wage employment	37	No data	52	48	27
% of administrative/ management positions	20	9	No data	No data	25
% of parliament or congress	25	?	13	11	6
Violence against women	15–40% report domestic violence; no rape/sexual assault data.	No rape/sexual assault or domestic violence data; no domestic violence, rape, or marital rape laws.	15% have experienced domestic violence; no marital rape laws; 216 rapes reported to police annually.	No rape/sexual assault or domestic violence data; no marital rape laws.	No rape/sexual assault or domestic violence data; no marital rape laws; honor killings occur.

Country	Mozambique	Myanmar (Burma)	Namibia	Nepal	Netherlands
Location	Southeastern Africa, bordering the Mozambique Channel, between South Africa and Tanzania	Southeastern Asia, bordering the Andaman Sea and the Bay of Bengal, between Bangladesh and Thailand	Southern Africa, bordering the South Atlantic Ocean, between Angola and South Africa	Southern Asia, between China and India	Western Europe, bordering the North Sea, between Belgium and Germany
Average age at marriage	22; 27% polygamous	22	No data; 13% polygamous	18	28
Education	28% literacy; 24% of college students; 50% of girls not in school	81% literacy; 64% of college students	81% literacy; 61% of college students	24% literacy; 24% of college students	99% literacy; 48% of college students
Life expectancy	39	59	44	60	81
Maternal deaths per 100,000 births	980	170	370	830	10
Average number of children	5.9	2.8	4.9	4.5	1.5
Contraceptive use (% of married women)	6	33	29	39	79
Abortion law	Health reasons	Only to save life of mother	Health reasons; rape; incest; fetal impairment	On request; sex selective abortion illegal	On request; 11 legal abortions per 100 pregnancies
% in non-agricultural wage employment	15	35	49	12	44
% of administrative/ management positions	12	12	21	9	17
% of parliament or congress	30	0	21	6	33
Violence against women	No rape/sexual assault or domestic violence data; no domestic violence or marital rape laws.	No rape/sexual assault or domestic violence data; no domestic violence or marital rape laws.	No rape/sexual assault or domestic violence data.	No rape/sexual assault or domestic violence data.	11–21% have experienced domestic violence; no marital rape laws; 1,526 rapes reported to police annually.

Country	New Caldonia	New Zealand	Nicaragua	Niger	Nigeria
Location	Oceania, islands in the South Pacific Ocean, east of Australia	Oceania, islands in the South Pacific Ocean, southeast of Australia	Middle America, bordering both the Caribbean Sea and the North Pacific Ocean, between Costa Rica and Honduras	Western Africa, southeast of Algeria	Western Africa, bordering the Gulf of Guinea, between Benin and Cameroon
Average age at marriage	28	27	20	17; 38% polygamous	19; 41% polygamous
Education	91% literacy	94% literacy; 54% of college students	64% literacy; 54% of college students	8% literacy; 77% of girls not in school	56% literacy
Life expectancy	78	81	72	46	52
Maternal deaths per 100,000 births	No data	15	250	920	1100
Average number of children	2.5	2.0	3.8	8	5.4
Contraceptive use (% of married women)	25	75	60	8	15
Abortion law	No data	Health reasons; incest; fetal impairment; 19 legal abortions per 100 pregnancies	Only to save life of mother; spousal/parental authorization required	Prohibited	Only to save life of mother
% in non-agricultural wage employment	No data	51	49	9	36
% of administrative/management positions	14	55	12	No data	6
% of parliament or congress	No data	28	21	1	4
Violence against women	No rape/sexual assault or domestic violence data.	20–35% have experienced domestic violence; no marital rape laws; over 800 rapes reported to police annually; 14% of women report having been sexually abused as girls.	21–69% have experienced domestic violence; no marital rape laws; 26% of women report having been sexually abused as girls.	No rape/sexual assault or domestic violence data; no domestic violence, rape, or marital rape laws; female genital cutting.	31% have experienced domestic violence; no rape/sexual assault data; no domestic violence or marital rape laws; no rape data; female genital cutting.

Country	Norway	Oman	Pakistan	Palau	Palestine
Location	Northern Europe, bordering the North Sea and the North Atlantic Ocean, west of Sweden	Middle East, bordering the Arabian Sea, Gulf of Oman, and Persian Gulf, between Yemen and UAE	Southern Asia, bordering the Arabian Sea, between India on the east and Iran and Afghanistan on the west and China in the north	Oceania, group of islands in the North Pacific Ocean, southeast of the Philippines	Middle East, bordering the Mediterranean Sea, between Egypt and Israel; occupied by Israel
Average age at marriage	29	19	22	No data	No data
Education	99% literacy; 56% of college students	62% literacy; 51% of college students	28% literacy	90% literacy	No data
Life expectancy	82	73	61	No data	74
Maternal deaths per 100,000 births	9	120	200	No data	No data
Average number of children	1.7	5.5	5.1	No data	5.6
Contraceptive use (% of married women)	74	24	24	No data	No data
Abortion law	On request; parental authorization required for minors	Prohibited	Health reasons	Prohibited	Prohibited
% in non-agricultural wage employment	48	25	8	No data	16
% administrative/ management positions	31	No data	4	32	No data
% of parliament or congress	36	A monarchy; no elected legislators	21	0	Occupied by Israel; no elected government
Violence against women	18–25% have experienced domestic violence; 424 rapes reported to police annually; 17% of women report having been sexually abused as girls.	No rape/sexual assault or domestic violence data; no domestic violence or marital rape laws.	80% have experienced domestic violence; no marital rape laws; rape victim charged with adultery and prosecuted unless male witnesses verify rape; 80% of jailed women were convicted of adultery; 2,920 rapes reported to police annually; dowry deaths and honor killings occur.	No rape/sexual assault or domestic violence data; no domestic violence laws.	52% have experienced domestic violence; no rape/sexual assault data; honor killings occur.

Country	Panama	Papua New Guinea	Paraguay	Peru	Philippines
Location	Middle America, bordering both the Caribbean Sea and the North Pacific Ocean, between Colombia and Costa Rica	Oceania, group of islands including the eastern half of the island of New Guinea between the Coral Sea and the South Pacific Ocean, east of Indonesia	Central South America, northeast of Argentina	Western South America, bordering the South Pacific Ocean, between Chile and Ecuador	Southeastern Asia, archipelago between the Philippine Sea and the South China Sea, east of Vietnam
Average age at marriage	22	21	22	23	24; divorce is illegal
Education	91% literacy; 60% of college students	68% literacy; 25% of college students	92% literacy; 51% of college students	85% literacy	95% literacy; 57% of college students
Life expectancy	77	59	73	72	72
Maternal deaths per 100,000 births	100	390	170	240	240
Average number of children	2.4	4.3	3.8	2.6	3.2
Contraceptive use (% of married women)	No data	26	57	64	46
Abortion law	Rape; fetal impairment; parental authorization required for minors	Only to save life of mother	Only to save life of mother	Health reasons	Prohibited
% in non-agricultural wage employment	42	24	38	35	42
% of administrative/management positions	27	No data	14	22	35
% of parliament or congress	10	1	8	18	17
Violence against women	No rape/sexual assault or domestic violence data; no marital rape laws.	67% have experienced domestic violence; no rape/sexual assault data; no domestic violence or marital rape laws.	10% have experienced domestic violence; no rape/sexual assault data; no marital rape laws.	31% have experienced domestic violence; no marital rape laws; rapist may go free if he agrees to marry victim; 4,807 rapes reported to police annually.	5–26% have experienced domestic violence; no rape/sexual assault data.

Country	Poland	Portugal	Puerto Rico	Qatar	Romania
Location	Central Europe, east of Germany	Southwestern Europe, bordering the North Atlantic Ocean, west of Spain	Caribbean, island between the Caribbean Sea and the North Atlantic Ocean, east of the Dominican Republic	Middle East, peninsula bordering the Persian Gulf and Saudi Arabia	Southeastern Europe, bordering the Black Sea, between Bulgaria and Ukraine
Average age at marriage	23	24	22	23	23
Education	99% literacy; 57% of college students	90% literacy; 56% of college students	88% literacy	83% literacy; 73% of college students	97% literacy; 50% of college students
Life expectancy	78	80	80	72	73
Maternal deaths per 100,000 births	12	12	No data	41	60
Average number of children	1.3	1.5	1.9	3.3	1.3
Contraceptive use (% of married women)	49	No data	78	43	64
Abortion law	Health reasons; rape; incest; fetal impairment; parental authorization required for minors	Health reasons; rape; incest; fetal impairment; parental authorization required for minors	On request	Health reasons; fetal impairment	On request
% in non-agricultural wage employment	47	47	39	14	46
% of administrative/ management positions	66	50	59	1	45
% of parliament or congress	20	19	U. S. territory	?	9
Violence against women	No domestic violence data; 2,262 rapes reported to police annually.	53% have experienced domestic violence; 551 rapes reported to police annually.	13–48% report domestic violence; no rape/sexual assault data.	No rape/sexual assault or domestic violence data; no domestic violence or marital rape laws.	No domestic violence data; no marital rape laws; 1,372 rapes reported to police annually.

Country	Russia	Rwanda	Samoa	Saudi Arabia	Senegal
Location	Northern Asia (though part west of the Urals is included with Europe),bordering the Arctic Ocean, between Europe and the North Pacific Ocean	Central Africa, east of Democratic Republic of the Congo	Oceania, group of islands in the South Pacific Ocean, about one-half of the way from Hawaii to New Zealand	Middle East, bordering the Persian Gulf and the Red Sea, north of Yemen	Western Africa, bordering the North Atlantic Ocean, between Guinea-Bissau and Mauritania
Average age at marriage	23; 65% divorce rate	21	25	22	20; 46% polygamous
Education	99% literacy; 53% of college students	60% literacy	98% literacy	67% literacy; 47% of college students	28% literacy
Life expectancy	73	42	74	74	56
Maternal deaths per 100,000 births	75	2,300	No data	23	1,200
Average number of children	1.1	5.8	4.2	5.5	5.1
Contraceptive use (% of married women)	73	13	43	32	13
Abortion law	On request; 63 legal abortions per 100 pregnancies	Health reasons	Health reasons	Health reasons; spousal/parental authorization required for minors	Prohibited
% in non-agricultural wage employment	50	17	No data	14	28
% of administrative/ management positions	No data	46	12	No data	4
% of parliament or congress	6	45	6	0	19
Violence against women	12,000 women die from domestic violence annually; 9,307 rapes reported to police annually; estimated 200,000 rapes occur annually; 25% of girls report unwanted sexual contact.	No rape/sexual assault or domestic violence data; no domestic violence, rape, or marital rape laws.	No rape/sexual assault or domestic violence data; no domestic violence, rape, or marital rape laws.	No rape/sexual assault or domestic violence data; no domestic violence, rape, or marital rape laws.	87% have experienced domestic violence; no rape/sexual assault data; no marital rape laws; female genital cutting practiced.

Country	Serbia - Montenegro	Seychelles	Sierra Leone	Singapore	Slovakia	Slovenia
Location	Southeastern Europe, bordering the Adriatic Sea, between Albania and Bosnia and Herzegovina	Eastern Africa, group of islands in the Indian Ocean, northeast of Madagascar	Western Africa, bordering the North Atlantic Ocean, between Guinea and Liberia	Southeastern Asia, islands between Malaysia and Indonesia	Central Europe, south of Poland	Central Europe, eastern Alps bordering the Adriatic Sea, between Austria and Croatia
Average age at marriage	24	24	18	27	21	26
Education	87% literacy	80% literacy	23% literacy	88% literacy; 46% of college students	99% literacy; 49% of college students	99% literacy; 57% of college students
Life expectancy	76	No data	42	80	78	80
Maternal deaths per 100,000 women	15	No data	2,100	9	14	17
Average number of children	1.6	No data	6.5	1.5	1.3	1.1
Contraceptive use (% of married women)	No data	No data	4	No data	74	No data
Abortion law	On request; parental authorization required for minors	Health reasons; rape; incest; fetal impairment	Health reasons	On request	On request	On request
% in non-agricultural wage employment	46	No data	32	47	52	48
% of administrative/ management positions	No data	29	8	36	60	23
% of parliament or congress	8	29	15	16	19	12
Violence against women	No rape/sexual assault or domestic violence data; no domestic violence or marital rape laws.	No rape/sexual assault or domestic violence data.	No rape/sexual assault or domestic violence data; no domestic violence or marital rape laws; female genital cutting practiced.	No domestic violence data; no marital rape laws; 103 rapes reported to police annually.	No domestic violence data; no marital rape laws; 173 rapes reported to police annually.	No domestic violence data; no domestic violence laws; 107 rapes reported to police annually.

Country	Solomon Islands	Somalia	South Africa	Spain	Sri Lanka
Location	Oceania, group of islands in the South Pacific Ocean, east of Papua New Guinea	Eastern Africa, bordering the Gulf of Aden and the Indian Ocean, east of Ethiopia	Southern Africa, at the southern tip of the continent of Africa	Southwest Europe, bordering the Bay of Biscay, Mediterranean Sea, North Atlantic Ocean, and Pyrenees Mountains, southwest of France	Southern Asia, island in the Indian Ocean, south of India
Average age at marriage	21	20	27	26	24
Education	No data	No data	84% literacy; 48% of college students	97% literacy; 53% of college students	89% literacy; 44% of college students
Life expectancy	71	51	48	82	76
Maternal deaths per 100,000 births		1,600	340	8	60
Average number of children	5.3	7.3	2.9	1.1	2.1
Contraceptive use (% of married women)	3	1	56	81	66
Abortion law	Only to save life of mother	Prohibited	On request	Health reasons; rape; incest; fetal impairment	Only to save life of mother
% in non-agricultural wage employment	24	28	39	39	47
% of administrative/ management positions	No data	No data	19	12	15
% of parliament or congress	0	0	28	23	4
Violence against women	No rape/sexual assault or domestic violence data; no domestic violence, rape, or marital rape laws.	No rape/sexual assault or domestic violence data; no domestic violence or marital rape laws; female genital cutting practiced.	16% have experienced domestic violence; 52,159 rapes reported to police annually; 1,500,000 rapes estimated to occur each year; 25% of females report that their first sexual experience was coerced.	In 2000, 22,000 cases of domestic violence reported to police; 22% of women report having been sexually abused as girls.	No domestic violence data; 909 rapes reported to police annually.

Country	Sudan	Suriname	Swaziland	Sweden	Switzerland	Syria
Location	Northern Africa, bordering the Red Sea, between Egypt and Eritrea	South America, bordering the North Atlantic Ocean, between French Guiana and Guyana in the north	Southern Africa, between Mozambique and South Africa	Northern Europe, between Finland and Norway	Central Europe, east of France, north of Italy	Middle East, bordering the Mediterranean Sea, between Lebanon and Turkey
Average age at marriage	24; 17% polygamous	No data	26	31; 64% divorce rate	27	22
Education	46% literacy	93% literacy; 53% of college students	79% literacy; 52% of college students	99% literacy; 56% of college students	99% literacy; 38% of college students	60% literacy; 39% of college students
Life expectancy	58	74	38	83	82	73
Maternal deaths per 100,000 births	1500	230	370	8	8	200
Average number of children	4.5	2.1	4.4	1.3	1.4	3.7
Contraceptive use (% of married women)	8	No data	20	No data	82	36
Abortion law	Only to save life of mother	Prohibited	Prohibited	On request; 25 legal abortions per 100 pregnancies	On request	Only to save life of mother; spousal/parental authorization required
% in non-agricultural wage employment	20	34	30	51	47	17
% administrative/management positions	2	10	15	59	29	3
% in parliament or congress	10	18	6	45	22	12
Violence against women	No rape/sexual assault or domestic violence data; no domestic violence or marital rape laws; female genital cutting practiced.	No rape/sexual assault or domestic violence data; no domestic violence, rape, or marital rape laws.	No rape/sexual assault or domestic violence data; no marital rape laws.	No domestic violence data; 1,308 rapes reported to police annually.	13–21% have experienced domestic violence; 370 rapes reported to police annually; 20% of women report having been sexually abused as girls.	No rape/sexual assault or domestic violence data; no domestic violence or marital rape laws.

Country	Tajikistan	Tanzania	Thailand	Timor-Leste	Togo
Location	Central Asia, west of China	Eastern Africa, bordering the Indian Ocean, between Kenya and Mozambique	Southeastern Asia, bordering the Andaman Sea and the Gulf of Thailand, southeast of Burma	Southeastern Asia, part of the Indonesian archipelago, north of Australia	Southeastern Asia, bordering the Andaman Sea and the Gulf of Thailand, southeast of Burma
Average age at marriage	21	21; 29% polygamous	24	No data	20; 43% polygamous
Education	99% literacy; 26% of college students	62% literacy; 20% of college students	94% literacy; 53% of college students	No data	43% literacy; 17% of college students
Life expectancy	71	52	74	51	53
Maternal deaths per 100,000 births	120	1,100	44	No data	980
Average number of children	2.9	5	2.0	3.9	5.4
Contraceptive use (% of married women)	21	25	72	No data	24
Abortion law	On request	Only to save life of the mother	Health reasons; rape; incest	No data	Prohibited
% in non-agricultural wage employment	52	33	47	28	47
% of administrative/ management positions	No data	No data	21	No data	8
% of parliament or congress	12	22	10	26	7
Violence against women	No rape/sexual assault or domestic violence data; no domestic violence or marital rape laws.	No domestic violence data; no marital rape laws; 1,576 rapes reported to police annually; female genital cutting practiced.	20% have experienced domestic violence; 3,726 rapes reported to police annually.	No rape/sexual assault or domestic violence data ; no rape or marital rape laws.	No rape/sexual assault or domestic violence data; no domestic violence or marital rape laws; female genital cutting practiced.

Country	Tonga	Trinidad & Tobago	Tunisia	Turkey	Turkmenistan
Location	Oceania, archipelago in the South Pacific Ocean, about two-thirds of the way from Hawaii to New Zealand	Caribbean, islands between the Caribbean Sea and the North Atlantic Ocean, northeast of Venezuela	Northern Africa, bordering the Mediterranean Sea, between Algeria and Libya	Southeastern Europe and Southwestern Asia (portion of Turkey west of the Bosporus is geographically part of Europe), bordering the Black Sea, between Bulgaria and Georgia, and bordering the Aegean Sea and the Mediterranean Sea, between Greece and Syria	Central Asia, bordering the Caspian Sea, Iran and Kazakhstan
Average age at marriage	25	22	25	22	24
Education	No data	97% literacy; 55% of college students	60% literacy; 45% of college students	77% literacy; 35% of college students	No recent data
Life expectancy	No data	77	72	73	70
Maternal deaths per 100,000 births	No data	65	70	55	65
Average number of children	No data	1.5	2.1	2.3	3.2
Contraceptive use (% of married women)	74	53	60	64	62
Abortion law	Prohibited	Health reasons	On request	On request; spousal/parental authorization required; 21 legal abortions per 100 pregnancies in England and Wales	On request; 26 legal abortions per 100 pregnancies
% in non-agricultural wage employment	No data	40	20	19	44
% of administrative/ management positions	5	42	9	6	No data
% of parliament or congress	?	25	12	4	26
Violence against women	No rape/sexual assault or domestic violence data; no marital rape laws.	No rape/sexual assault or domestic violence data; no domestic violence or marital rape laws.	No rape/sexual assault or domestic violence data; no marital rape laws.	58% have experienced domestic violence; no domestic violence or marital rape laws; 705 rapes reported to police annually; honor killings occur.	Honor killings; no domestic violence or marital rape laws.

Country	Uganda	Ukraine	United Arab Emirates	United Kingdom	United States
Location	Eastern Africa, west of Kenya	Eastern Europe, bordering the Black Sea, between Poland and Russia	Middle East, bordering the Gulf of Oman and the Persian Gulf, between Oman and Saudi Arabia	Western Europe, islands including the northern one-sixth of the island of Ireland between the North Atlantic Ocean and the North Sea, north-west of France	North America, bordering both the North Atlantic Ocean and the North Pacific Ocean, between Canada and Mexico
Average age at marriage	19; 30% polygamous	21; 63% divorce rate	23	26; 53% divorce rate	26; 49% divorce rate
Education	57% literacy; 37% of college students	99% literacy; 51% of college students	79% literacy; 72% of college students	99% literacy; 50% of college students	99% literacy; 56% of college students
Life expectancy	47	74	78	81	80
Maternal deaths per 100,000 women	1100	45	30	10	12
Average number of children	7	1.1	2.9	1.6	1.9
Contraceptive use (% of married women)	23	68	28	82	76
Abortion law	Only to save life of mother	On request	Only to save life of mother; spousal/ parental authorization required	Health reasons; rape; incest	On request; some states require parental authorization and/ or waiting periods
% in non-agricultural wage employment	43	53	14	50	48
% of administrative/ management positions	14	No data	2	33	44
% of parliament or congress	25	5	0	17	14
Violence against women	41% have experienced domestic violence; no domestic violence or marital rape laws; 268 rapes reported to police annually; female genital cutting practiced; honor killings occur.	No domestic violence data; no marital rape laws; 1,510 rapes reported to police annually.	No rape/sexual assault or domestic violence data; no domestic violence, rape, or marital rape laws.	25–30% have experienced domestic violence; 6,600 rapes reported to police annually; 50,000 rapes estimated to occur each year.	25–31% report domestic violence; 90,186 rapes reported to police annually; 700,000 rapes and sexual assaults esti-mated to occur each year; 15% of women raped before age 17; 21% of women report having been sexually abused as girls.

Country	Uruguay	Uzbekistan	Vanuatu	Venezuela	Vietnam
Location	Southern South America, bordering the South Atlantic Ocean, between Argentina and Brazil	Central Asia, north of Afghanistan	Oceania, group of islands in the South Pacific Ocean, about three-quarters of the way from Hawaii to Australia	Northern South America, bordering the Caribbean Sea and the North Atlantic Ocean, between Colombia and Guyana	Southeastern Asia, bordering the Gulf of Thailand, Gulf of Tonkin, and South China Sea, alongside China, Laos, and Cambodia
Average age at marriage	23	20	23	21	23
Education	98% literacy	84% literacy	No data	93% literacy	91% literacy
Life expectancy	79	73	71	77	72
Maternal deaths per 100,000 births	50	60	No data	43	95
Average number of children	2.3	2.3	4.3	2.7	2.3
Contraceptive use (% of married women)	No data	56	15	No data	75
Abortion law	Health reasons; rape; incest	On request	Health reasons	Only to save life of mother	On request
% in non-agricultural wage employment	46	38	No data	40	53
% administrative/ management positions	28	No data	13	24	No data
% of parliament or congress	12	7	2	10	27
Violence against women	No rape/sexual assault or domestic violence data; no marital rape laws; rapist may go free if he agrees to marry victim.	No rape/sexual assault or domestic violence data; no domestic violence or marital rape laws.	No rape/sexual assault or domestic violence data; no domestic violence, rape, or marital rape laws.	No rape/sexual assault or domestic violence data; no rape laws; 4,000 rapes reported to police annually.	No rape/sexual assault or domestic violence data; no domestic violence or marital rape laws.

Country	Yemen	Zambia	Zimbabwe
Location	Middle East, bordering the Arabian Sea, Gulf of Aden, and Red Sea, between Oman and Saudi Arabia	Southern Africa, east of Angola	Southern Africa, between South Africa and Zambia
Average age at marriage	19	17	21
Education	25% literacy; 13% of college students; 60% of girls not in school	74% literacy; 30% of college students	90% literacy; 21% of college students
Life expectancy	63	42	42
Maternal deaths per 100,000 births	850	890	610
Average number of children	7.6	5.7	4.5
Contraceptive use (% of married women)	21	25	55
Abortion law	Only to save life of mother	Health reasons; fetal impairment; socioeconomic grounds	Health reasons; rape; incest; fetal impairment
% in non-agricultural wage employment	6	36	20
% of administrative/ management positions	2	6	15
% of parliament or congress	.3	12	10
Violence against women	No rape/sexual assault or domestic violence data; no domestic violence or marital rape laws.	40% have experienced domestic violence; no rape/sexual assault data; no domestic violence or marital rape laws.	17–32% have experienced domestic violence; no domestic violence laws; 3,900 rapes reported to police annually.

Glossary

Abortion   Surgical or chemical means of terminating a pregnancy.

Accidental activism   When women in traditional roles are drawn into politics because the safety and health of their families or communities is threatened.

Affirmative action   Programs and policies that promote the entrance of women into better paying, traditionally male jobs.

AIDS   Acquired Autoimmune Deficiency Disease, a disease caused by the Human Immunodeficiency Virus (HIV) leading to a breakdown of the body's natural defenses and opportunistic infections.

Antinatalist policies   Government policies intended to reduce birth rates by encouraging or requiring that women limit their fertility.

Backlashes against feminism   Countermovements against feminism.

Bible   The primary text of the Christian religion containing both Old and New Testaments.

Bilateral aid   Country-to-country development aid.

Brideprice (*bridewealth* or *lobala*)   A practice where the groom gives money, goods, or livestock to the parents of the bride in return for her hand in marriage.

Buddhism   A nontheistic religion based on the teachings of the Prophet Buddha in the fifth or sixth century; found throughout the world, especially in Asia.

Canon   A religion's scriptures and texts.

Christianity   The Christian faith based on the life, death, and resurrection of Jesus Christ and the Bible.

Coercive antinatalism   Antinatalist programs that force, trick, or bribe people to undergo sterilization or use contraceptives that are high in effectiveness but have health risks.

Comparable worth policies   Policies that require the comparison of female and male jobs and the determination of pay based on the skill, experience and stress involved in the job.

Compensating differentials   Suggests that women's jobs pay less because they are easier, offer more pleasant work conditions, offer flexible hours, etc.

Compulsory heterosexuality   The idea that societies practically "require" heterosexuality by giving women few economic options outside of marriage, and by hiding the lesbian possibility.

Concrete ceiling   The dual burden of racism and sexism that prevents the promotion of women from traditionally disadvantaged groups.

Contraceptives and reproductive technologies   Methods and technologies used to prevent pregnancy, including barrier, hormonal, and permanent methods.

Convention on the Elimination of Discrimination Against Women (CEDAW)   A 1979 international treaty guaranteeing women's rights; also known as the Women's Convention.

Cultural globalization   The transnational migration of people, information, and consumer culture.

Cultural relativism   The notion that right and wrong are determined culturally.

Debt bondage   How women trafficked into sexual slavery get "stuck" because they must repay the costs of their travel and money paid to their families and pay for food, shelter, and clothing.

Declaration on the Elimination of Violence Against Women   Declaration passed by the UN General Assembly in 1993 that defines violence against women and calls on nation-states to alleviate it.

Development   The process of economic, political, or social growth in a nation.

Differential modeling   A mechanism of differential socialization whereby children learn appropriate gender behavior through observation.

Differential reinforcement   A mechanism of differential socialization whereby children learn appropriate gender behavior because they are rewarded for it.

Differential socialization   The process by which societies teach girl and boy children gender norms and roles.

Domestic violence   Physical, verbal, or emotional violence committed within the context of an intimate relationship.

Domestics   Maids, childcare providers, and caregivers for the elderly and disabled.

Dowry   Money or goods given to the groom or his family by the bride's family.

Dowry deaths   The staged death of wives by husbands or in-laws so that the husband can remarry, also called bride burnings.

Ecofeminism   Umbrella term for a variety of approaches that bridge feminist and environmental concerns.

Economic globalization   The transnational integration of world economies orchestrated by multinational corporations and financial institutions such as the World Bank.

Electoral system reform   Changes in the procedures by which representatives are elected such as quotas or the adoption of PL/PR systems.

Empowerment   The processes by which women gain power over their lives and the ability to bring about change in situations of gender inequality.

Equal pay legislation   Laws prohibiting gender pay discrimination.

Ethnocentrism   The tendency for people to place their own culture at the center of the world and to think that it is superior to others.

Female genital mutilation (FGM) or female genital cutting (FGC)   Procedures involving partial or total removal of the external female genitalia or other injury to the female genital organs for cultural or other non-medical reasons.

Femicide (female infanticide)   The killing of girl-children, either intentionally, or as a result of neglect.

Feminism   An approach committed to breaking down the structures that keep women lower in status and power.

Feminist spirituality movement   Variety of nonbiblical religions that include female images of the divine; also known as women's spirituality movement.

Feminist theology   The study of religious doctrines through a feminist "lens"; a theology concerned with the liberation of women from oppression.

Feminization of poverty   Refers to the larger number of women in poverty, relative to men.

First World nations   Nations that are industrialized and market based, also called the "North" due to their location predominately in the northern hemisphere.

Flexibilization   Requirement that countries be able to adjust to changes that affect the world economy; often entails structural adjustment programs.

Forced concubinage   The kidnapping of girls and women to wash, cook, serve, and have sex with soldiers and militia.

Formal labor sector   Formal employment counted by governments and included in national accounting systems.

Formal politics   Institutionalized politics such as voting, parliaments and congresses, and heads of state.

Free trade zones (FTZs) or Export Processing Zones (EPZs)   Areas in Third World countries established to attract transnational factories.

Gender and development approach (GAD)   Development approach that focuses explicitly on improving women's status, also called the empowerment approach.

Gender-based household divisions of labor   Describes the tendency for women to do more of the core household tasks and childcare.

Gender harassment   Type of sexual harassment characterized by verbal and nonverbal behavior that conveys insulting, hostile, and degrading attitudes toward women.

Gender mainstreaming   The inclusion of a gender perspective in all development activities, requires women's active participation in the development process.

Gender norms   Social rules regarding what is appropriate for each gender to do.

Gender occupational segregation   Explains the pay gap in terms of the fact that women tend to work in lower-paying sectors of the economy and hold lower ranks within the same occupational group.

Gender perspective on household labor   Argues that household labor is a symbolic representation of gender relations; household labor and child care are viewed as "women's work."

Gender pay gap   The common gap between male and female earnings with women generally receiving less pay.

Gender stereotypes   Beliefs about the qualities of each gender.

Gender wage discrimination   Paying women less because women's work is devalued, because it is assumed that her income is supplementary to her husband's, or because employers can get away with it and it increases their profits.

Gender wage gap   Describes the fact that employed women are generally paid less than employed men.

Genocidal rape   When rape is used to destroy an ethnic or political group perceived as the enemy.

Glass ceiling   Invisible barriers to the promotion and advancement of women into higher status, power positions.

Global feminism   The study of feminism cross-culturally based on an appreciation of women's cross-cultural similarities and differences.

Global feminism or transnational feminism   Feminist movements that span across nations, with a core belief that women are entitled to the same human rights as men.

Goddess spirituality   Pagan religions focused on goddess worship.

Government cabinets   The group of advisors to the head of state who frequently lead specific government agencies and wield considerable policy making power.

Grassroots organizations (GROs) Locally based groups that work to develop and improve the community.

Grassroots support organizations (GRSOs) Nationally or regionally based development assistance organizations that channel funds to grassroots organizations.

Hadith The sayings attributed to Muhammad. Individual sayings are called *ahadith*.

Hermeneutics The study of the principles of interpretation for religious texts.

Heterosexism Prejudice against homosexuals.

Hinduism A 6,000 year-old religion of India with numerous male and female deities.

Homophobia Fear of homosexuals.

Honor killing A tradition whereby a man is obliged to kill a close female blood relative if she does something that is believed to tarnish the family honor.

Horizontal occupational segregation Explains the pay gap in terms of the tendency for occupations mainly held by men to have substantially higher pay rates and status as compared to those mainly held by women.

Human capital approach Suggests that women get paid less because they are less skilled, less educated, or less experienced workers than men are.

Income-generating project A type of WID development project intended to provide opportunities for women to make money.

Informal politics Political actions including grassroots protests and political action organized by nongovernmental organizations.

Ideological explanations for gender differences in political activity Explains gender differences in political activity in terms of traditional gender beliefs that make women seem unsuitable for politics.

Informal labor sector Uncounted, "under the table" employment such as trading and selling at markets and work done on a contract basis in the home.

Islam Religion founded in the eighth century C.E., and based on the Prophet Muhammad's teachings.

Islamists Muslim fundamentalists who use strict scriptural interpretations to restrict women and resist Western influences.

Judaism The Jewish faith, which is based on study of the Torah and ritual practice as described in the Talmud.

Koran The primary text of Islam.

Leader prototype A culture's stereotypical view of what a leader should look like in terms of gender, ethnicity, class, and age.

Leadership categorization theory Suggests that gender and ethnic stereotypes affect whether we perceive individuals from various social categories to be suitable candidates for leadership roles.

Legal literacy Knowledge of one's legal rights and the means to defend those rights.

Leisure gap The common gap between the amount of leisure time women have relative to men; men have more leisure time than women.

Lesbian diversity Idea that because sexuality is socially constructed, there is no one way to be lesbian or to describe the lesbian experience.

Lesbian feminism Beliefs and practices based on the assumption that an erotic and/or emotional commitment to women and political resistance to patriarchy are connected.

Lesbian invisibility Tendency for cultures to deny lesbians' existence and for lesbians to live quiet, hidden lives.

Lesbian separatism A rare type of lesbian feminism emphasizing a complete rejection of patriarchy; may involve all-women communities and the avoidance of any relationship with men.

Lesbians Female homosexuals, women affectionately and sexually attracted to women.

Liberation theology Theology focused on freedom from oppression and the reduction of racism, classism, and sexism.

Macro power Power in the economic and political or public sphere of life.

Mail-order brides Women who use commercial organizations to arrange introductions and broker marriages with foreign men.

Masculine God-language Religious language in scriptures, prayers, and liturgy that suggests God is male.

Maternal mortality The death of a woman while pregnant or within forty-two days of termination of pregnancy from any cause related to or aggravated by the pregnancy or its management.

Maternalism Political activity that is an extension of women's role as wife and mother.

Matriarchy A society where women have greater power and status than men.

Micro power Power in the home or private sphere of life.

Military sexploitation of women When militaries permit and even encourage soldiers to buy the services of sex workers.

Modernization theory A traditional development approach focused on economic growth and a conversion to capitalist market economies.

Mujerista **theology** A Latin American feminist liberation theology with the goal of liberating Hispanic women.

Multiculturalism (Interculturalism) A perspective that emphasizes the understanding, accepting, and valuing of cultural differences between groups.

Multilateral aid Development aid funded by international agencies.

Muslims Name given to followers of Islam.

Obstetric fistula When prolonged and obstructed labor, especially in young women, tears tissues between the vaginal wall and the bladder or rectum resulting in incontinence, infections, and/or ulcerations.

Opportunistic rape   Occurs when men rape women during wartime, knowing it is unlikely they will face consequences.

Organizational tolerance   The degree to which an organization is perceived by employees to be insensitive or tolerant of sexual harassment; affects its frequency and severity.

Parliaments and congresses   Political bodies comprised of citizen representatives that create laws and policies.

Patriarchy   The economic, political, cultural, and legal structures that perpetuate gender inequality; also, a society where men have greater power and status.

Party list/proportional representation system   Electoral system where parties receive seats in proportion to the votes they receive and party lists and multi-member districts are common.

Political explanations for gender differences in political activity   Explain gender differences in political activity as arising from the culture and processes of formal political institutions.

Political insider or **climber**   Female political leader who attained power by working her way up through a party hierarchy.

Political literacy   Knowledge of the processes required for political participation.

Political outsider   Female political leader who entered politics from a grassroots citizen movement, chosen as an alternative to politics as usual.

Political rape   Rape used to punish individuals, families, or communities that hold different political views.

Political surrogate   Female political leader who serves as a "stand-in" for a deceased and/or martyred husband or father.

Pronatalist policies   Governmental policies intended to increase birth rates by reducing or banning contraception and abortion.

Practical gender interests   A motivation for women's movements that arises out of concerns about an immediate issue facing women.

Private sphere   The domestic domain of the home.

Private Use Value   Unpaid labor for the use of the family.

Prostitution   The selling of sexual services.

Public sphere   The public domain outside of the home.

Public Use Value   Labor exchanged for goods or money.

Quotas   Type of electoral reform where a certain number of seats or candidacies are reserved for women.

Rape   Forced sex against a person's will.

Reformist Efforts in Feminist Theology   Efforts to transform existing religions for greater gender equality.

Relative resources perspective on household labor   Emphasizes that women do more household labor to make up for their smaller monetary contribution to the household.

Reproductive choice   The extent to which women can freely choose from a variety of birth control methods.

Reproductive control   How much control a woman has over her sex life and her fertility, as well as her access to reproductive health care and safe abortion.

Revolutionary feminist theology   Umbrella term for efforts to create new religions free of patriarchy.

Second shift   Term describing how employed women frequently work one shift in paid work and another shift doing household labor before or after paid work.

Self-efficacy   The belief that your efforts will be effective.

Self-employed sector or Women's micro- and small-scale enterprises (WMSEs)   Other names for the informal labor sector intended to highlight its importance to economies.

Sexual exploitation or sexual objectification   When women are used as sexual objects for financial gain or pleasure without regard to them as people; the reduction of women to their bodies.

Sex-segregated religious practices   The notion that in most religions, women and men are expected to show their devotion to God differently and public religious roles and rituals are often designated as male.

Sex-selective abortion   The aborting of female fetuses when a son is desired.

Sex-role spillover theory   Suggests that sexual harassment occurs because traditional relationships between the genders overflow into the workplace.

Sexual coercion or *quid pro quo* sexual harassment   Type of sexual harassment where sex is required as a condition of employment or job rewards.

Sexual tourism   Tourism based on the travel of men from First World countries to Third World countries to buy cheap sex from exotic women.

Sex trafficking industry   A multibillion-dollar transnational industry that recruits and tricks women into sexual slavery.

Shari'ah (or ***sharia***)   Islamic law based on sayings attributed to Muhammad, often conservative and supportive of traditional gender roles.

Single-member district system   Electoral system where the winning candidates is the one with the most votes and there is only one seat per district.

Social protest   Community-based informal political activities around social problems such as hunger, war, pollution, and social justice.

Sociostructural explanations for gender differences in political activity   Explain gender differences in political activity in terms of social structures that reduce the "supply" of female candidates.

Son preference   When families value male children over female children.

State feminism   Government structures such as bureaus and agencies that are charged with addressing women's issues and equality.

State pseudofeminism   When government agencies created to ostensibly promote women's equality, actually promote traditional gender roles.

Strategic gender interests   A motivation for women's movements that arises out of a desire to bring about large-scale gender social change.

Structural adjustment programs (SAPs)   Government "belt-tightening" measures typically entailing cuts for social services, schools, hospitals, public transportation, and utilities.

Sustainable development   Development that promotes human well-being and dignity while regenerating and protecting the natural resource base.

Swara   A practice that involves handing over young girls and women to rival partners in order to settle conflicts.

Sweatshops   Businesses that violate wage, child labor, and safety standards and laws.

Sticky Floor   The idea that women are often relegated to the lowest paying jobs under the poorest work conditions.

Talmud   Sixty-three volumes of legal and theological teachings centering on the meaning of the Torah and the practice of Judaism; in addition to the Torah, one of the most important Jewish texts.

Third World feminist theology   Liberation theology emphasizing the multiple oppressions faced by Third World Women.

Third World nations (developing nations)   Nations that are less or non-industrialized nations, also called the "South" due to their location principally in the southern hemisphere.

Time availability perspective on household labor   Explains gendered divisions of household labor by suggesting that women have more time to perform household tasks due to less time in the paid workforce.

Transnational feminism   A feminism that spans across cultures, often based on a human rights perspective and relying on the Internet and women's conferences for networking.

Torah   The first five chapters of the Old Testament that make up one of the two most important Jewish texts.

Tripartite model of sexual harassment   Identifies three behavioral dimensions of sexual harassment: gender harassment, unwanted sexual attention, and sexual coercion.

United Nations (UN)   International organization with representatives from most of the world's nation-states; creates international law and guidelines, provides technical assistance.

Universal human rights   Inalienable rights possessed by all humans.

Universalism   The idea that all humans share the same inalienable rights, regardless of nationality, culture, gender, etc.

Unwanted sexual attention   Type of sexual harassment characterized by suggestive comments about a woman's body as well as unsolicited and unreciprocated sexual advances such as repeated requests for a kiss, a date, or sex.

Vedas   The primary Hindu scriptures.

Vertical occupational segregation   Explains the pay gap by noting that even when men and women have the same occupation, women tend to be represented in lower ranks than men within the same occupation.

Vienna Declaration and Programme of Action   Declaration from the 1993 Vienna human rights conference that documents women's rights abuses and provides recommendations.

War rape   The rape of women during wartime.

Welfare approach   A traditional development approach that considers women in terms of their traditional role as wife and mother.

Wicca   Pagan religion based on wiccan (witchcraft) traditions.

Womanist theology   An African American Christian feminist liberation theology reflecting Black women's social, religious, and cultural experiences.

Womanspaces   The "female-only" spaces provided by traditional religions; potentially a source of power, sharing, and integrity for women.

Womanspirit movement   Another name for feminist wicca; features group and meditative rituals emphasizing women's connectedness with the earth and nature.

Women in development (WID)   Development approach that includes women through income-generating projects, labor-saving technologies, and improving women's local resource access.

Women entrepreneurs   Women who start their own businesses.

Women's human rights perspective   A perspective emphasizing that regardless of culture, women and men are equally deserving of rights and freedoms; views abuses against women as human rights violations.

Women's movement   The sum of campaigns that address issues of concern to women.

Women's spirituality movement   Another name for feminist spirituality movement.

Women's suffrage   A name for women's voting rights.

References

Abdel Halim, A. M. 1995. Challenges to the application of international women's human rights in the Sudan. In *Human rights of women: National and international perspectives,* edited by R. J. Cook. Philadelphia: University of Pennsylvania Press.

Abdullah, H. 1995. Wifeism and activism: The Nigerian women's movements. In *The challenge of local feminisms: Women's movements in global perspective,* edited by A. Basu. Boulder, CO: Westview Press.

Abu Khalil, A. 1994. Women and electoral politics in Arab states. In *Electoral systems in comparative perspective: Their impact on women and minorities,* edited by W. Rule and J. F. Zimmerman. Westport, CT: Greenwood Press.

Acevedo, L. 1995. Feminist inroads in the study of women's work and development. In *Women in the Latin American development process,* edited by C. E. Bose and E. Acosta-Belen. Philadelphia: Temple University Press.

Acosta-Belen, E., and Bose, C. E. 1995. Colonialism, structural subordination, and empowerment: Women in the development process in Latin America and the Caribbean. In *Women in the Latin American development process,* edited by C. E. Bose and E. Acosta-Belen. Philadelphia: Temple University Press.

African Women's Development and Communications Network (FEMNET). 2001. Enhancing Ethiopian women's access to and control over land. http://www.law.emory.edu/WAL/Advocacy/Ethiopia.htm

Afshar, H. 1991. *Women, development, and survival in the Third World.* New York: Longman.

———. 1996. Islam and feminism: An analysis of political strategies. In *Feminism and Islam: Legal and literary perspectives,* edited by M. Yamani. New York: New York University Press.

Agent France Presse. 2002, September 24. U.S. to end supply of contraceptives to Philippines in 2004.

Ahmed, L. 2002. Gender and literacy in Islam. In *Nothing sacred: Women respond to religious fundamentalism and terror,* edited by B. Reed. New York: Thunder's Mouth Press/Nation Books.

Alan Guttmacher Institute. 1999. Abortion in context: United States and worldwide. http://www.agi-usa.org/pubs/ib_0599.html

Allen, P. G. 1992. *The sacred hoop: Recovering the feminine in American Indian traditions.* Boston: Beacon Press.

Allen, S. M., and A. J. Hawkins. 1999. Maternal gatekeeping: Mothers' beliefs and behaviors that inhibit greater father involvement in family work. *Journal of Marriage and Family, 61.*

Almeida Acosta, E., and M. E. Sanchez de Almeida. 1983. Psychological factors affecting change in women's role and status: A cross-cultural study. *International Journal of Psychology, 18.*

Alvarez, S. E. 1994. The (trans)formation of feminism(s) and gender politics in Brazil. In *The women's movement in Latin America: Participation and democracy.* 2d ed., edited by J. S. Jaquette. Boulder, CO: Westview Press.

American Medical Association. 1995. Council report: Female genital mutilation. *Journal of the American Medical Association, 274.*

Amin R., and Y. Li. 1997. NGO-promoted women's credit program, immunization coverage, and child mortality in rural Bangladesh. *Women and Health, 25.*

Amnesty International. 1990. *Women in the front line: Human rights violations against women.* New York: Author.

———. 1997a. *Breaking the silence: Human rights violations based on sexual orientation.* London: Author.

———. 1997b. *Pakistan: Women's human rights remain a dead letter.* http://www.amnesty.org/ailib/aipub/1997/ASA/33300797.htm

———. 2001. *Lesbians, human rights, and organizing on gender within AI and it LGBT network.* http://www.ai-lgbt.org/lesbian_issue.htm

———. 2002. *Pakistan: The Tribal Justice System in Pakistan.* http://web.amnesty.org/library/Index/eng ASA330242002

———. 2003. Female genital mutilation: A human rights information pack. http://www.amnesty.org/ailib/intcam/femgen/fgm1.htm

Amoah, E. 1987. Women, witches, and social change in Ghana. In *Speaking of faith: Global perspectives on women, religion, and social change,* edited by D. L. Eck and D. Jain. Philadelphia: New Society Publishers.

Anand, A. 1993. Introduction. In *The power to change: Women in the Third World redefine their environment.* London: Zed.

Anderson, B. 2002. Just another job? The commodification of domestic labor. In *Global woman: Nannies, maids, and sex workers in the new economy,* edited by B. Ehrenreich and A. R. Hochschild. New York: Metropolitan Books.

Anderson, J. 1994. Separatism, feminism, and the betrayal of reform. *Signs,* Winter, 437–448.

Anderson, N. F. 1993. Benazir Bhutto and dynastic politics: Her father's daughter, her people's sister. In *Women as national leaders ,* edited by M. A. Genovese. Newbury Park, CA: Sage.

Anderson, T. 1992. Summit weighs women's role in changing world. *Los Angeles Times,* July 10, A6.

Anker, R. 1998. *Gender and jobs: Sex segregation of occupations in the world.* Geneva: International Labour Organization.

Anson, O., A. Levenson, and D. Y. Bonneh. 1990. Gender and health on the kibbutz. *Sex Roles, 22,* 213–236.

Antrobus, P. 1991. Paper presented to the World Women's Congress for a Healthy Planet, Miami, FL.

Anwar, G. 1999. Reclaiming the religious center from a Muslim perspective: Theological alternatives to religious fundamentalism. In *Religious fundamentalisms and the human rights of women,* edited by C. W. Howland. New York: St. Martin's Press.

Archarya, K. 2001. Sterilisation in India. *Contemporary Review, 279,* 26–29.

Armstrong, K. 2002. Fundamentalism. In *Nothing sacred: Women respond to religious fundamentalism and terror,* edited by B. Reed. New York: Thunder's Mouth Press/Nation Books.

Armstrong, S. 2003. Not my daughter: Villages in Senegal say no to female cutting. *Ms.,* Summer, 22–23.

Arthur, R. H. 1987. The wisdom goddess and the masculinization of western religion. In *Women in the world's religions, past and present,* edited by U. King. New York: Paragon House.

Arungu-Olende, R. A. 1996. Kenya: Not just the literacy but wisdom. In *Sisterhood is global,* edited by R. Morgan. New York: Feminist Press.

As, B. 1996. Norway: More power to women. In *Sisterhood is global,* edited by R. Morgan. New York: Feminist Press.

Asian Women Workers Newsletter. 1992. Sexual harassment at work. *Women's International Network News, 18,* 46.

Associated Press. Bill would regulate mail-order bride business. *Los Angeles Times,* 6 July 2003, A23.

Atwood, N. C. 2001. Gender bias in families and its clinical implications for women. *Social work, 46,* 23–36.

Aulette, J. R. 2001. New roads to resistance: Polish feminists in the transition to democracy. In *Democratization and women's grassroots movements,* edited by J. M. Bystydzienski and J. Sekhon. Bloomington: Indiana University Press.

Bachofen, J. J. 1967. *Myth, religion, and mother right.* Princeton, NJ: Princeton University Press.

Bacon, D. 1997. Workers in maquiladoras from Tijuana to Juarez are fighting back against NAFTA-driven exploitation. *San Francisco Bay Guardian,* 5 March.

Bales, K. 2002. Because she looks like a child. In *Global woman: Nannies, maids, and sex workers in the new economy,* edited by B. Ehrenreich and A. R. Hochschild. New York: Metropolitan Books.

Bamberger, J. 1974. The myth of matriarchy: Why men rule in primitive society. In *Women, culture, and society,* edited by M. Z. Rosaldo and L. Lamphere. Stanford, CA: Stanford University Press.

Bancroft, A. 1987. Women in Buddhism. In *Women in the world's religions, past and present,* edited by U. King. New York: Paragon House.

Bandura, A. 1986. *Social foundations of thought and action.* Englewood Cliffs, NJ: Prentice-Hall.

Barak, A. 1997. Cross-cultural perspectives on sexual harassment. In *Sexual harassment: Theory, research, and treatment,* edited by W. O'Donohue. Boston: Allyn and Bacon.

Barnes, N. S. 1987. Buddhism. In *Women in world religions,* edited by A. Sharma. Albany: State University of New York Press.

———. 1994. Women in Buddhism. In *Today's woman in world religions,* edited by A. Sharma. Albany: State University of New York Press.

Baron, J. N., A. Davis-Blake, and W. T. Bielby. 1986. The structure of opportunity: How promotion ladders vary within and among organizations. *Administrative Science Quarterly, 31,* 248–273.

Barry, K. 1995. *The prostitution of sexuality.* New York: New York University Press.

Barstow, A. L. 1994. *Witchcraze: A new history of the European witch hunts.* New York: HarperCollins.

Baruch, G. K., and R. C. Barnett. 1986. Role quality, multiple role involvement, and psychological well-being in midlife women. *Journal of Personality and Social Psychology, 51,* 578–585.

———. 1987. Role quality and psychological well-being. In *Spouse, parent, and worker: On gender and multiple gender roles,* edited by F. J. Crosby. New Haven, CT: Yale University Press.

Basu, A., ed. 1995. *The challenge of local feminisms: Women's movements in global perspective.* Boulder, CO: Westview Press.

Batalova, J. A., and P. N. Cohen. 2002. Premarital cohabitation and housework: Couples in cross-national perspective. *Journal of Marriage and the Family, 64,* 743–756.

BBC News. 2002. Nigerian women's oil protest ends. 25 July. http://news.bbc.co.uk/1/hi/world/africa/ 2152264.stm

Beckman, P. R., and F. D'Amico. 1995. Conclusion: An end and a beginning. In *Women in world politics: An introduction,* edited by F. D'Amico and P. R. Beckman. Westport, CT: Bergin and Garvey.

Bem, S. L. 1993. *The lenses of gender: Transforming the debate on sexual inequality.* New Haven, CT: Yale University Press.

Beneria, L. 1998. On paid and unpaid work. *Radcliffe Quarterly.* Fall.

———, and M. Roldan. 1987. *The crossroads of class and gender: Industrial homework, subcontracting, and household dynamics in Mexico City.* Chicago: University of Chicago Press.

Berger, M. 1995. Key issues on women's access to and use of credit in the micro- and small-scale enterprise sector. In *Women in micro- and small-scale enterprise development,* edited by L. Divard and J. Havet. Boulder, CO: Westview Press.

Bergmann, B. R. 1989. Does the market for women's labor need fixing? *Journal of Economic Perspectives, 3,* 43–60.

Bernard, J. 1972. *The future of marriage.* New York: World.

———. 1987. *The female world from a global perspective.* Bloomington: Indiana University Press.

Berstein, S. 2000. Persistence brought abortion pill to U.S. *Los Angeles Times,* 5 November, A1, A24.

Bhatnagar, D. 1988. Professional women in organizations: New paradigms for research and action. *Sex Roles, 18,* 343–355.

Bhatt, E. 1995. Women and development alternatives: Micro- and-small-scale enterprises in India. In *Women in micro and small scale enterprise development,* edited by L. Divard and J. Havet. Boulder, CO: Westview Press.

Bhutto, B. 1989. *Daughter of destiny: An autobiography.* New York: Simon and Schuster.

Bianchi, S., M. A. Milkie, L. C. Sayer, and J. P. Robinson. 2000. *Social Forces, 79,* 191–229.

Biehl, J. 1991. *Rethinking ecofeminist politics.* Boston: South End Press.

Bjorkqvist, K., K. Osterman, and K. M. J. Lagerspetz. 1994. Sex differences in covert aggression among adults. *Aggressive Behavior, 20,* 27–33.

Blackwood, E. 1984. Sexuality and gender in certain Native American tribes: The case of cross-gender females. *Signs, 10,* 27–42.

———. 1986. Breaking the mirror: The construction of lesbianism and the anthropological discourse on homosexuality. In *The many faces of homosexuality: Anthropological approaches to homosexual behavior,* edited by E. Blackwood. New York: Harrington Park.

———, and S. E. Wieringa. 1999. *Same-sex relations and female desires.* New York: Columbia University Press.

———. 1999. Sapphic shadows. In *Same-sex relations and female desires,* edited by E. Blackwood and S. E. Wieringa. New York: Columbia University Press.

Blair, S. L., and Lichter, D. T. 1991. Measuring the division of household labor: Gender segregation of housework among American couples. *Journal of Family Issues, 12,* 91–113.

Blau, F. D., and M. A. Ferber. 1987. Occupations and earnings of women works. In *Working women: Past, present, future,* edited by K. S. Koziara, M. H. Moskow, and L. D. Tanner. Washington, DC: BNA Books.

Blau, F. D., and L. M. Kahn. 1996. Wage structure and gender earnings differentials: An international comparison. *Economica, 63,* 529–562.

Bloom-Feshbach, J. 1981. Historical perspectives on the father's role. In *The role of the father in child development,* edited by M. E. Lamb. New York: Wiley.

Blumberg, R. L. 1991. Income under female versus male control: Hypotheses from a theory of gender stratification and data from the Third World. In *Gender, family, and economy: The triple overlap,* edited by R. L. Blumberg. Newbury Park, CA: Sage.

———. 1995. Gender, microenterprise, performance, and power: Case studies from the Dominican Republic, Ecuador, Guatemala, and Swaziland. In *Women in the Latin American development process,* edited by C. E. Bose and E. Acosta-Belen. Philadelphia: Temple University Press.

Blumstein P., and P. Schwartz. 1991. In *Gender, family, and economy: The triple overlap,* edited by R. L. Blumberg. Newbury Park, CA: Sage.

Bonder, G., and M. Nari. 1995. The 30 percent quota law: A turning point for women's political participation in Argentina. In *A rising public voice: Women in politics worldwide,* edited by A. Brill. New York: Feminist Press.

Bonner, R. 2002. Pakistani group offers bleak view of Pakistan's rights record. *New York Times,* 29 March, A6.

Bonvillian, N. 2001. *Women and men: Cultural constructs of gender.* 3d ed. Upper Saddle River, NJ: Prentice Hall.

Boserup, E. 1970. *Women's role in economic development.* New York: St. Martin's Press.

Boston Women's Health Collective. 1992. *The new our bodies, ourselves.* New York: Simon and Schuster.

Boudreau, V. G. 1995. Corazon Aquino: Gender, class, and the people power president. In *Women in world politics: An introduction,* edited by F. D'Amico and P. R. Beckman. Westport, CT: Bergin and Garvey.

Brandell, S. G. 1998. FGM roundup. *Ms.,* May/June, 26.

Brandiotti, R., E. Charkiewicz, S. Hausler, and S. Wieringa. 1994. *Women, the environment, and sustainable development.* Santo Domingo, Dominican Republic: INSTRAW.

Braun, S. 1998. Mitsubishi to pay $34 million in sex harassment case. *Los Angeles Times,* 12 June, A1, A18, A19.

Braverman, L. 1991. The dilemma of housework: A feminist response to Gottman, Napier, and Pittman. *Journal of Marital and Family Therapy, 17,* 25–28.

Breinlinger, S., and C. Kelly. 1994. Women's responses to status inequality: A test of social identity theory. *Psychology of Women Quarterly, 18,* 1–16.

Brennan, D. 2002. Selling sex for visas: Sex tourism as a stepping stone to international migration. In *Global woman: Nannies, maids, and sex workers in the new economy,* edited by B. Ehrenreich and A. R. Hochschild. New York: Metropolitan Books.

Brenner, J. 1996. The best of times, the worst of times: Feminism in the United States. In *Mapping the women's movement: Feminist politics and social transformation in the North,* edited by M. Threlfall. London: Verso and New Left Review.

Brenner, O. C., J. Tomkiewicz, and V. E. Schein. 1989. The relationship between sex role stereotypes and requisite management characteristics revisited. *Academy of Management Journal, 32,* 662–669.

Brooks, D., and S. Goldberg. 2001. Gay and lesbian adoptive and foster care placements: Can they meet the needs of waiting children? *Social Work, 46,* 147–157.

Brownmiller, S. 1986. *Against our will.* New York: Simon and Schuster.

Bruce, J. 1995. The economics of motherhood. In *A commitment to the world's children: Perspectives on development for Beijing and beyond,* edited by N. Heyer. New York: UNIFEM.

Bryant, E. 2003. Glass ceiling thrives in French politics. *United Press International,* 14 October.

Bryceson, D. F. 1995. Wishful thinking: Theory and practice of western donor efforts to raise women's status in rural Africa. In *Women wielding the hoe: Lessons for feminist theory and development practice,* edited by D. F. Bryceson. Oxford: Berg Publishers.

Bullock, S. 1994. *Women and work.* London: Zed.

Bumiller, E. 1990. *May you be the mother of a hundred sons: A journey among the women of India.* New York: Random House.

Bunch, C. 1995. Transforming human rights from a feminist perspective. In *Women's rights, human rights: International feminist perspectives,* edited by J. Peters and A. Wolper. New York: Routledge.

———, and S. Fried, 1996. Beijing '95: Moving women's human rights from margin to center. *Signs,* Autumn, 200–204.

———, and S. Frost. 2000. Women's human rights: An introduction. http://www.cwgl.rutgers.edu/globalcenter/whr.html

Burke, R., and C. McKeen. 1988. Work and family: What we know and what we need to know. *Canadian Journal of Administrative Sciences, 5,* 30–40.

Burn, S. M. 1996. *The social psychology of gender.* New York: McGraw-Hill.

———. 2004. *Groups: Theory and Practice.* Belmont, CA: Wadsworth/Thomson Learning.

Buschman, J. K., and S. Lenart. 1996. "I am not a feminist, but . . .": College women, feminism, and negative experiences. *Political Psychology, 17,* 59–75.

Buss, D. M., and M. Barnes. 1986. Preferences in human mate selection. *Journal of Personality and Social Psychology, 50,* 559–570.

Buvinic, M. 1995. Women's income generation activities in Latin America and the Caribbean: A commentary. In *Seeds 2,* edited by A. Leonard. New York: Feminist Press.

———, C. Gwin, and L. M. Bates. 1996. *Investing in women: Progress and prospects for the World Bank.* Washington, DC: Johns Hopkins University Press.

Bystydzienski, J. M. 1992a. Introduction. In *Women transforming politics: Worldwide strategies for empowerment,* edited by J. Bystydzienski. Bloomington: Indiana University Press.

———. 1992b. Influence of women's culture on public policies in Norway. In *Women transforming politics: Worldwide strategies for empowerment,* edited by J. Bystydzienski. Bloomington: Indiana University Press.

———. 1994. Norway: Achieving world-record women's representation in government. In *Electoral systems in comparative perspective: Their impact on women and minorities,* edited by W. Rule and J. F. Zimmerman. Westport, CT: Greenwood Press.

———. 1995. *Women in electoral politics: Lessons from Norway.* Westport, CT: Praeger.

Cabal, L. 2003. Defending reproductive rights: Women's rights activists in Latin America should take to the courts. http://www.crlp.org/rfn_03_07_3.html

Cabezas, A. L. 2002. Tourism, sex work, and women's rights in the Dominican Republic. In *Globalization and human rights,* edited by A. Brysk. Berkeley, CA: University of California Press.

Calhoun, C. 1998. Taking seriously dual systems and sex. *Hypatia, 13,* 224–231.

Cannon, C. M. 1997. The Adams chronicle. *Working Woman,* October 24–27, 88, 91.

Cantor, A. 1995. *Jewish women, Jewish men: The legacy of patriarchy in Jewish life.* New York: Harper and Row.

Carillo, R. 1992. *Battered dreams: Violence against women as an obstacle to development.* New York: UNIFEM.

Carmody, D. L. 1974. *Women and world religions.* Nashville: Parthenon Press.

———. 1979. *Women and world religions.* Nashville: Abingdon.

———. 1989. *Women and world religions.* Englewood Cliffs, NJ: Prentice Hall.

———. 1991. *Religious woman: Contemporary reflections on eastern texts.* New York: Crossroad.

———. 1994. Today's Jewish women. In *Today's woman in world religions,* edited by A. Sharma. Albany: State University of New York Press.

Carras, M. C. 1995. Indira Gandhi: Gender and foreign policy. In *Women in world politics: An introduction,* edited by F. D'Amico and P. R. Beckman. Westport, CT: Bergin and Garvey.

Cartright, D. W., and A. Zander. 1968. *Group dynamics: Research and theory.* 3d ed. New York: Harper and Row.

Cath. 1995. Country report on lesbians in India. In *Unspoken rules: Sexual orientation and women's human rights,* edited by R. Rosenbloom. San Francisco: International Gay and Lesbian Human Rights Commission.

Cavin, S. 1985. *Lesbian origins.* San Francisco: Ism Press.

Center for American Women in Politics. 1997. The gender gap: Attitudes on public policy issues. www.rci.rutgers.edu/~cawp/Facts/ggapissues.pdf

Center for Reproductive Law and Policy. 2000. Reproductive rights 2000: Moving forward. New York, New York: Center for Reproductive Rights and Policy (CRLP).

———. 2003a. Female circumcision/Female genital mutilation (FC/FGM): Global laws and policies toward elimination. http://www.reproductiverights.org/pub_fac_fgmicpd.html

———. 2003b. The Global Gag Rule's Effects on NGOs in 56 countries. http://www.reproductiverights.org/pub_fac_ggreffects.html

———. 2003c. Peru's minister of health issues apology. http://www.crlp.org/ww_lac.html

Chafetz, J. S. 1990. *Gender equity: An integrated theory of stability and change.* Newbury Park, CA: Sage.

———. 1991. The gender division of labor and the reproduction of female disadvantage: Toward an integrated theory. In *Gender, family, and economy: The triple*

overlap, edited by R. L. Blumberg. Newbury Park, CA: Sage.

Chan, K-S., C. S-K. Tang, and W. Chan. 1999. Sexual harassment: A preliminary analysis of its effects on Hong Kong Chinese women in the workplace and academia. *Psychology of Women Quarterly, 23,* 661–672.

Chanan, G. 1992. *Out of the shadows: Local community action and the European community.* Dublin: European Foundation for the Improvement of Living and Working Conditions.

Chang, G. 2000. *Disposable domestics.* Cambridge, MA: South End Press.

Chant, S. 1997. Female employment in Puerto Vallarta: A case study. In *Gender, work, and tourism,* edited by M. T. Sinclair. London: Routledge.

———. 2003. *Gender in Latin America.* New Brunswick, NJ: Rutgers University Press.

Charles, M., and F. Hopflinger. 1992. Gender, culture, and the division of household labor: A replication of U.S. studies for the case of Switzerland. *Journal of Comparative Family Studies, 23,* 375–387.

Charlesworth, H. 1994. What are "women's international human rights"? In *Human rights of women,* edited by R. Cook. Philadelphia: University of Pennsylvania Press.

———. 1995. Human rights as men's rights. In *Women's rights, human rights: International feminist perspectives,* edited by J. Peters and A. Wolper. New York: Routledge.

———, Chinkin C., and Wright, S. 1991. Feminist approaches to international law. *The American Journal of International Law, 85,* 613–645.

Chen, M. A. 1995. Introduction. In *Seeds 2,* edited by A. Leonard. New York: Feminist Press.

Chesler, P. 1996. What is justice for a rape victim? *On the Issues,* Winter, 12–16, 56–57.

Chinchilla, N. S. 1994. Feminism, revolution, and democratic transitions in Nicaragua. In *The women's movement in Latin America: Participation and democracy,* edited by J. S. Jaquette. 2d ed. Boulder, CO: Westview Press.

Chinery-Hesse, M. 1995. Speech as Deputy Director-General, International Labour Office at the Fourth World Conference on Women. gopher.un.org/00/conf/fwcw/conf/una/_950906203352.txt

Chinkin C. M. 1993. Peace and force in international law. In *Reconceiving reality: Women and international law,* edited by D. G. Dallmeyer. New York: Asil.

———. 1999. Cultural relativism and international law. In *Religious fundamentalisms and the human rights of women,* edited by C. W. Howland. New York: St. Martin's Press.

Chodorow, N. 1978. *The reproduction of mothering: Psychoanalysis and the sociology of gender.* Berkeley: University of California Press.

Chow, E. N., and K. Chen. 1994. The impact of the one-child policy on women and the patriarchal family in the People's Republic of China. In *Women, the family, and policy,* edited by E. N. Chow and C. W. Berheide. Albany: State University of New York Press.

Chowdhury, N. 1994. Bangladesh: Gender issues and politics in a patriarchy. In *Women and politics worldwide,* edited by B. J. Nelson and N. Chowdhury. New Haven, CT: Yale University Press.

———, B. J. Nelson, K. A. Carver, N. J. Johnson, and P. L. O'Loughlin. 1994. Redefining politics: Patterns of women's political engagement from a global perspective. In *Women and politics worldwide,* edited by B. J. Nelson and N. Chowdhury. New Haven, CT: Yale University Press.

Christ, C. P., and J. Plaskow. 1979. Introduction: Womanspirit rising. In *Womanspirit rising: A feminist reader in religion,* edited by C. P. Christ and J. Plaskow. San Francisco: Harper and Row.

Chronicle of Higher Education. 2003. Report says gay and lesbian students face hostility on campuses. May 16. http://www.ngltf.org/library

Cianni, M., and B. Romberger. 1995. Perceived racial, ethnic, and gender differences in access to developmental experiences. *Group and Organization Management, 20,* 440–459.

Cisernos, S. 1996. Guadalupe the sex goddess. *Ms., 7,* 43–46.

Clark, B. 1995. Country report on lesbians in Zimbabwe. In *Unspoken rules: Sexual orientation and women's human rights,* edited by R. Rosenbloom. San Francisco: International Gay and Lesbian Human Rights Commission.

Cleveland, J. N., and K. McNamara. 1996. Understanding sexual harassment: Contributions from research on domestic violence and organizational change. In *Sexual harassment in the workplace: Perspectives, frontiers, and response strategies,* edited by M. S. Stockdale. Thousand Oaks, CA: Sage.

Col, J. 1993. Managing softly in turbulent times: Corazon C. Aquino, President of the Philippines. In *Women as national leaders,* edited by M. Genovese. Newbury Park, CA: Sage.

Collier, R., and J. Strasburg. 2002. Clothiers fold on sweatshop lawsuit. *San Francisco Chronicle,* September 7, A1.

Collins, P. H. 1990. *Black feminist thought: Knowledge, consciousness, and the politics of empowerment.* Boston: Irwin Hyman.

Cook, R. J. 1995. International human rights and women's reproductive health. In *Women's rights, human rights: International feminist perspectives,* edited by J. Peters and A. Wolper. New York: Routledge.

Cooley, M. 2003. U.S. health: Catholic hospitals refuse patients contraception. *Inter Press Service,* February 6.

Coomaraswamy, R. 1994. To bellow like a cow: Women, ethnicity, and the discourse of rights. In *Human rights of women,* edited by R. Cook. Philadelphia: University of Pennsylvania Press.

———. 1999. Different but free: Cultural relativism and women's rights as human rights. In *Religious fundamentalisms and the human rights of women,* edited by C. W. Howland. New York: St. Martin's Press.

Cooper, G. 1997. Lesbian mothers. *Networker,* July/August, 15.

Copelon, R. 1994. Intimate terror: Understanding domestic violence as torture. In *Human rights of women,* edited by R. Cook. Philadelphia: University of Pennsylvania Press.

———. 1995. War crimes: Reconceptualizing rape in time of war. In *Women's rights, human rights: International feminist perspectives,* edited by J. Peters and A. Wolper. New York: Routledge.

Corea, G. 1991. Depo-Provera and the politics of knowledge. In *Reconstructing Babylon,* edited by H. P. Hynes. Bloomington: Indiana University Press.

Coronel, S., and N. Rosca. 1993. For the boys: Filipinas expose years of sexual slavery by the U.S. and Japan. *Ms., 5,* 10–15.

Coughlin J. H. 2002. The rise of women entrepreneurs. Westport, CT: Quorum Books.

Crampton, S. M., J. W. Hodge, and J. M. Mishra. 1997. The Equal Pay Act: The first 30 years. *Public Personnel Management, 26,* 335–344.

Cray, C. 1997. Conducive to sexual harassment: The EEOC's case against Mitsubishi. *Multinational Monitor,* October, 24–26.

Crosby, F. J. 1991. *Juggling: The unexpected advantages of balancing career and home for women and their families.* New York: Free Press.

Curtius, M. 1995. Paying a high price for honor. *Los Angeles Times,* March 12, A1, A6.

Dahlburg, J. T., and B. Bearak. 1996. Pakistani president sacks Bhutto and government. *Los Angeles Times,* November 6, A1, A26.

D'Alusio, F., and P. Menzel. 1996. *Women in the material world.* New York: Random House.

Daly, M. 1971. After the death of God the Father. *Commonweal,* 12 March, 7–11.

———. 1973. *Beyond God the Father.* Boston: Beacon Press.

————. 1974. Theology after the demise of God the Father: A call for the castration of sexist religion. In *Sexist religion and women in the church: No more silence,* edited by A. L. Hageman. New York: Association Press.

————. 1985. *The church and the second sex.* 2d ed. Boston: Beacon Press.

D'Amico, F. 1995. Women as national leaders. In *Women in world politics: An introduction,* edited by F. D'Amico and P. R. Beckman. Westport, CT: Bergin and Garvey.

————. 1999. Women workers in the United Nations. In *Gender politics in global governance,* edited by M. K. Meyer and E. Prugl. Lanham, MD: Rowman and Littlefield.

————, and P. R. Beckman. 1995. *Women in world politics: An introduction.* Westport, CT: Bergin and Garvey.

Daniszewski, J. 1997. Egyptian women scarred by hate. *Los Angeles Times,* 3 May, A1, A8, A9.

Dankelman, I., and J. Davidson. 1988. *Women and environment in the Third World: Alliance for the future.* London: Earthscan.

————. 1991. Land: Women at the centre of the food crisis. In *Women and the environment: A reader on crisis and development in the Third World,* edited by S. Sontheimer. New York: Monthly Review Press.

Dansky, B. S., and D. G. Kilpatrick. 1997. Effects of sexual harassment. In *Sexual harassment: Theory, research, and treatment,* edited by W. O'Donohue. Boston: Allyn and Bacon.

Darcy, R., and C. M. Hyun. 1994. Women in the South Korean electoral system. In *Electoral systems in comparative perspective: Their impact on women and minorities,* edited by W. Rule and J. F. Zimmerman. Westport, CT: Greenwood Press.

Darling, J. 1995. The women who run Juchitán. *Los Angeles Times,* 31 March, A1, A11, A13.

Datta, R., and J. Kornberg. 2002. Introduction. In *Women in developing countries: Assessing strategies for empowerment,* edited by R. Datta and J. Kornberg. London: Lynne Rienner Publishers.

D'Augelli, A. R. 1992. Lesbian and gay male undergraduates' experiences of harassment and fear on campus. *Journal of Interpersonal Violence, 7,* 383–395.

Davidson, A. R., and E. Thomson. 1980. Cross-cultural studies of attitudes and beliefs. In *Handbook of cross-cultural psychology.* Vol. 5, edited by H. C. Triandis and W. W. Lambert. Boston: Allyn and Bacon.

Davis, E. G. 1971. *The first sex.* New York: Putnam.

Davis, R. H. 1997. *Women and power in parliamentary democracies: Cabinet appointments in Western Europe, 1968–1992.* Lincoln: University of Nebraska Press.

DAWN. 2003. Victim of 'Swara' custom acquitted: Sentence in murder case overturned. June 6. http://www.dawn.com/2003/06/06/nat30.htm

de Beauvoir, S. 1953. *The second sex.* New York: Alfred Knopf.

Degler, C. N. 1990. Darwinians confront gender; or, there is more to it than history. In *Theoretical perspectives on sexual difference,* edited by D. L. Rhode. New Haven, CT: Yale University Press.

Demick, B. 2002. Off-base behavior in Korea. *Los Angeles Times,* 26 September, A1, A15.

Desai, M. 2002. Transnational solidarity: Women's agency, structural adjustment, and globalization. In *Women's activism and globalization: Linking local struggles transnational politics,* edited by N. A. Naples and M. Desai. New York: Routledge.

————. 2001. India: Women's movements from nationalism to sustainable development. In *Women's rights: A global view,* edited by L. Walter. Westport, CN: Greenwood Press.

Deutsch, M., and H. B. Gerard. 1955. A study of normative and informational social influence on social judgment. *Journal of Abnormal and Social Psychology, 51,* 629–636.

Devine, P. G. 1995. Prejudice and out-group perception. In *Advanced social psychology,* edited by A. Tesser. New York: McGraw-Hill.

Devraj, R. 2003. Fiancée's rejection of a dowry reopens old debate. *Inter Press Service,* 28 May.

Dietz, M. 1985. Citizenship with a feminist face: The problem with maternal thinking. *Political theory, 13,* 19–37.

Dignard, L., and J. Havet. 1995. Introduction. In *Women in micro- and small-scale enterprise development,* edited by L. Divard and J. Havet. Boulder, CO: Westview Press.

Diner, H. 1975. *Mothers and Amazons.* New York: Julian Press.

Dinnerstein, D. 1976. *The rocking of the cradle and the ruling of the world.* London: Souvenir.

Dion, K. L., and R. A. Schuller. 1990. Ms. and the manager: A tale of two stereotypes. *Sex Roles, 22,* 569–577.

Dixon-Mueller, R. 1993. *Population policy and women's rights: Transforming reproductive choice.* Westport, CT: Praeger.

Domosh, M., and J. Seager. 2001. *Putting women in place: Feminist geographers make sense of the world.* New York: Guilford Press.

Dorf, J., and G. C. Perez. 1995. Discrimination and tolerance of difference: International lesbian human rights. In *Women's rights, human rights: International feminist perspectives,* edited by J. Peters and A. Wolper. New York: Routledge.

Doyle, P. M. 1974. Women and religion: Psychological and cultural implications. In *Religion and sexism: Images of woman in the Jewish and Christian traditions,* edited by R. R. Ruether. New York: Simon and Schuster.

Drury, C. 1994. *Christianity.* In *Women in religion,* edited by J. Holm. New York: St. Martin's Press.

Dubisch, J. 1993. "Foreign chickens" and other outsiders: Gender and community in Greece. *American Ethnologist, 20,* 272–287.

Duda, A., and M. Wuch. 1995. Country report on lesbians in Germany. In *Unspoken rules: Sexual orientation and women's human rights,* edited by R. Rosenbloom. San Francisco: International Gay and Lesbian Human Rights Commission.

Duin, J. 2001. Women break through the stained-glass ceiling. *Insight on the News, 17,* 26–30.

Duley, M. I., and S. Diduk. 1986. Women, colonialism, and development. In *The cross-cultural study of women: A comprehensive guide,* edited by M. I. Duley and M. I. Edwards. New York: Feminist Press.

———, and M. I. Edwards. 1986. *The cross-cultural study of women: A comprehensive guide.* New York: Feminist Press.

———, K. Sinclair, and M. I. Edwards. 1986. Biology vs. culture. In *The cross-cultural study of women: A comprehensive guide,* edited by M. I. Duley and M. I. Edwards. New York: Feminist Press.

Eagly, A. H. 1987. *Sex differences in social behavior: A social-role interpretation.* Hillsdale, NJ: Erlbaum.

———, S. J. Karau, and M. G. Makhijani. 1995. Gender and the effectiveness of leaders: A meta-analysis. *Journal of Personality and Social Psychology, 60,* 685–710.

Eck, D. L., and D. Jain. 1987. Introduction. *Speaking of faith: Global perspectives on women, religion, and social change.* Philadelphia: New Society Publishers.

Ehrenberg, M. 1989. *Women in prehistory.* Norman: University of Oklahoma Press.

Ehrenreich, B. 2002. Maid to order. In *Global woman: Nannies, maids, and sex workers in the new economy,* edited by B. Ehrenreich and A. R. Hochschild. New York: Metropolitan Books.

———, M. Dowie, and S. Minkin 1979. The charge: Gynocide, the accused: The United States government. *Mother Jones,* November, 32.

———, and A. R. Hochschild. 2002. Introduction. In *Global woman: Nannies, maids, and sex workers in the new economy,* edited by B. Ehrenreich and A. R. Hochschild. New York: Metropolitan Books.

Eisler, R. 1987. *The chalice and the blade.* San Francisco: Harper and Row.

El-Bakri, Z. B., and E. M. Kameir. 1983. Aspects of women's political participation in Sudan. *International Social Science Journal, 35,* 605–623.

El Dareer, A. 1982. *Woman, why do you weep?: Circumcision and its consequences.* London: Zed.

Elliot, L. 1996. Women, gender, feminism, and the environment. In *The gendered new world order,* edited by J. Turpin and L. A. Lorentzen. New York: Routledge.

el Saadawi, N. 1987. Toward women's power, nationally and internationally. In *Speaking of faith: Global perspectives on women, religion, and social change,* edited by D. L. Eck and D. Jain. Philadelphia: New Society Publishers.

Engle, P. L. 1993. Influences of mothers' and fathers' income on children's nutritional status in Guatemala. *Social Science and Medicine, 37,* 1303–1312.

———, and C. Breaux. 1994. *Is there a father instinct? Fathers' responsibility for children.* Report for the Population Council (New York) and the International Center for Research on Women (Washington, DC).

Enloe, C. 1989. *Bananas, beaches, and bases: Making feminist sense of international relations.* Berkeley: University of California Press.

———. 1995a. The globetrotting sneaker. *Ms., 6,* 10–15.

———. 1996. Spoils of war. *Ms., 6,* 15.

Everett, J. 1993. Indira Gandhi and the exercise of power. In M. A. Genovese, edited by, *Women as national leaders.* Newbury Park, CA: Sage.

Faderman, L. 1981. *Surpassing the love of men: Romantic friendship and love between women from the Renaissance to the present.* New York: William Morrow.

———. 1991. *Odd girls and twilight lovers: A history of lesbian life in twentieth century America.* New York: Columbia University Press.

———. 1997. Who hid lesbian history? *Journal of Lesbian Studies, 1,* 149-154.

Falbo, T., and L. A. Peplau. 1980. Power strategies in intimate relationships. *Journal of Personality and Social Psychology, 38,* 618–628.

Fang, D. 2003. The one-child policy is here to stay. *South China Morning Post,* 12 July, 7.

Farley, M. 1998. In Lugo Lake, marriage is a ticklish affair. *Los Angeles Times,* 26 December, A1, A5, A6.

———. 2003. Grass-roots donors fund U.N. agency: Two activists try to make up for the lost U.S. aid to the family planning body. *Los Angeles Times,* 2 May, A16.

Fathalla, M. F. 2002. Implementing the reproductive health approach. In *An agenda for the people: The UNFPA through three decades,* edited by N. Sadik. New York: New York University Press.

Fausto-Sterling, A. 1985. *The myths of gender.* New York: Basic Books.

Feijoo, M. D. C. 1998. Democratic participation and women in Argentina. In *Women and democracy: Latin America and Central and Eastern Europe,* edited by J. S.

Jaquette and S. L. Wolchik. Baltimore, MD: Johns Hopkins University Press.

Ferdman, B. 1995. Cultural identity and diversity in organizations: Bridging the gap between group differences and individual uniqueness. In *Diversity in organizations,* edited by M. M. Chemers, S. Oskamp, and M. A. Constanzo. Thousand Oaks, CA: Sage.

Ferguson, A. 1981. Patriarchy, sexual identity, and the sexual revolution. *Signs, 7,* 157–172.

——— . 1990. Is there a lesbian culture? In *Lesbian philosophies and cultures,* edited by J. Allen. Albany: State University of New York Press.

Ferree, M. M. 1987. Equality and autonomy: Feminist politics in the U.S. and West Germany. In *The women's movements of the U.S. and Western Europe,* edited by M. F. Katzenstein and C. M. Mueller. Philadelphia: Temple University Press.

Filer, R. 1985. Male-female wage differences: The importance of compensating differentials. *Industrial and Labor Relations Review, 38,* 426–437.

——— . 1989. Occupational segregation, compensating differentials, and comparable worth. In *Pay equity: Empirical inquiries,* edited by R. Michael, H. Hartmann, and B. O'Farrell. Washington, DC: National Academy.

Filkins, D. 1998. Writer risks threats, arrest on her return to Bangladesh. *Los Angeles Times,* 13 November, A5.

Fiorenza, E. S. 1979. Women in the early Christian movement. In *Womanspirit rising: A feminist reader in religion,* edited by C. P. Christ and J. Plaskow. New York: Harper and Row.

Fisher, J. 1996. Sustainable development and women: The role of NGOs. In *The gendered new world order: Militarism, development, and the environment,* edited by J. Turpin and L. A. Lorentzen. New York: Routledge.

Fitzgerald, L. F. 1993. Sexual harassment: Violence against women in the workplace. *American Psychologist, 48,* 1070–1076.

——— . 1997. But was it really sexual harassment?: Legal, behavioral, and psychological definitions of the workplace victimization of women. In *Sexual harassment: Theory, research, and treatment,* edited by W. O'Donohue. Boston: Allyn and Bacon.

Foek, A. 1997. Sweat-shop Barbie: Exploitation of Third World labor. *The Humanist, 57,* 9–13.

Food and Agriculture Organization. 1997a. *Q and A with Marie Randriamamonjy.* http://www.fao.org/news/1997/ 970304-e.htm

——— . 1997b. *Research and extension: A gender perspective.* http://www.fao.org/focus/e/Women/Extens-e.htm

——— . 1997c. *Women and land tenure.* http://www.fao.org/focus/e/Women/tenure-e.htm

——— . 1997d. *Women hold the key to food security.* http://www.fao.org/focus/e/Women/Wo-Hm-e.htm

——— . 1997e. *Women: Users, preservers and managers of agro-biodiversity.* http://www.fao.org/focus/e/Women/Biodiv-e.htm

——— . 1997f. *Women and water resources.* http://www.fao.org/focus/e/Women/Water-e.htm

——— . 2003a. *Gender and food security: Division of labour.* http://www.fao.org/gender/en/labb2-e.htm

——— . 2003b. *Gender and food security: Education, extension, and communication.* http://www.fao.org/gender/en/educ-e.htm

——— . 2003c. *Gender and food security: Forestry.* http://www.fao.org/gender/en/fore-e.htm

Forbes, G. H. 1987. *Women in modern India.* New York: Cambridge University Press.

Forrester, A. 1995. From stabilization to growth with equity: A case for financing women in development programs. In *Women and the United Nations,* edited by F. C. Steady and R. Toure. Rochester, VT: Schenkman Books.

Forsyth, D. 1999. *Group dynamics.* Pacific Grove, CA: ITP.

Frank, T. 1991. Irish leader decries narrow definition of women's success. *Providence, Rhode Island, Bulletin,* 20 October, E3.

Frankson, J. R. 1998. Getting our day in court. *Ms., 7,* May/June, 19.

Fraser, A. 1988. *The warrior queens: The legends and life of the women who have led their nations in war.* New York: Random House.

Fraser, A. S. 1987. *The U.N. Decade for Women: Documents and dialogue.* Boulder, CO: Westview Press.

Freedman, L. 1999. Finding our feet, standing our ground: Reproductive health activism in an era of rising fundamentalism and economic globalization. In *Religious fundamentalisms and the human rights of women,* edited by C. W. Howland. New York: St. Martin's Press.

Freedman, S. M., and Phillips, J. S. 1988. The changing nature of research on women at work. *Journal of Management, 14,* 231–251.

Freeman, C. 2000. *High tech and high heels in the global economy: Women, work and pink-collar identities in the Caribbean.* Durham, NC: Duke University Press.

Freeman, M. A. 1995. The human rights of women in the family: Issues and recommendations for implementation of the women's convention. In *Women's rights, human rights: International feminist perspectives,* edited by J. Peters and A. Wolper. New York: Routledge.

French, M. 1992. *The war against women.* New York: Simon and Schuster.

Friedman, E. 1995. Women's human rights: The emergence of a movement. In *Women's rights, human rights: International feminist perspectives*, edited by J. Peters and A. Wolper. New York: Routledge.

Friedman, R. C., and J. Downey. 1995. Internalized homophobia and the negative therapeutic reaction. *Journal of the American Academy of Psychoanalysis, 23*, 99–113.

Frisco, M. L., and K. Williams. 2003. Perceived housework equity, marital happiness, and divorce in dual-earner households. *Journal of Family Issues, 24*, 51–73.

Frohmann, A., and T. Valdes. 1995. Democracy in the country and in the home: The women's movement in Chile. In *The challenge of local feminisms: Women's movements in global perspective*, edited by A. Basu. Boulder, CO: Westview Press.

Frymer-Kensky, T. 1994. The Bible and women's studies. In *Feminist perspectives on Jewish studies*, edited by L. Davidman and S. Tenenbaum. New Haven, CT: Yale University Press.

Fuentes, A., and B. Ehrenreich. 1983. *Women in the global factory*. Boston, MA: South End Press.

Fujieda, M. 1995. Japan's first phase of feminism. In *Japanese women: New feminist perspectives on the past, present, and future*, edited by K. Fujimura-Fanselow and A. Kameda. New York: Feminist Press.

Gardini, W. 1987. The feminine aspect of God in Christianity. In *Women in the world's religions, past and present*, edited by U. King. New York: Paragon House.

Garnier, J. 1995. Country report on lesbians in Poland. In *Unspoken rules: Sexual orientation and women's human rights*, edited by R. Rosenbloom. San Francisco: International Gay and Lesbian Human Rights Commission.

Gay, J. 1986. "Mummies and babies" and friends of lovers in Lesotho. In *The many faces of homosexuality: Anthropological approaches to homosexual behavior*, edited by E. Blackwood. New York: Harrington Park.

Gebara, I., and M. C. Bingemer. 1994. Mary—Mother of God, mother of the poor. In *Feminist theology from the Third World*, edited by U. King. New York: Orbis.

Geis, F. L. 1993. Self-fulfilling prophecies: A social psychological view of gender. In *The psychology of gender*, edited by A. E. Beall and R. J. Sternberg. New York: Guilford Press.

Gelb, J. 1989. *Feminism and politics*. Berkeley: University of California Press.

Genovese, M. A. 1993. Margaret Thatcher and the politics of conviction leadership. In *Women as national leaders*, edited by M. A. Genovese. Newbury Park, CA: Sage.

Gentile, G. 2002. Group rips Disney over labor conditions in Bangladesh. *Associated Press State and Local Wire*, October 8.

Gerhart, M. 2003. Christianity. In *Her voice, her faith*, edited by A. Sharma and K. K. Young. Boulder, CO: Westview Press.

Ghorayshi, P. 1996. Women, paid work, and the family in the Islamic Republic of Iran. *Journal of Comparative Family Studies, 27*, 453–466.

Gimbutas, M. 1991. *The civilization of the goddess: The world of Old Europe*. San Francisco: Harper and Row.

Ginsberg, F. D., and R. Rapp. 1995. Introduction: Conceiving the new world order. In *Conceiving the new world order: The global politics of reproduction*, edited by F. D. Ginsberg and R. Rapp. Berkeley: University of California Press.

Glass, J., and V. Camarigg. 1992. Gender, parenthood, and job-family compatibility. *American Journal of Sociology, 98*, 131–151.

Glenn, E. N. 1992. From servitude to service work: Historical continuities in the racial division of paid reproductive labor. *Signs*, 1–43.

Glick, P. 1991. Trait-based and sex-based discrimination in occupational prestige, occupational salary, and hiring. *Sex Roles, 25*, 351–378.

———, C. Zion, and C. Nelson. 1988. What mediates sex discrimination in hiring decisions? *Journal of Personality and Social Psychology, 55*, 178–186.

Gold, S. 2003. Texas OKs disputed abortion legislation. *Los Angeles Times*, 22 May, A1, A18.

Golden, K. 1998. Rana Husseini: A voice for justice. *Ms., 9*, July/August, 36–39.

Gonzalez, M. B. 1995. Country report on lesbians in Nicaragua. In *Unspoken rules: Sexual orientation and women's human rights*, edited by R. Rosenbloom. San Francisco: International Gay and Lesbian Human Rights Commission.

Gonzalez, V., and K. Kampwirth. 2002. *Radical women in Latin America: Left and right*. University Park, PA: Pennsylvania State University.

Goodwin J. 1994. *Price of honor: Muslim women lift the veil of violence on the Islamic world*. Boston: Little, Brown.

Goodwin J. 1997. Prisoners of biology. *Utne Reader*, January/February, 66–71.

Gottlick, J. F. B. 2001. From the ground up: Women's organizations and democratization in Russia. In *Democratization and women's grassroots movements*, edited by J. M. Bystydzienski and J. Sekhon. Bloomington: Indiana University Press.

Greene, B. 1994. Lesbian women of color: Triple jeopardy. *Journal of Lesbian Studies, 1*, 109–147.

Griffin W. 2003. Goddess spirituality and wicca. In *Her voice, her faith*, edited by A. Sharma and K. K. Young. Boulder, CO: Westview Press.

Gross, R. M. 1979. Female God language in a Jewish context. In *Womanspirit rising: A feminist reader in religion,* edited by C. P. Christ and J. Plaskow. San Francisco: Harper and Row.

———. 1993. *Buddhism after patriarchy: A feminist history, analysis, and reconstruction of Buddhism.* Albany: State University of New York Press.

———. 1996. *Feminism and religion: An introduction.* Boston: Beacon Press.

———. 1999. Strategies for a feminist revalorization of Buddhism. In *Feminism and world religions,* edited by A. Sharma and K. K. Young. Albany: State University Press of New York, pp. 78–109.

———. 2003. Buddhism. In *Her voice, her faith,* edited by A. Sharma and K. K. Young. Boulder, CO: Westview Press.

Gruber, J. E. 1997. An epidemiology of sexual harassment: Evidence from North America and Europe. In *Sexual harassment: Theory, research, and treatment,* edited by W. O'Donohue. Boston: Allyn and Bacon.

———, M. Smith, and K. Kauppinen-Toropainen. 1996. Sexual harassment types and severity: Linking research and policy. In *Sexual harassment in the workplace: Perspectives, frontiers, and response strategies,* edited by M. S. Stockdale. Thousand Oaks, CA: Sage.

Gunderson, M. 1995. Comparable worth and gender discrimination: An international perspective. *WIN News, 21.*

Gupta, L. 1991. Kali the savior. In *After patriarchy: Feminist transformations of the world religions,* edited by P. Cooey, W. Eakin and J. McDaniel. Maryknoll, NY: Orbis.

Gutek, B. A., A. G. Cohen, and A. M. Konrad. 1990. Predicting social-sexual behavior at work: A contact hypothesis. *Academy of Management Journal, 33,* 560–577.

———, and M. P. Koss. 1993. Changed women and changed organizations: Consequences of and coping with sexual harassment. *Journal of Vocational Behavior, 42,* 28–48.

———, and B. Morash. 1982. Sex-ratios, sex-role spillover, and sexual harassment of women at work. *Journal of Social Issues, 38,* 55–74.

Haavio-Mannila, E. 1993. Family, work, and gender equality: A policy comparison of Scandinavia, the United States, and the former Soviet Union. *SIECUS Report, 21,* 1–5.

Hada, A. 1995. Domestic violence. In *Japanese women: New feminist perspectives on the past, present and future,* edited by K. Fujimura-Fanselow and A. Kameda. New York: Feminist Press.

Hadley, J. 1996. *Abortion: Between freedom and necessity.* Philadelphia: Temple University Press.

Hampson, D. 1987. Women, ordination and the Christian Church. In *Speaking of faith: Global perspectives on women, religion, and social change,* edited by D. L. Eck and D. Jain. Philadelphia: New Society Publishers.

———. 1990. *Theology and feminism.* Oxford: Basil Blackwell.

Hardy, E. 1996. Long-acting contraception in Brazil and the Dominican Republic. In *Coerced contraception? Moral and policy challenges of long-acting birth control,* edited by E. H. Moskowitz and B. Jennings. Washington, DC: Georgetown University Press.

Harris, K. 1995. Prime Minister Margaret Thatcher: The influence of her gender on her foreign policy. In *Women in politics: An introduction,* edited by F. D'Amico and P. R. Beckman. Westport, CT: Bergin and Garvey.

Hartmann, B. 1987. *Reproductive rights and reproductive wrongs.* New York: Harper and Row.

———. 1995. *Reproductive rights and wrongs: The global politics of population control.* Boston: South End Press.

Hartmann, H. 1984. The unhappy marriage of Marxism and feminism: Towards a more progressive union. In *Feminist frameworks: Alternative theoretical accounts of the relations between women and men,* edited by A. Jaggar and P. Rothenberg. New York: McGraw-Hill.

Hassan, R. 1991. Muslim women and post-patriarchal Islam. In *After patriarchy: Feminist transformations of the world religions,* edited by P. Cooey, W. Eakin and J. McDaniel. Maryknoll, NY: Orbis.

———. 1999. Feminism in Islam. In *Feminism and world religions,* edited by A. Sharma and K. K. Young. Albany: State University Press of New York.

———. 2003. Islam. In *Her voice, her faith,* edited by A. Sharma and K. K. Young. Boulder, CO: Westview Press.

Heilbroner, R. 1963. *The great ascent.* New York: Harper and Row.

Heilman, M. E., C. J. Block, R. F. Martell, and M. C. Simon. 1989. Has anything changed? Current conceptions of men, women, and managers. *Journal of Applied Psychology, 74,* 935–942.

———, and R. F. Martell. 1986. Exposure to successful women: Antidote to sex discrimination in applicant screening decisions? *Organizational Behavior and Human Decision Processes, 37,* 376–390.

Heise, L. L. 1995. Freedom close to home: The impact of violence against women on reproductive rights. In *Women's rights, human rights: International feminist perspectives,* edited by J. Peters and A. Wolper. New York: Routledge.

Helie-Lucas, M. A. 1993. Women living under Muslim laws. In *Ours by right: Women's rights as human rights,* edited by J. Kerr. Ottawa, Canada: North South Institute.

———. 1999. What is your tribe? Women's struggles and the construction of Muslimness. In *Religious fundamentalisms and the human rights of women,* edited by C. W. Howland. New York: St. Martin's Press.

Herald, The. 2003. Women and gender: Trafficking of women condemned. *Africa News,* 4 January.

Herbert, B. 1995. Not a living wage. *New York Times,* 9 October, A17.

———. 1996. From sweatshops to aerobics. *New York Times,* 26 June, A15.

———. 1997. Nike's boot camps. *New York Times,* 31 March, A15.

Hersch, J. 2003. Employment discrimination, economists, and the law. In *Women, family, and work,* edited by K. S. Moe. Oxford, UK: Blackwell.

Heschel, S. 2003. Judaism. In *Her voice, her faith,* edited by A. Sharma and K. K. Young. Boulder, CO: Westview Press.

Hesson-McInnis, M., and L. F. Fitzgerald. 1995. *Modeling sexual harassment.* Unpublished manuscript.

Hewlett, B. S. 1992. Husband-wife reciprocity and the father-infant relationship among Aka pygmies. In *Father-child relations: Cultural and biosocial contexts,* edited by B. S. Hewlett. New York: Aldine de Gruyter.

Heyzer, N. 2002. Women are key to development. In *An agenda for the people: The UNFPA through three decades,* edited by N. Sadik. New York: New York University Press.

Hochschild, A. R. 1989. *The second shift.* New York: Avon.

———. 2002. Love and gold. In *Global woman: Nannies, maids, and sex workers in the new economy,* edited by B. Ehrenreich and A. R. Hochschild. New York: Metropolitan Books.

Holm, J. 1994. Introduction. *Women in religion.* New York: St. Martin's Press.

Hom, S. K. 2001. China: First the problem of rights and law. In *Women's rights: A global view,* edited by L. Walter. Westport, CN: Greenwood Press.

Hong, L. K. 1987. Potential effects of the one-child policy on gender equality in the People's Republic of China. *Gender and Society, 1,* 317–326.

Hong, Z. 1995. The testimony of women writers: The situation of women in China today. In *Women's rights, human rights: International feminist perspectives,* edited by J. Peters and A. Wolper. New York: Routledge.

Hooijberg, R., and N. DiTomaso. 1996. Leadership in and of demographically diverse organizations. *Leadership Quarterly, 7,* 1–19.

Horney, K. 1967. *Feminine psychology.* New York: Norton.

Howard, J. A., P. Blumstein, and P. Schwartz. 1986. Sex, power, and influence tactics in intimate relationships. *Journal of Personality and Social Psychology, 51,* 102–109.

Howard, R. E. 1995. Women's rights and the right to development. In *Women's rights, human rights: International feminist perspectives,* edited by J. Peters and A. Wolper. New York: Routledge.

Hubbard, D., and C. Solomon, 1995. The many faces of feminism in Namibia. In *The challenge of local feminisms: Women's movements in global perspective,* edited by A. Basu. Boulder, CO: Westview Press.

Hulin C. L., L. F. Fitzgerald, and F. Drasgow. 1996. Organizational influences on sexual harassment. In *Sexual harassment in the workplace: Perspectives, frontiers, and response strategies,* edited by M. S. Stockdale. Thousand Oaks, CA: Sage.

Human Rights Watch. 1995. *The Human Rights Watch global report on women's human rights.* New York: Human Rights Watch.

———. 1998. *The women's rights project.* http://www.hrw.org/hrw/worldreport/Back-04.htm

———. 2000. Jordanian parliament supports impunity for honor killings. http://www.hrw.org/press/2000/01/jord0127.htm

———. 2000. Thousands of Thai women trafficked to Japan. http://www.hrw.org/press/2000/09/japan0921.htm

———. 2001a. Uzbekistan turns its back on battered women: Uzbek women forced to remain in violent marriages. http://www.hrw.org/press/2001/07/uzbekistan070.htm

———. 2001b. Integration of the human rights of women and the gender perspective: Violence against women and "honor crimes." http://www.hrw.org.press/2001/04/un_oral12_0405.htm

Hunger Project. 1997. 1997 Africa Prize for Leadership: Joyce Banda. http://www.thp.org/prize/97

Hyatt, S. 1992. *Putting bread on the table: The women's work of community activism.* West Yorkshire, UK: University of Bradford, Work and Gender Research Unit.

Ilgen, D. R., and M. A. Youtz. 1986. Factors affecting the evaluation and development of minorities in organizations. *Personnel and Human Resources Management, 4,* 307–337.

Ilyas, Q. S. M. 1990. Determinants of perceived role conflict among women in Bangladesh. *Sex Roles, 22,* 237–248.

International Gay and Lesbian Human Rights Association. 2003. *Where having sex is a crime: Criminalization and decriminalization of homosexual acts.* http://www.iglhrc.org

International Labour Association. 2003a. Women's labour factsheet. http://www.ilo.org/public/english/bureau/inf/download/women/pdf.factsheet.pdf

———. 2003b. *Time for equality at work.* http://www.ilo. org/public/english/standards/decl/publ/ reports/report4.htm

International Labour Organization. 1995. Press releases. http://www.essential.org/ilo/press_ releases/ ilo1.html

———. 1996a. Women swell ranks of working poor, says ILO. http://www.ilo.org/public/english/ 235press/pr/96-25.htm

———. 1996b. Gender issues in micro-enterprise development. http://www.ilo. org/public/ english/140femme/guides/enterpri.htm

———. 1997. Gender issues in workers' activities. http://www.ilo.org/public/ english/140femme/ guides/workers.htm

———. 1998. Will the glass ceiling ever be broken? Women in management: It's still lonely at the top. http://www.ilo.org/public/english/235press/ magazine/23/glass.htm

———. 2002. *Key indicators of the labour market 2001– 2002.* http://www.-ilo-mirror.cornell.edu/public/ english/employment/gems/eeo/download/KILM

International Research and Training Institute for the Advancement of Women (INSTRAW). 1991. Women, water, and sanitation. In *Women and the environment: A reader on crisis and development in the Third World, edited by* S. Sontheimer. New York: Monthly Review Press.

———. 1995. Measuring women's unpaid work. *Women's International Network News,* 21, 7–8.

Inter-Parliamentary Union. 2003a. *Women in national parliaments.* http://www.ipu.org/wmn-e/classif.htm

———. 2003b. *Rwanda leads world ranking of women in parliament.* http://www.ipu.org/press-e/gen176.htm

Irish Family Planning Association. http://www.ifpa.ie/ campaigns/abortion/iabst.html

Isasi-Diaz, A. M. 1994. The task of Hispanic women's liberation theology—*Mujeristas:* Who we are and what we are about. In *Feminist theology from the Third World,* edited by U. King. Maryknoll, NY: Orbis.

Ishii-Kuntz, M. 1993. Japanese fathers: Work demands and family roles. In *Men, work, and family,* edited by J. C. Hood. Newbury Park, CA: Sage.

Ishino, S., and N. Wakabayashi. 1995. Country report on lesbians in Japan. In *Unspoken rules: Sexual orientation and women's human rights,* edited by R. Rosenbloom. San Francisco: International Gay and Lesbian Human Rights Commission.

Jacobs, J. A., and R. Steinberg. 1990. Compensating differentials and the male-female wage gap: Evidence from the New York State Comparable Worth Study. *Social Forces,* 69, 439–468.

Jacobsen, J. P. 2003. The human capital explanation for the gender gap in earnings. In *Women, family, and work,* edited by K. S. Moe. Oxford, UK: Blackwell.

Jacobson, J. L. 1992. Women's reproductive health: The silent emergency. *New Frontiers in Education,* 22, 1–54.

Jacobson, M. B. 1981. You say potato and I say potahto: Attitudes toward feminism as a function of its subject-selected label. *Sex Roles,* 7, 349–354.

Jahan, R. 1995a. The elusive agenda: Mainstreaming women in development. In *Seeds 2,* edited by A. Leonard. New York: Feminist Press.

———. 1995b. Men in seclusion, women in public: Rokeya's dream and women's struggles in Bangladesh. In *The challenge of local feminisms: Women's movements in global perspective,* edited by A. Basu. Boulder, CO: Westview Press.

Jain S. 1991. Standing up for trees: Women's role in the Chipko movement. In *Women and the environment: A reader on crisis and development in the Third World,* edited by S. Sontheimer. New York: Monthly Review Press.

Jaising, I. 1995. Violence against women: The Indian perspective. In *Women's rights, human rights: International feminist perspectives,* edited by J. Peters and A. Wolper. New York: Routledge.

Jamison, L. 2003. Killing for 'honor': Legalized murder. *Amnesty Now,* Summer, 18–19.

Jankowiak, W. 1992. Father-child relations in urban China. In *Father-child relations: Cultural and biosocial contexts,* edited by B. S. Hewlett. New York: Aldine de Gruyter.

Jaquette, J. S. 1995. Losing the battle/winning the war: International politics, women's issues, and the 1980 mid-decade conference. In *Women, politics, and the United Nations,* edited by A. Winslow. Westport, CN: Greenwood Press.

———, and S. L. Wolchik. 1998. Women and democratization in Latin America and Central and Eastern Europe: A comparative introduction. In *Women and democracy: Latin America and Central and Eastern Europe,* edited by J. S. Jaquette and S. L. Wolchik. Baltimore: Johns Hopkins Press.

Jeffrey, D. 1996. Sweatshop update. *Ms.,* 6, 38.

Jenkins, P. 1988. *Mrs. Thatcher's revolution.* Cambridge, MA: Harvard University Press.

Jenson, J. 1995. Extending the boundaries of citizenship: Women's movements of Western Europe. In *The challenge of local feminisms, Women's movements in global perspective,* edited by A. Basu. Boulder, CO: Westview Press.

Johnson, P. 1976. Women and power: Toward a theory of effectiveness. *Journal of Social Issues,* 32, 99–110.

Johnson-Odim, C. 1991. Common themes, different contexts: Third World women and feminism. In

Third world women and the politics of feminism, edited by C. T. Mohanty, A. Russo, and L. Torres. Bloomington: Indiana University Press.

Jones, T. 1992. Summit weighs women's role in changing world. *Los Angeles Times,* 10 July, A6.

Kabilsingh, C. 1987. The future of the Bhikkhuni Samgha in Thailand. In *Speaking of faith: Global perspectives on women, religion, and social change,* edited by D. L. Eck and D. Jain. Philadelphia: New Society Publishers.

Kakuyama, T., M. L. Onglatco, Y. Tsuzuki, and T. Matsui. 2003. Organizational tolerance as a correlate of sexual harassment of Japanese working women. *Psychological Reports, 92,* 1268–1271.

Kalin R., and R. Tilby. 1978. Development and validation of a sex-role ideology scale. *Psychological Report, 42,* 731–738.

Kanno, N. 1991. The failure of Western family planning. In *Reconstructing Babylon: Essays on women and technology,* edited by H. P. Hynes. Bloomington: Indiana University Press.

———. 1996. Lesotho and Nepal: The failure of Western "family planning." In *Reconstructing Babylon: Essays on women and technology,* edited by H. P. Hynes. Washington, DC: Georgetown University Press.

Kanter, R. M. 1976. The impact of hierarchical structures on the work behavior of women and men. *Social Problems, 23,* 415–430.

Kapur, R. 1999. The two faces of secularism and women's rights in India. In *Religious fundamentalisms and the human rights of women,* edited by C. W. Howland. New York: St. Martin's Press.

Karides, M. 2002. Linking local efforts with global struggle: Trinidad's national union of domestic employees. In *Women's activism and globalization: Linking local struggles transnational politics,* edited by N. A. Naples and M. Desai. New York: Routledge.

Katumba, R., and W. Akute. 1993. Greening takes root. *The Power to Change.* London: Zed.

Katzenstein, M. F. 1987. Comparing the feminist movements of the United States and Western Europe: An overview. In *The women's movements of the United States and Central Europe: Consciousness, political opportunity, and public policy,* edited by M. F. Katzenstein and C. M. Mueller. Philadelphia: Temple University Press.

———. 1989. Organizing against violence: Strategies of the Indian women's movement. *Pacific Affairs, 62,* 53–71.

Kaur-Singh, K. 1994. Sikhism. In *Women in religion,* edited by J. Holm. New York: St. Martin's Press.

Kawashima, Y. 1995. Female workers: An overview of past and current trends. In *Japanese women: New feminist perspectives on the past, present and future,* edited by K.

Fujimura-Fanselow and A. Kameda. New York: Feminist Press.

Keck, M. E., and K. Sikkink. 1998. *Activists beyond borders: Transnational advocacy networks in international politics.* Ithaca, NY: Cornell University Press.

Kehoe, A. B. 1983. The shackles of tradition. In *The hidden half: Studies of plains Indian women,* edited by P. Albers and B. Medicine. Washington, DC: University Press of America.

Kemp, A., N. Madlala, A. Moodley, and E. Salo. 1995. The dawn of a new day: Redefining South African feminism. In *The challenge of local feminisms: Women's movements in global perspective,* edited by A. Basu. Boulder, CO: Westview Press.

Kendall. 1998. "When a woman loves a woman" in Lesotho: Love, sex, and the (Western) construction of homophobia. In *Boy-wives and female husbands: Studies of African homosexualities,* edited by S. O. Murray and W. Roscoe. New York: St. Martin's Press.

Kenrick, D. T., E. K. Sadalla, G. Groth, and M. R. Trost. 1990. Evolution, traits, and the stages of human courtship: Qualifying the parental investment model. *Journal of Personality, 58,* 97–116.

Kerig, P. K., Y. Y. Alyoshina, and A. S. Volovich. 1993. Gender-role socialization in contemporary Russia. *Psychology of Women Quarterly, 17,* 389–408.

Kernaghan, C. 1997. A living wage to end sweatshops. *San Francisco Examiner,* 30 April, A19.

Kerr, J. 1993. *Ours by right: Women's rights as human rights.* London: Zed.

Kilic, D., and G. Uncu. 1995. Turkey. In *Unspoken rules: Sexual orientation and women's human rights,* edited by R. Rosenbloom. San Francisco: International Gay and Lesbian Human Rights Commission.

King, L. 2002. Demographic trends, pronatalism, and nationalist ideologies in the late twentieth century. *Ethnic and Racial Studies, 25,* 367–389.

King, U. 1987. Goddesses, witches, androgyny and beyond? Feminism and the transformation of religious consciousness. In *Women in the world's religions, past and present,* edited by U. King. New York: Paragon House.

———. 1994. Introduction. In *Feminist theology from the Third World,* edited by U. King. Maryknoll, NY: Orbis.

King, W. C., Jr., E. W. Miles, and J. Kniska. 1991. Boys will be boys (and girls will be girls): The attribution of gender role stereotypes in a gaming situation. *Sex Roles, 25,* 607–623.

Kissling, F. 1999. Roman Catholic fundamentalism: What's sex (and power) got to do with it? In *Religious fundamentalisms and the human rights of women,* edited by C. W. Howland. New York: St. Martin's Press.

Knapp, D. E., and G. A. Kustis. 1996. The real "Disclosure": Sexual harassment and the bottom line. In *Sexual harassment in the workplace: Perspectives, frontiers, and response strategies*, edited by M. S. Stockdale. Thousand Oaks, CA: Sage.

Koen, K., and P. Terry. 1995. South Africa. In *Unspoken rules: Sexual orientation and women's human rights*, edited by R. Rosenbloom. San Francisco: International Gay and Lesbian Human Rights Commission.

Kojima, Y. 2001. In the business of cultural reproduction: Theoretical implications of the mail-order bride phenomenon. *Women's Studies International Forum, 24*, 199–210.

Kotter, L. 1995. Country report on lesbians in Estonia. In *Unspoken rules: Sexual orientation and women's human rights*, edited by R. Rosenbloom. San Francisco: International Gay and Lesbian Human Rights Commission.

Kumar, R. 1995. From Chipko to Sati: The contemporary Indian women's movement. In *The challenge of local feminisms: Women's movements in global perspective*, edited by A. Basu. Boulder, CO: Westview Press.

Kusha, H. R. 1995. Minority status of women in Islam: A debate between traditional and modern Islam. *Journal of the Institute of Muslim Minority Affairs, 11*, 58–72.

Kuzmanovic, J. 1995. Legacies of invisibility: Past silence, present violence against women in the former Yugoslavia. In *Women's rights, human rights: International feminist perspectives*, edited by J. Peters and A. Wolper. New York: Routledge.

LaBotz, D. 1993. Manufacturing poverty: The maquiladorization of Mexico. *Multinational Monitor*, May, 18–23.

Lafferty, E. 2003. Rise up Kuwaiti women 2007: The right to vote is postponed. *Ms., 13*, Summer, 24.

LaFromboise, T. D., A. M. Heyle, and E. J. Ozer. 1990. Changing and diverse roles of women in American Indian cultures. *Sex Roles, 22*, 455–486.

Lakeman, E. 1994. Comparing political opportunities in Great Britain and Ireland. In *Electoral systems in comparative perspective: Their impact on women and minorities*, edited by W. Rule and J. F. Zimmerman. Westport, CT: Greenwood Press.

Lamas, M., A. Martinez, M. L. Tarres, and E. Tunon. 1995. Building bridges: The growth of popular feminism in Mexico. In *The challenge of local feminisms: Women's movements in global perspective*, edited by A. Basu. Boulder, CO: Westview Press.

Lamb, M. E. 1981. Fathers and child development: An integrative overview. In *The role of the father in child development*, edited by M. E. Lamb. New York: Wiley.

Lang, P. 1998. Update: Still a woman's burden? *Ms., 7*, May/June, 21.

Larwood, L., E. Szwajkowski, and S. Rose. 1988. Sex and race discrimination resulting from manager-client relationships: Applying the rational bias theory of managerial discrimination. *Sex Roles, 18*, 9–29.

Lauter, D. 1995. EMILY's List: Overcoming barriers to political participation. In *A rising public voice: Women in politics worldwide*, edited by A. Brill. New York: Feminist Press.

Lazarowitz, E. 1997. Panel prepares to ok use of pill after thirty-year ban. *Los Angeles Times,* 22 February.

———. 1997. A woman's place now is in the sumo ring. *Los Angeles Times,* January, A1, A10.

Leacock, E. B. 1981. Women in an egalitarian society: The Montagnais-Naskapi of Canada. *Myths of male dominance.* New York: Monthly Review Press.

Lebra, T. S. 1984. *Japanese women: Constraint and fulfillment.* Honolulu: University of Hawaii.

Leisure, S. 1999. Exchanging participation for promise: Mobilization of women in Eritrea. In *Democratization and women's grassroots movements*, edited by J.M. Bystydzienski and J. Sekhon. Bloomington: Indiana University Press.

Lerner, G. 1986. *The creation of patriarchy* Vol. 1. New York: Oxford.

Leslie, J. 1983. Essence and existence: Women and religion in ancient Indian texts. In *Women's religious lives*, edited by P. Holden. London: Croom Helm.

Leslie, L. A., E. A. Anderson, and M. P. Branson. 1991. Responsibility for children: The role of gender and employment. *Journal of Family Issues, 12*, 197–210.

Lim, L. Y. C. 1990. Women's work in export factories: The politics of a cause. In *Persistent inequalities*, edited by I. Tinker. Oxford: Oxford University Press.

Lindau, R. 1993. A sexualized image of lesbians in Sweden. *Off Our Backs,* June, 10, 20.

Ling, Y., and A. Matsumo. 1992. Women's struggle for empowerment in Japan. In *Women transforming politics: Worldwide strategies for empowerment*, edited by J. Bystydzienski. Bloomington: Indiana University Press.

Lips, H. M. 1991. *Women, men, and power.* Mountain View, CA: Mayfield.

Lister, R. 2003. *Citizenship: Feminist perspectives.* 2d ed. New York: New York University Press.

Livingston, J. A. 1982. Responses to sexual harassment on the job: Legal, organizational, and individual actions. *Journal of Social Issues, 38*, 5–22.

Lochhead, C. 2003. Sex trade uses Bay Area to bring in women, kids. *San Francisco Chronicle,* 26 February, A3.

Lorentzen, L. A., and J. Turpin 1996. Introduction: The gendered new world order. In *The gendered new world order,* edited by J. Turpin and L. A. Lorentzen. New York: Routledge.

Low, B. S. 1989. Cross-cultural patterns in the training of children: An evolutionary perspective. *Journal of Comparative Psychology, 103,* 311–319.

Louie, M. C. Y. 2001. *Sweatshop warriors.* Cambridge, MA: South End Press.

Macan-Markar, M. 2001. Rights for women can stem the spread of HIV/AIDS. *SHAAN Online Interpress Service E-Zine on Gender and Human Rights.*

MacKinnon, C. A. 1979. The social causes of sexual harassment. In *Sexual harassment: Confrontations and decisions,* edited by E. Wall. Buffalo, NY: Prometheus Books.

———. 1989. *Toward a feminist theory of the state.* Cambridge, MA: Harvard University Press.

Macklin R. 1996. Cultural difference and long-acting contraception. In *Coerced contraception? Moral and policy challenges of long-acting birth control,* edited by E. H. Moskowitz and B. Jennings. Washington, DC: Georgetown University Press.

MacLeod, M. 2003. Out of the closet: Gays and lesbians wrestle with the pros and cons of "coming out" in their workplaces. *Hamilton Spectator,* 7 June, M12.

Magnier, M. 2002. Battery behind the shoji screen. *Los Angeles Times,* 29 January, A1, A5..

Maloney, C. 2004. A better future for Afghan women? *Ms.,* Spring, 33.

Mak, A., K. Hui, J. Poone, and M. A. King. 1995. Country report on lesbians in Argentina. In *Unspoken rules: Sexual orientation and women's human rights,* edited by R. Rosenbloom. San Francisco: International Gay and Lesbian Human Rights Commission.

Margolis, D. R. 1993. Women's movements around the world: Cross-cultural comparisons. *Gender and Society, 7,* 379–399.

Marin, M. S. 1995. Country report on lesbians in Argentina. In *Unspoken rules: Sexual orientation and women's human rights,* edited by R. Rosenbloom. San Francisco: International Gay and Lesbian Human Rights Commission.

Martin, V., and B. Apple. 2003. Burma uses rape against minorities; terrorizing refugees. *International Herald Tribune,* 25 April, 6–7.

Martinez, A. 1995. Country report on lesbians in Uruguay. In *Unspoken rules: Sexual orientation and women's human rights,* edited by R. Rosenbloom. San Francisco: International Gay and Lesbian Human Rights Commission.

Martinho, M. J. 1995. Country report on lesbians in Brazil. In *Unspoken rules: Sexual orientation and women's human rights,* edited by R. Rosenbloom. San

Francisco: International Gay and Lesbian Human Rights Commission.

———, and J. Gardner. 1983. A methodological review of sex-related access discrimination problems. *Sex Roles, 9,* 825–839.

Massengill, D., and N. DiMarco. 1979. Sex-role stereotypes and requisite management characteristics: A current replication. *Sex Roles, 5,* 561–569.

Matynia, E. 1995. Finding a voice: Women in post-communist Central Europe. In *The challenge of local feminisms: Women's movements in global perspective,* edited by A. Basu. Boulder, CO: Westview Press.

Mayell, H. 2002. Thousands of women killed for family "honor." *National Geographic News,* 12 February. http://news.nationalgeographic

Mayer, A. M. 1995a. Cultural particularism as a bar to women's rights: Reflections on the Middle Eastern experience. In *Women's rights, human rights: International feminist perspectives,* edited by J. Peters and A. Wolper. New York: Routledge.

———. 1995b. *Islam and human rights: Tradition and politics.* 2d ed. Boulder, CO: Westview Press.

Mazur, A.G. 2001. Introduction. *State feminism, women's movements, and job training.* London: Routledge.

Mbachu, D. 2003. Women activists in peaceful takeover of Nigerian oil site. *Associated Press,* 29 July.

Mbon, F. M. 1987. Women in African traditional religions. In *Women in the world's religions, past and present,* edited by U. King. New York: Paragon House.

McClelland, S. 2003. The mail-order bride business. *Maclean's, 115,* 48–52.

Meacham, D., and L. Shallet. 2002. Morning after pill: Chile grapples with sex. *Women's Health Journal,* Fall, 47–52.

Mead, M. 1935. *Sex and temperament in three primitive societies.* London: Morrow.

Meir, G. 1975. *My life.* New York: Putnam.

Mendez, J. B. 2002. Creating alternatives from a gender perspective: Transnational organizing for maquila workers' rights in Central America. In *Women's activism and globalization: Linking local struggles transnational politics,* edited by N. A. Naples and M. Desai. New York: Routledge.

Menon, S. A., and S. Kanekar. 1992. Attitudes toward sexual harassment of women in India. *Journal of Applied Social Psychology, 22,* 1940–1952.

Merchant, C. 1992. *Radical ecology: The search for a livable world.* New York: Routledge.

Mermel, A., and J. Simons, 1991. *Women and world development: An education and action guide.* Washington, DC: OEF International.

Mernissi, F. 1987. *The veil and the male elite: A feminist interpretation of women's rights in Islam.* Reading, MA: Addison-Wesley.

Mertus, J. 1995. State discriminatory family law and customary abuses. In *Women's rights, human rights: International feminist perspectives,* edited by J. Peters and A. Wolper. New York: Routledge.

Mikell, G. 1997. Introduction. In *African feminism: The politics of survival in sub-Saharan Africa,* edited by G. Mikell. Philadelphia: University of Pennsylvania Press.

Miller, M. A. L. 2002. Women and development in the Caribbean. In *Women in developing countries: Assessing strategies for empowerment,* edited by R. Datta and J. Kornberg. London: Lynne Rienner Publishers.

Minter, S. 1995. Country report on lesbians in the United States. In *Unspoken rules: Sexual orientation and women's human rights,* edited by R. Rosenbloom. San Francisco: International Gay and Lesbian Human Rights Commission.

Mirhosseini, A. 1995. After the revolution: Violations of women's human rights in Iran. In *Women's rights, human rights: International feminist perspectives,* edited by J. Peters and A. Wolper. New York: Routledge.

Mir-Hosseini, Z. 2001. Iran: Emerging women's voices. In *Women's rights: A global view,* edited by L. Walter. Westport, CN: Greenwood Press.

Moaveni, A., and S. Rotella. 2003. Iranian jurist wins Nobel Peace Prize. *Los Angeles Times,* 11 October, A1, A5.

Moghadam, V. M. 1991. Islamist movements and women's responses in the Middle East. *Gender and History, 3,* 268–284.

——— . 1999. Gender and globalization: Female labor and women's mobilization. *Journal of World-Systems Research, 5,* 367–388.

——— . 2003. *Modernizing women: Gender and social change in the Middle East.* 2d ed. Boulder: Lynne Rienner Publishers.

Mohanty, C. 1991. *Third World women and feminism.* Bloomington: Indiana University Press.

Molinelli, N. G. 1994. Argentina: The (no) ceteris paribus case. In *Electoral systems in comparative perspective: Their impact on women and minorities,* edited by W. Rule and J. F. Zimmerman. Westport, CT: Greenwood Press.

Molyneaux, M. 1985. Mobilization with emancipation? Women's interests, the state, and revolution in Nicaragua. *Feminist Studies, 11,* 227–255.

——— . 1996. Women's rights and international context in the post-communist states. In *Mapping the women's movement: Feminist politics and social transformation in the North,* edited by M. Threlfall. London: Verso and New Left Review.

Morgan, R. 1984. *Sisterhood is global.* New York: Feminist Press.

——— , ed. 1996. *Sisterhood is global.* 2d ed. New York: Feminist Press.

Morrison, A. M., and M. A. Von Glinow. 1990. Women and minorities in management. *American Psychologist, 45,* 200–208.

——— , R. P. White, and E. Van Velsor. 1987. *Breaking the glass ceiling: Can women reach the top of America's largest corporations?* New York: Addison Wesley.

Moser, C. 1989. Gender planning in the Third World: Meeting practical and strategical gender needs. *World Development, 17,* 1799–1825.

——— . 1995. From Nairobi to Beijing: The transition from women in development to gender and development. In *Seeds 2,* edited by A. Leonard. New York: Feminist Press.

Mosse, J. C. 1993. *Half the world, half a chance: An introduction to gender and development.* Oxford: Oxfam.

Munroe, R. L., and R. H. Munroe. 1975. *Cross-cultural human development.* Monterey, CA: Brooks Cole.

——— . 1992. Fathers in children's environments: A four culture study. In *Father-child relations: Cultural and biosocial contexts,* edited by B. S. Hewlett. New York: Aldine de Gruyter.

Murphy, D. E. 1998. Zimbabwe's gays go "out" at great risk. *Los Angeles Times,* 27 July, A1, A12.

——— . 1998. Africa's silent shame. *Los Angeles Times,* 16 August, A1, A20.

Murray, B. 1998. Psychology's voice in sexual harassment law. *American Psychological Association Monitor, 29,* 50–51.

Murrell, A. J. 1996. Sexual harassment and women of color: Issues, challenges, and future directions. In *Sexual harassment in the workplace: Perspectives, frontiers, and response strategies,* edited by M. S. Stockdale. Thousand Oaks, CA: Sage.

Mwamwenda, T. S., and L. A. Monyooe. 1997. Status of bridewealth in an African culture. *Journal of Social Psychology, 137,* 269–271.

Myers, D. G. 1998. *Social psychology.* 3d ed. New York: McGraw-Hill.

Naples, N. A. 2002. Changing the terms: Community activism, globalization, and the dilemmas of transnational praxis. In *Women's activism and globalization: Linking local struggles transnational politics,* edited by N. A. Naples and M. Desai. New York: Routledge.

Narayan, U. 1993. Paying the price of change: Women, modernization, and arranged marriages in India. In *Women's lives and public policy: The international experience,* edited by M. Turshen and B. Holcomb. Westport, CT: Greenwood Press.

Narayanan, V. 1999. Brimming with *Bhakti,* embodiments of *Shakti:* Devotees, deities, performers, reformers, and other women of power in the Hindu tradition. In *Feminism and world religions,* edited by A. Sharma and K. K. Young. Albany, NY: State University Press of New York.

———. 2003. Hinduism. In *Her voice, her faith,* edited by A. Sharma and K. K. Young. Boulder, CO: Westview Press.

Nauman, A. K., and M. Hutchison. 1997. The integration of women into the Mexican labor force since NAFTA. *American Behavioral Scientist, 40,* 950–956.

Navarro, M. 2001. Argentina: The long road to women's rights. In *Women's rights: A global view,* edited by L. Walter. Westport, CN: Greenwood Press.

Neft, N., and A. D. Levine. 1998. *Where women stand: An international report on the status of women in 140 countries 1997–1998.* New York: Random House.

Nelson, D. L., J. C. Quick, M. A. Hitt, and D. Moesel. 1990. Politics, lack of career progress, and work/home conflict: Stress and strain for working women. *Sex Roles, 23,* 169–184.

Ng, Vivien. 1996. Looking for lesbians in Chinese history. In *The new lesbian studies: Into the twenty-first century,* edited by B. Zimmerman and T. A. H. McNaron. New York: Feminist Press.

Niarchos, C. N. 1995. Women, war, and rape: Challenges facing the international tribunal for the former Yugoslavia. *Human Rights Quarterly, 17,* 649–690.

Niditch, S. 1991. Portrayals of women in the Hebrew Bible. In *Jewish women in historical perspective,* edited by J. Baskin. Detroit, MI: Wayne State University Press.

Niebur, G. 1996. The lay of the holy land. *Working woman.* November/December, 22.

Nikolic-Ristanovic, V. 1996. War and violence against women. In *The gendered new world order: Militarism, development and the environment,* edited by J. Turpin and L. A. Lorentzen. New York: Routledge.

Nkomo, S. M., and T. Cox, Jr. 1989. Gender differences in the upward mobility of black managers: Double whammy or double advantage? *Sex Roles, 21,* 825–839.

Noe, R. A. 1988. Women and mentoring: A review and research agenda. *Academy of Management Review, 13,* 65–78.

Norris, P., and J. Lovenduski, 1995. *Political recruitment, gender, race, and class in the British Parliament.* Cambridge: Cambridge University Press.

Nsamenang, B. A. 1992. Perceptions of parenting among the Nso of Cameroon. In *Father-child relations: Cultural and biosocial contexts,* edited by B. S. Hewlett. New York: Aldine de Gruyter.

Nur, R. 1995. Country report on lesbians in Malaysia. In *Unspoken rules: Sexual orientation and women's human rights,* edited by R. Rosenbloom. San Francisco: International Gay and Lesbian Human Rights Commission.

Nussbaum, M. 1992. Human functioning and social justice: In defense of Aristotelian essentialism. *Political Theory, 20,* 202–246.

Obiora, L. A. 2003. The little foxes that spoil the vine: Revisisting the feminist critique of female circumcision. In *African women and feminism: Reflecting on the politics of sisterhood,* edited by O. Oyewumi. Asmara, Eritrea: Africa World Press.

Oduol, W., and W. M. Kabira. 1995. In *The challenge of local feminisms: Women's movements in global perspective,* edited by A. Basu. Boulder, CO: Westview Press.

Olsen, C., ed. 1983. *The book of the goddess: Past and present.* New York: Crossroad.

Olson, J. E., and I. H. Frieze. 1987. Income determinants for women in business. In *Women and work: An annual review.* Vol. 2, edited by A. H. Stromberg, L. Larwood, and B. A. Gutek. Newbury Park, CA: Sage.

Opfell, O. S. 1993. *Women prime ministers and presidents.* Jefferson, NC: McFarland.

O'Regan, V. R. 2000. *Gender matters: Female policymakers' influence in industrialized nations.* New York: Praeger.

Orth, M. 1992. Proud Mary. *Vanity Fair,* July, 121–132.

Oxfam. 2002. Learning from Oxfam's experience of gender equality. *Links,* July, 1–3.

———. 2003. Taking a lead on gender equality. *Links,* May, 3-4.

Oyewumi, O. 2003. Introduction: Feminism, sisterhood, and other foreign relations. In *African women and feminism: Reflecting on the politics of sisterhood,* edited by O. Oyewumi. Asmara, Eritrea: Africa World Press.

Pablos, E. T. 1992. Women's struggles for empowerment in Mexico: Accomplishments, problems, and challenges. In *Women transforming politics: Worldwide strategies for empowerment,* edited by J. Bystydzienski. Bloomington: Indiana University Press.

Padavic, I., and B. Reskin. 2002. *Women and men at work.* 2d ed. Thousand Oaks, CA: Sage.

Pagelow, M. D. 1992. Adult victims of domestic violence. *Journal of Interpersonal Violence, 7,* 87–120.

Pagels, E. H. 1976. What became of God the Mother? Conflicting images of God in early Christianity. In *Womanspirit rising: A feminist reader in religion,* edited by C. P. Christ and J. Plaskow. San Francisco: Harper and Row.

Palmer, A. 1995. Country report on lesbians in Britain. In *Unspoken rules: Sexual orientation and women's human rights,* edited by R. Rosenbloom. San Francisco: International Gay and Lesbian Human Rights Commission.

Pan, P. P. 2002. China's one-child policy now a double standard: Limits and penalties applied unevenly. *Washington Post,* 20 August, A1.

Papanek, H. 1990. To each less than she needs, from each more than she can do: Allocations, entitlements, and value. In *Persistent inequalities,* edited by I. Tinker. Oxford: Oxford University Press.

Parrenas, R. S. 2001. *Servants of globalization: Women, migration, and domestic work.* Stanford, CA: Stanford University Press.

———. 2002. The care crisis in the Philippines: Children and transnational families in the new global economy. In *Global woman: Nannies, maids, and sex workers in the new economy,* edited by B. Ehrenreich and A. R. Hochschild. New York: Metropolitan Books.

Parvey, C. F. 1974. The theology and leadership of women in the New Testament. In *Religion and sexism: Images of woman in the Jewish and Christian traditions,* edited by R. R. Ruether. New York: Simon and Schuster.

Pateman, C. 1992. Equality, difference, subordination: The politics of motherhood and women's citizenship. In *Beyond equality and difference,* edited by G. Bock and S. James. London: Routledge.

Patterson, C. J., and R. E. Redding. 1996. Lesbian and gay families with children: Implications of social science research for policy. *Journal of Social Issues, 52,* 29–50.

Paul, D. Y. 1979. *Women in Buddhism: Images of the feminine in Mahayana tradition.* Berkeley: Asian Humanities Press.

Paxton, P., and S. Kunovich. 2003. Women's political representation: The importance of ideology. *Social Forces, 82,* 87–104.

Peach, L. J. 2002. *Women and world religions.* Upper Saddle River, NJ: Prentice Hall.

Pearce, T. O. 1996. Ethical issues in the importation of long-acting contraceptives to Nigeria. In *Coerced contraception? Moral and policy challenges of long-acting birth control,* edited by E. H. Moskowitz and B. Jennings. Washington, DC: Georgetown University Press.

Penelope, J. 1990. Introduction. RU12? In *Finding the lesbians: Personal accounts from around the world,* edited by J. Penelope and S. Valentine. Freedom, CA: Crossing Press.

Perez, G. C., and P. Jimenez. 1995. Country report on lesbians in Mexico. In *Unspoken rules: Sexual orientation and women's human rights,* edited by R. Rosenbloom. San Francisco: International Gay and Lesbian Human Rights Commission.

Perry, T. 2003. In liberated Kuwait, some still lack right to vote. *Los Angeles Times,* 9 March, A19.

Petchesky, R. P. 1984. *Abortion and women's choice.* New York: Longman.

Peters, J., and A. Wolper. 1995. Introduction. In *Women's rights, human rights: International feminist perspectives,* edited by J. Peters and A. Wolper. New York: Routledge.

Peterson, V. S., and A. S. Runyan. 1999. *Global gender issues.* 2d ed. Boulder, CO: Westview Press.

Pharr, S. 1988. Homophobia: A weapon of sexism. In *Issues in feminism,* 3d ed., edited by S. Ruth. Mountain View, CA: Mayfield.

Plaskow, J. 1991. *Standing again at Sinai.* San Francisco: HarperCollins.

Plata, M. I. 1994. Reproductive rights as human rights: The Colombian case. In *Human rights of women: National and international perspectives,* edited by R. J. Cook. Philadelphia: University of Pennsylvania Press.

Pleck, J. H. 1985. *Working wives/working husbands.* Beverly Hills, CA: Sage.

Pollit, K. 2002. Introduction. In *Nothing sacred: Women respond to religious fundamentalism and terror,* edited by B. Reed. New York: Thunder's Mouth Press/Nation Books.

Powell, G. N., and D. A. Butterfield. 1984. If "good managers" are masculine, what are "bad managers"? *Sex Roles, 10,* 477–484.

———, and L. A. Mainiero. 1992. Cross-currents in the river of time: Conceptualizing the complexities of women's careers. *Journal of Management, 18,* 215–237.

Posusney, M. P., and E. A. Doumato. 2003. Introduction: The mixed blessing of globalization. In *Women and globalization in the Arab Middle East: Gender economy and society,* edited by E. A. Doumato and M. P. Posusney. Boulder, CO: Lynne Rienner Publishers.

Prusak, B. P. 1974. Woman: Seductive siren and source of sin? In *Religion and sexism: Images of woman in the Jewish and Christian traditions,* edited by R. R. Ruether. New York: Simon and Schuster.

Pryor, J. B., J. L. Giedd, and K. B. Williams. 1995. A social psychological model for predicting sexual harassment. *Journal of Social Issues, 51,* 69–84.

Pyle, A. 2000. A collision of medicine and faith. *Los Angeles Times,* 3 January, A1, A16.

Pyne, H. H. 1995. AIDS and gender violence: The enslavement of Burmese women in the Thai sex industry. In *Women's rights, human rights: International feminist perspectives,* edited by J. Peters and A. Wolper. New York: Routledge.

Rachels, J. 1993. *The elements of moral philosophy.* 2d ed. New York: McGraw-Hill.

Ragins, B. R. 1999. Gender and mentoring relationships: A review and research agenda for the next decade. In

Handbook of gender and work, edited by G. N. Powell. Thousand Oaks, CA: Sage.

———, and E. Sundstrom. 1989. Gender and power in organizations: A longitudinal perspective. *Psychological Bulletin 105,* 51–88.

Rajesh, N. 1997. Working to death in Thailand. *Multinational Monitor,* July/August, 7–8.

Ramalingaswami, V., U. Jonsson, and R. Rohde. 1996. Commentary: The Asian Enigma. *The Progress of Nations 1996,* UNICEF.

Rao, A. 1995. The politics of gender and culture in international human rights discourse. In *Women's rights, human rights: International feminist perspectives,* edited by J. Peters and A. Wolper. New York: Routledge.

RAWA (Revolutionary Association of Women in Afghanistan). 2003. Afghan poor sell daughters as brides: Years of war, drought force some to give up young girls. http://rawa.fancymarketing.net/brides.htm

Ray, R. 1999. *Fields of protest: Women's movements in India.* Minneapolis: University of Minnesota Press.

Reanda, L. 1992. The commission on the status of women. In *The United Nations and human rights: A critical appraisal,* edited by P. Alston. Oxford: Oxford University Press.

Renzetti, C. M., and D. J. Curran. 1995. *Women, men, and society.* 3d ed. Boston: Allyn and Bacon.

Reske, H. J. 1995. Lesbianism at center of custody dispute. *American Bar Association Journal,* July, 28.

Rich, A. 1976. *Of woman born: Motherhood as experience and institution.* New York: Norton.

———. 1980. Compulsory heterosexuality and lesbian existence. *Signs, 5,* 631–660.

Ridgeway, C. L. 2001. Social status and group structure. In *Group processes,* edited by M. A. Hogg and S. Tinsdale. Oxford, UK: Blackwell.

Robinson, S. P. 1985. Hindu paradigms of women: Images and values. In *Women, religion, and social change,* edited by Y. Y. Haddad and E. B. Findly. Albany: State University of New York Press.

Rodin J., and J. R. Ickovics. 1990. Women's health: Review and research agenda as we approach the 21st century. *American Psychologist, 45,* 1018–1034.

Rodriquez, V. E. 2003. *Women in contemporary Mexican politics.* Austin: University of Texas Press.

Rogers, B. 1980. *The domestication of women: Discrimination in developing societies.* New York: St. Martin's Press.

Rogers, S. C. 1985. Gender in Southwestern France: The myth of male dominance revisited. *Anthropology, 9,* 65–86.

Rogers, S. G. 1982. Efforts towards women's development in Tanzania: Gender rhetoric vs. gender realities. *Women in Politics, 2,* 23–41.

Rogoff, B. 1981. The relation of age and sex to experiences during childhood in a highland community. *Anthropology UCLA, 11,* 25–41.

Rondon, E. 1995. Country report on lesbians in Colombia. In *Unspoken rules: Sexual orientation and women's human rights,* edited by R. Rosenbloom. San Francisco: International Gay and Lesbian Human Rights Commission.

Roopnarine, J. L., and M. Ahmeduzzaman. 1993. Puerto Rican fathers' involvement with their preschool-aged children. *Hispanic Journal of Behavioral Sciences, 15,* 96–107.

Rosaldo, M. Z. 1974. Women, culture, and society: A theoretical overview. In *Women, culture, and society,* edited by M. Z. Rosaldo and L. Lamphere. Stanford, CA: Stanford University Press.

———, and L. Lamphere. 1974. *Women, culture, and society.* Stanford, CA: Stanford University Press.

Rose, S. D. 1999. Christian fundamentalism: Patriarchy, sexuality, and human rights. In *Religious fundamentalisms and the human rights of women,* edited by C. W. Howland. New York: St. Martin's Press.

Rosenbloom, R. 1995. Introduction. In *Unspoken rules: Sexual orientation and women's human rights,* edited by R. Rosenbloom. San Francisco: International Gay and Lesbian Human Rights Commission.

Rosenthal, R., and D. B. Rubin. 1982. Further meta-analytic procedures for assessing cognitive gender differences. *Journal of Educational Psychology, 74,* 706–712.

Rourke, M. 1997. It must be what birth is like. *Los Angeles Times,* 22 October, E1, E6.

Rowbotham, S. 1996. Introduction: Mapping the women's movement. In *Mapping the women's movement: Feminist politics and social transformation in the North,* edited by M. Threlfall. London: Verso and New Left Review.

Ruan, F. F., and V. Bullough. 1992. Lesbianism in China. *Archives of Sexual Behavior, 21,* 217–228.

Ruether, R. R. 1985. *Womanguides: Readings toward a feminist theology,* Boston: Beacon Press.

———. 1974. *Religion and sexism: Images of woman in the Jewish and Christian traditions.* New York: Simon and Schuster.

———. 1999. Feminism in World Christianity. In *Feminism and world religions,* edited by A. Sharma and K. K. Young. Albany: State University Press of New York.

———. 2002. The war on women. In *Nothing sacred: Women respond to religious fundamentalism and terror,* edited by B. Reed. New York: Thunder's Mouth Press/Nation Books.

Rule, W. 1994. Parliaments of, by, and for the people: Except for women? In *Electoral systems in comparative perspective: Their impact on women and minorities,* edited by W. Rule and J. F. Zimmerman. Westport, CT: Greenwood Press.

Rupp, L. J. 1996. Finding the lesbians in lesbian history: Reflections on female same-sex sexuality in the western world. In *The new lesbian studies: Into the twenty-first century,* edited by B. Zimmerman and T. A. H. McNaron. New York: Feminist Press.

———. 1997. "Imagine my surprise": Women's relationships in historical perspective. *Journal of Lesbian Studies, 1,* 155–176.

Russell, G., and N. Radin. 1983. Increased paternal participation: The father's perspective. In *Fatherhood and family policy,* edited by M. E. Lamb and A. Sagi. Hillsdale, NJ: Erlbaum.

Ruth, S. 1995. *Issues in feminism.* 3d ed. Mountain View, CA: Mayfield.

Sachs, C. E. 1997. Introduction: Connecting women and the environment. In *Women working in the environment,* edited by C. E. Sachs. Washington, DC: Taylor and Francis.

Sacks, K. 1982. The case against universal subordination. *Sisters and wives: The past and future of sexual equality.* Urbana: University of Illinois Press.

Sadik, N. 2002. Preface. In *An agenda for the people: The UNFPA through three decades,* edited by N. Sadik. New York: New York University Press.

Safa, H. I. 1995. *The myth of the male breadwinner: Women and industrialization in the Caribbean.* Boulder, CO: Westview Press.

Saint-Germain, M. A. 1993. Women in power in Nicaragua: Myth and reality. In *Women as national leaders,* edited by M. A. Genovese. Newbury Park, CA: Sage.

———. 1989. Does their difference make a difference? The impact of women on public policy in the Arizona legislature. *Social Science Quarterly, 70,* 956–967.

Salinas, G. A. 1994. Women and politics: Gender relations in Bolivian political organizations and labor unions. In *Women and politics worldwide,* edited by B. J. Nelson and N. Chowdhury. New Haven, CT: Yale University Press.

Salzinger, L. 2003. *Genders in production: Making workers in Mexico's global factories.* Berkeley, CA: University of California Press.

Sanchez, L. 1993. Women's power and the gendered division of domestic labor in the third world. *Gender and Society, 7,* 434–459.

Sanday, P. R. 1974. Female status in the public domain. In *Women, culture, and society,* edited by M. Z. Rosaldo and L. Lamphere. Stanford, CA: Stanford University Press.

———. 1981. *Female power and male dominance: On the origins of sexual inequality.* Cambridge: Cambridge University Press.

Santiago, L. Q. 1995. Rebirthing *Babaye:* The women's movement in the Philippines. In *The challenge of local feminisms: Women's movements in global perspective,* edited by A. Basu. Boulder, CO: Westview Press.

Sarda, A. 1995. Country report on lesbians in Argentina. In *Unspoken rules: Sexual orientation and women's human rights,* edited by R. Rosenbloom. San Francisco: International Gay and Lesbian Human Rights Commission.

Sassen, S. 2002. Global cities and survival circuits. In *Global woman: Nannies, maids, and sex workers in the new economy,* edited by B. Ehrenreich and A. R. Hochschild. New York: Metropolitan Books.

Sawer, M. 1994. Locked out or locked in? Women and politics in Australia. In *Women and politics worldwide,* edited by B. J. Nelson and N. Chowdhury. New Haven, CT: Yale University Press.

Schein, V. E. 1973. The relationship between sex role stereotypes and requisite management characteristics. *Journal of Applied Psychology, 57,* 95–100.

———. 1975. The relationship between sex role stereotypes and requisite management characteristics among female managers. *Journal of Applied Psychology, 60,* 340–344.

———, and R. Mueller. 1992. Sex role stereotyping and requisite management characteristics: A cross-cultural look. *Journal of Organizational Behavior, 13,* 439–447.

———, R. Mueller, and C. Jacobson. 1989. The relationship between sex role stereotypes and requisite management characteristics among college students. *Sex Roles, 20,* 103–111.

Schneider, K. T., S. Swann, and L. F. Fitzgerald. 1997. Job-related and psychological effects of sexual harassment in the workplace: Empirical evidence from two organizations. *Journal of Applied Psychology, 82,* 401–415.

Schoepf, B. G. 1997. AIDS, gender, and sexuality during Africa's economic crisis. In *African feminism: The politics of survival in sub-Saharan Africa,* edited by G. Mikell. Philadelphia: University of Pennsylvania Press.

Schulman, G. B. 1974. View from the back of the synagogue. In *Sexist religion and women in the church,* edited by A. L. Hageman. New York: Association Press.

Seager, J. 1993. *Earth follies.* New York: Routledge.

———. 2003. *The Penguin atlas of women and the world.* London: Penguin.

Segal, L. 1987. *Is the future female? Troubled thoughts on contemporary feminism.* London: Virago.

Sekhon, J., and J. M. Bystydzienski. 2001. Conclusion. In *Democratization and women's grassroots movements,* edited by J. M. Bystydzienski and J. Sekhon. Bloomington: Indiana University Press.

Sen, G., and C. Grown. 1987. *Development crises and alternative visions.* New York: Monthly Review Press.

Sered, S. S. 1994. *Priestess, mother, sacred sister.* Oxford: Oxford University Press.

———. 1999. *Women of the sacred groves: Divine priestesses of Okinawa.* Oxford: Oxford University Press.

Shaaban, B. 1995. The muted voices of women interpreters. In *Faith and freedom: Women's rights in the Muslim world,* edited by M. Afkami. London: I. B. Tauris.

Shalev, C. 1995. Women in Israel: Fighting tradition. In *Women's rights, human rights: International feminist perspectives,* edited by J. Peters and A. Wolper. New York: Routledge.

Sherif, C. W. 1982. Needed concepts in the study of gender identity. *Psychology of Women Quarterly, 6,* 375–395.

Sherif, M., and C. Sherif. 1964. *Reference groups.* New York: Harper and Row.

Shiva, V. 1988. Interview. In *Women and environment in the Third World: Alliance for the future,* edited by I. Dankelman and J. Davidson. London: Earthscan.

———. 1989. *Staying alive: Women, ecology and development.* London: Zed.

———. 1994. *Closer to home: Women reconnect ecology, health and development worldwide.* Philadelphia: New Society Publishers.

———. 1996. Let us survive: Women, ecology, and development. In *Women healing earth: Third World women on ecology, feminism, and religion,* edited by R. R. Ruether. New York: Orbis.

Simmons, A. M. 1998. Abortion deaths in Nigeria attributed to archaic methods. *Los Angeles Times,* 29 December, A4.

Simons, M. 1996. U.N. court for the first time, defines rape as war crime. *New York Times,* 28 June, A1, A10.

Singapore Asian Christian Women's Conference. 1994. Summary statement on feminist Mariology. In *Feminist theology from the Third World,* edited by U. King. Maryknoll, NY: Orbis.

Slocum, S. 1975. Woman the gatherer: Male bias in anthropology. In *Toward an anthropology of women,* edited by R. R. Reiter. New York: Monthly Review Press.

Smith, J. I. 1987. Islam. In *Women in world religions,* edited by A. Sharma. Albany: State University of New York Press.

Snow, R. C. 1994. Each to her own: Investigating women's response to contraception. In *Power and decision: The social control of reproduction,* edited by G. Sen and R. C. Snow. Cambridge, MA: Harvard University Press.

Soares, V., A. A. Alcantara Costa, C. M. Buarque, D. D. Dora, and W. Sant'Anna. 1995. Brazilian feminism and women's movements: A two-way street. In *The challenge of local feminisms: Women's movements in global perspective,* edited by A. Basu. Boulder, CO: Westview Press.

Sonthcimer, S. 1991. *Women and the environment: A reader on crisis and development in the Third World.* New York: Monthly Review Press.

Stacey, J. 1983. *Patriarchy and social revolution in China.* Berkeley: University of California Press.

Stamatopoulou, E. 1995. Women's rights and the United Nations. In *Women's rights, human rights: International feminist perspectives,* edited by J. Peters and A. Wolper. New York: Routledge.

Stammer, L. B. 2001. Bishops ban sterilization services at all Catholic-affiliated hospitals. *Los Angeles Times,* 16 June, A1.

Starhawk. 1979. Witchcraft and women's culture. In *Womanspirit rising: A feminist reader in religion,* edited by C. P. Christ and J. Plaskow. New York: Harper and Row.

Stark, C. 1996. One woman's life in a sweatshop. *Bangor Daily News.* 22 October.

Stark, R. 1995. Reconstructing the rise of Christianity: The role of women. *Sociology of Religion, 56,* 229–244.

Staudt, K. 1995. Planting *Seeds 2* in the classroom. In *Seeds 2,* edited by A. Leonard. New York: Feminist Press.

Steady, F. C. 1995. Women and the environment in developing countries: The challenge of implementing Agenda 21. In *Women and the United Nations,* edited by F. C. Steady and R. Toure. Rochester, VT: Schenkman Books.

Stearns, J. 1998. *Gender and international relations: An introduction.* New Brunswick, NJ: Rutgers University Press.

Steinberg, R. 1988. Women, the state, and equal employment. In *Feminization of the labor force: Paradoxes and promises,* edited by J. Jenson, E. Hagen, and C. Ruddy. New York: Oxford University Press.

Stetson, D. M., and A. G. Mazur. 1995. Introduction. In *Comparative state feminism,* edited by D. M. Stetson and A. G. Mazur. Newbury Park, CA: Sage.

Stevens, G. E. 1984. Women in business: The view of future male and female managers. *Journal of Business Education, 59,* 314–317.

Stevens, P. E., and J. M. Hall. 1991. A critical historical analysis of the medical construction of lesbianism. *International Journal of Health Services, 21,* 291–307.

Stienstra, D. 1994. *Women's movements and international organizations.* New York: St. Martin's Press.

Stockard, J., and M. Johnson, 1979. The social origins of male dominance. *Sex Roles, 5,* 199–218.

Strange, C. 1990. Mothers on the march: Maternalism in women's protest for peace in North America and Western Europe, 1900–1985. In *Women and social protest,* edited by G. West and R. L. Blumberg. Oxford: Oxford University Press.

Stroh, L. K., J. M. Brett, and A. Reilly. 1992. All the right stuff: A comparison of female and male managers' career progression. *Journal of Applied Psychology, 77,* 251–260.

Strunsky, S. 2003. A young lesbian's stabbing death is far from resolved. Associated Press State and Local Newswire. 9 August.

Sturgeon, N. 1997. *Ecofeminist natures: Race, gender, feminist theory, and political action.* New York: Routledge.

Sugirtharajah, S. 1994. Hinduism. In *Women in religion,* edited by J. Holm. New York: St. Martin's Press.

Sugisaki, K. 1986. From the moon to the sun: Women's liberation in Japan. In *Women in the world: 1975–1985, the women's decade,* edited by L. B. Iglitzin and R. Ross. Santa Barbara, CA: ABC-Clio.

Sullins, P. 2000. The stained glass ceiling: Career attainment for women clergy. *Sociology of Religion, 61,* 243–277.

Sullivan, D. 1995. The public/private distinction in international human rights law. In *Women's rights, human rights: International feminist perspectives,* edited by J. Peters and A. Wolper. New York: Routledge.

Swers, M. L. 2002. *The difference women make: The policy impact of women in Congress.* Chicago: University of Chicago Press.

Tanaka, K. 1995. Work, education, and the family. In *Japanese women: New feminist perspectives on the past, present and future,* edited by K. Fujimura-Fanselow and A. Kameda. New York. Feminist Press.

Tarawan, K. 1995. Country report on lesbians in Thailand. In *Unspoken rules: Sexual orientation and women's human rights,* edited by R. Rosenbloom. San Francisco: International Gay and Lesbian Human Rights Commission.

Tavris, C., and C. Wade. 1984. *The longest war: Sex differences in perspective.* New York: Harcourt Brace Jovanovich.

Taylor, D. 2002. Women in search of peace. *The Guardian,* 22 January, 8.

Taylor, V., and L. J. Rupp. 1993. Women's culture and lesbian feminist activism: A reconsideration of cultural feminism. *Signs,* Autumn, 32–61.

Thomas, K. 1998. FGM watch. *Ms., 8,* March/April, 28.

Thomas, S. 1994. *How women legislate.* New York: Oxford University Press.

Thompson, S. 1993. Golda Meir: A very public life. In *Women as national leaders,* edited by M. A. Genovese. Newbury Park, CA: Sage.

Threlfall, M. 1996. Feminist politics and social change in Spain. In *Mapping the women's movement: Feminist politics and social transformation in the North,* edited by M. Threlfall. London: Verso and New Left Review.

Thurman, J. E., and G. Trah. 1990. Part-time work in international perspective. *International Labour Review, 129,* 23–40.

Times Wire Reports. 2002. Government faulted in report of sex slaves. *Los Angeles Times,* 9 December, A12.

———. 2003. Women protest being shut out of elections. *Los Angeles Times,* 6 July, A13.

Tinker, I. 1990. A context for the field and for the book. In *Persistent inequalities: Women and world development,* edited by I. Tinker. Oxford: Oxford University Press.

———. 1994. Women and community forestry in Nepal: Expectations and realities. *Society and Natural Resources, 7,* 367–381.

———. 1995. The human economy of microentrepreneurs. In *Women in micro- and small-scale enterprise development,* edited by L. Divard and J. Havet. Boulder, CO: Westview Press.

Todosijevic, J. 1995. Country report on lesbians in Serbia. In *Unspoken rules: Sexual orientation and women's human rights,* edited by R. Rosenbloom. San Francisco: International Gay and Lesbian Human Rights Commission.

Tomasevski, K. 1993. *Women and human rights.* London: Zed.

Toro, M. S. 1995. Popularizing women's human rights at the local level: A grassroots methodology for setting the international agenda. In *Women's rights, human rights: International feminist perspectives,* edited by J. Peters and A. Wolper. New York: Routledge.

Triandis, H. C. 1994. *Culture and social behavior.* New York: McGraw-Hill.

Trible, P. 1973. Eve and Adam: Genesis 2–3 reread. In *Womanspirit rising: A feminist reader in religion,* edited by C. P. Christ and J. Plaskow. New York: Harper and Row.

Trujillo, C. 1991. Chicana lesbians: Fear and loathing in the Chicano community. In *Women images and realities: A multicultural anthology,* edited by A. Kesselman, L. D. McNair, and N. Schniedewind. Mountain View, CA: Mayfield.

Tulananda, O., D. M. Young, and J. L. Roopnarine, 1994. Thai and American fathers' involvement with preschool-aged children. *Early Child Development and Care, 97,* 123–133.

Uchino, K. 1987. The status elevation process of Soto sect nuns in modern Japan. In *Speaking of faith: Global perspectives on women, religion, and social change,* edited by D. L. Eck and D. Jain. Philadelphia: New Society Publishers.

Umanksy, E. M. 1999. Feminism in Judaism. In *Feminism and world religions,* edited by A. Sharma and K. K. Young. Albany: State University Press of New York.

UNAIDS. 2003. Gender and HIV. http://www.unaids.org

UNIFEM. 1998. gopher://gopher.undp.org:70/00/unifem/polieco/poli/whr/cedaw/cadaswkit/wctp

———. 2001a. Shining a bright light: Monitoring a domestic violence law in Malaysia. http://www.unifem.undp.org/trustfund/malaysia.html

———. 2001b. Gender responsive budgets. http://www.unifem.org/index.php?f_page_pid=19

———. 2003a. Women's human rights: Addressing the gender dimensions of HIV/AIDS. http://www.unifem.org

———. 2003b. Women, gender, and HIV/AIDS in East and Southeast Asia. http://www.unifem.org

United Nations. 1985. *The state of the world's women.* Oxford: New Internationalist Publications.

———. 1988. *Compendium of international conventions concerning the status of women.* New York: Author.

———. 1989. *Violence against women in the family.* New York: Author.

———. 1991a. *Report of the working group on contemporary forms of slavery on its sixteenth session,* UN Doc. E/CN.4/Sub.2/1991/41 of August, paras. 1 and 3.

———. 1991b. *The world's women: Trends and statistics, 1970–1990.* New York: Author.

———. 1993. *Abortion politics: A global review, Volume II.* New York: Author.

———. 1994. Equal pay, urban women problems discussed by commission. *UN Chronicle,* August, 60–61.

———. 1996. *The United Nations and the advancement of women: 1945–1996.* New York: Author.

———. 1997a. *Human Development Report 1997.* New York: Author.

———. 1997b. *Work.* http://www.un.org/Depts/unsd/gender/sum5.htm

———. 1998. *Too young to die: Genes or gender?* New York: Author.

———. 1999. World survey on the role of women in development: Globalization, gender and work. New York: Author.

———. 2000. *The feminization of poverty.* http://www.un.org/womenwatch/daw/followup/session/presskit/fs1.htm

———. *The world's women 2000: Trends and Statistics.* New York: United Nations.

———. 2002. Physical abuse against women by an intimate partner. *The world's women 2000: Trends and statistics.* http://unstats.un.org

United Nations Conference on Trade and Development. 2001. Least developed countries 2001. http://r0.unctrd.org/engl/pub/ldcprofiles2001.en.htm

United Nations Development Programme. 1995. *Human development report.* Oxford: Oxford University Press.

———. 2003a. *Mainstreaming gender in water management.* http://www.undp.org/water/docs/resource-guide.pdf

———. 2003b. *Human development report 2003.* Oxford: Oxford University Press.

United Nations High Commissioner for Human Rights. 2002. *Fact sheet 23: Harmful practices affecting women and children.* http://www.unhchr.ch/html/menu6/2/fs23.htm#i

United Nations Integrated Regional Information Networks. 2003. *Zimbabwe: Focus on rape as a political weapon.* 8 April.

United Nations Population Fund. 2001. *Environmental sustainability.* http://www.unfpa.org/iss

———. 2002. *State of the World Population, 2002.* http://www.unfpa.org/swp/2002/english/ch5/page3.htm

———. 2003a. UNFPA in the news, Week of March 8-14. http://www.unfpa.org/news/news.cfm?ID=192

———. 2003b. *Fast facts on maternal mortality and morbidity.* http://www.unfpa.org/rh/mothers/facts.htm

———. 2003c. *34 million friends campaign.* http://www.unfpa.org/support/friends/34million.htm

———. 2003d. *Frequently Asked Questions about Female Genital Cutting.* http://www.unfpa.org/gender/faq_fgc.htm

———. 2003e. http://www.unfpa.org/intercenter/hopes/gap.htm

United Nations Statistics Division. 2003. *The world's women 2000: Trends and statistics, maternity leave benefits as of 1998.* http://unstats.un.org/unsd/demographic/ww2000/table5c.htm

U.S. Department of Justice. 2002. *Annual symposium on domestic violence.* http://www.ojp.usdoj.gov/vawo/nac/agremarks.htm

United States Department of Labor. 1997. *Facts on working women: Women in management.* http://www.dol.gov/dol/wb/public/wb_pubs/wmgt97.htm

U.S. Department of Labor, Bureau of Labor Statistics. 2002. *Highlights of women's earnings in 2001. Report 960.* http://www.bls.gov/cps/cpswom2001.pdf

Vahme-Sabz. 1995. Country report on lesbians in Iran. In *Unspoken rules: Sexual orientation and women's human rights,* edited by R. Rosenbloom. San Francisco, CA: International Gay and Lesbian Human Rights Commission.

Van Vianen, A. E. M., and T. M. Willemsen. 1992. The employment interview: The role of sex stereotypes in the evaluation of male and female job applicants in the Netherlands. *Journal of Applied Social Psychology, 22,* 471–491.

Vasudev, S., A. K. Menon, R. Vinayak, S. David, and K. Muralideharan. 2003. Groom showroom. *India Today,* 9 June, 64.

———, and M. Renuka. 2003. Rape! *India Today,* 48–56.

Via, E. J. 1987. Women in the gospel of Luke. In *Women in the world's religions, past and present,* edited by U. King. New York: Paragon House.

Vogel, L. 1983. *Marxism and the oppression of women: Toward a unitary theory.* New Brunswick, NJ: Rutgers University Press.

Waldfogel, J. 1997. The effect of children on women's wages. *American Sociological Review, 62,* 209–217.

Wallace, C. P. 1992. Doing business: new shots fired in Indonesia wage war. *Los Angeles Times,* 22 September, 2.

Walter, L. 2001. Introduction. In *Women's rights: A global view,* edited by L. Walter. Westport, CN: Greenwood Press.

Ward, K. B., and J. L. Pyle. 1995. Gender, industrialization, transnational corporations, and development: An overview of trends and patterns. In *Women in the Latin American development process,* edited by C. E. Bose and E. Acosta-Belen. Philadelphia: Temple University Press.

Waring, M. 1988. *If women counted: A new feminist economics.* New York: Harper and Row.

Watanabe, T. 1999. Sikhs celebrate major anniversary. *Los Angeles Times,* 10 April, B2.

Waters, E., and A. Posadskaya. 1995. Democracy without women is no democracy: Women's struggles in post-communist Russia. In *The challenge of local feminisms: Women's movements in global perspective,* edited by A. Basu. Boulder, CO: Westview Press.

Wax, E. 2003. A brutal legacy of Congo war. *Washington Post,* 25 October, A1, A17.

WEDO. 2003. *50/50 campaign.* http://www.wedo.org/fact_sheet_1.htm

Weissinger, C. 1993. Introduction: Going beyond and retaining charisma: Women's leadership in marginal religions. *Women's leadership in marginal religions: Explorations outside the mainstream.* Chicago: University of Illinois Press.

Wekker, G. 1993. Mati-ism and black lesbianism: Two ideal typical expressions of female homosexuality in Black communities of the Diaspora. *Journal of Homosexuality, 24,* 11–24.

Wells, B. L. 2002. Context, strategy, ground: Rural women organizing to confront local/global economic issues. In *Women's activism and globalization: Linking local struggles transnational politics,* edited by N. A. Naples and M. Desai. New York: Routledge.

West, G., and R. L. Blumberg. 1990. Reconstructing social protest from a feminist perspective. In *Women and social protest,* edited by G. West and R. L. Blumberg. New York: Oxford University Press.

West, L. 1999. The United Nations women's conferences and feminist politics. In *Gender politics in global governance,* edited by M. K. Meyer and E. Prugl.

Whitam, F. L., and R. M. Mathy. 1991. Childhood cross-gender behavior of homosexual females in Brazil, Peru, the Philippines, and the United States. *Archives of Sexual Behavior, 20,* 151–170.

Whiting, B. B., and C. P. Edwards. 1988. *Children of different worlds: The formation of social behavior.* Cambridge, MA: Harvard University Press.

Wilkinson, T. 1998. She seeks women's rights—quietly. *Los Angeles Times,* 7 October, A1, A6.

Williams, A. 2003. Sima Samar. *Ms.,* Winter, 37.

Williams, D. S. 1994. Womanist theology: Black women's voices. In *Feminist theology from the Third World,* edited by U. King. Maryknoll, NY: Orbis.

Williams, H. 1995. Violeta Barrios de Chamorro. In *Women in world politics: An introduction,* edited by F. D'Amico and P. R. Beckman. Westport, CT: Bergin and Garvey.

Williams, J. E., and D. L. Best. 1990a. *Measuring sex stereotypes: A thirty nation study.* Rev. ed. Beverly Hills, CA: Sage.

———. 1990b. *Sex and psyche: Gender and self viewed cross-culturally.* Beverly Hills, CA: Sage.

Willis, J. D. 1985. Nuns and benefactresses: The role of women in the development of Buddhism. In *Women, religion, and social change,* edited by Y. Y. Haddad and E. B. Findly. New York: State University of New York Press.

Wilshire, R. 1995. Gender in development: A critical issue for sustainable development. In *Women and the United Nations,* edited by F. C. Steady and R. Toure. Rochester, VT: Schenkman Books.

Wilson, E. O. 1978. *On human nature.* Cambridge, MA: Harvard University Press.

WIN. 1992. Sexual harassment at work. *Women's International Network News, 18,* 46–47.

———. 1993. Hong Kong: Sex discrimination in the work force. *Women's International Network News, 19,* 60.

———. 2003. UNIFEM: Women's political participation a most positive change. *Women's International Network News, 29,* 3.

Wolfe, L. R., and J. Tucker. 1995. Feminism lives: Building a multicultural women's movement in the United

States. In *The challenge of local feminisms: Women's movements in global perspective,* edited by A. Basu. Boulder, CO: Westview Press.

Women's Health Journal. 2002. Sexual and reproductive health and rights threatened in Peru.

Women's International Network News. 2000. Uganda: The facts about the tradition of bride price. Winter, *26.*

World Bank. 2001. Engendering development: Through gender equality in rights, resources, and voice. Oxford: Oxford University Press and the World Bank.

World Commission on Environment and Development. 1987. *Our common future.* Oxford: Oxford University Press.

World Health Organization. 2000. Female genital mutilation. Fact sheet no. 241. http://www.who.int/inf-fs/en/fact241.html

World in brief: Orthodox Jews pelt worshippers at Wall. 1997. *Los Angeles Times,* 12 June, A12.

World Resources Institute. 1994–95. *World resources: A guide to the global environment.* Oxford: Oxford University Press.

Wright, R. 1995a. Economic progress comes slow for women worldwide, UN study finds. *Detroit News.* 25 August. http://detnews.com/menu/stories/1469.htm

———. 1995b. *Los Angeles Times.* 27 August. http://detnews.com/menu/stories/1469.htm

Yee, S. 2003. Overcoming fear to fight sterilizations. *Los Angeles Times,* 3 March, A3.

Yoko, H. 1995. The path to gender equality in Japan. *Japan-Asia Quarterly Review, 25,* 18–19.

Yoshihama, M. 2002. Breaking the web of abuse and silence: Voices of battered women in Japan. *Social Work, 47,* 389–400.

Yoshizumi, K. 1995. Marriage and the family: Past and present. In *Japanese women: New feminist perspectives on the past, present, and future,* edited by K. Fujimura-Fanselow and A. Kameda. New York: Feminist Press.

Young, K. K. 1987. Hinduism. In *Women in world religions,* edited by A. Sharma. Albany: State University of New York Press.

———. 1994. Women in Hinduism. In *Today's woman in world religions,* edited by A. Sharma. Albany: State University of New York Press.

Youseff, N. H. 1995. Women's access to productive resources: The need for legal instruments to protect women's development rights. In *Women's rights, human rights: International feminist perspectives,* edited by J. Peters and A. Wolper. New York: Routledge.

Zaman, A. 2003. Turkey passes more reforms in quest for EU membership. *Los Angeles Times,* 20 June, A3.

Zhang, N., and W. Xu. 1995. Discovering the positive within the negative: The women's movement in a changing China. In *The challenge of local feminisms: Women's movements in global perspective,* edited by A. Basu. Boulder, CO: Westview Press.

Zimmerman, J. F. 1994. Equity in representation for women and minorities. In *Electoral systems in comparative perspective: Their impact on women and minorities,* edited by W. Rule and J. F. Zimmerman. Westport, CT: Greenwood Press.

Zimonjic, V. P. 2002. Rights—Yugoslavia: Women sold like sacks of potatoes. *Interpress Service,* 26 December, 26.

Zita, J. N. 1981. Historical amnesia and the lesbian continuum. *Signs, 7,* 172–187.

Index